PUBLISHED BY ALFRED A. KNOPF CANADA

Copyright © 1997 by Bill Richardson

All rights reserved under International and
Pan American Copyright Conventions. Published in
Canada by Alfred A. Knopf Canada, Toronto, in 1997.
Distributed by Random House of Canada Limited, Toronto.

Page 341 constitutes a continuation of the copyright page.

Canadian Cataloguing in Publication Data
Richardson, Bill
Scorned & beloved : dead of winter meetings with
Canadian eccentrics

ISBN 0-676-97079-6

1. Eccentrics and eccentricities - Canada - Biography.
I. Title.
II. Title: Scorned and beloved.

FC25.R52 1997   920.071   C97-9309883
F1005.R52 1997

Printed and bound in the United States of America

First Edition

Dead of Winter Meetings

SCORNED & BELOVED

with Canadian Eccentrics

BILL RICHARDSON

KNOPF

CANADA

For Wallace

• • •

"Scorned as Timber, Beloved of the Sky"
Title of a painting by Emily Carr

"Sometimes, however, a trip across
the country is just a trip across the country."
Rick Salutin, *The Globe and Mail*, Sept. 20, 1996

Contents

ELLY MAY
: *Entertainer, Toronto*

GLENN GOULD
: *Pianist, Toronto*

GLENN GOULD'S NEIGHBOURS
: *Tenants of Mount Pleasant Cemetery, Toronto*

ANNA BROWNELL JAMESON
: *Art Historian, Nineteenth-Century Travel Writer*

JOHN HENRY LEFROY
: *Nineteenth-Century Surveyor*

GEOFFREY PIMBLETT
: *Restaurateur, Queen Impersonator, Toronto*

ESTHER BRANDEAU
: *Cross-dresser, Traveller, Quebec City*

SARAH EMMA EDMONDS
: *Bible Salesman, Civil War Veteran, Cross-dresser, New Brunswick*

CHAS. S. ROBERTSON
: *Elocutionist, Kenabeek, Ontario*

GRENVILLE KLEISER
: *Master of the Universe and Author,* Fifteen Thousand Useful Phrases

DAME EDITH SITWELL
: *Author,* English Eccentrics

CHARLES DOMERY
: *Remarkable Glutton*

ST. SIMEON STYLITES
: *Pillar Sitter*

ST. SIMEON SALUS
: *Fool for God, Tectonic Clairvoyant, Dog Walker*

CHARLES HENRY DANIELLE
: *Dancing Master, Costumier, Proprietor of Octagon Castle, Paradise, Newfoundland*

S. G. COLLIER
: *Undertaker, St. John's*

FREDERICK A. BRAZILL
: *Heir to Charles Henry Danielle, Paradise*

CLARENCE WAUGH
: *Friend of Charles Henry Danielle*

PIERRE-LÉON AYOTTE
: *Farm Labourer, Trousers-Phobic, Ste-Geneviève-de-Batiscan, Quebec*

WILLIE FRANCIS FRASER
: *Learned to Dance in a Dream, Deepdale, Cape Breton Island*

MRS. JOYNER
: *Struck by Lightning, Souris, Manitoba*

MR. JOYNER
Her Husband, Souris
EDDIE R. SOURIS
Genealogist, Mouse Fancier, Traveller, Toronto
ST. MODOMNOC
Apiarist
FRED SAUER
Inventor, Charlottetown
GEORGE DOWIE
Convicted Murderer, Poet, Charlottetown
FRANCIS LONGWORTH
Sheriff, Charlottetown
NOAH
Flood Survivor, Wildlife Conservationist
NOAH'S FAMILY
Also on the Ark
MOGUL
Elephant
SAMUEL BEAN
Preacher, Physician, Cryptographer, Wellesley, Ontario
MERIT BEAN
Curmudgeon, Yarmouth
JEROME
Amnesiac, Double Amputee, Meteghan, Nova Scotia
ARTHUR THURSTON
Historian, Collector, Pigeon Keeper, Yarmouth
CAPTAIN REED
Commander of the Ill-Fated Royal Tar, *Saint John*
KEITH PELTON
Actor, Burned to Death with a Curling-Iron, Yarmouth
TONY CURTIS
Actor, Hunk
ROBERT GOULET
Singer, Hunk
JEAN ST-GERMAIN
Inventor, Mystic, Pyramid Builder, St-Simon-de-Bagot, Quebec
ALEX KOLANSKY
The Mad Trapper of the Whiteshell
NICK KOLANSKY
His Brother, Portage la Prairie
MARGARET MCDONALD
Muskrat Slayer, Cobden, Ontario
NELLEE JESSEE REID
Farm Labourer, Cross-dresser, Englehart, Ontario
JACK AND DONNA WRIGHT
Cat Fanciers, Kingston

DRAMATIS PERSONAE

JACK MARRIOTT
: *Photographer, Philosopher, Composer, Farmer, Cat Lover, Port Williams, Nova Scotia*

JOB
: *Resident of Heaven*

JEAN-PAUL SARTRE
: *Existentialist*

PAUL WUKETSEWITZ
: *Known as Paul Bog, Petersfield, Manitoba*

MICKEY DONOHOE
: *Paul Bog's Neighbour*

HECTOR MACKENZIE
: *Fiddler, Tour Guide, New Glasgow, Nova Scotia*

K.
: *Hermit, Nova Scotia*

GABRIEL DRUILLETTES
: *Jesuit, Quebec*

LAURA KAY PROPHET
: *Seer, Duck Fancier, Vancouver*

SYLVIE LONGPRÉ
: *Barbie Enthusiast, Repentigny, Quebec*

THE GREAT ANTONIO
: *World's Strongest Man, Montreal*

BILL JAMIESON
: *Collects Shrunken Heads, Toronto*

JOE DELANEY
: *Scarecrow Maker, Cheticamp, Cape Breton Island*

CLYDE FARNELL
: *Artist, Decorator, Cornerbrook, Newfoundland*

ALEXIS LAPOINTE
: *Half Man, Half Horse, La Malbaie, Quebec*

LETITIA J. REID
: *Graduate, 1928 Marvel School of Cosmetology, Regina*

THE MARVEL GIRLS
: *Her Classmates*

LILLIAN ALLING
: *Walked from New York to Siberia*

DAVID CURNICK
: *Teacher, Film Maker, Robin Hood Fan, Vancouver*

EMILY CARR
: *Painter, Writer, Victoria*

Fugue

So, you want to write a fugue,
You've got the urge to write a fugue,
You've got the nerve to write a fugue,
The only way to write one is to plunge right in and write one.
So go ahead.
— Glenn Gould, "The Anatomy of Fugue"

Elly May's eyelashes are beautifully groomed and expertly attached. Longer than long. Fracturers of time and space. Exquisite, extravagant receptors. At any minute they might register a distant seismic trembling, or crackle with radio waves beamed over light-years from a remote and intelligent corner of the universe. If you were to see one out of context — flaccid and strewn across the bar, say — you might mistake it for one of those cunning brushes waiters use, postprandially, for clearing crumbs from tables. When Elly May bats her lids, which is often, they generate a breeze that sets the candle flames to shimmying. These, as the inquisitor said to the heretic, are holy lashes. Everything about their architecture — their anti-gravitational sweep, their unlikely heft, their evidence of the divinely inspired human inventiveness we call Art — funnels attention heavenward. If a single, highly individuated snowflake were to precipitate itself from the grey forge of the December clouds, tumble down angle over unique angle, and expire, meltingly, on the thoughtfully combed expanse of one of these wide rakes, they would achieve transcendence. Mere lashes no longer, they would become Poetry. Unalloyed Poetry.

Elly May's eyes are brown and uncommonly wide. They may owe their preternatural dilation to the effort required to keep half a kilo of synthetic fur aloft. Or, it might be nothing more than one of the discreetly athletic requirements of voguing.

"Have you seen my Bette Davis?" she asks. I shake my head. We have only just met. I haven't had the chance to plumb her repertoire of tricks, which is evidently steppe-like in its expansiveness. It doesn't matter a jot that our acquaintance is so freshly minted. Elly May lowers her eyes to half-mast and lasers me with the same "where the hell have you been" regard she used when I asked her her name. It is surely no accident that avid is the mirror image of diva. As divas go, Elly May is the quintessence of avidity. She is accustomed to having her reputation parade before her, preceding even her hyperextended and feathery ocularia. She sighs the sigh of the worn-out and the righteous. In me, she sees, she has her work cut out for her.

"Then watch."

She stands, opens the full-length fur coat her mother gave her last year for Christmas. She squares her hands — her nails are magenta, her fingers festooned with gaudy, multifaceted glass bijoux — on her hips. They are so narrow, those hips! Even so, they are scarcely contained by the shiny vinyl swatch of her black miniskirt. It is a frock of her own design, and she says it began its life on earth as a tablecloth. No matter. It more than suits her. She looks like a million bucks. Elly May stretches her neck. Elly May angles her head. Elly May lifts her chin, and achieves the seemingly impossible by widening her eyes further still. She flares her nostrils to such cavernous good effect that I find myself momentarily thinking of the Chunnel. Every movement is acid-etched and arch. She lifts her fag to her lips, sucks, exhales both smoke and the inevitable camp expostulation.

"What a dump!"

New Year's Eve, 1996. Toronto, Ontario. "Dump" would be the operative word. Canada's largest city is labouring under the weight of its second meaningful snowfall in twenty-four hours.

The pavements are encumbered with soggy, treacherous slop, neither slush nor snow nor ice. The Inuit must have a name for it, but there is no noun in English. The language is lacy with such inadequacies. Speak, and you hear your own wind whistling through the lacunae. In this neither-here-nor-there climatic moment, when thaw and freeze battle for hegemony of the air, what aspires to snow hangs somewhere between liquidity and quiddity. Revellers, fishtailing after the sexy bait of midnight, squoosh and slip through the same weepy, abortive, churlish stuff that blighted the land God gave to Cain.

Here and there around the city, it must be said, are untrodden Edens, landscapes that are simply like picture prints from Currier and Ives. I spent a cheerful afternoon in the anaesthetically named Mount Pleasant Cemetery, where the snow dusting the graves and markers was a shroud (what else?), unblemished save for the ungual calling-cards of a few of the city's more contemplative deer. I had come to the cemetery on the first day of my travelling not to fawn, but to pay homage to Glenn Gould. His is a complex portfolio: pianist, composer, nocturnalist, pill popper, actor, documentarist, genius, legend, dead man, academic growth industry, eccentric. As I am the well-raised son of a very good mother, I phoned ahead to check on his availability.

"Good morning, thank you for calling Mount Pleasant Cemetery."

A male voice, warm and welcoming, but mercifully not unctuous.

"Good morning. I'm calling to confirm that Glenn Gould is interred at Mount Pleasant."

"Okay. Just a second while I change screens. I'll have to get out of 'point of sale.'"

I had not before this minute taken into account how computers have altered even the reassuringly pallid complexion of the funeral business. It was not a rosy dawning. Something shifted, then withered in and around my left chest. I knew in that moment that my life would never again be quite the same. Indeed, not even my death would be as I had imagined it.

"There we go! Now, you said Gould? That would be G - O..."

His voice trailed off into orthographic uncertainty. I gave him the spelling of both family and Christian name, and also provided the year of death.

"Nineteen eighty-two," I intoned, hoping I sounded appropriately sepulchral.

The tell-tale tapping of keys. A tense, digitized silence.

"Yup!" came the merry reply, jigging over the fibre-optic filaments that lay between us. "Here he is! Section thirty-eight, lot ten-fifty."

"Thank you. Can you tell me how long it takes to get there by cab? I'll be coming from downtown."

"Golly! I wouldn't know about that. You see, I'm from Whitby."

"Ah."

What else could I say? For I have never been to Whitby. For I detected in his voice something melancholy and confessional. For I could think of no other rejoinder.

"That was swell," I tell Elly May. And it was. I've seen more than a few Bette Davis impersonations in my time, and hers surely was among the best.

"And this," she says, clamping a full nelson on my attention, "who's this?"

She gives her frosted mane — a wig which has been teased until it is on the threshhold of outrage — a haughty toss, and follows through with a vixen moue. It is not a lot to go on, but I can't bear the idea of disappointing her.

"Can I see it again?"

She sighs the sigh of the afflicted and obliges.

"Oh. Oh, golly. Uh — is it Tina?"

"Baby!" she cries and smacks her palms with glee. "Oh, baby, you are so right! Tina! And I do Billie, and Sarah, and Aretha. I do Dionne, too. Did you know I did Dionne for Dionne once? It was at the Sheraton in Hamilton. I was entertaining there, just a one-night thing, just a favour for a friend, you know. I sang 'I'll Never Love This Way Again' and 'Do You Know the Way to San José.' Oh, you know, baby, I do them all, all the Dionne songs. 'That's What Friends Are For,' of course. Anyway, after I'd gone to my dressing room, there was this knock on the door, and there was my friend and she said, 'Elly May, I've brought you a surprise.' Well, I thought it would be a little brooch, you know, maybe a few roses, something like that. But no. She steps back, and standing there is Dionne Warwick. I mean, *Di*-onne *War*-wick! And you know what she said to me? She said, 'Honey, you do me better than I do me.' And I'll tell you, the both of us standing there, it was like we were two energies becoming one. Yes. Yes. Dionne Warwick. Hey, you want a cigarette?"

I demur, tell her I've quit, pick up her pack of Export A's with its "Smoking Can Kill You" warning, and study the grim chemical analysis.

"Wow. That's a whack of tar."

"Yeah, baby, but you know I need that tar. It keeps me looking the way I do. If I didn't have that tar, I'm afraid I'd wake up some morning looking like a little white boy and we couldn't have that! Uh-uh."

She takes a long drag and looks at me closely in the dim light.

"Hey. You know what you can do for those crow's feet? Spirit gum. You just put a little spirit gum around your eyes and it'll smooth those wrinkles away. You try it. You'll see."

Elly May, one of Dame Veracity's crueller handmaidens, had a point. My complexion is not without furrows. Mind, she wasn't seeing me at my moisturized best. The drying environs of Mount Pleasant had not bestowed anything like a benefice on my epidermis. If you visit this cemetery — and one day before you die you must — you should take a moment to stop at the office and pick up one of the easy-to-follow walking-tour maps. I squinted through cold-fogged lenses and tripped a hot fandango in the doorway, coaxing the snow from my boots' deep treads. The sweet fellow from Whitby was nowhere to be found, but an equally well-disposed woman named Mary Angel — it said so on the decorative plaque on her desk — happily gave me the guide to the graves of the erstwhile worthwhile and presently absent. Over the years, Mount Pleasant has been thickly sown with establishment skeletons. Here lie politicians, military types, industrialists, kingpins of commerce: rich white guys and their wives and families, all gone to seed. Timothy Eaton, William Lyon Mackenzie King, and Sir William James Gage are here. So are the Masseys, whose Greek revival mausoleum is a real showpiece. If it were transplanted wholesale to an upscale neighbourhood like Forest Hill, or Westmount, or Shaughnessy, it would handily fetch a price in the seven figures. Such ornate memorials are rare in this tony bone drop where, by and large, a Presbyterian austerity prevails: thoughtful, timeless design for a thoughtful, timeless place. *Life may be transient, darling, but taste is forever.*

Fresh air. Bright day. I was in a perambulatory mood. I took my time finding section thirty-eight, lot ten-fifty, gladly wandering the ploughed paths that bracket the ploughed-under. The Boylens. The Conways. The Millers and the Pattersons. The Staines. I marvelled at the commendable restraint of those epitaph writers who had resisted doing something whimsical with the Paynes, the Aikens, the Youngs, the Stillmans. To say nothing of the Scores. I passed by the insulin-discovering team of Banting and Best, and the well-tamped mound of Dr. Alan G. Brown, the inventor of Pablum. I turned the hackneyed phrase "the dead of winter" over and over in my mouth, contemplating how it took on a new flavour as I skirted the tombs of the Ballards, the Breckenridges, the Boultons, the Bennetts, the Blodgetts. There were the Greens. There were the Hills, whom not even the sound of music could revive.

And so I walked among the dead for an hour or more before I steered my ramble through neighbourhoods that were largely Asian, and finally found, masked by snow and a concealing wreath, the sought-after plot. The Gould memorial is tasteful and unassuming: a simple stone with a classic border — trailing roses — surrounding the most laconic of family summations.

Gould
Florence E.
July 26, 1975
Beloved Wife Of
Russel H. Gould
November 22, 1901 – January 4, 1996
Their Dearly Loved Son
Glenn H. Gould
October 4, 1982

He may have been one of the century's great pianists, but the exigencies of filial piety prescribe that he spend eternity with bottom billing. It is a modest memorial for so extravagant a talent. There is a small marker nearby, etched with the melancholy aria from the *Goldberg Variations*. Otherwise, nothing beside remains. All that is Gould is not glitter.

It had just gone noon. The snow, though not at all deep, was reasonably crisp and absolutely even. Its tracklessness was evidence that I was the family's only hogmanay visitor. I tried, unsuccessfully, to call to mind the specifics of the Scots tradition called "first footing." Does it not bode ill to find a fair-haired man on your stoop at the turning of the year? Here was fodder for concern. Then again, for the Goulds at least, how much worse can it get? A fledgling, graveside Sitka spruce — the very wood used in piano manufacture — cast a long shadow over the hallowed ground. A crow claxoned. A hardy, omniscient songbird whistled, "I see, I see, I see," in descending minor thirds. A jogger trotted along the nearby trail. She waved. I returned her salute. A funeral party of twenty-one vehicles, seventeen of which were minivans, followed a hearse into the nether reaches of Mount Pleasant. Then everything was still. All you could hear was the ripening of the day and the slow dancing of happy shades. The crematorium across the way was quiet, its chimneys cool.

Elly May jettisons smoke into the air at a forty-five-degree angle. She coughs and says, "Hey, baby. Who told you smoking was bad for you? Huh? Who told you? That's just what everybody wants you to think. Me, I'm fifty-one and it isn't hurting me. That's because I won't let it. You got to make up your own mind about this stuff, you know? Because everyone's different. Those lines around your eyes. You know what causes them? Worry. You're worried all the time. I can see it. I'm watching your face and I can see it. You get worried and you sort of screw up your face all tense-like, and you end up with those lines. You're worried about money. Worried about work. Worried about what people might think. You're worried about smoking. Ha! Me, I'm my own person, so I just don't pay any attention to that crap. I do what I like in this world, you hear what I'm saying? It's this way with me, baby. You can call me and call me, but chances are you won't find me at home and that's because I'm going to be out doing just exactly what I like, which is having fun with my friends. I won't stop having fun till they put me in my coffin. Hell, you can come and visit me then! I'll roll over! I'll make room!"

Graveyard visiting is a particular penchant, a "never the twain shall meet" recreation. You like it or you don't. It can be a great frustration to travel with someone who is otherwise disposed in this regard. It's annoying for the one to be forever pulling over so that the other can caper through the corpse field, and just as irritating for the aficionado of the fallen to be pulled away prematurely from his pleasures by a tooting horn or the short-tempered bark of impatience. I am of the mind that it's one of those aspects of being, like blood type, for which two people should be tested before they form a serious attachment. Conversion is not a realistic prospect. Those who are ill disposed towards a cemetery tour are unresponsive to tactics of suasion. For them, it will never be transcendent, never anything more than a dull break from the road; and is possibly a symptom of a dangerous morbidity. We who like nothing better than a

cadaverous meander cite any number of reasons for our enthusiasm. Genealogical research. Historical curiosity. The challenge
of creating spontaneous fictions by filling in the blanks between
birth and death. Incipient necrophilia. Me, I embrace the point-
lessness of the enterprise. When I stroll among headstone, angel,
and virgin, it is almost never with a specific goal or soul in
mind. I am merely enjoying the business of being. If I had to isolate a purpose, I would say it is to rinse my mind clean with a
wash of names — McCleary, Woo, Seaton, Anderson, Brandt.
The faceless, anonymous dead. Their random dates. The nullity
of their requirements. Now and then I'll be struck by the way a
wreath or flower offers up the tacit proof that memory and love
are active agents in the battered world. Sometimes I might be
visited by a line from *Hamlet*, or by a glimmer of something like
perspective. But this is nothing I long for, nothing I crave; which
is all to say that visiting Mount Pleasant with the specific intention of dropping in on Glenn was an aberrant moment in the
history of my relationship with the dead.

I think it was in the worthy pages of *Reader's Digest* — with its
tales of valour at sea and good clean jokes, its subtle tips for
keeping the magic in a marriage and biographical sketches of
Joe's organs — that I first heard about Glenn Gould. I would
have been nine or ten years old at the time, just beginning to
read material that was not meant specifically for children, and
just learning that I harboured a fondness for music. I suppose
it was because I came across his story at this developmental
stage — when the world was presenting itself on a new set of
terms — that it made such an impression and stuck with me. It
was full of anecdotes attesting to Gould's many peculiarities.
Much was made of his penchant for dressing in a heavy coat
and gloves in the heat of summer, of his idiosyncrasies and rituals in the recording studio and on the concert stage. The *Digest*
detailed his unnerving need to vocalize while he played, of the
guttural baritone that rumbled beneath the melody like an improvised continuo line. I read about the long, warm baptism to

which he treated his arms and hands before every performance, and about the battered chair he always used when playing. His father had tinkered with it, sawing, filing, and nailing, altering it to his genius son's specifications so that he could enjoy an easier relationship with gravity when he was wooing the gods with his virtuoso tinkling. The writer of this article recounted one of Gould's appearances with the New York Philharmonic, a performance of Brahms' Concerto in D Minor, and how Leonard Bernstein grew ever more vexed with the young Canadian's bizarre requirements, especially the way he kept the orchestra waiting while he adjusted his seat, taking forever to settle on a physical angle of attack. "Perhaps we could slice an inch off your *derrière*, Mr. Gould," said the fretful maestro. (Or words to that effect. I remember it only because it was the occasion of my first learning the word "derrière.") There were disagreements between soloist and conductor that were even more fundamental. Gould's interpretation was so very *outré*, so entirely abstracted from the traditional and time-tested conventions of performance that, before the concert, Bernstein publicly disassociated himself with what was to follow. Nonetheless, he is reported to have said after the fact, "There's no doubt about it. That nutcase is a genius."

Standing graveside, I fired up my Walkman and listened to an interview Gould gave in 1958, three years after the release of the Columbia recording of the *Goldberg Variations* had made him a huge international star. His conversational style is fluid and tangential, fugal really, an intricate braiding of ideas, conveyed on the buoyant and nuanced voice of an aesthete. He's confident, brash, funny at times, an expert mimic. He's unpredictable, unapologetic, uncompromising in his views — which are fascinating, sometimes infuriating. It's a wonder that anyone so young can be so self-possessed, so anchored in his opinions. Sometimes, his arrogance makes you want to say, "Oh, Glenn! Blow it out your *derrière*!" He's just so damn fussy with his tight-assed litany of wills and won'ts. He plays Chopin only in weak moments. The only operas he cares to hear are those by

Mozart and Strauss. Verdi makes him squirm, Puccini makes him squiggle. He never goes to concerts unless they are given by friends and he has to attend for diplomatic reasons. The tedious social obligations of touring exhaust him, just exhaust him. And as for performing itself — well, it is a vastly overrated enterprise. Still six years away from famously turning his back on the concert hall, he is even now staking out his preference for making recordings over giving live performances. The microphone, he finds, is a benevolent presence, but an audience is troublesome, inhibiting, and applause is misleading, sometimes even vicious. In the studio, there is no one to answer to, no one to please but oneself. Already he is envisioning the day when he will be able to achieve hermitage through the sanitary distancing made possible by technology.

He is not all prickly self-absorbtion, though. He is quite endearing when he speaks of his love for Canada. London, New York, Paris: any of those cities would be available to him, but Canada is not a place he'd care to abandon. When he says he feels something like a sense of debt to his homeland, I can't help but think how uncommon it has become to hear the country spoken of with tenderness, with passion even, in a moment that isn't fuelled by crisis. He is tired, he says. The demands of being Glenn Gould have drained him. Half-jokingly, he tell his interviewer that someone of his age can hardly sustain the rigorous pace required of sought-after artists. It's a peculiar remark for someone who is just twenty-six. In the here and now, it takes on a patina of irony, for in a relative way Gould was already middle-aged. He couldn't have known it, could never have imagined dying at fifty, a cerebral hemorrhage taking him down, one last big flash from the brain, an explosion of circuits, and then he was bound for the earth.

Gould once said that Toronto was among the few cities in which he could find peace of mind. A little less than a century before his birth, the English writer and art historian Anna Brownell Jameson, who possessed an *amour propre* of at least

Gouldian proportions, was not so well pleased. When she arrived from New York around Christmas-time, 1836, she wrote, "I see nothing but snow heaped up against my windows, not only without but within; I hear no sound but the tinkling of sleigh-bells and the occasional lowing of a poor half-starved cow, that, standing up to the knees in a snow-drift, presents herself at the door of a wretched little shanty opposite, and supplicates for a small modicum of hay." Nor was the English surveyor and military man John Henry Lefroy any more impressed a few years later. Even after he spent the better part of two years doing magnetic surveys in the western and northern hinterlands, Toronto failed to tug at the iron filings of his heart. In January 1845 he wrote to his sister Isabella that the city was socially deficient. "There is so little that deserves the name of conversation, so much egregious trifling, so much which makes me ashamed of my folly if I join in it, that I seldom leave a party without some secret self-reproach....The great defect in the lady society of Toronto, especially the young lady branch of it, is the want of character. There are very few who possess any one distinguishing taste, acquirement, or characteristic. One cannot be surprised at this considering the deficiencies of the colony in subjects and schools of taste, but it reduces conversation to trifles and matters of the moment."

Anyone seeking reassurances that the lady society of Toronto has come a long way in the 150 years since these two early travellers set down their impressions would need only spend New Year's Eve with Elly May and company at Pimblett's. This Cabbagetown restaurant and bar has the genial, slightly down-at-the-heels, flocked-wallpaper look of a cluttered Victorian bordello. It is chock-a-block with taxidermy: stag heads, tick-filled ducks, and mounted fish. There is a dusty Canada goose whose wings are spread in a sad posture of flight, and the goose forges a curious link between Elly May and Messy May. Messy May was a Vancouver drag queen. She reigned in days of yore. She is said to have invited friends for Christmas dinner and neglected to procure the requisite fowl. Messy May was unfazed. Resourceful to the nth degree, she simply doffed her heels, slipped on a pair of serviceable flats, and hustled her way along Robson Street to Stanley Park. There, any number of geese were floating about on Lost Lagoon. She surveyed the possibilities. She selected a bird that would look better on a platter than it did on the pond. Somehow, she dispatched it. Don't ask me how. The story is hazy on this point. Messy May trotted home with her prize under her arm. She plucked it as she went, scattering the feathers behind her. The police, alerted to the felony, simply followed the trail of discarded plumage. Not for nothing was she called "Messy."

At Pimblett's, a couple of cats, self-contained and still animate, wander from table to table, heedless of city by-laws. No one seems to mind. Everywhere you turn there are pictures of monarchs, past and present. One wall is hung with paintings of bathers, very Aubrey Beardsley. There are a couple of magnificent chandeliers, some imposing fireplace surrounds and mantels, a suit of armour, odds and ends of statuary, and *tchotchkes* too plentiful to name. The furnishings, the dishes and flatware, all the various trappings have a look of proud salvage. Much the same can be said for the clientele. Pimblett's patrons are an eclectic bunch. It's a popular gathering spot for monarchists, for transvestites, for transsexuals, for gay and straight Torontonians alike. Elly May is here to strut her stuff as one of three performers in the prelude to the midnight drag show that is a Pimblett's New Year's Eve tradition of long standing. She has changed costume five or six times now, first shedding her fur and black vinyl for a sequinned sheath, then for a skimpy little lamé number. She watches with some disdain while one of her colleagues varnishes her nails. "Oh her," she says, *sotto voce*, though perhaps not quite as *sotto voce* as absolute discretion might require, "she thinks she looks like Anne Murray. Does she look like Anne Murray to you? Ha! I don't think so!"

Well. Maybe Anne Murray on a bad day. Maybe Anne Murray after a lengthy bout with Asian flu. But so what? Put her on the stage and crank up "Snow Bird" or "Danny's Song," and disbelief will quickly settle into a state of blessed suspension. No one would dispute that Geoffrey Pimblett, the cheerful, eponymous owner of the joint, looks remarkably like the Queen. He has togged himself up in a gown and a sash and a tiara — one of several regal headpieces he has crafted out of soup tins and a prismatic array of costume jewellery. The queen get-up is one he likes to trot out on festive occasions and high holy days such as this. He often sports it for gay pride parades, or for special events staged by the Cabbagetown merchants' association. Tonight, his regalia is rather more slapdash than he would like. He has lingered too long in the kitchen, dishing up huge servings of roast beef, Yorkshire pudding, and trifle. Between times, he has been nipping over to the computer to make last-minute amendments to his New Year's speech. "Come on, old queen, move along," he mutters while navigating through his many tasks, and while hurrying to change. He is unable to locate a pair of matching gloves, and has to discard his falsies as they make the zipping of his frock impossible. Even so, he looks very much the part. He has no need of a wig as his own slate-coloured and very full head of hair is a fine approximation of the bob we see pictured on so many stamps and coins.

Elly May and company rise up on their spikes and teeter downstairs to the bar to do their show, while Geoffrey, alias Betty Windsor, takes the stage in the upper room that is the restaurant proper. There is prolonged applause when the queen mounts her dais. She crooks her arm and acknowledges her people with an understated wave. She adjusts her tiara and launches into her address. Something is awry with the queen's sound system. Everyone cranes forward, straining to hear. These are words worth hanging on, her insights, her benisons. Her lips move, but all we hear is Marilyn Monroe coming through the floorboards from the bar below. She is singing "Diamonds Are a Girl's Best Friend." The queen adjusts her paste diadem and takes it all in stride. She is too noble and well practised to let a little gaffe like this hang her up. Appearance counts for everything. Resilience is all. She soldiers on, not appearing to mind that she has lost her audience, that they have returned to attacking their trifle and to gossiping among themselves. Outside, it is snowing like blazes.

Glenn Gould tolerated Toronto well enough, but he loved the country north of the city, around Lake Simcoe. He loved it especially in the winter, when the trees were stripped down and careless of their secrets; when the cottagers were absent and the icy stillness in the air made the place seem all the more remote. In winter, at Lake Simcoe, it was the heated *froideur* of the music of Sibelius that spoke to him most ringingly. I would be hard-pressed to think of something more crystalline and lovely than Gould's performance of the andantino from Sibelius' Sonatine in E Major. It is heart-centred music, full of longing, moving beyond telling. If you listen to his recording, you will hear how he inhabits not just every note, but every space between every note. You can't help but believe that, in the moment of its playing, the whole structure of the piece, all its gentle mathematics, was as necessary to him as oxygen.

You would think better of me, I'm sure, if I could tell you it was the andantino, or even *Finlandia*, I thought to hum by way of tribute as I left his grave on this winter afternoon, on this last day of the year, with the clockwork Earth already rocketing closer to the sun. But the song that came to my mind and mouth was one made famous by a singer for whom Gould had a certain wry and surprising fondness, Petula Clark. I looked around to make sure I was alone and unobserved. I sang "Downtown," badly, but with all the feeling I could muster:

Just listen to the music of the traffic in the city
Linger on the sidewalk where the neon signs are pretty,
How can you lose?

The words thudded among the markers, sterile seeds on stony ground. My breath was the colour of a ghost. I clapped my hands together when I was done, thinking just to warm them, but the addled whacking rang out like the saddest applause the world has ever heard. It was time to say goodbye. It was getting late. Elly May, whom I had yet to meet, was studying her wardrobe, making hard and necessary choices. She was saying to herself, "Oh, baby, how can you lose?" while her closet shimmered and the day turned grey. Soon, she would settle on her vinyl miniskirt, wrap herself in her fur, kiss her mother goodbye. "Don't be late, son," the old lady would say. And Elly May would answer, "Don't be late yourself." She'd angle her wide-brimmed hat and pull it down low, give herself a final once-over in the mirror, bat her lovely lashes approvingly, and step out into the deepening dark, the deepening snow. Soon, all the city's neon would come into its own. As would Elly May. The night would grow heavy with possibility. And downtown was where it would happen. And downtown was where she needed to go.

Before We Go Further,
a Parenthetical Word

Pride and self-disgust served her
like first-aid surgeons on the battlefield.
— Grenville Kleiser, *Fifteen Thousand Useful Phrases*

I admit I have my hypocrisies. I can't deny that I maintain a running subscription to certain double standards. That I see these lapses for what they are, and acknowledge them, mitigates nothing. Such detached and self-critical lucidity gets me nowhere. I consider my imperfections. I know the sticky welling of remorse. Then, I continue on my merry, duplicitous way. I risk compounding the interest on whatever disdain this deficiency earns me by revealing that I am also godless. Perhaps it would be more precise to say I don't seek the sponsorship or intervention of a god who is affiliated with one of the major fraternities. I've been that way for years now. In fact, the one behavioural arena in which I stand resolute and steadfast, where hypocrisy is forbidden to enter, is my refusal to attend church, other than to put in an appearance at occasions that are largely social: weddings, funerals, concerts, fowl suppers, white elephant sales, and so on.

I am especially committed to this staunch and Calvinistically dour principle of non-attendance on high holy days. On those occasions I actually have to make a study of avoiding the place. For reasons of personal history, and because I like a crowd, and because I know all the verses to "O Come, All Ye Faithful," even the one about "Lo, he abhors not the Virgin's womb," I can count on feeling the strong tug of churchiness on Christmas Eve. I resist giving in to it. I can't bear the idea of being one of those fair-weather Christians who turns up when the living is easy. I figure that if I am not able to find my way clear to accepting some of the basic tenets of Christian belief, and I am not; if I can't carry the salvationist teachings of the faith in my heart on a day-by-day basis, and I can't; then I hardly deserve the pew space I'd usurp by putting in an appearance just when everything is so campy and garish and sodden with ceremony that it actually verges on being fun. A ritual is a ritual. It deserves respect in and of itself. You dishonour it if you take part with anything less than full and unqualified intent, and to do so wreaks havoc on the old karma. If it has no more meaning for you, has no more impact on your being and thinking than, say, yet another viewing of *It's a Wonderful Life*, then what's the point?

I suppose it's been ten years since I last did the Christmas Eve thing. I went with friends to an Anglican cathedral where all the observances are quite high church. I sat in the balcony and watched it unfold from above. I remember how, at the beginning, the choir and the celebrants and the sub-celebrants and associate sub-celebrants proceeded up the aisle, engulfed by the effulgent from the swinging censers, their progress measured by a heartfelt bellowing of "Joy to the World." Among them was a man I knew, a queen of high degree, who was also a very respectable high-school English teacher. He was in his glory. He had been given what I imagined to be a plum assignment, which was to carry the crucifix. He held it high before him, with the same expression on his puss that I had seen a few weeks earlier when I had been to his house for dinner. He had come to the table from the kitchen with a dessert soufflé that had risen so beautifully it had the look of a sacred relic. On Christmas Eve, as then, his pace was grave and stately, and with his long robes, white and red, hiding his footwork, he seemed almost to float, as though on water, towards his rendezvous with the Father, the Son, and the Holy Ghost. (Come to think of it, in candid moments he had often professed a fondness for threesomes.)

Now, this was a man who managed to be both prim and craggy at the same time. He was regimental in his bearing, and possessed a steely-eyed regard and stiff-upper-lip demeanour that has rarely been seen since the days of the Raj. In a personal ad he would describe himself as "straight-looking, straight-acting," and for all his fastidious prissiness, he was. He professed an aversion to displays of effeminacy, and wouldn't on a bet have donned such gay apparel as a slinky sheath festooned with sequins and bugle beads. However, studying him from above, noting how carefully he had arranged his hair to hide the beginnings of male-pattern baldness, I felt I understood the deeper reason he took so active a role in this pageantry, rather than contenting himself with the sidelines, and the status of believing observer. I felt sure that I was witnessing an act of sartorial sublimation. Some deep-seated urge to disport himself in garments with such beautiful names as camisole, negligée, peignoir, or in a gown of taffeta or of lace worked in colonnades and gussied up with flounces or in peau-de-soie, was satisfied by this wonderfully pompous display of chasuble, surplice, and cassock. Were he drawn to the Church for reasons of faith alone, straightforward attendance and adherence to rules and regulations would have scratched his religious itch. But no. He wanted a more visible and theatrical role. He wanted the assistance and complicity of the costume department. More than anything else, he wanted to swaddle himself in bright ecclesiastical drag and go for an after-dinner mince at midnight mass. And here he was, fully engaged. Oh, his countenance might have been a study in devotion, but I knew very well there was a smirk of delight bubbling not far below his sneer of cold command. He was working hard to keep it from breaking through and shattering his marmoreal visage. And why should he not be delighted? He was doing what he'd always craved. He was wearing a dress in public, and getting away with it, too. Not only that, his swishing was sanctified by the highest authority, by God himself. It was definitely a case of whirl without end, amen. I was seized by one of those uncontrollable fits that usually come over me at funerals when the kitsch of mourning becomes too much to bear. I had to make a great show of coughing into the Book of Common Prayer, in order to suppress my laughter.

I'm sorry I've burdened you with this. I've told you things that will make you think the less of me. But we are going to go on a long trip together, and you might as well know I am evil, evil, evil. Evil right to the core.

Not evil exactly, but certainly suspect, was Esther Brandeau, who got herself into hot water by preferring trousers to frocks and who declined to affiliate herself with the Church. Esther is popularly said to be the first Jew to arrive in Canada. She also bears the weight of being one of our first recorded cross-dressers. She was a pioneer of gender-role subversion. An early confounder of conventions of costume, Esther paved the way for the likes of Elly May, as well as for Sarah Emma Edmonds, who was born in New Brunswick in 1841. Sarah dressed as a boy from early childhood, and when she left home to take up work as an itinerant Bible seller, it was as Franklin Thompson that she went door to door. Franklin was also her *nom de guerre* when she enlisted as a private with Company F, 2nd Michigan Infantry, during the American Civil War. She served with distinction, survived the conflict, went on to marry and to raise three children, moved to Texas, and eventually revealed the truth of her soldier-boy identity. She was awarded, by a special act of Congress, a civil war pension, and was the only woman ever to receive one.

Esther was not so well compensated. When she put into the port of Quebec in September 1738, on board the ship *St. Michel*, she was dressed as a man, a boy really, and had successfully passed herself off as "Jacques La Fargue." Exactly how the ruse was discovered — a wrestling match, a bunk-room glimpse, an unwarranted interest on the part of Jacques in feminine hygiene products — I can't say. What is sure is that Esther, when her

true identity was revealed, was hauled before the local administration, and that a prolonged tizzy ensued.

And no wonder. Everything about her was wrong, plain
wrong. Everything about her was unsettling. For one thing,
there was her religion. Jews were forbidden by decree to set foot
in the colony. And then there was the question of her inappropriate choice of wardrobe. A proper woman of the day might
have come down the gangplank dressed modestly and practically in a sacque dress, apron, petticoat, and mob cap. She
might have accessorized the ensemble with a neat little fichu,
delicately knotted at the neck. But no, not Esther, who was presented to the intendant, Hocquart, and the naval secretary,
Varin, clothed in standard eighteenth-century mariners' duds:
the all-purpose linen trousers known as "slops," a jacket, a
waistcoat, a body shirt, a leather hat, and shoes with wide
silver buckles. They peppered her with *pourquois*, and the story
she had to tell about her life as a boy was a regular pageant
of misrepresentation.

To everything there is a beginning. Diane Tye, who teaches
in the Folklore Department at Memorial University in St. John's,
Newfoundland, wrote her dissertation about "local characters"
in her own home town of Amherst, Nova Scotia. In her data
gathering, she noted the way her informants would isolate a
specific event, often a mishap or trauma, and identify it as the
trigger or fuse that detonated some neighbour's quirk or eccentricity. So-and-so was perfectly "normal" until such-and-such
happened. Until he was gassed in the trenches. Until her fiancé
stood her up on their wedding day. Until the barbecue was
struck by lightning. And so on. Dr. Tye observed that finding
such a hook on which to hang a peculiarity provides a comfort,
of a sort. Not only does it offer an explanation as to the under-
lying reasons behind perceived aberrance, it also reinforces the
sense of inclusivity within community. We acknowledge that
someone has veered from the well-furrowed path. We seek to
know why. We find a way to accommodate the unusual behaviour that is theirs by virtue of some external intervention, either

deliberate malevolence or accidental mishap. And we receive the tacit assurance that we, too, will be taken care of, should we be gassed, dumped, or struck by a bolt from the blue, and find ourselves derailed as a consequence. In the case of Esther, the agents of change appear to have been a shipwreck and a ham sandwich. Here is the substance of her story, contained in a document signed by Varin, "Commissaire de la Marine," and dated September 15, 1738.

"This day…appeared Esther Brandeau, aged about twenty years, who embarked at La Rochelle as a passenger dressed in boy's clothes, under the name of Jacques La Fargue, on the vessel *St. Michel*, Sieur de Salaberry commander, and declared her name to be Esther Brandeau, daughter of David Brandeau, a Jew, trader, of St. Esprit, diocese of Daxe, near Bayonne, and that she is of the Jewish religion; that five years ago her father and mother placed her on a Dutch vessel, *Captain Geoffroy*, in order to send her to Amsterdam, to one of her aunts and to her brother; that the vessel having been lost on the bar of Bayonne, in the moon of April or May, 1733, she was happily brought safe to shore with one of the crew; that she was received by Catherine Churiau, a widow living at Biaris; that two weeks thereafter she started, dressed as a man, for Bordeaux, where she shipped as a boy, under the name of Pierre Alansiette, on a vessel commanded by Captain Bernard, destined for Nantes, that she returned on the same vessel to Bordeaux, and there shipped again in the same capacity on a Spanish vessel, *Captain Antonio*, for Nantes; that on reaching Nantes, she deserted and went to Rennes, where she took service as a boy at the house of one Augustin, a tailor, where she remained six months; that from Rennes she went to Clissoy, where she took service with Récollets as a servant and to run messages; that she remained three months in the convent and left without warning for St. Malo, where she found shelter at the house of a baker named Seruanne; that she next went to Vitré to get a place there and entered the service of Sr. de la Chapelle, an ex–captain of the infantry; that she left the situation because her health rendered her unable to watch the said Sr. de la Chapelle, who was always sick; that when returning to Nantes, and when one league from Noisel, she was taken for a thief and confined in the prison of Noisel aforesaid; that she was set free, after twenty-four hours, because it was found that a mistake had been made; that she then went to La Rochelle, where assuming the name of Jacques La Fargue, she took ship as a passenger on the said vessel, *St. Michel*.

"Upon which declaration we called upon the said Esther Brandeau to state for what reason she had so concealed her sex during five years. Whereupon she said: That when she escaped from shipwreck and reached Bayonne, she entered the house of Catherine Churiau, as above stated; that the latter made her eat pork and other meats the use whereof is forbidden among the Jews, and that she thereupon resolved not to return to her father and mother in order that she might enjoy the same liberty as the Christians."

In all my days, I have never once tried to conjure the forbidden flavour of liberty, but I can't imagine that it would ever register on my tastebuds as bacon. Why would it? Mine was a WASPy, Sunday-joint kind of upbringing and I was never estranged from the delights of pig flesh. Still, I wonder if Esther might not have been teasing her tribunal with her "give me pork chops or give me death" story, might not have been prevaricating, just a little. Surely the greater freedom was to be found in cutting herself loose from the shackles of girlhood, concealing her sex to safeguard herself against interference and tampering, and then taking to the road. A few months here, a few months there, another name, another situation, no ties to bind her, no fixed address. The allure, especially to a young person with a bent for adventure, could not have been so very different in the eighteenth century from today.

Perhaps by the time Esther reached Quebec, she had decided that the advantages of a Christian life didn't outweigh the dreary prospect of blistering her fingers on a rosary. In spite of her professed desire to enjoy the same freedoms as were accorded trinitarians who didn't give a hoot what they ate, Esther resisted the idea of conversion. She stayed in the colony a year, yawning at the priests who tried to instruct her, and generally proving herself a thorn in the hides of the governors, who didn't know what to do with her. She was lodged with nuns, she was put up in private homes, she was surrounded by the day-to-day rituals and trappings of Catholic devotion, but she resolutely refused to take the plunge. Her résumé, as cited above, suggests that she might have had difficulty applying herself to employment for any length of time. Hocquart and his cronies found her fickle and flighty, for sure, and finally they just gave up and packed her back across the Atlantic on *Le Comte de Matignon*. There is no record of what she wore as a going-away ensemble. No one can say what she did or became. France absorbed her. We can be confident, I think, that somehow she got by. If nothing else, she had learned the importance of keeping her options open. She hadn't spent all that time shipboard without learning something about navigating her way through the trickier shoals, and the older she got, the more confident she became that the tired old restrictions didn't apply in her case. There was nothing she couldn't do.

"Tell me," asked the boy, looking up from his Torah studies, "why you have never grown a beard like the other rabbis?"

"For the same reason Moses never grew wings. God gives to each of us only as much as we require. And not a whisker more. Now hush."

And the child went back to his scroll, well satisfied. He didn't care what the others said, wouldn't heed their suspicious whisperings, or believe for even a second those stories about covert cutlet gobbling. This was a holy man, and as far as he was concerned, no one could ever be as good and as wise as Reb Brandeau.

Begin

As men strip for a race,
so must an author strip for the race with time.
— Grenville Kleiser, *Fifteen Thousand Useful Phrases*

Imagine yourself stretched supine in a wintery field. This is Frostian snow, man. What words best describe it? Deep. Lovely. Dark. Though not necessarily in that order. You have given in to the childish impulse to make an angel, and now you lie quietly, bisecting a seraph of your own sculpting, hardening your hearing to the siren cries of cryogenics. You study the sky, study the indolent vapouring of two clouds through the blue and recumbent air. Within the grey striations of one cumulus puff you can make out the word ECCENTRIC. In the other, you are sure you can discern the comforting label CANADIAN. Slowly, slowly, they drift together. Each cloud absorbs the woolly mass of the other. There is a low rumble, a suspenseful pause, and then a gentle tumbling-down of names. When first I lay on my back and saw those clouds collide, Glenn Gould's was the second name to fall to earth. Chas. S. Robertson came first. I never met Chas. S. Robertson, never met any of his family. I have only the most circumstantial of evidence that once upon a time — round about sixty years ago — he lived in Kenabeek, Ontario. His is the name and that is the town stamped on the inside cover of a book which is now mine, a flea-market find. The book, *Fifteen Thousand Useful Phrases*, was written in 1917 by Grenville Kleiser. What a glorious moniker to trail! Grenville Kleiser! He was, according to the information on the jacket, the author of a great many texts which must have been intended mostly for elocutionists, or other *belles-lettres* dabblers. I mean such books as *Similes and Their Use*, *How to Read and Declaim*, *How to Argue and Win*, and *Humorous Hits and How to Hold an Audience*. I have not seen these fruits of his labour, but I'd bet none is as stirring, as juicy, as the book which is a bond between me and Chas. S. Robertson. *Fifteen Thousand Useful Phrases: A Practical Handbook of Pertinent Expressions, Striking Similes, Literary, Commercial, Conversational, and Oratorical Terms, for the Embellishment of Speech and Literature, and the Improvement of the Vocabulary of Those Persons Who Read, Write, and Speak English*. Fifteen thousand! An outlandish claim, but true! Not, understand, that I have taken the time or trouble to count and verify. What? Grenville Kleiser beef up the stats? I think not! Anyone called Grenville Kleiser deserves to be trusted, deeply, unconditionally, and always. Just imagine the work of it — Herculean! — assembling 15,000 phrases, all of equal utility; phrases that the happy reader can use to liven up business talk. Day-to-day talk. Literary talk. And so on.

A drowsy murmur floats into the air like thistledown.

Languid streams that cross softly, slowly, with a sound like smothered weeping.

Theories sprouted in his mind like mushrooms.

She flounders like a huge conger-eel in an ocean of dingy morality.

Each is a gem! And there are 14,996 more just like them!

Chas., who had the book before me, marked the phrases he found most useful. The pages are dense with his check marks and underlinings. Here and there he added a date. I wish I could have seen him on May 7, 1932, waiting on tenterhooks for his chance to insinuate *quaking and quivering like a short-haired puppy after a ducking* into any old conversation. Only a month before, he had amazed those around him by referring to *buried hopes rising from their sepulcher*. Over the course of 1933, he was able to embrace such circumlocutions as *into the purple sea the orange hues of heaven sunk silently* and *jealousies and animosities which pricked their sluggish blood to tingling*. But it was on July 8, 1934, that poor Chas. experienced his Grenville Kleiser–inspired apotheosis. It was on that day that Chas. let a simile be his umbrella. Or so it would seem. Dozens of phrases in the book are marked with that date. What was it that pushed him over the margins of the merely reasonable? What dark angel possessed his throat? By my reckoning — which, in the absence of contemporary accounts, I base on his annotations — he must have said:

> *Dear as remembered kisses after death, hers the loveliness of some tall white lily cut in marble, splendid, but chill. Her hair dropped on her pallid cheeks like sea-weed on a clam. Like Death, who rides upon a thought, and makes his way through temple, tower and palace; or, like a caged lion shaking the bars of his prison, shadowy faces, known in dream, pass as petals upon a stream. Bronze-green beetles tumbled over stones, and lay helpless on their backs with the air of an elderly clergy-man knocked down by an omnibus. Thy brown benignant eyes have sudden gleams of gladness and surprise, like woodland brooks that cross a sunlit spot. My love for thee is like the sovereign moon that rules the sea. The days have trampled me like armed men. Thou must wither, like a rose. This life is like a bubble blown up in the air. Your tongue is like a scarlet snake. Like two doves —*

July 8, 1934. It must have been quite a day in the life of Chas. S. Robertson, late of Kenabeek, Ontario, for it is the last date entered in *Fifteen Thousand Useful Phrases*. I can just see how Chas. spat them all out at once at the church picnic, stopping the box-lunch auction and the three-legged race, stopping everyone in his tracks, stopping them with his fragrant vomiting. And then he would have dropped his lemonade and just expired from the beauty of it all.

They didn't bother to hold an inquiry into his dramatic demise. It was obvious to everyone that plain old ecstasy did him in. Life was cheap back then, up there, and no one much saw the point in asking a lot of damn-fool questions when all was as clear as clear could be. They knew what to do. They closed his eyes. There was no need to soften his mask by curling his mouth into a smile. In fact, his last expression was one of such delighted goofiness that they had to rearrange his features so he looked more decorous, more appreciative of the gravity of the moment. They carried him home, dressed him in his one decent suit, and laid him out in his parlour. Word spread. Neighbours dropped by to pay their respects. It was generally agreed that he looked at peace. Several even remarked how the strawberry spot on his left cheek was less angry in death, which wasn't surprising since Chas. had tended towards the florid in life. Some of the ladies brought over pies and casseroles and jellied salads. It was a demonstration more of custom than of charity; there was no one so grief-stricken as to wring comfort from eating to excess. Chas. lived alone. He had not been in the habit of having people round, had not encouraged visitors. Hardly any of the mourners could think of when they'd last been invited to his place. A simple house. Neat. They were glad to see he'd kept it up, that he hadn't let things slide since his wife up and left with that Bible salesman all those years ago. No one knew how to track her down, and they wouldn't have thought it appropriate to contact her even if they did. She'd always had a wild way about her. Some recollected that he had a sister, but she had moved to California and had come to a bad end. Some thought she might even have been divorced. Poor Chas.! He'd had bad luck with women, that's all there was to it. His life had been touched by sadness. Still, it was a tidy death, as deaths go.

Fifteen Thousand Useful Phrases was on the kitchen table where last he left it, held open by the butter dish. Someone leaned over and read aloud the whole of the phrase Chas. had marked but had not managed to fully utter, his last amen, the interrupted coda of his glorious incantation. *Like two doves with silvery wings, let our souls fly.*

"You know," said Joseph Flanagan, who was Chas.'s nearest neighbour, "he was straight as an arrow till he got hold of that book."

"Till it got hold of him, you mean." That was Ethel Parker who had as much right to say so as anyone, since she had made a point of inviting Chas. over for Christmas and Easter dinners until her own husband had died, after which it wouldn't have been seemly. She picked up the book, opened it randomly, and read out one of the marked similes.

Rage, rage ye tears, that never more should creep like hounds about God's footstool.

A sour pill, that one. Ethel pursed her lips and handed it over to Joseph, who also read aloud.

Me on whose heart as a worm she trod.

And passed it on. One by one, the good folk of Kenabeek located a phrase Chas. had found useful. One by one, they spoke his eulogy.

Silence now is brooding like a gentle spirit o'er the still and pulseless world.

Her heart has grown icy as a fountain in fall.

Sorrowful eyes like those of a wearied kine spent from plowing.

The dead past flew away over the fens like a flight of wild swans.

Suddenly snuffed out in the middle of ambitious schemes.

All my life broke up, like some great river's ice at touch of spring.

He snatched furiously at breath like a tiger snatching at meat.

Life had been arrested, as the horologist, with interjected finger, arrests the beating of the clock.

They did not, when they were through, feel they knew him any better. His life had been a puzzle. When all was said and done — and now it was — there wasn't much to be gained from piecing it together. They buried Chas. on Sunday, and before the week was done they had cleared out his house. There was not much worth keeping. The remnants of his wife's wardrobe — curiously, he'd held onto a few of her things — and some of his more colourful shirts were earmarked for the quilting circle. His chipped butter dish, his several plates and shaving mug, and his few books went for jumble. *Fifteen Thousand Useful Phrases* was purchased at a church sale just before Thanksgiving by someone's city cousin, an English teacher who happened to be visiting and wasn't acquainted with its sad history. She thought it might have some utility in the classroom. For a while, it did. Then, it travelled. It must have had many owners in the interim between then and now, but it will never have another during my lifetime. I number it among my treasures. I will never let it go. As near as I know, it is the only memorial to Chas., one of this country's great, if little-celebrated, oddballs.

When I began confiding to friends, acquaintances, and colleagues that I planned to investigate and write about the lives of some Canadian eccentrics, a disconcerting number of them arched speculative brows and asked, "Are there any?" That they had never heard of Chas. S. Robertson or Grenville Kleiser was neither astonishing nor disappointing. These gentlemen are my personal heroes. For me, they *are as amusing as a litter of likely young pigs.* Although I believe they merit wider attention than they have received, I accommodate the sad and present certainty that they are long since *gone like a glow on the cloud at the close of day* and are pivotal to no one's mythology but my own. However, it surprised and rather pained me to have my project and its broader possibilities so summarily dismissed, *as ruthlessly as the hoof of a horse tramples on a rose* by chums who are, in the main, *fresh and unworn as the sea that breaks languidly beside them.* I read in my friends' supercilious rebukes the subtext that I was setting out on a fool's errand; that the concepts "Canadian" and "eccentric" were wholly foreign to each other and would find no point of intersection. I stress that these initial consultants were not dolts. They were — they are — good people, *as delightful to the mind as cool well-water to*

thirsty lips. They are responsible people, vigilant citizens, conscientious taxpayers, bearers of degrees from accredited post-
secondary institutions, holders of enormous mortgages taken
on for five-year spans at reasonable rates. They are people with
mutual funds, people who flock to seminars on how best to
squirrel away their hard-earned moolah for their retirements,
which they plan to begin in their mid-fifties. They are dedicated
consumers of culture. Oh hell, they are middle-aged, slightly
jaded, somewhat educated, faintly agnostic, mostly pink-skinned
city dwellers. They are people of my own tribe and they had
disappointed me. For them, the phrase "Canadian eccentric"
was oxymoronic, an exemplum of mutual exclusivity, *as un-
approachable as a star.* It was strange, depressing even, to see
implicit in this flippancy the way they subscribed to the frayed
old notion that Canadians have a genetic propensity to eschew
individualism, that we aspire as a nation only to a passive uni-
formity, that we trail clouds of blandness behind us where'er we
walk, that we are a self-effacing folk: mildly humorous, peace-
keeping, maple-tapping, syrup-sucking, snow-fort–building rus-
tics. Meek? Sure! Proud to be! But we'll have our reward, by
cracky! It'll take a team of apocalyptic horses to keep us from
inheriting the Kingdom of Heaven, bucko, just you wait and see!

"Are there any?" I would echo the doubters, feeling in the
moment *companionless as the last cloud of an expiring storm
whose thunder is its knell.* "Well, what about Glenn Gould?"

"Oh. Yes. Well. Him. I suppose Gould, yes. And Mackenzie
King. He was quite odd, wasn't he? Something to do with spir-
itualism, or his dog, or his mother, or Hitler. What was it? Did
his mother have an affair with Hitler? Did *he?* And then there
was Emily Carr. She kept that monkey. Gould, King, Carr. Who
else? Well, there's always my uncle. He's a real case. He spends
every weekend going to lawn sales, looking for back issues of
Majesty magazine. He never buys anything else. His basement
is stacked, floor to ceiling, with *Majesty* magazine. He also likes
to speak in rhyming couplets. Of course, he was born in England. That's the place to find eccentrics!"

That England holds a world monopoly on eccentricity was another refrain I often heard sung as I began to make my discreet domestic inquiries, *like a moral lighthouse in the midst of a dark and troubled sea*. I would not for one second think of drawing bead on the tenet that the old sod (an endearment to which I myself aspire) has proved itself, over the last thousand years or so, a rich loam for the cultivation of human curiosities. I doubt that any social precipitate other than one that has oozed up over the centuries in Britain could have produced such outstanding examples of eccentricity as those catalogued by Edith Sitwell in her aptly odd (and aptly titled) book, *English Eccentrics: A Gallery of Weird and Wonderful Men and Women*. To read her florid prose is rather like coming home to discover that one's favourite old auntie has mistakenly eaten a whole plateful of hash brownies and is free-associating all over the attic. Cutting a wide swath through a rich trove of sources — dispensing, by and large, with the tedious convention of acknowledging them — Dame Edith tells the story of Mr. Jemmy Hirst, a tanner who went hunting on a bull, with pigs instead of hounds, and who kept his coffin in his dining room and whose eventual funeral procession was attended by pipers and fiddlers. Their music sustained the exertions of the eight stout widows who bore the pall. Widows were engaged in this labour only because eight willing old maids could not be found. It was old maids he'd hoped to employ. She recounts dozens of other remarkable lives, including that of Lord Duffus, who was spirited away by fairies and found himself in the wine cellar of the King of France; and the reprobate Squire John (Mad Jack) Mytton, who liked to go duck hunting in the nude, and who set his nightshirt on fire to cure himself of hiccups.

So much weirdness has flourished in England's green and pleasant land that it sets a standard which is hard to match, let alone beat. What tales can Canadians trot out that will not pale to invisibility when held up against such flamboyant exploits detailed by Dame Edith? More *outré* still is the cast assembled by Henry Wilson and James Caulfield in a sadly neglected Victorian tract called *The Book of Wonderful Characters: Memoirs and Anecdotes of Remarkable and Eccentric Persons in All Ages and Countries*. What does Glenn Gould with his summertime over-coat and agitated humming have to say to Francis Battalia the stone-eater, or to Joseph Capper the enemy of flies? What are Emily Carr's spiny strangenesses compared with those of Eve Fleigen, who lived on the smell of flowers? And can Mackenzie King, who merely talked to the dead, so much as hold a flick-ering candle to Charles Domery, the remarkable glutton?

Domery was a Pole by birth and a soldier by profession. He fought for the French, was captured by the English after one of those overwrought Napoleonic confrontations, and brought as a POW to Liverpool. His dietary insatiability attracted the attention of his captors, and little wonder. His appetites were legendary. As an enlisted man, he would supplement his camp rations with whatever he could find that was remotely edible. He would graze on four or five pounds of grass every day. In one year, he is reported to have stuffed himself with 174 cats (skinned). His face was badly scratched, as he did not always scruple to kill them before ingesting them. He ate rats. He dined on dogs. He was observed, after the pitched battle that brought about his ship's surrender to the English, to pick up another man's leg — it was not attached, as it had been shot off — and to gnaw on it contentedly until it was snatched away by a sailor of more refined sensibility, who chucked the offal over-board. It was nothing to Domery to wolf down, in a single sit-ting, a bullock's liver, three pounds of candles, and a few pounds of beef.

Curious to see just how much grub this ravenous prisoner could put away without doing himself harm, a committee from the English Admiralty — made up, we must suppose, largely of men with too much time on their hands and unfettered access to the larder — conducted an experiment. On September 17, 1799, at 4 a.m., Domery was awakened and allowed to chow down on four pounds of raw cow's udder. At the more respect-able hour of 9.30 a.m., a small consortium of doctors and captains assembled and watched their prisoner go at breakfast in earnest.

"There was set before him five pounds of raw beef, and twelve tallow candles of a pound weight, and one bottle of porter; these he finished by half-past ten o'clock. At one o'clock there was again put before him five pounds of beef and one pound of candles, with three bottles of porter; at which time he was locked up in the room, and sentries placed at the windows to prevent his throwing away any of his provisions. At two o'clock he had nearly finished the whole of the candles, and a great part of the beef, but had neither evacuation by vomiting, stool, or urine; his skin was cool, and pulse regular, and [he was] in good spirits."

Glenn Gould, for his part, ate a moderate, low-fat diet.

"Aha!" my considerate detractors would cry, assailing me with *windy speech which hits all around the mark like a drunken carpenter.* "Our point exactly! We rest our case! Devotion to tofu is admirable, but not nearly so tasty a lure as a slab of raw bullock's liver. And while we're scattering nails in your path, let's ask another troublesome but necessary question. What do you mean by 'eccentric,' anyway? To define 'eccentric' don't you need to define 'normalcy'? Surely that puts you in the express lane to peril."

The words of the wise fall like the tolling of sweet, grave bells upon the soul. What could I do but shrug and let them fall? I had already made up my mind to proceed. In my heart of hearts, I never doubted for a second that all I had to do to drag up instances of eccentric people and places in Canada was to cast a wide-enough net. I was as confident as Christ at Tiberias that it would come back teeming. If there is one thing I've learned over the years I have spent listening to, and now and again working for, the radio services of our public broadcaster, the CBC, it is that the numbing onslaught of information, the noisy parade of news and commentary to which we are daily subjected, has not dulled our need to flesh out the verb "to be."

We are a people — or at least there are numbers of people among us — who like to take stock of our lives, to wrap them up and give them away as stories. There is still a hunger for narrative in the land, and all the anecdotal evidence presented to me over the years suggests we are as fond of receiving such gifts as we are of giving them. I have sometimes been in the happy and privileged position of having a pulpit from which to encourage such an exchange. Demonstrate an interest in the real and everyday lives of real and everyday people, and demonstrate that you will honour their lives simply by taking them seriously, and the stories will come, *fluent as a rill that wanders silver-footed down a hill.* I have learned enough about the imperative of narrative to know, or to be able to predict with some accuracy, that if you open yourself up to hearing the stories we like best to tell — the stories about the people in our families or neighbourhoods who distinguish themselves by their peculiarities, who perplex and delight us because they are so different from us — then willing tellers of tales will present themselves, and in numbers *impressive as a warrant of arrest for high treason.* Canada itself is so unlikely a proposition — this long, thin band of bickering population strung out necklace-like in clusters mainly across the southern reaches of a hugely ponderous land mass — that it wouldn't be so much of a stretch to attach the sobriquet "eccentric" to the political entity as a whole.

While no one, on anything like serious reflection, could cleave for long to the ridiculous credo that this is a country held together by a thin paste of devotion to monochromatic geniality, a country that by its very nature is inimical to displays of eccentricity, it would also be a mistake to think that the ferreting-out of stories scribbled in the margins will necessarily add an attractive gloss to our ideas of nationhood. Shout "eccentric" often enough into the air, and the words of John Stuart Mill will come walloping back as an echo. In *On Liberty* he wrote, "Precisely because the tyranny of opinion is such as to make eccentricity a reproach, it is desirable, in order to break through that tyranny, that people should be eccentric. Eccentricity has always abounded when and where strength of character has abounded; and the amount of eccentricity in a society has generally been proportional to the amount of genius, mental vigour, and moral courage it contained. That so few dare to be eccentric marks the chief danger of the time."

This is good stuff, delicious to cite and self-contained, exactly the sort of high-humanist pith a librarian would stitch up as a sampler, or a civil-liberties agency would get silk-screened onto tea towels or T-shirts to sell at fund-raisers. Because John Stuart Mill said it, and because most of us know that we should recognize his name even if we can't say particularly why, we impute to his sloganeering the quality of authority. Why? After all, he was only writing and it isn't as though writing doesn't have its own dumb-ass exigencies. He was as concerned with the balance and music of his words, as concerned with their aesthetic impact as he was with illuminating the Truth. Whatever *that* might be. He was riffing. He was on a roll. He was in love with the sound of his own sermonizing voice in his own head, and anyway he had a reputation to sustain. Opinion spewing was his whole *raison d'être*. What's more, he had bills to pay. He had a publisher sending threatening letters. He'd spent the advance. He had a headache, he was constipated, the milk was sour, the coal was gone, the cat knocked over the inkpot, the maid was surly, he thought he might have syphilis, God only knows, and 150 years later we nod sagely and say "Hmmmm. Yes. Yes."

I don't think there's any more reason to run Mill's flag up the pole and salute it than there is to embrace the like-minded but lesser-known words of Henry Wilson and James Caulfield, who attained the specious sanctity of print when they compiled the aforementioned *Book of Wonderful Characters*. It was their opinion that "we have nearly lost all, and are daily losing what little remains of our individuality; all people and all places seem now to be alike; and the railways are, no doubt, the principal cause of this change. For railway stations, all over the world, seem to have a strong, we might almost call it family, resemblance to each other...." No doubt the railways led to a certain homogenization, as did the expanding network of adequate roads, as did the proliferation of cars, as did the emergence of the many mind-grasping tentacles of media. Any agent that brings us closer together carries with it a certain pressure to conform. We are deeply social creatures, and we resist the urge to do anything that might set us apart from the group. But that same agent also bears on its back the opposite number, which is the more theatrical urge to stand apart from the throng. I am, I am, I am, beats the labouring heart. We harbour alongside our need to belong, perhaps in lesser measure, a need to assert selfhood; it is part of us, it is in our blood. We find a way to do it, even if only through so mild and private an expedient as wearing our underwear inside out. There is no one who could not be called, in some way, eccentric. A few are taken over by it. A few make it a life's work. They are conspicuous, easy to see. But look hard enough, and at just the right angle, and you will find other stories. They are everywhere. For my purposes, for better or worse, it is the stories that matter, in and of themselves. My responsibility is to query, to find, to listen, and to tell. I leave it to others to extrapolate clues as to the state of the nation.

I untoothed the venomous question of definition, that is, What does "eccentric" mean?, by shrugging it off. I have chosen not to worry about it. This was not so much a product of intellectual laziness — although I would never deny that my deficiencies of brain are many and that their number is on the rise — as it was of a decision not to be prescriptive or proscriptive, not to limit the field by presenting a series of fixed and numbered dots which, if joined, would make the picture of an eccentric. The dictionary was a sufficient anchor for me. "Eccentric." From the Latin *eccentricus*, out of the centre. Also the Greek *kentros*, the centre, and *ek*, out of. What could be more succinct or descriptive? I would search out stories of people whose lives veered away from the comfortable middle ground. I would collect stories of both the living and the dead. I would be broad in my definition of "Canadian," since the historical record is thick with names of personages whose extraordinary adventures took place somewhere in the country we now call Canada, and are of necessity part of our collective story, but who were not by nationality Canadian. I dispensed right away with any idea of all-embracing inclusivity. Even if such an inventory were possible, the end product would prove to be little more than an annotated list, possibly supplemented by illustrations, which is a snore-provoking prospect if ever there was one. Instead, I chose to rely on my favourite research methodology, which is to leave everything to chance and simply pay attention to rumour. I would inflate a trial balloon, inscribe it with a question, and float it right across the country. Who do you know who is or was eccentric? Feel free to nominate yourself. That would be the extent of my specificity. Whatever names were forwarded by those scattered individuals who just happened to hear of the project in whatever way and had the time or inclination to contact me would serve as the basis for my investigation. My job would be to check out reported sightings. I knew full well that the imperfections in such a technique would make social scientists and ethnographers run screaming from the room. So be it, I thought. They can write their own damn books to their own pernickety standards. Furthermore, I decided I would visit as many of the nominees as possible, which would require that I travel across the country. Considerations that were purely practical and professional dictated that I would do this during the months of January and February. While this is not the season most ideally suited to tripping about north of the 49th parallel, and while there was a general consensus among those most likely to benefit materially from my death that I was mad to even think about such an undertaking, I went ahead and booked the time off work. I got a post office box. I got an e-mail address. I gassed up the balloon, tested the prevailing winds, and sent it off. I sat back and waited for word.

The first letter to arrive came from an anonymous source in Regina. I transcribe it here in its every detail:

Today everybody who is CULTURED and EDUCATED is an eccentric, that is what I am called, because 90% of Canadians are uncultured and uneducated as well as unsophisticated and unrefined.

Canadians fuck into every hole they can get a handle on, kill their offsprings, murder and steal by breaking into other people's houses. THAT is CANADIAN CULTURE, and everybody who is vice from this and a bit sophisticated on top of it is an eccentric, because he does not fit into the norm.

So, here you are! Now you know Canadian eccentrism! And everybody is ridiculed by wearing necklase, earrings and a proper outfit is laughed at and called an ECCENTRIC.

Beside, what do you want with other people's stories? to make money by publishing a book from other people's material and gaining from it. You are a mental burgelar.

The veiled future bowed before me like a vision of promise. Any doubts I might have entertained about the viability of the project were blasted out of the clear blue sky with this finely nuanced missive from the heartland. *They broke into pieces and fell on the ground, like a silvery, shimmering shower of hail.* There was nowhere to go from here but up. I called the airline. I booked a ticket (one-way) to Toronto. I bought a pair of long johns and some Bermuda shorts. I polished my St. Christopher medal and began to collect all the Glenn Gould tapes I could muster. Before I knew it, December was at an end. *The gloom of winter dwelt on everything.* It was time to begin.

Chapter Four

A Folly in Paradise

...a fool layeth open his folly.
— Proverbs 13:16

I am Sleep's courtesan. His slave. His talisman and harem favourite. His elected slut and tart *du jour*. Don't ask how this came to pass, what I did to merit his attentions. I have no idea. It was nothing I asked for. I can only suppose that Sleep, passing others by, spotted me in the cradle and sniffed some ineffable quality that made his loins boil over. He stopped. He kissed me. He made me his. My one true lover. Lusty autocrat. Irascible demagogue. Unkind master. He metes out his humiliations willy-nilly, whether I'm at home or in the most public of circumstances. He'll have his way with me at a lecture or a play or a movie. At a dinner party, where I might turn from my interlocutor and fall face forward into the *crème caramel*. He has even intervened while I'm making love. He'll come calling any old time at all to assert his randy primacy. He is rapacious, voracious. Insatiable. I adore him. I hate him. I wouldn't have it any other way.

Sleep loves to travel. Buses, cars, trains, planes, it doesn't matter a damn. Directly we're in motion, my dauntless companion is all over me, suffocating me with caring. The poor sod sitting next to me, in 27B, has no idea that I am being raped as we climb towards 35,000 feet. How could he? I'm the soul of decorum. I neither struggle nor flinch. My seat-back is upright, my tabletop securely fastened. The *ceinture de sécurité* is neatly cinched. Everything tuckable is tucked. There are no outward signs of my appalling circumstances. This is a pity, for if my assigned partner in altitude understood all that was unfolding beside him, he would surely be more tolerant of the incursions of this stranger who lolls on his shoulder, trickling spittle and fetidly exhaling.

En route from Toronto to St. John's, Newfoundland. The year is new. The day is cold. The sky is clear. Somnolent before the wheels leave the tarmac, I dream that we are passing through the ghost of Glenn Gould. I know with a vain oneirocritical certainty that this is so, even though there is nothing about the apparition that's reminiscent of Gould in his terrestrial incarnation. His ghost is more "Star Trek" than Dickens, a vast and amorphous protoplasmic film. It is suspended in the stratosphere, like a jellyfish in a tidal pool. Phantoms are said to wander, but there is nothing transient about this spectre. No, it is fixed longitudinally in space. This is its permanent address. Exempt from even momentary appropriation, it doesn't care to budge or sidewind. The nose cone of the plane penetrates its midriff and it neither dissolves nor shatters nor rends, but stretches on and on, a kind of indefatigable taffy, dimensionless, self-regenerating, complete, linking the tangible earth with the limitless sky. Its only response to penetration is sonic: not a Jacob Marley rattling of chains, but a spill of voices, an articulate cascade like the one Gould orchestrated in his celebrated radio documentary, *The Idea of North*. It was a brilliant concept, a fugal composition for voices that was revolutionary in its day and remains both startling and wholly unlistenable, an aggregative and aggravating weave of narratives. Rising above the babble, I hear two clear phrases in a voice that might be my own. Old land, new country. Old land, new country. Then, the flight attendant's chirpy and reviving interrogative: Peanuts? How could so significant a ghost be exorcised with so mundane a spell? Much to the relief of 27B, I lurch awake and take the snack, wrest open the recalcitrant cellophane with my teeth, and down the pale, stale nuggets in a single gulp.

The word "saline" surfaces in my fudgy brain, borne along

on the salty wake of aftertaste. "Saline" morphs to "Salus," which comes from the Greek *salos*, which means foolish. "Salus" was the descriptor given to one of the St. Simeons. There were several of these, the most famous being the pillar-sitting hermit St. Simeon Stylites, who is said to have lived for thirty-seven years in the desert on a platform he installed atop a column. Originally, his pillar was ten feet tall. As word of his exploits got out, he was swarmed by copycat hermits, all of them eager for a piece of the action. The *arrivistes* were a nuisance. They set up their own columns in Simeon's sandy backyard and threatened his solitude. They intruded on his silence. They lobbed plea after plea in his direction. They wanted short-cuts to enlightenment. They wanted construction hints. There was nothing for it but to undertake renovations. Simeon built his pillar higher. And higher. And higher still. By the time he was done and his burnished soul was sundered from his flesh, he had a commanding view of the surrounding dunes from an altitude of sixty feet.

St. Simeon Salus is a lesser character in the Roman martyrologies. He was born in Egypt, round about 522, and lived a solitary life in the Sinai for twenty-nine years. Eventually, when he was about sixty, he made his way to the Syrian city of Emesa. There he had a ready audience for the antics that would one day make the hagiographers sit up and take note. Unlike his brother Stylites, he didn't tempt gravity. Nor would anyone have called him grounded. He was just about as flighty as they come. He became a fool for God. He could be seen wandering about the streets of Emesa, dragging a dead dog on a rope, babbling happily to himself, eating dirt. One day, thanks to that internal seismic measuring device with which cats and holy men are blessed, he sensed a terrible earthquake in the offing. He walked through the town, rapping with a lash on various columns (none of which, as near as we know, was sustaining the weight of high-flying hermits), and saying to them, "Thus saith the Lord: you will stay standing. Thus saith the Lord: you will fall down." And sure enough, when the earthquake rocked the foundations of Emesa in 588, it was with the columns just as Salus had said it would be. Iconographers have pictured him surrounded by children. The little ones watch wide-eyed while he huffs into a sixth-century balloon. Balloons, pillars, earthquakes, a willing fool: it all makes for an engaging story, but what I like best about Simeon Salus is that his feast day is July 1. Canada Day. Oh, Canada. There. Look. In the window, a pale, transparent face. My own, of course. Not so much a ghost as a Salus balloon caught up in the jet stream. Below, a curve of earth, an accidental amalgam of mineral and water, a blotter onto which we've spilled the idea of a country. A fool's paradise. The idea of north.

My mind canters in a pre-Newtonian corral. Laws of motion? Elementary concepts of physics? Feh! Don't even speak to me of such high-school fripperies! I choose to believe that a plane stays aloft because of an act of collective will. If, for even one second, all we passengers were to abandon our belief that these several tons of metal are capable of sustaining us at this height, we would plummet to earth like a buckshot-riddled mallard. And this country where I've been pleased to live my whole life long, and above which now I hang, is likewise nothing more than an act of imagination, of irrational belief. In these latter days, we're not much given to taking sustenance from imagination. We'd rather a diet of proof. We'd rather see and name every rivet. Nonetheless, the country holds. Against every reasonable expectation, and on the strength of imagination alone, so far, it holds. Old land. New country. I mouth these words to my shivering, exiled *doppelgänger*, close my eyes, and drift.

Whatever his other gifts, it must be said that Sleep is a lousy mime. Death is the only charade he can successfully pull off. Since Sleep left his vampire love bites on my neck when I was still floating in the rushes — and since I have been all these years his tasty bit, his cherished piece of tail — I have very often had to sit through performances of his single party piece. Little wonder, considering these influences, that I was precocious when it came to courting intimations of mortality. Anyone would think my mother had spent her pregnancy reading the drearier sermons of Donne. As a child, I would spend many happy hours imagining the circumstances that would see me pulling up to the door of the Hotel Terminus. A solitary soul, I played a private game. On hot summer afternoons, when the unhaltered south wind bucked its way over the flatlands, when I was bored with the more savoury recreations of dashing through the sprinkler and peeing onto anthills, I would position myself upright in the middle of the lawn, extend my arms to their fullest width, and spin around and around and around, a tubby gyroscope, before surrendering to the depredations of gravity. I'd collapse onto that well-tended square of green and urbanized prairie, let it absorb my giddiness while the vertigo-inducing inner-ear fluids splashed and settled in their delicate, Eustachian canals. I'd stare up at the same thin stretch of timpanic blue through which now I fly: a screen behind which God sat, conniving with His angels. To see them face to face! What a tempting prospect! So many questions would be answered. I would lie there and imagine my death, would turn face downward and inhale the earth, and think of all the possible ways and means of achieving ending, all the grim and pleasant catalogue.

How and where and why would it happen? A brakeless bus, a limping heart, a stumble on a high cliff, a rusty nail, irascible hiccups? Yes, even that was possible. I knew, for I'd seen it. When next-door Mr. Magnuson came down with the hiccups one morning, he and his wife just supposed he was drawing the wages of gobbling his oatmeal. No one would have guessed that before the week was out he would dig his own grave with his intemperate gulping, that he would hick [sic] the bucket without ever having recourse to Squire Mytton's drastic pyrotechnic therapy. Oh, yes. You didn't have to look far to see that Death would come. When and how were the only variables. I was full of childish impatience to know. Let it happen now, I would think, now, when I am as happy as this! But here I am, decades later, telling the tale. Dig in childhood's littered midden and you'll find the shards of shattered wishes. Come to think of it, I never got a pony, either.

The irony is that now that I am of an age when arteries can be counted on to implode, when rogue tumours (always the size of a golf ball or grapefruit) could rear up and overthrow the body's careful government, I am entirely unprepared for that great day's dawning. If this buoyant craft were to shudder and fall, achieving homonymic unity with the plain, I'd perish intestate. I've left no instructions, other than having once muttered something on the radio about how I'd rather be planted than incinerated. This prompted a woman from Qualicum Beach to send a note saying she hoped I would persevere in this line of thinking. Cremation, she told me, "is a horrid, painful happening. The extreme heat burns all your aura which will be the support, ground, in your new existence. No guardian angel can help you. It is your will which is supremely Godly. The two most awful acts God and heavenly angels cannot do anything about are suicide and cremation."

Heavens to Betsy! There are days when it's worth your life to open the mail. Still, it's always a good idea to hedge your bets. What if she was right? I had never bothered to pass the scoop along to someone with the power to influence the disposition of my remains. What were the chances my court-appointed executors would find her letter among my effects and put two and two together? I would put them on a par with the chances that, should I die in a car wreck, the celebrant at my service would think to speak the only words I care to have uttered in such an eventuality: He suffered and died under Pontiac pile-up.

"It is better to be ready to die and live than to die and not be ready," said Professor Charles Henry Danielle, whose end days were an encomium to just such morbid preparedness. He was born in the United States, but severed his links with the earth in Newfoundland. The Professor — for that is what he was called, both fondly and derisively by the people among whom he landed as an exotic alien and to whom he was always an object of considerable curiosity — died not where but as he wished. He boarded the coach for heaven at Octagon Castle, the eight-sided palazzo he had designed as a resort and erected on a pond near Irvine station, which was next door to Paradise, which was then about two hours by train from St. John's. He died in his own bed, with his customized coffin in an adjacent room. Danielle was a true Son of Salus, a *fin-de-siècle* crank who just managed, like Queen Victoria, to overlap the new century. His spirit flew the coop in the spring of 1902, when he was seventy-one and a half years old to the day, and just a couple of months shy of launching his seventh season as the island's most cele-brated hotelier.

It was neither an unexpected nor an untimely death. He himself had predicted it, and with eerie accuracy. A pioneer in the art of public relations, he customarily distributed, free of charge, a descriptive booklet, detailing for prospective cus-tomers the many delights afforded by a visit to the Octagon. "Pleasant rooms are provided, with a liberal table, and tourists may find here a peaceful home for a brief or a prolonged stay. The views from the Octagon are at once extensive and beauti-ful. A landscape for twenty miles in extent is presented to the eye, including Conception Bay, in which may, far into the Sum-mer, be seen icebergs, and lovely lakes, meadows and forests, with all the lights and shadows by which the sun lights up this beautiful land." And so on. At the end of the 1901 edition of his pamphlet, the Professor offered this adumbration: "It is more than probable, this spring booklet...will be the last from my pen that the intelligent public of Newfoundland will ever be amused at, or a lot of others disgusted with. I am a victim and a sufferer from a VERY BAD CASE of valvular heart trouble, and cannot live long, according to all medical opinions and my own knowledge of my condition....CHAS. H. DANIELLE. Octagon Castle. May 1st, 1901."

None of his readers was taken aback at this news. None was surprised. How could one expect otherwise? He had already hung on for more than his allotted span of three score and ten. He was living on borrowed time. The bloom was gone from his rose. Anyway, it was well known round about that Danielle's relationship with robust good health was at best flirtatious. Certain prophylactic measures might have sustained him. Anyone in his situation who had a vested interest in continuance could abjure activity, give himself over to leisurely days and tranquil nights punctuated by herbal infusions and recuperative meditations. But the Professor, a veteran showman, was undeterred by the thickening and slowing of his own vapours. In the best tradition of the show going on, he averted his gaze from the imminence of his ending. He welcomed excursionists from near and far to his castle for one last summer. As always, they came. As always, there was a crowd. The Professor was partial to self-aggrandizement through statistics, and by his own figuring and boasting: "The Octagon covers 3,750 square feet of ground; it has 10,180 square feet of inside floor surface. Allowing 18 square inches for each person, it can shelter 6,756 persons at one and the same time. There are 420 chairs in the Octagon and more are ordered. There are 84 windows in the Octagon, and 43 doors. The 3 lower front rooms are paneled, 4 feet from the floor, with 344 panels. There are 9,979 running feet of moulding in the building. Every foot of this moulding the Professor has gone over with 3 coats of Aspinal's enamel. It took 1,040 yards of wall cotton to cover the walls of the various rooms, and over 25,000 tacks to hold it there; 5,480 blocks of the best wallpaper cover the walls — no two blocks being alike. There are curiosities and artistic draperies to be seen at the Octagon that are to be seen nowhere else in Newfoundland, or at few other resorts on earth."

Oh, the measuring, the hammering, the fumes from the Aspinal's enamel! His poor old wheezing heart! By his reckoning, 9,927 visitors had come to the Octagon during the 1900 season, and he expected to entertain at least that many in this, his final go-round. Madness for a man in his condition! Surely his doctor told him so, surely even the servants, over whom he ran roughshod, ventured a word. He was heedless of their counsel. He forged on. All summer long he worked to ensure that the outdoor fêtes and picnics of the various societies, clubs, lodges, Sunday schools, and churches he suffered to come unto him went off without a hitch. Not only did he treat them splendidly when they arrived, but he immortalized their outings by stitching up "large Satin Banners, elaborately embroidered and bespangled in gold and silver [and bearing] symbolic letters of the gatherings they commemorate, so all may be read." Failing though he was, he didn't break with his custom of entertaining the Church of England orphans, turning over the grounds to them on a given afternoon, and sending them away with fond memories and pockets full of sweets. The Anglican teachers came to the castle, as was their custom. Temperance societies turned up, reassured by his promise that they would find the Octagon "as free from the sight, sound, taste or smell of spirits as the WCTU...the Bar-room and Wine-room will be locked and sealed if they but express the wish." The Odd Fellows put into port, as did the Dudley Lodge of the Sons of England, whose party numbered 200 people, and whose sentiments were in no way prohibitionist. "JOLLY DAY AT THE OCTAGON" read the next day's newspaper headline, and the accompanying story makes it clear that the verb "to stint" had been stricken from every Son of England's lexicon for the day. Directly the Sons (and, one imagines, their female adjuncts) arrived, they broke into teams and went at a football match "as if their lives depended on it." They played cricket, too, "the contesting teams being formed by W. Edney and J. Harris. Here, it was hard to decide who won for in the midst of the game tea was announced. Needless to say the Professor had done his best and was eminently successful. The delicacies obtainable at this season were soon disposed of and with appetites sharpened by the clear pure air of the country, full justice was done." They stayed late into the night, dancing to music provided by Professor Powers' band, and didn't allow their host to retire until well after midnight. They sang patriotic songs all the way home.

However deleterious the effects of these wee-hour revels on the Professor's leaky valves, it surely did the SOE a world of good to come to the Octagon and romp with such careless abandon. Ever since the century turned, the papers had been full of nothing but dreadful news. The Boer War. The Boxer Rebellion. The seductive, subversive whisperings of confederationists.

The world! The world! It was more than a healthy heart could bear, never mind one constricted and worn by years of hard work and disappointment. The Professor took in all this news — he must have read the papers, if only to scan them for news of himself — and still he pressed on. He wrote a little poem that made his life seem a regular breeze:

Just six things are requisite
    To make the Octagon sunny,
One is a cook, that is a cook,
    The other five are money.

Of course, there was much more to it. Simply inspecting the quality of the dusting would tax the strength of a young and healthy man. His was a house of many mansions. The ceiling in the rotunda was thirty feet high. There was a private dining room, a reading room, a smoking room, a music room, a bagatelle room, a card room, and a barn with room for eight horses. To prepare himself for his last innkeeping summer on earth, the Professor had supervised the construction of seven new salons, including "a Blue Chamber, a Pink Chamber, a Yellow Chamber, a Crimson Chamber, and a Lace Chamber, all true to their names and elaborately embellished. There is not a room in the Castle that is not furnished in satin draperies, with gold and silver trimmings. Even the rooms in the servants' quarters have satin window lambrequins, while their beds have the same spring, wool, and hair mattresses and furnishings as the rooms in the Octagon itself." The servants were an ongoing concern and required his vigilance. They were so well schooled in the domestic arts — taught by Danielle himself — that other grasping agencies were forever trying to lure them away with ridiculous offers.

Horticulture brought its demands and influence to bear. The Professor oversaw the cultivation of seventy-five gallons of strawberries, from choice new varieties of American plants, as well as the tending of the gardens that made it possible for the kitchen shelves to groan under the weight of 800 pounds of home-made jams. He made a daily tour of inspection to check on his four cold-storage plants to see that the hundred tons of lake ice he had put in store was sustaining itself against the beating of the August sun. Likewise, he ascertained that the miraculous beverage-cooling device he had installed — and there was not another one like it anywhere in Newfoundland — was keeping its frosty promise. Angered by accusations that he was watering down his milk, he issued a sensible disclaimer that his dairy herd, by way of some grievous congenital defect, had developed overly porous hides, thus allowing water in. To safe-guard against future leakage of rain into their milk, he had tiny bovine-friendly roofs constructed for their use. These he caused to be strapped onto the backs of the willing cows.

Summer took a powder. One morning he woke up, and it was *gone like tenants that quit without warning*. The touristic flood slowed to a trickle. He caught up on his correspondence. He continued to write away to fabric companies for free sam-ples, continued to plan how he would use their swatches to do over yet another room. With enough cunning, you could pro-ject the impression of tremendous opulence and wealth and do it on the cheap. Illusion, illusion, that was the thing! It was the promise and possibility of illusion that had sustained him, all these years. Now, however, his body was overtaking his will. It was a long winter. The Professor's powers dwindled steadily. According to his obituary in the St. John's *Evening Telegram*, he was under the constant care of Dr. Mackenzie, but was always acutely cognizant that his long-term prospects were far from cheery. He knew full well "that there was no medical agent that could save him, and had therefore made all preparations for his burial. His system became greatly weakened by lack of sleep. One peculiarity of his disease was that, when in a lying position or sleeping, a suffocating sensation would come in the throat, of which the sufferer is always in dread. On Thursday evening last there was a relapse and the Professor knew he could never rally again....Mr. S. G. Collier was called to the Octagon to receive instructions as to the burial. His casket was made by himself and was a magnificent piece of work."

The splendour of the coffin was well known and amply celebrated, and not just in St. John's or Carbonear or Harbour Grace, either. *Scenic Magazine*, published in Portland, Maine, had given over precious column inches to describing the Byzantine grandeur of Danielle's château, and of his coffin in particular. In an article published shortly before the Professor's death — too soon, really, for him to have enjoyed whatever tourist dollars that might have found their way to his counting-house on account of it — an American reporter draws back the curtain on what was certainly the most widely touted of the Octagon's many features. On the building's third floor, he writes, "is a large, square room that is kept locked; it is called the mortuary chamber. It is draped in black velvet embroidered in gold. In the center of this room is a catafalque, covered with black velvet trimmed in white satin, on which rests the most elaborate casket the writer has ever seen. The casket is covered with black satin beautifully embroidered in gold, while the interior is upholstered with 7,800 white satin shells. A fluted satin pillow filled with eiderdown is at the head, while a white satin shroud and golden slippers lie within, ready for the body of the strange man. All this burial outfit is the work of the man it is waiting for. At the head of the casket, hanging upon a wall, is a gilt frame encircling a sheet of paper on which is written, 'In the back of this Frame will be found Full instructions to be followed Immediately after my Death.'"

The Professor's hour came and went. The document was dislodged from the frame, and not for the first time, either. Vandals had snitched it on at least two previous occasions, had stolen the record of his wishes away and snickered at it with their friends in some foul-smelling bar. "Full," as it turned out, was too slight a word to bear on its back the heft of his instructions. They were the work of a controlling sensualist, a man who wanted more than anything to be both an active participant in his own laying-out and chief mourner at his own funeral. Mr. S. G. Collier, the undertaker, who had been a regular visitor to the Octagon over the years, who was indeed the president of the Dudley Lodge of the Sons of England, followed the five pages of instructions in their every finicky particular.

"1st My Body to be washed & dressed in a suit of new cotton Underclothing & a White top shirt & collar, the white Satin Shroud, which buttons up the back, in dressing the body do not roll it over with the face on the Table or bed, but place a pillow under the Head."

He furthermore admonishes that they be "careful that the mouth is closed with the head resting on a Pillow. Tie the feet with a bandage, so they will be upright & not spread....During the days & nights of my 'Waking' I particularly request & Hope there will be *none* of the Unseemly & out-of-place mirth which is too often a part of the last solemn rites here in Newfoundland."

Poor Danielle! A devout Christian, and an artist to boot, stranded on this barren rock, with no one to keep him company but a legion of party-mad, spirit-swilling, loutish heathen. He died on the first of May, and was shortly thereafter consigned to the clay. (Mercifully, his sustaining aura was spared the damaging heat of ovens.) On the day he reverted to dust, a Sunday, there were still tattered, wind-whipped ribbons, bright as flames, unbraiding themselves from various poles on various greens. Nubile Newfoundland maidens had wrapped them there, had capered and twined at the very hour of his leave-taking. None of them, we can safely guess, gave the embittered, dried-up man in his folly in Paradise a second's thought as she pranced around and around the phallic columns. The light touch of flesh as they passed under one another's arms made them long for a more significant pressing, for heat, for salt, for the taste of something like cod. His systems were shutting down, one after the other. He had just heart enough left to worry that some slatternly visitor — for this had been known to happen, and more than once, too — had climbed into his coffin during this time of his indisposition, had failed to wipe her shoes, had soiled the silken scallops. The cheek of it! The wench who would do such a thing was no better than the common trash who had snatched photographs from the wall and torn them into pieces; had stolen his silver jug, marked "Royal." All this had happened in his own home, under his very nose. Who knew what might be transpiring as he lay there, fighting for air. He would have clutched at his throat, had he had the strength to lift his hand. He felt himself suffocating, and this time it was for real. He tried to call out, but his voice was lost in the rattle that says finis. Somewhere nearby, the cool virgins skipped and twirled and sang "Tra la," and all the while their young blood simmered.

The funeral cortège was to come down Prescott Street. One can't help but feel sorry for Daniel Mulrooney, a sergeant of the Western Fire Station, who was buried on the same day. Officers came out for him, came out in all their regalia, and they tolled the fire bell, too. But Mulrooney's obsequies paled before the hoopla accorded the Professor, whose dying was acknowledged by the presence of representatives of the bar, the bench, the professions, commerce, the press, and many, many run-of-the-mill citizens. Oh, there was a crowd! Perhaps the organ grinder who had recently arrived from Port-aux-Basques with his monkey played to keep them all amused while they lined the pavement and waited. There was a long delay before the procession hove into view. Fathers held their children in the air so they could catch a glimpse of the man of the hour — his full head of hair, his imperious nose, his artistic beard, his spotless shroud — through the coffin's glass top. The neglected May Day ribbons crackled in the air as the spectators oohed and aahed at the splendour of it all. The ribbons still snapped as they headed home for tea. Some — no more than a few — might have reflected on the irony that, while the old fellow's death and disposal were incendiarily innocent, his life on earth had been dogged by fire. Fire would trail his legend, too, like a comet's tail. Thirteen years later, in circumstances some would call "mysterious," the Octagon would burn to the ground, and the stories of the enigmatic Danielle would be hauled out again, and undergo the fond regilding accorded to oft-told tales.

Octagon Castle was the last of Danielle's several Newfoundland hurrahs. It was opened in a grand ceremony held on June 18, 1896. *The Evening Telegram* recorded it as "a red-letter day.... Sir Wm. Whiteway [the premier of the colony] formally declared it open in the afternoon, at 4.30, in a few happy words in which he paid tribute to the manner in which the genial professor had exercised his energy and taste in placing such a lovely resort at the service of the public.... The wish of all seemed to be that success and prosperity might attend this venture of Mr. Danielle, to which the professor responded in his own inimitable manner. The gathering was immense, and the professor ably sustained his reputation as a caterer of the first water. Mr. Vey took some excellent photos of the proceedings. Prof. Powers' band discoursed sweet strains during the evening. Everybody and his wife was there, and boating and other amusements were indulged in during the day. We trust that this will be the commencement of a long reign for the 'Octagon' as one of the best holiday resorts that this country possesses, and a boon that the tired worker of this city will not forget to appreciate."

That Danielle was able to broker the construction of so stately a pleasure dome — the total cost was more than $20,000 — and that he could attract so sizeable and so eminent a crowd to its opening tell us something about his standing in the community. Keenly aware that he had a reputation to sustain, he spared no expense to equip the Octagon with every sybaritic accessory. Visitors stepped from the fresh Atlantic breeze into a torrid opium dreamscape, the rooms festooned with — in Danielle's own words — "hundreds of yards of satin, thousands of yards of tinsel, and hundreds and thousands of spangles." Of particular note was the honeymoon suite, described in one finely observant contemporary account as "a bower of satin, lace and plush, all dazzling in gold and silver, while on the bed is a quilt composed of small shells of satin, of every imaginable color, adroitly put together, each shell overlapping the other, like the scales of a fish, and not a stitch is visible. It took 2-1/2 years to complete this quilt; it contains 8,500 yards of satin and is valued at $700."

There were 19,832 individual pieces of fabric in that bed-spread. But however splendid the chamber, and however lavish its accoutrements, this intended site of maidenhead disposal became a focal point for the Professor's growing ennui and impatience with the stubborn refusal of the locals to live up to the standards he had set for them. Once, a young and blushing couple turned up at his door. Even though the ink was still wet on their marriage certificate, even though they stood on the cusp of *l'heure exquise*, they showed no sign of being anxious to consummate their union. They lingered overlong by the fire in one of the sumptuous downstairs parlours. Danielle, thinking they surely must be longing to steal away for a night of connubial bliss, but were too delicate to reveal their carnal eagerness, suggested subtly that he might show them where to "find the chamber." The bridegroom simply shrugged the kindness off, saying, "That's all right, sir, just show it to the woman, I'll do mine out the window." At one point, he is said to have thrown up his hands in despair at the paltry receipts he was able to bring in from renting to newlyweds. He declared he would turn the suite over to the rearing of hogs. He could make more money from pig husbandry than from piggish husbands.

Even if Newfoundland in the early years of the century was not populated by women who would fondly remember the night of their deflowering in the beautifully adorned room at the Octagon, the quilt, like the coffin, became an object of veneration and visitation for the castle's many day-trippers. Not only was Danielle a dab hand with needle and thread, not only was he an interior designer and caterer *par excellence*; he was a dancer. In fact, he was a dancer first and foremost. It was in this capacity, and as a teacher of the Terpsichorean arts, that he first presented himself to the people of Newfoundland. The precise date of his glorious advent on the rock is not certain. Michael Francis Harrington, who provided the entry on Danielle in the *Dictionary of Canadian Biography*, and has written about him elsewhere, suggests that he first turned up in St. John's in the 1860s, and that he might have been drawn there by news reports of Cyrus West Field, the quixotic American business-man who around that time was trying to lay a transatlantic cable to the island. While there seem to be no exact data on when and why he came, and how long he stayed initially, it is clear that this first excursion was the beginning of an "on again, off again" love–hate relationship with the place.

He was a man with ambi-tion, he was a man with in-sight, and he was a man with portable skills. He could dance, he could sew, and he was possessed of a zealous, persuasive theatricality. Little is known of his parentage or family. He said he was the youngest of six children, that his parents were Joseph and Isabelle, that he was born in Baltimore on November 1, 1830, and that he took to the boards at an early age. He was on the stage at fourteen,

Charles Henry Danielle as Neptune.

and claimed to have shortly thereafter founded a dancing acad-emy in Chicago. For a time, he worked in Brooklyn as a haber-dasher. By all accounts, he was endowed with evangelistic fervour, and was able to spread a great contagion of enthusiasm for the spectacles he was uniquely equipped to engineer. By

1872, he had dropped anchor in St. John's and acquired, through either lease or purchase, the use of the Victoria skating rink in Bannerman Park, near Government House on Military Road. Danielle was a gifted visionary. He looked into the blade-scarred ice and saw, clearly revealed in the frozen intricacy of its curlicues and whorls, certain signs that the edifice was intended for less pedestrian purposes than, say, curling. He took it over. He installed his enormous collection of costumes, each one a product of his own hand. He hired a printer to do up some posters, and he set about staging the first of the fancy-dress balls that made his name.

He knew from the start that this was a no-fail proposition. He brought his costumes and his haughty demeanour, his slightly Southern accent with its overlay of who-knows-where and his other maddening affectations, and he came to live among fisher folk, farmers, and small-time merchants, among prostitutes and hidebound school teachers, among lunatics. It was perfect! He understood that the rough and jagged surfaces of this place concealed a pliable underbelly and a heart that was soft and ripe for the plucking. His neighbours were cut from the coarsest of cloth, but by simple dint of being human, each and every one of them had a soul. One of the soul's essential properties is that it hungers after brighter shining. What better way to achieve this luminescence than through the arts? And what art could be more elevating than the dance? It was simple! And it was lucrative, too. There was a living to be made, just by working out a simple syllogistic sequence. Advertise yourself as a "Professor of the Terpsichorean arts" and you suggest to the public the possibility of dancing. Once you've created the possibility, you've also created the need. Don't give too much of yourself away. Let it be known through word and deed and rumour that you carry the credentials of one who is exotic, cultured, remote, all of which is to say, someone who is clearly a cut above the *hoi polloi*. Thus, you become a source of fascination and envy. Offer to share, for a reasonable fee, one of the skills that sets you apart from the throng, such as a knowledge of the dance, and you will attract some of the many who want in on your secret. Teach it, and your students will want to show off their new skills, to demonstrate to the world at large how like you they've become. Give them this opportunity through a fancy-dress ball, for which you conveniently will be able to rent the costumes, and *voilà*! Every Bob will clamour to be your uncle.

For six years, the Professor staged his carnivals and taught his classes. No student left his care without being able to execute a credible minuet, quadrille, polka, schottische, or waltz.

For six years, all went swimmingly. Then came the first of the fires that were to punctuate his latter days. On July 16, 1878, someone set the Victoria rink ablaze. Who could have done such a thing? And why? Someone eaten away by jealousy, perhaps. Someone who couldn't abide the sight of others having fun, who didn't know his right foot from his left, someone with an icy heart. All his sets, all his costumes, even his piano, was reduced to smouldering ruins. If there was just one hint of pewter in that black, black cloud, it was that he was insured. He collected his thousand pounds and left Newfoundland. Where did he go? Somewhere he'd be appreciated, that much we can count on. Somewhere the climate was amenable to the licking of wounds. Somewhere you could live comfortably for a long time on a thousand pounds.

Time heals. A Christian man forgives. It was ten years before islanders again had the benefit of his presence among them. His first words, on stepping off the gangplank, were "Is the fire out yet?" At least, this is how they have been recorded in the vast book of his apocrypha. What is sure is that on May 31, 1888, *The Evening Telegram* reported that Professor Danielle, "well and favorably known throughout Newfoundland as a teacher of dancing," had arrived on the steamer *Peruvian* and that he "will soon open classes in dancing and weekly assemblies. He is quartered at the Atlantic Hotel, where he will be pleased to see his old friends and pupils."

A week later, once he was reacclimatized to the reviving slap of the wind and the cobbles of the street; once he had adapted, as any traveller must, and as he was accustomed to doing, to the strange physics of a new hotel room, he went down to *The Evening Telegram* office and placed an ad. It ran, with some variation, for the next three weeks.

From this moment on, the public was kept well informed of Danielle's Terpsichoric progress. On September 1, 1888, the *Telegram* ran a breathless story about the Grand Juvenile Ball the Professor had held at the British Hall, an *amuse-gueule* meant to give the public a foretaste of the glorious feast to come. Danielle himself appeared as "Emperor William," and his pupils were togged up as Joan of Arc, the Queen of the Golden Realm, the Albino Prince, an Amazon, and an Italian Peasant. The paper notes that lucky Master Firth, who must have been a favourite of the moment, or gifted with an especially pretty turn of ankle, had been elected to play the page to Danielle's Emperor.

"The hall," writes the *Telegram*, "was brightly lit up and well ventilated all through the night, and it is needless to say that parents and friends of the pupils — large numbers of whom were present — as well as the young people themselves, were delighted with the evening's exhibition. Indeed, so enchanted were they with the fairy-like scene and the fascinating influences of the occasion, that many remained until midnight, and even then they seemed reluctant to tear themselves away.

"Some people are opposed to this kind of amusement; but, for the life of us, we never could see any great harm in it, when superintended by suitable persons."

Harmless, if superintended. How broad-minded! Doubtless this is what they said about skeet-shooting and fireworks, too. Danielle, we are to understand, was not "suitable," but by and large he was harmless enough. Whatever danger or threat he represented could be mitigated, defused by the presence and intervention of the conventionally respectable. He was an odd duck, amusing, but you wanted to keep an eye on him, just in case. Who could say what he might get up to when your back was turned, and it wouldn't do to leave him alone with the children, who were defenceless and impressionable, both. You could never tell when someone might come along and pipe them out of Hamelin.

The juvenile ball was a feast for the senses, but it turned to dust in the mouth when set next to the main event, the Oriental Ball. For the next several weeks, Danielle extolled the glories of "a mammoth night at the big city rink." The anticipated Babylonian excesses of the evening had *le tout* St. John's slavering with anticipation. This was going to be good! More than 2,000 people attended the event, including Governor and Mrs. Blake. The Governor was overheard to remark that, other than a production or two at the Drury Lane Theatre, it was the finest show of theatrics he'd ever witnessed. The critics waxed orgasmic. "The first tableau — the Japanese legation — was simply inimitable. As the dais slowly revolved, the posing of the different figures had the best possible effect, and during the entire scene the delighted audience frequently expressed their admiration. The second tableau — 'Mary, Queen of Scots,' was very impressive in all its details, especially the reading of the death warrant and the execution.... Not a hitch or disappointment occurred at any stage of the entertainment. Every part was admirably performed...."

When the reviews were in and the costumes put away, Danielle took himself off for a recuperative visit to Halifax. He had a right to be tuckered. He had been burning the candle at every available end. For almost two years he hunkered down, kept a low profile, hammered out the details of his reinvention. His next Newfoundland incarnation would be as a restaurateur. He launched a bistro called The Royal. It was a throbbing success until it was eaten by fire in the great conflagration of 1892 — the St. John's equivalent of London's 1666. It was a concussive blow, but the Professor didn't know the meaning of the word "daunted." Another smaller establishment, The Little Royal, rose from the ashes. In these two eateries, our hero was able to hone his culinary skills and exorcise the twin demons that possessed him: an irrepressible hospitality and an overweening need for executing handiwork. The press, for a time, was on his side. The papers advised the public that "Prof. Danielle, who has the nicest dining parlors in this city, is constantly adding improvements to his establishment, which not alone beautify the place but add to the convenience of his patrons. The skill of the Professor as a designer and decorator is unsurpassed. This fact is admitted by everybody. His latest work is a magnificent piano canopy composed of 90 tablets of different colored silks and satins exquisitely embroidered in gold and silver, no two designs being alike. The effect of this superb piece of work, as one enters the room, is simply indescribable. He has also on exhibition a beautiful mantel drape... which surpasses anything of the kind ever seen in this city. In the same room are some very attractive curtains and lambrequins, also a bed-spread representing the aurora borealis, all the work of the busy hands of the Professor."

Busy hands, it is well known, are not available to do the devil's work. Similarly, it is said that one good reason to build an octagonal house is to soften the corners, so Hell's governor will have no place to hide. It is tempting to speculate that the

Professor, whose energies were superhuman, might have struck a Faustian bargain somewhere along the line. Somewhere in his far-flung travels he cut a deal with old Nick. All that stands between Satan and satin is a single vowel and it is almost certain that, in a moment of weakness, Charles drew a pentangle in the snow and summoned the goatman forth. He said, "Listen here, good fellow. Give me your dancing shoes, and all the shiny fabric my heart desires, and you can have my soul when my body is done with it. You can waltz with me for all eternity, and what's more, you can lead."

"Agreed," said the evil one, who clicked his cloven heels and vanished, leaving sulphurous pocks in the deep, white drifts. And from that day forth, Charles Henry Danielle kept Lucifer at bay with his art and his industry. Not that the devil much cared. If there's one thing he's good at, it's biding his time. He watched Charles Henry at his petit point and laughed. He knew what to do. He had his own recreations. He made up spells by working out anagrams of his quarry's name.

> *Cheery liars handle Len,*
> *Helena's early children,*
> *Chilled hyenas relearn,*
> *Hen reached Nelly's lair,*
> *Chinese rarely lead* NHL.

And he planted contempt and rancour into some prominent hearts. He gave the Professor enemies, caused them to whisper calumnies against him. They called him a fool. One Member of Parliament said his satins and laces were nothing but "refuse." It was more than he could bear. He moved away from the city centre. He built a roadhouse on the shores of Quidi Vidi Lake and called it the Royal Lake Pavilion. Its dining room measured sixty-by-forty feet. It had eight magnificent columns supporting a ballroom overhead. It was a bower of beauty, and what did it get him? Contempt. Hot, unwatered, carbolic contempt.

"I was harassed," he would write in his 1901 booklet,

"hooted at, groaned at and barked at, and suffered nightly acts of vandalish destruction, and my servants were assaulted when getting water from the public lake, and all by the very man from whom I leased the land, and why? Why! because I ran a similar business to his and because I ran it thousands of miles superior to his.

"Then, in 1895, being unable to endure the persecutions at Quidi Vidi Lake any longer and remain outside of the insane asylum, I bought this property, tore down the Royal Lake Pavilion, carted it through town to the railway station, railroaded it and its plant to Irvine station, carted it again to the present Octagon grounds, tore down old buildings, and with a hundred thousand more feet of lumber I erected this magnificent Octagon Castle. Then my real heartaches only began, and they have lasted up to this writing, six years later, and all through ignorant, brutish jealousy."

He must have found more than occasional consolation in the beauty of his castle. Out of wood and glass, he built four storeys, eight sides, three wings, and a mansard roof. Some of the gabled windows were decorated with caribou antlers. He must have found solace in the wrought-iron furnace, which measured seven-by-three-by-three feet, which could boil two barrels at once, for dishwashing. It must have cheered him to stroll about the cricket grounds, and the open-air ballroom, and to consider the lake, which was alive with trout. He did not, however, take kindly to dogs. Dogs weren't welcome at the Octagon. Included on his list of dos and don'ts was "Don't bring any growlers with you; they keep me awake nights... I have [had] two sixty-five dollar satin draperies ruined by the inquisitiveness of dogs and this is enough for me to say, 'No Dogs.'"

He was a man of many parts and a man of many words. What were the last words he uttered, May 1, 1902? Alas, they are not recorded. What was the last sound to make its way through his ears to the still-sensible brain, as the net closed around him? It would have been just his luck to have been assailed by a terrible baying, a delighted howling welling in the throat of what only sounded like a dog. Outside his mortuary chamber, the devil was building a satanic head of steam, gearing himself up to lay claim to his prize.

"At 4.15 p.m. yesterday the news reached town of the death of Charles Henry Danielle, proprietor of the Octagon Castle at Irvine station.... The remains will be confined at the Octagon and remain there till 1 p.m. Sunday, when a special train will take it to the West End railway terminus. The casket will be left there, when friends can view the body through the glass lid.... Professor Danielle's death will be regretted by many. He, though eccentric, had many good traits of character and was well-liked by his friends around him. He was very fond of children..."

There was a funeral card. It reads:

> One precious to our hearts has gone,
>   The voice we loved is stilled,
> The place made vacant in our home
>   Can never more be filled.
> Our Father in His wisdom called
>   The boon His love had given;
> And though on earth the body lies,
>   The soul is safe in Heaven.

He was buried in the Church of England cemetery on Forest Road. I went to find him on the very day I arrived in St. John's. It's a very satisfactory graveyard, a few blocks from downtown, in a beautiful neighbourhood of quiet streets lined with stately homes. There is a wrought-iron gate that growls and clanks, and row upon row of eroding, slanted stones. This is a place where even at noon it's easy enough to believe in hauntings. I trudged along paths steeply banked with snow. I heard a crow, looked up to find it, and saw at the same time, in a hoary, thick-limbed elm, the Fellini-esque vision of three little boys in a simian mood, hanging by their legs from one of its branches, studying me, the blood rushing to their toques. I thought how that would have pleased the Professor, what with his fondness for youth and all. I searched and searched along the rows, but was unable to find the requisite mound. I sought out the sexton. He was hunched over a desk in a small outbuilding office. He reluctantly left his work — he was writing a letter of complaint to someone about a lobster he'd ordered for Christmas that hadn't been up to snuff — and led me where I needed to go. *En route*, he pointed out a gully they call, rather redundantly I thought, "Death Valley." This is a mass grave, an earthen blanket laid over those who were sliced and diced by one of the cholera pogroms that marauded its way with Cossack-like rapaciousness across the island. Whole families were wiped out in a few days. "Even now," he assured me with a dire nod towards the shallow depression, "we won't dig there. Won't risk setting something lose." This proscription may or may not stand up to medical scrutiny, but it certainly excites grunts of understanding and accord from a dark and reptilian corner of the brain.

"To the memory of Charles H. Danielle" is the simple inscription on the marble slab that covers his pretty bones and whatever might remain of the magnificent walnut coffin with its thousands of silken scallops, its golden slippers at the ready, and the Orphean lyre etched on the side. There are those who will tell you that stone absorbs sentiment and, if that is the case, someone who is psychically acute might be able to lay hands on the Professor's flat marker and still discern, especially on a warm day, something of the fever-pitch excitement that surrounded his burial. There were accounts of the event in the daily papers, but it was most lovingly and lavishly described by *The New York Post*. The predominant emotion, they say, was not so much grief as it was curiosity.

A carnival atmosphere pervaded overall as some 10,000 people massed along the processional route. They leaned from windows. They stood on roofs. They hung from telephone poles. They jostled on the sidewalks. Those who had cameras brought them along, and the air was alive with the sound of their clicking. There was a great deal of pushing and shoving. At one point, the bier was almost overturned. Individual will was lost in the clamour of the collective. The crowd began to move. They followed along behind the hearse. They practically pushed down the gates of the cemetery in order to watch the lowering. A vault had been built over the grave. They tore it down, bearing away the bricks as souvenirs of the day. It's a compelling picture, this graveside fracas, though here and there are details that make one question the absolute veracity of the report. For instance, we are told that at the head of the procession was "the Professor's body servant, dressed as a Bulgarian brigand and leading his pet dog." The costume would be absolutely in keeping with Danielle's wishes. But a dog? We think not.

Let us turn our attention towards the question of "the Professor's body servant." A couple of years after he opened the Octagon, the Professor granted an audience to an American journalist, who published the interview under the headline "WHO WILL BE THE HEIR OF THIS NEWFOUNDLAND HERMIT?" The writer caught Danielle in a confessional mood. Solicitous, even. He said, "I am practically all alone out here. When you see me, you see my whole family, and I don't fancy that any one else would take as much trouble with me after I have passed away as I have in anticipation of the actual event.... There is only one thing in the world I want. It would take a heap of trouble from my mind. I am well to do, and probably haven't many years to live. If I only had an heir! I'd like to adopt a well brought up, honest, intelligent American lad who would be a son to me and carry on this property after I am dead."

Enter Frederick A. Brazill, a young man of uncertain provenance. Brazill is a common-enough Newfoundland name, although it is more often spelled with a single "l." In fact, one of

Frederick A. Brazill by Danielle's coffin.

the first Europeans known to have drowned off the Newfoundland coast went by the surname Brazil, and he was so called
because he had travelled in South America. It seems unlikely,
given the regional prevalence of this family name, that Frederick was an American opportunist who made his way north
after reading the Professor's plangent plea. He was more likely
a local lad, possibly the son of someone in the SOE who had
been an occasional visitor to the Octagon. He was someone in
whom the perspicacious proprietor saw qualities he liked and
trusted. He was good-looking, that was for sure. In his photos,
he projects dapper self-confidence. In one portrait, he holds a
smoke in his left hand. He might be a youthful Noël Coward or
Ivor Novello or some such matinée idol. He was hired on as the
aging Professor's right-hand man, and before long was named
his heir. He was left Octagon Castle, "on condition that it be
conducted on the same lines as when the Professor was alive."
The building was not heavily mortgaged. At the hour of dissolution, his employer's aggregate debt on his $20,000 investment
was under a thousand dollars. Brazill was also entrusted with a
notebook, the title page of which was inscribed, in the Professor's own handwriting:

Book of Instructions and Information by C.H. Danielle for
the guidance of Frederick A. Brazill. Octagon Castle N.F.L.
November 14, 1900.

In this book, as clearly as in the funeral instructions he
placed in the frame behind his elaborate casket, we read writ
large the truth of this man's deeply controlling nature. Death
might come for us all, but there are those of us who cannot bear
the idea of loosening our grip on the world or on our loved ones.
The Professor's written legacy to Frederick includes homely
advice as to the handling of servants and the advisability of
keeping an adequate supply of firewood on hand in the winter
and ice in the summer, as well as more portentous, Polonius-like
words of counsel.

Keep this Book in your own possession & in such a safe place as to be able to put your hand upon it at any and all times & let it be your guide in all its bearings.

When death over takes me suddenly or after confinement to Bed, Lock all the doors of all the Rooms in the House & take possession of the Keys, there is no one who has the right to question your authority to do so....

Clear the Reading Room of its tables & chairs and have the body "Laid out" there, the Casket resting upon the Stool & drapery it now rests upon in the Mortuary Chamber. Keep the Body in the House "Waking" over two nights, or if possible for a Sunday funeral as more friends can attend on that day than any other....

My Sisters two Photos tacked to the Wall in my Bedroom, please place under the pillow in my Casket....

Keep Octagon Castle as clean and as reputable as you have known me to keep it. Add as little as possible to it until my Debt is cleared....

Order a wreath of Flowers from Mrs. Stein, to place upon the Casket, for I have few loving friends in this coldhearted country. Oh! how *different* it would be if I could be fortunate Enough to Die in my own country America, there I would be *burried* [*sic*] beneath flowers.

Mrs. Stein will send the bill to you, & you pay the same....

And so he ended, and so he was buried, with handsome Brazill (evidently) parading before the glass-topped coffin in the guise of a Bulgarian brigand, possibly with an incongruous dog in tow, and with six prominent men of the day — including, once again, the politician William Whiteway — bearing the pall. They walked slowly. They nodded at friends in the crowd. Now and then, one might have winked. They inhaled the pollen from Mrs. Stein's flowers. They tried not to sneeze. They unshouldered their burden, they doffed their hats, they bowed their heads, they said amen, they went home again, and they had supper. Brazill returned to the hotel. For a while, he kept it up. Then he sank without trace. When the Octagon burned in 1915, it was held in the name of R. Fowlow, of Trinity. A Mr. Poole was the proprietor. And that is where the story more or less peters out. More or less.

Most of the extant material about Danielle is housed in the archives of the Centre for Newfoundland Studies at Memorial University of Newfoundland. Bert Riggs, the archivist, has done a very admirable job of cataloguing, describing, and preserving what little remains, materially, of the Professor. However, in the Special Collections division of the St. John's Public Library, locked away in a little cash box, and bound with a pretty ribbon, is a small cache of letters and papers that fleshes out the story ever so slightly. There are two documents in Danielle's hand. One is a sort of work in progress, a rather paranoid account of his investigation into the kleptomaniacal tendencies of his servants. It's next to impossible to wring anything like sense from those pages, but my impression is that he decided to test the honesty of his domestics by leaving thick ham sandwiches and slices of cake round about the Octagon. Having baited the trap, he hid behind the arras, waiting to see who would bite and when and how often. Not surprisingly, these unclaimed foodstuffs didn't linger long. It gave him some satisfaction to see them eaten and to have his suspicions confirmed. There is also a more contained and cogent note, a single page written on the letterhead of Deer Lodge Farm, Montrose, Susquehanna County, Pennsylvania. It is dated September 18, 1881, and is addressed to a Mrs. Waugh. The Professor offers her his condolences. He has just received the news about "*Poor Clarence's* distressing *condition*," and begs her to keep him apprised of details as they emerge about her husband, that is, Clarence, and his unnamed pathology.

The rest of the letters were written in 1902 and 1903, all of them after the pivotal date of May 1, and all are addressed to Mr. Frederick A. Brazill. One is a note from Perry Claude Byron, who lived in New York, and apparently made his living as a theatrical photographer. It is dated September 25, 1902. He wrote, "Been very busy since we got home, have no time for such dances & singing as on that Thursday night when within the Castle's walls, but oft-times think of the fun we had.... Wish Mr. Lunt and I were with you...." From this we can garner that the Castle was not hung overlong with the black crêpe of mourning. There is also a letter from an American relative of the Professor's who wonders if there might not be a bibelot or two coming his way, now that the estate has been settled. The balance of the material, however, consists of letters from one C. H. Waugh, of Pittsfield, Massachusetts. This would be none other than Poor Clarence who in 1881 was laid low by that distressing condition but was luckily able to stave off its more lingering symptoms. We can suppose that Frederick uncovered Waugh's name and address among the Professor's effects, or that his particulars were included by Danielle on a list of those to be contacted after his death. Read through this one-sided correspondence — none of the letters from Brazill to Waugh is to be found here — and you get the sense that Frederick is pressing his benefactor's old friend for biographical details. Perhaps the Professor was as much a mystery to him as he was to any of the throng of 10,000 who mobbed his funeral. On July 12, 1902, Clarence replied to a letter he had received from the new owner of the Octagon:

"Dear Sir: Your interesting letter of July 5, 1902 received this day. The last letter Prof. Danielle wrote me was about two years ago. It was a very pathetic letter, telling me how much he had wept over the loss of my friendship, and how much he had thought of me over all these years. I first met him in Bridgeport, Conn. when I was teaching there, a principal in one of the city's grammar schools in 1866, and have known him ever since. He was a great lover of *men*. He used to hug and kiss them and want to *sleep* with them. I did not like this. But there was much about him I *did* like."

Aha. Yes. Men. Well. Is anyone surprised? Hands up whoever is surprised. Bachelorhood, embroidery, theatrics, tinsel, spangles, costumes, fits of temper, and a career in the hospitality industry: put it all together and the word "symptomatic" comes to mind. On July 16, Clarence wrote:

"I felt sure you would like to know someone well acquainted with Prof. Danielle, for it is best to know all we can of our valued friends. With all his glaring faults, did he have more of them than most of us? We are all imperfect, but in different ways. Our faults are different. For that reason, I exercise the broadest charity towards my fellow men, as I want the same for myself.

"But faults aside, I have always considered Prof. Danielle a *very remarkable man* — superior to nearly all other men. His ability, executiveness, his creative genius and art were sublime. His tender heart and charity to the poor were conspicuous throughout his life....He in early life was always infatuated with *men* — never women — and these *men* would work on his soft side to get all the *money* they could and then *drop* him — and he gave *freely*. They *bled* him. Only for that he would have become *a very wealthy man*."

It would be neither charitable nor kind, not even in the light of this information about the Professor's attraction to gold-digging bottom feeders, to cast aspersions on the purity of the motives and actions of Mr. Brazill, or to speculate that the Professor might actually have been in love with his ward. Only an outright bounder would won-

Charles Henry Danielle (seated) and Frederick A. Brazill.

der aloud whether the hunky Freddy might have had motives that were just ever so slightly on the ulterior side of honourable when he came knocking on the door of the Octagon, with an indulgent look on his face and his kitbag in hand. There is no concrete proof to suggest that he delayed marrying until after the death of his sugar daddy for fear of alienating the Professor's affections, which might have led to his being heaved out of the comfy castle. It is surely nothing more than a coincidence that directly the old man was gone he found himself a willing girl and put the honeymoon suite to its intended purpose. On August 28, 1902, Clarence — who would receive a piece of wedding cake by return mail — sends a note of congratulations to him and to "the dearest little girl in St. John's." In subsequent letters, he recalls how, once upon a time, the touch of his own beloved would send shock waves through him, would make him feel as though he had fallen from a two-storey building. Frederick must always remember that the love of a good woman is the greatest thing a man can have. "The dear creatures come high but we must have them and I never forget that my mother was a woman."

In other letters Clarence speaks of his health. It has remained rocky ever since the unpleasantness of 1881. He has just enough energy to tune and repair pianos. This is an avocation at which he is expert. Perhaps one day, he writes, he'll come for a visit and work his magic on uprights in Newfoundland. Would there be enough paying customers to make a trip north worth his while? In every missive, he always offers up another recollection of dear, departed, mixed-up Charles.

"When the lady and I were stopping at his home for a few days…he had arranged for *me* to sleep with *him*. Every *man* that *visited him* he wanted to *sleep* with him. Not being in the habit of sleeping with *any*one — not with my own wife even, nor with *any* person, I said, 'No, Charles, let me sleep *alone*.' Being short of *beds* he made me one up on the *floor* and I slept there *alone*. I am queer about that — can't sleep with anybody else, male or female."

Mr. Waugh also thanks Brazill for having sent him a copy of Danielle's last booklet. He must have paid special attention to page twenty-six. There he would have read, "I have scrap-books as big as family Bibles, filled to bursting with letters and press opinions, that locate me every day from 1848 until this day — such a record as no other man in this country can show. These records can be seen by any visitor to the Octagon, and, if I am not Charles Henry Danielle, I have stolen his life and records and the question is: Who am I?"

It is the query of a dyed-in-the-wool romantic who must have lived between the lines of stories like "Rumpelstiltskin" and *Parsifal*. He made a show of stanching the sly, suspicious whisperings about his genesis and habits, but his nature was so thoroughly theatrical that he might now and then have seeded with rumour the cloud that hung above his name. Ah, the conundrum of the name! Some mendacious bastard spread it about that "Danielle" was a transmogrification of "Dan O'Neill," a slanderous utterance which moved the Professor to say, "...if my name ever had been Dan Neill or Dan O'Neill, I would have swapped it for a dog, and killed the dog. My full name is Charles Henry Danielle, a much prettier name than Dan Neill.... If I am not Charles Henry Danielle, the question is: Who am I?"

Clarence Waugh — who, let's just come straight out and say it, was one of the all-time great killjoys, and a terrible priss to boot — knew the answer. He was only too happy to blurt it out, in his very first letter to Brazill, crying the truth as triumphantly as the miller's daughter in the fairy tale. Danielle's real name, he crows, was Charles Augustus Everson. He had it on the high authority of the Professor's brother-in-law, a cultured man with whom he was well acquainted. Yes! His real name was — Charles Augustus Everson! "Mr. Overton gave away his secret, and Prof. D. *wrote me* that *that name* was his *true* name.... Charles *wrote* me that he changed his name because he had danced himself into fame under the name of *Charles H. Danielle* and therefore *retained* it *afterwards*. (This was at Chicago.) But he was a born *mystic* and had his own secrets that he kept from his most intimate friends. He had a large cluster ring which he called *diamonds*, when in fact they were only imitations — yet he would *say* they were *genuine*. Of course I could not *trust* his *word* for *this* defect was *born in* him, and he could not be different — could not *help* it....He could cry like a child over the death of a bird. I have *known* him to weep over the death of a swallow. When I was about to marry he wanted to know if *his* love was not better. He *begged* of me *not to marry*. Of course, *this* showed an *abnormal mind*, but it was *born in* him; and what is *born in* a man will *stay* there till death. But he is dead — God bless him. C.H.W."

The little lake on which Danielle built his castle is still called Octagon Pond. You can take a cab there from St. John's for about $20. You should know, though, that there is precious little to see. A convenience store. A few hangar-like buildings, remnants of the one or two failed attempts to establish some light industry on the grounds where a castle once stood. In a normal January, the pond will be frozen. The snow might have been cleared from a small patch of ice in preparation for a hockey game. The children of Paradise will arrive with their sticks and their pucks and their skates, and chase each other around the crusty water where years and years ago, on an August afternoon, the Church of England orphans paddled, and tortured frogs. You won't be able to guess, from surveying the scene, where the Octagon stood. There is not a single sign of its galleries, its paintings, its banners, its kitchens and its banquet halls where, during any given summer, 2,969 meals would be offered up and 817 chickens and ducks would be roasted and served. Long gone is the guest book in which were inscribed such appreciations as "Excellent, magnificent, unequalled...Out of sight...Of all the places I have seen in the United States and other countries, nothing compares with this grandeur...Ingenuity and taste everywhere displayed...Three cheers for the Professor."

Three cheers for the Professor, who kept close track of numbers, and who by the end of the day had taught dancing in eighty-nine cities and towns to 16,831 persons; who had slept in 912 beds, who had travelled 51,833 miles, who had written

61,390 letters (where are they now?), and who finally managed to boil his life down to something that could be contained in an octagon. He is gone now, gone altogether. There is no sign of him, nor will there be again. His life was smoke and mirrors. No one had to show him how to vanish, and he knew when it was time to go. Stand by Octagon Pond in the winter and think of him inside the eight walls of his soon-to-be immolated palace, that Knossos of Newfoundland. Think of him stitching up his quilts, embroidering his hangings, working at his tatting, sitting at his loom. Think of the pricked fingers, the hunched shoulders, the eye strain, all the suffering in the name of art. Think of him rising from his work and surveying his domain, moving from room to room, looking from each of his eighty-four windows, taking in the magnificent far-off views, the big white fields and the big grey sea. Think of his full and aching heart; his deep, cold loneliness. Think of him listening, listening to see if he could distinguish in the wind the syllabizing hubbub of Beelzebub's desperate and incantatory anagramming:

> *Ye learn Hell's red chain!*
> *Die charnel, Hell yearns!*
> *A cheery Hell, sinner lad!*
> *Any Hellish reel, dancer!*

Think of him smiling, knowing that, as sure as he was born in Baltimore, the devil could never, not in a million years, guess his secret name.

Chapter
Five

Devil among the Tailors

But the Spirit of the Lord departed from Saul,
and an evil spirit from the Lord troubled him.
> — I Samuel 16:14

Sad sack Saul, then! An evil spirit come to roost where once the Lord had lived. This is not the kind of visitation to which anyone would willingly open the door. Even for the King of Israel, this was a problem. What to do? What to do? It was a lucky thing for him he could call on David, his personal Mr. Fix-It. David, the psalm singer. David, the giant killer. David, who was not only a dab hand with a slingshot, but also a music therapist with a specialty in exorcizing evil spirits. He knew what his king needed, and, what was more, he had the skills and materials to bring it off. He picked up his harp. He strummed a soothing song. Before you could say Nebuchadnezzar, "Saul was refreshed, and was well, and the evil spirit departed from him" (I Samuel 16:23).

The moral of the story is, never underestimate the power of the harp. It is the instrument of angels, and calms the mind as surely as a rose-scented breeze from the south. The psaltery will also do in a pinch, and the timbrel and the trumpet both have their sanctified uses. As for the fiddle — well, that's an instrument you want to handle with care. Be leery, dearie, of the fiddle. It's not for nothing they call it "the devil's box." They call it that because it's his invention. He's the one who thought it up. Are you surprised? You shouldn't be. Figure it. A slab of wood, strung with four tight filaments of gut. A hank of horsehair to stroke them till they squeal. Could anyone invent such a device had he not spent the better part of eternity assailed by clouds of sulphur and the screams of the damned? I think not.

The devil made the fiddle and he loved it right away. He never tired of playing it, and would have sawed at it without a break were it not for the administrative demands placed on him by his job. Even when he had to give full attention to the day-to-day running of Hell, he didn't set the contraption down, but carried it on his hip, as a mother carries a baby. It didn't take long before the fiddle came to feel like an extension of his body, an extra limb. He knew it proprioceptively. It became his language, his currency, his passport. He played it while clambering up the smoky flue that was his conduit to the world above. He played it as he wandered the earth, looking for frangible souls he could tempt with a jig or a reel. He played it at the Octagon while the Professor tatted or sewed up his costumes, sequin after sequin. He played it at Frederick Brazill's wedding, bowed all his favourite tunes: "Knocking at the Door," "Hell among The Yearlings," "Joy among The Darkies," and "Big Footed Coon." He laid into "Fat Meat and Dumplings," "Old Mother McCarthy," "Peaches and Cream," and "Soldier's Joy." He tried his hand at "Old Woman at the Well," "Ice on the Pump Handle," "Sugar in the Coffee," and "Ladies on the Steamboat." He teased them a little with "Turkey Knob," and by way of saying goodnight, he treated them to "Speed the Plow." "Speed the Plow" was his favourite. When he played "Speed the Plow," the sparks just flew.

Any fiddler knows that the quick tunes are so much flash and sparkle. They're not without their challenges, they're full of virtuoso turns, but it's the slow and tender melodies that really prove a player's mettle. If you play the fiddle, you know it's the lullabies and laments, with their transparent simplicity, that plumb the depth of your heart, that reveal your essence to the listener. The devil, who has an investment in keeping such qualities concealed, did not care for music with an easy lilt. Too namby-pamby, he said. Too soporific. It might be said that he lacked a sense of occasion, for he'd as readily play "Hogs in the Tater Patch" at a funeral or a christening as he would at a wedding or a barn-raising. Exactly what he played while standing beside the cradle of Pierre-Léon Ayotte is anyone's guess. "Joseph Won the Coated Fiddle" or "Silver Star Hornpipe." What is sure is that the baby didn't like it one little bit. It made him all sleepless and bilious. He erupted into a colicky fit, and that was what gave the devil his entrée.

Pierre-Léon Ayotte, who was born in 1845, spent his life in and around the rural environs of Ste-Geneviève-de-Batiscan, Quebec. It was a no-nonsense kind of place where most people lived off the avails of farming and forestry; where practicality was the byword; where men wore pants, women wore skirts, and that was that. Pierre-Léon distinguished himself from the crowd by wearing a *jaquette*. This was a curious garment that looked, from all accounts, like a nightshirt. It was simple in design, long-sleeved, unadorned except for the buttons that ran up the front, cardigan style. It was about the length of a nightshirt, and hung down over his knees and boot tops. So identified did he become with this get-up that he achieved his nickname, "Jaquette-à-Simon."

That the *jaquette* became his everyday attire grew out of his phobia about wearing trousers, an inconvenient kink dating back to his infancy. It was really his father who was to blame, his father who should have known better. It was he who opened the door to satanic influence. Once it was ajar, even that tiny crack, the fiddling devil couldn't wait to get in there and leave his mark. The story they told around Ste-Geneviève was that Pierre's mother heard her child sobbing in his cradle. She was occupied elsewhere in the house, and shouted to her husband to attend to the baby and his rocking. The elder Ayotte's nerves were on edge. This kid cried all the time, and surely it was a mother's job to comfort her baby. So, he refused. She bristled. They quarrelled. The devil, who likes such a scene, stood by, playing "Good for the Tongue." The baby bawled the louder. Finally, his father threw up his hands in rage and frustration and shouted, "Que le diable le berce d'abord!.," which is to say, "May the devil rock him then!" Hell's fiddler required no further invitation. He was in there like a dirty *jaquette*. From then on, the baby's cradle would rock and rock, seemingly of its own volition. The child was pacified, but the house was otherwise thrown into disarray. Dishes would fly from the cupboards, pictures rearranged themselves on the walls, even the barn was seen to shake and tremble, as though it were dancing to the strains of the "Findy Sickle Two Step."

No one doubted whose handiwork this was. Watching Pierre-Léon grow up — which is not to say mature — was like watching the linking of the letters that made the devil's signature. The boy became increasingly bizarre. He began stealing things — common, dumb household objects — and squirrelling them away. It satisfied a need, no one could say for what, least of all Pierre-Léon, who never learned to speak in anything other than a childish lisp. And then there was the question of his clothing, where his predilections were not at all *comme il faut*. He couldn't be made to dress properly. That *jaquette*! Many thought he needed only a stern hand and tried to force him into trousers. The breeches would be ripped to shreds within the hour. It was the devil's handiwork, there could be no doubt about that.

Word of his eccentricities spread and reached the ear of one Hubert Trépanier. He was an unscrupulous promoter, an impresario with an eye for the freakish. He convinced Pierre to run away with him to the circus. They went to New England and got onto the carnival circuit. They fell in with the bearded ladies and the Siamese twins, with the brainless babies floating in bottles, and the giants and the midgets and the man from whose forehead there sprouted horns. As if Pierre didn't know already about men with horns. He was exhibited as one who was possessed by satanic spirits, as the carrier of a cruel curse. "Come See Jaquette-à-Simon, the Man Whom the Devil Forbids to Wear Trousers!"

It was a short-lived adventure. The ruse was transparent. It was easy enough to expose. Some gamblers got together and decided to test the veracity of this outlandish claim. They placed their bets, then laid hold of Ayotte. They dressed him all in white, in a shirt and the hated pants. They blackened his hands with charcoal, they locked him in a room. When he emerged, his suit was in tatters, and dirtied all over with tell-tale soot. The devil's work? The smudges told a different tale. It had all the earmarks of a ruse, and not even a cunning one. Conclusions were drawn. Fingers were pointed. The jig was up, and a jig was what the devil played. "If I Hadn't Been a Fool, I Might Have Been a Lady," I think it was, or maybe "Shake the Bow."

Pierre-Léon must have been relieved. He slipped back into his beloved *jaquette* and hit the road for home. He spent the rest of his life as a labourer, laughed at by some, pitied by others. His reputation continued to grow, and he became in his own lifetime a figure of folkloric fun, a full-blooded fool, a cautionary tale. He died in 1907, at the age of sixty-one. You'll never guess who provided the music at the funeral. He played "Someone's at the Door." He played "Done Gone."

The sad story of poor Ayotte is told in the *Dictionary of Canadian Biography*, and has been recounted in a number of journal articles and novels. Lionel Dessureaux, writing in *Le Mauricien* in 1938, remembers how he became a kind of bogey man, and that the threat of a visitation from La Jaquette-à-Simon was used to quell children who refused to go to sleep. E. Z. Masicotte speculated in 1929 that Ayotte's strange comportment might have been the result of a prolonged childhood fever that left him damaged. Whether or not that was the genesis of his strangeness, I suspect that any qualified diagnostician could, if given all the facts of the case, attach a name to his condition. *A quoi bon?* would be the operative question. Me, I favour the supernatural explanation. I'm content with the fiddling hypothesis. If a reason must be found, it's as good as any other.

For the longest time, the devil kept the fiddle to himself. He was the only one who owned or played one. Somewhere along the line, the instrument fell into human hands. How this happened is anyone's guess, though I imagine it was part of a deal Beelzebub cut to secure the promise of some coal-rich soul he couldn't do without. Over time and use and travel, passed from mortal hand to mortal hand, the fiddle shed most traces of its fiery antecedents. Held to the chins of some players it still sounds like hell, of course, but overall it's taken on a much more benignant quality. In some lives, like that of Willie Francis Fraser, the fiddle has even proved something of a charm.

Mr. Fraser, who is verging on eighty, lives in Deepdale, on Cape Breton Island. He is not celebrated as a fiddler, but rather as an exponent of the related craft of step-dancing. He's been at it all his life and says he's danced in or on every hall, step, and bridge on the island of Cape Breton about ninety-nine times, usually with a fiddle playing along. When he was younger, and still working in the mines, he'd sometimes stay out most of the night dancing, then go underground with just a couple of hours' sleep. Such alacrity and indefatigability make him the artistic heir to Malcolm MacLean, who arrived from Scotland early in the nineteenth century. No sooner had Malcolm seen the shores of North America rise up on the horizon than he hurried below deck and put on his step-dancing togs, donned his top hat, and coattails, and fine buckled shoes. He was a man with a mission. He meant to teach his art to all and sundry in the New World, and it was his intention to launch in the second he stepped onto the pier. That would have been a landing to see: Malcolm MacLean, skipping and capering down the gangplank, clicking his heels in boyish anticipation of what was to come. He was sidetracked by petty considerations of land-clearing and house-building, but eventually was able to stake his intended vocational claim. He is said to have had the floor joists changed in his house three times before he was satisfied with the springiness of his dancing surface.

Willie Fraser doesn't know the name of the man who appeared to him in a dream over seventy years ago and taught him to dance. Perhaps it was the ghost of Malcolm MacLean, although, when I asked him to tell me the story and happened to use the word "ghost," he protested loudly that it wasn't a ghost at all. It was for real. It was true. And he should know, since he was there. It happened like this.

He was just a little boy, though older than Pierre-Léon had been when *his* life changed, maybe five, maybe six years old. He came down from his room one morning and his father, Simon, who was a terrific fiddler, asked him how he had slept. Willie Francis said fine, just fine, but that there had been this fellow in his room who had told him that he, Willie, was going to be a dancer and that he was there to teach him the steps. He was a good-looking young fellow, the dream man. He was dressed in a blue suit, white shirt, and tie. Willie was not alarmed. He felt no fear or threat. He took this visit in his stride, quite literally. He didn't ask the apparition any questions as to his name or provenance, he just paid attention to the dancing. And in the morning, he told his father all about it.

"Ah," said his pa, no more alarmed than his son had been, "let's see what you can do, then." He picked up his fiddle and he played a reel, and sure enough, the boy had learned his lessons well. It was amazing, the things he could do, and there wasn't just one step, either. The young man returned to him a few more times, and on each visit, he saw to it that Willie had five or six dances added to his repertoire. By the time he stopped appearing, he had laid the foundation for the "close to the floor" style that Willie Fraser still practises.

One day, I suppose, years and years from now, Willie might himself appear to some youngster in a dream. Happily, he's not waiting until he's passed beyond to start teaching. He passes on his learning in the here and now. He has made recent trips to the Hebrides in Scotland, and there he instructs the great-great-great-great-grandchildren of the immigrants who entered Canada with their toes tapping and their fiddles primed to sing. It's an act of repatriation, really, like returning an artifact to its tribe of origin. The lively ghost (if I may say so) of Malcolm MacLean must surely be pleased, for any dancer appreciates the beauty of a circle. Any dancer knows the object of the exercise is somehow to get back home.

Willie Francis Fraser's dancing gifts are heaven-sent. They're wakened when the devil's box is played; when *like a mist the music drifts from the silvery strings*. How that old devil must grit his teeth and swear when he hears what his pride and joy, his marvellous toy, has become. Damn, damn, damn! He should have known better than to give it away. "Old Fort Smith," "The Old Blue Tick," and "Eli Green's Cakewalk." He still plays them when he has a mind to kill some time, but it's just not the same. He'll play "8th of January," "Jennie Put the Kettle On," and "Bummer Reel." The mood he's in these days, he's especially fond of "Bummer Reel."

The devil, who likes to be in charge, doesn't usually take requests from the floor. But I've sent him a note and shot of dark rum and asked that he favour us with just one tune, something that will put us in the right frame of mind for what's to come.

"Fine," he said, knocking back the toddy. "But no more than one."

"Do you mind if we dance?" I asked, and he *began to laugh with that sibilant laugh that resembles the hiss of a serpent.*

"Do your damnedest. You'll never keep up!"

His bow is taut. His strings are tuned. Listen between the lines, and you're sure to hear him play. There it is now. Can you place the tune, make it out through the squawk and rasp of overtones? It's called "The Lightning Hornpipe."

Shock

...when thou walkest through the fire,
thou shalt not be burned; neither shall
the flame kindle upon thee.
— Isaiah 43:2

It was an afternoon late in June, the first really hot day of summer. The year was 1906. An electrical storm was cruising through the supercharged ions of the crackling lower atmosphere. It passed above the newly seeded fields of southwestern Manitoba, passed over the farming communities of Rivers and Brandon, passed over sleepy Minnedosa and the gentle rise of Riding Mountain. It grumbled. It spat. From time to time, it sparked, just small-time delinquency. By the time it got to Souris, which was where the Joyners lived, it was primed for headier mischief. It was ready to rumble.

Mrs. Joyner and her husband had taken rooms on the third floor, above the dry goods store. They moved in there after his threshing accident made farming an impossibility, and town the only available option. Everyone was amazed that they chose to install themselves in a place where he would have to cope with all those stairs. They shook their heads, even though they understood the why of it well enough. It was his way of showing he was still capable, that not so very much had changed, that he was still the man he had always been. Even though he was not. You just had to look at him to see that. It broke your heart, watching his slow and painful progress up and down those three flights. He was stubborn, though. He had always been stubborn. Proud, too.

The day of the electrical storm, the Joyners happened to be at home. Truth be told, home is where they usually were. When they went out, he complained that he was looked at, and that people felt sorry for him. He was right. They did. He couldn't abide their pity, so they kept mostly to themselves. It was hard on them both, though in different ways. They stayed indoors, three floors up, under a flat roof that was a magnet for the heat. Their place tended towards the stuffy, as you can imagine, so from the middle of June till the middle of September, depending on the vagaries of the season, they would leave the windows open. By the open window was where Mrs. Joyner liked to sit. The light was good there, and she felt more connected to the world beyond, less homesick and aware of her losses.

On the afternoon in question, when she was in her accustomed place, a breeze that was almost a gust joined them in the room. It was uncommonly warm and sudden. Mrs. Joyner looked up from her hemming. She was finishing off an apron, a gift for her favourite niece who had moved to Winnipeg just before Christmas and was now engaged to be married. This niece might have been her own daughter, they were that close. She herself had never had children, which was her only regret in life, other than her husband's misery. When she told the story of that afternoon — and she often would — Mrs. Joyner would remember that she noted the curtains fluttering back into place, that she looked beyond them to the darkening complexion of the sky, the deep and angry creases of its brow. It gave her a funny turn. She said as much to Mr. Joyner. He was seated across the room on the settee, his one leg propped up on a footstool, and she told him how she was feeling all queer and apprehensive. These were the first words either of them had uttered since breakfast. They had been married for thirty years, and a silence that was not always comfortable had grown up between them.

Directly she had spoken she wondered if this aberrant restlessness might not be another symptom of the onset of her change of life. She had been troubled latterly by inconvenient sweats and mood swings. It was a nuisance, but she wasn't overly concerned. She knew more or less what to expect, and in a way she was glad. A fat lot of good all that cramping and bleeding had done her, anyway. They'd tried and tried for a baby. In all those years, she had never missed her monthly visit from Nurse Blood. Now, she was drying up. She would have to do her best to be uncomplaining, to set a good example for her niece and the young women at the church. She still went to church. She went by herself most Sundays.

"I do feel queer," she said. "I feel queer all of a sudden. Hot, kind of."

Mr. Joyner raised his eyes from his book. He was reading Dickens, *Bleak House*. He used to read the Bible, but abandoned it after "the incident." That's what he called it. "The incident." He had always been a laconic man, given to understatement. He looked across the room and considered his wife for a moment or two before venturing the opinion that perhaps she felt unsettled because a finger of lightning had just tapped her on the shoulder. And as for feeling warm, well, that would be because she was, in fact, on fire. On June 23, 1906, *The Toronto Daily Star* reported that, by the time the blaze was extinguished, "it had burned a hole six inches in diameter into her clothes, to the flesh, though she herself was not injured and the lightning's work was not visible in any other respect."

And it was so. That night, when Mrs. Joyner sat at her vanity, pulling her brush through her long hair — there was very little grey in it yet, a fact which stirred up in her a pride she knew to be wholly irrational — she observed with some disappointment that she was utterly unchanged in her every aspect. One would think that so striking and nearly fatal an encounter would have left behind a visible souvenir. Scars. Stigmata. A limp to match her husband's. A miracle baby, floating in her shrinking womb. It seemed to her, on reflection, that in that quick and shocking instant, when her awareness had been elsewhere, her one and only life had been blasted up to its pinnacle, its apogee. In the blink of an eye she had gone from being the wife of a defeated, one-legged man to being a woman with her own remarkable, annunciatory tale to tell. She had been singled out by lightning and saved by God. Blessed was she among women. But while legend is fine and dandy, it's not as though you can hold it in your hand. From here on in, it would all be downhill. She was hardly fifty and already knew for a fact what the mourners at her funeral would whisper about among themselves. What kind of prescient certainty was that to haul around all the rest of her days? Was there nothing more to hope for? How could she top the split-second searing of this afternoon?

The only redemptive possibility was that lightning might strike twice. She left her mirror. She made three paces through the room, pussyfooting past her snoring husband. He had gone to bed early, worn out by all the excitement, by so many neighbours coming round to gape and to wonder. Of course, the uninvited company had to be served cold drinks, which meant they had run out of ice, which annoyed him. Worse still was that the ghost of his missing leg had chosen that night for one of its occasional hauntings. It was out there, stomping around the field where he'd left it, pining for its old attachments. How the bereaved stump ached! On top of everything else, he had one of those pollen-induced headaches that plagued him at this time of year. He'd taken one of his special draughts and was asleep within minutes. He didn't stir when Mrs. Joyner heaved up the high window and looked down at the dark and dusty streets of Souris. The air had a promising mugginess about it. She turned back to the bed and left the window open to the world and its infinite possibilities. She slid between the summer sheets, fanned her hair out on the pillow. She inhaled deeply, was rewarded by a faint whiff of lavender. She always kept a sachet in with her linens as she found the scent calming. She crossed her hands over her breasts and assumed a look of deep satisfaction. This was how she would like to be found. It was best to be ready. She thought of how upset her mother would have been had she known when she went to bed in her stained old nightgown that she would be dead in the morning, and it would be left to that pedlar to find her and raise the alarm. By the time she, Mrs. Joyner, heard about it and hurried over, half the town had been by to have a gander. As everyone knows, you can never tell what might happen when you're asleep or simply looking the other way. You can just never tell.

I was reminded of Mrs. Joyner on board the ferry for Prince Edward Island. I'd boarded at Cape Tormentine, New Brunswick, and there was nothing about my circumstances to suggest that she should surface in my meditations. It was a clear day in the middle of January. I had been listening to the radio, and the news was innocent of malevolent omens. True, hogs were having a hard time of it. A livestock report leaked word that things were gridlocked at the abbatoir. Porcine executions were running an hour behind schedule. As well, I learned that a card party in Tignish had been cancelled because one of the regular players had passed away, of natural causes, and that two lost dogs were found wandering in the vicinity of Summerside. Sad news, all this, but the world is a sad, sad place. Nothing I heard on the radio seemed so very much out of the ordinary as to contraindicate a voyage over water. Certainly there was no danger of lightning. So, whence came Mrs. Joyner? I'm ashamed to say it must have been eavesdropping that fired the synapses which caused her to breech and gulp for air.

"Where you headed?" one trucker asked another in the little ship's cafeteria. They were both eating ham sandwiches and I couldn't keep from wondering how long the pigs had lingered in the holding pen.

"Just up to Charlottetown. You?"

"Just out to Souris."

Aha! Souris! Hence the Joyner connection. I had never before been to P.E.I., and I was thrilled at the prospect of adding flesh to the bones of places about which I'd heard or read, of seeing if their reality measured up to my imagining. It was disappointing to hear these seasoned travellers shrug off their destinations so casually, demonstrating the indifference, if not the contempt, that is bred by familiarity.

"Just up to Charlatan. You?"

"Just out to Surrey."

That trucker said "Surrey" with such indifference that you knew for a fact he'd never thought about it with a fringe on the top. Still, I was glad to know something about the local inflection, glad to know that on P.E.I. Souris = Surrey. I should have hated to have stopped at a service station and spoiled one of those testosterone-scented under-the-hood discussions by manfully grunting, "Sure, top up the oil, and by the way is this the road to Souris?" pronouncing it as I might the French word for "mouse," tossing it off with that Continental flare for which I am celebrated near and far.

In Manitoba, where I grew up, they anglicize "Souris" even more tellingly. There, it is rendered as "Surris." When the reporter from *The Toronto Daily Star* contacted Mrs. Joyner for a horse's mouth rendering of the story of her miraculous escape, "Surris" would have been where she told him it had all transpired. Yes, she told him, that was right. It was in "Surris" that she lived and it was in "Surris" that she very nearly died. Wasn't that something? Didn't that just about beat all?

The peculiarity of regional vernacular must be well known to Mr. Eddy R. Souris, whom I happened to meet quite by chance one day in a downtown Toronto office lobby. He was a man of indeterminate age, sixty something I would say, pleasantly enough turned out, but unremarkable of stature or mien. He was clutching a manila envelope to his heart. He approached me, inquired after my name, then — seemingly satisfied, God knows why — reached into his envelope and drew forth a single-page brochure. In bold print at the top were the words "Mousing Around." I gathered straight away that this was something he had prepared and printed and with which he wanted to present me. It was a completely unsolicited show of largesse, which is a rare-enough occurrence these days. I thanked him for the proffered sheet, which I accepted. We exchanged a few words and then he walked away. He disappeared through the revolving doors and onto Front Street, leaving me to wonder whether everyone who crosses his path receives such a gift, or whether he spotted me across a crowded room and intuited that I might be interested in owning such a publication. Which, of course, I was. I have it before me now.

Under the "MOUSING AROUND" headline are drawings of two heraldic crests, one French, one Dutch. Each incorporates three mice into its symbology. "Mr. Eddy R. Souris, of Toronto, is fascinated by his surname," the text of his document begins. It goes on to explain that, through explorations both genealogic and geographic, he has pursued the name in all its forms: the German, Maus; the Dutch, Muis or Muys; and the Danish, Muus. The name can be traced back as far as 1462, when the lordship of Lavoud, in Limousin, was held by a French family called — you guessed it — Souris. Eddy "has personally visited twenty-seven localities named Souris. Three are towns, one each in P.E.I., Manitoba, and North Dakota. Others are rivers, or features such as valleys, parks, or hills. They are found in France, Belgium, Madagascar, the Seychelles, and in both North America and the Indian Ocean. Research has brought him knowledge of almost sixty places called Mouse, such as Mouse Creek, Alaska and five lakes of the name in Ontario alone."

I tried, without success and many times, to contact Mr. Souris after this one fated and all too brief encounter. I am sorry for this failure, because I would have liked to have looked more searchingly under the rock of his reasons. I would have liked to have visited his house, to see if his passion extends to home decoration. Would there be novelty door bells, toilet roll covers, wall clocks? Would he have china cabinets burgeoning with rank on rank of Beatrix Potter, Mother Goose, and Walt Disney figurines? What would be on his book shelves? *Of Mice and Men*? *The Mouse and His Child*? Might he keep pets? If so, how many? As it is, I can only reflect on the rarity of his character. How many of us carry our names around with us as thoughtlessly as we do our noses or chins, using them when they are required, regretting sometimes that they don't seem to suit us, but content for the most part to take them for granted? That

Eddy R. Souris, of Toronto, is so smitten with his own family name that he will make the effort to travel as far as Madagascar, just to deepen his connection with it, sets him apart. Whether or not he reaches a destination and thinks about it analytically, forms opinions about his whereabouts, compiles a check-list of pros and cons, takes pictures, and gathers up anecdotes to spin back home, I cannot tell you. I wouldn't be surprised to learn that it is enough for him to arrive, scent the air, confirm that such-and-such a place exists, read the road signs and maps that connect it to the idea of the mouse and therefore, by extension, to him, and then go right back to Toronto. It pleased me to think of Eddy, and the possibility that he might have been a passenger on this self-same ferry, the *Abegweit*, while he made his pilgrimage to Prince Edward Island to take a quick squinny at Souris.

Eddy R. Souris! I wanted more than anything to speak of him, and of Mrs. Joyner too, to the ham-eating truck drivers, but there was something about the serpentine tattoos of the one and the bristling tool belt of the other that made me feel all shy and marshmallowy inside. Sometimes, a shackling timidity comes upon me and I clam right up. Who can say why? It's always been thus with me. That's just the kind of boy I am. I kept my counsel, left them to their cruel lunch, and stepped onto the deck of the *Abegweit*. I stood there alone and stared out at the ice-caked water of the Northumberland Strait. It was very, very cold.

Abegweit, as any tourist brochure will tell you, was the name given to the island by the Mi'kmaq. It means "cradled on the waves," which is prettier and less irritatingly proprietary than "Prince Edward Island," or even "Ile St. Jean," which is what the French called it when they settled in. Abegweit was also a promising contender as a name for the fixed-link bridge which now connects P.E.I. to New Brunswick. That "Confederation" won out is not so surprising. It is a duller but certainly a safer choice; it is far from inappropriate as it is not without historical resonance; and Lord knows it's easy to remember.

One wonders if there might have been a survey that suggested some tourists would be reluctant to trust their families and vehicles to a miles-long bridge the name of which they couldn't reliably pronounce. There was a kind of pathos to be distilled from plying the waves on this January ferry to Borden, chugging along in plain view of the span that was soon to put such a brave little boat out of business. Poor old *Abegweit*! It sluiced blithely through the icy channel, coursing along towards superfluity, towards its own oblivion.

The fixed link is a faint and steely echo of the once-upon-a-time land bridge that connected the two provinces. Thousands of years ago, the assiduous tides managed to wear it away. When officials first raised the prospect of summoning forth the genie of engineering to redraft that old connection, there were countless arguments for and against the venture. Of course there were! How could it have been otherwise?

Predictably, these arguments were based on concerns that were aesthetic, environmental, or socio-economic. The pro-bridge faction said its completion would herald the dawning of a bright day for business on the island. Tourists, who have been flocking to the place for years in any case, would be even more inclined to make the trek if they didn't have to take a boat. The no-bridge contingent peered into the dark side of the crystal. They countered with the theory that local businesses would actually suffer. Islanders, they feared, would give in to the mercantile temptations of Moncton, whose malls and doughnut shops would become shockingly accessible. Worst of all, though, was the sense of threat best expressed in a bumper sticker: "Real islands don't have bridges." This most pervasive fear was the hardest to articulate, as it could be neither proved nor quantified. What if the link should rob the place of its essential "islandness"? What if P.E.I. should lose everything that its relative isolation (a word which is joined at the etymological hip with "island") has made possible?; if it sacrificed its gem-of-the-sea, rural, down-home, red-earthed, potato-cultivating, fiddle-playing, Anne-of-Green-Gables folksiness on the seductive but tarnished altar of cosmopolitanism and financial gain? Good-bye God, hello Mammon. The anti-bridge lobby wanted to see preserved the sentiments celebrated in that turn-of-the-century ditty "My Old Island Home."

Far away to the north lies a dear little island
A Garden 'tis called in the lap of the sea.
'Tis the home of the Pine tree, the Birch and the Maple,
A Garden of promise, a land fair to see.

"Oh yes, everyone has something to say about the bridge," an Island friend told me one Saturday morning as we walked about the lively Charlottetown farmers' market. "Even the bee-keepers are upset. They think it'll now be easier for swarms of killer bees to find their way here."

I confess that I snickered. This seemed so far-fetched, so desperate a reaching. Paranoid, even. In the moment, a vision swam up before me of secretive cells of these singularly anti-social insects stowing away in camper vans with Ontario plates. I saw scheming, stinging cabals concealed in the luggage of Japanese tourists. I imagined how they had all been coached to choreograph themselves at the moment of landing into swarms that were as hard as mailed fists, that they would take to the air, and throw down the gauntlet before the gatekeepers of every local hive, and then proceed to pound the shit right out of them. But further reflection brought back the memory of St. Modom-noc. The useful didacticism of his story is too often overlooked or forgotten, no doubt because his feast day falls one day before St. Valentine's, who has received a disproportionate amount of press over the years. Modomnoc was an Irish holy man of the sixth century, probably of royal lineage. He travelled to Pem-brokeshire, where he studied at Menevia, in the monastery headed up by David: the very David who went on to become patron saint of Wales. One of Modomnoc's duties among this clan Davidian was to serve them as bee wrangler. He would have become well acquainted with such curious and ancient apiary customs and beliefs as the one which posits that, when bees remove themselves from a hive, it is a sign that their owner is not long for this world. If a keeper died in Modomnoc's time, and his bees were still in place, the hive was draped in mourning, and a piece of funeral cake placed before its opening. As well, when a cadaver was removed from the house, the hives were turned away so that the bees would not witness the removal of the body. This tradition persisted well into the eighteenth century. Hazlitt quotes a story that appeared in the London newspaper *Argus*, September 13, 1790. It tells of the aftermath of the collapse of a rich old farmer who died and "just as the corpse was placed in the herse [*sic*], and the horsemen, to a large number, were drawn up in order for the procession of the funeral, a person called out, 'Turn the bees,' when a servant who had no knowledge of such a custom, instead of turning the hives about, lifted them up, and then laid them down on their sides. The bees, thus hastily invaded, instantly attacked and fastened on the horses and their riders. It was in vain they galloped off, the bees as precipitately followed, and left their stings as marks of their indignation. A general confusion took place, attended with loss of hats, wigs, &c., and the corpse during the conflict was left unattended; nor was it till after a considerable time that the funeral attendants could be rallied, in order to proceed to the interment of their deceased friend."

Modomnoc, having established a connection with his bees, and knowing what he knew about the hardiness of such relationships, could hardly have been surprised that they decided to share in his leave-taking when his studies were done, and he was dispatched back to Ireland. After he had bade the monks a fond farewell, and had hopped into his barque, he heard the familiar buzz of a pleasing, harmonious chorus. He looked up and, lo and behold, there were his bees, settling themselves around his single mast. There they clustered and there they remained, all the way over the sparkling Irish Sea. So it was that Modomnoc brought apiculture to Ireland. The moral of the story is that if bees are willing not only to accept a transfer, but to endure the rigours of so uncertain a voyage at their own expense, they would surely be happy to hitch a ride on faster and more reliable transport. If I were a bee-keeper on Prince Edward Island, I would make sure that certain pertinent clauses were added to my insurance policy.

"I have an opinion about the bridge," says Fred Sauer, who is a watchman by night, an inventor by day, and one of the best friends electricity has ever known. We are standing around in his Charlottetown kitchen, which looks nothing like any other kitchen I've ever seen. It is a circus of circuitry, a jungle thickly hung with brightly coloured wires, a canopy of vivid liana. We are standing because there is really no place to sit, other than on the well-loved La-Z-Boy rocker which is the throne from which Fred rules this, his wondrous, high-voltage kingdom. From time to time, a light flashes to indicate that something is going on elsewhere in the house. Perhaps the sump pump in the basement has kicked into action, for instance, or it may be that one of Fred's two dogs, a gallumphing big mutt called Marmaduke, has retired for a nap. "Big Dukie's in Bed" reads the masking-tape label stuck under one of a panel of eight red lights arranged along one wall. Big Dukie's bed is upstairs next to Fred's bed. Fred has a water-bed, likewise his dog. The canine version is an inner tube filled with water and covered with a blanket. As soon as Big Dukie — a good-natured, shepherd–Dobermann cross with a white muzzle and floppy, comical ears — takes his ponderous weight off his feet and stretches out on his little couch for a kip, the water rises through a tube and makes a circuit. Electricity takes over. Hot, sharp impulses fly along the intestinal twist of wires that are stretched and coiled behind the drywall, passing a baton from hand to electronic hand. The last runner hits the finish line and the light illumines. "Big Dukie's in Bed" is the message it broadcasts.

It might seem an invention of limited utility, but it's perfect for Fred, who has an eye for detail, and likes to keep close track of just about everything that's trackable. For instance, he has a digital counter he can look at to ascertain how many times Big Dukie and Twister — that's Marmaduke's companion pooch — use their doggie door. He has devised a way to determine how much heat his tenant uses, proportionate to overall energy consumption, which has not as much to do with sharing utility costs as with Fred's being able to do it. It's the kind of thing he likes to know, just as he likes to keep the half-dozen clocks in the house synchronized to the second. Similarly, there is no good reason to be sure that Big Dukie's in Bed, other than if bed is where he is, it means he isn't out roaming the neighbourhood, and Fred knows there's no need to activate his electronic dog whistle, which is another of his inventions.

"For the most part I approve of the bridge," says Fred, lighting his pipe from a furnace transformer he's mounted on the workbench near his rocker. A crazy line of sparks crackles between its two delicate prongs, and Fred assures me that they are the trusted agents for 10,000 volts. "That bridge is going to bring more tourist business, that's for sure. This summer will be a dandy if the weather is nice and people don't have to fool around with the boat. But at the same time as it'll bring business, you can bet that it'll bring more thieves. They won't have to wait around for an early morning boat, so they'll be able to come over, rob someone's shop, and get off the island in the middle of the night."

Since Fred is both a watchman and an inventor, he has, of course, been figuring out prophylactic measures businesses and warehouses could take to safeguard against an anticipated criminal invasion. He has come up with a robotic alarm system made up of a wild conglomeration of parts, including copper tubing and a spray of water and something along the lines of his furnace generator that would add 10,000 volts to the mix. It would be activated when someone broke through a window with malice aforethought. Not only would the feisty partnership of water and electricity stop him in his tracks, it would send him reeling back into a collage of spikes and shards and leave him begging for prison.

I ask if a receiving line with a 10,000-volt grip wouldn't effectively eliminate the need for the sharp objects, but Fred assures me that it is not so powerful a charge if handled correctly. Fred is a connoisseur of shocks. They are part of his quotidian experience, and he knows just how much the human body can withstand before it is dragged across damage's jagged threshold. He wonders if I'd like to feel a moderate jolt, just so I know what he's talking about. I decline.

P.E.I. looks so sleepy and docile in the wintertime as to make the presence of a criminal element seem incongruous. However, it has often been said, because it is self-evident and true, that history is repetitive. There is much to be learned about the perils of the present from studying the past. Charlottetown, for all its here-and-now placidity, has seen its share of unsavoury activity. In fact, the hotel where I put up was built on the site of the old gallows. A plaque in the lobby gives an abbreviated account of the city's last public hanging. It took place in 1869. George Dowie (also spelled Dowey) was the star of the show. He was born in Montreal and went to sea as a lad. He wound up as a steward on the *Clara Novello*. One of his shipmates was a man named Cullen, from Limerick. Late in November 1868, while on shore-leave in Charlottetown, they were embroiled in a midnight quarrel over a woman named Miss McQuarry. They fought it out in an alley-way. It came to a calamitous end when Dowie drew a knife and stabbed it into Cullen's heart.

Dr. Beer's coroner's jury rendered a verdict of "wilful murder." The matter went to the Supreme Court, where it was an open-and-shut case. The judge came down fast and he came down hard. This kind of heinous act would not be tolerated in his jurisdiction. The scroll containing the written verdict is available for viewing in the provincial archives in Charlottetown, and it makes for fascinating reading. The many ink blots suggest that the clerk of the Court couldn't wait to wade through the tedious prose of jurisprudence to get to the punchline, the glorious capper which condemns the dagger-happy Dowie to be "taken from hence to the place from whence you came and that from hence you be taken to Pownal Square in Charlottetown on Tuesday, the thirtieth day of March next, between the hours of six o'clock in the morning and six o'clock in the afternoon, where you are to be hanged by the neck till you are dead and may God almighty have mercy upon your soul."

Between the passing of sentence and the actual hanging, the newspaper *The Islander* was chock-a-block with disgruntled letters and editorials. While no one disputed Dowie's guilt, there was a bluster of discontent about the severity of the penalty and about the public nature of his intended earthly demissioning. Surely there was nothing to be gained from so macabre and gruesome an exercise! There were appeals, and stays of execution, and various delays. Finally, on April 6, when every route to clemency had been tried and found blocked, Dowie's sentence ended with a gory period.

By half-past noon, a crowd of 1,500 had gathered for the show. The volunteer militia was present, armed and ready. There had been rumours that Dowie's more radical sympathizers might try something rash. The tension hung in the air *like a swift eagle in the morning glare breasting the whirlwind with impetuous flight*. Every shoulder tensed as the prisoner was led from the jail. He blinked at the midday light, and held his manacled hands up to his eyes. He climbed the stairs to the platform and turned to acknowledge his audience. He looked emaciated, unshaven. There was a welling of pity in every heart. Poor lost soul! Wasn't he some mother's son? Some woman's husband? How had he come to this sorry end? The man he had killed was trash, no one would dispute that. The world was none the worse off for the loss of him, no one would dispute that. As for the woman who'd led him astray — well, she wasn't spoken of in polite society. It didn't seem right, it surely wasn't fair, it was enough to make you choke, and yet, and yet, and yet it was all so irresistible!

The throng pressed in, sucked towards the delicious vortex of punishment, vying for position, eager for proximity until they saw the twenty militiamen lift their rifles, saw the glint of the bayonets, and they all fell back, *hushed as a breathless lyre.* Then they caught sight of something curious, some activity in the wings. Who was that? Only a stage-hand. But what was he carrying? Why, a chair! He held it above his head. He hefted it with as much ceremony and dignity as he could muster, right up the gallows stairs. He set it down stage centre, in front of the drop, and motioned for Dowie to sit. The crowd muttered. This was most unusual. "Down in front," called latecomers, as they craned and scrambled for a better view. They saw the sheriff remove the manacles, saw him hand his prisoner a sheaf of paper. Dowie nodded his thanks and cleared his throat. He took a swig of water from a glass passed him by a prison official. He began to speak. No one had ever heard anything like it. They were held in thrall by the power of his oratory. Scant minutes before he was scheduled to swing, Dowie delivered himself of a stunning sermon. He spoke in a clarion voice that could be heard at the back of the stalls, heard clearly over the squalling of the babies and the bellowing of the chestnut-sellers. It was hard-hitting, no-holds-barred, confessional, cautionary stuff.

"During all my voyages and when I was in port, there was no sin of which I was not guilty....Thousands there are in the world whose record is as black and as heinous as mine — whose lives are as wild and as reckless — who never think of their God as their last end....Seafaring men! I would caution you to avoid such streets as Park Lane in London; Barrack Street in Liverpool; North Street in Boston; Baker Street in New York; Empire Street in New Orleans."

He went on in this vein for a very long time, speaking, related *The Islander*, "with wonderful fortitude and distinctness, only pausing occasionally to take a mouthful of cold water." Who wouldn't wax windy in such adverse circumstances? He knew what lay ahead. Every declamation delayed damnation. Dowie took his time. He thanked those who needed to be thanked (the constables who had been so attentive to his needs while incarcerated, his attorneys who had done their best), and forgave those who needed to be forgiven (the judge, the jury, the hangman). Once again, he advised young men to abandon vicious behaviour, and most especially drink. Then, by way of a peroration, and perhaps most remarkably of all, he launched into a poem of unsurpassingly tearful sentimentality. It was said afterwards that he wrote the whole opus himself, unaided and unencouraged, on the very eve of his execution. The whole opus runs to seventeen stanzas. Here are an illustrative few:

Weep my dear old mother weep
Let tears fall fast and free,
They will help ease your troubled heart
Of woe and agony....

Farewell, my mother, sad farewell,
Likewise my loving wife
I leave you poor and desolate
Within this world of strife....

And from each Christian heart then doth
A tearful prayer ascend
That Christ will take me to his home
Where Sabbaths never end.

He rose from his chair. The hangman turned his hand to his grisly work.

He is buried, I was told, in the Elm Street Cemetery on University Avenue. It's directly across from a laundromat and adjacent to a radiator repair shop. Look up from reading the stony register of the dead and you're struck by a billboard that says "Rust check." I had no luck turning over any trace of Dowie, but did note the prominent marker of Francis Longworth. Longworth was the sheriff who presided over the execution, and it was Longworth who bore the brunt of the blame for what was widely regarded as a badly handled job. In *The Islander* of April

16, 1869, he was given a chance to tell his side of the story, and the archly defensive tone of his writing leaves no doubt that he was feeling a great deal of heat. Little wonder. Public sympathy, in this case, was not with the law. Dowie had moved the people to fits of near rapture. If he was owed anything, it was surely the courtesy of a proper climax. But things went awry. Almost everything that could go wrong with a hanging did. There was no quick dispatch. It lasted for over an hour, a cruel, prolonged, hideous death. Word of the travesty spread, fanning the fires of community outrage. The officials were vilified. The Attorney General demanded an explanation. Sheriff Longworth's exhaustive account is a masterpiece of evasiveness.

It should be stressed at the outset, wrote Longworth, that there was nothing amiss with the gallows themselves. They were in tiptop shape, and all the requisite personnel had been lined up to do their dirty but necessary jobs. He had worked hard to find someone who could fill "the dreaded and unenviable post of hangman. The rope, which the day before I had procured, after searching Charlottetown from one end to the other, was apparently the best and most secure I could find." It must have been an aggravation to him, after all that time devoted to rope shopping, to see the twine break and the intended tumble fifteen feet to the earth below. The Sheriff admits that, while this did happen, there is no truth to the story that Dowie broke both his legs when he fell. He was shaken up, nothing more. He had a contusion on the side of his neck, and a minor case of rope burn. He was returned to his cell to regroup, and then they tried again. Dowie remounted the gallows without a fuss. He did not make a reprise of his speech. Once again the killing lever was thrown. From this point forward, says Longworth, the stories making the rounds are just bald lies, falsehoods from beginning to end. It was true that on the second try Dowie's feet touched the ground, and it was true that, strictly speaking, this might be a breach of hanging etiquette, but there was no doubt that he was dead at the moment of impact. His neck had been dislocated and he was beyond feeling pain. The reason he was then raised up and left to measure the blowing of the breeze for the next forty-five minutes had nothing to do with torturing the man or completing the process of strangulation. It was just done on the doctor's orders, and was strictly routine in such cases. And that, he says, is all there is to report. That, he hopes, will put minds to rest.

Fred Sauer lives just a block or two from where Longworth lies and Dowie is said to rest. When I read the story of that botched hanging, I thought how different it might have been, how much more humane, had someone with Fred's technical expertise been on hand. It would have gone off without a hitch. Fred, I imagined, would even have found a way of automating the procedure. He might even have stood on the other side of the square and worked the drop by way of remote control.

In Fred's house, doors swing and appliances leap into action as if by magic. He activates most everything with a garage-door opener he carries around in his shirt pocket. He can sit in his kitchen rocker and turn on the faucet at the sink, or open any one of the several cabinets he has built and installed around the room. Their doors swivel and lift noiselessly, mysteriously, as if they possess independence of will, to reveal the computers or television contained within. These, too, are coaxed into life with his all-purpose clicker. He can use it to open the under-the-sink cupboard where the garbage lives, or open and close the window. He can use it to start his lathe. The lathe is in a corner of the kitchen, which is not a usual place to find such a tool, but it looks very much at home there. Just about the only thing for which Fred does not use the garage-door opener is to open the garage door. There is no garage.

Fred lives on a little street that has a name but no sign. Save for the tractor parked in the driveway, his two-storey, wood-frame house is unremarkable from the outside. His father bought the tractor for $1,600 in 1955, which was also the year Fred was born. He came into the world on New Year's Eve. He grew up in Savage Harbour, where his parents, German immigrants, ran a hog operation. It was observing the pigs that led Fred to one of his opinions, which has to do with diet.

"One of the things about staying healthy is keeping your weight consistent. Even putting on a pound or two is already screwing up balances in various mechanisms. That's what your body is, a mechanism, and if you treat it like one it'll respond like one. We're always told to eat a cross-section of all these different foods in order to be healthy, but I think you should eat one, high-quality food substance every day. When we were raising pigs — and we were dealing with four or five hundred at a time — they ate the same food, all of them. It was good quality, and there was enough of it, not too much. We never overfed them. They grew fast. They were all healthy. And it clicked. The reason they use pigs for experiments is because their chemistry is similar to ours. It doesn't hurt a human not to eat a wide range of everything from the grocery store. We can get by on just a few things."

Fred, who is lithe and thin and sports a handsome goatee, sustains himself on hamburger, macaroni, and coffee. Especially coffee. He drinks lots and lots of coffee. He likes to add almond flavouring to the brew, and to this end he's recycled a soap dispenser from a dishwasher to squirt out a precisely measured amount of syrup into his cup. As well, he has devised a way to signal the coffee to start brewing downstairs in the kitchen while he is upstairs in the bedroom. Ask Fred why he doesn't avail himself of the timing device that is already built into most automatic coffee makers and he will explain, patiently, that his way gives him more control. He can get up when he feels like it and start the java bubbling, rather than feeling compelled to rise at, say, 7.20 because the coffee maker was set to kick into action at 7.30. It takes him, on average, ten minutes to get dressed. He used to be faster, but he has had to spend more time taking care of such pedestrian business since he lost his left arm.

It happened on May 11, 1977, in Ottawa. Fred had moved there to take a good job in a motorcycle repair shop. He was on his way to work, driving his Kawasaki 900, when he was broadsided by a taxi. The insurance adjusters apportioned the fault equally, but the weight of injury fell entirely on Fred. The impact damaged the brachial plexus nerves of the left arm, leaving it limp "like a big spaghetti hanging there. I woke up in the hospital about ten or eleven days after the accident."

He went back to Savage Harbour to convalesce. When he had adjusted somewhat to his loss, he found work as a mechanic, fixing lawnmowers in the summer and snowmobiles in the winter. In the spring of 1982, he had the arm amputated.

"I'd been talking to doctors about it for five years. I couldn't find any treatment to improve it or to do anything about the pain. I'd hoped amputation might improve that, but it hasn't changed much. That's the worst part of an amputation, the pain. It's like it's burning on fire all the time. The weather influences it, too. When the weather is miserable the pain is miserable."

Fred's arm is gone, but he carries the sensory memory of it. It's very detailed. He shows me with his right arm how he can feel his left arm angled in front of him. The hand really hurts, he says. Oddly, the thumb does not. He shows me where the thumb juts, comfortable and invisible, parallel to his lower ribs. Then he pulls the right arm away, creating a glum vacancy. He has a prosthesis, but says it's useless to him. "Let's just say it's not something the Terminator would use. I've thought of trying to design some kind of a hand, but it would cost hundreds of dollars a month just for the cables. You'd wear them out. God made the human body to repair itself all its life. But cables wear, so how long would it be useful?"

"When did you start inventing stuff?"

"I'd say I got serious about it after I stopped drinking."

"You drank a lot?"

"Yes. That started after the accident."

"Were you alcoholic?"

"I guess so, but it wasn't like I was out making trouble all the time. I'd drink with friends, or I'd drink alone. I preferred to drink alone. I'd sit here and listen to music and drink. Then, ten years later, the day came when I realized that I was going to lose my job if I kept it up. I stopped on St. Paddy's Day, 1987. I didn't need anyone to help me. My opinion is that if you want to do it right, you have to do it by yourself. And you have to find something to replace the booze. You have to do something else with the time."

Fred had always been good with his hands. Now, with that clarity of purpose that so often settles on people who are getting over drinking problems, he determined that he would find ways to be just as good with his hand. He would redirect the obsessive energy he'd put into boozing into finding ways to make life easier for himself. Perhaps he would also find ways to help others with his or a similar disability.

There is no doubt that Fred can lay claim to a particular brilliance. His gift, in addition to pure indomitability, is that he can strip away the limitations of form and function we place on commonplace objects, and see in them possibilities of usage that are obscure to most of us. No talent comes without a price, and Fred has had to pay for his by developing a high tolerance for clutter. Step into the foyer of his house and the first thing that meets the eye is a workbench piled high with a Babel of foundling mechanical bits, lying dormant and still, attending the day that Fred finds a way to reanimate them as part of some unlikely kinetic contrivance. If you were to turn to the left, and walk past the aquarium with the homespun feeding system, you would come to what I think is meant to be the living room, but which is completely inaccessible for anything like conventional living. It is piled chest deep with old turntables, toasters, blenders, kettles, coffee makers, and other such odds and sods: kitchen appliances that have seen better days, but are motherlodes of nifty bits Fred will be able to cannibalize for his inventions, such as the whatnot now under construction, which at this point consists of a pole with a bleach bottle on the top, and what I think is the motor from a tape deck. The basement of the house presents the kind of scene that must rise like a miasma in a fire marshal's nightmare. It is a rat's nest of wires, a tangle of mechanical dross, an accumulation of bags and papers. I wonder out loud if this garish weaving is entirely safe, but Fred shrugs off my concern. He has it under control. Unlike most people, he says, he understands electricity. He is close to it. He knows it's not some wild thing lurking out there, licking its lips, and waiting to pounce. He has it tamed. He knows precisely how it works.

Back in the kitchen he launders his mug before filling it up with more coffee. How do you wash your dishes at the sink when you have just one arm? Fred met the challenge with a motor from an old cash register and a dish-scrubbing brush he attached near the spiggot. When he turns on the water — this time he uses a foot pedal, rather than the aforementioned garage-door opener — the brush whirls around, doing the sinister work that would once have fallen to his missing arm. I notice that the kitchen cabinets are marked with stick-on numbers, one through five, and mention it in passing.

"What do those mean?" I am sure they must have some Kabbalistic significance in Fred's eccentric universe.

"What? The numbers? They're just numbers. Somebody gave them to me and I thought I should use them."

John Valerius was a German of the Upper Palatinate, born without arms in 1667. He developed uncommonly agile feet and he more than got by. There was nothing he couldn't do. With his feet and his toes he could play cards, throw dice, shave himself, fence with a rapier. He became a popular salon figure in London and on the Continent. He does not seem to have wanted for friends or social contacts. Like Valerius, Fred Sauer is a man of enormous talent and psychic reserve. Unlike Valerius, he has not found widespread acceptance for the work he has taken on in response to his disability. He has not been able to coax anyone who might make a difference to the wider dissemination of his inventions into taking them seriously, or even into coming by for a long chat and a good hard look at what he has to offer. It may be that his gadgets are just too particular to his own needs and situation. Certainly, they are unusual. They are every bit as idiosyncratic as the man who made them, as Fred, who could never be accused of feeling sorry for himself, but who has had, by any objective measure, a rough row to hoe in his life, and who freely admits to being lonely.

"I don't understand it. I'll invite people to come around and see the gadgets, I'll invite them four or five times, but no one wants to come near the place. I don't know if they're afraid of it, or of the dogs, or of me. I just don't know. I mean, no one comes to the door, the phone doesn't ring."

We spent just four hours together, over two days. Fred talked fluently and steadily that whole time, but of course there was much that was left unsaid. Two weeks would hardly have been sufficient, there was that much more that he wanted to tell me about his life, his philosophy, his work, his opinions. There were many other inventions, or adaptations, that he wanted to show me. There was so much more for me to learn about his oblique and useful way of looking at the world, about the way his right hand understood what his left hand longed to do. I've shown you just a tiny piece of his valiant, crazy heart.

Disgusting weather was blowing in off the Atlantic when I walked to my hotel. The wind howled *like the fierce fiend of a distempered dream* as I turned my steps back to my own temporary bed, which was made on the spot where the gallows once stood. What pinched face might I see peering down at me when I woke with a start in the thick of the night? The rain streamed down on the unfinished bridge. It thickened and turned to sleet in town. It swarmed. It stung. It fell fast on the pavements, and there became ice, and walking was tough on the Charlatan streets.

Ark

I have been thinking of the difference between
water and the waves on it.
— Kabir

Good old Noah. He was a just man, and perfect in his generations. The Bible tells us so. He was reliable, a paragon of
dependability. It was ever thus with him. "Noah is a careful boy
who follows instructions well." That was what his teachers
would chisel on his report cards. He was the kind of pupil they
liked. He was no trouble at all, and they could forget his name
the minute school dismissed for the summer. He didn't show
much of a predilection for the more academic subjects, so a
vocational counsellor suggested he should be channelled into
the technical stream. That was fine with his parents. They had
a studious daughter who looked to have all the makings of a
doctor or a lawyer and on whom they could heap their white-
collar expectations. It was fine with Noah, too. He was happiest
in the shop. He felt right at home there. It was where his particular intelligence flourished, where he felt most himself. He
understood instinctively the process of materials assemblage.
He always knew what had to be done and when. He never
fussed. He was slow, he was steady, he got the job done. It was
never innovative or visionary, but you knew for a fact that whatever he built was not going to come unseamed after a single use.
Nothing much seemed to worry or rile him. His blood pressure
was consistent, his bowels functioned like clockwork, he slept
eight hours a night, he never once thought about suicide. He

was obviously someone who would never succumb to a stress-related illness.

Noah grew up. He went out into the world. He continued along his measured, circumspect path. He got married right out of high school to a young woman who was the daughter of long-time friends of the family. They only ever quarrelled once, and that was after the birth of their third son. They couldn't agree on a name. She favoured Japheth. He wanted to call the boy Tom. He liked names of one syllable, and thought that Tom would work well with Shem and Ham, who were the baby's older brothers. He imagined them walking down the road, singing "Shem, Ham, Tom" to the tune of "Three Blind Mice." Japheth, he said, was too lispy. It was a name the lad might have to defend with his fists on the playground. The missus held firm. She had had a favourite uncle called Japheth who had died when she was young after being gored by an ox. Noah and his wife exchanged heated words. Finally, he gave in. The tears were too much to bear. All the same, he continued to think of Japheth as Tom, to call him that in the privacy of his own thoughts. He would call him Tom on his deathbed, although he would not lie there for a long, long time. That would not be until all the days of Noah tallied 950 years. The Bible tells us so.

Noah never had a job, exactly. It wasn't for want of trying, it was just that he didn't present well at interviews. He still managed. He kept his family fed, kept body and soul together by working on small contracts and making himself available to his neighbours as a handyman. Everyone knew you could count on Noah. He had all the right tools for all the right jobs. He knew a cubit from a ploughshare, and there was no one who could touch him when it came to working with gopher wood. He knew about pitch, too, knew how to get the really good stuff at a reasonable price, knew how to slather it on for maximum impermeability. There was no need to fret over the possibility of leakage when Noah was around. He had never been known to leave a chink or crevice unplugged.

"Must be a mid-life crisis," everyone said when they noticed him cupping his ear in the direction of the heavens, when he commenced nailing together his three-storey ark. "Do you spell that with a 'c' or a 'k'?" asked the reporter from the local rag who came by hoping for a "lighter side of the news" story he could use as filler. "And do you mind telling me your age?"

"Six hundred," answered the obliging Noah, but his mouth was full of nails, and the reporter understood him to say "fuck off." He left in a huff. He wrote a denunciatory rant and ran it as the lead story in the paper that was published the day before the long rains kicked in; before the waters began to prevail upon the earth. The neighbours read it and shook their heads. Poor Noah, he'd gone off the rails. It's always the quiet ones who surprise you. They turned to the weather forecast on page three. It was for "sunny skies, above-average temperatures." A few planned picnics.

The last thing Noah thought to make was a cribbage board. He was hesitant at first, because it hadn't been mentioned by the Lord as a piece of necessary equipment. However, by the time his precipitation-measuring device was showing an accumulated rainfall of fifteen cubits, and by the time even the mountain peaks were completely submerged, he was glad of this recreational foresight. So was his family. A spirited round or two offered them all a much-needed break from the tedium of shovelling manure. It was a way to kill time when there was no longer any need to beat down the poor drowning buggers who were trying to cling to the side of the ark. Noah had always thought of Japheth's wife as a flighty creature without a practical bone in her body, but it was she who thought to bring along earplugs to block out their screams, and for that he blessed her.

"When you have your sons," he said to her, "it might be nice if you called the first-born Tom."

She smiled, but noncommittally. She hadn't yet told him, had only begun to suspect herself, that there was a wiggling newt in the pond. She didn't want to heap still more trouble on the old fellow's plate by telling him she had already decided her baby would go by Gomer.

Noah stood the midnight watch, so he did his dreaming at noon. He would wake at two, flushed and troubled. He didn't even care to eat the lunch his wife kept covered and waiting in the warming oven. He was having disconcerting dreams about betrayal, about sabotage. Noah had lived long enough to know when to trust his dreams, and there was no question that this was one of great import. He saw that this floating refuge of all that was good and salvageable in the world had somehow come to harbour an agent of evil. How was this possible? The devil must have made his way onto the ark as part of the two-by-two procession, slipping past security in one of his many disguises. Noah would rise from his pallet and stride through the stalls and aviaries, stride among the things that walk and stalk and creep and leap, would study the features of various creatures, would look deep into the eyes of the goats, and the stoats, and the chattering apes, the hens, and the wrens and the slithering snakes. "Is it you?" he would whisper. "Is it you?" But of course, there was never any answer other than a seasick bleating, or a bone-weary whine.

For forty days and forty nights they bobbed around, until "every living substance was destroyed which was upon the face of the ground, both man and cattle, and the creeping things, and the fowl of the heaven." And another 150 days passed after that, while the winds blew and the waters were somewhat assuaged. Eventually, the favoured eight found themselves teetering on the tip of Ararat. At this point, Noah decided enough was enough. They couldn't go on like this for ever. He would have to strike a reconaissance mission, dispatch some trusty agent into the field to see if there was in fact any sign of a field. But who? To whom could he entrust so vital an assignment? He could not be too careful, especially given the opprobrious infiltration of which he had been warned in his dreams.

Now, Noah knew as well as you or I that there are only two animals whose shape is inimitable by Satan. One is the dove.

The other is the lamb. The only way he could be sure of side-stepping a potential snare would be to send one of them out in search of land. Which was it to be? The sweet little dove, all pale and frail, could never endure so arduous a charge, besides which he would miss her gentle cooing. The lamb was another story. The lamb was full of beans, bumptious, and always kicking up a fuss. He had energy to burn. Yes. He would be the one. It would be best to do it fast. Noah picked the fleecy thing up and carried him to the upper deck. He held him under his arm and galloped, nearly tripping on the hem of his robe as he took the stairs two at a time. There was no time to lose and he could not run the risk of reflection, lest he question the mettle of his intuition and stay his hand. If he did that, they would all be lost. He ran past the amazed Mrs. Japheth, who was stroking her swelling belly, ran past Shem and Ham, who were checking each other over for fleas, which had multiplied, and ran past his own wife, who was combing the angora rabbits to within an inch of their lives. (It was Noah's birthday coming up, and she had some mittens in mind.) He ran to the deck railing and hurled the struggling lamb into the green and churning sea. It cried and cried and swam around the ark, its four little hoofs churning up a froth the colour of ewe's milk. Noah had to hurl stones to drive it away. "Get out! Get going! God bless your journey! Come back with news!" he shouted as it paddled off, dragging its tail behind it, struggling to keep afloat against the relentless roll of the waves, and the heavy ballast of its sodden woolly coat.

God looked down from His Heaven and wept. Noah, His trusted simpleton, His old, industrious fool, His chosen one, had got it all wrong. The lamb, the lamb, the pretty little lamb! What a waste. He could not watch it suffering. He pointed a finger and smote it from on high. Only Mrs. Ham saw a slight puff of smoke rise up from the horizon. "Mirage," she said out loud, not knowing whence the word had come. It was the first time anyone had spoken it since the beginning of time. "Mirage," she said again, pleased with her own cunning coining. It would

be a fine name for a daughter. She would have told her shipmates all about this minor epiphany, but her attention was
diverted by a raucous blast, half trumpet, half wheeze, from the
bottom deck. It was the elephant, who inhabited the stall adjacent to the departed lamb. He sounded for all the world as if he
were laughing. God heard him, too, and felt something like suspicion catch in His infinite craw. He peered down through the
clouds, directed His X-ray vision through the floorboards of the
vessel. He located the source of the sound. His unassailable gaze
travelled the length of that snake of a trunk. He looked into the
great beast's eye, and saw soon enough what Noah had missed.

"Aha," said the Lord. "It's you. I ought to have guessed. Do
you have any idea what you've done? Because of you I had to
smite my sweet little pet, my precious doll, my favourite among
all my creatures. Well, laugh this off, you coal-eyed dung
machine! This is the way it will be with you and with all your
children and with your children's children's children, from
hence forward, all the days of their lives. This diaspora will not
end for you when the waves are worn out and the waters have
relinquished their hold on the land. Oh, no, my hearty. You will
be hunted, and captured, and killed. Your bodies will be torn
asunder and your parts dispersed the world around. And some
of you will die in cages. And some will die by water. On this I
set my seal!" And He took the blood of the wasted lamb and
smeared it all across the western sky.

"Nice sunset," said Ham to his wife.

"Hmmm," she said, although she wasn't really listening.
She was trying to remember her marvellous word. That night,
as Ham lay on top of her, she whispered strange sounds into the
dark. Collage. Triage. Steerage. None of them was right. None
of them would do. Oh, well. You couldn't force these things.
Perhaps it would come back to her in that no man's land
between waking and sleeping. It had worked for her before.
Only last month she'd remembered the whereabouts of a button hook that had been missing for weeks. What was it, what
was it? Peerage? Marriage? Marriage was close. Ham, who

always loved the little games she thought of to play in bed, traced her ear with his tongue and answered her with nonsense sounds, with nursery-rhyme syllables, before shouting out his own private, joyous word. He shuddered, collapsed, and rolled away. He was asleep within seconds. His chest heaved like the slow tumble of the waves. She closed her eyes, pulled the blanket up around her neck, and began to count sheep. Soon she was gone. Everyone slept except Noah. He was down in the cote, talking softly to the white-breasted dove, explaining what would happen next.

And God, as always, kept His word. Thus it was that the psalmist was able to write of ivory palaces. Thus it was that Solomon's throne was made of the stuff. Every three years Solomon's navy pulled into port, the ships spilling over with gold, silver, peacocks, apes, and tusks. "What shall we do with these?" his artisans would ask, holding up the vast elephantine scythes. "Oh, make me up another throne for the summer palace," Solomon would answer, hardly looking up from his writing. "Thy lips," he wrote, "O my spouse, drop as the honeycomb: honey and milk are under thy tongue; and the smell of thy garments is like the smell of Lebanon.... Awake O north wind; and come, thou south; blow upon my garden, that the spices thereof may flow out. Let my beloved come into his garden, and eat his pleasant fruits" (Song of Solomon 4:11, 16).

God never forgets. He's got a memory like — well, let's just say that He never forgets. Yea, verily, unto the present day you can see the working-out of His vengeful promise in cameo brooches, in key chains, in any number of carved trinkets: angels, monkeys, little Buddhas. You can see it in the delicate inlay work on furniture or guitars. You can see it in the eighty-eight keys strung across the thousands of pianos that in the nineteenth century were hauled across the Atlantic or around the Cape, all the way to Canada, where they were manoeuvred overland and hefted into the parlours of homesick immigrants: their link to all they had left behind, their link to more than they knew or imagined. Were it not for the incursions of the devil, none of this would have happened and the elephant Mogul would have lived a blissful life on the Serengeti plain, showering himself with dust, bellowing sweet hymns to the ponderous moon, servicing his harem. Were it not for the incursions of the devil, the elephant Mogul would never have found himself striking out across the Atlantic, paddling to distance himself from a burning ship, his cavernous sinuses clogged with smoke, his heart pounding with an urgency and a hope that had never before inhabited an elephant heart — namely, that he would find the strength to make it to the shores of New Brunswick.

I love a good pachyderm tale, and this one was brought to my attention in Yarmouth, Nova Scotia. Mogul has become part of local lore because Yarmouth was among the last towns to host him in all his magnificence. He fell victim to the family curse not long after leaving that South Shore port on board the good ship *Royal Tar*. That was in October 1836. He was part of a floating menagerie that was operated under the auspices of the Zoological Institute of Boston.

The story of the bizarre fate that befell that circus ship would be a fascinating digression, and a less disciplined writer than I would give in to the urge to tell it, right here and now. However, I had no more gone to Yarmouth to learn about the *Royal Tar* or about Mogul than I had gone there to learn about Mr. Bean. I mean Merit Bean, of course, not Samuel Bean. They are two quite separate stories. Samuel Bean, who claimed to have read the Bible sixty-five times, and who was a physician before he became a preacher, was born in Wilmot Township, Ontario, in 1842. As near as I know, he was never in Yarmouth, although he might have passed through *en route* to Cuba, where he drowned in 1904. Merit Bean is of much more recent vintage and had better luck with water, although just barely. He made a conspicuous entrance into Yarmouth shortly before Christmas in 1975. That was when he barged his house 200 miles across the Bay of Fundy from Cundy's Harbor, Maine. It was a very nice house, and Mr. Bean was attached to it, which is why he didn't want to just leave it behind when he started having set-tos with the Cundy's Harbor fishing co-operative about their wharf. It was a very nice wharf, too. The timbers they used were the best around, a hundred years old, and they blended in beautifully with the Howard Johnson's semi-trailer rig which was one of the principal components of the construction. The wharf measured ninety feet, and Mr. Bean's angry contention was that it had been positioned in such a way as to interfere with his view. "I never would have paid a nickel for this lot had the pier been here," he fumed to *The Bath Brunswick Times Record*. At this, the fishermen scoffed. "We could be two hundred feet longer before we would bother his view," one of them told *The Boston Globe*. "Two hundred feet longer!" he said, gesturing with his scaling knife at the contentious shoreline and derisively stamping his gumboots.

Merit Bean was described by locals as a bit of a mystery man. It was generally understood that he had done well for himself back in New Hampshire with his dealings in real estate and the lumber industry. God only knew why he had come to Cundy's Harbor or what contentment he hoped to find there. He bought some land on Quahog Bay and built a replica of a French farmhouse, seven rooms contained in a yellow frame. The roof was flared, curving up at the eaves. It had a stone front, and three gabled dormers, and was panelled inside with pumpkin-coloured pine. No wonder he didn't want to just pull up stakes and move on. No wonder he thought it worthwhile to run the place through with twin steel I-beams, heft it onto a barge he was renting for $3,000 a day, and steer it through the quarter-mile of ledges and wharves that stood between him and the open waters of the Bay of Fundy, with its uncertain winds and its punishing tides. On the other side lay the twenty-five acres he had bought in Markland, across the harbour from the town of Yarmouth. Mr. Bean had selected it after flying around in his private plane, up and down the Atlantic coast, surveying the scene from above like a dove, scouting about in the hope of finding an appropriate parcel of land. Nova Scotians, he was sure, would give him a warmer welcome than he had received in Maine. The talk around Cundy's Harbor was that he could have built a new and comparable home on those twenty-five Canadian acres for a third of what it was going to cost him to lift and float his treasured French farmhouse. There was great speculation as to whether or not he would ever get it as far as the Bay, the squeeze would be so tight. "He's different than anybody on this earth," the assistant co-op manager told the man from the *Globe*. "A lot of people are really going to be sorry when he goes."

And perhaps it was a sadness for them to say goodbye to Mr. Bean, to see the receding back of his house as the ocean-going tug — newly painted in Germany — hauled it and him away from them for ever. What would they have to talk about now? What would they have to gaze at from their ninety-foot wharf? Just an empty lot. Mr. Bean, for his part, was Lot-like and never looked back. What was done was done. He was fifty-three years old when he said goodbye to Maine and sailed for the north. He was fifty-three years old, which made him 547 years younger than Noah was when he set out on his journey of a lifetime.

Nathaniel Hawthorne was only eleven when he went to Maine. His sea-captain father had died of yellow fever, and his widowed mother was deeply mired in grief. They took a house deep in the woods and led a reclusive, sequestered life. Mrs. Hawthorne rarely stirred from her room. Nathaniel's own activity was restricted because of a foot injury, and so he acquired the habits of reading and solitude. He went on to college and then returned to Salem, where he had been born, a place that for him was full of ghosts. Here, his founding-family ancestors had ordered Quakers to be whipped and had sat in judgment at the witchcraft trials. He wrote to his mother, "I do not want to be a doctor to live by men's diseases, nor a minister to live by their sins, nor a lawyer to live by their quarrels. So I don't see there is anything left for me but to be an author." He continued to live hermetically while he studied the writer's trade. In the very year that Mogul the elephant swam panting, struggling against the downward tug of the cold Atlantic currents, Hawthorne was locked away, setting down the stories he would publish in 1837 as *Twice-Told Tales*. One of them, "Chippings With a Chisel," has to do with visits paid to the workshop of a Martha's Vineyard gravestone carver, "an elderly man, a descendant of the old Puritan family of Wigglesworth." He's an uncluttered character, but not by any stretch simple-minded. He has acquired a certain salty wisdom through his years of dealing with the recently bereaved, of chipping into marble slabs the names of the newly dead. The narrator spends time with Mr. Wigglesworth, observing the various comings and goings of his customers. "None of the applicants, I think, affected me more disagreeably than an old man who came, with his fourth wife hanging on his arm, to bespeak grave-stones for the three former occupants of his marriage-bed. I watched with some anxiety to see whether his remembrance of either were more affectionate than of the other two, but could discover no symptom of the kind....I shuddered at the gray polygamist, who had so utterly lost the holy sense of individuality in wedlock, that methought he was fain to reckon upon his fingers how many women who had once slept by his side were now sleeping in their graves. There was even — if I wrong him it is no great matter — a glance side-long at his living spouse, as if he were inclined to drive a thriftier bargain by bespeaking four grave-stones in a lot."

Physician–preacher Samuel Bean, who drowned thousands of leagues to the south of where Mogul fought his pitched and valiant battle against both the sea and divine will, and who was born five years after the publication of *Twice-Told Tales*, might have been labouring under the influence of "Chippings" when he commissioned the single stone that marks the grave of his first two wives, Henrietta Furry and Susanna Clegg. (Some sources say they were sisters.) His first marriage lasted only seven months. He took Susanna to wife shortly after Henrietta's death. Alas, she also found the strains of married life too much to bear — those doctors and their long hours — and proved herself to be just as eager as Henrietta to turn out the lights. In fact, the second Mrs. Bean died nineteen months to the day after the first. Henrietta and Susanna are buried side by each in the Rushes Cemetery, which is south of Crosshill, which is near Wellesley, Ontario, which is near Kitchener. Their marker has been much observed and admired. It has weathered badly, however, and in recent years a duplicate stone has been planted next to the original. The local carver — the Crosshill equivalent of Hawthorne's Mr. Wigglesworth — decorated it with a common funerary symbol of the day: a clenched hand, the index finger extended and pointing upwards. The text, however, is anything but common.

We deal individually with grief, as we need and must. Some weep, some sleep, some put the crypt back in cryptogram. Dr. Bean knew how to heal his broken heart. He sat down with a piece of paper and a quill and he got right to work on a puzzle, fifteen characters across and fifteen characters down. He was a peculiar chap, with a turn of mind that was both mischievous and mystic. He was two times a widower, and still he had the wherewithal to smile as he imagined future graveyard visitors doing a double take as they passed by his crafty arrangement of numbers and letters. This was a bone they could worry at for years and years to come!

Of course, he made sure the number seven figured prominently in the solution. He knew about the power of seven. He had grown up hearing that a sick man could be made whole if his shirt were dipped seven times in south-flowing water. He was well acquainted with the powers ascribed to the seventh son, or better yet, the seventh son of a seventh son: that his touch could cure scrofula, or that warts would vanish if you washed them in his baptismal water. As a Bible scholar, he knew that Elijah, atop Carmel, sent out his servant seven times to look for rain, knew that Elisha sent Naaman to wash in the river Jordan seven times, knew that when Jericho was taken they compassed the city seven times. Seven, then, gives you the key. Start at the top left-hand corner, and count seven letters in. Then, count seven letters down. Then, read from the centre in a zigzag counter-clockwise spiral.

> In memoriam Henrietta, 1st wife of S. Bean M.D. who died 27 Sep 1865 aged 23 years 2 months & 17 days & Susanna his 2nd wife who died 27th April 1867 aged 26 years 10 months & 15 days. 2 better wives 1 man never had. They were gifts from God but are now in Heaven. May God help me so to meet them there.

Dr. Bean's neighbours weren't so very surprised when they saw the stone. They had been more or less prepared for it by

Henrietta's memorial service. Then, they were presented with a black-edged funeral card on which was inscribed a similarly crafted brain teaser. Hardly anyone paid any attention to the eulogy, they were all so intent on deciphering the message.

In memoream Henriettah Furry Bean born in Penn. Married in Philadelphia to Samuel Bean M.D. & went with him to Canada leaving all her friends behind — died in Linwood the 27th of Sep. 1865 after an illness of 11 weeks aged 23 years 2 months & 17 days she was a model wife 1 of 1000 — Much regretted by her sorrowing husband & all who knew her — Was married 7 months & 10 days — Lived a godly life for 5 years & died happy in the Lord — Peace be to her ashes — So mote it be.

What did the townfolk think? Were they in any way suspicious about his short back-to-back marriages, about the truncated lives of the two has-Beans? Was it just bad luck, or did medicine play a part? A few of the locals must surely have wondered. He was plenty unusual, that Dr. Bean; he had all that easy access to poisons, and he would know just how to use them. In the end, they shelved such fruitless musings. They led precisely nowhere, and were convincingly invalidated by the evidence of his third marriage to Annie Wankmiller, which went on for thirty-four years. Happily, happily were they wed. Happily, happily did they live, in New York and in Iowa. And then he went to Cuba for his old-man-and-the-sea routine.

Dr. Sam divided public opinion, but there was no neighbourly equivocation about Merit of Maine. They couldn't abide him in Cundy's Harbor and he wasn't quick to endear himself to Yarmouthians, either, after he quite literally barged into their lives. The crew made good time getting from Cundy over Fundy on a Monday. The house was towed through the treacherous shoals and into the bay that evening, and by Tuesday midnight the tug's pilot could see the several unextinguished lights of Yarmouth, which is an early-to-bed kind of town. The barge drew near to the wharf, and that was the end of the smooth sailing. The wind picked up and dislodged the chimney, which crashed through the roof with its pagoda-style eaves, and sullied with plaster dust the pumpkin-hued panelling. There was a problem establishing an equitable relationship between the moorings and the tide, and when the tug of one met the too-taut resistance of the other, the enterprise was nearly pulled asunder. The cranes that were to actually hoist the building onto its new foundation site were delayed. A nasty gale blew up, the barge slipped its moorings and scuttled across the harbour, by which time a corner of the house had been split open, leaving the interior exposed to the lashings of the freezing, salty spray. The cranes arrived but got mired in the mud on the public access road to Bean's twenty-five acres, and when they were finally removed, the road was so badly chewed up as to be impassable, which vexed the new arrival's neighbours who were counting on being able to use the thoroughfare to get to and from their home, especially with Christmas coming on and whatnot. Not only had the cranes damaged their road and their property, Bean had been seen tampering with their lobster traps, shoving them out of his way, in strict violation of an unwritten code of maritime etiquette. Ask any Easterner to complete the sentence "Thou shalt not" and he or she will invariably respond with "dislodge another man's lobster traps." Strong words were bandied. The neighbours, who were not about to forgive him his trespassing, summoned the Mounties. Lawyers were soon on the scene. Writs were issued. Merit Bean had arrived in Canada.

That's just the way of it when you live in a harbour town. You get out of bed in the morning, step onto the porch to pick up the paper, and you're like as not to find yourself staring at some damn thing or other that wasn't there when you retired, something that started out in a distant elsewhere, and that the waves piggybacked to your door, overnight express. Sometimes it's a note in a cerulean bottle, or a bit of driftwood sculpted by the acid wash of the sea to look like the holy rood. Sometimes, it's a house on a barge and a cantankerous American. You just never know from one day to the next, and isn't that one of the reasons you live there? The shores around Yarmouth have seen their share of flotsam and jetsam, both the mundane and the obscure: ships' masts and timbers, tea chests, harp frames, glass floats, beaded evening gloves, monogrammed cigarette cases, horseshoes, a lamb skull of great antiquity, men with their legs amputated at the knees. Oh, yes. Even that. Among the citizens who were aghast at the antics of Mr. Bean were several who remembered the death in 1912 of Jerome, a transplant to nearby Meteghan. His obituary appeared in *The Yarmouth Herald* on April 23.

DEATH OF JEROME

This well-known but mysterious man of Meteghan died on Friday last. With his passing away disappears a most remarkable character in the Province, if not in the world. Although for upwards of half a century (we think since 1854) he has been living in Meteghan no one knows his name, his nationality, nor any particulars of his relatives. The family who took care of him have [sic] been receiving from the local Government the sum of $104 annually for his care. He was found on the shore by two men early one morning without legs, with his palate cut, moaning piteously. He was taken care of, and as he could not speak, his identity remains a mystery up to the present. He had apparently been an officer of some warship, as his garments led to this belief. He was then about 24 years old, so that he was about 82 years when he died.

There he lay, languishing on the beach, all of a morning early, legless, mute, a sack of damp biscuits and a jug of water nearby, a scene that might have been cooked up by Edgar Allan Poe while channelling the spirit of Omar Khayyám. He had only one sound in his repertoire, and his rescuers took it as a given that he was telling them his name. "Jerome, Jerome," is what they understood him to mumble, forcing the sounds out over his damaged palate. What? His name? Come now! Let us summon empathy to the fore, something the slack-jawed Meteghanians were excusably too stunned to manage. Let's put ourselves in the castaway's shoes, never minding for the moment that he had no need of them. Consider. If you had spent hours and hours, possibly even days, sprawled out on the sand and unable to walk or speak, defenceless against the crueller ministrations of the sun, the wind, the rain, would your name necessarily be the first piece of intelligence you would hasten to impart to the passers-by who were your only chance for worldly salvation? Or would you be more inclined to ask for something that would be truly useful?

"Cologne! Cologne!"

"A tome! A tome!"

How long it had been since he'd had a bath or something decent to read? But no. "Jerome, Jerome" was the consensus they reached that morning, standing over him while he wheezed on the sand, or so the story is told.

Who's to say, who's to say? It is, in film-business parlance, a story "with legs." It has stumped along smartly over the years, and there's no need to probe too deeply to understand why this might be so. You need only hear the story in its barest outline, as I first did — "and then there was Jerome who was washed up legless on the shore" — to willingly pick up the hook, lance your own lip, and beg to be reeled in. "Washed up legless on the shore." What could be more evocative? You'd have to be as senseless as granite to hear those words and not conjure an image of the beached half-man; not to see him there by day, stunned by the sun, crumpled where *the surf was like the advancing lines of an unknown enemy flinging itself upon the shore*; not to see him there at night, prone Jerome alone among the stones, when *the stars lay on the lapis-lazuli sky like white flower petals on still deep water*. It is a story that is magnificent for its sparseness, that begs for individual investiture. How and why did he? Who and where was he? It's because of everything we don't know that Jerome has become a twice-told, thrice-told, oft-told tale: oft-told, at least, in and around that part of the world where he spent more than half of his peculiar life. It is the absence of fact that lends Jerome his strength. It is because there is so little about him that is concrete that he floats. It's because he is a mystery that he became a legend. Leg end.

Jerome is a juicy bit of gossip, a chuckle in the endless dialogue between the land and the sea. The same could be said of Mogul, the circus elephant who went down with the ship, and whose last battle was in all ways elemental. The same could be said of Merit Bean, who turned up like a tortoise with his house on his back, and who didn't last long in Yarmouth; who went elsewhere to find whatever it was he was looking for, and who left behind the rumour that his strangeness was due to a brain tumour; who left behind his squabbled-over French farmhouse; who made like a pigeon and flew the coop.

Pigeons. Yes. Now I remember. Pigeons are the reason I'm telling you all this. It was because of those scruffy and ubiquitous birds that I went to Yarmouth in the first place. An explorer in search of a totem or an emblem to stitch on his standard could do worse than to settle on the pigeon. It would be a mistake to call these intrepid navigators "fly by night," as they are among those sensible birds that prefer to migrate during the day and orient their compasses to the sun. They are capable, if required, of finding their way after dark. Pigeon trainers with the U.S. Army were able to convince them to do just that during the First World War, thus increasing their chances of avoiding capture by taloned and enemy raptors.

One would think that their directional genius alone would be reason enough for us to venerate these motley birds. Unfortunately for pigeons, we have never been much inclined to value them just because they can distinguish one isthmus from another from a height of 6,000 feet. We shoo them from pedestals, rather than placing them there, not caring in the slightest that they are able to discern the subtle vibrations of even the slightest of ley lines and use them to find their way home. If ever an avian order stood to benefit from the interventions of a good

publicist, it would be the columbidae. Those among their number who can get away with being called "doves" have an easier
time of it, of course. Symbol of peace, of the Holy Ghost, a con-
venient rhyme for "love": all this dictates that we respond to
the soft syllable "dove" with a kind of warm fuzziness and generosity of spirit. When we read that doves were a favourite sacrifice on Old Testament altars, we wince. But the news that their
more maladroit cousins, the garden-variety columba, were
every bit as agreeable an offering elicits nothing but plain indifference, or possibly even a tiny twinge of gladness.

"And if the burnt sacrifice for his offering to the Lord be of
fowls, then he shall bring his offering of turtledoves, or of
young pigeons. And the priest shall bring it unto the altar, and
wring off his head, and burn it on the altar; and the blood
thereof shall be wrung out at the side of the altar: And he shall
pluck away his crop with his feathers, and cast it beside the
altar on the east part, by the place of the ashes: And he shall
cleave it with the wings thereof, but shall not divide it asunder:
and the priest shall burn it upon the altar, upon the wood that
is upon the fire: it is a burnt sacrifice, an offering made by fire,
of a sweet savour unto the Lord" (Leviticus 1:14–17).

In my hotel room in Yarmouth, I turned on the TV and
caught the end of a newscast about how the city of Moncton
had just introduced an ordinance making it illegal to feed
pigeons in public places. None of the council's reasons for
enacting this prohibition was startling, unusual, or particularly
unreasonable. The birds were a nuisance. They were a health
hazard. They were fouling public walkways. The population
was growing out of control. I watched and listened as the
reporter read through the predictable inventory of columba-
ceous crimes, knowing with sibylline certainty what was to
come next. And sure enough, the sequence cut to a park. There
was a man in a park and also in a parka. He was tossing corn,
a snowbound Demeter, and he was surrounded by a hundred
beating wings, spinning away from him like Catherine-wheel
sparks. He was the local pigeon man and when the camera cut

to a close-up, his face filled the screen. His knitted toque. His sad eyes behind smudged glasses. His nose, threatening to run. He was vowing defiance. The law was an ass, he would continue to feed his birds, it was winter, it was cold, they relied on him and on others with tender hearts and bags of grain, what would they do, what would they do, and what real harm was it, anyway? What harm?

I once lived down the street from a vacant lot in the west end of Vancouver. Every morning, an old woman came and stood by the sign that specifically forbade feeding the pigeons, and gleefully fed the pigeons. They would wait for her to come, this hungry feathered legion, in their dunnish coats with their greasy collars, with their ringed and snapping eyes, with their flawless sense of direction, all of them lined up, polite after a fashion, respecting an order of their own devising, kind of like rock fans camped out and lolling on the sidewalk in front of the box office on the night before tickets go on sale for a Stones concert. They perched on the rooftops of the nearby church, the apartment buildings, and houses, waiting and prating, cooing and pooing. Oh, how they loved to poo! It lay thick on the paving bricks, it marred the cars, they let it fly on the passers-by. It was terribly unpleasant. They had worked out a routine. It never varied. A posted sentry would send out word when their renegade benefactor turned the corner, and they would rise like a well-trained choir from their loft, and flutter down around her. She had bags of feed she bought at the pet-food store, and she talked to her soup-kitchen hangers-on as she doled out the grub. "Pigeons," I heard her say once, with a commendable sense of understatement, "yes, yes, my pigeons." It was irritating as all get-out, of course. Feelings ran high against her. There was no one in the neighbourhood who couldn't be relied upon to spell "psittacosis," that unfortunate chlamydial disorder activated by inhaling the microbial nastiness that thrives among pigeon (or parrot) feathers and droppings. It can bring on bouts of pneumonia, and in severe cases patients may require artificial ventilation. Pigeons can also play a role in transmitting aspergillosis, candidiasis, coccidiosis, cryptococcosis, encephalitis, erysipelas, histoplasmosis, Newcastle disease, salmonellosis, toxoplasmosis, tuberculosis, yersiniosis, helminths, ectoparasites, and that's not all. You'd want to think twice about accepting a blood transfusion if you knew a pigeon had been the donor. (Anyone who feels a need to plumb the subject should refer to Walter J. Weber's seminal work, *Health Hazards from Pigeons, Starlings, and English Sparrows*. It is an enlivening text, full of conversational ice-breakers. One's cocktail-party chatter is hugely enriched by the knowledge that Manson's eyeworm is a common parasite among pigeons, and that they often pick it up from chowing down on cockroaches.)

The old girl who came out every morning and fed the pigeons in contravention of the posted bylaw didn't give a hoot for toxicology. While it might have been galling to watch her give succour to these half-wit plague incubators, it was impossible not to admire her pluck. She had determination to burn, she had the strength of her convictions, and she simply didn't care about the parochial priorities of civic authorities. She certainly had the undivided attention of a great many pigeons. I'm not sure I would go so far as to say she had their love, but I don't doubt for a second that they had hers. I don't doubt for a second that she nourished them because she loved them. It was that simple, and that rich. She loved them, they were an outlet for her love, and perhaps she was able to believe, feeling the beat of their wings, that they loved her back.

"Well, they were like family. It was a relationship. You've got to have an emotional connection to something," says Arthur Thurston, explaining why he kept pigeons, and not just a few either. Mr. Thurston, who is a historian, author, and columnist, is well known in Yarmouth. He has often been in the papers and often for reasons other than his column, in which he describes events of historical interest in the area. In this regard, he has a rich vein to mine. Stories of shipwrecks alone could keep his engines stoked for years at a stretch. He is a prolific writer. He thinks that at this point in his career — he is nearly seventy

— he has written more than three million words. On the day I visited, he had just fired off a new batch of writing, including a piece about two Yarmouth boys who rode with Custer. There is no end to the stories you can find if you're willing to dig for them.

Arthur Thurston lives kitty corner to a funeral home, and next door to the synagogue. The synagogue is a handsome structure, built in 1906. These days, it is little used. The numbers in the congregation have dwindled, which is a familiar-enough scenario in small-town churches and temples the country over. It is still maintained, however, and stands as a reminder that Yarmouth, not so very long ago, was a cosmopolitan burg, a thriving mercantile centre, the second-largest shipping port in the country. While this is not to say that the present-day town is hanging on the precipice of ruin, it does seem very much the kind of place that is a monument to an earlier heyday. Having said that, I would add that it looks to be a very well-preserved monument, and that preservation of a noteable past seems to me a perfectly adequate *raison d'être* in the present moment. There are not many places of a similar size with so impressive a stock of heritage buildings. It is a pleasure, even in winter, with the wind whipping off the harbour, to stroll the streets and take in the houses, with their abundance of gingerbread and their elegant façades. Look to the rooftops and you will see a regular widow's cruse of widow's walks. Every block is a show-case of architectural fashion, Italianate, Second Empire, Georgian, as well as the various styles of revival: Greek, Gothic and Queen Anne. You can easily imagine how sea captains, returning from their far-flung travels, might have wanted to build a dwelling that would be, in effect, a souvenir, a home base that would capture something of the fancy of far away. They built their houses to withstand the insistent pressure of their own nostalgia, and they continue to bear up well under the weight of ours.

Arthur Thurston's family has been in Yarmouth for generations. He lives on a street that was laid out by and named for his great-uncle. The house in which he grew up and lived for sixty-one years stood on the same lot occupied by his present home, which is new and cottage-like. Its construction was organized by a consortium of concerned citizens who banded together to help him out after the family home was demolished in 1990. There's a cheerful, hand-lettered sign in the window — you can see it plainly from across the street — that says "Welcome Home Mr. Thurston." It seems to have been there for some time, which lends it an air of stubborn defiance. The window is also decorated with a Confederate flag. He likes to ask visitors if they are bothered by it. One of his abiding interests is the American Civil War, which he has often written about, in articles and in his books, such as *Tallahassee Skipper*. He has named his house "Tallahassee."

"I don't know why you want to see me," Mr. Thurston had told me on the phone when I'd called to see about an appointment and explained my little project. "I'm not eccentric at all. I can't think why anyone would say so! But you can come around if you wish. You know that I'm on oxygen?"

I'd heard that was the case, heard that he suffers from chronic asthma. But what I'd mostly heard about was pigeons. For all his three million words, for all his research, for all his hard and valuable work to keep local history a part of the continuum, it is with pigeons that his wider celebrity lies. Toss out Arthur Thurston's name to just about anybody in Yarmouth and they will say, pigeons, pigeons, Arthur and his pigeons. He kept them, you know, kept them for years, lots and lots of them, so many, many pigeons. They had the run of his house. They were everywhere. After a while, well, you can imagine. It was two and a half storeys, that house, and the upper window was always open, so in and out they flew. In and out. It had been different when his mother was alive; she was a bit of a neat freak, really. When she was alive she kept things in line. But after she was gone, the pigeons took over. It just got to be too much.

At first a few people complained, then more people complained. And it wasn't just the mess. It was Arthur, living like that. It wasn't just that they were angry about the birds, they were concerned for him. It couldn't go on. Something had to be done. So it was that the pigeons came to roost at the epicentre of a decade-long battle that was played out in the town-council chambers, in the papers, in the courts. Pigeons feathered a fracas in which just about everyone took part and took sides.

It seemed that the one person who couldn't say pigeons and problem in the same breath was Arthur Thurston. Arthur Thurston thought then what Arthur Thurston thinks now, which is that there wasn't any problem. There were only pigeons, and he was quite happy to have them living there, in his house, and living there in their hundreds. "Hundreds" is what everyone remembers. "Hundreds" is what the papers reported. He says there were considerably fewer. Dozens, perhaps. Anyway, what did it matter to anyone else? It was nobody's business but his own. But of course, it was. Finally, it fell to the Supreme Court of Nova Scotia to issue an ultimatum. Mr. Thurston was found guilty of housing-standards violations. On Hallowe'en day, 1989, the court declared that, unless he was able to clean his place up, unless he was able to bring it up to scratch within ninety days, the corporation would be within its rights to take possession and deal with the problem as the town elders saw fit. They could bulldoze, if they wanted to. They wanted to. The house in which Arthur Thurston was raised was razed ninety-four days later, on February 2, 1990.

So much attention was focused that day on Mr. Thurston's forced removal from his premises, and the demolition of his house, that hardly anyone thought to remark that it just happened to be the fourteenth anniversary of the great Ground Hog's Day storm, which was the worst recorded meteorological contretemps in the history of south-shore Nova Scotia. Boats and buildings were battered, insurance companies wept, streets became rivers on which people rowed. It was as though the flood had come again: not the flood of Genesis, mind, but the flood that is spoken of in Mi'kmaq legend. In that story, after a long and cleansing rain, a pigeon is dispatched from a boat that is the last remaining outpost of virtue. The bird flies and flies and finally finds not just any old piece of land, but the country we now call Canada. He lands, scouts around, scoops up a blueberry leaf as proof of his discovery (not, note, a maple leaf), and wings his way back to the vessel, where the holy people rejoice at this sign that drier days are near to hand. Then the pigeon perches on the prow, and guides them to that distant shore.

Three of that antediluvial navigator's descendants now live in Arthur Thurston's living room. They are caged, and look to be carefully attended. His cosy house (eight metres long and seven metres wide) is likewise well looked-after, cluttered but clean. It is redolent of bird, that sour, somewhat fecal smell, but it's an odour you adjust to. Mr. Thurston has not been well in recent years. His asthma has taken its toll, and he must be hooked up to a cumbersome oxygen-feeding system, which means that he's pretty much a shut-in. There's a hospital bed in the corner of the room, and various medications round about. He takes fifteen different pills as part of his daily regimen. A "meals on wheels" volunteer turns up with his lunch. For all these signs of invalidism, he's lively of mind; he continues to research and to clack out his column on his typewriter, and his famous memory is as prodigious as ever. He can rhyme off names and dates in Yarmouth history with Gatling-gun efficiency, his speech patterns punctuated by occasional pauses while the oxygen makes its way from tank to lungs. While I am there, a student phones asking for help with a history assignment. Mr. Thurston was for many years a high-school teacher, and is the very soul of consideration with his caller, suggesting this and that source or tack she might take, telling her tidbits about her own family's role in recent Yarmouth history.

"I know too much," he says with a chuckle, when he puts down the phone, "and I think that scares some people. I have all the dirt, you see. I know about who did what when and to whom, know about which wife from which respectable family had an affair with a boy scout. That makes them nervous. Did you say you're a writer? I am, too. My interests are history, especially of Yarmouth; the Civil War; guns and swords; and capital punishment. Have you read my books?"

I was sorry to say I had not, although it was not for want of trying. They are hard to come by, and even the Yarmouth bookstore didn't stock any of his nineteen titles. Arthur Thurston is proud, and justifiably so, of these fruits of his historical research. He has written about Nova Scotia flying aces, in *Bluenose Spitfires*. He has written about some of the Yarmouth County First World War dead, in *A Monument Speaks*. He is especially fascinated by the role Yarmouth played in the Civil War, when Yarmouth fast boats operated out of Saint John as Union blockade runners, ferrying supplies to the Confederate army in Wilmington and Charleston. Mr. Thurston is very happy to talk about his writing, as well as about his collection of vintage swords and pistols. Each of them has a distinguished pedigree. He has a sabre that was brandished in the Charge of the Light Brigade, and a sword that was worn by a Governor General of Bermuda. He has a handgun that was presented by Robert E. Lee to his son.

"How did you begin collecting guns and swords?"

"There was a sheriff here. A son of a bitch, a real prick. He had a big gun collection, and I wanted to outshine him. So I started collecting with a vengeance. I have one that belonged to Cornelius William Van Horne who built the CPR. He was presented with it a year after the railway was finished. It's very rare, a first of that calibre."

"Aren't you worried about security? These are valuable pieces."

"No. Anyone who came in here and tried to rob me would get a sabre through the butt, and not a very clean sabre, either."

"And how did you get interested in pigeons?"

"I thought you said you were a writer."

"I am. Well, I'm a sort of a writer. I'm more of a story gatherer."

"If you're a writer, why are you asking me about pigeons? Why aren't you asking me about writing?"

"Because of everything people have told me about you. I'm collecting stories about eccentrics, and you kept all those pigeons. That's not exactly usual, is it?"

"I'm not eccentric. I can't help it if people say so. They get nervous around me because I know so much more than they do."

"But the house. Didn't they tear down the house because of the pigeons?"

Silence. Then, "You must have seen my book *Tallahassee Skipper*. If you look under those papers you'll find a copy."

This was a conversation that made me feel profoundly uncomfortable. Cannibalistic. What was I doing here? Trying to trick him in some way? What was I expecting of this bright-eyed, white-tufted, intelligent, housebound man who didn't know me from Mogul, the sanctity of whose home I had invaded with my little notebook and my prying questions? How big a piece of him was I after? Oh come on, Arthur! Tell me how the pigeon shit was three feet deep in some places, that there were fifty to sixty dead birds around the house when it was finally demolished; tell me about the three oil heaters that were teetering on various chairs, about the blanket on the droppings-covered floor. Tell me, was that where you slept? That's what the provincial inspector for the Nova Scotia Society for the Prevention of Cruelty to Animals suggested in a letter to *The Chronicle-Herald*. It was published on February 28, 1990, a month after the demolition, and when the heated controversy about your ousting was still making the news around the province.

The house came down on a Friday. "'They're killing my pigeons,' he said as he watched his home fall." That was the sub-headline for an article that appeared in section B of Saturday's Halifax paper. It painted a piteous picture. A small group gathered to watch the demolition of the 120-year-old house. It took just a few minutes to effect its transformation to rubble. Some said that not all the birds, which were to have been removed and put in the care of the SPCA, were clear of the structure before the power shovels came in with their jaws wide open. Arthur Thurston watched from a police cruiser, powerless to stop the carnage. "How much blood do they want? How much blood is there in one human being?" Those are the Shy-lockian words he is reported to have cried out, buckling under the weight of his persecution. Some children brought him a pigeon whose leg had been mangled. He wrapped it in a hand-kerchief and held it close.

His first pigeon had also been hurt. It was given to him by Cecil Mangue, a golf pro at the course where Arthur used to play. (He was once an avid golfer, and still pays sufficient atten-tion to the game to know that one of his pigeons, Brownie, died on the day golf wizard Tiger Woods was born: December 30, 1975.) He named it Cephas, as in: "And he brought him to Jesus. And when Jesus beheld him, he said, Thou art Simon the son of Jona: thou shalt be called Cephas, which is by interpre-tation, A stone" (John 1:42). This much about his troubled life as a pigeon fancier Arthur Thurston told me. It was an ironic choice of names, given that it was the beginning of an obsession that led finally to the casting of the stones that brought his life crashing down around him.

The handling of the pigeon man of Yarmouth divided pub-lic opinion. There were those who said he had been given ample warning, time and again, that he had been advised of the possi-ble consequences of purposefully and wilfully ignoring instruc-tions to bring his house in line with standards clearly spelled out in city bylaws. He had been so careless about its mainte-nance that it was structurally unsound as well as unsanitary, and there was nothing for it but to call in the wreckers. Others thought the town-sanctioned action was unnecessarily severe, that the public-nuisance factor of the pigeons had been grossly exaggerated, that their guardian was a man who had chosen to follow a different path, and it was for that more than anything else that he was being punished. Among the Thurston support-ers was, and is, Sheriff Basil Pero. "People," he told me, "live their own lives in their own way, and if they're not hurting any-one they should be left alone." He was one of the prime movers in arranging a mortgage for "Tallahassee." Sheriff Pero feels that the RCMP, who had the responsibility for removing Mr. Thurston from his natal home, were heavy-handed in the extreme. Fred Hatfield, on the other hand, who is the editor of the venerable *Yarmouth Vanguard*, for which paper Mr. Thurston writes his column, and who was also there on the eventful day, says that the officers did an unpleasant job with considerable compassion. It's a question of hermeneutics, of interpretation. Stories change as they travel, which is how a legend grows.

Arthur Thurston, for all his expressed reluctance to talk about the pigeons of the past, still harbours so much anger about the events of February 2 that he can't hold back from a now-and-again need to vent. He can't help himself. It just comes up in conversation. He says that he owes his bad health to a small stroke he suffered when he was forcibly removed from the house. He talks of the various lawsuits he has launched or is planning to launch against the town. He still reports — as he did in the days following the demolition, when he was being pestered for comments — that some of his personal possessions, such as various papers and academic certificates, were stolen or hauled off to the dump with the detritus that was once his home. And that's not all. He knows more than he's saying. He can name names.

When the house was gone, Arthur Thurston lived in rented rooms and did a stint or two in hospital. He moved into his new digs at the end of March 1994. He's comfortable there. It looks like home. There's a calendar from Ernie's Bar & Grill tacked to the wall, as well as a few newspaper clippings, some of them about other pigeon lovers elsewhere in the country who have run afoul of authority. And there's a photograph of Arthur himself, taken by Fred Hatfield. He's standing outside the house that is no more, surrounded by his one-time flock.

After the old place came down, the birds remained in the neighbourhood. Of course. It was what they knew. Deprived of their habitual haunt, they sought out other nearby roosts. They clung to the eaves of the synagogue, heedless of the cruelties dealt them by the rabbis of yore. They swarmed all over the

Arthur Thurston.

neighbours' rooftops. They were more of a nuisance than ever before. Once again, the town elders gnashed their teeth. Solutions were considered, including hiring a Pied Piper to lure the winged vermin to some out-of-sight, out-of-mind, Never-Never Land. New Brunswick was mentioned as a possibility. Eventually, the birds agreed to disperse, seemingly of their own accord, and migrated to the waterfront. Mr. Thurston continued to see to the maintenance of the flock, paying for the feed which his supporters would distribute twice a week: six to eight forty-kilogram sacks of whole corn would be spread out on a grassy location. "I love them," Arthur Thurston said once, by way of explaining his devotion, "they're like little people. They've been my only life. Other than my writing, they're really all I have."

It is said that Noah first released his sweet dove into the sky above the endless sea on April 1. Poor old fool! The joke was on him, as the elephant knew very well. Perhaps he allowed himself a covert snicker when he heard the bird had come back, hungry and empty-beaked, her white breast heaving, so tuckered from her exertions that she could hardly keep to her perch with her little red feet. It was not until her second foray that she was able to find the tell-tale olive branch, and the reluctant mariners could finally count on bidding "ta ra ra" to Ararat. And the elephant might have laughed even then, knowing full well that all the purging had been for naught. They'd get back on dry land, they'd go forth and multiply, as directed, and things would go from bad to worse. It was human nature. God would be helpless to turn on the faucet again. He had set His rainbow in the sky as a sign of His dry-land covenant. So, har-de-har-har on all of them, and a plague on all their houses. Oh, that elephant, that rogue! Would he have been so careless, so conceited, if he could have imagined or in any way anticipated the fate of his great-, great-, umpteen-times-great-grandson; if he could have foreseen the agonies of Mogul, whose time has finally come?

Let us return to the *Royal Tar* and its unusual cargo, the Boston menagerie, that had just been exhibited at Yarmouth, had made another stop or two in Nova Scotia, and had boarded the ship at Saint John. It consisted of *a rare collection of Animals and Birds, many of which (taken at great hazard and expense by the Company's Hunters in India and Africa) have never been exhibited in this Province, among which are the Gnu, or horned horse, a rare specimen of nature's handiwork; — the Zebra, Pelican, Angola Goat, &c., &c., a very large Elephant, with a splendid Eastern 'Saddle,' Lions, Tigers, Monkeys, Hyenas, Dromedaries, &c., &c....The exercises of the highly trained Elephant Mogul — the leading of the wild beasts — the entering of the Lion's Cage; and the performances in the ring of the Monkey and Pony — form a truly astonishing and interesting exhibition.* Also berthed on the *Tar* were an anaconda, two golden pheasants, several species of talking parrots, and two Comic Negro Singers of celebrity.

Captain Reed was in command. She was a new ship, scarcely six months old. What's more, she was sturdy and fast, built to make the run between Saint John, New Brunswick, and New York City in just two and a half days, with all scheduled stops taken into account. The *Tar* weighed 400 tons, and no expense was spared in her outfitting. There were seventy-two passengers on board, and twenty-one crew members. They must have been looking forward to reaching their destination, and telling their families about how they had travelled with this menagerie. They required a lot of room, Mogul especially, and two of the lifeboats had been removed to enable their passage. Between them, and in a pinch, those boats could accommodate thirty passengers. But what were the chances of needing them? Perhaps it was this same optimism that obviated in the minds of the ship's owners any need for the prudent measure of insuring their $10,000 ship.

It was late October, and the weather had been rough. Captain Reed, facing a gale, and with the wind blowing hard from the northwest, thought it best to shelter behind Fox Island on Penobscot Bay. He asked that the boiler be filled, but through some carelessness on the part of the engineer, this order was never obeyed. Thus did the worm enter the bud. Before long, that boiler ran dry. Before long, it was red hot. Here is part of Captain Reed's own statement, as it appeared in *The Yarmouth Herald*, on November 4, 1836:

"The steam being down, after we had been at anchor about half an hour, the Boat was discovered to be on fire immediately over the boiler, under the deck; the cable was slipped instantly and the fire engine began to work, but in five minutes the men could not stand at the pump, which was below; the smoke nearly suffocating them; at this awful juncture, there was a rush for the boats, there being only two; sixteen of the passengers and crew took the largest boat, and went away before the wind, which blew so hard that they were afraid to bring her to. I got possession of the Jolly Boat, with two men; Mr. Sherwood, Mr. Fowler and a man from the Caravan jumped overboard and we picked them up."

Luckily, the U.S. revenue cutter *Veto* was in the same waters and was able to offer assistance to the distressed ship. The *Royal Tar* was in "a sheet of flame" by the time Captain Dyer was able to steer his vessel close enough to rescue forty passengers who would otherwise surely have perished, augmenting the final death toll of thirty-two: twenty-nine passengers and three crew. Among those who wound up as wave fodder was one of the animal keepers, who went down carrying $500 in coin. The fortunate ones made their way to Isle of Haut, nine miles distant, and there were taken in by Esquire Kimball. Mr. Stinson Patten, of Saint John, was among those who were sufficiently quick and devoted to self-preservation to be able to find a place in one of the two lifeboats. He offered this eye-witness account:

"We lost all our baggage and goods. A temporary raft was made of ladders and planks, on which some of the suffering people took refuge, but it was of little avail, as most of those who trusted to such a frail machine were precipitated into the sea and sank to rise no more. Many who had been driven overboard by the fire sustained themselves on parts of the wreck which had fallen overboard, but the violence of the sea and the cold soon terminated their earthly career. The horrors of the scene were truly appalling; the women threw their children overboard and jumped after them. The screams of these poor creatures at that time, added to the roaring of the two vexed elements, combined to produce a scene that beggars description and can only be conceived by those who have witnessed such scenes of horror. When the fire first burst through the deck such was its rapidity that the caravans immediately ignited, and so overpowering was the smoke and fire that the animals in their cages met an instantaneous death, as not a sound was heard from any one of them. The horses and camels were backed overboard, in hopes that they might reach the shore, but neither force nor any other means could induce the elephant to follow, and he remained, poor fellow, viewing the devastation, until the fire scorching him, he sprang over the side, and was seen striking out lustily for the shore with his trunk held high in the air."

For weeks after the *Tar* went down, the papers were full of follow-up stories and recriminations. How could such a travesty and tragedy have insinuated its way into the annals of seafaring? Who was responsible? Who would pay? And most of all, whatever happened to the elephant, Mogul, last seen striking out across the Atlantic — bravely, hopelessly — his trunk held high? In a way, it was because of Mogul that the fire was such an unmitigated disaster. It was feared that the deck would not be sturdy enough to support him. Wooden wedges had been driven in between the boiler and the deck, in order to bolster its carrying capacity. It was these wedges that first caught fire. Some sources reported that it was Mogul, when he crashed through the deck railing and flung his scorched hide into the sea, who took out the jerry-built raft made of ladders and timbers. What a magnificent image! Every person with vision who leaves this vale of tears must look on one earthly object and know that it is the last thing he or she will ever see. How grand it must have been to look up, to be captivated by the sight of a tumbling elephant, and then to see no more! Mogul swam off and left a wake that was frothy with hearsay. It was rumoured that he made it to shore, in the company of a pony. It was said that he had made his way to a grazing pasture, where he alarmed a herd of dairy cows. Someone heard he was safe and sound and had taken shelter in a farmer's barn.

The story of the burning *Tar* got wide play in Boston, a city where the zoological gardens would be the poorer for the losses incurred on a Canadian ship. *The Boston Transcript* even ran a long and elegaic poem of extraordinary quality. Alas, the name of the author has not survived the onslaught of the intervening years. The title, however, has come down to us. It is the *Royal Tar*. The last stanza reads as follows:

All — all had sunk in that wild sea
    Had human aid alone
Been left to combat with the breeze
    Of terror round them thrown;
But in the hour of deepest need
    A refuge was supplied,
And God his saving hand displayed
    Upon the whelming tide.

"And God his saving hand displayed upon the whelming tide." Did He? Well, perhaps. Perhaps for some. Not for Mogul, though. At least, I'd wager not. Not for Mogul who leapt from the fire and smashed through a raft and into the cold and sucking currents of the sea; who struck out for shore, his trunk held high, trumpeting useless defiance; Mogul, with his enormous feet reaching, reaching, reaching dumbly, hopelessly, reaching for something hard, for something warm, reaching for something like the plains of home, reaching, reaching, and trying so hard to remember them, all those hot, tall grasses, how they tickled his wrinkled knees, reaching and trying to remember the comfortable winds, his great wise mother, the smell of the herd, the colour of that impossible sun, half amber, half blood. Reaching. Reaching. He died reaching. If there was a pitiful or even a forgetful God above, his dying would have been eased by one final glimpse, one guttering memory of that paradise on earth. But all he saw was a filthy cage, and all he felt was the dash of the waves, and all he heard was a terrible laugh, completely foreign yet shocking in its familiarity, and then he heard no more. And he was no more seen, until he washed up on the shores of an island. Brimstone Island, as it happens. Oh, yes. It was Brimstone Island that received the bloated corpse, the stinking remains of all that was Mogul. A flock of doves fought over who would get to eat his eyes. The gulls and the crows lived for weeks on what the pigeons left behind. A high tide came and claimed the bones. And then, Mogul was utterly done. God would have chuckled, if He'd thought it was worth the effort of shaking His belly.

You wonder — how much is he making up?

I say — not much.

You wonder — how can I know what is true?

I say — there is one sure way.

You say — yes?

I say — Reader, meet us in Heaven.

Food for the Phoenix

...Behold, how great a matter a little fire kindleth!
And the tongue is a fire...
   — James 3:5–6

In memoriam Keith Pelton, burned to death at age 13,
Yarmouth, Nova Scotia, August 15, 1898

He died before his time, they always say. They always say, he died too young. When the brakes fail, when the rope frays, when the gun goes off while it's being cleaned, when the mezzanine collapses under the weight of the Christmas shoppers, they say, too young, and they say, too soon. He had his whole life before him, they always say, which wakens something niggling within me, which makes me want to beg to differ, which makes me want to say, no no no, the fact is his whole life was behind him. Whatever life he had was over and done. One dies when and as one dies. That's all there is to it. Nothing is as impartial or as disregarding of the calendar as the forces of termination.

Of course, I understand perfectly well that the reason we fall back on such smooth-edged platitudes is that they usher us into a comfort zone. When death comes and we hum, too young; when life ends and we croon, too soon, we are only making the gentle noises of assuagement, just as a mother might whisper lullay, lully to her baby. We mourn our own diminishing. With every loss, we are lessened. We are left to look wistfully into the west and say, "Oh, but we hardly knew ye."

Keith died in the morning, just before sunrise. He slipped away as the foolish birds of August were tuning their pipes, deked out once again by that thin glimmer in the east, by false dawn, their morning chorus a mourning chorus. By 8 a.m., the first of the neighbours knew, and the words "too young, too soon" began their door-to-door and over-the-fence passage. By noontime, the undertaker had visited and Keith's mother was on a mission of recovery. She went through the house, carrying the trug she used when picking flowers. She combed the place from top to bottom, went from room to room, gathering pieces and remnants of her son, *memento mori* for the reliquary she had in mind. In the kitchen, on the counter, she found a crust of bread, and a knife, sticky with raspberry jam. She had to shoo away a pair of wasps before she could pick it up. From the piano lectern she removed the sheet music for a song by Cecile Chaminade, "Les Fleurs Jetées." He had been at the piano that morning, had been practising when they left for their picnic. He had chosen to stay at home. There were many details that required his attention before his play premièred that night. He was mounting this new opus in honour of his brother and his brother's new bride, just arrived from California. "Hope the ants leave you be!" he called over his shoulder as they trooped out the door. Those were his last words, he with whom the ants and worms would soon have their way.

In the parlour, she found her son's illustrated copy of *Cinderella*. She picked it up gingerly, as though it might combust, and studied the picture of the transformed ash girl, radiant in a gossamer gown, in a candlelit ballroom, no present danger, not so much as a drop of wax on her gauzy, white raiment. There was a costume sketch between two of the leaves, Keith's work. She tucked it back into the book, being careful not to crease or tear its edges, and placed the book in her basket.

She went upstairs, counting the steps — one, two, three — gripping the banister with her right hand, holding her basket in the crook of her opposite elbow, trailing the left hand over the singe marks on the wallpaper. On the landing she found the slipper he had lost while he was tearing down the stairs. Eleven, twelve, thirteen, she summoned all her nerve as she reached the hallway, as she came to Keith's room. Here was his bed, with its precisely turned corners, his shirt and breeches folded on the comforter, the steamer trunk where he kept the makings of his costumes, the lid propped open, his little desk, the notebook in which he wrote his poems, the sun on the wall and the curtains, now scorched and ragged. Ash on the carpet. A tiara still on the dresser, and her face paint. The curling-iron on the floor, the hardwood scarred by the burn mark it left when it fell from the gas fire, a blemish that would never lift.

She set down her trug. She knelt to pick up the iron, testing it first, to see if it retained any of its killing warmth. It was cold, of course. Cold as a dagger. If only! She held it before her, a samurai sword, and liberated from her throat the hell-freezing howl that had been welling all morning, then sprawled on the floor, crying, crying, Keith, oh Keith, my own dear son, oh Keith, I hardly knew you.

I know him. I think I do. Keith Pelton, who was different from the other boys. All his short life he had been an animating force, leading the other children in games of dress-up, organizing the plays in which he would invariably take the lead. Everyone in the neighbourhood knew his name. Keith Pelton, who overnight would become "Poor Keith." Keith Pelton, who was burned to a crisp while dressed as Cinderella, who came to grief at four o'clock on an August afternoon. August: when the shimmering mid-month light breeds chimera; when the heat becomes so heavy it melts away sense and breeds unhealthy sensibility. Everything gets overripe. This was the season Keith's brother chose to come from California, with his new bride in tow. She was so lovely. He was so handsome. They were junior gods, newly come down from their warm Olympus. A celebration was called for! Keith would stage one of his famous spectacles. It would be *Cinderella*. What better way to honour this princess and her consort than with a fable about the transformative powers of love?

Keith massed his forces. It didn't take him more than an hour or two to find the ugly half-sisters, the cruel stepmother, the fairy godmother, the palace courtiers, the others. No one had to ask who would play Cinderella herself. He toiled late into the night, worked deftly and secretively on his sets and costumes. The *pièce de résistance*, the ball gown, heavy with seed pearls, thick with tulle, he saved till the end, knowing as he did that such a monumental robe would tax his every resource. His mother remarked on the bags under his eyes at breakfast that morning, told him that he should really think about getting some beauty rest if he wanted to win the heart of Prince Charming. That made them all laugh, Keith and his seven brothers and his new sister-in-law, too. They all chuckled at the pleasantry, all except his father, Stipendiary Sandford H. Pelton, who was beginning to wonder if Keith might not benefit from a year or two at a military academy.

Keith stayed at the piano for an hour after his family had left on their picnic. The Chaminade was transcendent music. It helped him forget he was stuck in Yarmouth, a town whose charms he had long since outgrown. Sometimes, he would go to the shore and stare into the east, wishing away the curve of the earth, imagining that he could see all the way to France. One day, and before too long, he would get out. He would be the toast of Paris. Yes, sooner rather than later, he would be the toast.

He went into the pantry, found a loaf of bread, cut off a thick slice, spread it generously with raspberry jam. The housemaid, who was polishing the silver, asked Master Keith how his play was coming along. She had secretly hoped he might have assigned her a part, something minor, a church mouse perhaps, something suitable for a country girl with no education but plenty of goodwill. She expected nothing more. She was thirty-three years old. She had always slept alone. She could not point to one moment of what she would call "glory" in her life.

Keith heard the word "play" and snapped out of his reverie. Goodness! He still had work to do. He hurried upstairs. He opened his trunk and took out his princess gown. He had come by it in a way that was not entirely above reproach. It had started out as a wedding dress, and it was meant for Alice Walcott. She had been engaged to the scion of a wealthy shipping family. It was tragic that she should have succumbed to meningitis just a few days before the wedding. She had just turned eighteen. Her mother became quite unhinged. She took the yards and yards of fabric that had been cut and shaped to her daughter's dimensions, but had not been fully seamed and were still pinned to the mannequin, down to the cemetery. She placed the dummy bride at the head of the grave, put it right where the marker would be planted. There the mannequin stood, its gorgeous flags blowing in the wind, a riveted ghost, an improbable scarecrow. No one knew quite what to do about it. It was sheer lunacy to sacrifice such beautiful stuff to the gnawing predations of the sun and the rain. At the same time, it didn't seem right to violate a mother's mourning by removing the totem. It was spooky, though. You had to admit it was spooky, and there was a tacit sense of relief when one morning word got round that the dress had disappeared.

Keith tried not to think of Alice in Heaven, looking down at him as he stripped off his own clothes and laid them neatly on the bed. He studied his body in the mirror. He liked what he saw. His chest was taking on some shape. His nipples were coming into their own. It would be worth paying the price of their present tenderness. The new tufts under his arms and down below were growing in nicely. He was happy with his hair, too. It was quite long, it was thick, and it had a healthy sheen to it. He was confident that he wouldn't go bald before his time, as his father had done. If only his locks had more curl to them! He sighed, but took some consolation in knowing that God did everything for a reason and that one could rely on art to assist nature in matters such as these. To this end, he had borrowed his mother's curling-iron. He hadn't exactly asked if he might help himself to this tool, nor had he received her approval for the loan of her rouge, her lipstick, or her kohl. He was certain she wouldn't mind. She would understand that no self-respecting

Cinderella could look anything but her best for the ball. He ignited the fire, placed the curling-iron to warm, and turned his attention to the dress.

Too young, they say. They say, too soon. He had his whole life before him, we hardly knew him. But I'm telling you, I do. I know exactly who he was, and I know just how it happened. He picked up the dress, held it before his naked body, studied the effect, this way, that way, in the mirror. He stepped into it, reminding himself that he would have to engage someone, maybe his new sister-in-law, to be his dresser, to help him with the hook-and-eye fastenings. It would be a bonding moment between them. Perhaps they would become good friends. He could tell already that she liked him. He imagined that one day she might share with him some of the more intimate details of her wedding night. Had his brother unfastened her dress, his hands moving slowly, deliberately down her back? Or had he torn it away, unseamed it in his eagerness? Keith giggled at the thought. He closed his eyes. He moved his hands over his chest, pressed himself under the lace. His imaginings shifted, and now he became the servant girl who rose up from the ashes. She had come to the ball. She had dazzled the prince. The slipper had fit. She had passed every test. There had been a big wedding feast. Now, at last, they were alone. His hands were at her back. Keith shivered at his touch. He knew just what to do. He mouthed the word "bride," then turned to offer up his lips. He opened his eyes then, and found himself staring into the face of Apollo. Apollo! He was the most beautiful thing Keith had ever seen. God of music, god of poetry, everything that was lovely and manly, all trussed up together in this one divine package! Apollo! Keith threw open his arms in wonder, in welcome, to draw in the god of fire, and it was in that moment of fitful exuberance that a fold of his dress brushed over the curling-iron and passed into the flame.

"It happened so fast, he burned so fast!" That was all the maid could say to the family when they came home from their picnic. She told them how he had come screaming down the stairs, told them how he ran right through the parlour, where she was buffing the monogrammed teapot. She grabbed a rug, chased him out the door, caught up with him on the walk, but by the time she was able to extinguish the flames, there was nothing to be done but to kneel beside him, kneel in his cinders. She was sorry. She was sorry.

Of course, she couldn't stay on. She just couldn't bear the thought of it, nor could she bear the idea of severing her connection with this family, how could she, they were bound for ever. Finally, it was decided that she would return to California with Keith's brother and his bride. Their house was so big! "Like a castle," she wrote in a letter home. She had never imagined that she would live in a castle. The day did not go by that she didn't think of Keith, or tell his story, to herself mostly, but sometimes to others. The nurses in the old folks' home, to which they sent her when she could no longer tend to her own needs, learned to stop listening when they heard her say "Keith." As her time drew near and her own light faded, she forgot his name. She died remembering not so much the burning boy himself, but the brilliant fire and the hot fury of his final flight. She died without ever having heard the word "apotheosis." The attending physician said he had never seen a corpse with eyes so bright. They were as bright as the pennies he pressed to her lids when finally those eyes were closed.

The Offending Hand

As though Pharoah should set the Israelites
to make a pin instead of a pyramid.
— Grenville Kleiser, *Fifteen Thousand Useful Phrases*

I have always been a late bloomer. Always. When I was thirteen, for instance, I knew nothing about anything. Absolutely
nothing at all. The first clue I had that something was up was
when I attended a special band workshop led by a Miss Perkins.
I was enthusiastic about learning to play the flute. Miss Perkins,
it was widely known, had been disappointed in love. She had
been engaged once, to a soldier. Unfortunately, her fiancé had
stopped a German bullet with his skull, at Dieppe or some such
place, and she had never recovered from the loss. From that day
forward, she harboured a deep resentment against all things
Teutonic. One manifestation of this lingering aversion was that
she refused to make any effort whatsoever to pronounce German words when they arose. As you can imagine, this was
something of a liability for a music teacher. On the day in question, which was the day I realized I had some catching-up to do,
she presented us with a sight reading exercise, a transcription of
a movement from the Bach cantata No. 140, "Wachet auf."

"All right, everyone," she said, "get out your instruments
and we'll all play 'Whack it off.'"

It was an offhand remark that precipitated a profoundly
adolescent moment. There was a charged silence in the room,
akin to the one that always settled in after a teacher said
"frigate," or else solemnly intoned "The curse is come upon

me!" when reading aloud from Tennyson's "The Lady of Shal-
lot." "Whack it off" echoed from the bells of the euphoniums,
bounced off the taut skin of the snare drums. There was a
snicker. Then the assembly collapsed into a wholesale guffaw. It
took Miss Perkins several minutes of baton rapping before she
was able to restore order. I was canny enough to know that
something of import had taken place, and canny enough to
make a show of snickering along with everyone else. But the
truth was, I didn't get it at all.

I attribute my naivety in this regard to the fact that I was a
solitary child, and out of the information loop. Whack it off.
What could it mean? Other boys of my age had learned about
their body's new and amazing tricks from cooperative older
brothers, or from experienced cousins visiting from out of town,
or at scout camp, where they were tutored under canvas. Night
after night, they would lie in their beds and practise their new
five-finger exercises, all the while imagining private conjugation
lessons with Mademoiselle Dubois, our French instructor, who
was dishy and young and newly arrived from Rimouski.

It wasn't that I didn't have a fantasy life. I did, but it was
hugely deficient and unproductive. I invented dreamy romances
that were based on B-movie plots. I would play them out in
geometry class, or between the covers while I waited for sleep
to come. There being no women available through the casting
agency of my imagination, I had to take the role of the heroine
myself. I had two favourite leading men. One was Tony Curtis.
The other was Robert Goulet. All the stories followed pretty
much the same scenario, with only slight variations to accommodate shifts in location. For example:

I have been captured by a band of Wild West brigands. They
have bound me hand and foot and tied me to a stake. They are
threatening to cut off my ear unless my father, a fabulously
wealthy rancher, pays an enormous ransom. For some reason,
he is reluctant to do so. I can't imagine why. The banditos are
at the end of their tether. They have waited long enough. Death
to the gringo scum! They are coming at me with a knife, they

are just about to make good on their terrible promise, when who should come riding over the crest of a hill, the sun at his back — straddling with his muscular thighs a lightning-quick white charger — with fire in his eyes and wearing a white stetson, too, but Tony Curtis. He fires his six-gun into the air, bang! bang! bang! and the outlaws all scatter, terrified. *Carumba!* The handsome rustler, the one who had been nice to me when the others weren't paying attention, jumps over a cactus as he makes his escape. He rips his trousers, and I can see a patch of his exposed flesh as he flees into the night. I feel a slight, incongruous pang of affection and loss, the well-documented hostage syndrome. Tony Curtis jumps down off his charger. He rushes over and unties me. He is so very solicitous of my well-being. He picks me up and places me before him on his saddle. He encircles me with his arms, so strong, and away we ride. And ride. And ride. And ride and ride and ride and ride and ride. And then I fall asleep.

Or, I am on the roof of a burning skyscraper. Someone, I don't know who, and I can't say why, has bound me hand and foot and tied me to an air shaft and left me there to die a terrible, excruciating death. The smoke is thick. The flames are near. The building is high. It's not looking good. Just then, who should appear out of nowhere, wearing a hard hat and a very tattered shirt, and smelling all of sweat and good intentions, but Robert Goulet! He sings "If Ever I Would Leave You" while he gnaws through the ropes with his immaculate white teeth, then scoops me up in his arms. He holds me tight to his torso; I can see myself reflected in his hard hat. I look so vulnerable and grateful and, happily, my hair is still in place, and with all the careless grace of a mighty stag, and carrying me as if I weighed nothing more than a cream puff, he leaps across the gaping chasm to the next building, then leaps to the next. And the next. And the next. And the next and the next and the next and the next. And then I fall asleep.

I always had the feeling that something else should happen, but I was never quite sure what that might be. Then came the fateful night I went off to bed with the ovens of desire stoked to bursting by a glorious evening of television watching. Not only had I thrilled to Robert Goulet on "The Ed Sullivan Show" — he had performed, I believe, "My Cup Runneth Over" — but I had seen Tony Curtis in a Sunday-night movie presentation of *Some Like It Hot*. I spread my legs on the cool sheets. I closed my eyes.

I have been captured by pygmy cannibals. They have stripped me and bound me hand and foot — what else? — and placed me in a pot of water. It's a steamy jungle scene, with the tom-toms going mad. The savages are dancing up a storm. The bones in their noses quiver as they hop, and they shake their spears at me in a way that bodes nothing but ill. They are just about to light the wood that will make the fire that will heat the water that will boil me alive, when the air is rent by a tremendous roar. The pygmies look up, astonished, alarmed, and who should they see crashing through the jungle but Robert Goulet, wearing a loin cloth, and riding atop an elephant. Holy doodle! Then there is another heart-stopping bellow, and all their heads swivel comically in the opposite direction. Look! If it isn't Tony Curtis, also wearing a loin cloth, and swinging through the trees on a vine, hollering like Tarzan. Well! This *is* my lucky day! Tony and Robert (as I know I can call them) arrive simultaneously and terrifyingly at the centre of the camp, and my captors scamper off into the forest, issuing little shrieks of alarm. The elephant, understanding that we want to be left alone, exits gracefully, stage right. Together, my heroes lift me out of the pot. I stand before them, naked and unashamed. This is paradise. I hardly know what to say to express my gratitude, my surprise, my deep affection for them both. Happily, emergency steps in and obviates the need for speech. A sickening wind, hot and sweet, has blown up out of nowhere. A ferocious tropical storm is brewing, and we're in terrible danger! But wait! Tony knows of a cave nearby where we could take shelter, but we can get there only by swinging through the trees. We'll have to share a vine! Fine with me, I say, let's go! The men hold me between them, they hold my naked body, I am the meat in their sand-wich, and we are in the air, we are as one, we are swinging from vine to vine, up and down, up and down, and on my back I feel the press of Robert Goulet's marmoreal chest, his muscles chis-elled by Bernini, and on my chest is the press of Tony Curtis's back, the intricate ladder of his spine, up and down, up and down, the wind is howling, and Robert, to make us all feel bet-ter, decides to offer the comfort of song, decides it is time to sing "The Impossible Dream," and we are swinging up and down, up and down, and when a torrid blast blows away their loin cloths, up and down, they say, oh well, that's the way it goes, up and down, that's the way it goes, I say, and now it isn't just Robert singing a capella, but a whole orchestra is playing along, soaring strings, and Robert's chest is rumbling, and my whole being vibrates with his baritone strains as he chants that he will follow his star, even if it's hopeless, and oh but it is hot, and oh but my body is slick with their sweat, and theirs with mine, and I decide that as long as there is an orchestra I might as well conduct, and I seem to have a baton in my hand, up and down, up and down, who can say where it came from, the baton I mean, it's as if I have waited my whole life just to wield this stick, and in the distance I can hear — what? no! yes! — the rumble of a volcano, oh my God, well, there is nothing to be done, we are on a charted course with destiny, we are swinging up and down towards the fiery crater, its perilous hissing is drowning out everything except the unquenchable Robert, who holds on tight to me, while my one unengaged hand is around Tony's waist, and with the other I coax the orchestra to greater and greater heights, up and down, up and down, it is all too much, I feel as though my DNA is uncurling, I feel as though I am replicating Tony's and Robert's cells, and nothing can stop what is going to happen now, whatever it is, we are on top of the volcano, we are passing right over it, and just as Robert bel-lows out that the unreachable star is nigh, it erupts and I can feel its molten lava spewing and then everything shudders and everything goes black. And that is the way it stayed until the sun rose on a new day in a new world that would never be quite the same again.

"In order to make strong babies," says the inventor Jean St-Germain, tugging at the magnificent shrubbery of his beard, "ejaculation must be preceded by at least one hour of physical affection. At least one hour." We are sitting in his sparsely furnished office, which is adjacent to his pyramid, which is at St-Simon-de-Bagot, which is not far from St-Hyacinthe, which is some sixty kilometres to the east of Montreal. You will see it if you are driving by. It is the only pyramid in St-Simon-de-Bagot. A large sign proclaims "Pyramids Are the Solution," an assertion that might provoke the Gertrude Steinian riposte, "Then what is the question?" The pyramid is part of a compound that also includes a restaurant (closed) in the shape of a flying saucer. The service, I gather, was provided robotically. Also advertised are a parachute school and facilities for something called Astro Golf. Even though it's all rather sad and deserted-looking in the winter — in the summer I'm sure it's a regular hive — I was delighted by what I found. I anticipated nothing more than a garden-variety pyramid. Certainly I'd never thought of a UFO, and never did it occur to me to expect a discussion of ejaculation, and in French, *en plus*! As M. St-Germain and I talk, it dawns on me that I have just said "ejaculation" in French for the first time, ever, in my life. I am amazed at the way it feels in my mouth, and at the way it makes me feel deeply, deeply homesick.

"At least one hour of physical affection is necessary to prepare the spermatozoa. Otherwise they will be weak. It is also helpful to eat many green vegetables."

"My! How do you know all this?"

"I have received this information from they who make human beings."

"Oh."

If anyone has earned a right to claim inside knowledge on how best to make durable infants, I suppose it would be Jean St-Germain. By the time he was thirty-six, he was the father of a dozen children. His starter fluid must have been adequately primed for the production of feisty babies, at least if we are to judge by the career path of one of his daughters. He tells me that she has recently enlisted with the RCMP and is part of an élite corps whose members serve as bodyguards to Prime Minister Jean Chrétien. I remark that she must be the sort of girl who can look after herself, and he agrees that this is so. The remaining eleven offspring are also launched and are forging successful lives for themselves out in the world.

Twelve children! Holy Dinah! This kind of fervent spawning was not at all uncommon among Québécois of an earlier, more Catholic generation. In our present and secular age, when the province's birth rate is at an all-time low and continues to decline, and when generally reliable birth control is easy to obtain, such prolificacy has become rare, anachronistic. *Ancien régime*, even. Of course, none of this clan building would have been possible without the cooperation of Mme. St-Germain, Adrienne, whom I did not meet, but of whom I read in Jean's autobiography. He wrote it in three weeks, in Florida, and published it himself in 1979 under the inspirational title *Lâche pas y'a toujours un moyen: Mes aventure, mes inventions*. It's a paean to his own perseverance, and I think he wrote it mostly as a way of dealing with people such as I, who come to ask questions like the ones I'm bent on asking. He tells of how he met Adrienne when he was a young skydiver, and how she used to hang around after his precipitous descents and help him fold up his parachute, and when he asked her to marry him he told her frankly what she could expect of him, which wasn't much, since he was broke, had no immediate prospects for earning any money, was overly fond of travel, wanted to be free, and in addition to all that had a notebook which contained the salient details (dates, places, names) of the 276 women with whom he had made love from the time he was seventeen until he was twenty-two. He showed it to her. You have to hand it to him. He wanted everything to be on the up-and-up. She digested all this.

"And you're choosing me among all of them?" she asked.

"Yes."

"Then I'm very happy."

From earliest childhood, Jean St-Germain demonstrated the inclinations that have been manifest throughout his developing career: an aversion to authority, a love of flying, a passion for risk taking, and a burning desire to invent stuff. An indifferent scholar from the get-go, he was forever skipping school to work on his own inspired projects. The community did not necessarily see these creative forays as benign. He ran afoul of the neighbours by pressing their pet cats into service as test pilots for his parachute contraptions. He would damage passing cars when his enormous kites fell prey to gravity. He would inflict injuries on pedestrians by running them down with hot-rods he'd hammered together out of whatever spare parts happened to be around. The police would be summoned. His parents despaired. Things went from bad to worse. He began to run away. He quit high school. Somewhere along the line, he took up the accordion. It looked like he would never amount to anything.

When he was sixteen, Jean St-Germain had his first near brush with big-time success. He was staying with one of his brothers and a sister-in-law. They bottle-fed their baby, and the poor mite was colicky and gassy because of the amount of air he ingested along with his milk. Ti-Jean, as his family called him, considered the problem for a few moments and had an inspiration. All that was required to make the baby comfortable during his meal was to eliminate the air problem. *Façile à faire!* He purchased some condoms, scrubbed them up, inserted one in a feeding bottle, filled the improvised balloon with formula, and gave it to the baby. When the child sucked up the liquid, the condom collapsed behind it, creating a seal. *Résultat:* no more air to trouble the heir. Thus did a high-school drop-out devise the prototype of the disposable baby bottle. All told, it took about three hours from conception through execution. "You have some genius in that head of yours," exclaimed an early appreciator of his brainchild. He knew he had a concept that was marketable, but couldn't quite figure what to do with it, which is a pity, since the disposable baby bottle was exactly the kind of modern aid the mothers of baby boomers craved, occupying as it does the same aesthetic rung as TV dinners, or Pampers. By rights, he should have made a fortune. At sixteen, though, what do you know? At sixteen, when you're in debt to your parents and you're carrying the burden of their disappointment besides, you won't necessarily hold out for the best deal. At sixteen, you'll take the money and run. Eventually, some sharp-eyed entrepreneur talked him into selling the patent for a thousand dollars. Eventually, it fell to Playtex to finally manufacture and market a bottle based on his design. They cleared considerably more than a thousand dollars.

If one were writing Jean St-Germain's life as a novel, this would be the moment one would have to choose a fictive fork to follow. Would he spend the rest of his life boring drunks in bars with the story of what might have been? Would he channel his bitterness into something warped and sociopathic, such as sneaking into pharmacies and lacing formula with strychnine? Would he collapse into weeping every time he saw a happy, swilling, gas-free baby? The truth, as is usually the case, is more pedestrian than fiction. The truth is that he happily took the thousand dollars, didn't look back, and simply trundled on. He joined the army, went to Europe, did a stint as a paratrooper, met the lovely Adrienne, and the two of them commenced having babies. Jean continued jimmying with this gizmo and that gizmo, inventing motor components, developing light aircraft and safety handles for snowmobiles, coming up with innovative milk jugs and children's toys, consolidating his reputation as an inventor and patent taker. Now and then he made some money. Now and then he took a bath. There were adversaries along the way. As he tells his story in *Lâche pas*, he was constantly doing battle with the banks, with various lawyers and politicians and safety inspectors and civic or aviation officials who simply couldn't see with his clarity of vision. He never lost faith in his own ability or sight of his own path.

Family life was important, too. Several of the St-Germain children were featured in an article that appeared in *National Geographic World*, in February 1982. Four of them — Daniel, Pierre, François, and Nathalie — appear on the cover. Daniel, wearing a vivid green flying-suit, a helmet and goggles, hovers in mid-air. He looks like a comic-book superhero, preparing to descend and lash out at a baddy. The other three, swathed in yellow, stand about the perimeter of what might be a brightly coloured circus tent and watch him fly. In fact, they were photographed while demonstrating the Aérodium, another of their father's inventions, which he designed and opened to the public in 1980. The Aérodium is a wind-tunnel affair where the emphasis is placed on vertical rather than horizontal thrust. St-Germain's first thought was that it would be useful to teach sky-divers how to handle themselves in a simulated free fall, but saw that it had a broader public application as an amusement-park attraction. After all, who hasn't dreamed of flying, free as a bird, spirit-like, without the shackling confines of a plane? The aspiring aviator gets decked out in an oversized Day-Glo flying-suit in a primary colour, as well as all kinds of protective padding. Then, she throws herself onto an upward draft created — at least in the prototype — by a propeller from a DC-3, and is hoisted aloft on a lusty column of air. Experienced flyers ride the upward current like happy swallows. First-timers are chucked around the room like poker chips, smashing into the walls until they get the hang of this windy levitation.

By the time of the advent of the Aérodium, Jean St-Germain was considerably more experienced in the rough-and-tumble legalistic world of rights, patents, and distribution. He sold the franchising rights to the Aérodium concept for a tidy sum. Rich as Pharaoh, and hardly over the threshold of middle age, Jean St-Germain turned his attention towards the construction of a pyramid.

Middle age. It is dangerous terrain. I often think there is little more pathetic than a man in mid-life, no matter how happy and well adjusted he seems. You can never tell, nor can he, what psychic malaise will come crashing, comet-like, through his window and damage him in his sleep. One day he wakes up, looks around, and realizes that the life he is living is both dreadful and real, that it has no sound, no fury, only nothingness, and that death or divorce is his only real prospect for change. How he longs for that distant season when *he radiated vigor and abundance like a happy child*. The dreams of his youth have *fallen like dead leaves on the highway*. Before long, he will grow *weak, like a shrunk cedar white with the hoar-frost*. He will be *wrinkled and scored like a dried apple*.

It's a grim time, there's no denying it, and it comes with its nutty, reactive pathology in tow. The biology of middle age prescribes that men fly off in one of two directions. Some will hunger after the world. They will gallop after the things of youth, thumbing their nose at mortality by buying absurdly flashy cars, having their love handles suctioned or their eyelids bolstered, and dallying with women half their age. Others — those who are inclined by nature to go more gentle into that good and relentless night — will seek hermitage. They will retire to basement workshops to sort endlessly through their accumulation of washers and screws, or they will construct little outbuildings in their backyards, slightly more vaunted versions of the clubhouses of their school days, those shacks hung with signs that warned "No Girls Allowed." I remember, while I was growing up, how a contemporary of my father's did this very thing. Night after night he hammered and sawed, building for himself what eventually evolved into an almost alarmingly pretty cottage, with a delicately painted trim, dainty shutters, and flouncy curtains. Night after night, once his project was done, this fellow — who must have been then my present age — would leave his house and whatever domestic strains might have been beating their wings around its rafters, and revel in the solitude of his little sanctuary. We could walk by and look at him there, could see him through the sheer drapes. It was like looking at a ghost, or a zoo exhibit: *homo sapiens in media vita*. He never appeared to do anything, not even to read. He just sat by himself, with a small lamp burning, and the evening settling around him. None of us children, I feel sure, saw him as a prophet of things to come.

As Jean St-Germain grew into middle age, his physical aspect became more and more prophet-like. With his long hair, and his burning bush of a beard, he was reminiscent of an illustration from a child's Old Testament. He was — still is — the very picture of a craggy desert Elijah or Jeremiah. It's a look he wears well, a look he has in some measure earned, since he once underwent a kind of John the Baptist stint in the wilderness. He took to the desert to keep a promise he made to God. One day, the story goes, he was testing out a light aircraft, a gyrocopter. Everthing went wrong. All systems were failing. It seemed hopeless. He was surely going to crash. He asked for assistance from on high. Get me out of this pickle, Jean prayed to God, and I promise that I'll come to Israel and visit You in the desert. ("*Si Tu me sors de ce pétrin, je promets d'aller te rendre visite dans le désert en Israel.*") Sure enough, a deep calm descended on him, and he knew exactly what he needed to do to bring his wonky craft safely back to earth. He did not forget. He was a man of his word. Shortly afterwards, he told Adrienne that she would have to look after things for a while. He had pressing business elsewhere. When she asked why he was going to Israel, he answered that he would tell her later, that for the time being she shouldn't ask questions.

His account of his journey across the sands from Beersheba to the Dead Sea presents the reader with a fascinating mélange of spirituality and sensuality. Not only does he dialogue directly with God, and learn the reason why there are such huge disparities between the rich and the poor, why the stars are at such a great remove from the earth, learn the truth about life after death, and the mystery of free will; he also spends the night in a Bedouin tent and makes love with two young girls, and winds up his voyage in a hotel room back in Beersheba with eight beautiful and bisexual women with whom he spends "une nuit sexuelle indescriptible." (I confess that when I read this I felt a wee pang of sympathy for Adrienne, back at home with who knows how many children and another bun in the oven. Readers of like sensibility might be relieved to learn, as I was, that, at a later juncture, Jean is able to converse directly with Jesus. When he asks the Saviour if it is wrong to make love to a woman other than one's own wife, he is assured that all is relative, and that he, Jean, is the only one who can pass judgment on himself. Since he not only recorded this tale of extravagant infidelity as part of a public record of his life, but did so in a book in which his wife is credited as "recherchiste," we can take it that Adrienne was at least as tolerant of his philandering as was Jesus.)

Given that he had not once, but twice, been privileged to sniff the rich breath of Divinity; and given that the success of his inventions, particularly the Aérodium, had made him a man of financial substance; and given that middle age and its "acting out" prerogatives were upon him, it is not so surprising that M. St-Germain would choose to build a temple expressive of his spiritual and fiscal achievements Why should it not take the form of a half-a-millon-dollar, 2.3-million-pound marble and granite pyramid? After all, these were the eighties, a period of great ecumenism, as well as a time when everyone was discovering that pyramids — albeit tiny ones — could sharpen razor blades, enhance the growth of house plants, effect the erasure of tumours, and bring the individual in closer touch with the cosmos. After the handsome *nouveau-égyptien* edifice was finished in 1982, and opened to the public as the first major installation in what was anticipated to be a kind of New Age Disneyland, St-Germain made personal weekly visits of about five minutes each to its inner chamber. There he would clear his mind, and enjoy the benefits of so concentrated a dose of magnetic energy. Early in 1983, to demonstrate its power as a high-frequency meditation chamber, he spent all night inside, and emerged with 2,000 written sequences of numbers between one and thirty-six to play on the roulette wheel of the Tropicana Hotel and Casino in Las Vegas. Thus armed, and with a thousand dollars in his pocket, he made another trip to another desert. It was his intention to see the thousand transformed into a million. At one point he was up by a hundred thousand dollars. However, by the evening's end, he had lost all but his original stake, a failure he attributed to being overtired after choosing the first thousand numbers.

I would recommend to anyone a visit to the dark inner sanctum of the St-Germain pyramid. It may not lead to an immediate lottery win, but it is a restful and pleasantly weird way to drop twenty-five bucks. An assistant will show you into a preparatory anteroom where you will remove your shoes and any metal objects you might be carrying or wearing: bracelets, belts, change, and the like. Metal interferes with the magnetic principle on which the whole thing operates and which I freely confess not to understand. Once you have sat for a calming few minutes, listening to environmental music (brooks, birds, quiet strings), with your feet resting upon a footstool that I think is meant to have a grounding effect, you will be ushered down a long and echoing candlelit corridor — stooping, because the ceiling is very low — until you emerge under the pointed dome of the pyramid itself. Here too, there is an evocative, flickering illumination that comes from many, many candles. It's terrifically pretty, it really is. The assistant will orient you, then leave you to stand or sit and receive the beneficial vibrations for fifteen minutes, at which point a gong will sound to let you know your time is up. The room is acoustically resonant, and she will tell you that you may sing, if you wish. I listened to the receding pit-a-pat of her footfalls as she padded away down the tunnel. When I was sure she was gone, I hummed a few trial notes. My voice rang pleasingly all around me. I tried and tried to think of an appropriate song, which I can never do when required. The only tunes that came to mind were "What I Did for Love" and "Lulu's Back in Town." I sang a quick chorus or two of each, made my way through as many verses of "Blowin' in the Wind" as I could remember, then sat quietly and waited for the gong.

Jean St-Germain eats lunch most days at a crowded strip-mall restaurant in St-Hyacinthe. It's full of folks on hour-long lunch breaks, many of whom are regulars, and many of whom greet him as he walks to his table. He's been coming here for years. They all have. I tag along with him, at his kind invitation, and when the waitress takes our order, he asks if she wouldn't mind bringing him an egg, not a cooked one, just an egg from the fridge, brown or white, it doesn't matter. There is a trick he wants to show me that will impart a clear and present tangible proof of his powers of mind. I don't much feel the need of such a demonstration, as I don't doubt for one second that he is a man of huge energy and varied accomplishment. The record speaks for itself. He has been incredibly fecund, with dozens more patents than he has children registered in his name, and he has made enormous whacks of cash over the years. By way of proving his solvency, he had earlier flashed before my eyes a letter from someone at Revenue Canada, an official with whom I gather he has been in fairly regular correspondence over the years. The bureaucrat was inquiring as to whether or not something might be done about paying off some of the interest that has been accruing on the St-Germain tax account. The amount mentioned — and this is interest, mind — was tens of thousands of dollars in excess of what most Canadians would consider a comfortable middle-class income. When I asked M. St-Germain if he was not concerned about the tax people, he chuckled. He has been playing a cat-and-mouse game with them for years now. Eventually, he'll render something unto Caesar, but he doesn't like to make it too easy. He believes inventors should be exempt from tax collection since they plough the money they earn right back into their creative enterprise.

"So you see," he said, "I am not really eccentric. My feet are solidly on the ground. I don't think an eccentric can owe that much in taxes!"

Though our acquaintance was short, and though he wasn't so very interested in answering my questions ("Vous verrez ça dans le livre"), and though much of what I have garnered about his life and thinking has come from his autobiography and from the magazine and newspaper pieces that have been published about him, I would still presume to say, on the basis of this slight evidence, that Jean St-Germain inhabits an ethical universe with parentheses wide and elastic enough to accommodate both a rooted Catholicism and such New Age philosophies as pyramid power. His chummy accord with Jesus lives alongside a *laissez-faire* attitude towards marital fidelity. He can take pride in his daughter who guards the physical person of the prime minister and at the same time revel in his sporting fondness for baiting her boss's cash collectors. The pyramid builder of St-Simon has a received philosophy about leading a good life that enables him to shelter such seeming contradictions under one roof; a code of conduct which has come his way via the same source that made manifest the business about an taking an hour for physical affection before giving in to ejaculation. The gist of his broader remarks, which I am both paraphrasing and translating, is that we are all the holders of moral bank accounts. We can fill them or deplete them as we wish, while we go about the business of whittling down the stump of our days. It does not matter if we give in to such base desires as the urge to smoke or to masturbate. (He was very specific about masturbation and smoking.) We won't be judged harshly for such laxness. However, we need to understand that, when we abuse ourselves in these ways, we demonstrate a lack of respect for the stuff of life. When we refrain from smoking, or from enjoying auto-erotic stimulation, and do so as a deliberate show of respect for the life with which we have been entrusted, then our moral bank accounts are topped up all over again. It is this awareness and this respect that are the keys to right living — at least, so I understood him to say. It is the kind of speculative moralizing that makes me feel a vice is being tightened around my temples.

The waitress brings an egg, as requested. She hands it to St-Germain.

"Qu'est-ce qu'il va faire?" she asks, and laughs. One senses there's not much he could do that would surprise her. He sets the *oeuf* down on the table on one of its elliptical ends, then tries to coax it into balancing, like a top.

"You are not supposed to be able to do this," he says, "but it is possible. You just need to be able to concentrate, to focus the mind. You just need to find the right point…"

And for the next ten minutes, while his soup cools, he gives the ovum the whole of his attention. He blots out the chatter and the clatter of a hundred other lunchers, and concentrates on making the egg stand at attention. I sit there quietly, hoping my expression betrays only rapt interest, even though I am mostly regretting the absence of placemats you can read.

Lâche pas is Jean St-Germain's motto. Don't give up. It's a dictum he applies to this kind of parlour trick, and to more momentous tasks, such as building the Aérodium or a pyramid. The present pyramid of St-Simon, splendid and useful though it may be, is not the pyramid of his grandest dreams. Several years ago, he announced his intentions to erect, right in his own back-yard, "la plus grande pyramide du monde." Yes, the biggest in the world, larger even than the great monument created by Cheops more than 4,000 years ago in the Egyptian sands. It would also be more inclusive. Cheops built his pyrmaid as a tomb for himself and a few of his closest friends. The St-Germain pyramid, which would measure about 1,000 feet at the base, and 500 feet in height, would accommodate, post-mortem, most of the present population of Canada on thirty-three of its forty-two levels. His plan was to have space for 22 million memorial urns. They would be arrayed, along with iden-tifying plaques, along the many corridors, and would be sold for fees ranging from $1,000 and $9,250. High rollers would be assigned to the upper levels of the structure, the view suites, I guess. Sales would be arranged through a non-profit organiza-tion called Citadelle de la Paix, and the money raised would underwrite the projected $750-million price tag attached to the concrete structure, as well as give a much-needed surge to the province's economy. As he explained to *La Presse*, in August 1988, "my great funerary pyramid I see as a source of life for future generations. Such a project shouldn't have a financial objective: it should be useful for all Québécois in such fields as health, education, ecology, and humanitarian work." Not the least-attractive feature of the pyramid would be a forty-two-ton prism that would be installed at the apex, and would project into the atmosphere, by way of skylights, a rainbow of luminous lights that would be very pretty indeed. Within, the ambience would be one of calm, peace, and serenity.

How can one help but admire this man for his tenacity and independence of spirit? Whatever else one might think about his philosophies, one has to commend his refusal to abandon, in spite of the drubbings meted out by age and experience, his passion for dreaming big. In his 1909 text *Ten Thousand Dreams Interpreted* — which reference source is nearly as necessary to my happiness and sense of well-being as *Fifteen Thousand Useful Phrases* — Gustavus Hindman Miller says that to dream of pyramids "denotes that many changes will come to you. If you scale them, you will journey along before you find the gratification of your desires." Whether Jean St-Germain received such warning prognosticatory signs, I can't tell you. However, it is a fact that construction of *la grande pyramide de St-Simon*, which he intended to go up right beside the Trans-Canada Highway halfway between Montreal and Quebec City, has been stalled, and for almost ten years now, by the conservationist truculence of the Agricultural Land Reserve (L'Office de Protection du Territoire Agricole). There is no sign that the long-standing dispute over land use is going to be solved any time soon. Ask him if he still plans to build his pyramid, and Jean St-Germain will tell you, quietly, almost shruggingly, yes. However, as it is a project that can't be realized in the short term, it has taken a back-burner position to his current undertaking, the erection of a 128-foot concrete cross in which he will house displays that will tell the story of religion. It's a relief to know that he has a channel for his energies. He is the kind of man who needs a project, a mission. He is now what he has always been: a man with his own sense of enigmatic purpose.

"I know why we are here," he tells me, as the waitress brings our cheque, "and I know where we are going. When the time is right, I will be able to say all I know."

"When will that be?"

"Maybe two months. Maybe two years. When the time is right to say, I will know."

It seems so long to wait! So much could be helped and planned if only one knew. Is it worthwhile having that dental work done? Is there any point in renegotiating the mortgage? Oh, well. Garrulous old Time, in tandem with Jean, will one day deign to tell. In the meantime, by way of a stopgap, by way of a promise, there is the egg, unassisted, holding its balance beside the ashtray, white and blameless as a dancer *en pointe*.

Jean has an appointment to keep. I want to get back to Montreal before a forecast snowstorm settles in. I head west, to the city of many restaurants, none of which looks even remotely like a flying saucer. He heads east, back to his parcel of land that could be made prettier only by the presence of the world's biggest pyramid. I turn on the radio, hoping for the weather. Instead, I get the news. In Albania, the announcer says, there is civil unrest in the wake of the collapse of a pyramid scheme. Civil unrest? Go figure! Here, at least, in this vicintiy, the disappointing dissolution of a pyramid doesn't disrupt the peace. I smile when I think of that. It makes me feel optimistic. It makes me feel that I am in Canada, after all.

● ● ●

Let a bear robbed of her whelps meet a man,
rather than a fool in his folly.
    — Proverbs 17:12

In *The Canadian Boy Scout* (1911), Robert Baden-Powell enjoined his disciples from smoking, telling dirty stories, reading trashy books, and looking at lewd pictures. Such indulgences are, he said, "very apt to lead a thoughtless boy into the temptation of self-abuse. This is a most dangerous thing for him, for should it become a habit it quickly destroys both health and spirits; he becomes feeble in body and mind, and often ends in a lunatic asylum."

He does not add "with hair on his palms," but might just as well have done so. In that same edition of his gospel, B.-P. warned that "many a tenderfoot has got lost on the prairie or the forest, and has never been seen again, through not having learned a little scouting, or what is called 'eye of the country,' when a boy."

"Eye of the country" is something I utterly failed to acquire during the long and terrible years I spent as a beret-wearing Powellian anchorite. Nor was I otherwise accomplished. My only badges were for my expertise in such womanly arts as housekeeping, singing, and reading. I may have been awarded one for philately, I'm not sure. I did my duty to God and the Queen, and tried to adhere to the most ringing of the many tenets, the one that demanded we Be Prepared. That was the total sum of my accomplishments. Knotting was an impossibility, as was campfire lighting, and the pivotal scouting skill of pathfinding eluded me altogether. It was neither within my reach or grasp. I had — I have — no innate sense of direction, and since every location-finding technique our leaders thought to teach us had to do with grasping for north, I felt no incentive to learn. North? What was the point in all that compass-reading, star-watching, moss-measuring, and sun-squinting if north was all it would net you? What was so all-fired great about north, anyway? What was there? An Arctic waste. A walrus or two. The Inuit, who have no word for love, which was all I craved. I could have cared less about north. It was the south that interested me. South was glamour, beaches, Hollywood, tans, bullfights, orange groves, hula dancers, torrid nights of romance. It was everything your little frozen heart could desire. During the Winnipeg winters, when south winds blew, I would face them head on, would welcome them, sniff them, longing for the scent of frangipani, of magnolia. Of otherness. Of elsewhere. For the most part, those winds were vicious and smelled like North

Dakota. But over time, if you managed to harden yourself against their full-frontal onslaught, you could learn to suss out a certain softness hidden deep beneath the bluster. At the cold south wind's remotest edges was the promise of something sweeter to come.

It was in such a southerly gale that I drove the fifty-four miles from my parents' home in the city to the pretty little town of Portage la Prairie. I went there to meet with Nick Kolansky. Nick owns a camping and fishing lodge in the Whiteshell. For years before that, he ran a popular family restaurant in Portage. Before that he was in the air force. And before that, when he was still a kid, he worked with his brother, Alex. Alex was a trapper for almost forty years. Finding out about Alex was why I went to Portage. It's an easy trip, even for someone as directionally challenged and tender-footed as I. You simply point your car in the general direction of Vancouver and step on the gas. You scarcely need to steer as you speed along the Trans-Canada. Early on a Sunday morning in February, there's no traffic to hold you up. The Sunday I went, there was only the gusting south wind, exercising its decorator prerogative, shoving the dry snow from one field to another, mindless of the highway that divides them. It's an amazing sight, all that snow blowing. It's the polar equivalent of a sandstorm, and in that geography, driving across the magnificent stretch of farm-friendly flatness, you can't help but think of tumbling topsoil, of the dust bowls of the last great Depression. Alex was born in Sundown, Manitoba, in 1914, but it's in the Depression that his story really starts.

Nick Kolansky and his wife, Evelyn, live in a comfortable bungalow on a quiet, sheltered street a few blocks from the railway line. Nick's many stories about his remarkable brother are well-loved party pieces, but Nick has the knack of making them fresh. He is a terrific storyteller, and as generous and gregarious a host as you could ever hope to find.

"When he started out, Alex lived the hard life. Everybody did, back then. The thirties. It was just the times. Alex would get a job in the fields at harvest; he'd get paid a dollar a day for twelve hours' worth of work. And then he'd ride the rails. He'd hop freights out of Winnipeg. He'd ride in a boxcar, or strap himself to the top. Three days he'd be up there, sometimes, going to B.C., to get a job in a lumber camp. Those trains would sometimes have a hard time getting through the tunnel. They'd be pouring out smoke. Alex told me about how he'd almost suffocate up there, there'd be nothing to breathe. He went into the bush in 1939. He liked that backwoods country. He applied for and got trapline number five. It ran for about 200 square miles in what is still the deepest part of that wilderness. It wasn't so much beaver he trapped back then, but lynx, weasels, fox, timber wolf, squirrels even. They were legholds, sure. It was a cruel way to make a living. But one thing about Alex is that even though he needed to take the animals, he never took any who lived around his own lake. No, they were his friends."

Talk to anyone who remembers Alex Kolansky, and you will be told this: that he was a man of extraordinary gentleness, of deep spirituality. He loved children. He forged a strong link with the land on which he lived, deep bush country, miles and miles from the nearest habitation. In his early years on the trapline, he'd go for months at a stretch without seeing or talking to another living soul. Animals were his society, and he got to know them well.

"The squirrel would come and have dinner with him every day," Nick remembered. "The wasps decided to build a nest in his cabin. He didn't bother them. They didn't bother him. And there was a bear that had a cave, about 200 yards from his cabin. Alex would go over to visit the bear. He'd go over in the winter and wake him up, and they'd just visit. Once, when he'd been away from the cabin for a few days, there'd been a forest fire. He got back and found these three little bear cubs, crying. The mother had been killed. So Alex made them some bannock with honey and milk and fed it to them and they stayed with him. He'd get in the canoe and they'd get in the canoe. He'd walk to the next lake and they'd follow him along, like puppies.

He slept with them in the camp, they kept him awake rolling on the floor and swatting each other. He lived with them all summer, and in the fall he found an old bear den and took them over there. He sealed them up and bid them farewell. This was, maybe, 1968. On the day before Christmas, I went down to visit him on the Skidoo. I told him I was taking him to Green Lake for Christmas dinner. He said, I'm not going to no Christmas dinner. I'm going to have Christmas dinner with the bears! And that's just what he did. He made up some bannock, honey, and milk. He went over to their cave. He woke them up. And he had Christmas dinner with the bears.

"And one time I remember, he'd finally managed to save around $500. He put it in a tin can, it was a baking-powder tin, and closed the lid. He buried it in the garbage pile. I had the restaurant by then, and Alex would sometimes come in the summers to help me out. He stayed with me for a couple of months. When he got back to his camp, he found the groundhog had decided to make a home where the can was, and he'd thrown it out. The bear came along and he wanted to know what was in the can and he chewed at it and the lid popped off and the south wind took all the money into the bush. All bills — fives, tens, twenties — all in the bush. Every time the wind came, it would blow it a little further into the bush. Alex went into the bush and started looking and he found everything but twenty or thirty dollars. Took him two weeks to find all his money."

Alex was a resourceful man. He made his own skis, out of birch planks, with soup tins for the tips. He made his own saw-mill and cut up the lumber to make his various shacks. He made a kind of waterwheel thingy, and an automatic washing machine. He was a religious man, too. He never worked on Sundays, and would close his traps on Saturday night. He smoked for a while, but gave it up. He never drank. He never, ever swore, and didn't appreciate hearing it from others. Nick remembers how his brother would clam up when they were out on the trapline together and Nick would use salty language.

Alex was never without a Bible, not even when he was riding the rails. He'd read it cover to cover several times. He was a compact man, just five-feet tall, 130 pounds, all muscle. Even after he lost his hand, he could heave his canoe up onto his shoulder, with one arm, like there was nothing to it. Even after he lost his hand, he would paddle his canoe, would gather wild rice, would operate his chainsaw. He ran his line and lived happily in the bush for thirty years after he lost his hand.

Alex Kolansky's story is fascinating by any measure, but it was the loss of the hand that cemented his legend, and earned him the nickname "The Mad Trapper of the Whiteshell." Different people to whom I've spoken have told me different stories. Some said he'd had an accident while chopping ice. Some had a darker tale to tell. Nick, who was the first person to see him after it happened, says this is the authoritative version:

"Alex, see, he was deeply religious. And when you're alone, and you read the Bible, you only have the one opinion that you yourself construct when you read a verse or chapter. Alex was carried away by the theory that if an eye offends you, pluck it out. If a hand offends you, cut it off. And of course, living alone, and being alone, and never seeing anyone, and only coming out once or twice a year, he never had anyone to set him right or contradict him. And his hand offended him. Well, he was playing with himself and he figured that wasn't right, so he read the Bible again and that's what it told him to do. On December 17, 1948, it was thirty-three below. I saw his calendar, he was marking down the temperatures. He was living at Cave Lake then. At thirty-three below, he tied a rope around the wrist to stop the blood circulation. He tied it tight, then he walked that way to the next lake. By the time he got back, he told me, he could put a knife through his hand anywhere. He had one of those big ice chisels — he used to chisel ice with it — and it weighed about nine pounds, maybe. He just put his hand on a block of wood and dropped the chisel down and the hand came right off. He shoved his arm in the fire to sear it. He had this big fire going.

"Eventually, someone heard about it, and they got hold of me, and in the spring of '49 I went down to see him. I finally made it to the camp with this pack-sack of food, and I found him skinning a beaver. He had a knife tied to the stub, and he was skinning a beaver. Well, I was tired and I didn't really know what had happened, didn't know what to expect. He was just so happy to see me! He jumped up and ran over and wanted to throw his arms around me and I looked at that knife and I thought he was going to kill me there and then. I thought, well, let him kill me, I haven't got any more strength left anyway. He untied his knife and I made supper and he wanted to talk, and I was so tired I was falling asleep, and he got a hold of the fiddle and he strapped on the bow, right on the stump, and he played for me. He could still play the guitar, too.

"That hand healed up. When I was there that time, I watched him take a knife and flick off the last piece of bone. He never saw anyone for it. He had a pack of those paper serviettes, and that's what he used for a dressing. He told me how he suffered. He told me I didn't know what pain was. He ran out of food. For a month he lived on prunes and wild rice. But he never regretted it. He was so deeply religious, so loyal to his thoughts. And he was completely rid of whatever had bothered him. He was at peace with the world. And after that, he started coming out more often."

A hard, holy story. Impossible not to try to fill in the blanks. Impossible not to imagine the sound in the forest.

Alex died in 1978. They found him in his cabin on Bernard Lake. The cause of death is uncertain. They think he may have choked on some bannock. He'd never seen a doctor once, not for any reason, and had never been sick a day in his life. Nick and a few friends cleaned out the cabin. They found a box full of receipts. He'd given five dollars a year to the Salvation Army. They found fifty dollars rolled up in the bread box, rainy-day money. They removed anything of importance, and burned the cabin down. A few years ago, a ski trail south of Big Whiteshell Lake was named the Kolansky Trail.

By the time I left Nick's and headed back to Winnipeg, the south wind had dropped any pretense of chumminess. It was howling over the Trans-Canada, and the snow was blinding. White-out. It was like driving home through the eye of the country, and all there was to fill it, all it could hope to see was every howling ghost that ever bothered to linger on the round and troubled earth.

Past Forgetting

Leave to the imagination the endless vista of possibilities.
— Grenville Kleiser, *Fifteen Thousand Useful Phrases*

Rumour is Death's dependable sidekick, the dogger of his steps. Strange, since they are such misbegotten companions. Magnetic opposites, really. Yin and yang. Death is light of foot, discreet. Rumour is a noisy batman. Death does his efficient work and hits the road. Rumour hangs around to sit shiva. His acrid waft lingers and lingers in the room. It's ever been thus. Even before the dear departed one has given himself over to the rigours of rigor, passing from *in extremis* to *in paradisum*; even before his insubstantial shade has peeled itself from the sucking exigencies of the flesh, his sad survivors have begun to expropriate his story, to turn it to their own purposes. Directly upon dispersal of the soul's properties, he becomes the sole property of the living, a sequence of dots they can connect in any old way they choose to make whatever picture they long to see. Well, what do the dead care, anyway? Not a thing! And we value them for their needlessness and pliability. Through them, we are made whole, wholer than we really are. Through them, we can magnify our own possibilities and foibles. We do this by turning them into legends. We make them our enduring delights.

I went to Englehart, Ontario, hoping to grasp a few tattered shreds of the ghost of the legendary Nellee Reid. To get to Englehart from Ottawa, you drive about 560 kilometres to the west and north along gouged and icy roads where the wind eggs the snow into capering, lane-obscuring *feux follets*. You drive along Highway 148, drive parallel to the Quebec border, pass through Cobden, and drive along the margins of Muskrat Lake, in whose unplumbed depths a serpentine monster is said to have set up house, and on whose shores the careless Champlain pitched his tent, leaving behind his astrolab when he decamped. For more than 300 years the instrument lay buried in the iron-rich earth, inhabited the whole time by its hankering for all that is north. It was hereabouts that the feisty Margaret McDonald engaged in a defiant act of self-defence which attracted the attention of the tabloid *The National Enquirer*, and will certainly earn her a place in the pantheon of Canadian school-book Amazons, alongside such stalwarts as daring Laura Secord, who famously used her cow as camouflage and almost single-handedly won the War of 1812; and the plucky Madeleine de Verchères, who, with her brother, Pierre, held off an Iroquois attack.

In the summer of 1996, Mrs. Margaret McDonald — who was then fifty-four and who is, according to *The National Enquirer*, a retired cook and a divorced mother of four — was making her way home after a peaceable night of bingo at the community hall. It was round about 10 p.m., a respectable time of the night for law-abiding souls to be out in the world, an hour of a summer night when, especially in the North, there is still enough light that no one need fear stumbling into harm's way. Margaret walked along contentedly enough. She was turning over in her mind the small triumphs and disappointments of the evening just gone, when her attention was drawn to a rustling in the bushes that lined the road. She paused to see what might be hiding in the greenery, stopped to peer into the darkening tangle of the branches, and it was then that she was set upon by a snapping and hissing muskrat: one of the sharp-toothed mammals for whom the lake is named. It all happened very quickly. There was no time to consider flight. In a trice, the varmint was upon her. Margaret swung at it with her purse, but missed. The muskrat must have felt the jet stream as it passed in front of its snout. It went straight for her ankle and lit in, causing Margaret to yelp with pain, panic, and drop her handbag.

Who knows how it all might have ended had she not been armed with a back-up weapon, a nylon bag containing six bingo dabbers, which are the implements used to mark the numbers on your card of record, and are each about the size and heft of a good-sized felt-tip marker?

"GRANNY FIGHTS OFF CRAZED MUSKRAT WITH BAG OF BINGO MARKERS" was the headline in the *Enquirer*. They ran two photographs, too, one of a muskrat and its gaping, menacing maw, and another of Margaret herself. She is shown in the high grass, squatting in a kind of sumo-wrestler pose, her hands on her thighs. Her face is set in a look of "so's your old man" bravado, as if she might be challenging any of the muskrat's kin to come at her and try the same trick. Every curve of her features, as Grenville Kleiser would say, *seems to express a fine arrogant acrimony and harsh truculence*. In her right hand, she holds a bag appliquéd with the slogan "I ❤ Bingo." This is the weapon she used to flail "the muskrat mugger" to death. She stunned him with her first whack, and then kept on swinging, blow after punishing blow, until there was hardly enough of him left to make one of those tacky steering-wheel mufflers. She comported herself with remarkable courage and aplomb throughout the entire ordeal, which left her *flushed with a suffusion that crimsoned her whole countenance*. "I was so worked up I had an angina attack that night and ended up in the hospital for three days. The bite didn't require stitches and, fortunately, the muskrat didn't have rabies." An ending which has about it the sanctity of happily-ever-after.

To get to Englehart from Cobden and dangerous Muskrat Lake, you drive through Pembroke, Deep River, and Chalk River, through Petawawa, through Mattawa, through any number of places whose names and mineral output or industrial *raison d'être* you memorized in elementary school. At North Bay, you switch your allegiance to Highway 11, trying not to be too unnerved by the jackknifed transport trucks, or by news reports of two fatalities on this very stretch of pavement in the last week. Turn off the radio. Choose a tape. Choose Leonard

Cohen. Drive through the pine, the blasted rock, through the snow the snow the snow. Sing. Sing along with Leonard. Sing about the enigmatic Suzanne. Call on the Sisters of Mercy. Drive and drive through Marten River and Temagami, drive through Earlton. Don't bother stopping to look at its zoo, which is closed for the season. Its inmates have been transferred to some warmer resort. A hulking, solitary buffalo statue guards the empty fields and cages, guards the trailer park next door. The buffalo faces east, and its hump, a furry scoliosis, is outlined with delicate fairy lights. When you clear Earlton, you can let yourself gear down. Relax your bison shoulders. You are almost there. Even if you miss the sign that announces it — Englehart, Population 1,700 — you will know you've arrived by the smoke. By day, by night, the waferboard plant — such a cosy, almost tasty name for so bland a commodity — expels into the sky a thick, phantasmic plume made in equal parts of effulgent and prayers: prayers for the health of the construction industry, for its enhanced appetite for waferboard; prayers for the prosperity and good health of the citizens of this shrinking town. Englehart, Englehart. Straight to Heaven go the prayers. To angel hearts, angel hearts.

Ten years ago — in one of those language-fuelled fits of ire that, sadly, have long been routine in our home and native land — Englehart declared itself unilingual. English heart. It is the woman who runs my hotel — and who also sells in the lobby a vast array of health foods, herbal cures, and religious tracts — who tells me so. She remembers how she and her husband, whose name happens to be French, were cold-shouldered when they arrived here, smack dab in the middle of that kerfuffle. She sloughs it off now, it's an old story, but from my outsider's point of view it seems an odd and rather confrontative decision to have made, however fractious the issue. After all, Earlton and New Liskeard to the south are largely French. Kirkland Lake and Timmins to the north both have sizeable Franco-Ontarian populations. And the province of Quebec is just a few scant kilometres to the east. Indeed, a cursory flip through the phone

book will reveal that a considerable number of Englehartian sur-
names are also Gallic in origin: all of which proves nothing, I
suppose, save that we humans are a clannish lot, and that sometimes we express our tribalism in ways that don't stand up to
scrutiny. Dorothy Dupuis, who grew up in this neighbourhood
in the fifties and lives here still, looks a little embarrassed when
I ask her about that chapter in the town's recent history, and I'm
immediately sorry I even brought it up, especially since I haven't
come here to cry "J'accuse" on behalf of national unity. At the
same time, it's hard to harmonize such apparent xenophobia
with the tolerance this place showed, more than forty years ago,
for a character as extravagant as Nellee Jessee Reid.

Dorothy is on the board of the Englehart & Area Historical
Museum. Its extensive collection of local artifacts is housed
in a handsome old schoolhouse on 6th Avenue. Like the zoo
in Earlton, the museum is closed pending the thaw. Even so,
Dorothy has kindly agreed to meet me here, the first Saturday
morning in February. She has even persuaded her second cousin,
Merlin Black, to join us. Dorothy is tiny, very slight. Her kins-
man is more portentous of stature, seventy-eight years old, fit,
with a powerful grip. Merlin began working at the age of twelve,
delivering groceries in a horse-drawn cart. It was often midnight by the time he made his last delivery, and he speaks nos-
talgically of the town as a thriving mercantile centre, back when
he was a boy. As a man, he spent his livelong days working on
the railroad. Merlin knows this place as well as anyone alive. As
we leaf through one of the museum's photograph albums, the
shifting images jump-start his keen recall. A portrait of some
once-upon-a-time town fathers moves him to sow wild oaths.
"Look at them. Bunch of goddam Conservative parasites. That's
what they were, sucking this town dry, sucking the blood right
out of it. Bunch of goddam Conservative parasites."

There's a picture of John Price, taken on the occasion of his
100th birthday. He is playing the accordion. John was a wart
charmer of local renown. Merlin sought his advice because he
had a hand that was fairly taken over with the things. They

were so bad and so populous he wore gloves to conceal the offending paw whenever he went out in public. John told him to take a census of the colonizers and record his findings on a slip of paper. Merlin counted them up and wrote 119. John placed the paper on a warming shelf above his stove.

"I thought there'd be a little more to it," says Merlin now, looking at the unblemished hand that betrays the story's ending, "but that was it. He sent me on my way. And the next day, when I took off my glove..."

There were many other remedies to which Merlin might have turned to clear his hand, although most are more cumbersome than John Price's efficacious conjuring. He might have found pins enough to stick in every wart, and then he would have had to put the pins in his pocket and carry them around until the wayward lumps disappeared. He could have taken a piece of meat — pork is preferred, though some will tell you any meat is fine, so long as it is rotten — and rubbed his blemishes with it while looking at the moon and saying "moony, moony"; then buried the meat, and his warts would have vanished commensurate with its decomposition. He might have rubbed the warts with a wedding ring, or with chalk, or with a penny, on which he would then have spat, and which he would then have buried. Rubbing them thoroughly with an onion, while invoking biblical names might have worked, as might have burning them one by one with a lighted match. He could have given away his warts by buffing them with a piece of flannel until they bled. Then, if he'd thrown away the cloth, the warts would have been passed on to whoever picked it up. There are also those who would have prescribed burning a cobweb over the wart, but best of all is to find a charmer such as Mr. Price. Charmers have different ways of working. Some will just look at the warts and wish them away; others rely on tokens, such as Mr. Price's required piece of paper.

I was fascinated by this story, as I have myself been troubled for years by plantar warts on my left foot. I have consulted several doctors and dermatologists for their best advice on how to rid myself of the things, but their prescriptions for removal have always struck me as so dire and crippling and invasive that I have preferred to tolerate their rooted presence. While passing through Garden Cove, Newfoundland, I happened to hear of a wart charmer named Don. Don had a good track record, I was told, and what's more he was able to charm warts over the phone. I wasted no time in calling him up. I had been warned that, for the magic to work, I must be sure not to offer him payment for his services, and I must be careful not to thank him. Talk of money or signs of gratitude would jinx the process.

"Hello, is this Don?"

"Yep."

"Don, my name is Bill. I understand you charm warts."

"Yep."

"Well, I have these plantar warts and I wondered if you might, well, you know, like, charm them?"

"How many?"

"Fourteen."

"Okay."

"Okay?"

"Okay."

"That's it?"

"Yep."

"Oh."

"I'll tell my sister."

"Your sister?"

"She charms 'em too."

"Great! Uh, okay! Bye!"

Click.

Our short chat was innocent of any discussion of money or thanks, and also of time frame. It might be that Don's remedy is very slow-acting. The fact is that as I write this, some six months after our session, there are seventeen plantar warts on my left foot. However, it is also a fact that no more than two days after Don and his sister unleashed the power of their charms in Garden Cove, Newfoundland, a wart that had been troubling my dog back in Vancouver, B.C., mysteriously and precipitously decamped from a toe on her left front foot. Coincidence? Reader, you decide.

We turn over the leaves in that Englehart Museum album until we come to the series of ten snapshots of Nellee Reid. Merlin has brought another picture from home to add to the community cache. Taken in 1942, it shows Nellee standing next to Merlin's brother, Elgin. We see them from the waist up. Elgin is dashing in his airman's uniform. Nellee is wearing a sort of Margaret Rutherford get-up: an Edwardian-style dress, amply ruffled, high collared, many buttoned. Nellee is corsetted, bust prominent, and sports a hat, which looks to be a kind of pelt which has been accessorized with a bone. The chapeau is pulled low on her brow, and Nellee's face beneath it, it must be said, is decidedly simian. There is something gross and excessive around the jaw line, either a case of the mumps or a monstrous overbite.

"Nellee had two sets of teeth," Dorothy remembers, "and that's what gave him that look. He was quite a sight. I was scared of him. His dresses were always covered with buttons, just buttons everywhere. He got around on a bicycle. Whenever I'd see him downtown, I'd hide behind my mother. I knew him a little when he was in the hospital. I was eleven and having my appendix out. Nellee was a patient there by that time. It was just before they sent him to North Bay. He always used to come into the women's ward. He'd come into the women's ward and crawl under the beds and hide there until they took him away. He had a birthday while he was there, and a bunch of the women got together and made him a dress. I remember that dress."

Here is Nellee astride his bicycle. He is in a sensible skirt cut just below the knee, a jacket with a *ceinture*, and a jaunty tam. A purse is slung on his shoulder. His shoes are dusty flats. Here is Nellee in an ankle-length, floral-patterned dress and a beribboned bonnet. He is outside a tarpaper shack, maybe in Tomstown, which is nearby Englehart, and he is feeding a few of his twenty-five cats. (After they removed him from Tomstown to

the hospital, it fell to the police to take care of the feline population. They did this so efficiently that they never had to make
a return visit.) Here is Nellee with
his striking white hair, long skirt,
and wide-tired bike, posing outside
a general store. A boy in the background stands at attention. He forces
his shoulders back. His shirt is un-
buttoned and you can see his navel.
Neither Dorothy nor Merlin can
identify the boy, or the suited gent
who appears in another picture.
Nellee is shaking the mystery man's
hand, looking up at him, smiling.
Here you can see clearly how tiny
Nellee was. It looks as though he is
receiving a prize. Best of show. Miss
Congeniality. I remark on how compact a person he was.

Nellee Jessee Reid.

"Oh, Nellee was small, but Nellee was strong," Merlin
says. "I knew him from the time I was a boy. He lived at our
place for a bit. There was nothing he couldn't do around the
farm. He used to labour for everyone around here, baling hay,
digging wells, whatever. He worked on the railroad for a time,
I know that. He fought in the Boer War. And he was smart. He
could talk and talk. He always wore dresses. Always. It didn't
matter where he was or what he was doing, a dress was what
he wore. I'm not sure where he got them. Maybe women gave
their cast-offs to him. He was trained as a millwright and they
can make anything, so it wouldn't surprise me to learn that he
sewed them up himself. I only ever once saw him in overalls,
and that was the day he went to court. He broke into someone's house."

"My mother told me he sometimes stole dresses, too," adds
Dorothy. "He'd steal them right off the line. It was for the
buttons."

Merlin concurred. "Yes, Nellee loved buttons. He was just covered in buttons. Beads, too. But you know, none of that stealing was malicious. If he broke into someone's house it was just because he needed something to eat. That's what I figure, anyway. It was a hard life he led, living way out in the bush like that. I remember what a relief it was to him when the pension came through, even though it was hardly more than a few dollars a month. I'd see him sometimes, hauling wood on his back. And he was old then, too. He was old when I first met him, when I was still a little boy. My God, when I think of it now! Why did he wear dresses? Well, he used to say that his mother had had five boys and he was the sixth. She simply decided she was going to have a girl, so she dressed him up as one. He said he just never lost the habit; that's the way he was. Everyone knew about Nellee. No one said much about it, not that I recall. It was different, then. People were more accepting. They helped each other. You had to, just to survive. What else? Oh, he was a big tobacco chewer. Must have poisoned his gums, all that juice. I wish I could tell you more. I wish sometimes I could get fifteen minutes with Nellee, just to clear a few things up."

Me, too. I ask a few questions to fill in some of the more conspicuous blanks. How old was Nellee when he died? Close to ninety. When did he die? Must have been in the early sixties. By then, he was in the mental hospital in North Bay. He'd become too much to handle at the local facility. And what about the spelling of his name? On some photos it appears as "Nellie." On others, "Nellee." Similarly, his surname. Reid? Or Read? And what was Nellee called before he was Nellee? Ah. Jack. He was Jack. Any known family? He had a brother who lived nearby, who worked for the sawmill and had a hook for a hand. At least, it was believed he was a brother. The two never saw each other. Merlin went to see this man when Nellee was very sick, before he went into hospital. He asked him if he was the brother of Nellee Reid, and the hook-hand man disavowed all knowledge. Merlin told him that that was too bad, because Nellee was terribly sick and if ever he needed help it was now.

The next day, someone alerted the RCMP to the situation, and they came and took Nellee away, and that was the beginning of his final chapter.

When the town of Englehart celebrated its fiftieth birthday in 1958, a group of archivally-minded citizens got together to compile a pocket history of the place. The book makes mention of several colourful characters of local renown, Nellee Reid among them. Nellee, it says, "was always well-informed about the happenings of the world, and apart from his phobia [*sic*] for wearing women's clothes, he appeared to be quite sensible." The life and times of Percy Legitt, a contemporary of Nellee's, are summed up thus: "Percy Legitt, the hermit from Savard, was well known in Englehart for the way he obtained lodging. His home was a tumble-down shack out in the country, but in order to keep warm during the long, cold winters, Percy would ride his bicycle into Englehart and heave a brick through the nearest store window — usually the liquor store. Since he had no way of paying the inevitable fines, he would spend the winter months as a guest at the crow bar hotel! *We know there are many others who deserve mention, but the time allotted us for this task has run out.*" (Italics are mine.) It is this last sentence that I find most telling and most frustrating. This is how we treat our history: casually, shruggingly, with no eye to the future. For the ostensible want of something as plentiful as time, so many names and stories have been lost, lost not just to the likes of me, a nosy parker who happens to be passing through, but lost to those who have a legitimate, profound connection to a place, even if that connection is anchored in something as banal and as random as the coincident accidents of birth and geography. Age comes and brings with it its particular hungers. We start to hanker for the past, and not just our own, either. As we gain perspective on our own stories — as the distance lengthens between our ever-shifting present age and our long ago fixed beginnings — we need to look at ourselves in the broader context of family and community. Even if this longing is not yet manifest in the individual, he or she should be able to look around and garner from example that it will one day come to roost, along with such geriatric inevitabilities as white hair and creaky knees.

Once, while I was visiting my parents in Winnipeg, I saw that my father was reading the local real estate paper. I asked him why, as I was sure he and my mother had no immediate plans to move or put their house up for sale. He told me that he just likes to keep abreast of the market, and that he was always curious to see if the house of his boyhood might be among the listings. That, he told me, was the very house he saw in his dreams, at least on those nights when a house was among the props his dreams required.

I see nothing sentimental or muddied about such nostalgia. It has less to do with a misty-eyed longing to capture the innocence of the past than with establishing connections, with creating the necessary linkages that give our lives their narrative sense and shape: the beginning, the middle, the developing end. Go into any library or archive anywhere in this country, and there you will see people, generally "of a certain age," cranking their way through microfilms of old newspapers, combing through birth and baptismal registers, absorbed by the work of learning and telling their family's or their community's own story. With this in mind, I have to say that I feel a twinge of sympathy for those erstwhile Englehartians, or their kin, who will turn up one day with their pencils sharpened and their hearts brimming with an eagerness to get a clear fix on their own compasses, only to learn that some of the best bits, the context-enriching curiosities, have been excluded from the record, and all because the allotted time ran out. True enough, they'll learn about Percy, learn at least that once he was, and that he committed petty felonies in order to have a warm place to sleep in the winter. And they'll have the redux version of Nellee as a bicycle-riding, tobacco-chewing codger who favoured frocks over overalls. But as for the *pourquoi* of their lives — well, if that's what they're after, they're out of luck.

Of course, this is not a situation that is unique to Englehart. It's everywhere the same. The fields of the past are richly layered with all the strata of everything that's been ploughed under before it was properly examined, before concerned conservationists had the chance to sift through and say: this is worth saving; this is worth holding up to the light; this merits elucidation through the simple question why? Merlin Black says he'd like to have fifteen minutes with Nellee, a mere quarter-hour to ask some of the same questions I would put to him, the questions nobody thought or wanted to ask Nellee in the moment, either because they were too polite, or too reserved, or because they didn't care, or because it just didn't seem to matter, or because they had more pressing concerns, or because it was none of their damn business. Nellee? What was to ask about Nellee? Nellee was there, had always been there, had always been the way he was; Nellee wore a dress, so what, that was Nellee's way, Nellee's thing, what was to fuss about Nellee, anyway, he was common as dirt, a farm labourer, a neighbourhood kook, a fringe-dweller; Nellee was no big deal.

Such bald acceptance is a legitimate way of accommodating the world. I do it myself with such things as household appliances. I have not devoted a minute of my life, which has already gone on for quite a long time, to understanding what it is that keeps a refrigerator cold. It's enough for me that it happens and that I can rely on it to protect the mayonnaise from bacterial invasion. But when it comes to questions of human comportment and behaviour, my inclinations are less complacent, and more speculative and analytical. Give me a bone like Nellee, and I will gnaw on it for all it's worth, even if it proves to be completely hollow, even if the flavour of its marrow is hallucinatory, a product of nothing more than my own overheated, needy imagination. Such leanings are not necessarily ingredients in a recipe for happy, healthy living. "Tu te complexe!" I remember some French friends saying to me once, in their wonderfully reflexive way, when they were swilling champagne and sucking back oysters and I was wrecking the party by knitting my brow over some insoluble thing or other. "This week," said a therapist I'd consulted in a fragile moment, never once suspecting that I'd be given homework assignments, "I'd like you to spend as much time as you can living outside your own head." What? And abandon my long habit of reading words backwards and making up lives for people I see on the bus or in the supermarket line-up? Forget it! I was cured. I never went back to therapy.

There are other traces of Nellee, though none of them is exactly fresh. An administrator at the North Bay Psychiatric Hospital, who asked that he not be named, told me that Jack Reid died on July 30, 1959. His birth year had been recorded as 1863. The usual patient-confidentiality regulations restrict access to records or other information. There are a few clippings in a file in the Englehart library, including an article by a journalist named Ian Ball. A handwritten addendum to the piece attributes it, incorrectly, to the The Temiskaming Speaker, July 31, 1958. It contains some intriguing notes, including the startling information that Nellee got his start as a full-time cross-dresser when he was a boy, and happened to be playing the bagpipes on the balcony of a hotel in Woodstock, Ontario. He was wearing a kilt, of course, and his appearance and performance so impressed the owner of a travelling circus, that Nellee was hired on and billed as "The World's Only Girl Bagpipe Player." Nellee got to like wearing a kilt, and as time went on, his taste in costumes matured to "fancy dresses, fashionable suits, charming hats. Even when he enlisted for the Boer War he refused to surrender his individuality: he joined a highland regiment. After the war he became, by turns, farmer, lumberman, construction hand, prospector and railroad fireman. He was an object of derision for his colleagues, but he stuck by his skirts. When he married the daughter of a circus performer (she was later killed in a railroad accident) he was resplendent in the frilliest costume he could buy....Apart from dress-making, he has only one other hobby: cats. If it weren't for the attraction of his appearance, Nellee Jessee Reid would probably be known as the Cat Man. He always has at least a dozen around the house and, believe it or not, he trains them to hunt rabbits."

Earl Houghton, who now lives in London, Ontario, grew up in the Englehart area, and he knew Nellee well. Nellee was a regular guest at the Houghton house. For years he came around for both lunch and supper. He would sit in the kitchen and talk and talk, telling stories about his Boer War adventures and his far-flung travels. He was always loquacious. Earl says that his mouth was swollen not because he had a double set of teeth, but because his gums had been so badly poisoned. He imagines that his parents were one of the few constants in Nellee's life. They were his friends, or at least they were accepting of him and generous towards him. Nellee would order dresses from their Eaton's mail-order catalogue. Once, he received some fur cuffs he didn't like. He sent them back with a note saying something like, "Nellee has an old bull he could kill that would make better cuffs than these." Eaton's responded by sending him in exchange the very best they had.

Nellee was lucky to have the Houghtons, as there were many others he'd alienated with his fits of temper. He was often on the outs with people who'd hired him to do odd jobs, and there were times when he showed a vindictive streak. Perhaps he'd strip a wagon of its wheels, or set a living room on fire, an act of vengeance for a slight that might be real or imagined.

As Earl tells it, "He was smart as a whip and could be dangerous. He had a fight with a neighbour who'd given him a job looking after his horses, and not long after that the man was found dead in his house. These were early days, rough and tough, and policing wasn't what it is now. No charges were ever laid, but Dad figured he'd been strangled, and I guess he figured he knew who'd done it, too."

Earl remembers the cats, and agrees that rabbit was the mainstay of their diet. It was Nellee who did the hunting, however. He'd pick off the bunnies with his rifle, open them up, and leave them for the cats to devour. After a season of this, the ground would be thick with rabbit fur. Nellee was also known to take random pot-shots at passers-by, for no apparent reason. Earl himself once came under fire, and had to take cover in a ditch until Nellee's trigger-happy urges were satisfied. He can't say why Nellee should have launched such a volley. He was unpredictable, and he wasn't necessarily harmless, but he was absolutely himself. He was Nellee, and there was no one like him.

"I have never known an eccentric like him in my lifetime," said Mr. Houghton when we spoke by phone, "and we knew he was, of course; knew he was eccentric. But over time he just grew on us, like grass, and we never really got into why he was the way he was."

And that's about all. That's everything that's left of Nellee Jessee Reid, the cross-dressing, itinerant farm worker, the skirt-wearing ditch digger, the cat fancier who might have been a murderer. That's everything I have been able to find, in any case. I rather wanted to prolong my stay in Englehart, in part to see if I could mine some new Nellee nugget, and in part to see who would win the 1997 Bachelor of the Year Contest. The eleven finalists were featured in a full-page spread of the *The Temiskaming Speaker* on January 29. Most of them had been nominated, or so I would guess, by family and friends who had submitted their names along with photos and short biographical sketches. There was Gilles, age 28, "outdoorsy, 'built' and a real 'slush puppy.'" There was Keith, 24, who "likes animals and driving around in his car." Trinh, at 23, "enjoys loud music," and Robert, 52, who had evidently put forward his own name, wrote: "I enjoy being a bachelor. I go to all the bingos." I wished with all my heart that I were an area resident, and therefore eligible to vote for Charles, age 46, a pleasant-looking man in a plaid shirt, posed against pine panelling, and whose write-up, in its entirety, read: "He never had a girlfriend all his life and he is our son." Charles, I felt, needed my support. I wondered if there might not be some point in calling him up, some pretext for phoning, wondered if he might have something revelatory to say about Nellee, or other pertinent information he might care to share. In the end, I thought better of it and decided simply to wish him well telepathically as I headed out of town. I wondered how long the Bachelor of the Year Contest had been a part of the social life of Englehart, Earlton, and New Liskeard; wondered if Nellee himself had ever entered, submitting maybe one of the photos I saw of him in the museum. What would he have had to say for himself? "This button-stealing manure shoveller loves nothing more than the sound of a well-chewed plug landing squarely in a spitoon, and the rustle of his own petticoats as he goes upstairs to bed. Can he bake a cherry pie? You bet, and he sews a straight seam to boot!"

Nellee, Nellee. I am thinking of you as I drive south, *en route* to Sudbury. It's later than would be ideal for such a long journey, a Grenville Kleiser hour of the day, *an evening of great silences and spaces*, wholly tranquil with *piles of golden clouds just peering above the horizon, the blue bowl of the sky, all glorious with the blaze of a million worlds, the empurpled hills standing up, solemn and sharp, out of the green gold air* and *the evening star silvery and solitary on the girdle of the early night*. I am thinking of you, Nellee, as I pass a billboard advertising a lingerie shop in Earlton, thinking of you and wondering if you might not have enjoyed having a teddy or some such garment. It is not a picture on which I especially care to dwell, and I take a small detour a few miles down the highway to look at Tomstown. It was named not for cats, as you might expect, but for a turn-of-the-century squatter who was known as "Uncle Tom." Now that I have seen it, I can report that the story of its naming is all there is to say on the subject of present-day Tomstown. There is no plaque marking the place where Nellee's shack once stood, no sign of any kitty descendants from his once-glorious pride, no sign of the bicycle Nellee rode up and down the sandy roads, his labourer's legs still strong at nearly ninety, pumping hard under his beautiful buttoned dresses. Pumping hard, like his strangely inclined, oddly angled heart. Angel heart, angel heart. Once again, I am travelling, driving and driving, listening with all my being for anything that sounds like news, anything that sounds like a rumour of you.

Some Good Shepherds

For he keeps the Lord's watch in
the night against the adversary.
For he counteracts the powers of darkness
by his electrical skin and glaring eyes.
    — Christopher Smart, "My Cat, Jeoffrey"

There's Alex, there's Stinky, there's Buddie and Billy, there's
Blindy and Sam, and there's Pain-in-the-Ass. There's Fat Fuck
and Tigger and Squeaky and Whisky and Smoothie and Freddy
and Pinky and Tom. There's Muffin and Stubby and Smokey
and Holly, there's Tortoise and Spooky and Lucky and Stray.
There's Pumpkin and Softy and Yankee and Yappy and Split
Face, there's Cooner and Sky and the three they call Boots. Boots
1. Boots 2. Boots 3. There's Tinkerbell. There's Catherine, who
has no teeth. And there's Angel, who's the favourite.

Angel is pure white. Of course she is. What else would you
expect of an Angel? Angel looks Persian. Angel is a princess.
Angel has her own potty. Angel eats from a dish that is hers
alone. Angel dines in the laundry room, next to the washer and
dryer. Their thundering guts heave and turn and jive all the livelong day, from Sabbath to Sabbath, as Donna Wright launders
every towel and blanket and slip-cover and throw rug in her
house. This is just one of the chores she strings together to make
a twelve- to fifteen-hour working day, which is how long it takes
to keep ahead of the fur and spit and dander and other excreta
which are the inevitable, unavoidable, and excusable deposits
of the more than 400 cats currently in residence in their house

and in whose choir Angel and Catherine and Tinkerbell and Boots 3, 2, and 1, etc., are just a few of the singers.

"Dogs just don't want to come in," says Jack Wright, who is Donna's husband, and who loves every bit as much as she the pitter-patter of 1,600 feet around the house, which, by the way, is an average-size bungalow on a quiet street not far from Queen's University in Kingston, Ontario. Every day, Jack and Donna prise the tops from 180 tins of cat food and pour out 14 kilos of kibble. These are the amounts required to load up the feeding stations strategically placed in most of the rooms. Other than Angel, who is pampered, the cats eat communally. They keep hydrated by sipping from big bowls of ice water. The ice is important, because cats like their liquids well chilled, and a trough warms quickly with the friction of 400 lapping tongues. Likewise, there are plenty of litter boxes round about, the maintenance of which calls to mind the nursery rhyme about seven maids sweeping for seven years. What with the feeding and the cleaning and the vaccinating and the vetting and all the various sundry expenses and capital costs that are incurred by keeping such an ark afloat, the Wrights figure their annual cat bill can be rounded off to something in the vicinity of $110,000. And that doesn't take into account the cost of the turkeys Donna cooks and carves and portions out to her purring brood on festive days such as Christmas, on which occasion they also receive individually wrapped toys.

I turned up at their house unannounced one afternoon in February. I am not a dropping-in kind of visitor, don't like being dropped-in on myself. However, as I had been unable to raise the Wrights on the phone, and as I had only a few hours in Kingston, and as I was eager to see this house about which I'd heard so much, I thought I would set protocol aside, and take my chances on finding them both at home and in a receiving mood. Donna answered the door with a mop in one hand, a cigarette in the other. I explained what I was about, and she was happy to let me in and show me around their operation. I think she must have been relieved to find out that I wasn't yet another desperate soul with yet another cat needing succour and care. The Wrights are famous for never turning an orphan away, and thousands of feline foundlings have been given sanctuary in their home since first they began their missionary work in 1969.

"Oh, come on in, dear," she said, "come on in. It's a good thing you didn't stop by this morning, I just can't see people in the morning, the place is a terrible mess in the morning. Come on in."

I took a deep gulp of air and stepped across the threshold. I confess that I had steeled myself against this moment. I have a cat myself, just one cat, a sweet black cat whom I adore, and who adores me in turn, and without whom there would be no point in going on. I comb her and pet her and feed her and dole out her favourite treats, which happen to be dog biscuits. She rides on my shoulder and she sleeps between my legs and she nibbles on my wrists and she serenades both me and her private god with tuneful hymns of her own composing. We have a good, solid relationship. We are in love. For all that, I am sorry to confess that there have been times when I have been too busy or preoccupied or lame-brained and have forgotten for a day or three about tending to her litter box. It's shocking, but it's true, and I know about the high, ammoniac wafts that rise from the tray of Jonny Cat when it has been less than scrupulously sifted. I know about the limits of those highly touted green, odour-fighting pellets with which the stuff is laced. And it was the prospect of such a full-frontal olfactory assault, but magnified several hundred times, that aroused my fear and trepidation as I entered their hallway, stepped over and around the half-dozen cats who were slaloming between my ankles, and walked into a place that was, much to my surprise, *as peaceful as a village cricket green on Sunday.*

There was an odour in the air, to be sure, but it was more of cleanser than of the acrid ripening that signals cat pee. It was different, the smellscape, but not objectionable, not off-putting. Keep 400 of anything in a smallish house — 400 cool water-melons, say — and I submit that there will be a redolence that reflects that particular presence. The point is that it wasn't what met the nose that was amazing or memorable. It was the visuals that were overwhelming. The first thing anyone will tell you about Jack and Donna Wright is that they give shelter to hundreds of cats, so naturally, it was hundreds of cats that I was prepared to see. But it is impossible to imagine what "hundreds of cats" look like, contained as a group in a small space, until you actually bear witness to the way they move in slow and solemn procession over every available flat surface of the house, kaleidoscopic, a stunning and shifting geometry of whisker and tail.

There were cats in the hallway, cats on the stairs, cats on the tables, and cats on the chairs. There were rusts, greys, blacks, whites, stripes; there was every patchwork permutation and combination of colouring represented among the cats on the microwave, the stove, the counter, and in the cupboards. On the kitchen table alone, which was layered with a couple of towels, I counted seventeen cats. Who would have imagined a kitchen table could have accommodated seventeen cats, curled up so placidly? They looked like commas, spilled from a typographer's tray.

I spent a very pleasant hour or so with the Wrights. I lost track of how many cats scaled my legs, or nuzzled my chin, or purred in my ear. "Which one is this?" I asked, as I felt the tidy grip of claw, and the brush of tail against my cheek. Some cat had just slipped from the top of the fridge and was straddling my shoulders, stole-like, the length of its warm body against my neck.

"Squeaky. That one's Squeaky."

"Do they all have names?"

"Oh, yes. They have to be registered with the city."

"And I imagine they all have personality traits?"

"Sure they do. Over there — that's Sam. Sam just loves Hostess Ripple Chips. And there, that's Pumpkin. Pumpkin has a thing for pork. They all have their stories. You get to know pretty quickly what they're like."

"Do they ever fight? You would think that with so many cats there'd be spats all the time."

"Almost never. Animal psychologists say that, if you have more than twenty-five animals contained in a space, you've got trouble. But they all get along, mostly. It gets tense when there are kittens. One cat will try to steal another's kittens and then we'll have a fight."

"Do they ever go out?"

"There's a fenced area out the back of the house, like a gazebo. They can go out there safely."

"Do they ever escape?"

"Once, somebody cut through the fence. I don't know who, some kind of animal-liberation activist, I guess. There was a knock on the door. I answered, and it was a nun. She asked, 'Are those your cats?' And all the roofs, all around, were just covered with cats."

"It's a big responsibility, four hundred cats."

"Oh, God. Oh, it sure is."

"Do you ever get away? On vacation?"

"Donna got away once, for a day. That was when she went on "The Phil Donahue Show." She called home every hour or so to check on her babies."

Jack and Donna have often been on television. They've made the news in Japan, in the United States, and in France, as well as in Canada. They have been featured in magazines and newspapers, and in tabloids such as *The National Enquirer*. Such exposure will usually bring in some donations, which is a good thing, since the house-painting business that sustains them has suffered of late, and there have been more than a few times when the demands placed on them by their 400 dependents have brought them close to the financial brink. The problem is, every time the Wrights are advertised to the world as the couple who just can't say no to a cat in need, they can count on taking delivery of the one commodity for which they have no further need. Cats have been packed up and sent north across the border. Bulk orders of cats have arrived from the country,

shipped to the city by owners who didn't know where else to
turn when they had to leave their farms.

"Could you not just say no?"

"Where else are they going to go? We just can't stand the
thought of them being hurt or euthanized."

"But it's taken over your whole life."

"I know, I know," says Donna, whose every day is spent
mopping, washing, feeding, cleaning, petting. "Sometimes you
think it'll make you crazy. We can't get away. Who's going to
look after them? I cry just about every day in the summertime.
But who else is going to do it?"

Cats and cats and still more cats. Sitting in the sink, sprawling on the sofa, spilling from the settee and the sills. What can
it be like there at night, when everything's settled and still? When
everything's settled and everything's still, what is it like at night?
How many cats are on the bed of Jack and Donna Wright?

"I'd say forty, wouldn't you Jack?"

"At least. Oh, at least."

Their delicate paws tucked under their chests. The neat,
quick beat of their small and happy hearts. The rumble of their
breathing. The low and flickering wattage of their dreams.

It has been Jack and Donna Wright's experience — and they
should know — that a cat, when it is ready to die, will seek you
out. It will come to you. It wants you as a vigil sitter. When Jack
Marriott's cat came to him for the last time, it was already dead.
Then again, so was Jack.

The cat was called Po. Old Po. White Po. Deaf Po. One-
eyed Po. He and Jack are buried in the Starr's Point Cemetery,
near Wolfville, Nova Scotia. Only Jack's name is mentioned on
the marker, but Po is with him. Although I wasn't there to witness the interment, I have it on good authority that this is so.
Jack and Po went down together, nestled side by each in a satin-
lined, yellow pine coffin, which was just the right length but
unnecessarily deep. There's a photo of the pair of them sequestered there. It's about as still a still life as anyone could imagine:

dead man, dead cat, each insensible to the other's presence, but looking nonetheless pleased with the arrangement, somehow, like two old friends snuggling up for a chaste wee nap. Jack is wrapped up in a favourite blanket, and Po is cuddled on his left chest, guarding his silent heart. Once they were arranged in the casket; once the lid was hammered down, and their earthly remains were lowered into the ground, everyone who braved the winter day to attend the service took a turn heaping dirt on the coffin. A local fellow had designed and built it, a cabinet maker, and it had stood for years in Jack's parlour. Likewise, the stone had been in place for some time, chiselled with both his birth year, 1888, and death year, 1988. That Jack Marriott caused the year of his demise to be literally carved in stone before the fact tells us how confident he was that he would live to be a centenarian. As it turned out, he died on December 28, 1986. Even though he was ready to go — he'd horrified his friends by asking them to help him die by driving a knitting needle through his ribs — it must have been a disappointment to him that his ferry across the Styx turned up two years in advance of its anticipated run. 1888–1988. Such a nice round number! Such gestalt! Luckily for Jack, the same friends who declined to pierce his heart — or to smother him with a pillow, or to set him on the edge of his bed and help him fall face forward onto the floor — saw to it that the stone was not altered to conform to the death certificate. Thanks to his friends, Jack was granted his hundred-year wish, at least insofar as the most visible and weather-resistant of the public records was concerned.

Jack's friends. He more than relied on their kindness. He demanded it. He orchestrated it. His attention-getting ploys were both transparent and effective. For the most part, he got his way. He was, in the words of one man who knew him, who was his neighbour, and who didn't like him, "an irascible old bastard." Irascible is one of many words that might be used to parse the man. Controlling, lascivious, fanciful, deluded, brilliant, charming, manipulative, and aggravating could also serve. David Sheppard, a high-school teacher in Wolfville, alerted me to Jack's story in a letter dated July 14, 1996, which would have been Jack's 108th birthday. I quote it here in part.

"In response to your request for material about Canadian eccentrics, I am sending you this manuscript about Henry John Burton Marriott, an Englishman who came to Canada in 1921 and settled into an unconventional life in the Annapolis Valley of Nova Scotia. I was Jack's best male friend, his secretary and agent, as well as the executor of his estate. His station in life was Artist, but the realities of his life meant he worked as a clerk, a farmer, a customs officer. Nothing meant more to him than his music, his photography, his enjoyment of Nature. He kept detailed diaries for fifty years. There are paradoxes in his life, which was, in some ways, a failure. He believed he achieved true happiness and friendship, but he paid a terrible price in lost friends, a dysfunctional and lost family, and personal disability. He believed his music and photography to be exemplary yet some of his critics are kind to use words like mediocre. He contributed to his community by organizing community theatre, concerts, picnics, spelling bees and the like, yet they ostracized him because he took nude pictures of women and girls. He believed that human friendship was the greatest Truth there was, yet by the end of his life he had decided that cats were vastly superior to humans as friends. Believing in the freedom of the individual, he determined that his death would be based on *his* dictates, not those of the status quo. The cat and the coffin story are the epitome of this individualism."

I went to Port Williams, near Wolfville, and spent a long and very pleasant evening hearing stories about Jack Marriott from David Sheppard and Jennie Sheito. Jennie also knew him well. She was his close neighbour, and was involved with his care in the last years of his life. She and her husband, Allen, literally bought into their relationship with Jack. He sold them his house on the condition that he be allowed to remain there undisturbed and unmolested until his death or failing health dictated his removal. Now, it has been restored it to its full Georgian splendour. It's a provincial heritage site, and they run it as the Planters' Barracks Inn. If ever you visit, you must ask to look at the "before" pictures. They will give you graphic insight not only into what is possible with hammer, nail, and elbow grease, but into the world of Jack Marriott. No life is simple. Jack's was not only longer than most, it was notably more baroque and variegated. His story is daunting in its complexities, but in order to set the cat and the coffin in context, here is a vastly pared-down version, gleaned from my conversation with David and Jennie.

Eighteen eighty-eight. Jack is born into a straight-laced Victorian family that was part of the emerging upper middle class. His father was a financier with a seat on the London stock exchange. Jack was a dreamer. He spent his time painting, sketching, writing, composing music, or cycling around the countryside. He fell under the influence of Maeterlinck. He adored Beethoven. They were the masters he venerated his whole life long. There was nothing in his temperament to suggest that he would make a success of the job his father found him when he left school. For sixteen years he worked as a clerk in the Bank of England, a dead-end job for which he was patently unsuited, and in which he had no hope of advancing. He married a young woman named Leila Talbot, of whom his family disapproved. When Jack was thirty-two and Leila twenty-eight, they had decided that they should take their two daughters and seek their fortune away from England. They settled on Canada and sailed from Liverpool on April 15, 1921, on the S.S. *Sachem*. They came to Port Williams, where they bought the house they would call "Acaciacroft" for about $7,500.

Jack thought he would be able to make a living as an orchardist, selling the Valley's famous apples. When that proved impossible, he took to fur farming. He raised foxes and chinchillas, and still the family barely scraped by. There were other setbacks. Their children embodied the lesson that there's nothing quite so cruel and capricious as genetics. Jack had failed to acquire his father's business sense, but he had inherited, recessively, the family diabetes. He was not affected, but both his daughters were, and severely, too. They were among the first insulin users in Canada. The drug didn't come cheap, and this compounded the family's stress level. It didn't take long for the community to come around to the opinion that Jack was ineffectual, flighty, a poor provider.

When the girls grew up and left home, the marriage dissolved. Leila moved on. Jack stayed put and lived alone in Acaciacroft for over forty years. At the age of fifty, he secured a job as a customs officer. It was not demanding work and he earned a decent wage. There was time to develop other hobbies, photography in particular. He took thousands of yearbook portraits for Acadia University. That was useful, innocuous work. He won his infamy by taking nude portraits of young women. Jack always insisted that his work was completely above board, that there was always a chaperone present, that he never importuned his models. Nonetheless, tongues wagged. It was a small, rural community, after all. He became someone to watch out for, someone to avoid. A dirty old man. The neighbourhood pornographer. At one point, he was banned from a local tea room. Still, for all his notoriety, he managed to find models. He would be smitten with some of them, would photograph them, and write about them obsessively.

There was Joyce, who was fifteen when he fell in love with her. Then there was Mary Lou. Others followed. Always, he said, the relationships were Platonic.

Fifteen cats kept Jack company at Acaciacroft in his declining years. Fifteen was the number he required, he said, in order to sustain his diet. He lived for years on a broth made from chicken necks he purchased in bulk from a nearby processing plant. He would take thirty-three necks —

Jack Marriott, Po, and Beethoven.

and it was always thirty-three — and stew them. These he would feed to the cats. He sustained himself on the broth, using it as a stock for a soup that he would keep on the go for weeks on end, adding more water, and another batch of necks as required.

From the road, Acaciacroft looked like a haunted house: a magnificent, crumbling edifice surrounded by shrubs and every noxious weed native to Nova Scotia. Young people were attracted to it, and to Jack. They saw him as an old Bohemian, saw his house as a place to crash. Some came to take advantage, to rob him of his stamps and coins. Others helped out. Jack was already quite blind when David Sheppard met him. He needed "a secretary," someone to read to him, to write the letters he would dictate. Sheppard — Jack always called him by his surname — took on the job. At the beginning, he visited once a week, stopping by to chat, to jot down a letter or two. Jack, however, exerted a powerful fascination, and as time went by, his increasing demands began to take precedence for Sheppard over the needs of his own family.

"In a sense," said Sheppard, "I was suckered. He made it so that I was absolutely essential to him. He could be incredibly insensitive. When my mother died, I didn't go to visit him as scheduled, and he didn't understand at all. It was completely irrelevant to him that she had died. He couldn't see past the fact that it was a day that we were meant to have been together, and I hadn't come. That was one of the days it almost ended, as it had for so many of his friends. But I'm a bit of an odd bird myself, and I said, 'I'm going to stick this out. You're not going to drive me away like you did everyone else.'"

Jack was ninety-four when blindness and ill health finally forced his hand, and he had to move to a care facility. Sheppard, dogged as ever, visited him every day. They settled into a routine that revolved around reading aloud from the diaries that Jack had kept from the time he was a young man. Day after day, they would review his life, his philosophies, his loves, his disappointments. It took them fourteen months to get through the dozens of little notebooks.

For every good reason, death was more and more on Jack's mind. He spent many happy hours with Sheppard, planning his funeral. "We could spend a whole Sunday afternoon talking about his pallbearers, and he would change them at his whim. I pride myself on keeping promises and I agreed that he would have a hand-dug grave, that there would be no backhoe used, that he wouldn't be embalmed, that there would be no formal display of the body, that he would be lowered into the ground by hand. It was one thing to promise that I would take his photograph. But he wanted to be buried naked. I asked, why naked, and he said he wanted everyone to stand around in a circle and place their hands on him. I said, 'Jack, your daughter Joan is in her late seventies. If she comes to the funeral and I have the lid off that casket and you're naked, she's going to be shocked.' He said that was just what he wanted. I said, 'Jack, I can do everything but bury you naked. I'll photograph you, I'll put the flowers on the grave, I'll put the things you want in the casket, like the picture of Joyce and the special grey blanket and the cat, but I just can't see burying you naked.'"

Jack's plan had been to die at home. He saw just how it would be. He would be lifted from his bed before rigor set in, carried downstairs, and placed in the waiting coffin. From there it would be just a short hop across the midsummer fields to the Starr's Point Cemetery, his waiting gravestone, and his view of the Minas Basin. He knew that a fast burial would be required if he wanted to sidestep the indignity of embalming. He was not someone who would gladly suffer hitches. He did not take his illness or the nursing home into account when he began to visualize his funeral; nor did it ever occur to him that he would die in the winter, when the ground would be frozen, making it impossible to dig a grave by hand, or that the graveyard itself might be inaccessible, the whole operation therefore requiring more than the thirty-six hours the health department will allow before a body has to be buried, burned, or shot full of preservatives. It was up to Sheppard to raise these troublesome possibilities.

"Jack, what if you die in the winter?"

"Why, you could carry the casket in on a sled, leave it there, I'd freeze solid, and you could bury me in the spring."

"No one will want to look at the casket all winter, Jack. And anyway, what about the coyotes?"

"Coyotes?"

"Sure, they'd get in there and drag you all over the dyke."

"Then I'll just have to die in the summer."

When Jack was removed to the nursing home, and the ongoing maintenance of his cats proved impossible, a local handyman was hired to take care of them, which he did, one by one by one. Finally, only Old Po was left, the sole inhabitant of the huge house. Jennie came to feed him, but he was going mad with loneliness. It was a dilemma. As Jack wanted the cat as a coffin buddy, and as there was no way to coordinate the two deaths, it was decided that Po would be put down and frozen, then exhumed for the funeral, a kitty cube in waiting. David Sheppard remembers — and who could forget? — how he took the cat in to be needled, and handed the vet a freezer bag. "I told him to tuck the cat up nicely so that nothing would break off. I took him home and placed him in our freezer, with the frozen strawberries, the hamburger, the vegetables. From time to time, Jack would ask me how his deceased pet was doing, and I would say he looked fine, even though he was a mass of matted fur with ice, freezer burn, and a grotesque look of horror on his face. When Jack learned that my family was upset about having Po next to the strawberries, he told me to get a second small freezer, and gave me the money to do so. I bought one second-hand, transferred the cat, then one day noticed a pool around the base. It had broken down, so Po went back in with the strawberries."

As Jack was no longer able to write, but wanted to document his life to the last, he began to make his diary entries on a tape recorder. When he spilled milk on his machine and it short-circuited, and when he was too weak to push the buttons, his visitors were encouraged to record their thoughts and observations so that some kind of diary, however scant, could be maintained to the end.

"Good visit. Talked about memories."

"Seemed out of it."

"He's wearing his teeth and can speak clearer."

"Jack well today. I visited his cemetery plot and reported how his stone looks. He was pleased to hear how nice the Starr's Point Cemetery is."

Towards the end, he was often in pain. It was then that he began to think longingly of knitting needles and pillows. But thankfully, his systems shut down one by one, of their own accord, and he surrendered himself peacefully, and with grace.

The weather was mild for the end of December. The grave was easily opened. Sheppard, as per their agreement, laid out the corpse. True to his word, he did not let Jack go to earth naked. He dressed the shell of his friend, wrapped him in his old blanket, placed him in the coffin, and then remembered Po.

"The one thing none of us had taken into account was how long it would take to thaw a cat. He was a big cat, too. We considered the microwave, but we just couldn't do it. There was nothing I could do but get him from the freezer and put him in the coffin with that dreadful look on his face. I like to think that maybe he thawed into a fond embrace."

"Jack was a misfit in many ways," said Jennie, as our evening wound down. "He seemed to be in the wrong time and place. He would have loved his funeral, though, the way the clouds parted and that light came down from the sky."

Sheppard said, "He thought the most important thing in the world was friendship, and I don't think he had any idea how many people despised him. Certainly we were completely shocked by the number of people who turned up at the funeral. There must have been 150. There were very few of the young people he'd attracted, they'd been gone for years. Mostly, they were people he'd known in the forties and fifties. Almost no one to whom he left things has ever claimed them. He was someone who had a great deal of talent, and none of it ever really went anywhere. In the end, I don't think you can say that he really left a legacy."

"No," said Jennie, "which is sad. He could have accomplished so much. In some ways, his life was like the ultimate failure."

In some ways, perhaps. On the other hand, we talked about Jack Marriott for three solid hours, and could easily have gone on. If his life didn't measure up to his own grandiose plans for it; if the world never saw or understood the full range of his imagined genius, he nevertheless, with all his vanity and all his silliness, left a seemingly inexhaustible supply of anecdotes, stories, and speculation. These have no *material* worth, but perhaps they are enough. And though his family life might have been a failure, and the passions of his middle and old age unrequited, and even misdirected, it's certainly true that he touched David Sheppard's life in a profound and lasting way. It was Sheppard who delivered the eulogy. At Jack's suggestion, he read from the diaries, including this excerpt from 1969:

"I drive back alone in the rain and think how good life is. I have dreamed and dreamed that life could be good and happy and sensible, but was afraid to believe my dream.... Surely the end of my life is coming, for what more is there? For all has come to my life that I have looked for, all the joy and beauty and sense that I have dreamed of; it has come bit by bit and then suddenly [it was] completed. There is no more. I want no more. I see everything now, I think. I feel nearer to the real truth and to the real God than ever before..."

And what is all this pother about?
The piquancy of the pageant of life
Awaiting his summons to the eternal silence

Job's Excellent Vacation

Mark me, and be astonished . . .
— Book of Job 21:5

Job and Jean-Paul Sartre met one day at the gym. They were on adjacent treadmills. Job said, "Hey, J.-P.! Walking, walking, going nowhere. Remind you of anything?" Jean-Paul squinted at him over his copy of *Le Monde*. He pursed his lizard lips and grunted by way of acknowledgment. He had never been one for banter, and ever since the introduction of the Heaven-wide smoking ban, he'd been on the testy side. Job pressed on, undeterred. He was enjoying an endorphine-generated high, and was momentarily insensible to signs of either suffering or indifference. He cranked his speed up a couple of notches and asked, "So, tell me J.-P., how are you finding all this nothingness? Is it everything you imagined it might be?" Jean-Paul folded his paper and calibrated his machine down to zero. He knew a losing battle when he saw one. Not that he was surprised. It was always like this with these biblical celebrities. They just wanted to drive a tent-peg into your heart, pin you down, and have at you hammer and tongs. Yammer, yammer, yammer, they never knew when to quit. Once a proselytizer always a proselytizer. The only one of that crowd he found even passingly tolerable was the Apostle Paul. He was appealing in his austerity, but also looked as though he'd once known how to have a good time. It was a combination of traits Sartre had always admired.

"*Franchement, mon ami*," said Jean-Paul, dismounting from what he and his weight-room buddy William Blake privately called "the dark satanic mill"; "*franchement*, I'd rather the Champs-Elysées than the Elyssian Fields."

"Miss the old stomping grounds, eh?"

"Ah, oui. La nostalgie de la boue."

"Say what?"

"Longing for the mud. Hard to translate exactly. It's a French kind of thing. *Au revoir.*"

"A la prochaine!" chimed Job, rather pleased that he had such a phrase available to him.

"Sainte vierge, qu' il n'y aura pas une prochaine!"

"Say what?" asked Job. But J.-P. feigned not to hear. He had picked up his towel and was heading for the steam room.

"*Nostalgie de la boue. Nostalgie de la boue,*" Job repeated to himself as he moved to the StairMaster. "I must remember to make a note of that. *Nostalgie de la boue.*" He was forever borrowing books from the library on how to increase his word power. He knew it was important to work new additions to his vocabulary into day-to-day chat as often as possible. It was the only way they would ever take hold. There had even been occasions when he would misrepresent the absolute truth or steer a conversation off on wild tangents just to have the chance to lob a bright new ball into his interlocutor's court. Mendacious. Egregious. Cotyloid. Polymorphous. Disingenuous. It was amazing, the things that would come out of his mouth.

"You're quiet, Job," God remarked that night when they met for their weekly chess game. "Anything wrong?"

"Yes, well, you know. Just a little *nostalgie de la boue.*"

"Those old muddy cravings. Well, that's easy enough to fix. It's been a while since you've had a break from Heaven, with its uniformly egg-white walls and its relentlessly temperate climes. It can be a tad monochromatic here, it's true. How'd you like a working vacation? There's a particular assignment I have in mind."

"Oh?" Job asked, rather hesitantly. The last time he'd been sent on a "particular assignment" he'd wound up dying on St. Helena, the consequence of slow poisoning. Or so he believed.

Worse still was that he'd spent that whole lifetime perfecting his French only to have it all wiped out when he was X-rayed prior to re-entry.

"Ever heard of Manitoba?"

"Can't say it rings a bell."

"You'll love it. It's a friendly place with ample recreational possibilities, and all the mud you'd want to see in a lifetime. And it's a short-term posting as these things go."

"How short?"

"Eighty, maybe. Ninety at the max."

"Are we talking dog years?"

"Not this time."

"What ever happened to three score and ten?"

"Improved health care. Don't fret. It'll fly by. You'll hardly know you've been away."

"What about my plants? My goldfish?"

"I'll see they're looked after. Checkmate."

So it was that Job descended once again to go to and fro on the earth, to walk up and down upon it. And once again, as was his well-established wont, he wandered hand in hand with bad luck. Even the most advanced and practised of souls, when they slip back into the atmosphere, experience a wholesale letting-go, a generalized forgetting of everything they've learned in Paradise. Over the course of their time on earth, the more refined among them will slowly recover a few of the more ringing eternal tenets and verities. It took Job fully half the length of his most recent tenure on the planet to get back to something that even approximated his name. He started out as Wuketsewitz, and eventually wound up with Bog. Paul Bog. If ever there was a life that could be understood as a prescription to counteract the effects of *nostalgie de la boue* it would be his. Back in Heaven, during his debriefing, Job would use the word "ruderal" to describe his Manitoba incarnation. For twenty years, he lived under a manure pile near Petersfield, about 100 kilometres north of Winnipeg, in the neighbourhood of Winnipeg Beach. I went there to hear the story of his life from Mickey

Donohoe, in whose barn Paul spent the last six winters of his life, who knew Paul Bog as well as anyone, and who in many ways has become the guardian of his story.

My conversation with Mickey took place — as was so often the case on this trip — over coffee, in a kitchen. The safe, domestic heart of the house. A good place for storytelling. Mickey was rather more cautious than most of the other narrators I met, and I wasn't sure if his diffidence was a product of shyness, or concern that I would in some way misappropriate his information. I had the clear sense that he had made deliberate choices about what he would and would not divulge. As it was also evident that Paul Bog was a man for whom he felt and feels a genuine fondness and kinship, I can understand well enough why he might have been so protective, even proprietary, about the Bog legend. After all, it was to Mickey that Paul had confided, in bits and pieces, his sad and bizarre story. Mickey, I imagine, feels he carries the responsibility of stewardship. He is the living repository of this eccentric man's memory. He was one of the locals who saw to it that the road to Paul's place was renamed Paul Bog Road.

Paul Wuketsewitz's story, before he came to Canada, and before he became Paul Bog, is sketchy. We have it only in broad strokes. He was born early in the century in Austria. According to Mickey, he lived in Vienna and had a secure (and rather prognosticatory) job working in the city's sewer system. Somehow, for some reason, he was cheated by his family out of his rightful share of his inheritance. Around the time of that considerable discouragement, he fell prey to the ministrations of an immigration propagandist who made him believe that a homesteading life on the Canadian flatlands would be like heaven on earth.

"He came here in the late twenties, thinking he would find the land of milk and honey," said Mickey. "He got here and there was nothing. He went to Saskatchewan and was employed on a farm. He was there for about two years and he asked the farmer to hold onto his wages. Then the Depression came along, the farmer went out of business, and he lost everything, so there was no way Paul was able to get the money out of him. I also heard he had a girl once, but she ran off with a neighbour. I don't know if he was married to her, but he did not like women at all. If a lady happened to walk into the barn he'd get mad.

"He came here early in the thirties. He'd got this piece of land, somehow. He came out here in the wintertime and had to stay with a neighbour and his wife. They had some kind of falling-out. I think it was because the woman was afraid of him, because of the hatred in his eyes. I'm sure they had a conflict and he had to get out. I'm awfully sure of that."

Mickey's sense is that Paul was a loner during those early years. His relationships with his neighbours were civil, for the most part, but distant. With some he had ongoing feuds. There are stories that he would chase unwanted visitors off his property with a pitchfork. He built a small house. He lived as a subsistence farmer, relying on fairly primitive, but reliable, agricultural techniques. He had a team of horses and a wagon, but got around the countryside on an old bicycle, the tires filled with twine, not air. He'd ride eleven miles to the store, even in the wintertime. And all that time he was Wuketsewitz. It was a fire that brought about the circumstances that earned him the nickname "Bog."

"His place burned down in 1960 on New Year's. I'm awfully sure it happened on the first of January. His place burned down and that was when he moved underground. He moved in with his two horses. He'd dug a shelter for them under the manure pile, a shelter for the horses."

(What follows is a transcription of our conversation. My first question is a marvel of journalistic acumen.)

"What's a manure pile look like?"

"Like a pile of manure."

"Like a mound?"

"Yeah. It's a mound."

"Would that have been a usual thing? To dig underneath one and keep horses there?"

"No. But heck, it was excellent. Hot in the winter. Insulation. You're out of the wind."

"How deep? It must have been deep to accommodate horses."

"Yeah. I was in there a lot. Just one of the horses was left there by that time. The steps he had were straight up and down and even now I'm not able to imagine how he got his horse in and out. Up is easy, but to go down!"

"What were the horse's names?"

"The horses didn't have names. One of his horses died in the summertime. Paul asked a local trucker to come over and pick up his horse and haul it into Winnipeg for him. He goes over and it's all chopped up in pieces and it's about two weeks old and it's the summer! The guy with the truck said, Paul I'm not takin' that. So he ate his horse the rest of the summer."

"He ate the horse?"

"He ate the horse."

"Oh. Well, what did it look like down there? Was there any light?"

"No, there was nothing. To open the door was a big thing. To open it from the inside was a big job. You'd give it a pull and the whole thing would fall down the steps and it would take him half an hour to haul it back up. He put sticks and hay around it. For heat, he had a drum and a pipe through the

Paul Bog in front of his manure pile.

top. There wasn't much down there. He had whatever he needed. There was a post in the middle to hold the horse off to the side, and he used to lie on the straw right beside the horse. But the post had to be there so that if the animal moved in the night he wouldn't land up on top of him. And he had cats, too. Oodles of cats. As long as I knew him he always had a bunch."

"How did he feed them?"

"In those days I don't know. But after I got to know him, when he was living in my barn, they ate the same thing he ate."

"What was that?"

"Evaporated milk, eggs, tea, coffee, sugar, rice, beans all in one pot. He'd mix it all up and he'd eat that for one week, in the summertime too. Then when it was empty, he'd make himself up another bunch of everything in one pot. Bag of tea, half a pound of coffee, half a bag of sugar."

"He'd heat it up?"

"At my place he used to heat it up for a day. Then off went the heat and he'd eat out of that big pot with a knife. He'd just scoop in there with this big knife that he had. It must have been okay. He was eighty-six when he died."

"Did you ever taste it?"

"No. I wouldn't taste that. In the summertime? In the heat? Almost a week old? I wouldn't ever try that."

"What did it smell like in his house?"

"Not awfully bad. On the smoky side. The manure from the horse I don't mind at all. Mostly just smoke and the horse."

"How often did the horse get out?"

"In the spring he went out. In the fall he came in."

"Did the horse seem okay?"

"Oh, yeah."

"How long did Paul stay underground?"

"A long time. Twenty years. And then the manure pile burned down. At the time he didn't have his last horse any more, he'd eaten him too. The place burned down in the fall, in the cold, and that was when he moved to my barn. He was there for about six years, but only in the winter."

"His place burned?"

"Yeah. The fire department ended up there, and an ambulance, and they hauled him away and he got mad. I mean, him, he was excellent, but the police were there too, and they just threw him in the ambulance, took him to the hospital. Two hours after that he had an argument in there and he said, 'I'm goin' home!' They dropped him off here at the farm. He just told me, 'I'm gonna come to your barn, now.' He didn't ask me or anything! I said, 'Okay, Paul.' He asked if I had a spade; then he asked me to go with him back to his house. The fire was all out now. Everything was all under water, you know, what with the fire department being there. He started lookin' around and he said to me, 'Here. Dig here. There's something down there.' So I dug there for most of the afternoon. Then I hit something. It was a garbage bag. Then another. They were both full of money. We went back to the barn and I set him up there for the night. And in the morning when I went back he had all his money, individual bills, lying all over the floor, drying, because of course they got so soaked. He had $34,000! It was old, some of that money. It was all excellent, all straight in lines up and down.

"That afternoon, I talked to a few of the neighbours, because I didn't want that much money there in the barn. I told him he had to take it to the bank, and he said he wouldn't. Finally I convinced him and made arrangements with the bank manager to meet me at the door at 10 a.m. exactly. I told him to be sure to be ready because this old guy's unpredictable. So at 10.00 sharp I was at the bank with the old guy and these bags of money. The manager opens up the door and the old guy goes running in behind the counter. And I'm after him because he's not supposed to be there, and the manager is after me because I'm not supposed to be there, and we were snaking around all through the bank with his bags full of money. Finally it was all arranged for us to go down in the basement. There was a teller at the table to take the money, but Paul wasn't going to hand it over all at once. He did it a handful at a time. It was all he owned. He knew exactly how much he had — although he was out by $5. He had $5 more than he thought."

"Did he ever spend any money?"

"On groceries, and he liked a drink."

"Did he ever buy clothes?"

"Not clothes. Not as far as I know."

"He wore the same stuff all the time?"

"Oh, yeah. The socks were unbelievable. Those he had to buy, maybe about two pairs a year. When he needed extra socks, he'd just add. He never took his old ones off. At the end, I took eight pairs of socks off him, and the only ones that were okay was the outside pair. All the rest were completely gone from the ankles down. And another thing I had to do that I don't think anyone ever had to do before was to potty-train an eighty-year-old man. The first time he'd ever had to use a toilet was when he moved into my barn. Before, he'd just go outside. I don't know. I mean, if the horse can do it...I told him at the start that on a dairy farm you can't leave a mess around, not any human mess. And I had to show him, from one end to the other, what he had to do in the toilet. I sat down and showed him how, and when I got up he looked, and understood, and then I showed him how to operate the flush. After that, he was okay."

"What kind of a set-up did you have for him in the barn?"

"It was excellent for him. It's a nice barn, huge, with an office in it, and other rooms that were excellent. It was all heated electrically. The heater was in the wall. One day I went in and noticed there were ashes on the floor. It happened like that for a few days, these ashes on the floor, and it turned out that the way he checked to see if the heater was on was to throw in a hunk of paper. If it burned, it was on."

"This was in the winter. Where was he in the summer?"

"He re-dug into the manure pile, this time into the side. It was about four feet wide, eight feet long, six feet high. No, it wouldn't have been that high because I had to duck down when I went in."

"Very cramped!"

"Yeah. One time at my place I gave him a dog, a little one, and he liked it. In the springtime he took it home. In the fall he stayed there too long, out in the cold, him and the cats and that dog all in the little room. When I went to see him I saw the dog wasn't there. I asked him where it was, and he said it had died. I said, 'Well, Paul, how?' And he didn't want to tell me. Finally, he said, 'A stick on the head! No room here for me, my cats, my dog. I kill dog!'"

"What happened to the cats when he went back and forth?"

"He moved with all his cats. They were wild. He'd haul them all over in a bag. Boy, that was something! But he was able to do it, and without anything on his hands. I helped him once, holding the bag, and those cats would scream, and they'd be trying to eat you from inside the bag, and him, he'd be reaching around behind the stove and he'd burn his hand and they'd be chewing at him, but he'd just keep grabbin' his cats, and then he had a bag full of screaming, fighting cats, eight or nine of them."

"Did he read?"

"At my place I used to catch him sometimes, reading. I'd go out after supper to look at the cows, and there he'd be in the dark with the newspaper opened up. Another thing was his handwriting, the finest I've ever seen. Whenever he had to sign his name it would be a half-hour job, everything had to be just so, all these accent marks above every other letter. But boy, did that man have a signature! It was just perfect. Unbelievable."

"How'd he die?"

"Old age."

"Was it fast?"

"Yeah. He was excellent, and then one day in the fall I noticed that the pot on the stove was still the same height every day, and he was not up and around as much. The next day I asked a nurse to come and look at him, and he was on the poor side then. I called the RCMP to make sure I wouldn't get in any trouble. They came out and took a look and then they phoned the ambulance and took him in. I had to go to the hospital with him, or else there was no way to take him. I told him I'd be back after milking. That night after supper he died, there in the hospital."

At this point, tears well. Mickey says, "Shit, it's hard talking about this old bugger!" He gets a Kleenex, continues the story.

"I told him I'd be back after milking and to wait for me. So I got there and the nurses were at the door, and they said,

'Hurry up, he's wild, there's something wrong!' And I went in there, and put his hand on mine. And he crawled up my arm with his fingers — like this — and grabbed me, kind of pulled me down, and kissed me on the cheek and then he died. December 2, 1987."

"He loved you, Mickey."

"Yeah. It took him a long time to let me know that he wanted me to lean down to him, and then he gave me a goddam kiss on the cheek and then he died."

A long silence. "What happened to his money?"

"Oh, now that's a story. You're not going to believe this. Of course he'd never made a will. They found some relatives back in Europe, and it all went to them, every last dollar. It went to a bunch of strangers who didn't know anything about him."

Finis Paul Bog, whose life is done, whose money is gone, whose house has become someone's fertile garden. Bog is done. A road bears his name. Bog is over. Close the strange, sad circle.

Earth, and What I Found There: A Post-Mortem, Written in Compliance with the Requirements of the Sabbatical Assessment Committee and Respectfully Submitted by Me, Job.

I will write this quickly and succinctly, in the hope that I will be forgiven whatever stylistic lapses might arise as a consequence of haste. Speed is essential, as I must set this down before the forgetting sets in, as I know it must, according to plan. Already, some of the details are hazy, which must be all to the good, if I can judge my time on earth by the condition of my nails. Praise the Lord, for the mercy of His methods! Still, there is enough man-think left in me to find it strange that so much is gone from me, after so extended a stretch in the field. My assignment lasted eighty-six years, that is, by standard terrestrial measurement. As God is quick to point out, however, time is a crude construct when one of your inventions is eternity, and the whole stretch of my absence didn't give Him time enough to belch or blink. Not that God has ever been known to do either.

But enough of this dilly-dallying. The question I must answer is, essentially, what did I do on my vacation? Well, truth be told, I can't say that it was exactly restful. There was little enough of what anyone would call "leisure." No tanning on the golden sands, no volleyball on the beach, no drinks bedecked with little umbrellas. I had a rough time of it, especially at the beginning. There was deceit, betrayal, disappointment, poverty. There was misanthropy, and I don't refer here to my own. That was easy enough for me to put up with. There was hunger, cold, discomfort, loneliness, and pent-up sexual longing. There was English. I never had an easy time with English. There was a kind of wilful blinkeredness. For the longest time, I understand now, I led what you'd have to call an unexamined life. For this I offer no apology. "What's my purpose here?" is largely a question of the comfortable middle class, as you will quickly realize if ever you find yourself in a situation where you have to think of ways to cook up rotting horse flesh. Oh, I know, I know. I should have been able to rise above it. I should have been buoyed by philosophy, like that know-it-all Boethius, and so on and so forth. I confess, I allowed myself to be sidetracked by brute, physical difficulty. The winters were ugly. The cupboards were bare. It wasn't until I had the notion that I might just as well live under the dung heap that things started looking up, or at least began to fall into perspective. There's nothing like a pile of shit to focus the mind, and that was a good lesson to learn, however late in the day it might have dawned.

"It's a nice place you've got here," said God, the one time He passed through.

"It's cosy," I said, "and the overhead is low."

"Yes," said God, "I can see that's the case."

"And it's not so bad living in close proximity to a horse."

"I've always said it's a wise idea to be close to one's eventual lunch."

"And here's the best thing, God. The way I figure it, I can thank this heap of manure for making me who I am. It's given me an identity. I have become the Bog Man. Paul Bog, they call me, and not always with cheer in their hearts. There are those who mock me. There are those who turn their backs. There are even those who have tried to rob me, though never more than once. That's a pitchfork over in the corner, and I can wield it with an aplomb that would make Satan himself think twice about pillaging my sacks full of loot. I am despised and rejected. But those who have known me will never forget me, if only because I am everything they are not, and everything they could so easily become. How far is anyone from the dung heap, God? Not so very far, as near as I can figure it."

"Ah. So you've acquired a *raison d'être*."

"Don't you get all fancy with me, God. Not down here."

"I mean, you've uncovered a purpose, Job."

"Bog."

"Bog, of course."

And indeed that's exactly what I found on earth. A purpose. It might have been odd, and it might have been obscure, but no one could ever call it small. On earth I found purpose, and along the way I found peace, of a kind. It was a here-and-there kind of happenstance, I grant you, but every now and again, I found peace. Peace and purpose, and in rare moments, though often enough to be significant, I saw the certain evidence of goodwill. Once, before I died, there was something I wouldn't hesitate to call love. Unstinting, unthinking love. It was all I required. It is all anyone needs. Love came, and it was time to take my leave. Just a kiss and goodbye. And that's about it. That is all I have to report. I have been gone. Once again, I've returned. My name is Job. At last, I am home.

Through the Hermitage Window

There is a shadow there that sings and calls
But not for you.
　　— Charlotte Mew, "The Forest Road"

There should be a word in English to describe the state of mild apprehension that comes over the solitary traveller when he opens the door to his hotel room — with a key, with a card — and steps from the public forum of the hallway into what will be his hermitage for the night. From the moment of his first arrival at the inn, from the very instant he sets foot over that threshold and braves the lobby, he has been plugged in to a source of low-voltage angst. There is so much that can go awry, so many niggling interrogatives: Will there be a vacancy? Will it be affordable? Will the credit card still have room in its heart to accommodate one more swipe through that know-it-all fiscal verifier? Will the desk clerk size you up with her practised eye and know that you are a fraud, that you have no business being here, that travel for you is just a masquerade, an avoidance, that you should really be in school with the rest of the kids? Who do you think you are, playing truant like this? You are on the road only because you are running from something, which you know to be true, even though you can't say exactly what. Will she test you in some way when you ask for the corporate rate, will she think "Corporate, my ass!" and demand a few stock tips, or say that she will have to check with your boss, or your mother, before she can give you a preferred tariff; will she roll her eyes at the hovering bellman who is asking if he can take your bags, and, if you let him have his way with your suit-cases, will there be the agonizing ride in the elevator while you make small talk, and he calls you "sir," making you feel as if you were in your forties or something, which of course you are? And after all that, will you have to tip him, and find that you only have a twenty that you will feel obliged to press on him in a cavalier, offhand way, as though money oozes by way of osmosis into your wallet from your right buttock, which is made of not of flesh but of crisp, surplus bills? If you decline, will he curl his lip and sneer at you when your back is turned and you lumber off to your room, which now you stand out-side, having just opened the door? Will this be the time you find a corpse in the bathtub?

Of course, there is nothing. There is always nothing. You fumble for the light switch and illumine a room you've never seen but is just as you knew it would be, a room that is in most ways indistinguishable from the one you were in last night, and the night before that, and the night before that, in a different city, in a different town, in a different province. *Déjà, déjà, déjà vu*: not the gift of prophecy, just the unwavering regard of habit. Look, look.

Look and see. See if you can find any trace whatsoever of the last person or persons to occupy this room. Chances are you won't. Every whiff of them has been expunged. No curly hairs in the tub, no cigarette butts in the ashtray, no favourite passages underlined in the Gideon Bible, no helpful notes sharing intelli-gence on the quirks of the shower or the thermostat, or advis-ing you to avoid the conditioner, because it will just make your hair greasy. There is no communal dream book in which the transient residents of, say, room 310 at the Old Orchard Inn in Wolfville, can jot down the wellings of their subconscious for the amusement and delectation of others. It's all so tidy! The sheets are bleached, the towels hang in regimental lines, every-thing is arranged to make you believe that no one has gone here before, that all the bedding and so on is newly purchased from the Bay. Why should the weary pilgrim tarnish his dreams of

Canterbury by meditating for even a second on the hundreds of passers-through who have used the very mattress on which he stretches out, face down, inhaling the Sanforized freshness of the puckered quilting; used it, and not always for the most savoury of purposes? Why should he exacerbate the loneliness of the road by imagining how eager and maybe adulterous lovers have romped on this very bedspread, not even waiting to pull it back and slide between the sheets before carrying out their sweaty exertions? Before screwing their brains out?

The most overt administrative acknowledgment of the hotel room's illicit potential is the selection of skin flicks which a broad-minded management makes available for about nine bucks a pop. I have occasionally viewed these on my various travels, never out of sociological interest, but more because of some untargeted randiness that required a focus. Of course, these movies are the most innocuous of pornographic excursions, as predictable and as involving as the compulsory-figures portion of a skating competition, or the dressage event of an equestrian meet. They all seem to be shot poolside, or in an adjacent cabana somewhere in California, and everyone looks pretty much the same, and performs pretty much the same acts in pretty much the same order with pretty much the same effect. The soundtracks are also indistinguishable one from the other. Once, I was lying in bed reading, and heard the tell-tale moans and the signifying drone of the synthesized strings and the drum machine bleeding through the wall from the room next to mine. Out of perverse solidarity I put down my book, picked up the remote, and surfed the naughty waves till I found the matching soundscape. An attractive young couple were splayed on top of an office desk, and flailed there happily. She still had her heels on, a remarkable oversight, potentially damaging to the shiny gloss of varnish beneath the blotter. I regretted missing the opening sequence, as I couldn't imagine the circumstances leading up to such a moment. I felt a strange bond, a weird communion of the road with whoever was watching beyond the eastern wall. I half wondered if I might be part of a group process, if the resident of the room on the western side might have heard my television and switched on, and if the same scene was possibly being repeated all down the long hall, that we were all part of a voyeuristic daisy-chain. I thought of how, if I were ever to make a porn movie, I would start it with just such a scene, and imagined for longer than was strictly necessary how I would develop the plot. I might very well have wasted an hour or more in such fruitless contemplation had not some Presbyterian angel whispered admonitions to the contrary in my ear. I turned off the movie, abandoned my next-door soul mate to his miscreant pleasures, and returned to my book, which was the SAS *Survival Guide*.

One measure of my dull ineptitude is that when I was preparing to make my dead-of-winter visits to Canadian eccentrics, I spent more more time fretting about what I would take to read than what I would take to wear. Travel guides, histories, biographies, poetry, diverting novels: I weighed the virtue of many genres and made my selections. On the day before I left Vancouver, I was wrestling with whether or not it would be worthwhile to pack along the *Dictionary of Canadian Biography*, which is a reference tool I have long cherished. I opened Volume One randomly, looking for some sign or advice, and there scanned the story of Anne de Noüe. Anne, who was a fellow, was born under the sign of Leo, near Rheims in 1587. He spent some time in the court of Henry IV, where he was known as "the handsome page." Around the age of twenty-five, he decided the Jesuit life was just the ticket, and signed up. Eventually, his duties took him to New France. He didn't find it an altogether commodious place. He was apparently a skilled angler, which stood him in good stead with his fish-loving colleagues, but was totally inept at learning the Native languages, and was never fully appreciative of their way of life. In 1646, while trekking through snow to administer the sacrament to the garrison at Sorel, he was overtaken by a blizzard and lost his way. He was found, kneeling, bare-headed, frozen solid, six miles upstream from his intended destination. His eyes were turned towards Heaven, as though in chilly supplication. A sad last turning of the handsome page. *Sic transit pulchritude.*

I had sought a sign, and sure enough I received one, a timely reminder that I was travelling to *le vrai Canada* at an intemperate time of year. With Anne's frosty finish in mind, I decided it would be prudent to leave the thirteen thick volumes of the DCB behind, and take instead some combination underwear, which is just about as bulky, and many times more confusing. The thermal suit I purchased — the first I've ever owned — came in a package with no instructions or schematic diagram. It took me the better part of an hour to figure out how such voluminous undies were actually applied, and longer still to acclimatize myself to looking like an overextended icing bag. For the first two weeks of my travelling, the weather in the East was relatively mild, and the unflattering swaddling lay wadded away under the tomes I couldn't bear to leave behind. It wasn't until I went to pay a call on a hermit who lives in the deep backwoods of Nova Scotia that I thought the time had come to forgo frivolous fears of fashion *faux pas* in favour of forestalling frigidity. When I exhumed the lumpen undies from my valise, they disgorged from their deep and many folds the SAS *Survival Guide.* How odd! I vaguely recalled buying it, couldn't remember packing it.

Ostensibly, this palm-sized book is meant to comfort élite airmen whose planes go down in Antarctic wastes or in the jungles of Borneo. It's full of diagrams showing how to signal a passing ship, or dig a trench latrine, or give yourself the Heimlich manoeuvre by hurling yourself against a stump. The point is that the SAS *Guide* was concealed in my thermal suit, and it pleased the heck out of me to for once find a useful tool folded up in my underwear. As I am not impervious to such cosmic *billets doux*, I pocketed the thing, and headed out to meet the hermit, K.

Hector MacKenzie, bless him, had agreed to be my guide. He is one of an informal ad hoc group that looks out for K. Hector is a well-known fiddle player in and around Pictou

County. He has deep roots there. He was born in the same house as his great-grandfather, and on the same day to boot. The old man was also called Hector. In fact, five MacKenzie lads over succeeding generations have carried that name. He lives with his wife, Eleanor, in a pretty house on the highway, not far from New Glasgow. They moved there a few years ago from a place called Salt Springs, leaving the handsome manse house where they spent most of their married life and raised their children. Their property was expropriated for road construction. They harbour no resentment about this forced displacement. They are happy where they've landed. It's a bright and comfy place, with a wood stove in the kitchen, and a glassed-in front room that gets so warm on a sunny winter's day that there's no need to bother cranking up the heat.

Hector had been puttering about in his workshop, sorting through the material accumulation of the years, winnowing oddments for a future garage sale. There were the usual small appliances, in varying states of repair. There were books and board games. There was a black bear, a real one, rearing up on his hind legs, a look of permanent surprise on his face. "Make me an offer!" he said, when I admired it, and I would have, were the road ahead of me not so long and fraught with uncertainty. Some things were not for barter, such as his scale model of the MacKenzie castle, and the sundry taxidermy treasures he and Eleanor have carted home from the far-flung travels they've enjoyed in retirement. On the day I visited, Eleanor was seeing to the renewal of their passports, preparatory to going to Venezuela. From other trips south, they've brought back a coiled cobra, twined around a pole, a turtle's head, mounted on a plaque, and a stuffed armadillo. Protruding from one wall was the hind end of a deer with a red light-bulb stuck in its butt hole. Plug it in and the light flashes. Adjacent to this arresting conversation piece hung a big framed photograph, a treasured memento, not for sale at any price, a blown-up colour shot of a bearded man sitting outside a tiny cabin, playing what is plainly a homespun guitar.

"That's him," said Hector. "That's K. Must have been taken twenty years ago. He looks pretty clean, there. I knew him from the time he was a teenager. He was always a little strange. He had this big dog with him all the time, and they'd just disappear into the woods, wouldn't come back for a couple of days. He was always musical and a good fiddle player. So was his father. Him they called Fiddle Foot."

Eleanor poured tea and set out slices of excellent Christmas fruit cake while Hector traced for me the outline of the hermit's progress. It's a simple story. More than fifty years ago, K. became an unwilling army conscript. He was on a troop train, *en route* to Halifax, from where he would have been shipped to war. The train made brief stops at stations and sidings. It was during one of these halts, somewhere around Salem, that K. decided once and for all that the battlegrounds of Europe and the forced camaraderie of service life were not for him. So, he slipped away. He took his army-issue Enfield rifle and high-tailed it into the woods. This was the landscape of his childhood, as familiar to him as the ridges of his teeth against his tongue. He knew of an abandoned cabin, a shanty on the shores of a little lake where his only company would be the trout. It was miles and miles from anything or anyone. That was where he went. That was where he holed up. And that was where he stayed. And stayed. For a long time, no one knew anything of his whereabouts. He hunted. He fished. The forest provided. He had no need of money or commerce. He had no need of medicine. If he was unwell — which he almost never was — he knew what plants, what barks to use to fix himself up. His only real requirement at the beginning was to lie low. In time, of course, the news got out. People in the community round about came to know of him. They accommodated him — it wasn't as if he was a stranger, someone from away. He was different, true; but he still belonged. And anyway, what harm had he done? If word of his whereabouts filtered back to the army, the authorities never bothered following up. Time passed and the tension eased. The war was long done. Over the years, K. moved from fugitive to fixture. He kept mostly to himself and was left alone, although he wasn't averse to social contact when it was required. He got by. He maintained a trapline and his rifle, could sell furs or venison or moose if he needed some money. Sometimes, he'd carve axe handles.

"How old is he?"

"I don't really know. I'd say he's probably got a year or two on me and I'm seventy-eight."

"That's old to be living alone in the woods."

"It is, though he's always been fit as a fiddle. You'll see that he's pretty bright, considering all the time he's spent alone. Lately, there's been some concern about K. from the social services people. Some folks have even got together and built him this nice little place, not too far from where he's been. It's a good set-up, brand new, closer to the road and to help if he needs it, closer to the store where he gets his groceries. Every so often, he picks up a few staples, flour, rice, tea, and so on. The storekeeper looks out for him, keeps track of everything on a running tab. Problem is, he's just not interested in moving. They're having a devil of a time convincing him he should. You'll see when we get up there. By the way, have you got a four-wheel drive?"

With one penetrating question, Hector had pierced right to the heart of my rented Mystique's every inadequacy. "Well, not to worry. We should be able to manage, long as the road's not too slicky underneath."

Hector suited up, and I took a covert squinny at the *SAS Survival Guide*'s directions for cooking reptiles. "Gut, then cook in their skins. Place in hot embers, turning continually. When skin splits, meat can be removed and boiled." I glanced at the stuffed armadillo, its baleful regard, then helped myself to another slice of fruit cake and off we went.

"Take a right," said Hector, as we passed the place where a bootlegger had his operation back when Hector was a boy. "Left now," he directed as we skirted the field where there's a Mac-Kenzie cemetery, and where every tenant save one belongs to Hector's clan.

"Yep," he said, "All except for one."

There was a lo-o-o-ng pause.

"You're going to make me ask, aren't you, Hector?"

"Hatch." He chuckled. "A foreigner by the name of Hatch."

How Hatch perished I have no idea, but the name called to mind a heart-rending and highly instructive tale I had read in the *Canadian Alpine Journal* of 1908. That was the year Mary E. Crawford, M.D., had written about the advantages of mountain climbing for women. "There is no recreation which, in all its aspects of surrounding and exercise, will bring about a quicker rejuvenation of worn-out nerves, tired brains, and flabby muscles than mountaineering. It is for women one of the new things under the sun and every fresh mountain is a new delight. Ennui has no place in the vocabulary of the woman who climbs, the words which rout it are enthusiasm and exhilaration. Diseases of the imagination cannot be discovered anywhere on a mountain side, where Nature asserts herself so grandly to the consciousness and with such insistence that the 'ego' with its troubles sinks out of sight."

One young woman who took Dr. Crawford's words to heart was Miss Helen Hatch, of Lethbridge. She was part of the Alpine Club's annual summer camp, which opened on Wednesday, July 8, 1908. The camp was pitched at the summit of the Rogers Pass, at 4,350 feet. Miss Hatch was not an utter novice when it came to mountaineering. In fact, just that spring she had made her way up the Crow's Nest Mountain. The climb that was to be her last, which she undertook with a party from the club, went up the northwest face of Mount Avalanche. The outing was supervised by experienced climbers, and what happened to Helen was freakish in the extreme. What happened to Helen happened before the real climbing began. The group was making its way towards the mountain and had to pass across a snow-filled couloir. They were not yet roped together, as there was nothing about their circumstances or environment suggesting that such a precaution might be necessary. Oliver Wheeler, a youth himself, but a veteran climber, went ahead first, to see if the snow was conducive to crossing. Miss Hatch, exhilarated by the altitude, by the surfeit of fresh air, by the novelty of snow in July, ignored his exhortations to remain back. She chirped, "I am coming. Look out now!" Then she took a little hop and slid on the snow. She "lost her footing and, as Oliver reached the bottom, went by him with tremendous velocity. Hearing her call he checked himself, turned swiftly and grabbed for her. Alas! she had gone wide and he only touched her outstretched hand. She passed on down the slope from ledge to ledge, gathering velocity as she fell and, at a depth of 120 feet, dropped over the final ledge, twenty feet perpendicular, to the snow-filled couloir. She had not uttered a sound and must have fainted at the moment she realized what had happened....A charming and plucky young life had been thrown away owing to a moment of impetuosity."

Plucky, impetuous Helen! Her death in the summer ice provides a grim but satisfying bookend to the fiery finish of Keith Pelton, who died ten years earlier in Yarmouth. Her body, *pale and grave as a sculptured nun*, was lifted from the snow where it lay *pillowed upon its alabaster arms like a child o'erwearied with sweet toil*, and was conveyed on a crude litter back to the base camp. No doubt the Alpinists, over whose summer this untoward incident must have cast a dreadful pall, derived some comfort from telling one another that she'd fainted dead away as soon as her slide commenced and that she couldn't have known what hit her; or rather, what she hit, as she died when she smashed into some projecting rock spurs. I prefer to think that her final moments were in no way anaesthetized, and that her blood was awash with dopamine, or whatever other chemical agent the cells churn out in moments of thrill and danger. Death is never graceful, but to have been so fully alive at the moment of life's ending must have felt like being touched by grace, or something like it.

Helen's story took on a cautionary note as Hector and I slid past the graveyard on our snowy route. With each turn the road became less roadlike. We passed the little house that was built with K. in mind, stopped, and got out to check it over. It was, as Hector had described, a charming chalet, with a sleeping loft, and propane heat and fridge, in a pretty wooded copse. The snow around it was unsullied by footfall. There was no sign that K. had been there, sniffing out his new digs. We drove on and on, and when the path finally petered out altogether, we left the car and prepared to strike out through the trackless woods. A pick-up truck hove into view. The driver, a burly, bearded fellow named Sterling, had followed us down the road. He is also part of the network that keeps an eye out for K.'s well-being. Satisfied that we were not up to mischief, he waved us on our way. Into the woods we went, the soon-to-be-octogenarian Hector bounding along ahead of me with rabbity alacrity, leaping over rivulets gone crusty around their margins, under pine boughs drooping with snow. Within minutes, my long johns were damp with sweat. The *SAS Guide*'s hypothermic warnings pulsed against my girdled groin. At one point, I slipped on a rock and my foot went into a brook.

"Did you get your foot wet?"

"Oh, maybe just a little." I had the idea that this was not a good thing, and Hector quickly confirmed my suspicions.

"Oh, lordy. Oh, lordy. We'd better get you to K.'s and get that dried out!"

I was visited by the memory of being eliminated from a spelling bee by the word "gangrene." Would it again prove my undoing, I wondered as we hurried on, passing all kinds of animal footprints which the *SAS Guide* could certainly have helped me identify had I only the time to refer to it. We hurried on, and in short order, we were there.

K.'s pine-log shack — it's really a lean-to — is in a kind of Lake Isle of Innisfree setting: deep woods, deep peace. Smoke from the tin chimney suggested he might be home. Hector pointed out the fresh cross-country ski tracks. It looked like K. had been on a jaunt of his own. One curious architectural feature of his place is the tree that years ago fell squarely onto K.'s roof, which is plastic sheeting covered with corrugated metal.

For reasons that are either philosophic or aesthetic, K. chose not to move the wasted trunk. It lies there, in the dent of its own making, at a forty-five-degree angle. The shack has no door. Entrance and egress take place through the window on which Hector hammered to announce our arrival. "K.! K.! Are you there, boy? It's me, it's Hector, can we see you?" A pause, a shuffling within, the grating of the window, and then there he was, our hermit, squinting into the light.

Once, I saw a baby born. I had never witnessed anything quite so overwhelming as when the hidden head emerged from the vulvic cave, followed by the shoulders, and then the greasy pell-mell tumble of that new life into the world. That is the image that came to me while watching K. exit his house through his window: head, shoulders, the long, accordion unfolding of his body, and then, there he was before us in the snow: tall, thin, and wiry, his flexibility no doubt sustained by his years of slipping in and out through so modest an aperture. He wore a long blue parka, green gumboots, a sweater of indeterminate, subfusc hue, and matching trousers. His beard and hair were long and wild in the best hermit tradition, and the whole of his being seemed bound together by soot. He was, without a doubt, the sootiest man I have ever seen. He didn't seem surprised or discomfitted to see Hector there, nor to see that he'd brought along a stranger. He shook us each by the hand, and did so with uncommon delicacy, crooking his pinky first around Hector's little finger, then mine.

"Afternoon, K.! I brought you a visitor. He's come all the way from Vancouver!"

"Oh, yes."

"How do you do?" I said, betraying my gift for originality.

"Oh, yes."

"Well, K.! Can we come in? Can you show us your place? The young fellow got his foot wet; he'd better dry his shoe by your stove."

"Oh, yes."

We all piled back through the window into the cabin, a

single room scarcely big enough to accommodate the crowd. Even with one it would feel jammed. It was dim in there in the middle of the day. There was a bench, a cot, and what I took to be the selfsame Enfield rifle K. carried when he skipped the train and went AWOL all those years ago. There were snowshoes, a kerosene lantern, a few cooking tools, and a bucket of sloppy-looking stuff Hector pointed out to me as sourdough starter. It was warm, almost oppressively close. There was an improvised stove dug into the dirt floor, and the rich smell of wood smoke, as heady as I've ever known it, almost asphyxiating at first.

This was turning out to be a day resonant with historical association, for the thick air in K.'s parlour, and the way my eyes teared at the beginning of our visit, summoned up the story of Gabriel Druillettes. Born near Limoges in 1610, he was another of the early Jesuit missionaries, a contemporary of the unfortunate Anne de Noüe. Unlike the handsome page, Gabriel adapted quickly to Indian ways. He was a resourceful fellow. If he felt peckish and there was no ready game in sight, he would boil up the thongs of his snowshoes and chow down on leather. One year, he followed the Montagnais on their winter hunting expeditions. The smoky lodges damaged his eyes. Over time he went blind, and had to be led about by a child who was assigned to him for that purpose. An old medicine woman said she could fix him up, and — in what might be the first recorded cataract operation in Canada — proceeded to scrape at his corneas with a rusty knife. Of course, it was terribly painful and ineffectual both. Finally, he assembled the Christian Montagnais around him, and celebrated a mass of the Virgin Mary. Even before he was done, his sight was miraculously restored. K.'s eyes, I was pleased to see, were bright, and his vision seemed unimpaired. Indeed, apart from his deep griminess — or maybe because of his deep griminess — he seemed remarkably sound overall. I would never have imagined him to be eighty, and Hector told me that a public health nurse who went to examine him as part of the campaign to move him to his new digs was amazed by his level of fitness.

I removed my dampened shoe and set it beside the stove, relieved to find my sock quite dry. We all three sat in companionable silence for a few minutes, just enjoying the sight of one another. K. tamped some tobacco into a long pipe, lit up, drew slowly, showed no curiosity about why we'd intruded on his solitude. Hector spoke first.

"We've just been up looking at your new place. Have you been there lately? They've got it fixed up real nice for you."

"Uh-huh. Mmmmm. Yes."

"Why, I think it would be grand to live there. So much space, right there in the woods. It's close to the store, K. They've got a big woodpile, all cut and stacked and ready. I'd move in there myself if I could. I'd move in tomorrow. Don't you think you should maybe take your stuff over there?"

"Hmmmmm. Well. No. No, I don't think so. No. I'm not much for moving, you know. Not in the winter. Afraid I could catch something. Afraid I could catch a chill. Bad at my age. A chill. No."

"But there's a good heating system up there, K. They've got it all set up with propane."

"Hmmmmmm. Yes. Understand it explodes from time to time."

Hector shrugged, rolled his eyes, grinned. It was just as he thought it would be. The hermit was not for moving. There was another stretch of quiet. I noticed many damp and mouldering books around, and picked up an old volume from the *Reader's Digest* condensed-novel series. It was positioned beneath the window-sill and covered in boot marks.

"You like to read?" I asked.

"Yes. Oh, yes. I've read all these books. I read the Bible most every Sunday. Know how many times the word 'howl' has been used in the Bible? Four. Yes, I read the Bible, and I remember amperisms."

"Amperisms?"

"You know. Little — what would you call them? Little sayings. Robert Louis Stevenson, he said that a purpose in life is the greatest treasure a man can own. Yes. I often wonder what he meant by that."

"Well, I'm not sure…"

"And G. K. Chesterton, he said that the best thing about miracles was that they sometimes happen. Hmmmmmmm. I often wonder what he meant by that."

"Chesterton said that?"

"Chesterton, yes. And Mark Twain, a woman once said to him that she had both a headache and a toothache and could anything be worse, and he said, yes, rheumatism and St. Vitus's dance. Yes. I like that. Did you ever hear tell of Pan?"

"Pan? Yes. Yes, I guess so. I remember a story about how he chased a nymph and she prayed to be saved from him and was turned into a reed. Pan cut her to make his flute."

"Is that so? Huh! I often wonder if I might not see him here," and he looked out into the woods. "Yes. Pan."

We sat and listened again to the attenuated quiet. It was very pleasant, and I just didn't feel like wrecking the moment with prying questions. What would I want to ask, anyway? I could see how he lived. I could see that he was content. I could see his wry humour in the way he deflected suggestions that he'd be better off elsewhere. No doubt there are thousands of stories he could tell about the life he has chosen to live, abstracted from any regular intercourse with human society, but he was not the sort of man who was going to open up to a stranger, to someone from away with no more than an afternoon to spend. It was enough to be there, and to enjoy the moment. Then Hector spoke. "K.'s quite a fiddle player, aren't you, K.? Remember how I came here once with my grandson and you played and we all danced? Why don't you play something for us?"

"It's broken."

"Well, how about the guitar, then? Could you play us something on the guitar?"

And much to my surprise, he agreed. He took down the guitar he'd made for himself, God knows with what tools, and played this wonderful, bluesy, loopy tune. It was his own composition, and there was nothing about it that was linear or thematic or familiar. It was absolutely original and beautiful. As was he. It was music that belonged wholly to that place. As did he. I taped it and played it back for him. He listened carefully, nodded approvingly. He filled his pipe, looked out his window. I imagined him there, hours after we would be gone, strumming his songs in the smoky dark. I imagined him looking from his window in the morning, studying the fresh prints in the snow. Strange ones. Nothing a member of the Special Air Service would be able to identify, not even by thumbing through that helpful guide. Not bear nor wild cat, not raccoon nor prairie dog. No, no. These would be the crazy calling-cards of the great god Pan, all melting, all tangled. For you should know that his cloven feet are hot as coals, and when he passed by in the thick of the night, he just couldn't keep himself from dancing.

Chapter Fourteen

A Woman Clothed with the Sun

And to the woman were given two wings of a great eagle,
that she might fly into the wilderness...
   — Revelation 12:14

There are not many words to which I can point and say with
assurance that such was the time and place, such were the circumstances that reigned when this new notch was carved in my
vocabulary. "Derrière" is one such instance, as I have already
said. "Nostalgia" is another. When I turned adolescent, and
every certainty was rattled or shaken loose, I began to read
poetry with the kind of feverish devotion I'd once brought to
the Hardy Boys and Enid Blyton. I can't say why. It just happened. Perhaps it was in part genetic, as my father was also partial to the stuff, and in part environmental, as we had a few
starter anthologies around the house, as well as editions of such
stalwart rhymesters as Kipling and Service and Longfellow and
Omar Khayyám. The home collection that quickly became my
favourite was a squat, fat book called *A Little Treasury of
Modern Poetry*, edited by Oscar Williams. It was published in
1946, and it remains to this day a solid, representative culling
of English and American poetry of the first half of the century.
Certain poems I committed to memory. "The Elephant Is Slow
to Mate," by D.H. Lawrence, "Recuerdo," by Edna St. Vincent
Millay, and Helen Hoyt's "Rain at Night," with its desperate
and fateful final cry, "O love, I had forgot that we must die," a

line which could have been improved only by the addition of an exclamation point.

One summer afternoon, flipping idly through the tubby *Little Treasury*, looking for something lush and improbable to learn by heart, I found a leaf pressed between two pages. It was an autumn leaf, plucked from the cotoneaster that grew by the side of the house. It was tiny and many-hued, orange and red with streaks of yellow. I picked it up, and remembered very clearly that it was I who had placed it there, half a lifetime (i.e., six years) before. I'd intended it as part of a display, a school project of the kind every child who lives in a part of the world where the foliage turns colour must have undertaken at one time or another. Why this leaf had not made the final cut I couldn't guess. Perhaps simply because it had been overlooked, or because there wasn't enough room on the dry-cleaner's cardboard onto which the fallen beauties were attached, or because there was a prettier inclusion from the same bush, or because I was uncertain about how to spell "cotoneaster." I held that leaf in my tender, hairless palm and remembered those far-off, simpler times, when life was unencumbered by the difficulties that were beginning to beset me. A delicious wave of something new washed over me, a dumb longing to reclaim what could never be retrieved. I looked down at the page (227) against which the leaf had languished all those years and read the first lines of the poem printed there — "My soul stands at the window of my room, / And I ten thousand miles away" — then took in its title: "Nostalgia." By Karl Shapiro. Nostalgia. What a soft, pretty word! I went to the dictionary, and was amazed at the dumb, happy accident that caused me to place such a souvenir in such a spot; that had caused me to find it, in that specific then-and-there, to teach me something for which I was past ready. It was a perfect moment. I understood, even then, that I had been given a gift. Could there be a more convincing way of learning the word "nostalgia"? I can't think of one, if there is.

Wallace Stevens and Marianne Moore joined Shapiro in the *Little Treasury*, as did Yeats, Auden, Delmore Schwartz, and

Robinson Jeffers. There was a Jeffers poem I loved and worked hard to learn. In "Cassandra," he aligns the neglected and misapprehended poet with the sad prophetess, who was doomed never to be believed.

> ...Poor bitch, be wise.
> No: you'll still mumble in a corner a crust of truth, to men
> And gods disgusting. — You and I, Cassandra.

This was heady stuff. Unfortunately, there was never an occasion to show off publicly my memorizing of this or other poems. I would speak them to myself in my room, cast them out to my own pimply, pale reflection, captive in the dresser mirror. How I loved to say the words, "Poor bitch be wise," giving the hard, explosive consonants a Gielgudian oomph, savouring especially the outlaw syllable "bitch," a word that in those days would guarantee severe censure and possibly suspension if you were to speak it too loudly on the school playground. "You and I, Cassandra," I would intone after a dramatic pause, forcing my voice into its lowest register, and feel in that instant connected, umbilically, to that great assembly of artists who, over time, have been scorned and dishonoured in their own countries. I was thrilled to be among them! How lucky I was, I thought to myself, then; how lucky to be such close kin to Robinson Jeffers, how lucky to be a player in the Cassandra league. How lucky, lucky, lucky to be me!

"Of course, psychics make mistakes all the time!" says the seer Laura Kay Prophet, who is wiser than Cassandra, as she is not freighted with the expectation that she will always be believed, nor with the conviction that she will always be right. "All the time!" she reaffirms, making a gentle grab for the fledgling robin who has come to roost on her blonde hair. "I know, because believe me, I've made them all!"

She spills this confession while we are talking in her tiny room in a modest, downtown hotel. It's a hard-times kind of place where the enterprising desk clerks have been known to take advantage of a long-term guest's week-long absence by renting out his room on an hour-by-hour basis to hookers and their tricks. The hallways are wide, but scuzzy and ill-lit. The carpets are a colour not found in nature, and have not been swept or vacuumed in a very long time. But step from the common area into Laura Kay's place, and all the Dickensian gloom metamorphoses into Beatrix Potter cheerfulness. Her cubby is cluttered, but tidy and feminine-looking. It measures, I would guess, nine-by-thirteen feet. There's a long vine, I think a philodendron, trailing along one wall. She has a single bed, a pint-size fridge, a sink, a wardrobe, a chair, a coat tree. The several square feet

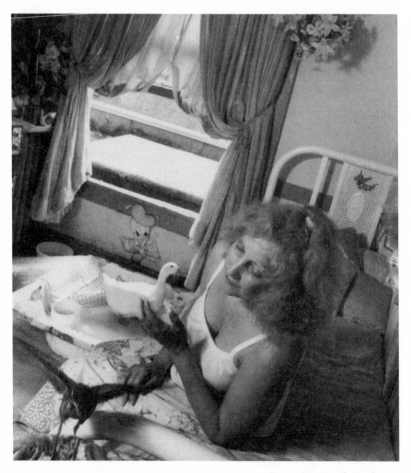

Laura Kay Prophet at home.

of floor space which are uncolonized by such necessary oddments as these are piled high, in an orderly way, with miscel-
laneous possessions. So are the one or two flat and elevated
surfaces. There's not really so very much stuff, but the minute
space available to it gives the impression of volume.

Laura Kay has tried to beautify her room over the four years
of her tenure by painting the walls and hanging pictures and
cultivating plants and so on. She has finally given up on such
decorating initiatives because every time she gets things just
the way she likes them, a bathtub will overflow upstairs, and
there'll be a flood that will come through the ceiling and ruin
everything, and she'll have to fight with the management to get
it all put right, so really, what's the point? She doesn't like to
press too hard, because she can't risk eviction. Finding another
place would be difficult, since Laura Kay comes with landlord-
aggravating encumbrances and attachments, of which the robin,
with its speckled breast and its cunning trill, is a transient
example. The robin was given to her a week or so ago by a couple of winos who found it after it fell from its nest. They brought
it to her to nurture. Besides the hookers, there are lots of winos
on this stretch of Granville Street, and many of them have tender hearts. A few know about Laura's way with birds. They
have brought her starlings before, too. The robin won't be here
much longer, as it is only a few days shy of being able to fend
for itself. It has made tremendous progress with its flying technique. It flutters about from corner to corner quite happily, with
little recuperative station stops such as the one it has just made
on Laura Kay's noggin. Laura takes the bird on her finger. It
looks her in the eye, leans back its little head, and gargles.

"She's hungry again. Do you want to feed her?"

"Sure."

This is just like a petting zoo! Laura takes a bag of wieners
from her fridge, removes one, slices off a sliver. She shows me
how to break it into pinhead-size pieces and foist the dainty
morsels directly down the robin's throat, which is not as easy to
do as she makes it seem. Then she cuts the remaining meat into

bigger cubes and offers them to Bob. Bob, who is a duck, all dressed in white like a first-communicant, and with a bright yellow bill, gets up out of her wading pool, shakes her little tail, and marches over for her treat, not even breaking stride to noisily expel a stream of liquid brown shit. I am having an education. For one thing, I am surprised at the size of the bird. It's dimensions verge on the goose-ish. That ducks are hot-dog eaters is also a revelation to me. What's more, I have never before seen one excrete at such close quarters. I'm amazed as all heck at the rapid liquidity of the operation, and even though my first thought is that this is surely the kind of incident that might invite managerial wrath, I decide it is my role as a guest to radiate nonchalance, as though this is something that is part of my everyday life as a convinced city dweller. As it turns out, the mess is in no way a problem. It's part and parcel of living with a duck, which I guess I should have figured. It goes with the territory. This, of course, is why the floor of the room is covered with plastic sheeting. Laura rips off a length of paper towel from a roll she keeps handy for just such mishaps, and wipes it up. Presto, it's gone, you'd never know it had been there. As I said, her place is scrupulously neat, and the duck, as it turns out, is as vigilant about such sanitary concerns as is her mistress.

"All my kids are well trained, that's for sure," Laura boasts as she disposes of the towel. "They like cleanliness around them. When we're going along the sidewalk and Bobby makes a poo, she stands right beside it and quacks till I come back to clean it up. Excuse me," she says, and interrupts the flow of the conversation to offer a smidgen of chocolate to her gerbil. Apparently, it is in need of such small consolations as this, for it has been depressed since it was displaced from a more palatial cage by the arrival of two chinchillas. A baby robin, an adult duck and its wading pool, two chinchillas in a stately pleasure dome, a pining gerbil in reduced circumstances, Laura Kay, and me: what a jolly confabulation on a weekday afternoon! Oh — there are also some goldfish, paddling in a largish aquarium.

Laura Kay Prophet and her duck — sometimes, ducks —

have been a fixture in downtown Vancouver for years now. I first met her in 1992. At that time, she was mostly seen on fashionable Robson Street. She would set up shop on the sidewalk in a sheltered spot where she would not obstruct pedestrian traffic, and hang a little placard to advertise her services as a clairvoyante. The duck, an eye-catching prop as well as a faithful companion, would watch from the buggy in which Laura used to push him to and from work. I happened to be living nearby, and would often pass her on my perambulations round about the neighbourhood. I grew accustomed to seeing her there, and came to regard her as one of the more colourful pieces of the urban jigsaw, like the one-tune harmonica player, and the tanned man who sat day after day at the same table outside the same coffee shop, conventionally dressed but for women's shoes and pantyhose, and the twins who looked like the Pillsbury Doughboy and who still wore quilted parkas when most people had switched to shorts. I would see the occasional passer-by stop to seek advice from the sidewalk psychic: tourists with video cameras wanting something out of the ordinary to show the folks back home, or packs of frisky young girls from the suburbs having a giggle with their friends before getting the bus back to Surrey, and so on.

I had recently misplaced my boyfriend and was holding open auditions to secure a replacement. One night, heading home from a song-and-dance session with a promising candidate, I saw Laura Kay sitting in a jeweller's doorway, with her duck at her side, and with time on her hands. I had spoken to her before, just to say hello, or to talk with her about my dog, of whom she was fond, and once I had taken one of her brochures. They were tiny and blue, and contained a capsulized version of her story, beginning with the sentence, "Laura Kay Prophet, a spinster, was born in Sudbury in 1941." That night, when I thought that love might be in the air, was the first time I'd stopped to inquire what the future might hold.

"What's his name?" she asked, when I had explained something of the investigation I hoped she would undertake.

I told her. She took out a pencil and a pad of paper, and began to sketch a goofy cartoon with quick short lines. She talked while she drew.

"Oh! He's *nice*-looking. Strong chin?"

"Yes."

"Dark hair?"

"Yes."

"Very nice! Very, very — Oh. Oh, well. Too bad. Not him. No. Nothing's going to happen."

And she was right, just as she was right the next time, and the next time, and the next. I began to make a habit of seeking her counsel whenever romantic attachment loomed, and always it was the same routine with the same result. The pencil, the pad, the quick cartoon, a wistful smile and a business-like shake of the head. Nope! Not this time. She never apologized for delivering up such sad news, and there was no reason why she should have done so. If it wasn't what I wanted to hear, well, that was nothing to do with her. She was just the messenger, innocent of judgment and malice. She said what she saw or heard — from what source came this news I was never sure — and it was up to the client to believe or disregard as he or she saw fit.

You and I, Cassandra.

Time passed. I formed an attachment with someone about whom I never sought psychic advice. We moved from the neighbourhood. For a couple of years, I saw nothing of Laura Kay. Sometimes I wondered idly where she might be living — when I first met her she and her menagerie were boarding at the Y — and if she was even still in town. During our conversations she had told me that she saw very clearly how she was not long for the city, that she would soon buy a winning lottery ticket, would become an overnight mogul, a millionaire ten times over, and would move to the country. There, she would have a big house, and use it to provide shelter for the families who would be devastated by the earthquake she also knew was in the offing. In this prediction, at least, she was in complete accord with the conventional wisdom offered up by geophysicists, *vis-à-vis* the tectonic future of the West Coast. Laura's specific vision had a Hollywood intensity about it. She saw how Nelson Street (a major east–west thoroughfare) would become a corridor of flames because of exploding gas lines. She saw sheets of plate glass detaching themselves from post-modern skyscrapers all throughout the downtown area, and falling like jagged guillotine blades, delivering fatal nicks to the unfortunates walking beneath. Her eyes, as she told me this, had a fixed and staring quality, as though she might be watching a disaster movie. I remember thinking that it was not so very unlikely a scenario, and was actually jarred into putting together an earthquake survival kit, which, if memory serves, consisted of several bottles of Perrier and many tins of smoked oysters. I was better prepared for unexpected company than for the trembling of the ground, but that's always been my little way. Several people suggested I should track her down when I began my eccentrics hunt. I wrote "Find Laura Kay" on my mental "to do" list. Over the next several months, it would surface for review, then sink again.

Late in the fall of 1996, troubled by a word-processing–induced numbness in my left arm, I began some massage therapy treatments. I was walking along Robson Street after the first of these sessions, heading east towards the office in the vaguely altered state of mind that can settle on one after being forcefully and corporally manipulated by a complete stranger. I was floating over the pavement, calm as a clam, meditating on the koan "The medium is the massage," when, at the corner of Granville Street, I crossed paths with a woman carrying a shopping bag across which was emblazoned the single word "Bliss." This was almost as happy an encounter as my long-ago meeting with "nostalgia." The cosmos hummed all the louder when she passed me by, and who should prove to be travelling in her slipstream but Laura Kay Prophet, looking as blonde and as fresh and as sweet as ever she did. Laura Kay, with her amazingly youthful skin, and her sweet, sweet smile, as *bright as the*

coming forth of the morning, in the cloud of an early shower.
The medium and the massage. You could have knocked me over
with a feather.

Feathers were once an important part of her psychic regalia.
That was back in the days of Harvey, who was her duck before
Webster and Holly, who were her ducks before Bob. "God
always gives me ducks," she tells me, while preparing a tomato
and lettuce salad for Bob, "and He always gives me miracle
ducks. Even though I love them, I sometimes say, 'God, why
me? Why ducks?' They cost me a fortune, and not just in
money, either. I pay the price of my privacy. It's like having a little baby. You can never be away from them, and you can't just
trust any sitter to look after them. Believe me, there are things
I'd rather be doing than spending my whole day wiping up duck
shit, but I'm never gone for more than two hours, and when we
go out together we have to walk. You can't take a duck on the
bus. I could in Calgary, but not here. Not in Vancouver."

It was while living in Calgary, in 1980, back in the days
when she had an apartment in a nice high-rise, that Laura Kay
hooked up with Harvey. He was the first of the several fowls
who have complicated and enriched her life on earth. She pref-
aces her story with the caveat that it might sound crazy, but this
is exactly how it happened. Laura learned through a dream that
she would have a duck who would be both magic and lucky.
One day she visited a hatchery. Baby ducks were being pulled
from the incubator. The operations supervisor would not let her
take just one chick. He told her she must leave with two. She
selected a runt who was cute, but who was destined not to live
for more than a few weeks. The hatchery man insisted she take
a big bruiser of a duckling he picked out for her, and this was
Harvey. It was not long before Harvey began to show just how
wondrous a creature he was. For one thing, he seemed to live in
a state of perpetual moult. He was forever shedding his feathers, of which he had a great many more than the average duck.
He could easily cast off a hundred on any given day. As well,
these feathers turned out to be more than commonly lucky. The

first of Harvey's miracles was that people's wishes came true when they made them on his feathers.

"If I told you some of the things, you wouldn't believe me."

"Try me."

"Okay, but you have to remember that these are miracles, and miracles don't make sense. You have to remember that nothing is impossible, just improbable."

And she tells about how wishes made on Harvey's feathers brought together young lovers. She tells about an old lady who'd been sick all winter and who was finally well enough to go out and who started going to bingo again, and who always lost until she got a feather, at which point she began to win every time. She won so much and she won so often that she came back for more feathers. She would take them to the games and share her luck, would rub Harvey's plumage on the shoulders of the people playing around her, and they started winning, too. And once — this was after she and Harvey moved to Vancouver — she got to talking to some boys who were skating on the Robson Square rink. One told her that he had a wish, but that it was impossible. "Only improbable," she assured him, and he went home with a Harvey token. A few months later, he found her again, and told her what had happened. His mother had died, and the impossible wish he had made on the feather had been to see her again, just once more. He was having a terrible time at school. One day he came home, downtrodden and discouraged and full of hurt, and there was his mother. She was standing before him, "as real as if she could have been real, as if he could touch her and everything, and she said, 'Everything is going to be all right, dear, I'm always with you, even though you can't see me, and you know I love you.' And then she just sort of evaporated."

Harvey also had the miracle of healing. Once, for instance, Laura and Harvey were in a welfare office in Vancouver, and they met a little girl who was wearing winter gloves, even though it was the middle of summer. Laura always knew when to expect a healing episode, because a deep, booming voice would alert her before she left the house that one was scheduled for that day. She had had such a warning and sensed that this child was to be the recipient of the miracle. Laura approached her.

"Would you like to pet the duck? He's magic, you know."

Her father wasn't keen. He explained that for the last several months the child had been plagued by blisters on the backs of both her hands. The little girl removed one glove, and there were indeed lesions that were horrible to behold. The doctors had been powerless to help.

"But I still told her to pet him, to feel his nice feathers. Harvey was just full of healing energy. His feet and his bill were unbelievably hot with it, like they were on fire, and when people were around he'd just squat and let them touch him, sometimes several at a time. It was like he was meditating. He did a lot of meditating, even at home, and this whistling sound would come out of him, kind of like: O-o-o-o-o. O-o-o-o-o. Anyway, he sat there, very still, and she petted him, and she laughed, and the next day I got a phone call from her mother. I'd given the father a card with my number. She told me that when the little girl got up that next morning her hands were healed. Her mother said, 'Jesus healed you. Praise the Lord.' And her daughter said, 'No, it wasn't Jesus. It was Harvey the Duck.' And you know, it never occurred to me to get their last name or telephone number to ask them if we could publicize this and do the media thing, so that I could maybe make some money. I mean, these ducks eat me out of house and home. They are terribly wasteful. Really, there are times when I wind up eating their leftovers!

"Harvey's third miracle was that he came to talk. I'd always known he was going to, but I couldn't understand how. It didn't make sense to me. The first few times I thought I was hearing things, but he did learn to say his name. He would say 'Harv, Harv.' And if I left the room, he'd go 'Mom! Mom!' And if you gave him a treat, he'd say 'W-o-o-o-w.' Of course, he didn't do it every time; when the media were around he'd never say it."

Harvey died in her arms on his sixth birthday, in April

1986. His spirit returned to her almost immediately in the form of a baby pigeon someone brought her to look after, although she didn't know at the time the baby bird was a revenant. It was only afterwards, when she thought of how it had gone straight away for Harvey's favourite toys, and how it shared Harvey's habit of watching her out of one eye, that she understood he had returned to her as a sign, a reassurance that their connection was far from severed. In the very near future, Harvey will be with her again, first as Harvey II, and then as Harvey III. Harvey III will be the big miracle, his healing power intensified many times over.

For the nonce, though, there is Bob, who has the miracle of tears. When Bob began to ovulate, she had a very hard time of it. Her eyes would stream for half an hour before and half an hour after laying an egg. The vet has witnessed this anomaly, and even tried to take a photograph of it, but for some reason wasn't able to. And before Bob, there was the tandem team of Webster and Holly. They came along in 1988, and were given to her by a couple of kids who couldn't properly see to their needs. Both ducks were gravely ill when they came to Laura, but she nurtured them till they were whole, and well enough to fulfil their rakish destinies.

"I had a dream they were coming, and I knew the male would be called Webster. Now, the spirits had told me that he was going to be an artist, and I thought, 'Oh great, he's going to make some great little abstracts and I'll get some money off of them.' One day I said to him, 'You're supposed to be an artist, so paint a picture.' And all I did was to put down the background. I spread it on a big paper with my hand, and he walked through the paint, and when he finished there was an amazing painting, with himself at the top, as a duck, but he was a duck that had artist clothes on: the baggy trousers, and the belt hanging. That was like his penis. He was oversexed. I felt sorry for Holly. He drew Holly facing him as a pretty girl, because she was beautiful. That was all she had going for her. She was not sweet-tempered, she was always bitching about something. Then there was a picture of me, kind of looming at the side, and you could see their special cup, the one with the Christmas goose on it, and he did the vines we had in the kitchen then. I was amazed at the detail. I mean, there was muscle tone! I can't even paint that well, and I'm quite a good artist. It took him about three minutes. He always did a poor piddle on the paper first, so I'd have to wipe it up. It would make a smear, which would become part of the painting, and also his signature!"

Laura Kay shows me a photograph of one of Webster's paintings, and with her guidance I can see how it looks sort of like a clown. She is skilled at interpreting this kind of symbology, since the cartoons she draws as a vehicle for expressing her clairvoyance look like so much hen scratch until she tells you what the various lines and curlicues signify. This she will do in a voice that is, by her own description, like a little girl's. There is much about Laura that is childlike, but she is not an innocent. She has lived for years in this flophouse hotel on a dangerous street, has seen plenty of unsavoury comings and goings, and has developed the set of survival skills you require when you live on and from the streets. There was a time when she supported herself as an exotic dancer, doing a Salome routine with seven veils. She's nobody's fool, she knows where to find the bottom line, and she can look after herself. At the same time, she has managed to hang on to an essential optimism that is both charming and, in some ways, alarming. She has made her little room into an enchanted forest where miracles are commonplace, a place of hanging vines, singing robins, magic ducks, flouncy curtains, and granted wishes. It is a mean place with which she has done her best and that she knows is just a stop along the way to something altogether more glorious. "I've got no damn past that's interesting," she says, "and my present is hell, so the future is all I've got to look forward to. I say, hey! there are better days ahead."

In fact, her past, as she relates it, is far from dull. It has about it the fairy-tale quality of her here and now, and like many such tales it contains more than a whiff of adversity. Once upon a time there was a pretty little girl called Betty. Her father was in the navy. The family travelled. They moved every year until she was five or so. Then, they settled in Edmonton, where her memories really begin. Some are happy. Many are not. Her mother liked to flirt, and when she flirted it was with intent. When her father found out she was sleeping around, he'd be furious. Her mother learned to save herself by diverting his anger. She would push little Betty at the raging man. He liked to beat her with his belt. Years and years later, she would say that it was as if there was something almost sexual about those whippings. He would take the strap to her while she lay naked on his bed. She couldn't understand why her parents treated her like this. She did her best to be good. She worked hard at being good. She loved them, but, over time, her heart grew full of rage.

One night, when she lay in her own bed, covered in welts, she had the first of two white-light experiences. An angel, maybe it was even God, came into her room and enveloped her in a warm, loving hug. The light spoke to her in a voice that was deep, fatherly, and genuine. Betty understood instinctively then that the man who beat her was not her real father. No, it was this kind visitor who was her true parent. He had come to show her how her life was going to be. He showed her everything, and it was like watching a movie. She saw that she would have to stay nearby her parents for the first thirty years of her life, even though they would abuse her and call her "it." She saw how they would treat her like a slave, like Cinderella, saw how her mother would try to keep her down, would not allow her to grow up. She saw that she would eventually get away from them and forge her own life. She understood that she was there to serve them as scapegoat, that their cruelty came from their own deep unhappiness, their own frustrated longings. The angel offered her this insight, and all the rage melted from her heart. In the morning, every welt had vanished. It was as if they had never been there.

Betty was a pretty child, with ringlets in her hair. She had lots of energy. She took dance classes and gave recitals. In the sixth grade, she choreographed a ballet for her class that won a prize in a festival. She was fond of singing, and could make her voice heard at the back of the room, without need of amplification. She excelled in athletics, especially the fifty-yard dash. She won track trophies for the school. She was a fine badminton player, unbeatable, even by the boys. She had such stamina and drive that she slept only for a few hours each night. When she grew up and left school, she got a job in an office. She moved from her parents' house into her own apartment, although they did their best to keep their hooks in her. Finally, in order to escape, she had an affair with a man she didn't love, and moved away to Calgary. It didn't last, but it served its purpose. At the age of thirty, she was rid of the family that had never been hers. It happened just as the white light had shown her it would. To make the severance complete, she decided to change her name. She'd had a dream. In this dream there was a big hall full of people, and she was coming up out of the audience to address the crowd. A deep, manly voice announced, "Ladies and gentlemen, the prophet Laura Kay!" He was lifting the veil on what was to be. Her real life could now begin.

After Laura Kay Prophet has told me about her early days, she looks at me and says something that makes me wonder if she might be in league with Elly May, who back in Toronto had confided in me the cosmetic usefulness of spirit gum. "Those lines around your eyes. You know, they're exactly the same as the lines I have. Those are the markings of someone for whom nothing happens in the right time. You see the same thing with a lot of movie stars and big shots. We're the kind of people who come not to have Christmas like everybody else, but to celebrate it in a different way. We're the ones who don't work the usual day jobs. I love stories about people who become something after being nothing, about people whose big chance came along at the worst possible moment, but they made it. Those people have our markings. There are other people with hardly any lines at all, or they might have itty-bitty short lines only.

They're the ones who go to school in the right years, they get courting in the right year, they have the baby in the right year, they get their business developed in the right year, and they drop dead in the right year. Everything happens like it's supposed to! But with us, it doesn't."

Laura Kay thinks a lot about timing, and no wonder. Coming up with an accurate schedule of events is a psychic's greatest challenge. It's one thing to be able to see a sequence of happenings before it unfolds, but pinpointing when that sequence begins and ends and how much time elapses between acts is something else altogether. I am sympathetic to this difficulty, for as Laura and I are talking, I find I have some difficulty keeping track of the chronology of her life and career. Our conversation ricochets so frequently off the signposts of the past, the present, and the future that I'm never sure in what direction I should be looking to see the action. However, I think I have it right when I say that around the time she was preparing to leave Edmonton and discard her family, Laura began to have some health problems. She found her energy was quickly depleted. She lost her motor skills. Sometimes, she couldn't bring a fork to her mouth. There would be days on end when she couldn't get out of bed, when she was so weak she could scarcely raise her arm. She began to have difficulty breathing and swallowing. Sometimes, her vision would blur to the point that she was effectively blind. Her hearing was no longer acute. She would soil herself when she coughed or sneezed. Then she would be well again, although for shorter and shorter periods of time. Doctors, she says, dismissed her complaints, or couldn't come up with a diagnosis. Eventually, she stopped seeking their advice. What good was it doing?

One day, in 1979, when her condition was as bleak as it had ever been, she was visited again by the white light. Again, she was shown the movie of her life. This time, she saw that it was to include these magic ducks, and that many, many miracles would be worked through her agency. She would be the focus of intense media scrutiny. And in order that she be able to sustain all this activity, she would be made well. It would not happen hocus-pocus, holus-bolus all at once, but gradually, in stages and degrees. She was told that she would soon meet a man in a wheelchair, and that if she found out what afflicted him, she would have the name of her illness.

The healing began as soon as the white light left her. It wasn't long before she was up and around. One day, in a nearby park, she met a man in wheelchair. On inquiry, he told her that he had multiple sclerosis. His symptoms were identical to her own. She had never heard of MS before, but was satisfied from his description that his pathology matched her own and that this was indeed the illness from which she had suffered. She was not concerned when he said there was no known cure, for she had the assurance of the angel to the contrary. That was more than fifteen years ago, and the healing is not yet complete. On the day of our meeting, she looks very well, lively, enthusiastic, full of beans. She still has bad days when she must stay in bed, but says her energy reserves are much more quickly replenished. Her breathing is noticeably laboured; it comes sometimes in gasps, and she must use a ventilator to handle the congestion in her lungs and bronchia. One day, though, the affliction will be lifted from her absolutely, and her remission will become permanent. This she deeply believes. This she has been shown. And she has to get her full strength back soon, because she has so much to accomplish before the end of the millennium.

In the present, she is occupied with a foundation she has established, Duck Soup. Through it, she would like to raise money and awareness to ease the plight of the homeless. But if the movie of her life, shown her all those years ago, holds true to the plot as she remembers it, she will soon have much, much more on her plate. She sees that her big lottery win will happen in the near future, and it will be followed by her move to the country. She looks forward to that, to moving into a place where she will have room for all her animals, where she doesn't have to scrub out the fridge and the stove, and clean up the mess from the last people before she can be comfortable. After the country move comes the earthquake. Then she will have to spearhead her humanitarian relief efforts. That will use up most of her money. There will be changes in the feathered personnel, too. Bob, she sees, will pass on. Then Harvey II will materialize. He won't last long, but will die (in a gas leak, she says) to make way for the big miracle of Harvey III. This duck's arrival will usher in a golden age of spiritual growth and renewal, when she will have to deal with the demands put on her by the wide public acclaim that will come her way when she is a celebrated guru, bringing her message of peace and reconciliation to audiences around the world. She sees that she will get caught up in some bad business deals, and at some point will be married to a man she calls "Prince Charming." This is not just a fond endearment, for he is actually of royal blood. He too, she has been shown, will treat her badly. It's a mixed bag, that's for sure, but there is no way out of any of this for Laura Kay. This is the work she is destined to do. She has seen the life she is meant to lead.

"How would you feel," she asks, "if you knew that you were born just to fulfil a prophecy in the Bible for a bunch of weird people who have to see it to believe it?" The prophecy she believes she was born to make flesh is that of Revelation (12:1–2, 5): "And there appeared a great wonder in heaven; a woman clothed with the sun, and the moon under her feet, and upon her head a crown of twelve stars: And she being with child cried, travailing in birth, and pained to be delivered....And she brought forth a man child, who was to rule all nations with a rod of iron: and her child was caught up unto God, and to his throne."

"You don't even know," she says, "the miracles that are going to happen to me. I've already had one. It happened when I was six, and that was walking on air. I've never been able to do it since, although I've been able to levitate off the scale to get myself down by five or six pounds. I know that I am here to walk on air again, and I do it during the time I am preg-a-nant with twins, and Harvey III, yellow as he can be, is walking on air behind me. Harvey III is not a reincarnation of Harvey I and II, but an actual resurrection. He is found by that fountain that's between Christ Church Cathedral and the government building with the number 666, and the man who finds him starts breathing fire as soon as he picks him up. I've seen the headline, 'Fire-breathing Man Finds Duck.' When we walk on air, we are in Toronto, and it's a cold, miserable day. It's standing room only, and you see all the cameras flashing as we walk. I've got this pretty yellow dress, and long ringlets."

"Laura, how old are you now?"

"Fifty-six and a half."

"But pregnancy isn't something that usually happens after you're say, fifty. I mean, unless you really work at it."

"Oh, I know. And I know it sounds crazy. But it's going to happen. I'll be strong and healthy, too. I'll have twins, but the girl will die. The boy will grow up to be a leader among men. He'll marry, and I won't like his wife. I'll die, alone in my bed, at the age of eighty-two. Oh, there'll be lots else, too. So many miracles! You know, my life is full of miracles."

I think about the impossibility–improbability ratio, and look out her window. It gives onto the alley. The view is of brick and of pigeons. It might be bleak, but this room — with its greenery and its wildlife, with its little robin who throbs with new life — has something of the oasis about it. It is peaceful here. Sometimes, the more raucous sounds of Granville Street filter in. A car horn. A harsh curse. Now, an ambulance speeds by, siren howling. It speeds past the drunks and the addicts and the hookers and the runaways, speeds past the doctors and the notaries and the stenos, speeds past everyone doing what we all of us do, in our time, in our way, while we're here, which is nothing more than trying to get by. It speeds past the cheap repertory cinemas where Laura likes to go when she can get a break from Bob, with her emotional and gustatory demands. None of the offerings at any of these theatres is as inventive or as promising as the movie of her future, the pageant of her days yet to come. Nonetheless, she goes and watches the movie of someone else's life for two hours. That's as long as she can risk being away from her duck, but so much can happen in that time. A robin could fall from its nest. A prince might arrive in the lobby, with her name on his lips. Her lottery number might be drawn. She could step back into the street and find the world totally rearranged. She might step into the rainy afternoon only to find she has been given eagle wings to take her to the wilderness. She might step into the chill of the night and find she is a woman clothed with the sun.

La Belle et La Bête

She looked like the picture of a young rapt saint,
lost in heavenly musing.
— Grenville Kleiser, *Fifteen Thousand Useful Phrases*

When I am feeling limber of neck or when the chiropractor tells me I must, I give my head a yogic twist. I look over one shoulder or the other, and study the steady retreat of the present moment. On such Lot's-wife occasions as these, with the panorama of the past in plain view, I like to reflect on my days on earth. Sometimes, I remember a game I enjoyed as a child, a diversion I made up when I was passing through a cumulative-thinking phase. It was a silly solipsistic pastime called "How Much? How Many?" To play, you simply ask yourself as many total-tally questions as you can before you collapse laughing. For example, in my life to date, how much money have I made, how much have I spent, how many people have I met, how many miles have I walked, how many words have I read, spoken, written? You press on in this vein, and the laughter typically comes when you reach the bodily fluid questions. It's always a great time-waster, and I enjoy it until I get around to wondering how many brain cells I've lost, and if they could be amassed and laid end to end would they equal the distance to Moscow, to the moon, or to Mercury. At this point, "How much? How many?" ceases to be amusing, and I hurry to reswivel my head.

The horror! All those brain cells, dead and done, and God only knows what they've taken away with them. So many years in school, and what have I retained of the specific theorems, formulae, and equations I worked so hard to master? What about the dates? The Diet of Worms. The Defenestration of Prague. Where have they gone? Once they were inscribed on the register, but try as I might, I can no longer call them up. Even the nine times-table eludes me, most days. I squeeze and squeeze the constipated medulla, and all that oozes from between its folds is the first stanza of "Excelsior" and four lines of dialogue from a seventh-grade French text I think was called *Parler et lire*.

«Paul et Louise, comment vont-ils?»

«Paul va fort bien, mais Louise est malade.»

«Que c'est dommage!»

«Oh, ce n'est pas grave.»

This dumb blandishment, so seemingly forgettable, was a feature of my very first French lesson. As such, it's taken on a symbolic weight that is disproportionate to its straightforward meaning and narrow import. Over the years, it's become a key I use to unlock the door to what little French remains from the days when I could actually get by. I repeat those few lines over and over, a mantra, a spell, concentrating on their rhythm, their music. I use them to prime the pump, and to invoke the spirits of Paul *et* Louise. Whenever I am in Montreal, I ask them to stand up for me and assist me as I try to negotiate my way through the world in a language that is not my own.

Why I persist with this, I'll never know. *The whole truth, naked, cold, and fatal as a patriot's blade* is that, as a linguistic lubricant, such an exercise is completely ineffective. Paul *et* Louise are of limited utility. They are interested only in talking about their respective states of health. What good are they to me when I have to engage the desk clerk in a mangled back-and-forth about whether or not my room is equipped to handle the requirements of a modem? "Que c'est dommage!" I say when she tells me that, no, their phone lines can't accommodate such a pesky innovation and that, furthermore, the last pernicious asshole who tried to send or receive an e-mail in his room brought the whole system down and caused considerable inconvenience to the hotel management, the other guests, and the phone company, too. "Oh! C'est grave!" I say, sympathetically, and she nods agreement before saying in English, "So don't try it, okay?"

Hélas! It's always this way for me in Montreal, a city that is pretty much my whole experience of Quebec. My conversational partners will put up with my blundering for a minute or two, and then slip into an easy, vernacular English. It invariably happens, and I invariably take it as a stiff rebuke. Would it be too much to play along? I have always been a convinced federalist and booster of official bilingualism. I want to do my bit to sustain the cultural underpinnings of the nation, want to show myself willing to make an extraordinary effort to keep the union from coming unseamed. But every time I am rebuffed, terrible red-neck whinings of the kind usually heard on private radio phone-in shows in Calgary insinuate themselves into my thoughts. "Well, phooey on you, Quebec," I come perilously close to saying. "If no one on your side of the linguistic divide is willing to play along, then what's the point in even trying? Go ahead and cash in your sovereignty chips for all I care!" But then I rally. Ever the optimist, I press on, and continue to measure out my Montreal days in encounters of four lines or less.

"Pourriez-vous me dire où se trouve l'Université de McGill?"

"Oh, sure, just a few blocks further on."

"Merci."

"No prob."

Or:

"Excusez-moi, monsieur, le métro, est-il loin d'ici?"

"Nope. There's the entrance over there."

"Ah, oui. Je vois bien. Merci, monsieur. Vous êtes très gentil. Prière agréer l'expression de mes sentiments les plus respectueux."

"Glad to be of help! Where ya from? Berlin or something?"

Given this history, and my exquisite sensitivity to the mere perception of a slight, you can readily imagine my delight when I called up Sylvie Longpré to request a viewing of her many Barbie dolls, and learned that she speaks almost no English. "Fort bien!" I said, and I meant it, too.

"Pourriez-vous m'expliquer comment je faire pour aller à Repentigny?" I asked the young woman at the car rental. Repentigny is the suburb where Sylvie lives.

"Repentigny? Oh, God. No one goes there. Why would anyone want to go to Repentigny?"

"J'y vais pour voir Barbie."

"Barbie? In this snow? It's your funeral, I guess. Go east on Sherbrooke. It'll take you right there. Eventually."

She was such a supercilious know-it-all that I almost hated to credit how her adumbrations were not without foundation, meteorologically speaking. However, by the time I was willing to say uncle, I was stuck smack dab in the middle of an industrial wasteland, in a blinding blizzard, in an absurdly long line of traffic that was *creeping like a snail, unwillingly to school.* To make things worse, Paul *et* Louise — who were in the back seat — were joined by the ghost of Grenville Kleiser. He was spunky and full of beans and eager to demonstrate that there are many more useful phrases available to conscientious users of the language than the famous 15,000 on which his reputation rests. *The car is like one segment of a parasitic worm clogging the intestine of the highway,* he sang, turning down the radio in order that I might hear him the better. *The traffic-bound drivers are squirming like young rabbits, eager for release from the magician's top hat. All the world is wearing a veil as white and as sticky as that of a young noviciate emptying a honeycomb.*

I was an hour and a half late getting to Sylvie's house. "Je suis désolé d'être tellement en retard," I began, but she kindly deflected all my sorry bleatings by making *ce n'est pas grave* noises. She apologized herself for the inconvenience of the weather, assuming total responsibility for it, the way we all will when we meet someone from away in less than clement circumstances. Sylvie is a lively woman, vibrant and gracious, radiant with good health. She broadcasts the kind of energy that belongs to someone whose reserves are regularly replenished by such vigorous activities as snowmobiling, which she adores. In the summer, she goes boating, and drives her four-by-four on lost and rutted roads. We met on a Friday evening, and she was as perky and outgoing as any human being has a right to be, especially after a long work week of teaching business principles. Her long blonde hair was swept back and held in place with barrettes. Her attractive face had a tan-in-a-tube bronziness about it, and she was very prettily dressed. She wore a navel-exposing white angora halter-top — it was a puffy, girlish aureole, like a dandelion seed-pod — and leopard-skin tights cinched at her tiny waist. She had on open-toed sandals, and she looked exactly like Barbie. Exactly.

In 1995, David Weeks published a book called *Eccentrics: A Study of Sanity and Strangeness*. Dr. Weeks, an American neuro-psychologist working in Edinburgh, observed that psychiatric literature has by and large overlooked eccentricity as a discrete and discernible condition. Three out of four of the best-known standard texts, he noted, made no mention of eccentricity whatsoever, and it had never been described clinically. He set out to remedy the situation, and brought the weight of scientific method to bear on his investigation. My mythopoeic reliance on luck, rumour, and coincidence pales next to his standardized methods of data gathering and analysis. I tried to avoid "in general" reductions, tried to avoid drawing conclusions, while he identifies particular descriptors or signposts of eccentric behaviour. These included devotion to nonconforming behaviour, and a supercharged sense of creativity, curiosity, and idealism. He found that eccentrics often had more than one obsession, were intelligent and confident in their opinions, had peculiar eating habits or living arrangements, were more often single than partnered, and were frequently bad spellers. I suppose I saw signs of many of these symptoms on my travels, save for the spelling, for which ability I didn't have the nerve or foresight to test. I was also struck by the presence of animal companions — cats, in particular — and by the use of clutter as decorating technique; I visited many amply strewn rooms. However, while it piques my interest to see such characteristics spelled out in a list, I remain stubbornly resistant to the idea of delineating an eccentric "norm." It pleased me to see that, if such a thing could be said to exist, Sylvie Longpré deviates from it in several key respects.

Repentigny is a suburb unremarakble in everything save its expansiveness. Sylvie and her co-vivant live on a quiet street in a very spiffy and neatly organized split-level house. It is tasteful in its appointments, subdued even, and you would never be able to guess from a cursory look around the living room or dining room or kitchen anything of the depths of Sylvie's obsession, which has to do with Barbie. There are no framed pictures of Barbie on the walls, no Barbies propped up on chairs, none of the many publications of interest to Barbie aficionados — collector's magazines, sales catalogues, lavish commemorative albums, and so on — fanned on the coffee table. You might note that her boyfriend, Pierre, who is trim, handsome, and neatly coiffed, looks more than a little like Ken. But you won't get the whole picture until he has disappeared downstairs to play with his sound equipment, and Sylvie has led you into the guest bedroom that is Barbie Central. The atmosphere there is hushed and reverential, as it should be. This is her sanctuary. This is where she becomes her truest self: a priestess venerating a goddess who is infinite in her incarnations, and in whose being the perfection of all possibilities is manifest. Barbie complete. Barbie regenerative. Barbie forever.

Now, there are plenty of Barbie enthusiasts in the world. I've met several of them, women and men both. They have Web sites and newsletters. They hold international conferences. They talk knowledgably and often about the arcane minutiae that is the basis of their shared experience: such things as dates of issue and regional variants in product and the small defects of packaging that can greatly enhance the value of a doll. Packaging overall is important. Take Barbie from her box, and the second she hits the air, her value goes down by twenty per cent. They all know the Barbie gospel, know that she was first marketed by Mattel in 1959 (one year after the birth of Sylvie), and right from the beginning she was a hit. Right from the beginning, she was desired. Of course she was! Everything about her appealed to collectors with a populist sensibility. As collectibles go, she is pretty darn democratic. There is enough "Barbie-ana" that is accessible and cheap to allow anyone to make a start, and there is enough that is rare and far-flung and impossibly expensive that you always have something to hope for, a reason to persist in your quest, a Grail to hold in your sights. You can be as expansive or as focused as you wish, for Barbie is bigger than Barbie alone. Barbie is also Ken and Skipper and Midge and Francie and Ellie and Teresa and Julia and Steven and all the other friends and hangers-on of diverse colours and abilities that she has admitted to her magic circle over the years. Barbie is All Of Us, and herein lies the reason behind her tremendous and enduring, her almost mystical magnetism. She is perfect, immaculate, and eternal. She is sister and mother, sun and moon. She is yin and yang, animus and anima. She is every ethnicity, she is all things womanly, the universal feminine principle. She is the source of our nourishment, though not one single drop of milk has ever been wrung from her impossibly conical, rigid

Sylvie Longpré in Barbie Land.

breasts. She is the ideal date, though never has a tongue — not Ken's, not even her own — slipped between her lips. Why would she need a tongue? Her communication is instant and telepathic. Intact and impenetrable, she is the fecund virgin who never stops giving birth. She is the tangle of incongruities that makes perfect sense. She is logic and confusion. She is Love. In a word, she is Barbie.

As we entered the temple, Sylvie apologized for certain lamentable absences. Some of her dolls, the rarest of the rare, were on loan to an important toy show at Olympic Stadium. She sat on the floor and motioned for me to do likewise. This was not as straightforward as it sounds. It required very careful positioning. There was not a surfeit of unstaked turf. There were collectible Barbies beaming from their boxes, and there were the free-range Barbies who were out and about, striding fearlessly through the world. Here was Barbie in one of her several dream houses, casually dressed as though for a picnic, coming down a spiral staircase to greet her friends, all of them looking up at her adoringly. There was Barbie emerging from a stable into her corral, a cowgirl for all seasons, and with roping and branding on her mind. If she were to be diverted from her purpose (which could never happen, her concentration is that pure), and if she were to look to her right or to her left, she would see herself laughing in a snowmobile, or speeding along in a flashy car. She would see herself swaddled in surgical greens, ready to perform a delicate surgery, or dressed for a wedding, her own, of course. Flight attendant, lawyer, teacher, lifeguard, missionary: there was nothing she couldn't do or be, since, for Barbie, thought and action are one. She only has to wish for it, and it is so. Ballerina Barbie, Hawaiian Barbie, Superstar Barbie, Beach Fun Barbie, Equestrienne Barbie, Disco Barbie, Club California Barbie, Gold Medal Skier Barbie, they were all there. It was grand! In the middle of January, in the middle of Repentigny, I'd fallen down the rabbit hole and ended up in Barbie Land, in the country of one citizen. I felt overcome with the same vertigo that seizes me when I look in one of those image-duplicating fun-house mirrors. I put down my right hand to steady myself and felt the digging of ten perfect toes against my palm. To whom could they belong? Why, to Barbie, of course. And what was she wearing? A pretty angora halter-top sweater, leopard-skin tights, and sandals. Her hair was held back with barrettes. *Déjà vu*. Where had I seen such an outfit before?

Outside, the storm raged. Inside, Sylvie talked, and the torrent of her words had a "leaves that before the wild hurricane fly" quality to them. She had so much to say about Barbie, so much to show me. Look at this one, see how her legs bend, that's what makes her special. And with this one it's the bangs that are important, and with this one it's her bubble cut. There were Barbies from every land, Australian Barbie, Korean Barbie, even Inuit Barbie. Every so often I would ask a question in my misshapen French, and Sylvie would graciously answer, though sometimes a mist of puzzlement would cloud her blue eyes, as though I had posed a non sequitur. Which probably I had, a consequence of not having taken in everything that had gone before. Sylvie's speech was rapid and colloquial. Still, I think I got the gist of it.

It was her mother, Audette, who launched Sylvie on her Barbie path when she was a little girl. That's a familiar story. Millions could tell it. Unlike most of her contemporaries, Sylvie never passed out of the phase, never lost her fondness for the doll. Her fascination began to compound as she grew older and she started acquiring more and more Barbies (and Skipper and Midge and all the gang) along with their licensed accessories. Nor was this so very bizarre. If one has the constitution of a collector, then that acquisitive urge will find an out. Teaspoons, vintage aircraft, salt and pepper shakers, Barbies: there's nothing that distinguishes one from the other in any moral or procedural sense. Whatever the object of your affection, you develop a keen eye, and a specialized, spongy intelligence, a breadth of knowledge, and a cool savvy.

Sylvie is steeped in Barbie lore. She knows every pertinent detail about Barbie's early days as a fashion queen, knows that her "Gay Parisienne" outfit was a pin-dot taffeta bubble dress in deep blue, along with a veiled hat in blue tulle, a rabbit-fur stole, long white tricot gloves, open-toed pumps, pearls and matching earrings, and a gold velvet clutch. Ask and she will be able to tell you about Ken's bath-time "Terry Tog" assemblage that came out in 1961: the blue terry robe with the "K" monogram, the white briefs, the tie belt, the blue sponge, the bar of pink soap, the razor, the comb, the slippers. She will know about how the "His" on his towel washed out if you weren't careful. You could not stump her with a question pertaining to the components of the "Leather Limelight" ensemble, or Francie's "Fur-Out" costume. Sylvie knows it all.

I liked Sylvie very much. I was charmed by her, completely caught up in the leghold trap of her enthusiasm. I was struck by her intelligence and good humour, but mostly by her depth of feeling. She spoke so lovingly, so breathlessly about Barbie, and about all the confections within her collection. Her eyes at times would roll back in her head as she described the profound, the really sensual pleasure that was hers when she found an elusive doll or wardrobe item to supplement her huge holdings. Listening to Sylvie talk was like witnessing the donning of a mantle of holiness, like watching a transcendent moment in *The Song of Bernadette*. But what really sets her apart from the garden-variety Barbie enthusiast is that the doll has become her role model. Unlike Pinocchio, the puppet/doll who wanted to become a real live boy, Sylvie, a flesh-and-blood woman, wants to become a real Barbie. More than a doll, she is an object of emulation. The angora sweater/leopard-skin tights combo was just one of many Barbie-inspired ensembles Sylvie owns, and costume is not the whole extent of it.

Every waking day, when she goes out into the world, Sylvie does her best to lead a Barbie kind of life. She gets up in the morning and fixes her hair. She owns several wigs, made in Italy, that she can style to match the Barbie do of the moment. She goes to her closet and decides what to wear. Many of her clothes have been made by her mother and are exact duplicates, in their every particular, of Barbie's outfits. She has done her best to match the jewellery too, as well as the shoes, the handbags. She also has some of the more exotic collations, that are not strictly suitable as classroom attire, like the all-white, all-fur trappings of Snow Queen Barbie. Before Sylvie leaves for work, she must walk her two dogs, Charlie and Stinger. They are Afghan hounds, which she acquired after Barbie turned up on the shelves with Afghan hounds. She kisses Pierre–cum–Ken goodbye and gets into her car. It is a Corvette. You needn't wonder why she drives a Corvette.

"But don't people think you're crazy?" I asked.

"Sure, they do! They have every right to think I'm crazy, just as I have every right to do what makes me happy. It's just the way I am. I see someone I admire and I want to become that person. I study every detail — her walk, her make-up, her style of dress — and then I copy it. I've just always loved Barbie. I feel comfortable in her skin. I make friends this way. It makes people smile. Children love it. Sometimes, I even go to visit them in the hospital. You should hear the little girls when they see Barbie come in the door. You should hear how they laugh!" She laughed herself and *let the soft waves of her deep hair fall like flowers from Paradise.*

Another "symptom" of eccentricity, or at least one that I observed, is a "greater than average need to exert control over an environment." Think of Charles Henry Danielle, determined to manipulate every detail of his laying-out and his funeral. Think of Fred Sauer, with the happy clutter of his inventions and his need to know whether or not Big Dukie's in Bed. Think of Glenn Gould, how he guarded his own privacy, shut people out, and called his friends at his own convenience, at two, three, four in the morning. Think of Sylvie Longpré, with her great sense of fun and style, and her commanding eye for detail, investing her considerable energy and imagination in the decorating of her temple, and in the crafting of a world where perfection is, in fact, attainable; a Barbie world where no hair is ever out of place, no nail is ever chipped, no dream is ever dashed. Barbie is a garden where fantasies grow. Barbie is a moulded palimpsest on which Sylvie can write the story of her own life. Why not have what Barbie has: independence; loyal friends; fast cars; great hair; a good man with limited ambition, a sculpted chest, and rock-hard thighs; and her own body that will never, ever change? All this, and universal adoration, too. Life as Icon is not without its appeal.

Sylvie told me as I was leaving, and as I was apologizing yet again for my broken French, that she wishes she had more English. She feels trapped, sometimes, for where can she go outside of Quebec and feel confident that she will be understood? The U.S. is problematic, no one speaks her language there. She was planning to attend a big Barbie congress in Detroit, and she wondered how that would go, how easy a time she would have of it. Heavens, even Toronto would be dodgy from the point of view of language. Not that her life is ever dull when she just stays put. Far from it! She can get in her Corvette any old time and head out of town, get in some off-road motoring, some snowmobiling, some boating. And there will always be subliminal escapes via Barbie. Barbie is an astronaut. Barbie is a time traveller. Barbie thinks nothing of changing the colour of her skin. Barbie adapts herself to any linguistic circumstance. Barbie does everything except get older. What if she did? What would she look like at forty? Fifty? What would be the complexion of Pensioner Barbie? Through Sylvie Longpré, goddess made woman, come to live on earth among us as Barbie's exact contemporary, we might yet find out. I told her *merci*, I wished her *bonne nuit. She seemed happy as a wave that dances on the sea.*

Outside, deep snow. Inside, the lights clicked off in the dream house. I watched them wink out, one by one by one. I wondered, as I stood in the dark and scraped the ice from the windshield with a credit card, what it was about Sylvie — other than language — that made her seem so very Quebec. Could she exist anywhere else? Was she, just maybe, a product of the "distinct society" about which we've heard so very, very much?

Oh-oh! Distinct society! It had been my hope that nowhere in these pages would I use those words in tandem, and now I've gone and done it. May I say how sorry I am? I thought I'd make it through without such a spillage. Anyone who spends more than five minutes in Canada and who pays even the scantiest attention to the ongoing and incredibly tedious bun toss that passes for secessionist–federalist dialogue in this country will appreciate how the rhetorical moo of "distinct society" can coax the gag reflex into dancing a hornpipe. Like most of the catch-phrases that are conceived by policy wonks, gestated in think-tanks, and then forced upon the public for suckling, "distinct society" has come to mean too much and too little. It is intended, of course, to have some bearing on the thwarted aspirations and disputations of Quebec. But by now, so many politicians and patriots and academics and commentators have passed that way and sown their seed in its soil, and so much has grown from it that is hybrid and out of control, that it has become impossible to penetrate the brambles. "Distinct society." What does it mean? Language, religion, the Napoleonic Code, the ready availability of the cholesterolic mess called "poutine," the creative use of greystone, shelves of liquor in the grocery stores, the absence of newspaper boxes on the streets of Montreal, and the fact that you can't turn right on a red but can still smoke in a restaurant: any of these might be trotted out to demonstrate that this place is essentially different from the rest of the country. Just try it, though, and see what a hoo-ha ensues! See what a lot of scrabbling and hoarding and bean-counting and recrimination-tossing gets loosed. It's been going on for centuries. It will never, ever change. Every goddam year we're subjected to yet another take on "Hey, ho, away we go, donkey riding, donkey riding." It makes one pine for Greenland.

I am one of those Canadians who has never lived in the province of Quebec but for whom an open-handed and unstinting acceptance of the notion of "distinct society" has never been a question, issue, problem. Lamentably, I am also a simpleton whose opinion counts for nothing, and properly so. I can't explain my feelings in this regard in a way that will make any difference to anyone. I go to Quebec and my response to the place is both psychic and visceral. Distinct? Sure it is! But I could never support the ringings in my ear or the rumblings in my gut that tell me this is so in a debate or other public forum, could never validate them in the way one must by pointing to the demonstrable or the quantifiable. What do I feel? *Je ne sais quoi*. It's the surge beneath my feet, the direction of the wind, the colour of the river, the slant of sleet and snow. And more than anything else, it's the clothes on people's backs.

Yes, when all is said and done, it's fashion more than anything that makes my barometer of distinctiveness point to "really, really, really different." I walk along St-Denis or St-Laurent, look in the stores and the restaurants, study what people are wearing, and time and time again it is driven home to me that, even if I could speak flawless, Quebec-accented French, I would never belong here. Not only am I too Anglo in speech and outlook, I am too dumpy by half, too much of a shlump, and there is nothing God nor make-over specialist could do to change that. I hasten to add that this is not a class distinction, not some white-collar Sunday-afternoon-at-the-gallery, Saturday-night-on-the-Main phenomenon. I notice it everywhere: on the Metro, in the library, even here, in a dough-nut shop on Beaubien, in Montreal's gritty east side. The place is inhabited by senior citizens, women for the most part. Each and every one of them sports something deliberately distinctive, like a pretty aquamarine scarf, or a shocking-pink tam, or a slightly outlandish set of spectacles: cat's eyes, rhinestones. They are fun-loving gals and you can tell from their easy banter with the waitresses that they are regulars here. They are gossiping avidly about the tabloid news. While I wait to make the rendezvous that has brought me to this unlikely place — unlikely for me, anyway; I don't even like doughnuts — I eavesdrop on their to and fro, and learn more than I ever thought I might about the pop diva Céline Dion and her alleged difficulties achieving gravidity.

"She needs to put on weight!" says one.

"She needs to spend more time at home!" says another.

"Her husband is not so young any more!" says a third, and they all fall about, cackling.

Distinct society? Can anyone imagine a clutch of women of similar age and circumstances sitting in a Salisbury House in Winnipeg or a Tim Horton's in Ottawa and carrying on in the same clucking and maternal and uproarious way about Alanis Morissette? Or Anne Murray, God save us. It would never happen. They could never care enough. Québécois(es) are legendary for their loyalty to their home-grown talent. They ply their indigenous celebrities with all the fawning courtesies and teasing disrespect that elsewhere in the world would be accorded only to royalty and truly international film stars. So caught up am I in the tragedy of Céline and her putative infertility that I don't even feel the earth tremble when the man I am here to meet comes through the door, surveys the scene, and makes his way in my direction. He knows where to go. It doesn't take him a second to spot the stranger, the one who obviously doesn't belong, the one who smells like an Englishman. With a Fee, and a Fie, and a Fo, and Fum, he comes, he comes, he comes, he comes, a Golem of a man who, seen from a satellite, might be mistaken for a European principality. Mountainous Andorra, maybe. He comes lumbering in my direction, rending the air before him, pushing his mass through the narrow spaces between the tables like an ice-breaker smashing its way through the floes.

Enter the Great Antonio, senior citizen, neighbourhood landmark, and living legend. Enter the Great Antonio, with his ankle-length, Rasta-thick braid tucked inside his blue parka, and the Ionic columns of his legs contained by an enormity of denim. Enter the Great Antonio, The World's Strongest Man, all 510 pounds of him, the very man who once fought eighteen wrestlers in a single ring in Fort Worth, Texas. And won. Enter the Great Antonio with his green garbage bag full of newspaper clippings tucked under his arm, the Great Antonio, six feet, four inches, who claims to be descended from extraterrestrials, who is as tough and as unplaned and as lumpen as a meteor latterly fallen to earth. With his white haystack of a beard and his gorgeous turnip of a nose (*covered with vegetation in wild luxuriance*) he might be a root cellar made animate. He is a force of nature, he is the reason we have the word "monolithic," he is hoarily alpine, he is his very own distinct society, and he has come here for one reason only. He has come here to talk. To me. He has come here to talk to me in English.

"Hello," I say brightly, "you must be the Great Antonio."

"YES! I am G-r-r-r-r-e-e-e-a-a-a-t ANTONIO!"

All of his verbal artillery is high decibel and rapid fire, but certain words seem to shoot from him with the weight and velocity of cannon balls. I hold my smile and extend my hand. He ignores it. He yanks back the table as far as it will go without toppling over the doughnut eaters who are adjacent to us. He wedges himself in next to the wall, squeezes into a space that is scarcely wide enough to accommodate both him and his shadow, and hovers for an instant over the long banquette that is about to receive the gift of his bulk. He lets gravity take over, shudders into a hunkering posture, quivers as he lands and his mass spreads out like a jelly salad, untimely sprung from its mould onto a too-warm plate. He begins to fuss with his bag, muttering as he removes its rolled and wadded contents. I try to pick up the conversation, and am taken aback at the sound of my voice as it falls from my mouth. I am nauseatingly chipper, and I start to blather with the forced cheerfulness of a dental assistant reassuring a patient before a root canal.

"It's so good to meet you, everyone has told me so much about you. Can I get you a cup of coffee? A doughnut, maybe?"

"NO! Not now COFFEE! Coffee LATER! Now, you SIT! You SIT, I SHOW!"

"Heh, heh, heh. Why, sure!"

In short order, his biography lies before me. The table is stacked, is overbrimming with prunings from the world press. There are sheaves and sheaves of clippings, originals, photocopies, all well examined, some smudgy with thumb prints, some tattooed with coffee stains. They impressively document the glorious life and expansive career of Antonio Barichievich, known to all and sundry as the Great Antonio. He was born in Yugoslavia in 1925, came to Canada in 1946, and began to work right away at his chosen vocation, which is that of Strong Man. Those were the days when it was not an overcrowded field — unlike today, when steroids are as readily available as Popsicles — and word of his deeds of derring-do spread quickly. He was soon well known in Montreal and beyond for his feats

The Great Antonio with Liza Minnelli.

of strength, nerve, and endurance. A dyed-in-the-wool exhibitionist, he liked nothing better than to show off in public. He wasn't — isn't — the kind of guy who could be satisfied hidden away in some gym, bench-pressing 500 pounds with only a few muscle-bound buddies to look on and applaud his brawny displays. No, he wanted to be out on the street, as visible as possible, attracting an appreciative crowd by doing something big and outlandish and unlikely, such as pulling something really, really heavy. Such as a loaded bus.

Buses, in fact, were his specialty, his habit. Sometimes, several buses were corralled so that he could prove his prowess.

On at least one occasion there were as many as four linked together. There are photos — he has them — of the Great Antonio yoked to a colossal bracelet on which buses are the only charms, straining as he pulls them down the road, his face a study of joyous agony and maniacal intent. This was how Samson looked when he prepared to pull down the pillars and wreak havoc on the Philistines, you can count on it. The G.A. performed this stunt so often, to such acclaim, and with such aplomb, that there was a time when one could hardly say "The

The Great Antonio (left) captures the attention of Sophia Loren.

Great Antonio" without pronouncing "bus" in the same breath. The two concepts became regionally synonymous. You can test this by mentioning his name to anyone who has lived in Montreal since the war, and who takes public transportation. They will know exactly who he is, and they will almost certainly say, "Oh, yeah. I was late for a movie once because of him. It was the strangest thing. I was taking the bus, and all of a sudden the driver just came to a dead stop, right in the middle of St-Catherine. There was kind of commotion up front, and it turned out to be the Great Antonio. He'd step into the road and stop these buses and attach a chain and haul it along for a block or two. Then, he'd pass the hat. I think he also sold postcards of himself. That was a long time ago. Isn't he dead?"

Many Montrealers to whom I mentioned his name wondered if Antonio had passed from the world. Absolutely not! He is very much among us, and, what's more, he remains preternaturally vigorous. At seventy-two, he is no longer interested in dragging buses up and down St-Catherine with a chain, but you could never call him inactive. Spreading his own legend is pretty much a full-time job. In fact, simply maintaining the archive is a chore to tax a strong man. So much paper! His is a well-documented life, amazingly so, really. No one gets that kind of slavering attention from news hounds unless he is deliberate about casting out attractive lures. Anyone who cared to court the attention of the media would be well advised to take a page from Great Antonio's book. As recipes for fame go, his is easy to follow. Stop a bus, attach a chain, haul the thing down the street, and every journalist in town will beat a path to your door. Pull four buses and they'll make a return visit. Pull four elephants — somewhere along the line he claims to have done that, too — and you can pretty much join the press club.

"EVEN AS A BOY, GREAT ANTONIO WAS A TITAN"

"STUNNED AUDIENCE WATCHES ANTONIO EAT 25 CHICKENS"

"GREAT ANTONIO — HIS MUSCLE IS 10 HORSEPOWER"

"THE GREAT ANTONIO TAKES A BUS"

The headlines just keep on spilling, one after the other, all of them clamouring to be heard after their confinement in the green garbage bag. All the clippings tell more or less the same story. International travel. Meetings with celebrities. Movie roles in films that required convincing autochtones, such as *Quest for Fire* and *The Abominable Snowman*. As Antonio shows off his impressive collection of cullings, one by one by one, he annotates the stories in his associative, rambling, stream-of-consciousness style. He gets very loud. A Strong Man show 'n' yell unfolds right there, in the middle of Montreal in the middle of the afternoon in the middle of Dunkin' Donuts. He is uninhibited by middle-class, born-of-therapy conventions like "respect for personal space and boundaries." He exudes a sense of proprietorship in this place, which is one of his regular haunts. He lives nearby, and this is where he comes "to take a meeting." All the other regulars are habituated to his tail-fanning displays and pay him no mind. They continue to gossip about Céline, and are unmoved by his voluble exuberance. Apparently, they've seen and heard it all before. As his monologue — and it is a monologue; he won't brook questions while he's talking about himself — gathers momentum, his language becomes harder to penetrate, not so much because of his accent but because his sentences swallow one another, eliding together as he thunders out the litany of his accomplishments. One thing that emerges from his prolix spewing is that he is especially proud of his foreign press, and his close encounters with movie stars.

"Here, here, ANTONIO in JAPAN, I go Japan FOUR times, pull buses for 14 MILLION people, 14 MILLION, you understand, POPE he get 50,000, MADONNA she get 60,000, Antonio he get 14 MILLION, MADONNA she come to Montreal, she want to MEET me, but I OUT of town, too BAD, some day maybe I GO to Los Angeles meet MADONNA, here is Antonio with MICHAEL JACKSON, he come here, much, MUCH security, MANY, many BODYGUARD, I only ONE he let in to SEE him, there is picture, he SMART man, very intelligent, people TALK about him, I DON'T give a SHIT what he does, I don't give a FUCK he very smart guy, there is Antonio with JOHNNY CARSON, with SOPHIA LOREN, with GREEK lady, what her name, NANA MOUSKOURI, yes, I, the GREAT ANTONIO, strongest man in WORLD, I pull buses with my HAIR, I never tell anyone how I get such STRONG hair, this a SECRET, old woman taught me, she TOLD me I come from EXTRATERRESTRIALS, maybe some day NASA come test my HAIR, test my BLOOD see why I got such strong blood, my BLOOD too strong for PEOPLE on this PLANET, one day the GREAT ANTONIO perform in Little Rock, PERFORM for CLINTON, I try to get him to COME to Montreal, he come SOON to see ME, see, here, SEE, I get this LETTER from his WIFE."

He pushes this piece of rare correspondence at me. I read it while he rears up and goes, at last, to get some coffee.

June 15, 1993

Dear Mr. Barichievich:

Thank you for inviting President Clinton to visit Montreal, Quebec. The President asked me to convey his appreciation for your kind invitation and to apologize for being unable to make a commitment to your request at this time.

During the Clinton–Gore campaign, the President had the opportunity to visit many towns and cities across our nation. Now, as he implements a national agenda to move our country forward, he does not have the opportunity to travel to as many places as he would like. However, the President is committed to staying in touch with the concerns of the American people. He hopes this will include a visit to Montreal.

Please be assured that I will keep your letter on file for further consideration. Your continued interest and support are both encouraged and appreciated.

Sincerely,

Marcia L. Hale, Assistant to the President

Director of Scheduling and Advance

Oh, dear. Oh, dear. Oh, dear. Marcia Hale, who obviously graduated in Tactful Studies from some Ivy League school, did herself proud with this reply to what must have been a bizarre invitation; though probably no more bizarre than many that fly over the White House transom. What "concerns of the American people" might be addressed by an audience with the Great Antonio? Would the President come to Dunkin' Donuts and use his considerable powers of persuasion to convince The World's Strongest Man to part with his hermetic and closely guarded formula for making his hair so strong he can use it to pull a bus? Well, why not? He does have an impressive mop, and surely such a secret might have a role to play in the development of post–cold war, national-defence strategies.

While Antonio is tanking up at the coffee counter, I begin to rehearse my "it's been swell but I gotta hit the road now" spiel. I've listened for more than an hour to what is plainly a well practised rant and feel that I know what it is to be a punching bag. I am completely enervated. I am flaccid and drained. I hear the words "sad and empty as a bereft belfry from which the bats have recently flown," and look around for Grenville, but he is nowhere to be found. A bad sign. When Kleiserisms surface in the absence of the master, you know you need a nap in the worst possible way. It's time to say goodbye, for there is nothing to be gained from lingering.

Such questions as I've tried to ask the Great Antonio during those rare spaces that opened up when he breached and gasped for air he has ignored or deflected with a wave of his paw. I think I get the picture, now. Strong man past his prime, grappling to come to terms with his present reality, anchored in the past, reliving his glory days, obsessed with his own record. In fact, he is not dissimilar from many men who are retired and struggle to find a way to reconcile their memorable then with their lacklustre now. I was reminded of a study I saw described somewhere, which had to do with a particularly male need for approval. Some scientists figured out how to lavish on rats the kinds of compliments only rats appreciate. They did this with a group of male rats and they did this with a group of female rats. The treatment went on long enough for rats of both sexes to get used to it, to like it, to think of it as the norm, to believe that life was just one big flattering banquet. Then, without warning or reason, the source of approval — whatever it was — was cauterized. The well-spring dried up. The rats no longer received external signs of approbation. And what happened? Well, the girls shrugged and got on with their lives. They looked within and found they had resources enough to adapt to the change. Not the boys, though. The boys languished. The boys got depressed. The boys thought that life wasn't worth living. I wouldn't be surprised to learn that some of them tried to enlist in experiments where they would be fed known carcinogens, if only to get it over with. If only to end the pain.

What can we extrapolate from this? How vast is the chasm between rat and man? Is the Great Antonio, "descending from extraterrestrial universal champion of the world," merely demonstrating a biological imperative when he saws so endlessly on his one-string fiddle? Does he just want reassurance that he is remembered, that he is still loved? There's nothing wrong with that. There's nothing wrong with that at all. And perhaps it's not so surprising that he chooses to dwell in the marble halls of his halcyon days. He trails a magnificent past, that's for sure, and God knows he worked hard for whatever rewards he has received, as any of the bus-pulling photos can attest. He worked hard with what he had, with strength, nerve, and more than a little gall. What did Liza Minnelli, Sophia Loren, Clint Eastwood, or Luciano Pavarotti think when this self-confessed scion of space creatures — who lists on his CV such accomplishments as "lifts 2 horses from the ground and kills many animals with his bare hands," and who claims in the same sentence to be a "dancing playboy" — muscled into their post-concert or film-festival parties and cosied up close for a photo opportunity? Doubtless they were surprised or amused, maybe even slightly alarmed, in the minute. An hour later, they'd have forgotten all about it. Another fan. Another photo. Ho-hum. None of them know, nor would they care, that the Great Antonio now carries around their smiling faces in his green garbage bag, and passes them out with indiscriminate abandon to total strangers in the Dunkin' Donuts on Beaubien.

When the Great Antonio returns to his seat, I begin to excuse myself, to make the usual "it was a pleasure" noises. I put Sophia and Liza and Clint and Johnny Carson into my bag. I stand to go and again extend my hand. This time he takes it, and I notice what very fine fingers he has. Huge, yes, but beautifully shaped and proportioned. They're smooth, too. Pianist fingers. Painter fingers. We shake, gravely, but when I try to reclaim my hand from his firm, firm grip, he doesn't let go. Instead, he gives a gentle tug. Gentle for him, that is. Gentle for a man who used to pull four buses and could still grind my bones to make his bread if he chose to. Which is the subtext of the gesture, I'm sure. *I am the GREAT Antonio and YOU are but a FEATHER! See?* He tugs, gently, and I am caught off guard, all balance is gone. Powerless to stop myself, I fall forward, or start to. I teeter. I totter. I am on my way to landing, squarely in the coffee spills and the doughnut crumbs, which would be an ignominious end to our meeting. There's a moment of giddy disequilibrium before I meet the resistance of his steadying hand, and he shoves me back in the contrary direction, just as gently as he had tugged me down, and lo and behold I am again on my feet. It is over in a second. No camera could have caught it, and for that I'm sorry. I would like to be able to send him a picture. I would like him to remember that once we met.

Still and Moving Images

My friends…expended much eloquence —
eloquence wasted in vain! —
in endeavouring to dissuade me
from a winter journey to Canada.
— Anna Brownell Jameson, *Winter Studies and Summer
Rambles in Canada*

Two days before I was scheduled to hit the road, when the
stores were still teeming with post-Christmas bargain hunters, I
was overtaken by the urgent need to acquire supplies for my
journey. The simple act of packing had drawn my attention to
some of the gaps in my readiness, and idle fantasizing about
whatever perils might await me as I sailed over the edge of the
world accounted for some of the perceived, and more far-
fetched, oversights. While I stopped short of including on my
"must get" list a barrel of salt cod and a score of limes, I saw
with feverish clarity that I would certainly have to invest in
more than just combination underwear if I hoped to incur a
minimum of psychic and physical damage over my two-months
voyage. The prospect and the dread of leaving behind all that
was familiar somehow stripped me of the remembrance that
this is a world where remote jungle tribes have Coke machines
and Metallica T-shirts, and that therefore I would surely be able
to find a tube of toothpaste or a stationer in, say, St. John's.
Such are the fitful delusions that settle upon the anticipatory
traveller, *as gently as the flower gives forth its perfume*, and it
was under their influence that I sallied forth on my charger,

Acquisitive. There was much that I required. I was intent on finding notebooks of several sizes and configurations, as well as pens in many colours, figuring that I would devise some codified and efficient way of record-keeping that would make such an investment worthwhile. I had to seek out such toiletries as bath balms and moisturizers and exfoliants, so that I could keep ahead of the dead and flaking skin cells that are so much a part of our northern winter, particularly in the drier climes. I needed new gloves, and a good winter hat, one of those seen-at-the-Kremlin models with the ursine earflaps. I had to have boots, for heaven's sake, boots that would cushion my feet (with their resident plantar warts) from the treacherous ice and snow I knew I would find everywhere in abundance, and yet be stylish enough so as not to attract hateful stares if worn out for dinner on St-Denis. And then there was the suitcase! None of the five or six valises available to me at home had anything like the requisite number of pockets, compartments, straps, wheels, and there was no doubt in my mind that I would need a bag that was fully loaded with every option.

I cut a wide swath through a mall in downtown Vancouver, sucking up supplies with all the indiscriminate and merry abandon of a black hole with its first credit card. I was on the verge of heading home — already courting a hernia with the poundage of my purchases — when I passed a camera counter, and lingered just long enough for the persuasive salesman to send out his suctioning tentacles. Five minutes later, I was the proud owner of a Pentax Espio Jr. with AF Zoom, an autofocus window, a self-timer lamp, and an infinity landscape button. This camera is about the size of my kneecap and is fully twice as smart and self-actualized as I'll ever be. It adapts itself instantly to any light, any place, any situation, with no fuss, no fear, no flash. It is unfailingly honest, and demonstrates no inclination to stretch or completely realign the facts to suit its own purposes. It is what I hope to be when I grow up.

Why I allowed myself to be persuaded that this was a gadget without which I couldn't live another day, I can't say. Of course, there was every good reason to take along a camera on an excursion such as the one before me, and many advisers had told me that I must. On the other hand, my incompetence as a photographer is so pronounced and has so often been proven that it could almost be called a disability. Cameras have always been a mystery to me, and the capacity to peer through a lens, compose a photo, press a button, and come up with anything that looks even remotely like the intended subject simply does not live in me. Anyone unfamiliar with our world, and who might try to understand it by leafing through my albums, would surmise that the planet is populated by beings whose heads end at the eyebrows, and who are ghostly in their smudginess.

"I guarantee you," said the clerk to whom I had explained all this, as he rang up the Espio Jr., "that all you'll need to do with this little baby is point and shoot, and you'll have professional-quality pictures every time." So convincingly did he deliver this assertion, and with such an authentic air of *bonhomie*, and so completely had my brain given itself over to the particular dementia engendered by dallying too long at the Christmas-week sales, that I actually believed him. I remembered that salesman and his windy promises just a few days later, as I prepared for my point-and-shoot début. This was in Toronto's Mount Pleasant Cemetery, where, you will recall, I had gone to stand before the grave of Glenn Gould. The dead don't squirm, which is one of the qualities that recommend them to novice shutterbugs.

I sized up the headstone through the view-finder, and wondered how long it had taken the earliest photographers to start chasing after images that were either sexual or death-related: seaside bathing beauties showing a bit of cleavage; Auntie in her coffin with her hands folded over her breasts. And I thought of how sex and death are the active agents in every photograph: you smile for the camera, you seduce it, are seduced by it, then you freeze the moment, defeat time, live forever as you are. This cosmic and wide-ranging line of inquiry brought on a Zen-ish state, that white-hot purity of thought that presages transcendence. I began to feel I had attained a mystic oneness with Glenn, and that, when my film was developed, I would see not just the grave itself, but the translucent form of its most famous tenant, looking on with detached humour. Just as I was poised to click the shutter, and take what I hoped would be the first picture of many, the Espio leapt from my hands with Tosca-like élan and decisiveness, and plummeted to the snow. I'm very much afraid that I might have said "Fuck!" or something quite like it, right there on sacred ground and with all the dear departed lying round about, helpless to stop their ears. I picked up the Pentax, brushed it off, tried to blow the powder out of its crevices, and hoped against hope that no permanent damage had been done to its red eye–reduction flash button or zooming lever. The lens was completely misted over, but nonetheless I prepared to shoot a second time. Once again, the camera slipped — flew is more like it — from my hands. Now, I am fumble-fingered, but not so maladroit as all that. This was a ton-of-bricks message from the beyond, if ever I've received one. These were the spirits flipping me a bird. Back off, Mr. Paparazzi Man, they said in their loudest spirit voices. Back off and leave us in peace! And I did just that.

It was too late for the Espio, though, and in some ways it was too late for me. Mild, but irreversible, damage had been done. Certain claims had been laid. The fog never did relinquish its hold on the autofocus window. I never did assimilate the miracle that is the infinity landscape button. Nor was I ever able to shake the feeling, from that moment on, that I was travelling in the company of ghosts. There were times over the next couple of months, especially when I was driving, that I felt they were sitting beside me, distracting me from my autofocus, pointing me towards an infinity landscape.

I am exactly the sort of driver after whom the recruitment officers for Death and Son come running, their attaché cases bulging with offers of immediate and permanent employment, all the while touting the advantages of their generous benefits packages. I am exactly the sort of driver who, if he were inclined to use one of those automotive air fresheners, would look for the scent called "Whiffs of Mortality." I am exactly the sort of driver who shouldn't drive at all and who, for the most part, doesn't. It's not that I drive too fast, or drive too slow, or take unnecessary risks, or lean from the window to whistle at construction workers. No, I am a cautious driver, a courteous driver, a defensive driver. Above all, I am an aware driver: too aware for my own good.

Every time I get behind the wheel of a car I'm invaded by the oppressive certainty that I am a weak, mortal creature who is at the helm of an instrument of potential mass destruction. The question "what if?" is never far from the surface of my awareness. What if vital cables snap, what if a wheel becomes disengaged, what if a swarm of killer bees flies through the window? Such terrible apocalyptic visions as these occupy a corner of my eye, *like a dew-drop, ill-fitted to sustain unkindly shocks.* Even more likely than a mechanical foul-up is the momentary lapse of attention or a failure of the fallible flesh that will lead to a slaughter of the innocents. Children in school buses, babies in strollers, old people in wheelchairs, young lovers planning their weddings while enjoying a cappuccino in a sidewalk café: any of these are potential victims of the stroke or seizure or unstoppable sneezing fit or detached retina that might take me while I am in charge of a ton or two of sculpted metal, filled with litre upon litre of volatile liquid. What good would such prophylactic agents as a red light, a crossing guard, a two-inch curb do in such a circumstance? These things happen. They happen every day. Why take a chance? Walk, don't drive along Tranquillity Street, and happiness will be yours.

I had stupidly hoped that I would be able to make my dead-of-winter crossing of the country without recourse to the automobile. I imagined following a light-hearted, Kerouacian trajectory. I saw myself in the plush embrace of a Greyhound seat, chug-chug-chugging along two-lane country roads, admiring the picturesque farms and the pokey little villages, their red barns and tall steeples glimpsed across white, unsullied fields.

My predominant emotion would be wistfulness: kind of lonely, yet kind of not; kind of detached, yet kind of engaged. I would incline my head against the window, expel hot breath on the plexiglass, and write haiku in the mist. Delicious! Now and again, I would take one of my several notebooks and jot down something exquisite in a legible hand, something aphoristic and Kleiserian:

> *Like a locomotive engine with unsound lungs*
> *Like a long arrow through the dark the train is darting*
> *Like a troop of boys let loose from school,*
> *the adventurers went by.*

But I was wrong. Oh, how I was wrong. *Bienvenue au Canada*, land of impossible bus connections and no trains whatsoever. Once I was into the thick of it, a rental car proved the only sensible option. All the ghosts who trailed me clapped their insubstantial hands. They tumbled into the backseat. I turned the key. I drove. Someone — not I — took a few pictures. Shall we see the phantom slides? Lights please. Thank you. Begin.

CLICK

Oh. This is a good one, yes. I remember this very well. January 6, 1997. Sydney, Nova Scotia. If I look a little bleary-eyed, it's because I've just got off the ferry from Newfoundland. An all-nighter. Look at that weather! Execrable. Slush by the cupful from a dung-coloured sky. That's Mert, my cab driver. He's taking me to the car-rental place. Mert's radio is blaring. It has to be loud because he's deaf, or getting that way. The announcer reads a chilly litany of school closures, event cancellations.

"I guess the driving's going to be pretty bad on the highway."

"Eh?"

"I said — I GUESS THE DRIVING'S GOING TO BE PRETTY BAD!"

"Ah, no. Piece of cake! Take 'er easy and you'll be fine!"

Mert squints through the woolly blanket of sleet, notices a stop sign, tries to brake, and sails right on through.

"Whoops! Guess I've forgotten how to drive in this stuff. I've just moved back from California."

"What were you doing in California?"

"Eh?"

"IN CALIFORNIA! WHAT WERE YOU DOING?"

"Tuning pianos. What's your name?"

"Bill."

"Eh?"

I look out at the harbour and think about Bill Jamieson, a local man whom I never met, but of whom I've read, and who has very recently gone to his reward. He took part in a New Year's Day "polar bear swim," and the sad aftermath was reported in the St. John's *Evening Telegram*.

"Bill Jamieson, 65, was one of 29 people who dunked themselves in the harbor at nearby South Bar in –7 degree temperatures watched by more than 1000 people.

"Jamieson stepped out of the water, went to his truck, got dressed and drove to the local firehall before he collapsed behind the wheel. Attempts to revive him failed and he was pronounced dead in hospital and his body released.

"Eddie MacDougall was with his friend when they went into the water near South Bar wharf where the waters were relatively calm....

"'I have no doubt in my mind it is the way he wanted to go,' said MacDougall."

"So, Phil, what brings you to Cape Breton?"

"I'm writing — I'M WRITING A BOOK ABOUT ECCENTRICS!"

"Ha! Like who?"

"Like a man — A MAN WHO COLLECTS SHRUNKEN HEADS!"

"No kidding? Who's that?"

"BILL JAMIESON!"

"Bill Jamieson. Bill Jamieson. Where've I heard that name before?"

CLICK

Here we are in Bill Jamieson's apartment. This Bill Jamieson, unlike the other, still maintains his flesh-and-blood status. He's in his early forties, and he lives in downtown Toronto, and we're going to look at his shrunken heads, of which he has a dozen or so. First, take a gander around these rooms. Gorgeous, no? Such deep colours, these golds, these reds. Such eclecticism, so much stuff! A Tamara de Lempicka print, a big carved mahogany palm tree (from some night club in Cuba, apparently), and many beautiful Art Deco pieces, including a sideboard for which I'd give up a kidney, lamps, statues, mirrors, a collection of microphones that make for very unusual accent pieces. All that gilt and chrome, all those sleek lines that are so much a product of a highly rarefied and European sensibility achieve a surprising homogeneity with his various jungle artifacts: the leopard skins, the zebra rug, the elephant foot, the tribal masks, the ostrich. Bridging the gap between the Deco pieces and the shrunken heads (we're getting there, be patient!) is the funerary collection. There's a coffin (again!) in the hallway; there's a grotesque dagger with a human hip joint for a handle; and in the bedroom, affixed to the wall, is the back end of a Victorian hearse, ingeniously adapted to serve as a salt-water aquarium. That's a pretty angel fish that dangles dead centre, all languorous and calm, not a care in the world, hanging as though suspended by a silken thread, hanging as easily as might a shrivelled head from the belt of an Amazonian tribesman.

"Different cultures hunted heads for different reasons," Bill will gladly tell you, "but for the most part, they were trophies. You can see why. They're light and easy to carry and everybody has one."

Had one, anyway. There's no denying their portability: by the hair; by the ears; or bowling ball–style, with your fingers inserted into nostrils and mouth. Truth be told, you'd have a hard time getting an index finger or thumb into these mouths, as they have been stitched shut, crudely, after the fashion of the day. Let's move in for a closer look. There, you can see them, the heads that is, daydreaming under their bell jars. They are about the size of and about as wizened as last fall's potatoes. You can lift up the glass if you'd like. Be prepared for a light and musty odour, an earthy, cellarish, old-potato smell. This is so different from the smell of Bill's Egyptian mummy head, which is thousands of years old, and is still lightly scented with the spices used in its embalming. Be informed that all these *objets de mort* are the real thing, not some fun-house knock-offs. You have to be careful, when you're in the market for shrunken heads especially, not to be taken in by the fakes, of which there are plenty out there. Do you want to know a sure way of distinguishing a real shrunken head from a bogus one? The nose hair. You just can't fake the nose hair.

Bill Jamieson became interested in head-hunting culture when he went to the Amazon on a kind of Carlos Castaneda pursuit of a powerful herbal hallucinogen called *ayahuasca*. It is ingested as part of the spiritual observances of the Jivaro tribe, in Ecuador. *Ayahuasca* opens the door from this world to the next, and the next, and the next. It is apparently dynamite stuff. Bill immersed himself in Jivaro lore, learning about the tribe's unstinting ferocity, and its reputation for nicking the heads of enemies at the slightest provocation. Such larceny was outlawed in the twenties, but is said to have been carried out until much more recently. Bill, who was touched by this, began to collect his heads after he returned to Toronto. He placed a discreet ad in the paper. It said something like "Authentic Shrunken Heads Wanted." The phone began to ring. His head-hunting career was under way.

Each of the heads is different. Wrinkled and stitched and stunned as they are, you can get a sense of individuality of appearance. Something lingers of happier days in the humid rain forest. Most of these relics have brown skin in common, and all of them look surprised. Taken aback. This is especially true of the one blotchy and pale-skinned model. He is a man who looks to have had Celtic antecedents. His moustache is red, and there is something about the whole set of his countenance that suggests he just can't believe this is happening to him. Him! Of all people! Why did they never warn him about such an eventuality when he was at Eton? Mommy will be so upset! Daddy will be — WHACK!

CLICK

What a lucky boy I am! Bill Jamieson gave me this T-shirt as I was leaving his place. That's me, modelling it. Pardon? Yes, I know a day or two at the gym wouldn't be time misspent, thank you very much for pointing it out. The front of the shirt is decorated with a shrunken head. On the back is the recipe:

Beheading

The warrior cut off his enemy's head with a lance as close to the shoulders as possible.

Removal of the Skull

He cut a vertical slit at the back of the head and peeled the skin from the skull. The eyes, lips, and back of the neck were then sewn shut.

Shrinking

He soaked and simmered the boneless head in a pot of hot chichipi plant juice for about 2 hours, reducing it to about one third of its natural size.

Drying and Hardening

He placed hot rocks in the head cavity while he smoothed the face with a small stone to preserve its natural proportions. He filled the cavity with hot sand when the head and neck became too small for stones to complete the drying process.

Blackening

He suspended the head in the smoke of a fire all night.

Polishing

He washed the hair and rubbed the skin with a cloth to make
it shine.

Apparently, the whole operation took about twenty hours
from beginning to end. Should you care to try it sometime, you
might be interested in these complementary instructions for
cooking brain, which appear in the aforementioned *SAS
Survival Guide*: "Skin head and boil, simmering for ninety minutes. Strip all flesh from the skull including the eyes, tongue and
ears. Blood: collect in a container and leave covered until a clear
liquid comes to the top. When separation seems complete drain
it off. Dry the residue by the fire to form a firm cake. Use to
enrich soups and stews."

And now you know.

CLICK

What? Another picture of me? This was also taken on Cape
Breton Island. I'm on my way to Cheticamp, and have stopped
to stretch my legs by the side of the road. The car is a white
Mystique, which is fitting for one of my colour and sensibility.
I'm looking skyward because I'm counting crows. One crow for
sorrow, two for joy, three for a wedding, four for a boy, five for
silver, six for gold, seven crows a secret, never to be told. Which
is fine and dandy as far as it goes. But what about eight? What
does that get you? Eight crows a cream puff? Eight crows a lay-
off notice? Eight crows a flat tire, a bad cold, a runny omelette,
a wooden nickel? Eight crows a shin splint? If there's anything
of prognosticatory value to be wrung from counting crows,
eight is the number I need, since there is an octave of the birds
(just the black keys) perched in their formal attire along the utility wire that runs parallel to the highway, near the field where
Joe Delaney's scarecrows are hibernating.

In the summer, they would never be so bold, those crows,
not when the field is full of scary totems, more than a hundred

scarecrows, some in rags, some in tags, some dressed as Marilyn Monroe. Joe Delaney, who was well known in the Cheticamp area as a *bon vivant*, a community organizer, and as the janitor at the high school, put up a few scarecrows in 1984, just as a way of diverting birds from a vegetable patch. They attracted the attention of passers-by, who would stop to talk, which appealed to Joe's gregarious nature. The next year, he planted a whole garden of scarecrows, with stuffed-stocking faces and decked out in a wild array of Sally Ann chic, each bearing a card stating the character's name and occupation. Word of his enterprise spread. Tourists began to flock. There were more than 18,000 visitors in 1986.

Then came the massacre. "Le massacre de 1986." Vandals came in the night. They unseamed the scarecrows from stem to stern, from nave to chops. They left the field strewn with parts. Incomprehensible! "They really did it dirty," remembers Joe's daughter, Ethel. "The only one who was left standing was a scarecrow called Rory. For a while, our father was very discouraged. But he began to get messages of support from all over the world. So, he decided to rebuild. He was inspired by Rory. Rory lead the charge."

Joe Delaney died on February 7, 1996. Ethel and her brothers decided to keep up the scarecrow field, as a tribute to their father, and to stick with their father's free-admission policy. But it's a lot of work. They make nothing from it, and there is considerable outlay. How long can it go on, one wonders, without the singular devotion of the man whose odd inspiration it was?

CLICK

A brief detour here for a cautionary tale. We are in the Humber Heights district of Cornerbrook, Newfoundland, standing inside what is left of the Sticks and Stones House. This small bungalow was Clyde Farnell's castle and fantasy world. It was his recreation. It was his oblique pathway to reconciliation.

Mr. Farnell was born in 1919 and died around the time of

the scarecrow massacre. For many years, his life was circum-
scribed by the ordinary. He was a married man with five children.
He was a worker, with jobs on the railway and as a carpenter.
In his spare time he sketched and painted, as many will. He was
a foot-soldier in the army of the day-to-day, marching, marching, and all the while, something was simmering. The lid blew
off the pot in the mid-sixties after the death of his wife, Leta.
When he was on his own, everything began to change. Perhaps
it stopped mattering to him what people might think. Perhaps
he woke up one morning and understood that names would
never hurt him. As if to prove it, he began gathering sticks and
stones. Using these as design elements, he undertook a wholesale transformation of his home environment.

The stones were pebbles, culled from the beach. The sticks,
which were the most conspicuous element of his new household
aesthetic, were once the spines of Popsicles. Over the years, he
used hundreds of thousands of Popsicle sticks to line the walls
of his house. He would pay neighbourhood children some nom-
inal amount to gather them up and bring them to him. Then, he
cut them, shaped them, and arranged them in various patterns.
The basic effect was that of a mosaic. When they were burnished
a tawny gold, it was a sight to behold. He began to add on layers, arranging sticks on sticks in floral patterns, geometric
shapes, and star clusters. These he painted a variety of shades.
The pebbles were incorporated into his stick configurations,
and used throughout the house to provide a granular texture.

I like to think of him placing the very first stick, think of
him standing back to study the result, and understanding that
yes, yes, it would work. The die was cast. There was nothing for
him to do but press on. When the foundation of sticks was laid,
Mr. Farnell proceeded to cover almost every square inch of that
corrugated foundation with something of his own creation:
paintings, collages, found objects. There were nautical scenes
and forest scenes, there were many, many renderings of flowers.
Often they were relief pieces, three-dimensional, incorporating
all manner of found objects, from matchsticks to hub-caps,

from busted spectacles to shell casings. Some of the pieces, the paintings in particular, were magnificent pieces of folk art, whimsical and altogether original. When they were all hung in one smallish dwelling — and there were thousands vying for space on the wall — it must have been dizzying to survey, and for some years, the Sticks and Stones House was a popular tourist attraction in Cornerbrook.

Sadly, the family was unable to maintain it for many years after Mr. Farnell's death. They just couldn't keep up with the maintenance and the staffing requirements, and so closed the house and broke up the collection. Now, there is hardly anything left. The bathroom is still more or less intact, and it is a thing of such weird beauty that it breaks your heart to think of what has been lost.

It breaks your heart to think of Mr. Farnell, working out what I suppose to have been his deeper purpose. He was blinded in one eye by a flying Popsicle stick when he was a child. In the subsequent years, he had ample time to reflect on what he had lost, to sift through the layers of anger, regret, resignation. I like to think that what he did in his home was to find a constructive way to bend his oppressor and assailant to his will. He built a palace of Byzantine splendour from dangerous dross. It was more reconciliation than revenge. The innocuous wand that plucked out his eye is not destroyed but transformed, and made to please the eye that remains. That the tangible record of Clyde Farnell's obsession, his one-of-a-kind inventiveness, the key to his secret oddness, has been removed from us is a terrible thing. It is not his family's fault, of course. They are living people with practical needs and concerns. But someone should have done something. Someone should have had both eyes open. Someone should have seen.

CLICK

Back to Cape Breton and Joe Delaney's field. A scarecrow's work is seasonal. When summer's done and the tourists disperse, their job is over. A period of hiatus ensues. This is a picture of the metal trailer where they come to sleep, huddled together in this rude shed. Huddled together all winter along, against the wind, a tangle of fabric and stocking and stick. Huddled together, while, outside, the harsh crows bark and palaver. Nine of them now. Nine crows a murder.

If ever there came a time, during their long hibernation, when these loony effigies would want to spring to life, it would be at Lent. In this part of the world, the solemn weeks leading up to Easter are broken by an observance called *mi-câreme*, that is, "midway through Lent." At *mi-câreme*, all the fasting and introspection of that austere season is set aside for a carnival night. People dress up, as at Hallowe'en. They go from house to house. They drink, they dance, they carry on. The object is to keep your identity hidden. The object is to kick up your heels. The object is to thumb your nose at the sacred, to confound propriety. It's purely pagan. It's purely fun, and Joe Delaney's scarecrows have a part to play.

Visitors from away, who come to see them in their summertime field, will be charmed by that unlikely congregation. The crazy hats, the fright wigs, the hobo clothes will make people chuckle and reach for their cameras. But Joe also intended his genial dummies as *mi-câreme* symbols. They have more on their stocking-stuffed minds than frightening crows. In fact, they are dressed up for the express purpose of going door to door as *mi-câreme* celebrants. They are reminders that we require the profane to remember the sacred; that in the midst of all that is holy, you must be ready to invite the devil into your house for a dance. Make him dizzy with a fast spin around the floor, and then send him packing. Joe's scarecrows have a transcendent purpose. They are symbolic, a present reminder of tradition and custom. And we all know how fragile a thing tradition can be in the absence of such touchstones.

Now they doze. Chances are they'll sleep right through *mi-câreme*. And in the spring, when the ground has thawed, Joe's kids will resurrect them, and plant them firmly in the earth.

They have to be well anchored, or they will fall victim to one of the area's dependable vandals, the wind.

In Canada we aren't much given to christening our winds. We content ourselves with generic terms like "squall" or "storm" and leave to others such lovely words as "mistral" or "hubbub"; "libeccio" or "Ox's Eye." Here, in this part of Cape Breton, the wind has a such a personality, they've claimed it with a name. It is *le suete*, so called because it blows from the south east: *le sud-est. Suete* is pronounced as "sweat." A hard-scrabble word for a hard-scrabble place. This is a wind that foments its revolutions in the dips and whorls of the worn-down hills. It uses them like the tubing in a brass instrument to pitch its frigid ululations. In the wintertime, it can stampede over the rise at speeds of over 250 kilometres an hour. Houses have to be built against its tantrums, with double shingling, with no windows giving onto the southeast. Even so, from time to time, one will blow right off its foundation and be tumbled down a hill. There's a terrible beauty in such a blow, to be sure, and I am thrilled to think I am experiencing it firsthand as I prepare to make my way south. A great howling wind is careening through Cheticamp, tearing over the fields and around the House of Sleeping Scarecrows.

"Is this *le suete*?" I ask the gas-station attendant, who laughs and laughs. How could I mistake this tickling breeze for that cold slug in the chops? How could I look at a midget and see such a giant? No, no, no, this is not a wind, not a wind at all! I ought to have been around last week! That was when there was a wind!

The story of my life to date: a week too early, or a week too late. In spite of his derision, I can't believe this is the puniest wind he's ever known. Look how it blows the snow! It rattles the car as I pull away from the pump. A trash can is being tossed along the street. The wind has even driven away the crows. Nine have become none. No. Wait. Not quite. There's one, hurling herself against the gale. One crow sorrow. Surely not! Don't let this be the case! In the name of Joe and Rory and the *mi-câreme*, in the name of the hibernating scarecrows, in the name of all that is good and all that is pagan, don't let it end with sorrow! I scan the sky and find another, far across the field, it is true, flying out to sea, but visible nonetheless. It is flying out to sea, where it will bring some mariner bad luck if it passes over his bow. He will look up and see just one crow, and head back to port. But for now, there are two crows and they are mine. Two crows joy. I give my attention to the highway. For the time being, I am through with the sky. It has told me as much as I need to hear or know.

CLICK

The white Mystique can't go on forever, and that is a lesson most of us in the middle class in this country could stand to learn, as the century winds down. I left my Mystique in Halifax. In Ottawa, I picked up a black Cavalier. "Would you like a black Cavalier, Mr. Richardson?" they asked me at the rental place, and believe you me, I had to bite my tongue.

Just the day before, I'd been in Montreal. It was a Sunday, a very cold and windy afternoon, and I'd slipped my way along the rutted, icy roads of the Cimetière Notre-Dame-des-Neiges in Montreal. There was no one in particular I cared to find. I'd simply had one of those hankerings only a graveyard visit will satisfy. Stung by the wind and defeated by the dreadful condition of the pathways, I took shelter in the foyer of the administrative offices, and availed myself of their CD-ROM information services. Post-modern death is a marvel of convenience. The curious passer-by can take a digitized tour of the new mausoleum (accompanied by Handelian music that is aptly funereal), or check into the cost of burial, or locate any extant grave by punching in the name of the tenant. Self-indulgent as always, I looked to see if there were any Bill or William Richardsons on the register. Delighted to find there was none, and thinking I might one day be the first, I printed out the price list. "Cremation done in the presence of the family — $165.00." A bargain! Why, so scant a sum would hardly buy you dinner out. Eternity at Notre-Dame-des-Neiges! An attractive and affordable option. One could do worse, and that's for sure.

Here's the thing. Spend too much time consorting with Death's many concubines, and he thinks you want to be numbered among them. After all, there's always room for one more in his harem. Now, advance the clock, two weeks hence. The picture is of another Sunday drive. Coming down from Sudbury, I stop in Parry Sound for lunch, the one open restaurant, all pub food. I order up the "suicide wings," get back in the black Cavalier, head in the direction of Gravenhurst. I listen to a tape, Shawn Colvin's *A Few Small Repairs*. The roads are slippery, a consequence of the thaw-and-freeze syndrome, as well as freezing rain. I drive slowly, pass through the village of Beatrice, and start to think of Dante. Halfway down the road of life. Lost in a dark wood. Abandon hope all ye who enter here. All that shit. Shawn Colvin is singing "Suicide Alley." I give a little belch, enjoy a gaseous memory of lunch, and the phrase "spread your suicide wings" rises up from the brain's tight folds. I chuckle at the melodrama of it all, to say nothing of the idea of going to Gravenhurst in a rental car. Grave in Hertz. It's all too perfect! Who arranges these things? I press on the brakes while approaching a curve, steer too wide, and the rear end of the Cavalier catches in some slush on the shoulder. A law of motion asserts itself and the car chucks itself into the opposite lane, mercifully nothing oncoming, then back, mercifully nothing behind, then half spins around, then whirls in the opposite direction, seems to pick up speed in spite of my braking. I am asking myself, what is the rule, what is the rule, is it steer into or away from the spin? But neither seems to work, the Cavalier is only going faster, there is nothing but motion and a noise which is the sound of treaded rubber on ice, sand, salt, asphalt, and someone's voice calling out "Jesus!" and the car is hurtling off the road, a crazy trajectory, a second's suspension as it takes to the air and then smashes itself starboard into an enveloping drift, and there is nothing but white against the windshield, nothing but the gunning of the engine as it tries to regain its primacy, the ferocious roar of the two front wheels, spinning, spinning, throwing up the snow. Shawn is still singing, wry and unconcerned. I find the key. Even when the engine is extinguished, the roar lingers in the air a second or two. An echo. Shock, manifesting itself sonically. A howl from some dark quarter. And then — peace. Peace. In less than a minute, I will be standing on the road, waving down a minivan, noting how I missed smashing into the guard rail by mere inches. In an hour I will be at my hotel, and able to appreciate more fully than ever before the beauties of the phrase "came out of it without a scratch." Even the black Cavalier will be unscarred. But in the moment, there is only this deep quiet, only this vista that is nothing but white. A few months from now, I will attribute the fact that I can write down this story to pure, dumb luck, to random rescue. But in the moment, it is like looking at a landscape of mercy, like gazing into the still and blameless heart of something I could never bring myself to believe in, and never hope to again. Our Lady of the snows. Notre-Dame-des-Neiges.

CLICK

Which were the winter roads they drove? Where did they think to go? How can you follow the black Cavalier who leaves no tracks in the snow? Never a track and never a trace to show he was there or here, and none can travel as far as fast as the coal-black Cavalier. No one. Nowhere. No how. Not you. Not me. Not the Great Antonio, with his extraterrestrial connections. Not even Alexis Lapointe could outpace him, and it was his celerity that won him celebrity. Alexis was as much horse as he was man. Or, so they said. Running was so much his game that he was known far and wide as "Alexis Le Trotteur." He was the *surcheval*, the superhorse of La Malbaie. He was said to have had the legs of a horse, with knees and hips that were jointed like a horse's. He had the heart of a horse, the lungs of a horse, the tongue of a horse. He smelled like a horse, and he cantered like a horse. When he was preparing to run, he would throw back his head and he would whinny like a horse. He had a whip with which he would administer a purposeful self-flagellation. When he had heated his chevaline juices to a near boil, when he had worked himself into a good old froth, he would break into a gallop and run like the wind, covering huge distances in a single stride, never flagging, scarcely touching the ground, like Poppy, the Flying Horse of the North, who was his mane-bearing alter ego. He ran against men who were on foot and on bicycle, and he won. He ran against horses, the fastest and best, and he won. Why, he even outpaced Roger Savard's famous grey horse in a race over the ice. The snow was no impediment to him. Once, he ran fourteen miles over winter roads, whinny-ing all the way, covering the distance in just thirty-five minutes, and all for the sake of fetching a forgotten fiddle so a fête could begin. In true Paul Bunyan fashion, he was able to win contests against trains, speeding alongside, and dashing in front of them, laughing and careless, with hardly a bead of sweat weighing down his withers. That kind of hubris exacts its wages. It was a locomotive that took him out, when he was sixty-five. Some say he was clipped while making one of his intrepid, daredevil cross-overs, and tripped mid-canter on a railway tie. The more credible story is that he was loping across a railway bridge, in man-mode, and didn't hear the approach of the engine until it was too late. Both versions converge on the outcome. His legs were severed and he died a few hours later, his horse-coloured blood drained into the snow, his ghost limbs churning, churn-ing, and the black Cavalier breathing hard down his neck.

Alexis Le Trotteur died in January 1924. Four years later, and more than a thousand miles to the west, Letitia J. Reed joined her twenty-seven classmates and their teacher in a photo-grapher's studio. Ready ladies? Smile!

CLICK

Thank you. This will be our last slide. May I draw your atten-tion to the figure who sits smack dab in the middle, the matron with the rounded edges. That would be the teacher. She's in her mid-forties, or so I'd guess. Her name is Mrs. Johnston. Some of the girls who surround her — the worker bees clustered about the queen — are called Viola, Olga, Phyllis, Pauline, Olive, Tessie, Okie, Lillie, and Hatley. They have left Estevan, Indian Head, North Battleford, Swift Current, and other little Saskatchewan towns and farms; have said goodbye to their families and friends and struck out on their own, putting their girlhoods behind them. They have come to Regina, come to the capital to be formed. They have come for vocational training.

The Graduating Class of the Marvel School of Cosmetology, 1928.

How old are they? Young, for the most part. Sixteen. Seventeen. They are young, but not frivolous. No, they are foresightful and cautious. They are not counting on anything: not counting on inheriting the farm, not counting on the death of a rich aunt that comes in good time, not counting on finding some man who will tend to their needs. They have come here to prepare themselves as best they can for whatever curves life — and their lives stretch on and on before them — might throw.

They are young, but they already haul behind them the ponderous weight of ambition and disappointment. Of course they do. You can't live even so short a time as they without having your heart broken at least once, without knowing the forward impetus that comes from mourning or regret. You can't live that long without catching a glimmer of what you might be, if you just have the nerve to seize the chance when it comes along. The turf that lies between heartbreak and hope is fertile. That is the ground they have come to Regina to till. Now, after months of hard work, they have arrived. They are the ladies of the graduating class of the Marvel School of Cosmetology, freshly minted experts in hairdressing and beauty culture, fully equipped and qualified to go into the world and practise haircutting, shampooing, marcelling, and permanent waving. "December 13, 1928. Photog. appt. 11.00. Wear whites!" That might have been the note Letitia wrote to herself in her daybook. December 13, 1928, is the date on a diploma that swears, in a fine calligraphic hand, that she has satisfied the requirements of Marvel's "Beauty Course Complete."

Oh, the Marvel girls! Look at them, wise and vestal virgins, priestesses of Venus, all dressed in their blameless acolyte robes, with their hair marcelled to a fare-thee-well, and little kiss-curls punctuating their foreheads just above their pencilled brows. They are the fulfilment of prophecies set down long ago in Kleiser's Holy Book.

> Her cheeks are like the blushing cloud
> Her eyes, glimmering star-like in her pale face
> Her lashes like fans upon her cheek
> Her little lips are tremulous as brook-water is
> Her skin was as the bark of birches
> Her two white hands, like swans on a frozen lake

All the days of the months just gone have been leading up to this moment. They know one another so well, know the contours of every classmate's face: the plane of cheekbone, the arc of

brow, the droop of chin, the faint line of moustache, the shadow
of a nose. They have been one another's guinea pigs. They have
willingly surrendered themselves, to one another, to a Platonic
ideal, to the suffering that is the midwife of beauty. They came
as disciples. Now they are apostles, with a mission. With a
gospel to spread. They are the Marvel girls, and they will never
forget it. It is 1928, and they are primed and eager to stride out
into the dangerous world, the jazz world, the talking-picture
world, the flapper world, the nothing-is-impossible world. Their
autograph books are full of fond and hopeful inscriptions.

> A half a yard of Georgia crêpe
> A facial and a curl
> Chiffon stockings, eyes that lure,
> Behold! The Marvel girl!

What would they have thought had they looked over their
shoulders and seen what was tearing along to catch them up:
the dust bowl, the drought, the Depression?

> Choose not your friends from outward show
> For the feathers float and the pearls lie low.

What would the Marvel girls have thought, as they arranged
themselves in their ranks in that studio; as they perched on the
tiered benches, on that December day, in that overheated room,
the air electric with static charge and thick with the grime that
had settled over the years on the plush draperies, the trailing,
trellised plants that were the photographer's dependable backdrop; what would they have thought as they engaged the camera, as they inhaled the several subtle scents of one another's
talcum, or rose-water spray; what would they have thought had
they known that one day their portrait would finish up in an
antique store on Main Street in Vancouver; that it would come
into the hands of a complete stranger who would fall in love
with them, who would spend much, much more time than he

properly ought, looking into their soft and frozen faces; who would invent their lives?

(See the sweet-faced girl with the long raven hair flipped at the shoulders? She almost failed to get her qualification because she missed two weeks of classes after her father hanged himself in the barn. She had to work hard to catch up when she came back. Nail care she found especially difficult. She just couldn't wrap her mind around nail care.

The girl kneeling on the bear-skin rug? She would tell her landlady she was going out for a malted and all the time she was sneaking into speakeasies. Only last night she caught the eye of a visiting bootlegger with important Mob connections, and she'll be living in Chicago before the year is out.

The two plump girls seated behind the speakeasy moll have formed a special attachment and they think they might go off to Paris together. If not Paris, somewhere, anywhere that's not here. When you have a pot of rouge and you can give a permanent wave, the waves will part before you.

The tall girl, standing on the left, the one with the crimped-up locks, will become a nun, will forswear all vanity, will take her vows in a firm, steadfast voice, but will secretly paint her toenails different colours — red, pink, coral, magenta, turquoise — will do so all her life, and no one will find out until 1981, when she dies at the age of seventy-six, and the removal of her shoes will start the breath of scandal wafting through the convent.

And the heavy-set girl who stands in the third row, at the extreme right of the photograph, the practical-looking young woman who seems to keep herself to herself? She's the one whose name no one could remember. She's the one at whom the photographer took one look and fell in love.)

Cows like apples
Pigs like squash
I like you, Hatley,
I do, by gosh.

Viola, Olga, Phyllis, Pauline, Olive, Tessie, Okie, Lillie, and Hatley. I know their names because Letitia noted them on the back of the photograph. She must have done so in her old age, not long before her death, not long before her goods would be parcelled up and sold at an estate sale, which was how she and her sisters came into my care and keeping. She must have done so in her old age when her memory was failing her and many names had been sundered from faces, as only half the girls are identified. Of course, Letitia did not inscribe her own name. Modesty forbade. Besides, what would have been the point in pointing herself out? She knew perfectly well who she was.

> Any girl would be gay
> In a classy coupé
> In a taxi they all can be jolly.
> But the regular girl
> Is the one who can smile
> While you're taking her home in a trolley.

Which is Letitia? Where is she sitting? Standing? Did she seek out the comfort of the centre? Or did she draw her strength from the edge? It's the girls on the margins I wonder about most, the girls who lean away from the firm but gentle hand, the kindly governance of Mrs. Johnston; who seek to enliven her tried-and-true prescription for beauty with their own saucy combinations. I wonder especially about the siren seated on the far left, at the very end of the second row. Her sceptical glance, her haughty demeanour, her been-around-the-block look that says "Don't give me that watch-the-birdie crap, mister, I've seen your kind before, I've got your number, and your birdie just ain't worth watching!"

I love her two kiss-curls, like tiny, crumpled horns. Check out the Clara Bow mouth, the gypsy hoops that are her ear-rings, and that gold chain around her neck. From whom was it a gift? What does she remember when she puts it on? She is angled away from the group. She cannot wait for this to be over.

She cannot wait for this suffocation to end, for her life to begin. Her heart is rattling the bars of its cage. It is too big to be contained by convention, by expectation. Her suitcase is packed. She has set it down just out of camera range. As soon as she hears the shutter snap, she will be out the door. Before the others have stopped blinking from the flash, she will have disappeared.

In the garden of your friendship
Keep a warm and sunny spot
Where my fondest wish may blossom
It is this — forget-me-not.

Years later, Letitia would look back at the Marvel girls. She would remember how she chased Clara Bow (that is what she will call her, in the absence of a name) out of the studio when she saw how she had left her autograph book lying on the floor. She ran after her, into the snowy December street, called Clara! Clara! But Clara only stopped to light a cigarette. She tossed the match over her shoulder and never looked back. Letitia watched as she receded into the future, watched the relentless retreat of her muskrat coat, her seamed stockings, her battered valise, her pert little bob; watched until she turned the corner, and that was the end of her. She left no forwarding address. She never turned up for the reunions. Letitia would sometimes dream of her, of Clara, and in her dreams she was walking, always walking. Clara walking, brisk and purposeful, but with no destination in mind. Walking through the world as if she owned it. Walking as if she were born to it. Walking as if she didn't care that the girls all talked about her when they realized she was gone. Who did she think she was? Little Miss All the Nerve! Little Miss High and Mighty! Little Miss Vanish Into Thin Air! Why, she didn't even trouble to sign my book, and after all that time I spent on her cuticles!

Think of us now
Think of us ever

Think of the gang
We are Marvel, forever.

"Ready ladies? Smile!"

CLICK

And then, it was done. Then, it was over. Then, she was gone.

The Forest Primeval

This is the forest primeval; but where are the hearts...
— Longfellow, "Evangeline"

Clara was not alone. In 1928, Lillian Alling — pronounced "ailing" — was likewise walking. One foot in front of the other, for 5,000 miles. Walking, walking, never balking, merrily on she rolled.

"Lillian Alling, steadfast, unfailing, where does your garden grow?" That was what the lonely telegraph linesmen demanded of her as she hiked past their cabins, through the dense British Columbia forest, as fixed on the north as any compass.

"Siberia" was her answer.

"Where are you off to, miss?" asked the police when they stopped her from travelling in the deep-snow country of the Bulkley Valley, alone in the dead of winter.

"Siberia! Let me go. Let me go. I am going to Siberia."

At the New York Public Library, they had been no less incredulous when she told them her plan.

"You want to walk where?"

The librarian was certain she had misheard, or had not been able to make out the request through the young woman's Eastern European accent. Was she Russian? Polish?

"Siberia," answered Lillian, a little too loudly. "Siberia," she whispered, and she carried every available map to the long, varnished table in the hushed reference room. She spread them out. She took out her pencil and notebook. She began to plot her route.

She left New York in the spring of 1927. What was she leaving behind? The throbbing metropolis. Her job as a maid. The usual disappointments. She never said why she turned her back on the bustle and the promise of the city, never said why she had come there in the first place. Adventure, let's suppose. Rumour. Because it was there.

"Siberia" was the answer she gave to anyone who asked as she walked west. Through Chicago, St. Paul, up to Winnipeg, and west across the prairies. Thirty miles a day she walked, in her simple brown skirt and shirt, her sensible boots. If she sang "Val-da-ree, Val-da-rah" as she walked with her knapsack on her back, no one thought to write it down. "Siberia" was Lillian Alling's constant refrain as she walked, through the foothills, over the mountains, all the way to Vancouver. Then she veered north, bearing straight for the Bering Strait. She followed the Cariboo Wagon Road, walked through Ashcroft, Hundred Mile House, 150 Mile House, Quesnel, Prince George, New Hazelton, and Hazelton. She was a thousand miles south of Dawson when she joined up with the telegraph line. Imagine the surprise of the linesmen who heard "Siberia" when she turned up at their cabin doors, thin, ragged, and on fire with determination. Of course she was mad. Why else would she do such a thing? She had to be stopped, she had to be reported, at least. The police were summoned. Questions were asked.

"What do you eat?"

"Berries. Bark."

"Why do you carry that iron bar?"

"Protection."

"Against animals?"

"Against men."

"Where are you going, miss?"

"Siberia."

They took her in. For her own good, they said, they sent her back to Vancouver. She spent a couple of months in jail, serving a sentence for vagrancy. On her release, she got a kitchen job in a restaurant. Spring came, and she put on her walking boots. By mid-July 1928, she was back in Smithers. This time, she would not be deterred.

Lillian Alling followed the line, and the telegraph messages scuttled above her. Telegraph Creek, Sheslay, Nahlin, Nakina, Pike River, Atlin, Carcross, Whitehorse, Fort Selkirk. When she reached Dawson, early in October, she was wearing a different style of men's shoe on each foot. She wintered there. She got a job, slinging hash. She bought a boat and fixed it up. She waited for the thaw. Sometimes, during the twenty-two-hour nights, the northern lights would sing, and Lillian would join in the chorus. Siberia. Siberia.

In the spring of 1929, she launched her skiff and set off up the Yukon River. She was 1,600 miles from the Bering Sea. And that is where her story peters out. There were rumours that she was seen pushing a two-wheeled cart, somewhere near Teller, Alaska. There were rumours that she was apprehended by authorities on the other side. Nothing is known for sure, though. Some say she was homesick, inhabited by a desperate longing for her family, country, language. Some say she was driven half-mad by a love that went wrong. She offered no explanation other than Siberia. When all is said and done, the only certainty is that one day she set out walking.

For a while she had a dog, Bruno. One of the linesmen gave him to her as a guardian and gift. He was a pack dog, and she loved him, but he drank from a poisoned stream and died. It broke her heart. She had him skinned and tanned, and when last she was seen, she was carrying Bruno — who was beyond cure but nonetheless cured — with her, schlepping his pelt on her back. Lillian Alling, what was she trailing, what did she have to show? Her tattered skirt streaked with sweat and dirt and the corpse of a dog in tow. She dragged him behind her, just as St. Simeon Salus had done with his no-name dog, wandering and babbling along the streets of Emesa, 1,600 years before. God's dear fools. Salus and his children. All his sons, and all his daughters, all their funny little ways. Look what I found, Ma! He followed me home. Can I keep him?

July 1, 1997. Just a few hours ago, and for the last time, the Union Jack was lowered in Hong Kong. Never one to shrink from jumping on a bandwagon, I, too, have reverted to china. As recently as last year, it would have been paper plates, disposable forks, and a plastic tumbler of cheap champagne. Not today, though. Not any more. I have acquired standards to which I cleave. I have an image to uphold. Middle-aged. Stodgy. Conservative. Establishment. I have worked hard for this, and I have no intention of throwing it away. Do without china? Unthinkable. Why, if someone should saunter through this meadow and see me eating my Canada Day/St. Simeon Salus picnic from something ersatz like, say, Chinette, I don't know what I'd do. Word would get out. I know it would. There'd be no point in going on.

What a varied array of delicacies I've assembled on my grandmother's Blue Mikado. What a colourful assortment of comestibles! Hummus. Dolmades. Roasted peppers: red, yellow, and orange. A fragrant bread laced with olives and sun-dried tomatoes. Smoked trout. Roasted chicken (free-range) with a tasty little pepper and garlic condiment on the side. A runny Brie (French). A good Fumé Blanc (Californian). Some lemon sorbet, insulated against the warmth of the day with an ice-pack. However did privilege get such a bad name when it's this much fun? My grin is so wide you can see my gums. Which I note is "smug" spelled backwards. Which may or may not be significant. I read less into such coincidences than was once the case.

I am not absolutely alone. My shaggy old dog is with me. She lies beside me, doing her celebrated impersonation of a bath mat. She is not so very long for this world, and I have promised her that she will be spared the post-mortem indignities foisted on their animals by Lillian and Simeon. She gave no outward sign of gladness at this news, though I am confident that in her heart she rejoiced. There are some cows who graze nearby, safely contained in their pasture by an electrified fence. They call to mind Emily Carr, who wrote in *The Book of Small* of how she would sing to the denizens of the cow-yard.

"When Small began to sing the old cow's nose-line shot from straight down to straight out, her chin rose into the air, her jaws rolled. The harder Small sang, the harder the cow chewed and the faster she twiddled her ears around as if stirring the song into the food to be rechewed in the cud along with her breakfast."

How grand it would have been to have had Emily here today. It would be grander still had Glenn Gould been able to come along for the ride. They were both dog fanciers, and Glenn was also known to serenade cows. He turned his back on sold-out concert halls, would not perform for an adoring and paying public, but would happily croon to a select audience on the hoof. There's a photograph of him doing just that in Peter F. Ostwald's book, *Glenn Gould: The Ecstasy and Tragedy of Genius*. It's a fuzzy-edged shot snapped by the soprano Roxolana Roslak. Glenn is perched on a rock, in a field. He wears his overcoat and familiar peaked cap while he vocalizes for some appreciative bovine fans. This was on Manitoulin Island, a place that exerted an Edenic tug on Gould. He fantasized that one day he would buy a farm there and establish a retirement home for beasts who were past their prime.

In fact, my cows — I hold them now in proprietary regard — have been getting the Gould treatment this afternoon. I have brought along a tape-deck and the soundtrack to *Thirty-two Short Films About Glenn Gould*. It contains his performances of music by Strauss, Beethoven, Sibelius, Hindemith, Prokofiev, Schoenberg, as well as several selections by J. S. Bach. Now and again you can hear his guttural, trademark "dum-dum-dumming" rumbling through. I am obliged to say that the cattle have not been visibly stirred by his lowing. Nor do they seem responsive to the quintessentially sixties sound of "Downtown." Its inclusion on an otherwise classical album is a tribute to Glenn's fondness for Petula Clark.

Downtown. Manitoulin Island. For Gould, they both held Utopian possibilities. Me, I'm a downtown kind of boy. Mine is not a voice fit for crying in the wilderness. Even to so pastoral a place as this — this meadow on the forest edge, only half an hour from the city — I bring along the trappings of urbanity. I find my peace in concrete and crowds, in fumes and noise. Not for me the forest primeval. Though I admire it in the abstract, and appreciate the important role it plays in the maintenance of the biosphere, and value it as a symbol, there is little that makes me as nervous as a thick tangle of trees. It has ever been thus. As a little child, I would listen to the story of Hansel and Gretel and squirm when they left the safety of their home, when they turned their backs on comfort and civilization and entered that dark and pathless wood. *Don't do it! So much that's bad can happen in there! You don't know what you're up against! Bears, bogs, badgers, witches! You'll get lost! Fools! Fools!* This was what I'd want to shout, to warn them, even though I knew perfectly well it would all work out fine, just fine, in the end. Similarly, the many legends of Robin Hood, and his merry men in Sherwood, made me feel more agitated than elated, and all because of the setting. I could see that it was an expedient environment for a bunch of well-intentioned outlaws, but I couldn't help but wish that they had found some other, more citified place for their redistribution-of-resources initiative. I would have been so much more comfortable, so much more willing to absorb their socialist message, had they robbed from the rich and given to the poor in Chelsea, say. Or Soho. Even downtown Nottingham would have done.

Despite this deep-rooted aversion, I experienced a twinge of sadness when I read in *The New York Times*, on April 8, 1994, an article with the headline "SHADES OF ROBIN! FOREST MAY BE SOLD." The story had to do with the hue and cry that erupted over the then Conservative government's plan to privatize the management of England's woodlands and heaths, including Sherwood Forest. Not that there was much left to manage in Sherwood. Most of the oak, birch, and yew that gave shelter to Robin and company was gone. Where there was any vegetation at all, it tended to be clusters of Mediterranean pine that had been imported after the Great War. By and large, the land had been given over to settlement and industry. It made me glum to think of all the gullible and disappointed pilgrims who must surely visit Nottinghamshire every year, only to have their mind's-eye vision of this brooding, mythic shadowland dashed beyond repair. It made me glum because it reminded me of David Curnick, who will always be linked in my mind with Robin Hood, and who died on January 31, 1994. He was — is — the only murder victim I've ever known.

I cannot say I knew him well. We were peripheral to each other's lives. We met through friends of friends, would intersect at parties and on the street. For a couple of years we lived a few blocks apart and we'd bump into each other fairly regularly. These meetings always took place by chance, never by design, but they happened often enough that our acquaintanceship became more than nodding. David was on the short side, about five feet, six inches, and puckish, the kind of person about whom you'd be tempted to use the phrase "elfin twinkle." He was bright and friendly. He had a keen sense of humour. He was articulate. By the time I met him he was in his mid-forties and had had a varied career. He'd been active as a film maker, had written and/or produced several low-budget features. I'd never seen these, and was under the impression that they had either been held up for years in post-production limbo, or had had only a very limited release. As well, he done some work with the National Film Board. It wasn't lucrative, and he kept body and soul together with a half-time job teaching English at Gladstone Secondary School on Vancouver's east side. He had been there for years, and was well known throughout the school for his unconventional approach to classroom management and for the musical extravaganzas he staged every year. These were elaborate, choreographed mime shows, which featured students lip-synching along with popular tunes.

David had much to recommend him, but he always made me edgy. Wary, sort of. When we had our occasional collisions, he would throw me off balance with the way he could steer the chat away from the bland pleasantries that are usual in such encounters into a voluble disquisition about what was new and vital in his ongoing research into the life and times of Robin Hood. There was an inevitability about the conversational drift that I found both engaging and dispiriting. With David, it was Robin Hood this, Robin Hood that, Robin Hood round the Maypole. He just loved, loved, loved Robin Hood. Ever since his childhood days in England, ever since he first saw the 1950s television series starring Richard Greene, Robin had been his governing passion. It grew with him. It followed him to Canada. He became an avid collector of films and videos and books and articles and visual representations of the Sherwood legends. It spilled over into his every undertaking. While it was lovely to see someone in whom a childhood enthusiasm had not withered, and while this youthful sprightliness inhabiting a middle-aged man presented a charming incongruity, I sniffed a depressing air of hopelessness about his obsession. He was always laying plans, big plans, which had Robin Hood paving David Curnick's path to the glory and recognition he had been denied, and somehow those plans never came to fruition. Of smoke there was plenty, but there was never a sign of flame in the forest.

Whenever I saw him, he would bring me up to date on the Robin Hood documentary he wanted to make but which was caught in a state of perpetual delay. He would give me the latest news about a book he planned to write. He had been talking about the damn thing for years. It was a project on a grand scale, the "definitive" examination of screen treatments of the Robin legend. It was a good idea, and as a film maker and self-made Sherwood Forest authority, he was ideally positioned to bring it off. To his credit, he did more than merely talk about it. He sent query letters to many publishers and received several encouraging expressions of interest. He travelled to England and interviewed some of the actors, directors, and producers who had been involved with film and television presentations of the Sherwood legends. He met and maintained a friendly correspondence with Alan Wheatley, Nickolas Grace, Sidney Cole,

Paul Eddington, and Patricia Driscoll, among others. In 1985, he visited Bristol and landed a walk-on role as a peasant in one of the episodes of *Robin of Sherwood.*

David Curnick aloft as a merry man.

He prepared, and prepared and prepared, but never got around to doing. He was like someone who winds and winds a jack-in-the-box that refuses to pop. David was not oblivious to the tragi-comic aspects of his quixotic tilting. There's a current of irony in the annual report he sent to his various correspondents and confederates, and in which he summarized his progress to date on the book that never was.

"August, 1990. How time flies. Eight years since I contacted most of you and told you of my plans. You'd think I was writing some kind of Decline and Fall."

"August 1991. It seemed that ten whole weeks of summer would provide me with so much time to work on 'the book.' Alas, I was wrong."

"May 1992. Well, I have to reluctantly admit that this is the 10th anniversary of my pronouncement that a book on Robin

Hood in film and on television was happening. I carry on, each year inexorably moving towards…what?"

Looking back from this temporal vantage point — the feast day of St. Simeon Salus, 1997 — I see how there was something dear about all this fudging and delaying and hoping. Something sweet. But at the time, I'm afraid I dismissed David as a bit of a flake, as one of those would-be writers who was more talk than typing; who bag on endlessly about how they long to string words together but never get down to the hard slog of it.

Of course, when I heard David had been murdered, I was jolted by stupid guilt. *I once thought badly of him, and now he is dead.* As if there were some causal connection. As if fondness would have made a difference. I had not seen him for some time. He had moved from the neighbourhood, and it had been a year at least since I had spoken to or of him. At such a remove I responded to the news of his violent passing with more shock than grief. I didn't know him well enough to mourn. But of course I was curious. Murder victims are never people one knows. How could this have happened to David? He was not innocuous, exactly, but he hardly seemed a candidate for harm. How on earth? However on earth?

When I began my winter's wandering, when I undertook to write about Canadian eccentrics, I determined that Rumour would be the pillar of fire I would follow to narrative's promised land. My methodology, such as it was, was passive and reactive. I would make it known, as best I could, that I was looking for stories. I would wait for word to come. Then, I would follow up on proffered leads. In this regard, David Curnick is an aberrant inclusion in the gallery. No one mentioned his name to me. No one spoke of his qualities or nominated him for inclusion. He surfaced in my own meditations early on, and I determined that he would find a place here. In some ways, for me, he came to personify the pleasures and perils of a life abstracted from the centre. Two poles exerted their influence on his compass: the scorned and the beloved.

We admire people who give rein to their passions and obsessions, who fly in the face of convention, who have easy access to an id unmediated by a prissy, stultifying ego. We need them. You could say they have a societal utility. They shake up the old order. They remind us that our familiar priorities, whether personal or political, are arbitrary; the product of unthinking convention, and nothing more. We cherish these outsized characters because they amplify qualities we each of us possess in some small measure. And we love them because they give us stories. When all is said and done, it is stories that keep us buoyant.

On the other hand, we are suspicious of such psychic spaciousness. It makes us uneasy. It can be messy and inconvenient. We like to know that there are mavericks and rule-breakers among us, but we want them at a tidy remove. We want them across the block and down the street. We are fearful of the contact that leads to contagion. All that "in your face" passion and volubility quickly wears thin. It's like a hot wind, pleasant and novel for a short while, but shrivelling and unnerving in the long run.

I knew him only slightly, but David Curnick stirred in me a strong reaction. He muddied my waters with both fascination and aversion. The more I thought about his eccentricities — his Robin Hood obsession especially — the more I wanted to learn about his story. His fanciful life. His brutal end. I would not have been able to venture into such hard territory had I not had the cooperation of three men who knew him well and whose friendship he valued. I am indebted to Graham Peat, who was the executor of his estate, and who kindly gave me access to his files and papers; to Dennis Pilon, who was one of David's students and who is now completing his doctoral work in political science at York University; and to Larry Killick, who was a long-time colleague at Gladstone Secondary School.

Larry, like most of the teachers at Gladstone, knew about David's all-embracing fondness for Robin Hood. David left full-time teaching in 1984, in favour of a half-time position, with the intention of devoting himself to the famous book. As well, he wanted to focus his attentions on a music business he had run for some years, a disc-jockey service, called Robin Hood Mobile Sound. The students were likewise apprised of his passion for all things Sherwood. Anyone who had Mr. C. as an English teacher soon learned that all his roads led to Nottinghamshire. He found ways of working the stories and films — especially the Richard Greene series — into his lesson plans. He justified their inclusion, when he was required to, by saying that folklore and mythology were part of the curriculum, and that the Robin stories were central to Anglo-Saxon traditions. The screen presentations, he said, enriched his students' vocabularies and were wonderful examples of tightly written narrative. And yes, there were quizzes.

Larry, like most of the teachers at Gladstone, knew that David was gay. He was discreet, but not secretive about his sexuality. He had written letters to the editor in support of gay causes. Some of his films had homoerotic themes. He belonged to an educators' gay and lesbian advocacy group. From all reports, he did not share this aspect of his life with his students, at least not in a direct way. Some may have drawn their own conclusions. Dennis Pilon recalls that there was a distinct campiness to his choice of classroom decorations, and his annual lip-synch extravaganzas held certain clues, particular drag-show references, for those who chose to find them. David had dallied with drag, had done a turn or two on stage in a club called BJ's. It was a lark, nothing more. It never became a lifestyle.

Larry was one of only a very few teachers at Gladstone who knew that David had once run a gay dating service called — no surprise here — Sherwood Forest Personal Introductions. That was in the mid-seventies. He may have matched a few true loves, but his interest was mostly in getting dates for himself. When he sold the business, he placed a running personal advertisement in a now-defunct sex-trade rag called *Star*. When that paper floundered, he transferred his allegiance to a weekly called *Buy & Sell*. He developed a niche-marketing strategy, and composed an ad that was a friendly, non-threatening come-on directed towards bisexual men, or to nominally straight fellows who might be in the mood for some experimentation. He used the usual catch phrases. First-timers welcome. Don't be shy. Give it a try. Call the Hotline. That was what he called it. The Hotline.

"David," remembers Dennis Pilon, "was a fan of all things British, a true Anglophile. It wasn't just Robin Hood. He loved such comedy series as *Yes, Minister*, and the *Carry On* movies. He was also very keen on espionage, especially the James Bond books and films. When he set up his Hotline, he actually installed a red telephone. Over the twenty years that he ran this service he met an astonishing number of men. More than anyone would have thought possible. Some would come over once, some more often.

"David never felt he was very good at presenting himself as an attractive commodity on the meat market, so he looked for other ways to meet sex partners. Like many people who spend years longing and never achieving, he got very fixed ideas about what he found attractive. He never got into that dialectic of sex, when your whole sense of attraction changes, when you discover that your partners don't have to be muscled, or hairless, or whatever. He became set in his ways. He liked big guys, muscular guys, Italianate guys. He liked them to be sort of menacing, but not very much so. He liked the illusion of rough trade, but was certainly not into getting hurt or pushed around. He was severe with anyone who got out of place, and he developed a remarkable set of skills for knowing who might be trouble."

Dennis and Graham Peat and David were part of a group of friends who would meet every Sunday for brunch. Often, David would regale them with stories of the "studs" he had met over the phone and whom he subsequently entertained in his home. These tales were received with a mixture of fascination and horror. Both Dennis and Graham warned David, as did Larry Killick in whom he also confided some of his adventures, that he was treading on thin ice. He was almost fifty. He was not a paragon of athleticism. He was putting himself in harm's way. David countered that he had taken the risks into account and that he took precautions to safeguard his person. He set an alarm when his visitors arrived, so that it would go off when they left unless he disarmed it. He kept a baseball bat under his bed.

He was lucky. Once or twice he had to eject a gentleman caller who was drunk and disorderly. Otherwise, there were no problems. There were plenty of guys who wanted what he offered, and for twenty years he enjoyed an active no-fuss, no-muss, no-obligations sex life. Little wonder he felt confident. He even began covertly videotaping his encounters, concealing a camera with a wide-angle lens in a stereo stand. His brunch buddies didn't mince words when they learned of this development. They told him such a tactic was both foolish and reprehensible. Many of the men he was meeting were insecure about their sexuality. Confidence, for them, was paramount. He was betraying a trust, and he was risking terrible consequences if he should be caught. David heard these concerns, but persisted. He had no intention of ever showing the tapes he made, and he further rationalized his actions by citing reasons of security. What if he were to be robbed? The videos could help identify the thief.

"POLICE THINK VICTIM KNEW HIS MURDERER"

That was the headline in the *Province* on February 2, 1994. And the police, it turned out, were right in their surmise. His name was Darin Young. David didn't know him well, but they had met on at least three occasions. They saw each other on the night of the murder, when Darin stabbed David repeatedly, in his own home, with one of his own kitchen knives, and they had seen each other earlier in that same week. Some six or seven years had elapsed between their second meeting and their first. They got together through the Hotline. Graham Peat remembers that David told him about that first meeting. He remembers that his friend was concerned. There was something about Darin that wasn't quite right. For one thing, he seemed rather young, even though he claimed to be nineteen. David was always, by every account, scrupulous about meeting only with callers who were of legal age. He activated his trouble-sensing radar, and his instincts proved spot-on. The boy called him again, not long after their first encounter. He'd changed his story. Now he claimed to be under age. He threatened to go to the police and lay charges of molestation unless they could agree on a cash settlement. David declined to play along. Darin never followed through. He disappeared.

When he resurfaced, some years later, he was fresh out of jail. He had served time for several misdemeanours, including violent misconduct. There was no longer any question of his majority. He was older, twenty-six, and his appearance was radically different.

"TATTOOED MAN SOUGHT IN SLAYING"

That was the headline in *The Province* on February 11, 1994. Why did Darin seek David out after so troubled a parting? Had he held him in his head the whole time of his incarceration? Or did he just happen on the ad again when he was flipping through the personals section of *Buy & Sell*, and call him up for old time's sake? On such arcane points as these, no one is clear. All that is sure is that they had a reunion. David, who was always sharing of such information, told his brunch companions that Darin was back on the scene, told them that he was now tattooed from stem to stern. They warned him against having any further contact. They told him the young man was surely disturbed, that he was bound to be trouble. "But he's terribly exciting" was David's answer.

Dennis Pilon says that David would engage in fantasy play with his Hotline friends. He would construct scenarios and have his friends act them out. He would ask them to pose for him, flex their muscles, encourage them to come at him in a threatening, but not too threatening, way. When Darin Young dropped by for the last time, on January 31, 1994, he went along with the prescribed scenario until it came time to turn on his host with mock menace. Then, he abandoned any pretense of play acting.

He left the apartment with David's wallet and chequebook. By the time the neighbours came to investigate the alarm, it was too late. "It's a terrible thing to happen at your own front door," one condo owner told a reporter, and she was surely right. The papers reported that David was stabbed more than a hundred times. And all the while, the video camera was taking it in. An unblinking eye. A terrible record. His final film.

David had been right all along about the utility of such evidence. In the end, he helped capture his own killer. The police released images from the tape to the papers. Darin's picture — his long hair, his muscled chest, his many tattoos — was published all over the country. He turned himself in in Kelowna, pleaded guilty, and was once again confined. Dennis and Graham attended the sentencing.

"David," said Dennis, "was my oldest friend, one of my best friends, and I miss him all the time. When I went to that sentencing though, all I could think was that there were two victims. Two tragedies. There was David, of course. And there was Darin. Here was someone who came from a background of terrible abuse, who was in and out of foster homes, who had sustained a head injury, who never really stood a chance, who held tremendous anger, and who, on top of everything else, got stuck with this uncertainty about his own sexuality in a society that hates gay people. And now where is he? In jail. And what kind of help will he get there? And in ten years when he's out, what's going to happen?"

What one wants, of course, is closure. What one wants is what one can't have, and that is the answer to the variations on the question: why? Why would anyone stab someone a hundred times? Why would David have willingly put himself in so vulnerable a situation with so dangerous a predator? Fatalism? Thrill seeking? Or was it just misplaced trust? A bad call? That's not so unlikely. Many of us can look back on an encounter that made perfect sense in the moment, and been appalled that it ever took place; shuddered at the prospect of what might have been.

It would not have been out of character for David to have met Darin with the hope of some kind of reconciliation in mind. Each of his friends told me, independently, that David was pathologically reluctant to let go of people who had passed through his orbit, to release them, or allow them to slip from his grasp and life. He knew that he could alienate people. He was always doing battle with some imagined foe, and he was argumentative and controlling by nature. He would fight with his friends, would give or take offence. There would be a sundering, a cooling off, and then a *rapprochement*. He would make overtures of friendship that were pleading, toadying almost. It was a familiar pattern. It happened time and again. He couldn't bear the weight of contempt. He wanted nothing more than acceptance. He wanted everyone to be his friend. He wanted to belong. He wanted to be part of a band of merry men.

Why did he love Robin Hood and the boys of Sherwood so much? Pick your reason. Because they were anti-authoritarian, and David felt he had been squashed by people who were in power. Because they stood up for the little guy. Because they looked great in tights. Mostly, all his friends agree, it was because they were naughty and got away with it.

David Curnick was a man who was lucky in his friends. They cared for him, watched out for him. They speak well of his accomplishments as both an artist and a teacher. They would like to see his films get wider attention. They were pleased when his family established a scholarship in his name. They want to see his memory and the several truths of his life preserved. They loved him for who and what he was. They loved him for his passion. For his naughtiness.

David was an adoring fan of Brenda Lee, Connie Francis, and Petula Clark. I imagine he might have enjoyed this little outing; would have enjoyed spending an afternoon here on the edge of these brooding woods — thicker than Sherwood — with Petula reprising yet again her hit of 1964. "Downtown," she sings, and it sounds like a good idea. This picnic is done. The country is another year older. St. Simeon Salus Day is withering on the vine. Even the cattle have taken a powder. I've always wanted to be able to say I wrote till the cows came home. Now I can.

Let's call it a day. It's time. The forest primeval is no longer content to hold back its shadows. It's sending them out in our direction. Look, look. Now they come. You can hear their steady jackboot tread. Their merciless advance. I shiver and do what I always do in moments of psychic distress. I close my eyes and think of Kipling ("The Way Through the Woods"):

> They shut the road through the woods
> Seventy years ago.
> Weather and rain have undone it again,
> And now you would never know
> There was once a road through the woods
> Before they planted the trees.

Seventy years ago. Nineteen twenty-seven. The year Lillian Alling began her walking. The year Letitia Reed made her big decision, sat down at her desk and wrote, "To Whom It May Concern, I am interested to know more about the courses offered by the Marvel School of Cosmetology. I enclose a stamped, self-addressed envelope for your reply." Nineteen twenty-seven. The year Marius Barbeau, who would later write down the story of Alexis Le Trotteur, recommended that Emily Carr's paintings be considered as part of an exhibition of West Coast art at the National Gallery of Canada. Nineteen twenty-seven was the year the Gallery director, Eric Brown, went to Victoria to visit Emily and see her work. He was overwhelmed — as millions of us have been since — by their energy and heft and vibrancy. He was charmed by the round little woman who had seen the forest in so particular and striking a way, and who lived with her dogs and her monkey called Woo, and was funny and quick and odd, and embittered. At his request, she composed an autobiographical sketch. In 1927 she wrote:

"When I sent to an exhibition they dishonoured my work in every way, putting it behind things, under shelves, or on the ceiling. My friends begged me to go back to my old way of painting, but [as] I had tasted the joys of a bigger way it would have been impossible had I wanted to, which I did not. When ever I could afford it I went up north among the Indians and the woods and forgot all about everything in the joy of those lonely wonderful places, I decided to make as good a representative collection of those old villages and wonderful totem poles as I could, for the love of the people, and the love of the places, and the love of the art, whether anybody liked them or not I did not care a bean.

"I painted them to please myself in my own way…"

The joys of a bigger life. Emily Carr achieved greatness before anyone had ever heard of her, but I don't suppose she could have known or imagined, as she wrote those anxious and defensive words, that her greatness was about to lead to fame. She was on the cusp of success. She would go to the east, and step into the warm light of approbation. She would feel the seductive tug of the centre. But she knew who she was, and where she belonged. She would never relinquish her claim on the margins. She would always be, in every way, eccentric.

In 1935, as though to renew those joyous, big-life vows, she painted *Scorned as Timber, Beloved of the Sky*. A tall and spindly fir is all that remains in a harvested forest. It was not worth the bother of cutting, not worth dulling the saw. There was no paper in it, no lumber. They passed it over. They left it where it stood, whole and uncompromised, paying the price of purposeful selfhood. Which is loneliness. Which is happiness. Which is communion with the sky. Scorned and beloved.

The breathless hours like phantoms stole away.

There's nothing left to do but pack away our feast. See? We've devoured so much, and so much still remains. It will always be like this. We need never fear famine. We need never know want. We can eat till we are bursting and our hunger will always be intact. We will always know the joy of wanting more. Praise the holy hunger in this blessed, blessed land. Praise as well the ending of this odd and lucky road. Amen, good friends, and thanks for coming. For look, now. Look. We are home.

An Alphabet of Suggested Kleiserisms for the Use of Critics

All the lesser lights paled into insignificance
As fresh and invigorating as a sea breeze
Browsing at will on all the uplands of knowledge and thought
A charming air of vigor and vitality
Comment of rare and delightful flavor
A cunning intellect patiently diverting every circumstance to its design
Delicious throngs of sensations
Endowed with all those faculties that can make the world a garden of enchantment
Every phrase is like the flash of a scimitar
Felicitousness in the choice and exquisiteness in the collocation of words
The flawless triumph of art
The fruit of vast and heroic labors
A gay exuberance of ambition
Generosity pushed to prudence
A heart from which noble sentiments sprang like sparks from an anvil
His words gave a curious satisfaction, as when a coin, tested, rings true gold
An ideal as sublime and comprehensive as the horizon
Ideas which spread with the speed of light
The idiosyncratic peculiarities of thought
Judging without waiting to ponder over bulky tomes
Justifiable in certain exigencies
Keen power of calculation and unhesitating audacity

A large, rich, copious human endowment

A man of matchless modesty and refinement

The maximum of attainable and communicable truth

The meticulous observation of facts

No longer shall slander's venomed spite crawl like a snake
across his perfect name

Occasional flashes of tenderness and love

The oscillations of human genius

Plaudits of the unlettered mob

Prodigal of discriminating epithets

The purging sunlight of clear poetry

Questions and answers sounding like a continuous popping
of corks

Quickened and enriched by new contacts with life and truth

Refreshing as descending rains to sunburnt climes

The romantic ardor of a generous mind

A spacious sense of the amplitude of life's possibilities

Startling leaps over vast gulfs of time

Through the riot of his senses, like a silver blaze, ran the
legend

Touched every moment with shifting and enchanting beauty

Unforced and unstudied depth of feeling

Uplifting the soul as on dovelike wings

Voices that charm the ear and echo with a subtle resonance in
the soul

Volcanic upheavings of imprisoned passions

Words were flashing like brilliant birds through the boughs
overhead

Wrought of an emotion infectious and splendidly dangerous

Yearning tenderness

Zealous in the cause he affected to serve

Notes

I have made frequent and conspicuous use of Grenville Kleiser's forgotten masterpiece, *Fifteen Thousand Useful Phrases* (New York: Funk & Wagnalls, 1917). Kleiserisms are italicized throughout. Overwrought figures of speech that appear in roman type are, alas, my own. The *Dictionary of Canadian Biography* (Toronto: University of Toronto Press) was an invaluable resource. Biblical quotations are from the King James version.

1. Fugue

In writing about my childhood recollections of Glenn Gould (the *Reader's Digest* connection) I am not reporting facts but am giving an accurate account of my memories. As these are well over thirty years old, I would not be surprised to learn that they are not correct in their every biographical detail. Glenn Gould's appreciation of Petula Clark, "The Search for Petula Clark," appeared in *High Fidelity*, November 1967. It was reprinted in *The Glenn Gould Reader*, edited by Tim Page (Toronto: Lester & Orpen Dennys, 1984). His remarks about Toronto, originally part of a film-documentary script, were also anthologized by Mr. Page. Anna Brownell Jameson's *Winter Studies and Summer Rambles in Canada* was published in 1838, and released as part of McClelland & Stewart's "New Canadian Library" in 1990. *In Search of the Magnetic North: A Soldier–Surveyor's Letters from the North-west 1843–44*, by John Henry Lefroy (edited by George F. Stanley), was published by Macmillan, 1955. My thanks to Robert Rothon and Myron Plett for telling me about Messy May, whose story is included on their Tides of Men Web site.

2. Before We Go Further, a Parenthetical Word

The story of Esther Brandeau has been told in many different ways and places over the years. She is mentioned in Volume 2 of the *Dictionary of Canadian Biography*, and B. G. Sack's *The History of the Jews in Canada* (Montreal: Harvest House, 1964). Thanks to Thomas Walter Brooks, of Gravenhurst, Ontario, for the information on Sarah Emma Edmonds. Mr. Brooks is an American Civil War historian, and a keen participant in Civil War re-enactments. He is well known in Gravenhurst, Ontario, where he can often be seen riding about the town on his horse. They are an arresting sight at the Tim Horton's Drive-Thru, especially as Tom wears a Confederate army uniform every day of the year except Hallowe'en. Tom Brooks is the author (with Michael Dan Jones) of *Lee's Foreign Legion: A History of the 10th Louisiana Infantry.*

3. Begin
Chas. S. Robertson, of Kenabeek, Ontario, was the owner of what is now my copy of *Fifteen Thousand Useful Phrases*, and he did indeed mark particular similes with dates. Otherwise, I know nothing of his biography, and his story — as the reader will surely have deduced — is a fiction. Edith Sitwell's *English Eccentrics: A Gallery of Weird and Wonderful Men and Women* (Harmondsworth: Penguin Books, 1971) was first published by Faber & Faber in 1933. Henry Wilson and James Caulfield published *The Book of Wonderful Characters* in 1876 (London: Reeves). Glenn Gould's diet is discussed, in part, in Peter F. Ostwald's *Glenn Gould: The Ecstasy and Tragedy of Genius* (New York: W. W. Norton, 1997).

4. A Folly in Paradise
Any good hagiography, such as *Butler's Lives of the Saints* (4 vols), will make mention of the Simeons Stylites and Salus. For information on Charles Henry Danielle, I am especially grateful to Bert Riggs, archivist at the Centre for Newfoundland Studies at Memorial University. In reconstructing Danielle's story, I used the various clippings, brochures, etc. contained in the centre's files. I also used newspaper accounts; the papers of the day were full of stories about the goings-on at Octagon Castle. I made ample use of Danielle's own brochures. Both the *Dictionary of Canadian Biography* and *The Encyclopedia of Newfoundland and Labrador* have useful entries. As just one side of the Waugh/Brazill correspondence has been preserved (so far as I know), I can only guess at how these two men came into contact with each other in the first place. The italicized words in my text appear as underlinings in Waugh's letters. I found his candour about Danielle's

love of men surprising and moving. One of the Professor's fancy boys, he says, was a dentist, Dr. Harry Burnett. "Charles *worshipped* him. He was good looking and Charles' money was paid out for him like *water*. Charles afterwards told me that for all his kindness Burnett treated him like a *thief*. Charles got him there & introduced him & wrote out a fine lecture for him and afterwards Burnett made lots of money. You must have heard Charles speak of him. All of Charles' friends went back on him sooner or later."

The odd document in which Danielle, seemingly teetering on the brink of paranoia, writes of testing his servants' honesty reads, in part: "Believing that Mrs. Ryan is still stealing from me for Mr. Porter and others, toadying to their favours & opinions, I today, June 24 sent Adam McCamby & Mr. F. Brazill up in Porter's Room to see what was there from my Larder & this is their report. To wit, 2 sections of Rhubarb Pie, a lot of Rhubarb Jam, Half Doz Long's Biscuits all on a plate." Danielle instigated further investigations on July 15 and 27, on August 15, 26, 27, and 28, on which occasions his agents discovered bread, ham, chicken, and fancy cake. I don't know what punishments were meted out to the miscreants, but Mrs. Porter must have been forgiven her complicity as she was remembered in the will.

5. Devil among the Tailors

"Devil Among the Tailors" is a fiddle tune. All the tunes named are traditional, and are among those collected in *The Old Time Fiddler's Repertory*, Vol. 2. Compiled and edited by R.P. Christeson (Columbia: University of Missouri Press, 1984). The story of Pierre-Léon Ayotte appears in Volume 13 of the *Dictionary of Canadian Biography*. I did not interview Willie Francis Fraser in person, but spoke to him on the phone. His childhood visitation was reported by Bruce Erskine in the Halifax *Chronicle-Herald*, January 10, 1997. The story of Malcolm MacLean I learned from Barrie Fraser, of East Lake Ainslie, Nova Scotia. He related it in a letter he sent to the CBC Stereo program "As You Like It."

6. Shock

That a Mrs. Joyner was brushed by lightning, while in her room, and that she was unharmed, was reported in *The Toronto Daily Star*, June 23, 1906. The other facts of her life are unknown to me, and her story is an invention. I met Mr. Eddy R. Souris in the lobby of the CBC building in Toronto, in November 1996. I have been unsuccessful in my efforts to contact him, and wish him well in his mousing around. The lyrics to "My Old Island Home" were written by Janette McLeod Morrison. The story of Modomnoc, who brought apiculture to Ireland, is contained in David Hugh Farmer's *The Oxford Dictionary of Saints* (Oxford: Oxford University Press, 1978). Hazlitt relates the story of the funeral party turned topsy-turvy by bees in his *Dictionary of Faiths & Folklore*, first published in 1905 by Reeves and Turner. Robert Dowie's story was assembled from material made available to me by the Prince Edward Island archives, as well as from contemporary accounts, reported in *The Islander*.

7. Ark

For dove and pigeon lore, I am indebted to Miriam Rothschild's *Butterfly Cooing Like a Dove* (New York: Doubleday, 1991) and to Iona Opie and Moira Tatem's *A Dictionary of Superstitions* (Oxford: Oxford University Press, 1989). Walter J. Weber's *Health Hazards from Pigeons, Starlings, and English Sparrows* was published in 1979 by Thomson Publications of Fresno, California. The curious tale of Merit Bean is taken from newspaper accounts (particularly *The Boston Globe*) kindly provided by the Yarmouth County Museum Archives. The story of Samuel Bean and the cryptogram gravestone is well known in the Kitchener–Waterloo area. The story of the *Royal Tar* and Mogul, the elephant, was cobbled together from 836 newspaper accounts of the disaster published in Boston, Yarmouth, and Halifax.

8. Food for the Phoenix

I have based my story of the sad death of Keith Pelton on an account contained in *Yarmouth Past and Present: A Book of Reminiscences* by J. Murray Lawson, published in 1902.

9. The Offending Hand

Lâche pas y'a toujours un moyen, by Jean St-Germain (Drummondville, Quebec: Les Editions Indépendantes, 1979.) The pyramid is located between St-Hyacinthe and Drummondville at 1447, rang St-Georges. This description of the forbidden pyramid, meant to be the largest in the world and scotched by the agricultural land reserve, was given in *La Presse*, August 24, 1988. "Pour financer cet audacieux projet, la corporation Citadelle de la paix prévoit vendre des emplacements pour des urnes funéraires de $1,000 à $9,250, les prix variants selon la hauteur achetée par la famille éplorée. Tout de béton, la pryamide comprendra 42 étages, dont 33 contiendront les 22 millions d'urnes. L'occupation des étages supérieurs n'est pas encore déterminée, mais il pourra servir, entre autres utilisations, de salles de recueillement pour les familles des disparus, etc. Au sommet, précise Saint-Germain, on trouvera un prisme de 42 tonnes qui projettra, par un puits de lumière jusqu'à la base, un arc-en-ciel de rayons lumineux d'y plus bel effet."

Alex Kolansky probably became fixated on Mark 9:43. "And if thy hand offend thee, cut it off: it is better for thee to enter into life maimed, than having two hands to go into hell, into the fire that never shall be quenched." How different his life might have been had Ecclesiastes, 11:6 become the focus of his attention: "In the morning, sow thy seed, and in the evening withhold not thine hand."

The Canadian Boy Scout, by Robert Baden-Powell (Toronto: Morang, 1911).

10. Past Forgetting
Margaret MacDonald's tale of bravery appeared in *The National Enquirer* in the summer of 1996.

There are, of course, many ways of charming a wart. A good source of spells and devices is Helen Creighton's *Bluenose Magic: Popular Beliefs and Superstitions in Nova Scotia* (Toronto: Ryerson Press, 1968).

I was fascinated by the possibility that Chas. S. Robertson, former owner of *Fifteen Thousand Useful Phrases,* might have known Nellee, inasmuch as Kenabeek is just miles from Englehart. While I was in the neighbourhood, I also looked into a letter I had received from one Mrs. Edna Hip, of Nanaimo. She wrote: "Growing up in Sudbury, I knew a number of eccentric individuals, as you can well imagine. Certainly the most eccentric of them all was an old farmer, Lester Kinos, who lived just south of the city. Old Les was as smart as they come, and was normal in all ways except for one peculiar trait. He believed the letter 'F' should be a vowel. He'd argue about this with anyone who cared to listen, and he even converted a few of the naysayers to his point of view. It was his plan to hold a civic plebiscite on this issue one day, but that never came about. 'Sure, I'm just an farmer,' he'd say, 'an farmer and an fool with lifelong ambition. But I have an dream,' he'd say, 'no wait…A dream…a dream to achieve justice for the letter 'F', the most misunderstood of all vowels.' Les's eccentric ways amused even old Roger Hope, the roofing contractor who wanted to replace capitalism with a small piece of wood."

Kinos is indeed a name that turns up in the Sudbury directory — it's of Finnish origin — and I called all of them to see if any knew of old Les, who was fond of "F." Everyone to whom I spoke disavowed knowledge. As there is no phone listing for Mrs. Hip, and as letters to her address (on a street that does exist) were returned, I have sadly and reluctantly come to smell a rat.

12. Some Good Shepherds
Jack Marriott's diaries, photos, and sundry papers have been housed in the Public Archives of Nova Scotia as the H.J.B. Marriott collection.

13. Job's Excellent Vacation
Paul Bog's story was reported in *People of the Interlake*, by Andrew Blicq, with photographs by Ken Gigliotti (Winnipeg: Turnstone, 1986). As well, there was an account of his life and times in *The Selkirk Journal*, June 24, 1996, written by Donna Delaurier.

14. Through the Hermitage Window
To protect his privacy, I have not revealed the name or location of the hermit K. The sad story of Helen Hatch and her icy plunge can be found in *The Canadian Alpine Journal* in its report of the 1908 camp.

15. A Woman Clothed with the Sun
A Little Treasury of Modern Poetry, edited by Oscar Williams, was published by Charles Scribner & Sons, 1949.

16. *La Belle et la Bête*
Eccentrics: A Study of Sanity and Strangeness is by David Weeks and Jamie James (New York: Villard Books, 1995).

17. Still and Moving Images
Alexis Le Trotteur, by Jean-Claude Larouche (Montreal: Editions du Jour, 1971).
The Kingdom of Saguenay, by Marius Barbeau (Toronto: Macmillan, 1936).

I found the photo of the Marvel girls in a store called Gardens Antique. A graduation diploma was part of the lot acquired by the store owners at an estate sale. The certificate was issued to Letitia J. Reed, and I have supposed that the photograph was also hers. The verses I copied or adapted from an autograph book that belonged to Lillian Godden. Lillian lived in Harbour Grace, Newfoundland. The Godden house was purchased and restored by Jerry Dick, who now runs it as the Garrison House Inn. Lillian lived in Boston for a time, and was part of a group of young women called "The Modern Priscillas." Most of the autographs are dated 1926 and were inscribed by other Priscillas.

18. The Forest Primeval

Lillian Alling's story is comparatively recent and often revisited. Even so, it has become impossible to separate fact from supposition and lore. It is not even clear whether she was Russian or Polish. What seems certain is that she started her journey in New York, and that she walked a very long way. I have based my truncated version of her story on materials supplied by the B.C. Provincial Archives and the Vancouver Public Library. For more comprehensive accounts of her extraordinary travels, see *Pioneer Days in British Columbia*, vol. 2, edited by Art Downs; "Lillian Alling," by Win Shivlock in *B.C. Historical News*, Winter 1992–93; and "The Long Trail to Home, Sweet Home," by J. Wellsford Mills, in *The Shoulder Strap*, vol. 1, no. 6. Emily Carr's *The Book of Small* was published by Irwin in 1942. Her biographical sketch, written in 1927 for Eric Brown, is quoted in *Emily Carr: A Biography*, by Maria Tippet (Toronto: Stoddart, 1979). Graham Peat, executor of the David Curnick estate, hopes to place his papers with the Special Collections Division of the UBC Library.

Acknowledgments

I thank from the bottom of my heart the men and women who agreed to be interviewed and profiled in this book. Meeting them was a privilege, and I am keenly aware that I have been able to draw attention to only a tiny aspect of their rich, rich lives.

My thanks to Louise Dennys and everyone at Knopf Canada, most particularly to the incredibly calm and patient Diane Martin who suggested this project to me, and on whose editorial guidance I have leaned rather heavily. Never did I see her flinch. Thanks, as always, to my agent, Dacia Moss. My friend and colleague Marg Meikle, who was born to organize, was an invaluable associate and collaborator during the information-gathering portion of the project, and ran Eccentrics Command Central while I was on the road. My partner, Wallace Robinson, kept the home fires burning and was the first to hear about it when I was frazzled nearly beyond repair. Sue Wagner was also a tremendous support, in many ways. I am grateful for research assistance received from Cathrine Wanczycki, formerly of Ottawa and now living in Vancouver; and from James Calnan.

I am indebted to my colleagues at CBC Radio, Stereo, and Television all across the country who provided many tips and leads. Thanks especially to my Vancouver co-workers who tolerated and accommodated my long absence and my subsequent distraction.

I was the fortunate recipient of kind assistance from librarians, archivists, and library workers at The Centre for Newfoundland Studies, Memorial University (Bert Riggs and Anne Hart); the St. John's Public Library (Joan Grandy); the Yarmouth County Museum Archives (Laura Bradley); the Argyle Township Court House Archives (Peter Crowell and Carmen Phinney); the Amherst Public Library (Beverly Prue); the Public Archives of Nova Scotia; the Halifax Public Library; the Public Archives of Prince Edward Island (Sharon Clark); McGill University Library; the Archives of the Canadian Jewish Congress (Janice Rosen); the McCord Museum of Canadian History (Eva

Burnham, Jacqueline Ross); the library of the Montreal *Gazette*; The National Library and National Archives of Canada (Sandra Bell and Mary Bond); the Toronto Public Library; Queen's University Library and Archives; the Provincial Archives of Manitoba; the Manitoba Legislative Library; the Winnipeg Public Library; the Saskatoon Public Library; the Moose Jaw Public Library; the library of the Whyte Museum of the Canadian Rockies; the Vancouver Public Library; and the British Columbia Provincial Archives (Ann ten Cate).

Thanks abounding to the following individuals for kindness shown along the way and for information freely given. In Newfoundland, thanks to Diane Tye and Phil Hiscocks of the Folklore Department at Memorial University of Newfoundland, and to Linda Badcock, Historic Sites Officer of the Department of Tourism and Culture, Government of Newfoundland and Labrador; to Kathie Housser, Ray Guy, Marjorie Doyle, John Gushue, Martha Muzychka, all in St. John's; to Jerry Dick and Company (fun-time guys, every one!) in Harbour Grace; to Johanna Rocco, of Garden Cove; and to Gilbert E. Higgins, of Stephenville. In Nova Scotia, thanks to Beatrice Desveaux, Lester Marchand, and the family of Joe Delaney, all in the Cheticamp area; to Hector and Eleanor MacKenzie, in Salem; in Amherst, to John McKay; in Wolfville, to David Sheppard and Jennie Sheito; in Halifax, to Stephen Archibald and Sheila Stevenson; and, in Yarmouth, to Brian Medel, Fred Hatfield, and Basil Pero. On Prince Edward Island, thanks to Annie Thurlow, Reg Porter, and Ed MacDonald. In Quebec, thanks to André Picard, Jim Boothroyd, and Philip Szporer, all in Montreal; and to Carol Froimovitch, in Chelsea. In Ottawa, thanks to Bridget Barber and Charles Gordon; in Englehart, to Jan Borecki, Dorothy Dupuis, and Merlin Black; also to Earl Houghton, in London; in Gravenhurst, to Tom Brooks and to the very kind people who stopped to extricate me from the snowpile at the side of the road and whose names I carelessly forgot to write down; in Guelph, to Richard Gorrie and the amazing Dr. Thut; in Toronto, to the gorgeous Elly May, to Geoffrey Pimblett and the staff of his restaurant, to the staff of Mount Pleasant Cemetery, to Robert Dante, Bert Archer, and Dennis Pilon, and to whoever abandoned his or her copy of *Fifteen Thousand Useful Phrases* that I might have it for my own. In Winnipeg, thanks as always to my parents, Stan and Peggy Richardson, for their quiet tolerance and hospitality; in Portage la Prairie, to Nick Kolansky; and, in Brandon, to Fred McGuinness. Thanks to Pat

Armstrong, of Sturgis, Saskatchewan, for a very pleasant afternoon; to Guy and Margaret Vanderhaeghe, in Saskatoon, for a very pleasant evening; to Moon Mullin, in Moose Jaw, for his amazing stories and the long loan of his tapes; and, in Willow Bunch, to M. Campagne, who took me on a tour of the closed museum and filled in some of the blanks concerning the Beaupré giant. In Vancouver, thanks particularly to bill bissett (thanks for the room, bill), Rosamund Norbury, Graham Peat, and Larry Killick.

Although I never aspired to anything like a comprehensive, coast-to-coast survey, I was disappointed to find that there were stories I had fully intended to include in *Scorned & Beloved*, but was unable to accommodate in so small a volume. I thank very much the following people who took the time to meet with me and willingly told me about their lives. Randy Lieb, a painter, writer, and fisherman who lives with his young family on Woody Island, in Placentia Bay. Randy, his wife, and their two daughters are the only full-time residents of an island that was depopulated during the resettlement. They live in a remarkable stone house of Randy's own design and construction. He was a very generous host when I visited there in November 1996. I thank as well the inventor and evangelist Lewis Roberts, of Bareneed, Newfoundland; the journalist and poet Elizabeth Cran, of Tignish, Prince Edward Island; Isabel Bayly, of Chelsea, Quebec, who is an authority in the area of wetlands conservation, and who welcomes a great many raccoons to her porch every summer and who described herself as "a brown paper wrapper of a person" but most certainly is not; and Margaret Kemper, of Ottawa, a writer, photographer, and homemaker who is a dedicated advocate of water conservation. During her life as Margaret Trudeau, she ruffled a great many feathers with the "dangerous spontaneity" she brought to her duties as Prime Minister's Wife. Thanks as well to Ron Ward, of Janetville, Ontario, who showed me his incredible parrots and spoke at some length about his ideas for deficit reduction. I am disappointed not to have found space for the story of Robert Dante, bullwhip master, publisher, and sado-masochist, and would have loved to have written about the late Noulan Cauchon. He was a city planner and dress reformer whose fearless, public showing of his knees, in Ottawa, in 1930, made it possible for men to wear short pants in the Capital, in the summer. I spent an entertaining morning with Kevin Torfason, in Peterborough. Kevin, who is not yet thirty, introduced the wearing of knee-britches to his Ottawa high school only a few years ago, and now creates fabulous period costumes which he sometimes wears around town. In Winnipeg, I visited with the family of Victor Leathers, who was for many years a professor of French at the University of Winnipeg, and who was recognized by students, staff, and faculty alike as an eccentric. Similarly, I wish I could have told the story of the late Ralfe J. Clench, whose many peculiarities endeared him to the community of Queen's University, and some of whose traces I sniffed out in Kingston. It was a pleasure to visit with Tam Bachalo in Portage la Prairie, and to hear about how she preserves Celtic pagan rituals, and about her aversion to wearing footwear. Jerry Kaiser, of Baildon, Saskatchewan, who lives just a few miles down the road from where the famous Sukanen "dust ship" is moored, spoke eloquently about his connection to the land, and showed me his beautiful, whimsical folk-art pieces. It had been my intention to write about the late mountaineer and snow appreciator Norman Bethune Sanson, who is a legend around Banff. And I had a lovely afternoon with Shawn Haley and his wife, Ellie, near Red Deer, Alberta, looking at their collection of Day of the Dead artifacts.

Similarly, space will not allow me to acknowledge individually the several hundred people who were generous enough with their time and information to contact me and tell me about eccentric personalities whose stories they thought I should investigate. I thank them each and every one, heartily, for steering me in all directions at once, and for helping me put the lie to a certitude of Reginald Hines, who, in his book *Hitchings Worthies: Four Centuries of English Life* (1932), said, "The age of the Eccentrics is over. We do not breed them nowadays. The world that made them possible has passed away." It is not. We do. We are living in it.

The impalpable presence of the new century rose like a vast empty house through which no human feet had walked.

Bill Richardson is a bestselling writer and broadcaster, currently the host of "Richardson's Roundup" on CBC Radio One. He is the author of *The Bachelor Brothers' Bed & Breakfast* (winner of the Stephen Leacock Memorial Medal for Humour); *The Bachelor Brothers' Bed & Breakfast Pillow Book*; and *The Bachelor Brothers' Bedside Companion*. He lives in Vancouver.

LAST STAND AT KHE SANH

LAST STAND AT KHE SANH

The US Marines' Finest Hour in Vietnam

GREGG JONES

DA CAPO PRESS
A Member of the Perseus Books Group

Set in 11.25 point Adobe Caslon Pro by The Perseus Books Group

Library of Congress Cataloging-in-Publication Data
Jones, Gregg, 1959–
    Last stand at Khe Sanh : the U.S. Marines' finest hour in Vietnam /
Gregg Jones. — First Da Capo Press edition.
        pages cm
    Includes bibliographical references and index.
    ISBN 978-0-306-82139-4 (hardcover) — ISBN 978-0-306-82140-0
(e-book)
    1. Khe Sanh, Battle of, Vietnam, 1968. 2. United States. Marine
Corps—History—Vietnam War, 1961–1975. I. Title.
    DS557.8.K5J66 2014
    959.704'3450973—dc23
                                                        2013045206

ISBN: 978-0-306-82372-5 (paperback)
First Da Capo Press edition 2014
First Da Capo Press paperback edition 2015

Published by Da Capo Press
A Member of the Perseus Books Group
www.dacapopress.com

Da Capo Press books are available at special discounts for bulk purchases in
the U.S. by corporations, institutions, and other organizations. For more
information, please contact the Special Markets Department at the Perseus
Books Group, 2300 Chestnut Street, Suite 200, Philadelphia, PA 19103, or
call (800) 810-4145, ext. 5000, or e-mail
special.markets@perseusbooks.com.

To those who fought at Khe Sanh, living and dead.

CONTENTS

MAPS

ACKNOWLEDGMENTS

One of the great joys at the end of a long journey such as this is having the opportunity to publicly thank the people who inspired, assisted, and sustained me along the way.

Dennis Mannion and Michael O'Hara introduced me to the brotherhood of Khe Sanh veterans, and over three years entrusted me with their personal stories, introduced me to comrades, read chapter drafts, and offered friendship, counsel, and encouragement. Tom Quigley was the third Khe Sanh veteran to enter my life, and he further enriched this book by sharing his story and persuading reticent comrades to do the same. I can only hope that Dennis, Michael, and Tom consider this book worthy of their generous efforts on my behalf.

Among the larger community of Khe Sanh veterans and family members is a core group of wonderful people who graced my life along the way: Ken Rodgers and his wife, Betty; Ray Stubbe; Paul Knight; Tom Esslinger; James Feasel; Michael Coonan; Bill Martin; William Smith; Edward Feldman; Dan Fisher; Ken Pipes; Ken Warner; Michael Archer; Earle Breeding; Larry McCartney; Dave Norton; Don Shanley; John Roberts; Charles (Toby) Rushforth; Greg and Constance Gibbons; Jim Kaylor; Michael Barry; Maurice Casey; Chuck Chamberlin; Bruce Geiger; Paul Longgrear; and the late James Finnegan. Mike Fishbaugh is an exceptionally kind soul and unsung hero of the Khe Sanh Veterans Association, and on several occasions he shared documents from the National Personnel Records Center in St. Louis, Missouri.

David Powell covered Khe Sanh as a young freelance news photographer in early 1968, and we became friends during many interviews, phone conversations, and emails. I am deeply appreciative that Dave has allowed me to share with readers of this book several of his extraordinary images from Khe Sanh Combat Base and Hill 881 South.

I would like to thank and acknowledge all those who shared their memories in interviews, conversations, emails, and written submissions: Arnold Alderete; Adam Alexander; Richard Allen; Charles Almy; David Althoff; Joe Amodeo; Michael Archer; James Armbrust; Michael Barry; Clifford Braisted; Earle G. Breeding; Calvin E. Bright; Jim Caccavo; Maurice Casey; Charles Chamberlin; George Chapman; John Cicala; Bruce Clarke; Michael Coonan; John Corbett; David Doehrman; Rich Donaghy; Richard Dworsky; George Einhorn; Nick Elardo; Tom Esslinger; James Feasel; Edward Feldman; Lynn Fifer; James O. Finnegan; William Gay; Bruce Geiger; Robert Genty; Lionel Guerra; Jack Haigwood; Joe Harrigan; Billy Joe Hill; Richard Hillmann; Norman Jasper; Keith Kapple; James Kaylor; Neil Kenny; Paul Knight; Lacey Lahren; Larry LeClaire; Guy Leonard; Paul Longgrear; Kevin Macaulay; Dennis Mannion; Bill Martin; Dave McCall; Larry McCartney; Howard McKinnis; Lewis S. Messer II; Ted Mickelson; Ray Milligan; David Norton; Michael O'Hara; Raul Orozco; Steve Orr; Robert Pagano; John Pessoni; Michael Pike; Kenneth W. Pipes; David Powell; Glenn Prentice; Tom Quigley; Henry (Mac) Radcliffe; John Rauch; Mike Reath; Jose Reyes; John Roberts; Ken Rodgers; George (Greg) Rudell; Charles Rushforth; John Sabol; Miguel Salinas; Lawrence Seavy Cioffi; Don Shanley; James Sigman; William Smith; Ron Smith; David Steinberg; Ray Stubbe; Daniel Sullivan; Mark Swearengen; F. J. Taylor; Jim Thomas; Robert Tipton; Craig Tourte; Matthew Walsh; Ken Warner; Ed Welchel; Steve Wiese; and Michael Worth.

Foreign correspondent Seth Mydans was a friend and mentor during my formative years as a journalist in Southeast Asia, and we shared many adventures in Vietnam, Cambodia, Thailand, Indonesia, and the Philippines over three decades. Seth's careful and enthusiastic reading of the completed manuscript of *Last Stand at Khe Sanh* made this a better book, and reminded me of the joy and passion he always brought to his work as a foreign correspondent. The readers of the *New York Times* were fortunate to have had Seth as their window into the war-scarred nations of Indochina for three decades, and I was fortunate that our paths crossed.

Dr. Charles P. Neimeyer and the staff of the United States Marine

Corps History Division provided kind assistance during my research forays into the various collections housed in Quantico, Virginia. A special thanks to Quantico archivist Greg Cina for his efforts on my behalf
on this book and the one before, spanning an epic century of Marine
Corps history. At the National Archives and Records Administration in
College Park, Maryland, archivist Nathaniel Patch provided valuable insights, as did NARA archivist Paul Brown. A chance meeting at the National Archives brought me into contact with Navy veteran Ralph J. Fries
of Escondido, California, who imparted his knowledge on Navy corpsmen in Vietnam.

I would like to thank Dr. Steve Maxner and his staff at the Vietnam
Center and Archive at Texas Tech University in Lubbock, Texas, for their
magnificent contributions to the work of Vietnam War research over the
past quarter-century. Their vast online collection enabled me to contin-
uously backstop and expand on the work I did in my interviews and my
research at the National Archives and Marine Corps archives, and I am
grateful to have had access to this wonderful resource.

Marine Corps reference historian and blogger Beth Crumley shared
her expertise on Marine helicopter operations in I Corps and other facets
of Khe Sanh history, and she also introduced me to legendary CH-46 pilot David Althoff. Donna Elliott shared contacts acquired during her im-
passioned search for her missing brother, Staff Sergeant Jerry W. Elliott,
who went missing outside Khe Sanh village on the afternoon of January 21, 1968. My thanks as well to geriatric psychiatrist Kevin Gray, for
his encouragement and observations about the impact of post-traumatic
stress disorder on Vietnam veterans.

I owe a great debt to Robert Pisor, Eric Hammel, John Prados, and
Ray Stubbe, whose trail-blazing books on Khe Sanh served as faithful
companions throughout this journey. Ray's attraction to Khe Sanh began
in the summer of 1967, when he was assigned to the Marine combat base
as a Navy chaplain. Between the time of his arrival and his departure in
February 1968, Ray explored much of the Khe Sanh area and immersed
himself in the local culture and history. He would eventually transform
his diary into a 1,500-page manuscript, which became the core of *Valley
of Decision*, co-authored with John Prados, as well as other books, articles, speeches, and sermons. Ray became my friend and ad hoc archivist

during this project, imparting his encyclopedic knowledge in letters and frequent phone conversations. He not only illuminated various aspects of Khe Sanh history, but also shared obscure documents and interview transcripts as I wrestled with sundry research and writing challenges. I am grateful beyond words.

A number of Khe Sanh veterans have filled gaps in the historical record by writing compelling memoirs. Particularly useful to me were the Khe Sanh books written by Michael Archer, Bruce B. G. Clarke, John Corbett, William Craig, James Finnegan, Barry Fixler, and Ernest Spencer. Vietnam veteran Jack Wells generously sent me a copy of *Class of '67*, his moving tribute to his classmates from Marine Corps Basic School Class 6–67, including Khe Sanh veteran Terence (Terry) Roach.

I'm grateful to Tom Turner for aiding my research in the genealogy collection housed at the Haggard Library in Plano, Texas. My thanks as well to the following institutions where I found quiet corners to write: Southern Methodist University's Fondren Library Center in Dallas, Texas; Brookhaven College Library in Dallas, Texas; McLennan Community College Library in Waco, Texas; and Collin College Library in Frisco, Texas.

My friend Jon Eig was an early sounding board as I contemplated a book on Khe Sanh in the fall of 2010, and his advice was impeccable. Brent Howard at Penguin's New American Library imprint encouraged my ruminations about a Khe Sanh book and continued to urge me on, even after a rival publishing house acquired the project. Gary Jacobson offered valuable feedback on several early chapters. Doug Swanson took time from his own projects to offer encouragement, read parts of the manuscript, and commune about books, family life, and other topics. Writing sage George Getschow has been a friend and supporter, inspiring me and countless others through the Mayborn Literary Nonfiction Conference in Grapevine, Texas.

Friends and colleagues from various chapters in my life have sustained me with their words and deeds, and I offer special thanks to the following: Steve LeVine and his wife, Nurilda Nurlybayeva; Pat Benic; Alan Berlow; Chris Billing; Jay Branegan; William Branigin; John Carroll; Rick Hornik; David Lamb; Tom Lansner; John Schidlovsky; and Mike Theiler. Many thanks as well to my agent, Jim Donovan, for his work in finding a good home for this book, and for his friendship and counsel in the years since.

The home that Jim found was Da Capo Press, and I am grateful to the professionals at Da Capo and Perseus Books who have shepherded *Last Stand at Khe Sanh* from proposal to publication. My editor, Robert Pigeon, has been a wonderful pillar of support throughout. My heartfelt thanks as well to project editor Cisca Schreefel, copyeditor Michele Wynn, designer Brent Wilcox, and publicist Kate Burke.

Finally, and most important of all, I wish to thank and acknowledge the three people at the center of my universe: my wife of nearly three decades, Ali Nucum Jones; our teenage son, Chris; and my brother, Steve. Without your love and support, none of this would be possible.

INTRODUCTION

During the first months of 1968, Americans were transfixed by the confrontation between US and North Vietnamese Army (NVA) forces at a remote Marine combat base in South Vietnam called Khe Sanh. President Lyndon Johnson feared a disastrous defeat, like the one that had driven the French from Vietnam in 1954. "I don't want any damn Dien Bien Phu," he groused, recalling the French debacle. General William Westmoreland, the supreme American commander in Vietnam, assured his commander in chief: Khe Sanh will not become another Dien Bien Phu. Privately, the general harbored doubts. He ordered his staff to study how the French had lost at Dien Bien Phu, and whether he might now be forced to use tactical nuclear weapons to stave off a crushing defeat.

Over time, Khe Sanh would become perhaps the most emblematic confrontation of the Vietnam War—the centerpiece of Michael Herr's classic book, *Dispatches*, a focal point of Bruce Springsteen's haunting post-Vietnam anthem, "Born in the USA," and the subject of countless other books, articles, paintings, songs, and exhibits.

For war critics and news correspondents, Khe Sanh was a metaphor for the Vietnam War's strategic folly and tactical deceptions: 6,000 US Marines forced to defend an isolated base that General Westmoreland had deemed indispensable, only to abandon it after hundreds of Americans were sacrificed in its defense.

So what really happened at Khe Sanh? What was it like for the young Americans who were there? How has Khe Sanh shaped and scarred their lives? How accurate is the history that has been written about this epic confrontation of the Vietnam War? These were the questions that guided me as I set out on this journey.

• • •

I celebrated my ninth birthday in April 1968, and though I don't have any specific memories of reading about the battle of Khe Sanh or the Tet Offensive, I was certainly aware of the rising death toll in Vietnam and the antiwar protests that were spreading across America. That August, after the local summer baseball league games had ended, I squeezed into the backseat of our 1964 Chevy Impala with my older brother and sister and we set off to the east on a family vacation. Our ultimate destination was Washington, DC, but I persuaded my parents to stop at several Civil War battlefields in our path, and so we hopscotched from Appomattox Court House in southern Virginia, to Richmond (with a side trip to Colonial Williamsburg), and then on to Fredericksburg before finally reaching the nation's capital.

Each day, our journey into America's past was jolted back to the present by newscasts and headlines about the widening war in Vietnam. In Washington, we visited the monuments and toured the White House, where President Johnson was in his final months of office, having announced in late March, amid the mounting antiwar protests, that he wouldn't run for reelection.

We made our way to Arlington National Cemetery and climbed the hallowed slopes, stopping at President John F. Kennedy's grave site before reaching the breathtaking vantage point of the Custis-Lee Mansion.

We couldn't help but notice all the fresh graves around us. And then, as my father captured the scene with his Brownie eight-millimeter camera, we watched in solemn silence as a flag-draped coffin passed on a horse-drawn caisson and, some minutes later, listened reverently as the mournful sound of "Taps" echoed over the hills.

• • •

Back home in Missouri, my family followed events in Vietnam on the *CBS Evening News* and in our local newspaper. Every so often, the paper wrote about some hometown boy who had died in America's service in Indochina. Eventually, fourteen young men from my hometown of about 15,000 people would die in Vietnam.

I read everything I could about the Vietnam War as the years passed. As a twenty-five-year-old journalist in 1984, just nine years after the war ended, I was drawn to Southeast Asia. Eventually, I would spend ten years there, spread over three decades.

At every opportunity, I visited Vietnam—Saigon, Hanoi, Hue, Quang Tri City, Bien Hoa, Cu Chi, Tay Ninh, My Lai, Street Without Joy, all the places I'd read about in my personal quest to understand the war that had claimed the lives of 58,000 Americans. I traveled along much of Route 1 as it followed the coast of the former South Vietnam, and, with Vietnam veteran Chuck Searcy, I ventured up Route 9, to the Khe Sanh area, just south of the old demilitarized zone (DMZ) that had divided Vietnam into the Communist north and American-supported south from 1954 until 1975. In my travels, I interviewed former North Vietnamese Army soldiers, Viet Cong guerrillas, and veterans of the Army of the Republic of South Vietnam (ARVN). I spoke with refugees who had fled Vietnam and returned, and those who had tried to escape Communist rule but never made it out. I visited a vast ARVN cemetery north of Saigon that the war's victors had allowed to fall into shameful disrepair, and I spoke with villagers along the northern fringe of the former DMZ who continued to die and suffer hideous injuries from unexploded ordnance left behind by the battle of Khe Sanh and the American bombing campaign known as Rolling Thunder.

Ultimately, I wanted to write something about the Vietnam War that would rise above the rancorous politics that had poisoned America during the conflict and in the decades since. I wanted to write a book that would capture the experience of ordinary young Americans thrown into these extraordinary events in Vietnam, a tragic sideshow of the Cold War between the United States and the Soviet Union. I decided to tell the story of the legendary confrontation at Khe Sanh in early 1968—the human story of the young Americans who were thrust into this pivotal moment in the Vietnam War.

• • •

Americans began dying at Khe Sanh in 1964, and they would continue dying there long after the siege was declared broken in April 1968. The Hill Fights at Khe Sanh in the spring of 1967 cost the lives of more than 150 US Marines and introduced Americans to the infamous terrain features known as 881 North, 881 South, and 861. To fully develop the storytelling, I limited my scope in this book, focusing on the four-month period from January through April 1968. The men who served at Khe Sanh before and after the siege months have my deepest respect, and my apologies for not being able to tell their stories.

I also focused largely on the American experience at Khe Sanh. It became clear to me early on that there were so many interesting characters and dramatic events involving US forces during these four months at Khe Sanh that it would be impossible to write a book of reasonable length and do justice to the stories of the North Vietnamese and South Vietnamese soldiers who fought at Khe Sanh. I look forward to reading about their experiences at Khe Sanh in future books.

For so long, it was unfashionable to speak favorably about the service of Americans in Vietnam or to acknowledge their sacrifices. Our recent wars in Iraq and Afghanistan have made it clear that it is possible to debate the wisdom of a war, or even actively oppose it, without denigrating the men and women who answer the nation's call. For those who served at Khe Sanh, and elsewhere in Vietnam, this courtesy is long overdue.

CHINA

● Dien Bien Phu

○ **Hanoi**

**NORTH
VIETNAM**

*Gulf of
Tonkin*

○ **Vientiane**

L A O S

Nakhon
Phanom ●

Demilitarized Zone (DMZ)

● Khe Sanh

Hue ●
● Phu Bai

● Da Nang

I Corps

THAILAND

II Corps

○ **Bangkok**

C A M B O D I A

**SOUTH
VIETNAM**

● Cam Ranh

○ **Phnom Penh** ○

III Corps

*Gulf of
Thailand*

Mekong River

○ **Saigon**

South China Sea

IV Corps

**AMERICA'S WAR IN INDOCHINA
1968**

NORTHERN I CORPS
1968

AIRSTRIP

Rao Quan River

ALPHA 1/26 (USMC)

37TH RANGERS (ARVN)

BRAVO 1/26
(USMC)

MAIN
AMMO
DUMP

1/26
COC

CHARLIE
BATTERY
1/13

BRAVO
3RD
RECON

26TH
MARINES
COC

Garbage
Dump

WATER
POINT

CBMU-301
(Seabees)

CHARLIE 1/26 (USMC)

CHARLIE
MED

GRAVES
REGISTRATION

MILITARY ROAD (UNUSED)

TO ROUTE 9

TO ROUTE 9

MAIN ACCESS ROAD

1/26 AID
STATION

DELTA 1/26
(USMC)

4.2-INCH
MORTARS

ALPHA
BATTERY
1/13

FOB-3
(MACV-SOG)

1/13
ARTILLERY
CP

3RD TANKS

155MM GUNS

3/26 CP

LIMA 3/26 (USMC)

DROP
ZONE

KHE SANH COMBAT BASE
1968

500 Feet

January 17, 1968

The Marines splashed across the shallow stream in single file, wide eyes scanning the steamy jungle for soldiers of the North Vietnamese Army. They were only nine in number, American teenagers and young men in their early twenties, formed into a squad assigned to India Company of the 3rd Battalion, 26th Marine Regiment.

Roaming up and down the column was the smoothly athletic squad leader, Corporal Ken Warner, nineteen years old, an avid surfer, baseball player, and Dodgers fan from Long Beach, California. A few hours earlier, he had led his men down from the Marine garrison atop the hill that rose steeply at their backs. The terrain feature was designated 881 South on Marine topographic maps, and it was the first line of defense for Khe Sanh Combat Base, a remote outpost from which US Marines and Special Forces sparred with enemy troops as they funneled into South Vietnam from the nearby Ho Chi Minh Trail in Laos.

The Americans had been trying for weeks to get a fix on two North Vietnamese Army divisions that had slipped into the area, but they had found only tantalizing hints of the nearly 20,000 enemy soldiers. Warner's patrol was part of the daily effort to find the elusive NVA, or at least make sure they didn't sneak up on the Marines atop 881 South or at the combat base at Khe Sanh, five miles to the southeast.

There were 540,000 American military personnel in Vietnam in January 1968, and Ken Warner's journey from the beaches of Southern

California to the jungles of South Vietnam could have been the story of just about any of them. He was the son of a housewife and a World War II Navy veteran who worked on the docks of Los Angeles harbor as a longshoreman, and life was good. At Robert A. Millikan High School in Long Beach, Ken had played center field on the baseball team and spent most weekends and holidays surfing with his buddies off Baja California. After studying Indochina in a high school history class, he had concluded that the American war was a noble crusade to save the people of South Vietnam from godless communism. He joined the Marines shortly after graduation, and after six months of training as a rifleman, flew to Vietnam with a planeload of replacement Marines.

In April 1967, within a month of his arrival, Warner saw his first action. During a firefight, a corpsman had asked him to look after a wounded Marine from another platoon while he tended to other casualties. Warner knelt over the Marine and tried to stanch the bleeding from a gut wound, but there wasn't much that could be done, so he ended up holding the guy in his lap, telling him over and over, "You're going to be okay." The Marine kept looking into Warner's blue eyes, then glancing away, never uttering a word, and then he died. Unsure of the proper protocol, Warner laid the dead Marine in the tall grass and crawled toward the gunfire.

Like most low-level Marines, Warner wasn't privy to the strategic deliberations underway at the headquarters of America's supreme commander in Vietnam, General William Westmoreland, or the captured intelligence that pointed to an escalating war. Grunts like Warner knew nothing of the June meeting of North Vietnam's ruling Lao Dong Party politburo and its conclusion that the time had come to deliver "a decisive blow" to "force the U.S. to accept military defeat" in Vietnam.[1] All Warner and his buddies knew was that the fighting was getting heavier, and life in the northern border provinces—I Corps, it was called—was getting more dangerous.

Unknown to Warner and his comrades, the ambitious North Vietnamese "1967–68 Winter-Spring Campaign" was underway.

For one terrible week in September, Warner and other Marines had hunkered down in their trenches and fighting holes at the small Marine combat base at Con Thien while the North Vietnamese pounded them.

When the artillery stopped, the Marines had fought off human-wave ground attacks that were broken only after some of the NVA troops had reached the American trench line. Warner lost his squad leader in the fighting, a veteran sergeant who had helped him survive his early months in Vietnam. The laid-back Southern California teenager grew a little bit older, a little wiser, a little harder.

India Company had suffered heavy losses at Con Thien, so the outfit was pulled out of combat for a few weeks to replenish its ranks with newly arrived replacements—FNGs ("fucking new guys") in the Marine patois that Warner had learned from the old-timers. Warner was given command of a squad, and in early December, India was dispatched to the Marine combat base at Khe Sanh, in the far northwestern corner of South Vietnam. On December 26, Warner and his comrades took over the Marine outpost on 881 South, where they could look out into Laos, seven miles to the west, and take up the search for the North Vietnamese troops pouring into the area.

Now, as his men pushed through the tall grass that clotted the stream at the base of 881 South, Warner dropped to the back of the column to make sure no one slipped up behind them.

His point man had broken through the wall of vegetation into a small clearing, which the other Marines were now approaching. Warner was the last to step from the water onto dry ground, and as he did, he heard something behind him.

Splash, splash, splash. And then silence.

Somebody was following them.

Warner sounded a wordless warning to his squad. Hand signals flashed, and the Marines began circling around the edge of the clearing. Within a few steps, they found warm cooking fires. They had walked into an NVA campsite.

The jungle around them was now unnaturally silent. The Marines exchanged worried glances.

Warner got his company commander, Captain William Dabney, on the radio. The squad leader whispered a situation report, even as he braced for the ear-splitting sound of gunfire and explosions.

"I'm going to send guys down the hill," Dabney said in a low voice. "Can you start back up?"[2]

Everyone looked at Warner, wondering how they were going to get out of this mess alive. The Californian pointed to the Marine at the head of his squad, motioning for him to move back across the stream and up the slope of 881 South.

Warner and his men moved as stealthily as they could through the elephant grass and water, but it was too late for that. Warner felt eyes watching them as they moved. He could almost see the NVA around him in the bush, fingers on triggers, poised to fire.

The Marines reached dry ground, and still the North Vietnamese had not attacked. The Americans started up the slope, and as each step carried them farther away from danger, relief swept the column.[3] Why had the enemy soldiers let them live? Warner and his men were baffled, but giddy at their escape.

Ken Warner and his men had been lucky. The NVA soldiers were almost ready to strike the Americans at Khe Sanh, but not quite, and their ambitious plan envisioned far greater victories than the slaughter of nine Marines on patrol.[4]

PART I

CHAPTER 1

Death in the Tall Grass

In the minutes before the operation began, the Marines made small talk. They spoke of food and home, girlfriends and wives, and the time left in their thirteen-month combat tours with the Marines in Vietnam.

The sun broke above the misty green peaks of South Vietnam's most distant corner, revealing a scene of deceptive tranquillity. A thick blanket of fog engulfed all but the highest hill masses, and in the soft early light they appeared like islands awash in cottony white waves. Somewhere beneath that spectral sea, less than a mile north of the Marines as they geared up on Hill 881 South, soldiers of the North Vietnamese Army's 325C Division waited in bunkers and fighting holes hidden in the tall grass.

It was Saturday morning, January 20, 1968.

Hill 881 South (designated by its height in meters) was the farthest outpost of the Marine combat base at Khe Sanh, nearly four miles to the southeast.[1] The hilltop stronghold stood like a sentinel overlooking the border with Laos, and the vital supply lines that the North Vietnamese used to funnel men and materiel into South Vietnam. Over the past week, the Marines of India Company, 3rd Battalion, 26th Marine Regiment, had made contact with the enemy nearly every time they left the hill and started up the slope to their north. Intelligence reports placed two NVA divisions around Khe Sanh, roughly 20,000 men—more than three times the total number of Marines around Khe Sanh.

India's commander, Captain William Dabney, wanted to see what was out there, and he was taking no chances. He ordered his entire company, about 175 men, to gear up. Their destination: a multi-fingered ridgeline a mile to the north—Hill 881 North on Marine topographic maps.

The pre-mission banter by short-timers made Navy corpsman Mike Ray homesick. He had been in Vietnam barely sixty days, which meant he wouldn't get home for another eleven months—unless he was killed or wounded. He was twenty years old, an Iowa farm boy assigned to India's 3rd Platoon, and he missed his wife and young son. He finished a breakfast of canned C-rations and headed to his bunker to check his aid bag one final time. He wanted to make sure he had enough battle dressings, tourniquets, and morphine, in case they ran into trouble. When his bag was ready, Ray scribbled a farewell note to his family, folded the paper, and slipped it into his personal gear.[2]

The platoons formed around 8:00 a.m., and a half hour later, on Bill Dabney's command, the men of India Company made their way through the perimeter wire and headed down the steep north face of 881 South, in search of the North Vietnamese Army.

• • •

For an ambitious officer like Captain William Howard Dabney, a thirty-three-year-old Virginian hungry for combat and glory, Khe Sanh Combat Base had seemed like the perfect posting. It was only fifteen miles south of the demilitarized zone that divided Vietnam into Communist and non-Communist nations, and seven miles from Laos, where the Ho Chi Minh Trail was bustling with North Vietnamese troops headed south to fight the Americans. The enemy was close, and the colonels and generals who might cramp Dabney's aggressive style weren't.

In Marine parlance, Dabney was a "mustang," a former enlisted man who had clawed his way up to the officer corps. He had joined the Marines in 1953, after flunking out of Yale University, and made sergeant before completing his enlistment. He entered Virginia Military Institute, graduated with a degree in English in the spring of 1960, and a few weeks later reentered the Marines as a second lieutenant.

Even in the macho world of the United States Marine Corps, Dabney turned heads. He was six feet four inches, handsome, square-jawed. He was a charming storyteller, with a born leader's grace and confidence. He had burnished his mystique by marrying Virginia Puller, the daughter of America's most famous Marine, retired general Lewis "Chesty" Puller.

When he arrived in Vietnam in September 1967, Dabney was a senior captain, but still waiting to command a Marine rifle company before moving up to major. He got his company within days of arriving in Vietnam but promptly lost it after clashing with his battalion commanding officer (CO).[3] Dabney got a second crack at it before the month was out and took the reins of India Company, 3rd Battalion, 26th Marines.

After several weeks of operations, Dabney and his men, in mid-December, flew to Khe Sanh, where he led the company on a weeklong 3/26 battalion sweep toward the border with Laos and back. The Marines made no contact with the North Vietnamese, but Dabney sensed the presence of the enemy all around. The day after Christmas, he led his men out to the battle-scarred stronghold of 881 South.

The hill that Dabney and his men now called home—along with two neighboring hill masses, 881 North and 861—had been the scene of a fierce two-week battle the previous spring in which 155 Marines had perished and another 425 had been wounded, engagements that became known as the Hill Fights of Khe Sanh. The Marines had attacked the hills with World War II–style frontal assaults, but they were thrown back by enemy troops firing from bunkers and camouflaged holes. American artillery and air strikes pounded the enemy positions, and the Marines awoke one morning to find that the North Vietnamese had slipped away.[4]

Dabney's Marines took over the former enemy redoubt on 881 South and commenced daily patrols in search of enemy troops. They made no contact for the first three weeks, but the signs of a major enemy presence had become unmistakable over the past week.

The previous day, a Marine recon patrol had made heavy contact with the NVA on 881 North and needed help breaking off the fight and getting its wounded out. Dabney's 3rd Platoon had rushed to the scene of the firefight and gotten their comrades to safety, but the recon boys had lost a radio and code sheets, a worrisome turn of events for the Americans.

Dabney's 1st Platoon had gone back in search of the lost radio and code sheets the previous day, January 19, with Corporal Ken Warner's squad in the lead. Warner was pushing his men forward through tall elephant grass about 1:30 p.m. when he and the Marine immediately to his front, Gary Joliet, heard the sound of rustling grass to their right. Joliet turned to his left and flashed Warner a quizzical look, as if to say: *What was that?* Before Warner could react, they heard more movement in the grass. Joliet had started to turn back toward the unseen danger when the grass exploded with automatic-weapons fire from the improvised North Vietnamese ambush.

Joliet dropped to the ground with three bullets in his back, and the Marine behind Warner fell wounded, but the big Southern Californian somehow survived the opening barrage without a scratch. After a hard ninety-minute fight, the Marines were able to break contact and withdraw under the cover of air strikes and artillery fire. It was something of a miracle that only one Marine was killed: Warner's M-60 machine gunner, Private First Class Leonard Lee Newton, a nineteen-year-old from Stockton, California, had waged a courageous duel with an NVA machine gunner on the slope above him until he fell dead with a bullet through the eye.

Now, Captain Dabney led his men off his hill and headed north, toward the rugged slopes stained with the fresh blood of US Marines.[5]

• • •

It was 1,500 feet from the American perimeter on 881 South to the base of the hill, and on the morning of January 20, the 30° slope was so slippery from fog and winter rains that the Marines had to grab at brush and small trees to avoid tumbling to the bottom. Grunts and curses sounded along the line, along with the clank of equipment, as men lost their footing.

India Company's slow and noisy progress worried Private Michael Pike, an eighteen-year-old Marine from Southern California. He had arrived in Vietnam only eight days earlier, and this was his first patrol.[6] He had stuffed the pockets of his jungle utilities with cans of C-rations, filled three or four canteens of water, and draped himself with bandoliers of M-16 magazines and a few hand grenades. As the new guy, Pike got the honor of carrying two white phosphorus rounds for the platoon's 3.5-inch rocket launcher. He was handed a hard-plastic backpack with the two rounds inside and told: strap it on.[7]

As they made their way down the hill, the Marines entered the fog cover that had appeared as a cottony sea from far above. They finally reached the bottom, then waded into a rushing stream that wound around the hill. Second Platoon rifleman Robert Tipton, a nineteen-year-old from Florida, knelt to fill his canteen before rejoining the column as it splashed ahead through soggy ground. The Marines moved cautiously through the thick fog.[8]

• • •

After crossing the stream, India Company split into two columns and began to move up parallel fingers of the hill, about 500 yards apart, climbing toward the crest of 881 North. Leading the left column was India's 1st Platoon, commanded by Second Lieutenant Harry F. "Rick" Fromme Jr., a twenty-four-year-old from Jacksonville, Florida; he was followed by Bill Dabney and his small command group and India's 2nd Platoon, led by Second Lieutenant Michael H. Thomas, a twenty-five-year-old from Pawnee, Oklahoma.[9] On the right, angling toward an almost identical grass-cloaked finger, was India's 1st Platoon, led by Second Lieutenant Thomas D. Brindley of St. Paul, Minnesota, a twenty-four-year-old who had played college hockey in Colorado before quitting to enlist in the Marines.

The 3rd Platoon moved hard uphill through the thick elephant grass. At the head of the column was Brindley's veteran point man, Private First Class James Collins. A muscular, bull-necked farm boy from the cornfields of central Illinois, Collins was only five days shy of his twenty-third birthday. He was at the end of his thirteen months in Vietnam and was packed and ready to leave 881 South. As a short-timer, Collins could have skipped the patrol. But when his buddies shoved off, there he was, leading the column.

At the rear of Brindley's column were seven reconnaissance Marines. Code-named Team Barkwood, they had been dispatched from Khe Sanh late the previous afternoon, with orders to slip away from the column and recover the radio and code sheets left at the scene of the ambush two days earlier. The team was led by Lance Corporal Charles William Bryan, a high school football player and Boy Scout back home in McKinney, Texas. After basic training, Bryan had volunteered to become a reconnaissance Marine, trained to prowl the jungles in small teams of a dozen men or less in search of enemy troops. He had married his high school sweetheart before heading to Vietnam at the end of September 1967. Assigned to Bravo Company, 3rd Reconnaissance Battalion, Bryan joined the outfit at Khe Sanh. He was popular with his recon buddies because he was a nice guy, he did his job well, and he shared the chocolate-chip cookies his young wife, Deidra, regularly sent.[10] And now, he and his team were impatiently plodding up the hillside at the rear of Tom Brindley's platoon.

Progress was agonizingly slow as the Marines carefully measured each step in the thick fog. Finally, Brindley and his men emerged into sunlight. Near the rear of the column, Team Barkwood's radioman, Robert "PJ" Pagano, a nineteen-year-old from White Plains, New York, gazed up ahead and suppressed a laugh. Only the helmets of the 3rd Platoon grunts were visible above the tall grass, and they looked like turtles bobbing along in a sea of green.

Pagano's reverie was shattered by a familiar sound.

Pop-pop-pop-pop. Pop-pop-pop-pop.

The helmets disappeared.

• • •

By the time Jim Collins spotted the well-camouflaged enemy fighting holes, it was too late. The Vietnamese fired first, and the point man from Illinois fell in the opening volley.[11]

Lieutenant Brindley advanced with his 2nd Squad and directed fire toward the suspected NVA positions that had pinned down his lead elements. The roar of machine guns mixed with the crack of assault rifles and the *whoosh-boom* of Communist rocket-propelled grenades. Bullets snapped and whined through the elephant grass. Enemy soldiers were on both sides of the Americans, firing their weapons and tossing grenades.

"Doc, up!"

Corpsman Mike Ray heard the cry above the noise and felt sick. He was paralyzed by fear, and then his training kicked in. He crawled forward, still terrified, but focused on finding and treating fallen Marines. The first man he found was his squad leader, a sergeant from the hills of Kentucky who loved to sing and strum his guitar on quiet nights. His chin had been ripped from his face. Ray handed the sergeant a large battle dressing to stanch the flow of blood, telling him to get back down the hill.[12]

Ray moved ahead and found a young Marine sprawled in the grass. A piece of grenade shrapnel had struck the man below his left eye and ripped through the roof of his mouth, exiting through his chin. Ray dressed the wounds as best he could and pointed the Marine down the trail.

The corpsman was still snaking his way up the trail when the order to fall back swept through the grass. Panicked Marines popped up and scuttled past in a low crouch, dropping and kicking rifle magazines and grenades as they ran. Ray joined the rush.[13] The spooked Marines ran until they reached a small plateau, a safe distance from the murderous enemy fire.

Ray was still catching his breath from the frantic retreat when a gravely injured Marine was laid at his feet. It was the fallen point man. Ray and another corpsman tried cardiopulmonary resuscitation (CPR), but there was no response. Jim Collins would be making the trip back to Illinois in a military-issue coffin.[14]

• • •

Bill Dabney had watched through field glasses as the fight began, and he quickly saw that Brindley's platoon was pinned down by North Vietnamese fire from a knoll about six hundred feet up the hill. Dabney radioed his young lieutenant: break contact and pull back with your wounded. He also ordered his executive officer, First Lieutenant Richard Foley Jr., attached to Brindley's platoon, to set up an emergency landing zone (LZ) for medevac choppers.

Within minutes, the LZ was secured, and a helicopter settled into the tiny clearing. Several seriously wounded Marines were carried aboard, along with the body of Jim Collins. As the medevac bird thundered off to the east, Lieutenant Foley and his artillery forward observer (FO) radioed coordinates that were quickly forwarded to waiting artillery batteries at Khe Sanh and mortar teams back on 881 South. The North Vietnamese positions above them erupted with explosions.[15]

• • •

On Bill Dabney's command, two squads of Lieutenant Rick Fromme's 1st Platoon on the western finger were maneuvering into position to enfilade the North Vietnamese that had pinned down Brindley's platoon. Fromme's men were thirty yards from the top of a knoll, charging ahead in a skirmish line, when the grass around them exploded with the roar of automatic weapons and rocket-propelled grenades (RPGs). Crisscrossing rounds from NVA .51-caliber machine guns and AK-47 rifles ripped into the legs and torsos of the charging Marines, dropping twenty young Americans in seconds.

Among those falling in the first volley was squad leader Ken Warner. Hot metal from an exploding RPG round had sliced his face and hip and gouged a gaping hole in his right shoulder. Bleeding heavily, Warner couldn't pinpoint the enemy soldiers hidden in the tall grass. He couldn't even see the Marines who had fallen around him, but he could hear their screams and cries of pain.[16]

Fromme's platoon was now completely focused on escaping the enemy killing zone. Murderous NVA machine-gun fire raked the Americans from the left flank. Fromme and several of his men laid down covering fire so corpsmen and other Marines could get their wounded down the hill.

Nearby, the men of Corporal Michael Elrod's 3rd Squad ran for their lives, one at a time, while comrades fired in the direction of the concealed North Vietnamese. Elrod was the only one left when three NVA soldiers charged him. He fired a final round, then sprinted after his men. A bullet smashed into Elrod's heel and ankle, and he collapsed to the ground. He started crawling and didn't stop until he reached the perimeter of Dabney's reserve force down the hill.[17]

For wounded squad leader Ken Warner, there was no easy way out. He ordered two men to help ambulatory casualties crawl away from the fire while he took responsibility for his most seriously wounded Marine, rifleman Bob Coniff, bleeding heavily from both legs. Grabbing Coniff under his armpits, Warner hugged the ground and began dragging the Marine through the tall grass. North Vietnamese machine-gun fire scythed the slope around them, drawn by the swaying grass as Warner forced his way through the thick vegetation.[18]

Their progress was agonizingly slow, measured in inches, and Warner was growing weak from blood loss and exhaustion. He could no longer hear any Marines nearby. He spotted a tree and dragged himself and his comrade beneath it and leaned against the trunk. Cradling Coniff in his lap, Warner said good-bye to his parents and waited to die. As he accepted his fate, he felt a strange calmness come over him, and his brain flashed a simple command: *Just keep going.*[19]

The wounded Marine resumed the torturous retreat through the heavy grass, pulling his even more seriously injured comrade along with him. After an agonizing forty-five minutes, the sound of gunfire and explosions had faded.[20] Warner willed himself on—*just a little more, just a little more.* Finally, a beautiful sight came into view: the cordon formed by the Marines of Mike Thomas's 2nd Platoon.

Ken Warner was among the last Marines from the left column to reach safety. As a corpsman began treating Bob Coniff, Warner did a quick head count. He and his men were a bloody mess, but the entire squad had made it back down the slope.[21] There was more to the miracle: in Fromme's assault, twenty-one Marines had been wounded, some critically, but they would all make it off the hill alive.

• • •

Mike Thomas had been moving his 2nd Platoon Marines through a small clearing down the slope when the left column came under attack. Private Michael Pike had just walked into the opening when an NVA machine gun fired from about 300 yards off to the left. Pike hit the deck as machine-gun rounds kicked dirt into his face.[22] A sergeant screamed at Pike. "Marine, get your ass up!" Pike scrambled for cover at the edge of the clearing.

In seconds, the platoon's 3.5-inch rocketman screwed together the two halves of his weapon, and another Marine grabbed one of the white phosphorus rounds from Pike's plastic backpack and shoved it in the launcher tube. The rocketman took aim, and a round roared westward and exploded in the distance. As white smoke boiled from the point of impact, a North Vietnamese soldier staggered from a camouflaged bunker. A Marine sniper stepped up and laid his rifle across the rocketman's shoulder. Peering through his scope, he dropped the enemy fighter with one shot.[23]

Within a few minutes, blood-soaked Marines from Fromme's platoon had clawed their way through the elephant grass and into the 2nd Platoon perimeter. A corpsman began pulling wounded men into a bomb crater. He dressed their wounds and tried to calm them.

A Marine CH-46 helicopter—*Frosty Gold* of Marine Medium Helicopter Squadron 262 (HMM-262)—whomped in from the east, banked and turned toward a makeshift LZ alongside the casualty collection point. Under heavy enemy fire, pilot Bob Ropelewski, a twenty-five-year-old captain from Erie, Pennsylvania, slowly backed into the hill. As the ramp of his Sea Knight touched the steep slope, rifleman James Schemelia put his arm around a wounded Marine and walked him inside the helicopter. They were moving toward the front when NVA machine-gun rounds ripped through the fuselage and severed the fuel line. The helicopter burst into flames.[24]

Fighting to control the crippled aircraft, Ropelewski careened toward the streambed below. Schemelia grabbed the wounded Marine he had just helped aboard, pushed him out the back, and jumped after him.[25] Ropelewski, his co-pilot, crew chief, and gunner all managed to bail out in the seconds before the helicopter crashed into the draw about fifty yards below.[26]

Within minutes, Fromme's Marines found Ropelewski and his co-pilot, Steve Stegich. They were waiting with .45 pistols drawn, poised to shoot it out if the North Vietnamese got there first. The Marines also recovered the crew chief and door gunner, injured but alive. James Schemelia had survived serious injury, and he dragged himself out of the heavy brush, found his wounded comrade, and helped him back to the bomb crater to await another medevac aircraft.[27]

• • •

About 2:00 p.m., as Bill Dabney's men fought for their lives, an extraordinary drama was unfolding at Khe Sanh Combat Base. A North Vietnamese lieutenant armed with an AK-47 rifle stepped from the jungle beyond the eastern perimeter, dropped his weapon, and surrendered.[28]

Marines hustled the uniformed Vietnamese back inside the base for interrogation, where he quickly confirmed American intelligence reports that two NVA divisions were drawn up around Khe Sanh. The prisoner was fed up with army life, and offered an even more chilling revelation: North Vietnamese troops were poised to strike the American outpost on Hill 861 that night. Once that objective had been seized, he said, they would move against Khe Sanh Combat Base.[29]

•   •   •

As friendly artillery pounded the North Vietnamese positions on 881 North, Tom Brindley's shaken Marines—the right hand of Dabney's thrust—had regrouped down the slope from the scene of their encounter. They had lost ten men, nine of them wounded and one dead. But Bill Dabney had no intention of walking away from this fight. When the friendly artillery fire tapered off, the order was passed: prepare to take the enemy strongpoint.[30]

The men of 3rd Platoon formed a skirmish line. Bill Bryan and his recon team anchored Brindley's right flank.

"Fix bayonets," Brindley ordered.

Almost as one, the heads of the recon Marines snapped toward the platoon commander. *Fix what?* PJ Pagano thought to himself.[31] Most recon Marines didn't even carry bayonets.

Brindley walked up and down the line, encouraging each man with a knock on the back.[32] On Brindley's shouted command, the Marines started up the hill.

Within seconds, enemy fire ripped through the grass and over the heads of the Americans. The Marines fired their rifles from the hip, like John Wayne in movies they had watched as kids. With Brindley in the lead, waving his .45 pistol, the Marines hit the first row of North Vietnamese fighting holes and broke the enemy line with a flurry of grenade explosions, automatic rifle fire, and bayonet thrusts. The Marines surged ahead and were able to seize the crest of the knoll in close combat with the remaining NVA.

Spilling over the crest, the Marines came under heavy fire from North Vietnamese troops down the reverse slope and to their east. Brindley ran back and forth along the line, pausing long enough to inform Dabney by radio that his men had taken their objective but had lost most of their noncoms and were running low on ammunition.

Seconds later, a rifle round slammed into Tom Brindley's chest. Mortally wounded, he gave one final command: "Keep low, keep going, and stay on line."[33]

• • •

On Brindley's right, Bill Bryan's recon team had tried to flank the NVA position but had run headlong into a small enemy force. The Americans scattered the opposing soldiers and were charging up the hill when they were caught in a murderous crossfire: friendly mortar fire and small arms rounds from the rear, and enemy machine guns and small arms from the front. Pagano had just called off the mortar fire when an M-16 round slammed into the back of his leg, and he fell to the ground.[34]

Lying on his back, Pagano felt an AK-47 round whizz by his head. It ripped through the left arm and shoulder of the team's deputy commander, Lionel Guerra. A new Barkwood team member took one look at the two wounded veterans, dropped his gear, and bolted down the hill.

Bill Bryan appeared in the grass to Pagano's right. "Stay there," the team leader yelled. "I'll come over."[35]

As bullets and grenades ripped the grass from all directions, Pagano lay on his back and worked the radio. He asked friendly units down the hill to hold their fire. He called in artillery support and requested medevac choppers. His hands became numb from the loss of blood, and it became increasingly difficult to key his radio handset. The numbness spread to his chest and face. He was bleeding to death.

Bill Bryan charged through the grass and dived to the ground next to Pagano. "Don't worry, PJ, you're not going to die," Bryan said. The team leader propped himself up on his elbows and was tearing open a battle dressing with his teeth when the crack of an AK-47 sounded nearby. Bryan slumped to the dirt, face first. A bullet had ripped through his armpit and into his chest.

"Bryan, are you okay?" Pagano asked.

"Hit bad," the Texan gasped. "Going to die."[36]

Bill Bryan's head slowly sagged onto Pagano's legs.

• • •

With Brindley and his noncoms down, Dabney ordered Lieutenant Richard Foley up the hill to take command of the 3rd Platoon. The

Marines had formed a tight circle in anticipation of a North Vietnamese counterattack, which aerial observers reported was about to hit them. Only seconds before the NVA surged over the crest, friendly jets screamed to the rescue, dumping high explosives and napalm on the charging enemy force. The Marines bounced like rag dolls as bombs exploded and napalm fireballs boiled into the sky, but the enemy charge was shattered.[37]

• • •

PJ Pagano was lying in the grass several yards east of Brindley's perimeter when the jets made their run. He could hear voices on the radio trying to reach his team, but he was too weak to respond. The lifeless body of Bill Bryan lay across his legs. Pagano stared up at the beautiful blue sky and waited to die.

A Marine F-4 Phantom jet suddenly roared directly overhead, so low that Pagano could see the rivets on its fuselage and feel the heat from its engine. On its second pass, Pagano watched two napalm canisters drop from the jet's wings and tumble toward him. He closed his eyes, covered his face, and waited for the jellied gasoline to incinerate him. But the canisters whooshed past and exploded just over the crest.

Pagano next heard two helicopter pilots talking over his frequency. "Have you been monitoring Barkwood?" one pilot asked.

"Yes, that was a sad situation," the other replied.

Pagano suddenly realized: *They think we're dead.*[38]

• • •

Tom Brindley's shattered platoon had been saved by the air strikes, at least for a few minutes, but the Marines remained pinned down by heavy NVA fire. Bill Dabney now ordered Mike Thomas to take half his platoon and maneuver from the left flank over to Brindley's trapped survivors. Thomas quickly covered the 500 yards that separated the two columns and found Brindley's men. He reinforced the perimeter and began organizing the evacuation of the wounded down the hill.

When it became clear that the team of recon Marines was missing, Thomas led the search through the tall grass to the east. One by one, he and his men found the lost Marines and carried them to safety, until only two remained missing: team leader Bill Bryan and radio operator PJ Pagano.

As Thomas lay in the grass with his men, he received a radio report with the location of the two missing Marines. Blood streamed from a painful facial wound Thomas had suffered, but he insisted on leading the final rescue. The young lieutenant was rising from the grass when he was hit again: one bullet struck him in the head; another tore through his midsection, sliced through corpsman Mike Ray's shoulder, and struck a third Marine in the ankle. Mike Thomas collapsed to the ground, mortally wounded.[39]

• • •

In the tall grass nearby, PJ Pagano had mustered his last bit of strength to let his comrades know that he was alive. He positioned the handset near his ear and pressed his head down on the talk button. "All stations this net, this is Barkwood," Pagano said. "Be advised this station is up."

A few minutes passed before Pagano got a response.

"Barkwood, this is Rainbelt Six Actual." It was Bill Dabney. "I've got six Marines here who have volunteered to come up and get you. You up for it?"[40]

Signals were arranged: the rescue party would stay on Pagano's frequency and ask him to fire two quick shots from his M-16 rifle every so often to guide them. Pagano's hands were so numb that it took all his strength to pull the trigger, but he managed to fire two sets of shots on command. On his third attempt, the rifle bolt locked open. He was out of rounds.

Dark clouds had moved in, and it was beginning to rain. If night fell, Pagano knew he would bleed to death or be killed by NVA soldiers. He heard a rustling in the grass nearby and tensed. The grass parted, revealing the grimy face of a Marine.

"Are you Barkwood?" Sergeant Daniel Jessup casually asked.[41]

Yes, Pagano confirmed.

"What about him?" the Marine asked. He nodded at the Barkwood team leader, still draped over Pagano's legs.

"He's dead," Pagano replied. As he finally allowed himself to accept the terrible truth, Pagano fought to suppress a scream. Bill Bryan, the finest of men and Marines, was dead.

Three Marines, including one of Pagano's wounded teammates, had found the Barkwood radio operator. They cut off Pagano's pack and began dragging him down the hill, a few inches at a time, as the NVA blasted the moving grass. The LZ finally came into sight. Pagano was loaded aboard a medevac helicopter with other casualties, and the bird made its escape under heavy NVA fire.[42]

• • •

Around 3:00 p.m., Bill Dabney had received a radio transmission from the battalion commander: break contact and get your men back to 881 South. There was no explanation—it was always assumed that the NVA was monitoring transmissions, so the less said, the better. Only later that night would Dabney learn about the North Vietnamese defector and his revelations about an imminent attack.

Dabney argued that he could take 881 North if he got reinforcements. His request was denied.[43] By late afternoon, Dabney had accounted for all his men and gotten the most seriously wounded off the hill. He had lost forty-two men in the day's fighting, one-fourth of his force, including seven dead or mortally wounded. The big Virginian gave the order to withdraw.

As the exhausted Marines retraced their steps down the parallel fingers, helicopter gunships and attack jets pinned the North Vietnamese in place. Night was approaching when the last Marine of India Company filed back inside the wire of the outpost on 881 South.[44]

• • •

During the course of the long day, the mood on 881 South had darkened as India's losses had mounted.[45] Lieutenant Tom Esslinger, a twenty-four-year-old Yale University graduate from Ephrata, Pennsylvania, had choppered up to the hill with 3rd Battalion's Mike Company, which was assigned to hold the outpost while Dabney confronted the NVA.[46] Esslinger had joined a group of senior officers as they watched the operation from atop Dabney's bunker.

As the fight raged, the officers sat on the bunker roof in lawn chairs and puffed cigars. Esslinger had watched admiringly through binoculars as Lieutenant Mike Thomas, a close friend, dashed around the lower slopes of 881 North, oblivious to the enemy fire. But as the hours passed, Esslinger's awe had turned to horror after he witnessed the death of Tom Brindley, another good friend and former classmate, and then Mike Thomas.

Esslinger had ducked inside Dabney's bunker, where he broke down and wept.[47]

Now, with the North Vietnamese all around, the mourning of fallen friends and comrades would have to wait. Tom Esslinger helped ready Mike Company for battle, while the men of India Company made similar preparations on their half of the hill. The long day drew to a close on Hill 881 South with the familiar figure of Captain Bill Dabney moving through the darkness, checking his lines, bucking up his men. The great confrontation at Khe Sanh was underway.

CHAPTER 2

The Battle of Hill 861

As the Marines on 881 South awaited the enemy, North Vietnamese sappers moved through the darkness and fog about one and one-half miles to the east. With practiced stealth, they closed on the American outpost on Hill 861—the advance elements of a four-hundred-man NVA assault force poised to strike the Marines of Kilo Company, 3/26.

Approximately twenty paces beyond the northern perimeter of the American stronghold, two Marines were the first to hear the enemy approach. They had drawn listening post (LP) duty on this night and were hiding in a clump of grass, waiting to sound the alarm if the enemy attacked. Periodically, the platoon radio operator called for a situation report, a heart-stopping request on nights when the enemy was about. It would suffice for the LP leader to key his mike a specified number of times, if everything was okay. "If there ain't no jive, give me five," the platoon radioman might instruct. Or: "If you're home free, give me three."[1]

The North Vietnamese troops closing on the hill—the 6th Battalion of the 325C Division's 2nd Regiment—had orders to overrun the American outpost. The 150 Marines and Navy corpsmen assigned to Kilo Company, 3rd Battalion of the 26th Marine Regiment, had orders to stop them.

Back home, the country might be coming apart at the seams over the war in Vietnam and civil rights, but the American melting pot was alive and well in Kilo Company. The Corps had taken young men from every conceivable background—Northerners and Southerners, blacks and whites, jocks and scholars, high school dropouts and college boys—and had broken them down and rebuilt them as peerless warriors, bound by a sense of brotherhood and purpose that transcended race and class and regional pride. It was fashionable in the Army to look down on the Marines and mock their *oorah* bravado, their claims of being stronger and tougher and faster than anyone else defending Old Glory. But for those who had been through boot camp at Parris Island or San Diego or Officer Candidates School at Quantico, the transformation was as real as air or sunlight. They were, and would forever be, United States Marines, guided by an uncomplicated creed: *Semper Fidelis*—Always Faithful, with an emphasis on Always.

The Marine Corps had taken disparate souls like Lance Corporal Dennis Mannion, a garrulous twenty-two-year-old Notre Dame dropout and son of a Connecticut FBI agent, and Sergeant Miguel Salinas, a thirty-eight-year-old Korean War veteran and worldly merchant seaman of humble Mexican migrant stock, and transformed them into highly skilled components of the killing machine that was Kilo Company. The Corps had taken a pair of mismatched twenty-year-olds named Ted Mickelson and Dave Rozelle—the former a short (and short-tempered) Mormon cowboy from Wyoming and the latter a tall, sweet-natured agnostic from Scranton, Pennsylvania—and forged them into a fine M-60 machine-gun team anchoring Kilo's eastern perimeter. The Corps had elevated college-educated men like twenty-four-year-old Norman Jasper from the cornfields of Illinois to company command and more recent graduates, like Benjamin Steve Fordham, the son of an American business executive in Mexico, to platoon leadership.

Holding it all together were career Marines like Melvin Rimel, Kilo's revered gunnery sergeant. At six foot three and 240 pounds, the native of Dawson, Pennsylvania, had earned the nickname Bull as a fledgling Marine recruit at Parris Island in 1953. To members of his family, he was a beloved son, brother, husband, and father of four. Now thirty-three, with fifteen years in the Marine Corps, Rimel was a "lifer," but he was larger than life. For young Marines, Rimel was a surrogate father, tough but fair, and he taught them how to be a Marine.[2]

The two Kilo Marines out on LP duty off the north end of 861 were another unlikely pair, a Louisiana Cajun named Bondurant and a wise-cracking Northern black named Diehl, but the finely honed process of Marine Corps acculturation wasn't foremost in their minds as they listened to the enemy sappers creeping toward their hiding place.

Their radio crackled to life with a reprieve: Captain Jasper wanted all LPs back inside the wire. Bondurant and Diehl ran for their lives. The shaken Marines sprinted back inside the Kilo perimeter, spewing a torrent of oaths. "Motherfucker!" one exclaimed. "There's all kinds of gooks out there!"[3]

• • •

The two Marines weren't exaggerating. The night came alive with the sounds of NVA sappers as they low-crawled up the slope toward the northern perimeter of the American outpost. The approach was gentler there, almost flat in places, whereas the hill dropped off steeply to the east and west.

The American stronghold on Hill 861 measured nearly four hundred yards north to south and about 150 yards east to west. The hill sloped upward toward the north and crested a little over fifty yards above the trench line as it snaked around the northern perimeter. Captain Jasper's command bunker—several layers of sandbags piled around dirt-filled barrels—sat near the crest. The helicopter landing zone was down the hill to the south.

Several sandbagged machine-gun bunkers had been carved into the outer wall of the trench line, spaced every twenty-five yards or so. In between were the fighting positions of Kilo's riflemen. Sergeant Miguel Salinas was positioned with his M-60 machine gun at a crucial point on the northern trench line, overlooking the main entrance to the outpost.

To slow an enemy assault force, the Americans had built an outer barrier anchored by three rows of triple concertina wire, a regular barbed wire fence and swaths of "tangle foot"—tautly stretched barbed wire laid out in a checkerboard pattern a few inches off the ground. Scattered among the tangle foot and concertina were pressure-detonated mines and trip flares that would burn brightly when triggered. Beyond the wire were command-detonated Claymore mines, positioned to spray ball bearings in a deadly fan-shaped pattern toward an assault force, and homemade anti-personnel weapons fashioned from twenty-five pound rolls of barbed wire packed with C4 plastic explosives and a blasting cap.[4]

Now, Miguel Salinas and his 1st Platoon comrades listened to the enemy sappers as they went about their work sizing up the outer American defenses—probing, digging up mines, and snipping wire. The Marines could hear the *tap-tap-tap* of bamboo signal sticks and see pinholes of light flickering on and off like fireflies as the sappers communicated with each other and with the assault forces moving into place behind them. The Marines occasionally tossed grenades toward the sounds and flashes of light. As the tension built, they yelled taunts and insults at their adversaries.[5]

Sometime after 9:00 p.m., Captain Jasper ordered Kilo's artillery forward observer, Dennis Mannion, down to the northern perimeter to see if he could put artillery on the NVA sappers. Mannion and his radio operator, Dave Kron, found the mood tense among the Marines.[6] The enemy sappers were now only thirty or forty yards away, so close that the Americans could hear the high-pitched, singsong tones of spoken Vietnamese. The sappers seemed nonchalant, chatting, even laughing. Other sounds carried through the fog: the slap of a rifle sling hitting the weapon's wooden stock; the *"Shhhhhhhhhh"* of an enemy soldier trying to quiet his comrades; and, strangest of all, a Donald Duck–like noise followed by laughter.[7] The concertina wire hummed as the North Vietnamese shook it, perhaps testing whether it was electrified or rigged with explosives.[8] There were metallic pings as taut coils of concertina were snipped and sprang back into place. The Americans threw more grenades, and the occasional screams or moans of injured North Vietnamese soldiers carried through the night.[9]

It was quickly clear to Mannion that the NVA had crept too close for an artillery strike. He returned to his fighting hole above the 1st Platoon positions and reported his assessment to Captain Jasper.[10] Twice more, Mannion and his radioman made their way down to the front wire to check the situation. They had just returned to their fighting hole after their final trip down to the front line when a figure took shape in the mist. They tensed, and Mannion barked a challenge.

A voice like that of a radio disc jockey sang out, announcing the call letters of a Florida radio station and a balmy weather report. It was corpsman Malcolm Mole, an aspiring DJ from DeLand, Florida. The cheery Mole had crept up the hill to use the latrine the Marines had carved into the slope near Mannion's bunker.

Laughing at Mole's comic relief, Mannion called out in mock anger. "Oh, Doc, come on! Give me a break!"[11]

• • •

Sometime around 12:30 a.m. on January 21, 1968, an RPG round streaked over Miguel Salinas and his 1st Platoon comrades on the northern perimeter of 861 and exploded on the crest of the hill behind them.[12] A green flare lit the night as RPG rounds whooshed in from North Vietnamese positions to the west, smashing into Captain Jasper's command post, machine-gun bunkers, and other key points. Rockets slammed into the hill, one after another, and enemy mortars bisected the hill with rounds that marched along a north-south axis, spraying deadly shrapnel in all directions. Machine-gun rounds and green tracers stitched the darkness.

In the eerie half-light of illumination flares and exploding shells, the Marines of the 1st Platoon could see dozens of NVA soldiers charging toward them, blowing gaps in the wire with Bangalore torpedoes and throwing bamboo mats and ladders over the tangle foot and concertina coils.[13] Miguel Salinas opened fire with his M-60, and other Marines up and down the northern line tossed grenades and emptied M-16 magazines into the enemy charge. Some of the attackers got tangled in the wire and thrashed about as they tried to break free.[14] The screams of wounded NVA troops and Marines mingled with exclamations and warnings of new threats. Salinas screamed in Spanish and bounced around the trench line like a fighting cock.[15]

Several enemy soldiers reached the trench line around Salinas's machine gun, and the fight became a desperate hand-to-hand struggle. A black Marine took up an exposed position atop the machine-gun bunker, pointed his M-16 at the charging NVA soldiers, and pulled the trigger. A Marine from Denver, Colorado, emptied his magazine into the mob, then slashed and stabbed the attackers with a switchblade. Salinas clubbed three or four with his rifle and shot one in the midsection at close range.[16]

Just as suddenly as it began, the attack rolled past Salinas and his comrades. Dead and dying NVA soldiers lay all around them—in the trench line, in the wire, and on the torn ground beyond. Several North Vietnamese soldiers had jumped the trench line and headed up the hill toward Captain Jasper's command post. A few others had made it into the trench on either side of the 1st Platoon line, and they now headed deeper into the American outpost.

• • •

Around midnight, Captain Jasper had dispatched Dennis Mannion to the southern end of the hill to check out reports from the 2nd Platoon that NVA troops were in the elephant grass beyond the western perimeter wire. Jasper instructed the artillery forward observer to confirm the sighting and call in artillery on the enemy soldiers if possible.[17]

Arriving at the 2nd Platoon command post, Mannion peered into the darkness with binoculars, but he couldn't see or hear anything. As he was standing there, scanning the grass-cloaked draw beneath the hill's western perimeter, a green flare spangled the sky. On cue, the entire northwest corner of the hill came under fire from RPGs, rockets, mortars, machine guns, and small arms positioned on ridgelines to the west and north. Mannion and his radioman, Dave Kron, headed toward their fighting position overlooking the northern perimeter, working their way up the road that ran from the LZ to Captain Jasper's command post in the middle of the hill. The entire northern end of the hill was getting hammered by mortars and RPGs, so they veered to their right, moving in a low crouch toward the northeast. Ahead, they could see the silhouette of the command post, backlit by the flash of explosions and the intermittent light of flares that floated slowly to the ground on tiny parachutes.

As they got closer, Mannion could see a body sprawled on the ground outside the command post (CP): it was Kilo's beloved gunnery sergeant, Melvin Rimel. He was lying on his back, eyes open, his massive body pierced and broken by an enemy shell.[18] Mannion knelt at the side of the great Marine and, with his thumbs, gently closed Rimel's eyes.

Tears of shock and disbelief ran down Mannion's cheeks as he stifled a wave of panic: *Oh my God, if they could kill Gunny Rimel, we're all going to die.*[19] From his vantage point, Mannion could see that an RPG or a mortar had demolished the command post. There was no sign of Captain Jasper or anyone else in the command group.

Mannion collected himself and began to formulate a plan. He *had* to get back to the northern end of the hill to call in artillery and see with his own eyes where the rounds were landing or else the NVA could move up reinforcements at will and overrun the outpost. But the hail of bullets, RPGs, and shells had turned the area around his fighting position into a death zone. Even now, as he hunkered with his radioman in the open, they could hear shrapnel whiz by and clang off the steel engineering stakes that anchored bunker walls and perimeter wire. They would have to find another route.

Crouching low to the ground, Mannion and Kron retraced their steps to the LZ and found their way to a small bunker along the western trench line. "Get Charlie 1/13," Mannion ordered, one of the batteries at Khe Sanh Combat Base. "We're going to start calling in artillery."

Kron dialed in the frequency and was stunned by what he heard. "Listen to this," he said, putting the handset to his comrade's ear. Mannion could hear the voices of North Vietnamese soldiers. They were jamming the frequency to block communications between the Americans on 861 and their artillery support.

With their efforts to call in artillery temporarily thwarted, Mannion and Kron started up the western trench line. Every ten or twelve feet, they passed a Marine standing at his post, rifle pointed outward. There were no enemy troops visible to the west, but the Marines occasionally tossed grenades into the shadows to make sure NVA assault forces weren't creeping up on their positions. Mannion asked each Marine they encountered: Is there a man to your right? Each time the answer was yes, and so they kept moving up the trench.

Periodically, when they could get a clear frequency, the two Americans paused to call in coordinates for artillery. When they were unable to get through, alert officers down at the base were firing missions on Mannion's preregistered targets to the west and northwest of the hill.

About an hour had passed since the opening salvo launching the attack, and the intensity of the enemy barrage had ebbed at times. Suddenly, a thunderous explosion rocked the hill, and a greenish-yellow fireball boiled into the sky above the north end. The 106-millimeter recoilless rifle bunker to the left of Mannion's fighting hole had taken a direct hit, and it was now gone.

Mannion and Kron finally worked their way up to the northwest corner of the perimeter. The acrid smell of gunpowder from NVA grenades and shells hung heavily in the air. A Marine bunker came into view, and they could hear and see that a machine gunner was firing short bursts, with every sixth or seventh round a red tracer that streaked toward the northwest. As the two Marines crept close to the bunker, Mannion yelled the gunner's name. "It's Dennis," Mannion called out.

The machine gunner fired a burst, then called back, "Okay."

Mannion and Kron ducked into the bunker, stepping on hundreds of shell casings that littered the floor. "Where's your crew?" Mannion asked.

"I don't know," the gunner replied. "They took off."

"Are there gooks out there?"

The M-60 gunner wasn't sure what was lurking in the fog, but he had a more immediate concern. "They're all up and down this trench line," he warned.

Mannion was stunned. "They're in here?"

"Fuck, yeah," the gunner said. "There's one guy right outside in the trench line. I think he got hit by his own grenade."

Mannion turned the subdued beam of his red-lens flashlight toward the bunker entrance and spotted the small crater from a grenade blast just outside. He stole a quick glance up the trench line and could see a North Vietnamese soldier, sprawled on his stomach, no more than two feet away.

Mannion turned back to the gunner. "Is the guy dead?"

"I think he's wounded, but I don't think he's dead."

"Well, we've got to get up around the corner," Mannion said firmly. He turned to his radioman. "Give me your .45."

Kron handed him the pistol. Squatting down in the bunker's entrance, Mannion slowly stretched his body out into the trench. Lying half on his side, he reached to his left. He touched the enemy soldier's shoulder, then his head. The injured man jerked away. Mannion thrust the pistol forward and fired four times.[20]

Bidding good luck to the machine gunner, Mannion and Kron cautiously continued up the trench line. They came to an abandoned bunker that overlooked the flat area where the North Vietnamese assault had first hit the Marines. Heavy enemy fire from outside the wire prevented them from going any further.

The two Americans eased back out of the line of fire and slipped into a cut in the trench wall. From there, Dennis Mannion and Dave Kron began calling in more artillery and adjusting the fire onto the NVA positions to their west and northwest.[21]

• • •

When the North Vietnamese attack got underway, Captain Norman Jasper, the Kilo commander, was standing in the fighting hole alongside his command bunker near the crest of 861. Ringed by a chest-high wall of sandbags, the hole was near one of the hill's two 106-millimeter recoilless rifle bunkers, carved into the rim of a bomb crater above the northwest trench line. As the NVA barrage pounded the hill, Jasper kept in touch with his platoon commanders and the battalion staff by radio, popping his head above the sandbags periodically to see for himself what was going on or to yell instructions to the Marines in his area.[22]

The cry of "Corpsman!" soon sounded around him. Five Navy corpsmen had been assigned to Kilo Company. One of the two corpsmen with Jasper's command group, aspiring disc jockey Malcolm Mole, scampered down the hill in response to a shout for aid. An RPG round streaked across the slope and exploded, killing the twenty-year-old from Florida.[23]

In the quavering half-light of exploding shells and flares, Jasper and his command group worked the radios and directed fire. When word of a breach in the northern line filtered back up the hill, Jasper radioed 2nd Platoon along the southern and western perimeter: get some men up the hill to plug the breach. Four riflemen and two men from a 4.2-inch mortar team hustled up the slope to join the desperate fight being waged by Miguel Salinas and his comrades.

• • •

M-60 gunner Ted Mickelson and Lance Corporal Dave Rozelle, a twenty-year-old from Scranton, Pennsylvania, heard and saw the assault unfold from their machine-gun bunker on the northeast trench line. It was a nonstop light show of exploding shells and flares, RPGs and trac-ers. It all vaguely reminded Mickelson of a fierce lightning storm out on his family's Wyoming ranch—except it was louder and more terrifying than any storm he had experienced.

While Mickelson peered out through the bunker's front firing port, watching for an enemy assault on the wire below him, Rozelle stood at the rear entrance, facing westward, to make sure that NVA troops didn't surprise them from behind. A 120-millimeter rocket screamed in from the west and slammed into the slope behind them, and a blinding flash filled the bunker. Mickelson turned back toward the sound and saw Rozelle silhouetted in the bunker entrance. The big Pennsylvanian slowly sank onto a bench along the bunker's back wall. Mickelson heard a sound like water gushing from a faucet. It was blood pouring from Rozelle's femoral arteries, severed by shrapnel or debris.

Mickelson rushed to Rozelle and held him.

"I'm sorry, Ted," Rozelle said. "I'm sorry I didn't kill a gook."[24] And then he died.

• • •

Over on the western trench line, Private First Class Paul Robert Bellamy, a big, easygoing nineteen-year-old from Portland, Oregon, lay dying with a terrible wound. A piece of shrapnel had blown out the right side of his head, but it hadn't killed him. He sat with his back against the trench wall, conversing cogently with his friends as his last minutes slipped away.[25]

• • •

After breaching the northern wire, the NVA assault troops who made it past the 1st Platoon trench line fanned out down the hill. Some, like the one Dennis Mannion encountered, had headed down the western trench line in an attempt to take out the American machine guns. A few took off for the Kilo command post and the interior of the outpost, where they were killed or captured by Marines. One of these enemy soldiers may have fired the shot that found nineteen-year-old Curtis B. Bugger of Kearns, Utah, an assistant machine gunner, killing him in the western trench line with a bullet to the head.

The leader of Bugger's gun team was a Marine from Oklahoma named Billy Ray Moffett, and he continued to blast away at the North Vietnamese off the northwest corner of the hill. Even after his assistant gunner had been killed and his bunker had come under assault from NVA machine guns, mortars, and RPGs, Moffett remained at his post, pouring fire into the main enemy avenue of attack.[26]

• • •

Well-placed enemy mortar fire had taken a heavy toll on the Kilo command group. Gunnery Sergeant Melvin Rimel had been killed, and First Sergeant Bernard Goddard seriously wounded when a piece of shrapnel had sliced his carotid artery. (Goddard fought on with a finger pressed against the torn artery so he wouldn't bleed to death.)[27] Captain Jasper was next.

About ninety minutes into the fight, Jasper was standing outside his command bunker when a flurry of NVA mortar rounds slammed into the hill. Thrown into the air by the force of the blast, Jasper landed in a heap about ten feet away. A piece of shrapnel had struck his cheek below his left eye, which began to swell shut. Another mortar round exploded close to him, and once again he was hurled through the air. Hot shrapnel tore into his right arm and shoulder, and other metal fragments burrowed under his sleeveless flak jacket and lodged in his chest.

Not long afterward, a third mortar round knocked Jasper flying. A piece of shrapnel penetrated his right knee and smaller fragments peppered his buttocks. He landed on a corpsman wounded by the same blast. "Treat your wounds," the Kilo commander told the corpsman. "Then you can treat mine."[28]

• • •

Twenty-five hundred yards to the west, the Marines of India and Mike Companies waited in their trenches for the expected NVA assault to roll up the slopes of Hill 881 South.

Most of the 3/26 battalion staff had remained on the hill after India's daylong fight on 881 North. Clustered in Captain Bill Dabney's command bunker, they followed Kilo's increasingly desperate situation over the battalion radio net. From their vantage point, they could see and hear the deadly NVA barrage that pounded 861—flashes of light in the eastern sky, followed a second or two later by muffled explosions.

Around 2:00 a.m., the radio in Dabney's bunker that had been tuned to the 3/26 battalion net crackled to life. A frantic voice transmitting from 861 cut through the static. "We're being overrun! Command group is all down!"[29]

Major Matthew Caulfield, the battalion operations officer, took the handset. "A Marine unit doesn't get overrun," Caulfield coolly replied. "Now calm down and tell me what is really happening."

The frantic voice belonged to Jasper's executive officer, First Lieutenant Jerry N. Saulsberry. The fear in Saulsberry's voice was palpable as he laid out the grim situation.

"Get your gunny," Caulfield said. "Make sure you rely on him."[30]

"The gunny is dead," Saulsberry replied.

"Get your first sergeant," Caulfield said, mindful of Ben Goddard's stellar reputation.

"He's dying," came the response. (Goddard, in fact, would live.)

Caulfield, a charming Irishman, summoned all his powers of inspiration to steel the overwhelmed lieutenant. "Now Jerry, I know you can do this," Caulfield exhorted. "I want you to take that ball and run with it!"[31]

There was silence on the other end. Finally, Saulsberry responded in a weak voice.

"Run? Did you say *run*, sir?"

"No, no, Jerry!" Caulfield shouted back into the handset. "You gotta stay right there!"

• • •

Jerry Saulsberry held his ground, and so did the rest of Kilo Company as the 3/26 battalion staff mobilized the formidable American firepower in support of Hill 861. With the assistance of Kilo artillery forward observer Dennis Mannion, still huddled along the northwest trench line of 861, a fierce counterbarrage began to saturate the areas where North Vietnamese reinforcements were massing and heavy weapons had been positioned.[32] The tide of battle began to turn.

Under Dabney's direction, the 81-millimeter mortars on 881 South maintained a furious pace. Dabney pulled riflemen from his trenches to keep a steady supply of rounds flowing to the gunners. When the 81 tubes began to glow red-hot and ignite propellant bags before the rounds could be fired, Dabney organized his men to cool one tube with water while the other was being fired.[33] The Marines soon emptied all the hill's canteens and jerry cans, so Dabney ordered his men to pour their stores of fruit juice on the overheated mortars. When the fruit juice ran out, Dabney lined up his men by platoon and the Marines took turns urinating on the tube. By dawn, the Marines on 881 South had fired nearly 1,000 81-millimeter mortar rounds and several hundred 105-millimeter howitzer rounds in support of 861.[34]

The first hint of dawn found the men of Kilo Company shaken and bloodied, but still in control of the hill. During the night, the North Vietnamese assault commander had been overheard in a radio transmission, screaming for his reserves to join the attack.[35] But the American response had been swift and decisive, from the riflemen and machine gunners on 861 to the artillery crews at 881 South, Khe Sanh, and Camp Carroll, further east along Route 9. Dead and dying North Vietnamese soldiers now littered the slopes of 861 and nearby terrain. The NVA attack had been broken.

● ● ●

After surviving the initial NVA assault, Miguel Salinas and the men of Kilo's 1st Platoon counted their losses and regrouped. Several had been wounded and two killed. The firing tapered off, and the haggard Marines began to move about the trench line.

Salinas knelt down to examine the NVA soldier he had shot at close range during the first minutes of the battle. The man looked neater than the other dead NVA troops he could see caught in the wire and outside the trench line. Salinas found a Catholic rosary in one of the dead man's pockets. In another, he found a cheap plastic wallet with a photograph of the soldier with his wife and young daughter, and a letter the soldier had written.

Salinas couldn't speak or read Vietnamese, but he later had the letter translated by a Communist defector. In it, the North Vietnamese soldier was asking his commanding officer for a leave so he might return home to visit his sick wife. For Salinas, it was a rare glimpse of the humanity on the other side of the savage conflict in Vietnam—a poignant reminder that the NVA soldiers, for all their fearsome reputation, were just like the young Americans on Hill 861 in at least one respect: they were sons and husbands and fathers, and they were frightened and homesick as they joined the battle at Khe Sanh.[36]

• • •

On the hill's northwest corner, Dennis Mannion and Dave Kron emerged from the hole where they had spent the night calling in artillery missions and retraced their steps down the western trench line. They came upon the NVA soldier that Mannion had shot outside the machine-gun bunker. Mannion made a mental note of the enemy soldier's attire: sneakers, greenish-tan shirt and pants, cartridge belt, and pith helmet.

Further down the trench line, Mannion and Kron cautiously made their way to the middle of the hill, and then, in a low crouch, started up the slope toward the Kilo command post. They saw Gunny Rimel's body lying in the dirt off to the right. Near their fighting hole on the hill's northern rim they saw four or five badly mangled NVA dead in an old bomb crater. Below them, a dozen or more NVA soldiers lay sprawled in and under the perimeter wire.[37]

Over on the northeast side of the hill, after hours of incessant noise—explosions, gunfire, and the rattle of his machine gun as he sprayed the darkness with nearly 10,000 rounds—Ted Mickelson was struck by the silence that engulfed the outpost. The calm was abruptly broken by the moaning of a wounded Marine, a recoilless rifleman, lying in the fighting hole a few feet behind Mickelson, his bloody body bristling with flechette rounds that had blown up when the 106 bunker had taken a direct hit. A corpsman arrived and went to work on the wounded Marine.[38]

• • •

The final drama of the attack on Hill 861 occurred as dawn broke. One of the NVA soldiers who had breached the 1st Platoon lines had taken refuge in a phone booth–size latrine on the northern end of the hill. He had neatly laid out his ammunition and food—rice and dried fish—and waited for his final showdown with the Americans. Marines closed in on the lone enemy holdout from three sides, pouring rounds into the wooden structure. The soldier died in a flurry of gunfire, the last casualty of the battle for Hill 861.[39]

• • •

On Hill 881 South, Captain Bill Dabney and the men of India and Mike Companies welcomed the news that their comrades on 861 had survived the night. India Company had burned through most of its M-16 ammo and 81-millimeter mortar rounds over the previous twenty-four hours. Several casualties from the fighting on 881 North still needed to be evacuated down to Khe Sanh.[40] Dabney radioed for helicopter support at first light, and a bird soon swooped low over the hill and settled onto one of the hill's two LZs. Two or three Marines on stretchers were loaded aboard the chopper, along with a couple of walking wounded.

Several hundred yards away, North Vietnamese artillery spotters had watched the helicopter land and had seen the throng of Marines spilling onto the LZ to offload cargo and load the wounded. An NVA 120-millimeter mortar team took aim and dropped a round down the tube.

The roar of the departing chopper's engine and thrashing rotors hid the sound of the enemy rounds leaving their tubes. Just off the LZ, Captain Dabney was standing with his company supply clerk, Private First Class Terry Melvin Johnson, when the first one hit. Dabney jumped into one hole, and Johnson into another. A round landed in Johnson's hole, killing him instantly.[41]

• • •

About 5:30 a.m., as the North Vietnamese assault on Hill 861 sputtered to a close, the Marines on the battered hill were startled by an ominous sound to the southwest, toward the border with Laos, about seven miles away.

BOOM-BOOM-BOOM.
BOOM-BOOM-BOOM.
BOOM-BOOM-BOOM.

A few seconds later, they heard the sound of explosions southeast of their position. Forward observer Dennis Mannion looked at his radio operator. He recognized the sounds of big artillery guns firing, and he knew what it meant.

Khe Sanh Combat Base was under attack.[42]

CHAPTER 3

"Get Up and Man Your Position!"

The final hours of January 20, 1968, found Lance Corporal Michael O'Hara cradling a shotgun as he walked point for a column of Marines that slipped out the east end of Khe Sanh Combat Base and headed into the nearby jungle to set a night ambush. The nineteen-year-old rifleman had been vaguely aware of the heightened activity at the combat base during the day, but like most of the nearly 6,000 Americans at Khe Sanh, he knew nothing of the worried deliberations underway in the regimental command bunker in the heart of the sprawling stronghold.

At the center of those deliberations was Colonel David Lownds, commander of the 26th Marines and Khe Sanh Combat Base. The World War II veteran had spent the first hours of his day preoccupied by India Company's operation to 881 North, and then two important guests had arrived by air. Lownds had devoted the late morning and early afternoon to his visitors, Brigadier General Phillip B. Davidson, military intelligence chief for America's supreme commander in Vietnam, General William Westmoreland, and Colonel Kenneth J. Houghton, chief of intelligence for the III Marine Amphibious Force. He had briefed them on the local situation and showed them Khe Sanh's defenses, but both had come away convinced that Lownds had badly underestimated the enemy threat and had failed to prepare his men sufficiently for the looming confrontation.[1] Before leaving, the intelligence chiefs learned about the surrender of the

North Vietnamese lieutenant and his revelations about Communist plans to attack the Americans that night.[2]

Late afternoon at the combat base had seen a flurry of activity as medevac choppers had arrived, bearing wounded and dead Marines from Bill Dabney's desperate fight on 881 North. As night fell, Marines on watch duty peered into the darkness from Khe Sanh's trench line. Others prepared for listening-post and night-ambush assignments outside the wire. Among them was the contingent from Bravo Company, 1st Battalion, 26th Marines, that included Michael O'Hara. They had slipped into the jungle south of Bravo Company's lines and laid out Claymore mines and fields of fire, then settled into the underbrush to await their prey.

● ● ●

Back in rural southern Indiana, Michael O'Hara had loved horses and hunting, but becoming a Marine had been his lifelong dream. He was still in elementary school when his older brother by seven years, Wayne, had joined the Corps. Young Michael had spent many a Saturday at the local movie house, watching John Wayne war movies and World War II newsreels about real-life Marine heroes.[3] In a pouring rain in late April 1967, O'Hara had hitchhiked to Bloomington, Indiana, where he enlisted in the Marine Corps. He was eighteen years old.

In early October 1967, O'Hara found himself in Okinawa, Japan, filling out a will and life-insurance forms before boarding a Vietnam-bound Continental Airlines chartered jet packed with replacement Marines. As the aircraft descended through the clouds over Da Nang, jungle-cloaked mountains loomed black and ominous. The raucous Marines fell silent.

A few days later, with his newly issued M-16 rifle in hand, O'Hara boarded a big transport helicopter in Phu Bai. It was a sunny day and a brilliant landscape unfolded below—green mountains, silver waterfalls, lush tropical forests. It was the most beautiful place he had ever seen. About thirty minutes later, the chopper settled onto the runway at Khe Sanh Combat Base in a cloud of red dust, and O'Hara and other wide-eyed Marines grabbed their gear and scuttled away from the thrashing rotors. It was October 11, 1967.

Assigned to the 2nd Platoon of Bravo Company, 1st Battalion, 26th

Marines, O'Hara found the reception less than warm. The Marines had all lost friends, and they weren't eager to make new ones. A few days later, O'Hara and the rest of Bravo Company walked up to Hill 881 South.

O'Hara and a buddy named Don Quinn shared a cramped bunker carved into the side of the hill. The day after they arrived, it rained harder than anything O'Hara had ever witnessed. One wet, miserable day followed another. O'Hara and his buddy fashioned beds out of artillery ammunition boxes, but sleep was hard to come by. All night long, thirty feet from O'Hara's bunker, a 105-millimeter howitzer fired occasional "harassment and interdiction" rounds at suspected enemy infiltration routes.

Hill duty around Khe Sanh was uncomfortable but seldom fatal in the fall of 1967. One day, O'Hara was out on a company-size patrol hacking its way through a wall of the razor-sharp grass when the column abruptly halted. He heard the captain issue a terse command.

"Sniper up."

O'Hara stiffened. *Oh, shit. This is it.*

In a low voice, the captain admonished the sniper. "If you miss him, corporal, you'll be a private when you go to bed tonight."

A shot exploded over O'Hara's head. He braced for the enemy's answer, but it never came. Instead of shooting an NVA soldier, the sniper had bagged a five-point deer. The weary Marines slogged back up Hill 881 South with their prize, and the deer was butchered and chunks of fresh meat tossed into a simmering caldron. That night the men of Bravo Company feasted on the first hot chow they had eaten since arriving on the hill a month earlier.

When they weren't patrolling, the Marines kept busy with mind-numbing work details. They filled sandbags, shored up their crude bunkers, and burned off the contents of half-barrel latrines casually referred to as "shitters." Most afternoons they got an hour to change clothes, dry socks, wash up, and write letters home.

At night they took turns standing watch, or they slipped outside the wire-enclosed perimeter to set ambushes. Worst of all was listening-post duty. A fire team of four Marines would creep into the bush a hundred yards or so outside the wire and hunker down for the night, waiting to sound the alarm should the NVA attack.

One night, O'Hara led a fire team off the east side of 881 South for

LP duty. They had set their Claymore mines in a driving rain and were huddled under a poncho awaiting daylight. The Marines suddenly heard noises between their position and the perimeter wire. O'Hara radioed the command post. "Any friendly troops in our area?" he asked in a low voice.

"Negative," came the response.

The voices came closer. O'Hara's heart pounded. Should he shoot the men? At the last possible second, he whispered an order to hold fire, and the strangers passed by a few feet away.

Some minutes later, the strangers approached once more. Again O'Hara radioed his platoon commander. "Are you *sure* there are no other friendlies outside the wire?"

The reply was emphatic: "No friendlies."

Once again, O'Hara hesitated, and he allowed the shadowy figures to pass.

Back inside the outpost after daylight, O'Hara reported the strange events. A chill ran down his spine when he was informed that another Bravo platoon had sent men out on a night ambush. O'Hara had come within an eyelash of killing his comrades.

The day after Christmas, Bravo Company had rotated off 881 South and returned to the combat base. They took over the portion of the Khe Sanh perimeter designated as Gray Sector, which wrapped around the eastern end of the runway and continued around the southeastern perimeter of the base. By mid-January, the word was out that they were going to get hit by the North Vietnamese, and it was going to be big.

Now, O'Hara and about a dozen men from Bravo Company crouched in the darkness south of the base perimeter wire, waiting for enemy soldiers to walk into their trap. Squad leader Quiles Ray Jacobs, from Compton, California, scanned the low hills ahead through an AN/PVS-2 Starlight scope. A large group of enemy soldiers came into focus in the scope's greenish light: they were hard at work, digging mortar pits. Jacobs radioed the information back to base, and a terse response hissed over the radio: get back ASAP.[4]

They made it back safely, and O'Hara returned to the tent he shared with several other Marines. He stretched out on his cot, worn out by the months of hill duty and a recent bout of dysentery he had contracted after drinking untreated water during a patrol. But he was still keyed up by the ambush duty, and sleep did not come easily.

O'Hara had finally drifted off when he awoke abruptly to the sound of explosions.[5] Groggy and confused, he heard what sounded like bedsheets being ripped. A surge of adrenalin cleared his head, and he realized he was hearing artillery shrapnel tearing through his tent. Grabbing his shotgun, O'Hara bolted outside. At the tent entrance, he collided head-on with another Marine, and they fell to the ground—O'Hara unhurt, the other Marine torn into pieces by an enemy shell. O'Hara dived headlong into the nearest trench.

Every Marine at Khe Sanh had been instructed to find his fighting position and be ready to repel an enemy ground assault in the event of an enemy bombardment. Now, O'Hara and other Marines up and down the line huddled in the trench, paralyzed by fear. Shells and rockets shook the earth, tossing the terrified Americans off the ground and slamming them into the trench walls. Nothing in the John Wayne movies had prepared them for this.[6]

• • •

At 5:30 a.m., Tom Quigley was in the Bravo Company command bunker, nearing the end of his overnight radio watch. The nineteen-year-old corporal was signing his name to a letter he had written a friend when two booms sounded in the distance.

Captain Ken Pipes, the Bravo commander, sat up on his cot. "Was that incoming?" he asked.[7]

"Hell no, captain," drawled an old sergeant from Georgia.

The words had barely left the sergeant's mouth when two explosions crashed outside the bunker.

Rounds fired from North Vietnamese rocket batteries and artillery positioned as far away as Co Roc massif in Laos, eight miles to the west, quickly took out key installations across the base. One NVA round scored a direct hit on the main ammunition dump, detonating shells, grenades, small-arms rounds, and tear gas in spectacular fashion and unleashing secondary explosions that would continue for two days.[8]

Not far from Quigley, Michael O'Hara lay in the trench line as artillery shells and rockets rained down. He felt a sharp pain in his buttocks and looked up to see Corporal Ron Ryan, a big redhead with a handlebar mustache, poised to give him another kick. "Get up and man your position!" Ryan yelled.[9] The M-60 machine gunner in O'Hara's area, Ryan seemed oblivious to the shells as he coolly walked the trench, delivering well-placed kicks to get other frightened Marines on their feet and ready to resist the expected enemy ground assault.

After pulling first watch on the Bravo lines the night before, Lance Corporal Ken Rodgers, a twenty-one-year-old from Casa Grande, Arizona, had slept soundly until the opening rounds jolted him awake. He heard somebody yelling "incoming!" and scrambled into the trench. He was lying on his stomach when something thumped into his back. "I'm hit!" Rodgers yelled.

A Marine who ran to his aid burst into laughter. "They're just dirt clods," he said. "Get up!"[10]

Twenty-two-year-old Navy corpsman John Cicala of Detroit, Michigan, had been running through the trench toward the screams of wounded Marines when everything went black. He awoke on his back and heard someone shout, "Where the fuck is that corpsman?"[11] Cicala felt around in the dark and found his steel-pot helmet. Embedded in it were the fins of a mortar round. Cicala slapped the helmet on his head and hurried toward the screams.

He would forever remember the first man he treated that morning, a young Marine named Jimmy Kirk, whose name and face were etched into his memory because it was the most horrific injury that Cicala had yet encountered in Vietnam. The explosion of the ammo dump had nearly sheared off one of Kirk's legs below the knee. Cicala stanched the bleeding as best he could and swathed the torn limb in a battle dressing before moving on to the next wounded Marine.

Tear gas from the burning ammunition dump soon enveloped the Bravo command bunker, and radioman Tom Quigley now paid the price for having left his gas mask in his tent. Amid his tears, he could hear the terrifying sound of shrapnel shredding the air. Rounds hit closer and closer to the command post. Captain Pipes finally ordered everyone in the bunker to head for the trenches. In the frantic scramble, Quigley got his cartridge belt tangled in a communications wire, and when he finally freed himself, he slithered into a mortar pit.[12]

For the next hour, a handful of frightened Marines crouched in the pit, surrounded by artillery shells. Convinced they were dead men regardless, the men carelessly lit cigarettes and puffed away, flicking their ashes into a shell case. When the enemy fire briefly eased, Quigley and his companions piled into their trench line and waited for the enemy to hit the wire.[13]

• • •

Along the southern edge of the Khe Sanh runway, Navy doctor Edward Feldman was fast asleep in his tent when the attack began. He knew he needed to get to the aid station of the 1st Battalion, 26th Marines, to treat casualties, but his hands shook so badly that he couldn't tie his boots.[14]

Feldman had grown up in midtown Manhattan in New York City, where his father was a manager at a local textile mill and his mother taught school. His comfortable childhood was made even happier by the fact that Manhattan's frequent military parades rolled right past his doorstep. His young imagination was fired by the sight of soldiers and sailors strutting past to pounding drums and the stirring strains of Sousa marches. When he wasn't cheering parades, he loved to watch war movies over and over again at a neighborhood theater.

When he was fourteen, Feldman moved with his family out to the leafy Forest Hills neighborhood in Queens. He graduated from high school in 1958 and earned a pharmacy degree from Columbia University four years later. He thought about seeking a Marine Corps commission but instead married his high school sweetheart and entered medical school in Kansas City, Missouri. In 1966, he graduated as a doctor of osteopathy and began a yearlong internship in Detroit, Michigan.

Feldman found it difficult to focus on his medical career with the United States at war in Southeast Asia, so he entered the Navy as a lieutenant in August 1967 and began hounding a Pentagon contact for an assignment to Vietnam. Feldman's orders came through in November, and eight days before Christmas, he arrived in Da Nang. Before the day was out, he was patching up wounded Marines at a field hospital in Phu Bai. On January 3, 1968, he flew to Khe Sanh to take up a temporary assignment as surgeon for the 1st Battalion of the 26th Marines.

Now, as the barrage of enemy shells merged into an ear-splitting roar,

Feldman finally got his boots tied, grabbed his M-16 and gas mask, and pulled aside the Army blanket that served as the blackout curtain for his tent. Two steps outside was a smoking shell hole the size of a small car. Fifty feet away, the battalion aid station was a pile of fire and rubble.

Feldman sprinted toward the casualty holding bunker, which had been hit but was still usable. The eight Navy corpsmen and three Marine runners on his team were already inside. While some of the corpsmen salvaged supplies from the burning tents, Feldman and the others tended to Marines with shrapnel wounds and cuts from flying debris.

A few minutes later, several Marines arrived with a wounded comrade. Feldman examined the injured Marine and found what looked like a metal pipe protruding from his abdomen. It was the fuse assembly of a mortar round, and it had plunged into the side of Private First Class Robert Mussari without exploding.

Feldman and the Marines carried Mussari to a far corner of the bunker and erected a small blast wall of sandbags around him. Feldman started an intravenous drip and struck up a conversation with Mussari, a nineteen-year-old from Scranton, Pennsylvania, to keep him calm and still. "You're going to be fine," the surgeon assured the injured Marine, far from certain whether he could make good on that promise.[15]

Feldman removed his flak jacket to free his movements and took off his helmet so it wouldn't fall on the wounded Marine or the mortar round. Electric power had been knocked out by the enemy barrage, so Navy corpsman Roger Tillotson taped together four flashlights and held them over the patient as Feldman prepared to begin the operation. There was no time to find surgical gloves in all the rubble, and Feldman couldn't use a scalpel or other surgical instruments—metal-on-metal contact might detonate the round. He would have to do the operation with his bare fingers.

Slowly stretching his body over the blast wall until he could touch Mussari, Feldman placed his fingers around the cylindrical fuse assembly and gently worked his way deeper into the Marine's torn abdomen, carefully freeing cauterized tissue and blood vessels. After fifteen minutes of work, Feldman felt the projectile's rounded nose. He made sure he had separated all the surrounding tissue, then gently held Mussari's intestines in place while a Marine staff sergeant, thirty-year-old Ronald

Sniegowski, slowly lifted the fuse assembly from the patient's body. As Sniegowski gingerly carried the explosive projectile outside for disposal, Feldman packed the wound with gauze.

Dawn was breaking as Bobby Mussari was loaded onto an all-terrain vehicle and driven to the base hospital, Charlie Med, to join the growing queue of wounded Marines awaiting evacuation. Edward Feldman returned to the work of patching up injured Marines, caring for another sixty men before the day was out.[16]

• • •

On the eastern perimeter, Lance Corporal Ken Rodgers had pulled himself together after his brush with the dirt clods and was dispatched down the trench line to check on Bravo's 1st Platoon by the ammo dump that had exploded. He was shocked by the almost surreal scene that appeared through the distorted lens of his gas mask. Unexploded artillery shells, bullets, and other debris littered the trench line and covered the Marines who had sought shelter there. Some of the men had suffered deep cuts, abrasions, and broken bones from big 155-millimeter rounds that had been hurled from the dump and dropped onto them where they lay.[17]

Over at Charlie Med, wounded India Company squad leader Ken Warner had reacted to the opening salvo by grabbing the badly injured comrade he had saved on 881 North the previous day and pulling him into the closest trench.[18]

Ambulance driver Dan Sullivan was searching for casualties around the burning ammunition dump when a howitzer round flung through the air by a secondary explosion smashed into his ambulance and blew up. The explosion shredded all four tires, shattered the windshield, and spattered Sullivan's flak jacket with shrapnel, but the twenty-year-old from Roxbury, Massachusetts, was unhurt. Sullivan, who was already on his second tour in Vietnam, spent the rest of the morning picking up wounded and dead Marines.[19]

On the south side of the runway, the men of Bravo Company, 3rd Recon, were on standby to plug any breach in the Khe Sanh perimeter.[20] Ray Milligan had been in many tight spots on recon missions, but he had never felt such penetrating fear as he did during the opening NVA barrage. He huddled in a bunker with his comrades, head between his legs, waiting to get blown to pieces.[21]

Over in the southwest corner of the base, 4.2-inch mortar crewman Billy Joe Hill awoke to the shriek of incoming rocket and artillery rounds. He and the other men assigned to artillery and mortar units took their positions in gun pits around the base and began to fire at suspected enemy positions.[22]

Second Lieutenant William Smith Jr., twenty-four years old, had just gone into his sleeping bunker for a nap when the North Vietnamese artillery and rockets hit the base. As the fire support coordinator for the 1st Battalion, 26th Marines, Smith worked at the side of the battalion commander, Lieutenant Colonel James B. Wilkinson, coordinating artillery and air strikes. His world at Khe Sanh revolved around the 1st Battalion command bunker and his nearby sleeping bunker, a rough affair built from sandbags and scrap wood, christened the Womb.

The sound of the incoming rounds sent Smith and his comrades in the Womb diving to the bunker floor. They grabbed their packs and ran out the door two at a time, crab-sprinting in a low crouch to the 1st Battalion command bunker, about forty yards away. When it was his turn, Smith bolted down the dirt street for the battalion command post. He was looking to the east, toward Ammo Dump No. 1, when he saw what looked like a greenish-yellow tsunami rushing toward him. It was the shock wave from the dump as it exploded. The force hurled Smith through the air, and he came to rest against a tent stake. Shaken but unhurt, he jumped up and sprinted the final yards to the command bunker.

The atmosphere inside was one of controlled chaos as the battalion staff tried to gather situation reports and preliminary casualty figures. Radios crackled and hissed with reports from platoon leaders and company commanders. Everyone assumed that the enemy barrage was prep fire for a ground attack.[23]

When the NVA assault got rolling, it would be Smith's job to coordinate with the frontline forward observers to call in air strikes and artillery missions on the enemy forces. Smith and his team had preregistered artillery and mortar coordinates so that every platoon and company commander could instantaneously summon precise fire. If Khe

Sanh did get overrun, Smith was poised to make the North Vietnamese pay dearly for the prize.[24]

• • •

Near the runway, twenty-one-year-old Navy Seabee Lewis "Sam" Messer of Gardner, Kansas, had spent most of January 20 partying with his buddies. The occasion had been the birthday of one of their fellow Seabees, and they had kept the drunken celebration going through most of the day and well into the night before retiring into their fortified bunker. (The Seabees had two fortified sleeping bunkers; the larger one, known as the Alamo Hilton, was favored by visiting news correspondents.)

Messer was supposed to go on kitchen duty at 5:00 a.m. on the morning of January 21, but the Seabee on watch had awakened him late. He took off down the road to the east toward the chow hall, pulling on his clothes as he ran, knowing he was going to catch hell from the duty sergeant. He was bent low to the ground, tying his boots, when the first rockets screamed from the sky and the air erupted with flying shrapnel, splinters, and debris.[25] Messer dived into the nearest hole.

When he had calmed his nerves, he started working his way back to his fighting hole to get his rifle and await the NVA attack. He would crawl or dart to a hole or section of trench, smoke a cigarette to steel his nerves, and then continue on. It took four hours, but he finally made it back to his comrades.[26]

• • •

Over in the Bravo Company, 1/26, sector Corporal Steve Wiese, nineteen, a speedy track and football athlete back home in Redlands, California, had been through enough firefights and artillery barrages to know what was coming next: the NVA would break from cover and charge the wire. Waiting for that moment was worse than enduring the incoming artillery. When the enemy barrage finally tapered off after a couple of hours, Wiese yelled at his buddies to get ready.[27]

The Marines peered out through the smoke and dust and last traces of fog, searching for the first wave of North Vietnamese assault troops. Thirty minutes passed, then an hour, still without any sign of an NVA attack.

The Americans began to cautiously emerge from their trenches and bunkers. Remarkably, the 1st Battalion, 26th Marines, reported only one man killed and thirty-eight wounded in the barrage. While officers prepared casualty reports and damage assessments, teams of Marines armed with garden rakes removed a three-inch layer of shrapnel from the area near the ammunition dump.[28] Others filled sandbags, deepened trenches and fighting holes, and shored up bunkers with sandbags and runway matting. Sam Messer and other Seabees went to work patching holes in the aluminum runway to allow transports to land with badly needed ammunition and supplies. As the men worked, ordnance from the burning ammo dump whined and exploded, fraying already raw nerves.

Sporadic NVA shelling resumed, and the Marines again piled into their trenches and bunkers. The pattern would be repeated throughout the day, and the days that followed.

Over in the Bravo Company, 1/26, lines, Steve Wiese remained vigilant for the North Vietnamese assault. He felt the nervous anticipation each time the latest round of enemy shelling stopped, and he kept scanning the edge of the jungle for any sign of the enemy charge. They were out there, and they were going to strike. Wiese and his comrades at Khe Sanh were now certain of that.[29]

CHAPTER 4

Khe Sanh Village

After weeks of stealth and subterfuge aimed at avoiding contact with the Americans, several thousand North Vietnamese soldiers in the vicinity of Khe Sanh Combat Base burst from their concealed bivouacs during the long night of January 20–21. Among the NVA troops on the move were the six hundred soldiers of the 66th Regiment of the 304th Division, a storied unit that had fought the North Vietnamese Army's first full-blown battle against the Americans at the Ia Drang Valley in November 1965. Now, moving through the fog and darkness around Khe Sanh in the early hours of January 21, they prepared to attack the Saigon government's Huong Hoa district headquarters, three miles south of the combat base, in the village of Khe Sanh.

The North Vietnamese troops assigned to attack Khe Sanh village—members of the 66th Regiment's 7th Battalion—were running late. It was a portentous development, for every minute of delay increased the likelihood that daylight would arrive before they could overrun the 175 Americans, South Vietnamese, and Bru tribesmen defending the fortified district compound. Hard experience had taught the North Vietnamese the inherent risks in a daylight challenge to the Americans, when their adversary's formidable artillery and aircraft could be fully marshaled. Every man and woman wearing the uniform of the North Vietnamese Army had learned to fear US airpower, especially the B-52 bombers that stalked the skies miles above them—unseen and unheard until the jungles erupted in apocalyptic fire and explosions. For those directly beneath the Arc Lights, as the Americans called their B-52 strikes, it would be as though they never existed. Those fortunate enough to find themselves at the edge of the blast radius would emerge from the cataclysm with blood pouring from ears and noses.[1]

The men of the 7th Battalion had narrowly avoided such a fate only the previous day. Just before the North Vietnamese soldiers began the final leg of their march to Khe Sanh village at midday of January 20, US B-52 bombers had carried out an Arc Light strike in their path. Entering the target box soon afterward, the 7th Battalion troops found a landscape of shattered trees and scorched earth, devoid of landmarks and trails. It was hard slogging through the jumbled earth and debris, and "many elements became lost."[2] Nightfall found the troops miles from their staging points, slowed even further by the thickening fog.

At 4:00 a.m., forty-five minutes before the attack on the district headquarters at Khe Sanh was to get underway, blocking forces were still getting into position. Precious minutes were lost while an NVA platoon slipped through the jungle north of Route 9, past a Bru hamlet of straw-thatched huts, and took up positions on Hill 471, about a mile south of the American base. Other NVA forces had been moving into position to ambush any attempt to reinforce the district headquarters once the attack began: one platoon was lying in wait at the junction of Route 9 and the access road to the base, near an old French fort that the US Special Forces had occupied until a few months earlier; another NVA platoon had prepared an ambush along Route 9 west of the village.[3]

A few minutes past 5:00 a.m., the morning calm was shattered by the sound of artillery rounds and rockets leaving their tubes, followed by muffled explosions from the direction of the main American stronghold. The bombardment of Khe Sanh Combat Base was underway, yet the soldiers of the NVA 7th Battalion were still not quite ready.

Around 5:30 a.m., the lead elements of the North Vietnamese assault force triggered trip flares along the western edge of the district headquarters complex. The darkness erupted with the ear-splitting explosions of mortars and rocket-propelled grenades, and the rattle of machine guns and automatic rifles.[4] The men of the NVA 7th Battalion surged toward the perimeter wire of the Khe Sanh village compound.

• • •

Captain Bruce B. G. Clarke of the US Army reacted instinctively when the trip flares erupted a few paces west of his command bunker inside the district compound: he grabbed a radio, got Khe Sanh Combat Base on the line, and began calling out preregistered artillery coordinates.[5] Before long, "variable timed" rounds fired by Marine artillery batteries at the base began detonating about twenty feet above the North Vietnamese troops who now swarmed the district compound's western perimeter.

A 1965 West Point graduate from Kansas, five days shy of his twenty-fifth birthday, Clarke led a four-man US Army advisory team assigned to Huong Hoa district headquarters. He and his team shared the compound with about twenty-five US Marines, seventy-five Bru tribal militiamen, and about seventy Vietnamese officers and soldiers—all nominally under the command of Clarke's counterpart, the Huong Hoa district chief, South Vietnamese Army captain Tinh A-Nhi.[6]

Near the front of the compound, Clarke's team members quickly determined that they were under heavy fire from a Buddhist pagoda just outside the western perimeter wire. Sergeant First Class Jim Perry, an Army medic who had worked at Walter Reed Army Hospital in Washington, DC, before deploying to Vietnam, blasted away at the pagoda with an Al Capone–era Thompson submachine gun.[7]

From trenches and bunkers around the compound's northern end, Marines and Bru fighters fired at muzzle blasts and silhouettes briefly illuminated by shell bursts.[8] The Marines were members of Combined Action Company (CAC) Oscar, the creation of a special counterinsurgency program in which Marine squads functioned like Army Special Forces A-teams. The Khe Sanh village contingent was commanded by a Marine mustang, First Lieutenant Thomas G. Stamper, and its forces were spread thin among three locations: the Oscar-1 platoon and headquarters detachment was based inside the district compound; Oscar-2 was dug in roughly 200 yards to the west along Route 9; and Oscar-3 was located in a Bru hamlet between the village and the combat base.

While the American and Bru forces battled the main North Vietnamese assault along the western perimeter, Captain Nhi's militiamen turned back a threat from the east mounted by NVA soldiers who slipped through a coffee plantation and took cover behind a US Agency for International Development food warehouse. From a concealed bunker atop the warehouse, Nhi's men broke the attack by dropping grenades onto the unsuspecting North Vietnamese soldiers.[9]

Other NVA soldiers fired on the compound from across Route 9, from a restaurant the Americans had wryly nicknamed Howard Johnson's. Small groups of enemy troops charged across the highway toward the northern perimeter, only to be killed by an M-60 machine gun manned by Corporal Verner R. Russell, a Marine from Poplar Bluff, Missouri.[10]

For ninety minutes, the North Vietnamese pounded and probed, but the compound's defenders held firm as night gave way to a gray dawn.

• • •

Along the western perimeter, Corporal Howard McKinnis, a twenty-year-old Oklahoman who had dropped out of college to join the Marine Corps, was peering into the swirling fog, searching for targets, when an explosion knocked him to the bottom of his trench. A high-explosive artillery round had nearly taken him out.[11]

McKinnis jumped to his feet, ready to fight off a wave of North Vietnamese attackers, but all he could see was swirling fog. A quick check revealed that his limbs were intact and he had suffered nothing worse than a "damn good headache."[12] His two Bru comrades weren't as lucky: one was dead, the other bleeding from shrapnel in his knee.

Sergeant John Balanco, a twenty-two-year-old Marine from Oakland, California, dropped into the fighting hole and announced that enemy troops were pressuring Captain Nhi's forces in an old earthen fort that anchored the compound's southern defenses. Could McKinnis lend a hand? McKinnis fell in behind Balanco, and they darted off through the maze of bunkers and trenches. Another Marine, Lance Corporal C. E. "Butch" Still, joined them, and the trio of Americans dashed into the triangle-shaped fort held by sixty frightened soldiers of the South Vietnamese 915th Regional Force.

McKinnis had barely settled into the western trench when at least a hundred North Vietnamese soldiers burst from a tree line about eighty yards away. McKinnis fired in short bursts, sometimes flipping to full automatic when he spotted several enemy soldiers bunched together. The NVA fighters fired from the hip as they ran, not pausing to aim. They closed on the fort as the defenders emptied their magazines, reloaded, and emptied them again. At thirty feet out, only a few enemy soldiers remained on their feet. And then, just shy of the fort, the last one fell.[13]

• • •

On the western fringe of Khe Sanh village, the men of Oscar-2—a Marine sergeant, eleven Marine riflemen, ten Bru Popular Force militiamen, and a Navy corpsman—were engaged in their own desperate fight for survival.

Among the unlikely warriors was an aspiring Southern Baptist preacher from the Texas Panhandle, twenty-four-year-old Navy corpsman John Roberts. On his first full day in Vietnam in July 1967, Roberts was nearly blown up during an enemy artillery barrage. On his second day, the truck driver who was taking Roberts and some Marines up Route 9 to Khe Sanh fell asleep and ran off the road. Roberts broke some ribs but continued on to the Marine combat base, where another truck shuttled him to the outskirts of Khe Sanh village. There Roberts found the Marines of CAC Oscar-2 saddling up for a patrol. Grab your medical bag, doc, he was told, and so he did. By the time he straggled back into camp later that afternoon, Roberts had discovered that Vietnam's emerald jungles weren't nearly as enchanting as they appeared from the air.[14]

Roberts did not adapt easily to his new life as a combat corpsman. He lost weight, lived in fear of being maimed, captured, or killed, and pined for his wife and unborn child back in Texas. During a supply run to Khe Sanh Combat Base, he sought out Protestant chaplain Ray Stubbe, and they talked and prayed. The Communists can kill your body, Stubbe counseled, but they can't kill your spirit. Roberts returned to Khe Sanh village at peace with himself and his situation, and threw himself into his perilous work.

Now, as gunfire and explosions shattered the darkness around him, Roberts heard the cry "Corpsman up!" and rushed to the Oscar-2 command bunker. Sergeant Roy Harper had been peering into the darkness through his firing port when a Communist RPG round had exploded and a piece of shrapnel had sliced into his face. Roberts found the Oscar-2 commander bathed in blood, with his eyeball dangling on his cheek. The corpsman carefully put the eyeball back in its socket and applied a pressure bandage, and Harper rejoined the fight.

Another Oscar-2 Marine, Corporal Dan Sullivan, shook off the concussion of an exploding enemy round and began returning fire with his M-16 rifle. He emptied one magazine, then another and another. When the rifle jammed, he switched to a Browning Automatic Rifle.[15]

Communist assault troops closed on the outpost, elusive shapes in the half-light of explosions and muzzle flashes. A Marine private first class exposed himself to enemy fire to hurl grenades and curses at the charging North Vietnamese. At one point, Roberts came almost face-to-face with an enemy fighter charging the wire. Squeezing a long burst from his M-16, Roberts nearly cut the man in two.[16]

After two hours of fighting, the men of Oscar-2 were running low on ammunition, and most had suffered at least superficial shrapnel wounds from grenades and RPGs. But the arrival of daylight seemed to spook the enemy troops. They fell back, leaving behind the bodies of dozens of comrades, torn and bloodied forms, tangled in the perimeter wire and scattered across the ground beyond.[17]

• • •

The initial North Vietnamese attacks on the district compound and the Oscar-2 outpost had failed. The remnants of the 7th Battalion had faded back into clumps of trees and jungle to tend to their wounded and await reinforcements.

Inside the district compound, Jim Perry, the advisory team medic, had transformed his bunker at the front of the headquarters building into a medical station. He had braved enemy fire to treat the wounded, carrying the most seriously injured back to his bunker.[18] Captain Bruce Clarke chain-smoked unfiltered Camel cigarettes while continuing to call in artillery strikes. Sergeant John Balanco had shrugged off multiple shrapnel wounds to continue with his rounds, surviving several near misses with the incoming RPG and mortar fire as he delivered ammunition and encouragement to the compound's defenders.

Late in the morning, Clarke made his way to the compound's southern sector to check the defenses in the area where Howard McKinnis had helped fight off an enemy charge. Clarke slipped inside an unmanned bunker and peered out just in time to see a North Vietnamese sapper crawling toward the perimeter wire in front of him. The sapper had a long pole with a block of explosives attached to the end. The Army captain pointed his sawed-off M-79 grenade launcher at the man and squeezed the trigger. A flechette round packed with steel darts ripped the enemy soldier in two.[19]

Around midday, the skies over Khe Sanh village had cleared just enough for a Marine forward air controller (FAC) to make his way to the battlefield in a small spotter plane. Two flights of jets followed, unleashing bombs and napalm on a tree line sheltering NVA soldiers.[20] But just as suddenly as he had appeared, the Marine FAC flew off. "Sorry," he radioed Clarke. "That's all I can do for you."[21]

Clarke relayed an urgent appeal to his boss, Robert Brewer, the senior Military Assistance Command, Vietnam (MACV) provincial adviser in Quang Tri City, thirty miles to the east. (Brewer's position was a cover for his activities as a CIA operative.) About half an hour later, a tiny Cessna O-1E "Bird Dog" spotter plane appeared over Khe Sanh village. In the cockpit was Captain Ward Britt, a US Air Force forward air controller who had picked his way through a maze of peaks and valleys to reach the battlefield.

For the remainder of the afternoon, Britt diverted aircraft from missions along the Ho Chi Minh Trail to attack targets around the embattled outpost.[22] Flying below the minimum ceiling—a risk the fighter pilots were not required to take—a succession of jets dropped bombs and napalm on targets that Britt had marked with white phosphorus rockets or smoke grenades he tossed out of his cockpit window.[23]

In the district compound's command bunker, Captain Nhi relayed radio intercepts about Communist reinforcements on the way, which Clarke promptly forwarded to Britt. One such North Vietnamese radio transmission included an urgent plea for a full company of medics and stretcher bearers.[24] With each new report, Britt would bank to the southwest and circle the area, braving nearly constant ground fire, until he found the enemy troops advancing toward the village. In minutes, a new flight of American aircraft would arrive and eliminate the threat, buying a little more time for the defenders of Khe Sanh village.[25]

• • •

By late afternoon, the situation inside the district compound was grim. Ammunition and medical supplies were running low, and some eleven South Vietnamese and Bru fighters were dead and twenty-nine wounded. Even worse, NVA reinforcements were on the way to deliver the coup de grâce.

Captain Clarke and Lieutenant Stamper had begun asking the Marine combat base for reinforcements and ammunition around midday, but heavy enemy fire had prevented helicopters from landing. One had managed to pass over the compound and push out a couple of boxes of ammunition for the M-1 and M-2 rifles carried by the indigenous forces, but that was it.

Under a standing contingency plan, Colonel David Lownds had dispatched reinforcements from Khe Sanh Combat base, but the Marines had been recalled before reaching the village because of fears of an NVA ambush. Intent on conserving forces to defend the base, the Marines had made a cold-blooded decision: the defenders of Khe Sanh village were on their own.

Bruce Clarke's boss, Quang Tri Province senior adviser Robert Brewer, began working his considerable contacts to resupply the embattled district compound, with mixed results. One chopper managed to offload ammunition and supplies while braving heavy NVA fire coming and going, but four other attempts were driven away. Brewer's deputy, Lieutenant Colonel Joseph Seymoe, a forty-one-year-old West Pointer from Waco, Texas, volunteered to lead a combat assault that would deliver supplies and fifty South Vietnamese soldiers. Late in the afternoon, ten helicopters of the 282nd Assault Helicopter Company—the Black Cats—headed west from Quang Tri: five loaded with troops; two bearing ammunition, medical supplies, and water; and three Huey gunships acting as heavily armed escorts.

In the fading light, twenty-year-old pilot Gerald "Mac" McKinsey eased the lead helicopter inside an old French fort at the junction of Route 9 and the access road to Khe Sanh Combat Base, about three-fourths of a mile east of the village. As the skids touched the ground, a platoon of North Vietnamese troops burst from camouflaged holes and opened fire.

McKinsey had gotten his aircraft about ten feet off the ground and was nosing forward when an NVA squad leader, Tran Dinh Ky, rose to his feet and fired an RPG. The rocket slammed into the chopper's midsection, and the aircraft plunged to the ground and came to a rest upside down at the base of the hill. McKinsey and the flight commander, Captain Tommy Stiner, escaped through the shattered windshield, but the mission commander, Lieutenant Colonel Seymoe, was pinned in the chopper's twisted carcass. There was no sign of the crew chief or gunner.[26]

As NVA troops headed down the slope toward the crash site, two trailing Hueys landed near the burning wreckage and three men jumped off to aid their comrades. The first Huey took off after recovering Stiner's crew chief. The second aircraft quickly abandoned the rescue and lifted off, leaving behind gunner Jerry Elliott. He was never seen again.[27]

Enemy troops closed on the downed helicopter, and McKinsey fell mortally wounded with a bullet to the head. After concluding that Seymoe was dead, Stiner and a crewman from one of the Hueys, Danny Williams, made a run for it. The two Americans made it to the Oscar-3 outpost near the combat base after a harrowing all-night trek.[28]

Back at the Khe Sanh village compound, Captain Bruce Clarke received a terse update on the relief expedition. "We didn't get the troops on the ground," one of the pilots of the aborted mission radioed, with no elaboration on the disaster that had just unfolded. "We're gone."[29]

• • •

In the command bunker of the 26th Marines, radio operator Steve Orr, from Sacramento, California, had followed the unfolding drama in Khe Sanh village with growing horror. Orr's best friend, Michael Archer, from Oakland, California, was in the Huong Hoa district compound as one of the temporary radio operators who rotated from the combat base every few days to help out Lieutenant Stamper at CAC Oscar. Orr and another comrade had been next in line to replace Archer and radioman Steve Tidwell, and now he feared he would never see his friends again. He had spoken on the radio with Archer several times during the day, and Archer had kept asking whether relief was on the way. "Yeah, yeah, we're going to come get you," Orr had assured his friend. Now, after overhearing Colonel Lownds and Lieutenant Colonel James Wilkinson, commander of the 1/26, make their fateful decision to recall the relief force, Orr didn't have the heart to tell his friends that help wasn't coming.[30]

• • •

As the battle for Khe Sanh village continued throughout the day, the Marines on Hill 861 braced for another NVA attack. The mangled bodies of North Vietnamese soldiers lay scattered around the hill. Others lay tangled in the perimeter wire or crumpled in the cleared areas beyond. A patrol that ventured outside the wire found more dead soldiers, piles of bloody bandages, and blood trails into the jungle.[31]

Around midday, the fog had finally cleared and helicopters arrived with crates of ammunition, medical supplies, and reinforcements. Dead and wounded Americans were loaded aboard for the return flight to the combat base. Among the living were Captain Norman Jasper and First Sergeant Bernard Goddard, still holding his perforated carotid artery to keep from bleeding to death, as well as six or seven North Vietnamese prisoners, all wounded and so small that two had been strapped to each stretcher.[32]

Among the new arrivals was a pair of young Navy corpsmen, both in-country barely a month. Larry LeClaire, twenty-one, hailed from New Orleans, Louisiana; his friend Christian Feit, twenty, was from the tiny borough of Smethport in the rugged hills of northern Pennsylvania. As LeClaire and Feit burst out of a CH-34 helicopter, Marines yelled, "Get in the trench! Get in the trench!" The corpsmen dashed into a slit in the ground flanked by crates of mortar shells.[33]

A group of Marines arrived at the LZ with a dead comrade wrapped in a poncho liner. As the somber procession passed, Gunnery Sergeant Melvin Rimel's arm slipped out from beneath the liner. LeClaire's eyes were drawn to the big Marine's left hand, and the wedding band that glistened on his finger.[34]

• • •

Throughout the day, Americans at the combat base and the hill outposts had spotted NVA troops moving about with impunity, setting up mortars, sniping, shelling. Every arriving aircraft at the base drew enemy fire, as did the mere sight of two or more Marines.[35]

Darkness brought fears of an enemy human-wave assault. The defenders of 881 South reported heavy movement north of the hill. At the base, jittery Marines of Lima Company, 3/26, opened fire on an enemy unit moving near their position west of the runway.[36]

Around 11:00 p.m., Bill Dabney's Marines on 881 South were hit by automatic weapons and mortar fire, and an enemy ground assault seemed at hand. At 11:30 p.m., an illumination round burst over the hill, another harbinger of a North Vietnamese attack, or so it seemed. But midnight came and went without an assault, and the weary Marines could only wait.

• • •

At the Marine Oscar-2 outpost on the western outskirts of Khe Sanh village, hopes of holding off another assault had faded. The small band of Marines and corpsman John Roberts had resolved to kill as many North Vietnamese as they could before dying.[37]

But fortune smiled on the Americans when the nightly fog failed to arrive. In the starlit skies, a Douglas AC-47 gunship—the vaunted Spooky—arrived to keep watch over the embattled defenders of Khe Sanh village. The aircraft crew dropped illumination flares that exposed North Vietnamese forces as they massed for an attack and then proceeded to slaughter the enemy soldiers with their moaning miniguns.

On the ground, the defenders watched the awesome spectacle and awaited the North Vietnamese. A sparring match ensued, with Captain Clarke calling in an artillery mission for each sniper round fired in their direction. At one point, the ground shook and the southern sky flashed as a flight of B-52 bombers unleashed an Arc Light strike on NVA forces moving north to join the battle.[38]

• • •

Dawn broke clear and crisp over Khe Sanh village on Monday, January 22. The weary defenders had remained in their fighting holes, bunkers, and trenches throughout the night, guns and grenades at the ready, but the North Vietnamese attack never came.

Sunrise had raised spirits, but uncertainty still hung over the compound. Nothing had been heard from the Oscar-2 outpost for hours. As the bleary-eyed soldiers at the district headquarters maintained their vigil, a commotion swept the lines. A formation of armed men came into sight, approaching the compound from the west, along Route 9.

There were shouts, unintelligible at first before the words could be made out. "Don't fire! We're coming in!"[39] It was the Marines of Oscar-2.

The front gate was flung open, and the defenders of the district compound welcomed the bloodied Marines and Bru fighters.

The uncontested movement of the Oscar-2 force raised the question: Where were the North Vietnamese? Patrols slipped out of the compound and found shocking scenes of carnage: there were a hundred or more dead enemy soldiers, blood trails, and scores of abandoned weapons. While patrols searched for the North Vietnamese, a UH-34 chopper from Marine Medium Helicopter Squadron 362 (HMM-362), the "Ugly Angels," evacuated thirty-eight wounded men in seven shuttle flights to the combat base.[40]

The safe passage of the Oscar-2 Marines and the discovery of the North Vietnamese pullback had unleashed jubilation among the defenders of Khe Sanh village.[41] But a pair of radio transmissions quickly shattered the mood. Colonel Lownds informed Captain Clarke that the compound had been deemed indefensible, so the Marines would no longer provide artillery support—a death sentence for Clarke and his men if they stayed.[42] Around the same time, Sergeant Balanco was ordered to prepare the CAC Oscar Marines for evacuation—without their Bru fighters. Later that morning, the Marines boarded helicopters that ferried them back to the base.[43]

After much agonized discussion between the senior provincial adviser, Robert Brewer, and his South Vietnamese counterpart, Quang Tri Province chief General Ngo Quang Truong, Clarke was ordered to evacuate the district headquarters.[44]

Refusing a seat on an evacuation helicopter, Clarke organized an orderly withdrawal to Khe Sanh Combat Base with Captain Nhi and his South Vietnamese and Bru fighters. The column passed through an area teeming with North Vietnamese troops and marched into the Special Forces compound without the loss of a single man.

In the fight for Khe Sanh village, the vaunted NVA 66th Regiment had suffered 154 killed and 486 wounded, among them the commander of the 7th Battalion.[45] Twelve South Vietnamese soldiers and seven Bru had been killed and twenty-five wounded. Miraculously, not a single American died in the battle.

As night fell on January 22, NVA troops claimed the district headquarters compound that they had failed to take in battle. It was a bitter turn of events for Bruce Clarke and his Army comrades at Forward Operating Base 3 (FOB-3) along the southwestern perimeter of Khe Sanh Combat Base. The fall of the first district government in South Vietnam had damaged the prestige of the Saigon government and its American backers, and it put the Special Forces camp at Lang Vei, along Route 9 west of Khe Sanh, in an untenable position. But the American lines of defense at Khe Sanh had been tightened, and for a badly outnumbered force, the consolidation made tactical sense.

General William Westmoreland had placed a high-risk bet that American artillery and air power would save the Marines at Khe Sanh, even in a confrontation with a much larger enemy force. Now, with the opening engagements concluded, General Vo Nguyen Giap and the formidable North Vietnamese force that had converged on Khe Sanh were poised to put Westmoreland's gamble to the test.*

---

* Scholarship over the past decade has revealed General Giap's objections to key elements of the North Vietnamese plan to win the war in 1968. In particular, Giap opposed widespread attacks on South Vietnamese cities—the so-called Tet Offensive—but was overruled by Communist Party leader Le Duan and other comrades. It is likely no coincidence that Giap sought medical treatment in Hungary in the fall of 1967, and didn't return to Hanoi until early February 1968—after the move against Khe Sanh and the Tet Offensive had begun. See Merle L. Pribbenow II, "General Vo Nguyen Giap and the Mysterious Evolution of the Plan for the 1968 Tet Offensive," *Journal of Vietnamese Studies*, Vol. 3, No. 2 (Summer 2008), pp. 1–33. I have written this account as events were viewed by the American military command and President Johnson: as a showdown with the mastermind of Dien Bien Phu, General Giap. I am grateful to Dr. George C. Herring, Alumni Professor of History Emeritus at the University of Kentucky, for bringing to my attention these revelations.

CHAPTER 5

Muscle Shoals

In the blue skies over Khe Sanh Combat Base on Monday, January 22, an unfamiliar craft had joined the usual assortment of military transports, spotter planes, and helicopters that plied the crowded air space of Quang Tri Province. An astute observer would have noted that the new arrival was a twin-engine P-2 Neptune, developed for the Navy by Lockheed in World War II, and it was far removed from its usual maritime duty of anti-submarine patrols.

The precise nature of the Neptune's business over Khe Sanh and the reason that its familiar gray-and-white color scheme had been painted jungle-green was a closely guarded military secret. Only a select few in the American chain of command knew that this particular plane was one of a dozen Neptunes that had been plucked from an Arizona boneyard, fitted with old Norden bombsights and given the innocuous designation of Observation Group 67 (VO-67).[1] Fewer still knew that for the past two months, the squadron had been flying out of a remote base in Nakhon Phanom, Thailand, part of a top-secret effort to stem the flow of North Vietnamese troops and supplies to southern battlefields, and that only three days earlier the VO-67 crews had been ordered by America's supreme commander in Vietnam to turn their full attention to the defense of Khe Sanh.[2]

With 20,000 North Vietnamese soldiers now surrounding the 6,000 Americans at Khe Sanh, and another 20,000 enemy troops nearby, General William Westmoreland was marshaling every conceivable weapon for a decisive confrontation. The centerpiece of his plan to deal the North Vietnamese a crippling blow was a coordinated campaign of massive air strikes and artillery missions, a veritable waterfall of destructive power bearing an evocative code name: Operation Niagara.[3]

A myriad of intelligence sources had been tapped to build an exhaustive target list for the campaign. And now, with the help of the low-flying Neptunes of VO-67 and a squadron of CH-3 "Jolly Green Giant" helicopters flying out of the same remote base, Westmoreland aimed to bolster Niagara with a secret weapon nearly two years in the making.

• • •

From the beginning of America's escalation of the war, US commanders had sought to stop North Vietnam from arming and supplying Communist forces in the South. In March 1965, US commanders had launched a systematic bombing campaign—Rolling Thunder—to force an end to North Vietnamese intervention. But even as the bombing expanded to a lengthening list of strategic targets, doubts about the campaign's ultimate success persisted in Washington.[4]

One of Rolling Thunder's early skeptics was US Secretary of Defense Robert McNamara. In early 1966, the former Ford Motor Company president read a deputy's memo that underscored the bombing campaign's mixed results. The memo also noted a proposal by Harvard Law School professor Roger Fisher to build a "border barrier" that would quarantine South Vietnam from Communist infiltration. Despite the misgivings of his military chiefs, McNamara ordered the Army to begin work on a system of "route and trail interdiction devices."[5]

McNamara also asked a group of civilian weapons experts to study the feasibility of a high-tech fence that could block the influx of North Vietnamese troops and supplies. The forty-seven scientists assigned to the project were collectively known as the Jason Division, named for the leader of the Argonauts in Greek mythology. In August, they submitted four reports that highlighted the disappointing bombing results and endorsed construction of an anti-infiltration barrier across northern Laos and South Vietnam. McNamara ordered work on a barrier fence to proceed.

By the fall of 1967, McNamara's "Strong Point Obstacle System" was fast becoming a reality. US Marines in the northern I Corps sector of South Vietnam had occupied a line of outposts that stretched along Route 9, from the coast westward to Khe Sanh. The final piece awaiting deployment was a network of electronic sensors that would allow the Americans to track and destroy North Vietnamese trucks and troops entering South Vietnam.[6] As part of that effort, the United States also embarked on a more sophisticated effort to cut the taproot of the Communist resupply network, the Truong Son Strategic Supply Route in eastern Laos, the series of jungle roads and tracks better known to Americans as the Ho Chi Minh Trail.

In November, twelve Navy crews flying modified P-2 Neptunes arrived at the Royal Thai Air Force base that would serve as nerve center for the clandestine Operation Muscle Shoals (later changed to Igloo White). Known to American covert operators as "the end of the line at the edge of the world," Nakhon Phanom lay in far northeastern Thailand, nine miles from the Mekong River, which formed the border with Laos.[7] The newly arrived crews of VO-67 had been trained to use World War II Norden bombsights to drop camouflaged electronic sensors along infiltration routes.

McNamara's scientists had drawn on naval anti-submarine warfare and oil-industry technology to devise the sensors for Muscle Shoals. Most were cylinder shaped, three to four feet in length, and weighed less than twenty pounds. Radio transmitters would relay sounds and seismic data to an EC-121B aircraft orbiting overhead, which would pass the data to a secret facility in Nakhon Phanom packed with the latest IBM mainframe computers. If everything worked as planned, data analysts in Thailand would be passing real-time information from activated sensors to US operational commanders in South Vietnam—all within thirty to forty-five minutes.[8]

In their first days at Nakhon Phanom, VO-67 pilots familiarized themselves with North Vietnamese infiltration routes and anti-aircraft batteries by flying combat missions with Air Force forward air controllers along the Ho Chi Minh Trail in Laos. Most of the VO-67 pilots had backgrounds similar to that of Commander Adam Alexander, an Ohio native who had joined the Navy after graduating from high school in spring 1948. He had earned his pilot's wings in 1950 and saw six months of combat in Korea as navigator on a PB4Y2, the Navy version of the B-24 bomber. Now thirty-seven years old, with nearly two decades of Navy service, Alexander had never undertaken an assignment so shrouded in mystery as VO-67.[9]

On November 25, the first VO-67 Neptunes took off from Nakhon Phanom to field test the Muscle Shoals program. They began by seeding the jungle with small anti-personnel "gravel" and "button" mines, cracker-size pieces of fabric that exploded on contact and activated acoustic sensors. They also dropped sensors of two varieties: seismic detectors modeled on oil-industry geophones and acoustic devices developed from US Navy anti-submarine sonobuoys.

The microphone-equipped acoustic sensors, known as Acoubuoys, had been designed to drift into the treetops on camouflaged parachutes. The seismic devices—ADSIDs (Air Delivered Seismic Intrusion Detectors)—had a weighted spike on one end and were designed to stick in the ground like a lawn dart. To effectively transmit vibrations from passing trucks or troops, the seismic sensors had to be dropped in carefully plotted strings within thirty feet of the targeted trail or track.

With North Vietnamese truck traffic through eastern Laos soaring by a factor of five in the closing months of 1967, Muscle Shoals had been rushed into the field. It was hardly surprising that "a nightmare of fault[y] detections, analysis, and correction" plagued its early weeks of operation.[10] But the sensors worked—sometimes too well, the analysts discovered, as the devices picked up the sounds of tigers, rock apes, and American air strikes. The glitches were resolved, and by December 7, Muscle Shoals was fully operational in eastern Laos and providing real-time reports for US units.

The successful deployment of the Muscle Shoals sensors could not have come at a better time for General Westmoreland and his plan to engage North Vietnamese forces in a decisive confrontation. On January 19, Westmoreland ordered VO-67 to shift its focus from the Ho Chi Minh Trail to Khe Sanh. The following day, in treetop-level missions, fixed-wing Neptunes and CH-3 helicopters began laying strings of sensors on the approaches to Khe Sanh.[11]

Defense Secretary McNamara and his scientists had envisioned

Muscle Shoals as an anti-infiltration device rather than a tactical weapon in a fluid combat setting. Sensor analysts in Nakhom Phanom were still fine-tuning the best methods for deploying and interpreting the devices as the North Vietnamese forces closed around Khe Sanh.

Now, as the battle got underway, the sensors emerged as a wild card with enormous potential. General Giap had committed three divisions of his finest troops to the move against Khe Sanh in the belief that they could mass and maneuver undetected under the cover of fog and darkness. What if the sensors stripped away that cover and denied North Vietnamese forces their critical advantages in mobility and stealth? General Westmoreland and the small group of Americans privy to the Muscle Shoals program aimed to find out.

CHAPTER 6

The Walking Dead

K he Sanh's days as a sleepy backwater had ended abruptly with the battles of January 20–21. Now, from Hill 881 South and Lang Vei in the west, to Hill 558 northeast of the combat base, the North Vietnamese went about the work of wearing down and bleeding the Americans. During daylight hours, the North Vietnamese pounded the base and its outposts with artillery, rockets, and mortars and harassed them with snipers. At night, NVA soldiers crept up on listening posts and probed the perimeter wire of the base and outposts, setting off trip flares, cutting wire barriers, tossing grenades, and staging hit-and-run attacks.[1]

In a surreal development for the frazzled Americans atop Hill 861, a Marine Corps field historian armed with a reel-to-reel tape recorder stepped off a resupply chopper the day after the North Vietnamese attack and spent nearly forty minutes conducting interviews with eight men. As fighter jets roared overhead and dropped bombs on the nearby ridgelines, the Marines recalled their experiences in the battle.

Among those telling their stories was the modest machine gunner from Oklahoma, Corporal Billy Ray Moffett, who had risen to the challenge in his first fight, pouring machine-gun rounds into the NVA attackers even as his gun attracted heavy enemy fire. "I was scared shitless," Moffett said softly. "There's no way getting around that. I don't think anybody was as cool as they should have been. It was hell, really."[2]

• • •

At Khe Sanh Combat Base, January 22 had begun with a predawn probe by the North Vietnamese at the western end of the base. Marines of Lima Company, 3/26, had spotted twenty-five to thirty-five North Vietnamese soldiers crawling toward their wire and opened up with M-79 grenade launchers and light anti-tank weapons. When the firing stopped after a few minutes, the NVA force was seen dragging the bodies of comrades off to the southwest.

Groups of North Vietnamese troops, some as large as seventy to ninety men and some carrying large packs, were occasionally spotted moving through clearings and along ridgelines.[3] Along the eastern and southeast perimeter of the American base, the Marines of Bravo Company, 1/26, found themselves in a war of nerves with NVA snipers firing from the surrounding jungle. At one point, a sniper unleashed half a dozen rounds and the Marines responded with automatic weapons and M-79 grenades. When the sniper resumed firing about twenty minutes later, the Marines called in an artillery strike on his suspected position, and the firing stopped.[4]

NVA artillery fire continued to pound away at the command bunker occupied by Colonel David Lownds and his 26th Marines staff. Nearby, a row of plywood-reinforced tents that had housed the base commissary, the post office, and other facilities lay in ruins. The area looked like a ghost town, deserted "except for an occasional man nervously running from one place to another."[5] Around 10:00 a.m., a North Vietnamese artillery round screamed from the sky and exploded outside a regimental communications workshop. When the smoke and dust settled, a pair of twenty-year-old Marines lay dead.[6]

The attack on Khe Sanh village the previous day had triggered a terrified exodus, and Vietnamese and Bru civilians had fled to the combat base with what few belongings they could carry. Lownds had refused entry to the refugees, fearing that enemy soldiers or spies might be among them.

On the morning of January 22, a frightened crowd of about 1,500 Vietnamese and ethnic Bru—young and old; men, women, and children—still huddled at the main gate. Hurried discussions between American and South Vietnamese officials produced an agreement to evacuate the Vietnamese, but not the Bru. The South Vietnamese I Corps commander, General Hoang Xuan Lam, insisted there was no place for the minority refugees, so they were told to return to their homes, now a no-man's-land between the combat base and the converging North Vietnamese troops.[7] The virtual abandonment of the Bru people at Khe Sanh stands as a sordid chapter for the Americans and South Vietnamese, ultimately leading to the deaths of as many as several thousand men, women, and children caught in the escalating battle.

Throughout January 22, transport planes and helicopters landed at the combat base to offload medical supplies and ammunition, flying out with loads of Vietnamese civilians. More than 1,100 noncombatants would be safely evacuated from Khe Sanh in this fashion over the next twenty-four hours. Late in the afternoon, shuttle flights of transport helicopters began to arrive and disgorge ranks of Marines—the men of the 1st Battalion, 9th Marines, rushed to Khe Sanh to bolster its defenses.

Darkness arrived, and the defenders of Khe Sanh once again braced for a ground attack. Shortly after 7:00 p.m., the first nighttime listening-post teams filed outside the perimeter wire, and over the next forty-five minutes, eight other teams of three to five Marines slipped into the bush. Inside the wire, two twenty-five-man reaction forces were briefed and readied for action.[8]

Soon enough the night came alive with the sounds of enemy movements. Around 10:00 p.m., Bravo Company, 1/26, reported seeing lights and hearing "heavy noise" and the "sounds of heavy digging" in front of their lines. Just after 11:00 p.m., a Charlie Company, 1/26, Marine peering through a Starlight scope spotted four North Vietnamese soldiers on his perimeter wire. A friendly artillery illumination round was fired, exposing a small group of NVA soldiers but no larger attack. The Marines opened up with M-16 rifles and an M-79 grenade launcher, and the North Vietnamese soldiers scrambled for cover, leaving behind a dead comrade in the wire.[9] The firing ended, and the tense wait resumed.

• • •

Shortly after 5:00 a.m. on Tuesday, January 23, the weary listening-post teams made their way back inside the base. Daylight patrols were readied to begin the work of checking perimeter wires for cuts or explosives laid by enemy sappers and to locate enemy trenches or signs of an impending attack. Later in the morning, the day's first fixed-wing transports and heli-copters began to arrive with pallets of ammunition, medical supplies, and boxes of C-rations. Four large crates addressed to "Fifth Graves Registra-tion Team, Khe Sanh," were also unloaded. Inside were 4,000 pounds of body bags.[10]

As supplies and reinforcements arrived, Colonel Lownds and his su-periors pored over maps and prepared to reposition troops in anticipa-tion of the next North Vietnamese move. A top priority was finding a place for the newly arrived men of the 1st Battalion, 9th Marines.

The battalion had been in nearly constant combat in Vietnam since December 1966, and its hard-luck reputation had earned it a grim moniker: the "Walking Dead." In February 1967, the battalion had been accompanied by the acclaimed French war correspondent Bernard Fall, whose two classic books on Vietnam had included *Hell in a Very Small Place*, on the French defeat at Dien Bien Phu. Fall had been with Alpha Company, 1/9, on February 21, 1967, as it patrolled the Communist en-clave north of Hue known as the "Street Without Joy" (the title of Fall's other book about the French war in Vietnam). In the deepening after-noon shadows that day, Fall stepped on a land mine that killed him, along with two Marines.[11]

A far bloodier day in the summer of 1967 had etched the battalion's name in Marine Corps history. On July 2, Alpha and Bravo companies of the 1/9 had kicked off Operation Buffalo by pushing up Highway 561 along the DMZ near Con Thien, about thirty miles northeast of Khe Sanh. The Marines had been ambushed by a large North Vietnamese force, and Bravo Company was decimated, its company commander, two platoon leaders, and artillery forward observer among the dead. The sur-vivors hung on until the arrival of reinforcements, among them a coura-geous young Virginian by the name of Captain Henry "Mac" Radcliffe. By nightfall, Alpha and Bravo Companies had sustained the heaviest single-day losses incurred by the Marines in Vietnam: 84 men killed (in-cluding eight Navy corpsmen), 190 wounded, and nine missing. Mac Radcliffe earned a Silver Star and command of Alpha Company.

In the aftermath of the July bloodletting, the ranks of the 1/9 had been replenished with scores of young replacements. Command of the battal-ion had been given to Colonel John F. Mitchell, who had earned a Silver

Star as a young platoon commander at the Chosin Reservoir in Korea. Seventeen years later, arriving at Khe Sanh with a coveted general's star in his sights, Mitchell's youthful pluck and self-confidence had taken on the hues of arrogance.

Now, in the rising morning light on January 23, Mitchell and the Marines of the Walking Dead marched away from the Khe Sanh perimeter and took up positions on high ground about a mile to the southwest, around a rock quarry dug by Seabees during runway work at the combat base the previous summer.

• • •

Colonel Lownds had welcomed his temporarily detached 2nd Battalion back to Khe Sanh one week earlier, and now the outfit's Echo Company was also on the move. Its assignment was to shore up the northern approach to the base by fortifying a spur about 200 yards northeast of Hill 861.

For Captain Earle Breeding, Echo's up-from-the-ranks commanding officer, the move was a welcome opportunity to prove his mettle as a combat commander. A native of Washington, DC, and the neighboring Maryland suburbs, the thirty-four-year-old Breeding had first joined the Marine Corps in 1952, when tight finances and his father's illness had forced him to drop out of college.[12] After serving out his enlistment, Breeding had enrolled at the University of New Mexico in 1956 with an eye on returning to the Corps as an officer.

Breeding reentered the Marines as a second lieutenant in the spring of 1961, and he had risen to captain by the summer of 1967, when he finally got his long-sought orders for Vietnam. He arrived at 3rd Marine Division headquarters in Phu Bai to discover that he was destined for anti-tank duty but wangled a coveted infantry command by plying personnel officers with bottles of prized whiskey. He was assigned to the 2nd Battalion, 26th Marines, and soon landed command of Echo Company.[13]

After arriving at Khe Sanh in mid-January, Breeding had led Echo Company up to the high ground north of the combat base, to Hill 558, where he began running patrols along the Rao Quan River. Breeding and his boys were still operating around 558 when the North Vietnamese struck on January 21. Now, Breeding prepared to lead his men to their new digs on a strategically valuable piece of land just east of Kilo Company's outpost on Hill 861.

On a straight line, Echo Company's destination lay only about a mile southwest of Hill 558, but the terrain was steep and broken, with sharp elephant grass and vegetation. The Marines set out around 8:00 a.m. on the morning of January 22, but the march quickly bogged down. The grass was so thick that the men on point became exhausted after hacking away at the wall of vegetation for only five or ten minutes.[14] It was the coolest time of the year around Khe Sanh, but daytime temperatures still ranged into the high seventies, and the oppressive tropical humidity made it feel much hotter.

Among the suffering, sweat-soaked Marines pushing through the hills was a raw-boned nineteen-year-old rifleman named David Norton. A former high school football halfback and defensive back, Norton had grown up in a good family in Charlotte, North Carolina. As a teenager, he had closely followed the news about America's deepening role in Vietnam. In his final weeks of high school, he and some friends decided to enlist in the Marine Corps.[15]

In the spring of 1967, Norton was undergoing advanced combat infantry training at Camp Pendleton in Southern California when the bloody Hill Fights unfolded on the slopes of Hill 861 and 881 North and South around Khe Sanh. A premonition came over him one day as he read a news article about the fighting on Hill 861. Norton announced to his fellow Marines, "I'm going to be right there."[16] Now, five months into his Vietnam tour, Norton and his comrades were struggling to scale the slopes of this infamous hill mass.

Late afternoon of January 22 found the men of Echo Company still clawing their way up the steep eastern slope of the spur soon to be known as Hill 861 Alpha. It was a grueling slog even for the fittest and toughest men in the company, like the 1st Platoon's rocketman, David McCall.

Nineteen years old, a wiry five feet eight inches and 145 pounds, "Big Dave" McCall had been a star athlete back home in Minneapolis, Kansas, lettering in four sports.[17] He enlisted in the Marines and arrived in Vietnam on November 10, 1967, the 192nd birthday of the Marine Corps. In his two months in Vietnam, McCall had experienced the usual mix of firefights, night ambushes, and boring guard duty. Early in his tour, he had dozed off on night watch and suddenly felt someone beside him. He opened his eyes to find a lieutenant in his face. "If I was a gook, you'd be dead," the lieutenant said quietly, and then walked away. From that moment on, asleep or on watch, McCall never let anyone get close without his knowing about it.

Night was falling when the exhausted Marines finally reached their destination. Much to their dismay, 861 Alpha was overgrown with high elephant grass and lacked fields of fire and natural defensive positions. If the enemy decided to attack, they would be in trouble, but the boys of Echo Company were too tired and angry to care. They made a perimeter, then "basically just sat down."[18]

In the darkness and gathering fog, Earle Breeding checked his ragged lines, such as they were, and returned to his makeshift command post to wait out the night. His radio operators had suffered more than most after lugging their PRC-25 field units as well as their personal gear, an extra 23.5 pounds weighing on every step, and they were out almost as soon as they hit the ground. Taking pity on the exhausted men, Breeding let them sleep, and he slipped the radio piece in his ear. If they made it through the night, they could worry about clearing and fortifying 861 Alpha tomorrow.[19]

CHAPTER 7

"Should We Withdraw from Khe Sanh?"

The legendary North Vietnamese general Vo Nguyen Giap would spend the final decades of his life assuring foreign interviewers that his campaign against Khe Sanh in 1968 was never intended to duplicate his victory over the French at Dien Bien Phu. It was a declaration of transparent self-interest, especially given how events played out, but critics of General William Westmoreland would seize on Giap's pronouncements as confirmation that the North Vietnamese at Khe Sanh merely sought to divert American attention away from urban centers in advance of Tet holiday attacks. The truth about North Vietnamese objectives will probably never be known with certainty, but Giap's commitment of three reinforced divisions to the opening stage of the Khe Sanh campaign was certainly more than was necessary for an effective ruse.

The Khe Sanh campaign was all part of an elaborate master plan, TCK-TKN, which laid out the end game against the Americans as a three-act drama. NVA forces had executed Phase I in the late summer and fall of 1967, launching attacks against remote targets like Con Thien, the Marine combat base along the DMZ. The strikes were aimed at drawing US forces out of the population centers and inducing Westmoreland to "launch operations along South Vietnam's borders," according to Phillip Davidson, Westmoreland's intelligence chief at the time.

By the final days of January 1968, Communist forces were nearly ready to launch Phase II of Giap's plan, coordinated attacks on South Vietnamese cities, which were supposed to inspire a sympathetic population to rise up against the American-backed government.

At Khe Sanh, the ground was already being laid for the climactic Phase III, "a large-unit conventional battle," with Khe Sanh the logical target.[1]

• • •

Whether Giap planned the campaign against Khe Sanh as a ruse or a decisive blow, his opening moves certainly evoked his signature triumph against the French.

After the French had reclaimed the valley of Dien Bien Phu in the far northwestern corner of Vietnam in November 1953, Giap's Communist Viet Minh forces had methodically encircled the enemy stronghold and bombarded it from the commanding heights. On March 13, 1954, the Viet Minh began reducing French strong points at Dien Bien Phu in human wave attacks. Simultaneously, Giap's anti-aircraft batteries began choking off French aerial resupply efforts. On May 7, after fifty-five days of fighting, the doomed outpost surrendered.

At Khe Sanh, Giap had initiated a stealth encirclement of the Americans in early January 1968, and the opening attacks of January 20–21 began the process of driving in American defenses from the north and the south. He had wholly committed two divisions—about 20,000 troops—to the effort: elements of the 304th Division had moved against Khe Sanh village from the south, while units of the 325C had hit Hill 861 from the north. A regiment of the 324th Division had been positioned within fifteen miles of Khe Sanh to perform supply duties, and the 320th Division, another 10,000 men, was less than a day's march northeast of Khe Sanh.[2]

The North Vietnamese struck again on the evening of January 23 by overrunning a Laotian Army outpost at Ban Houei Sane, fourteen miles west of Khe Sanh. The Americans quickly learned from survivors that Communist forces had used Soviet-made PT-76 light tanks in the attack, the NVA's first armor-backed assault of the war. With the district headquarters at Khe Sanh village and Ban Houei Sane in their hands, the

North Vietnamese now set their sights on the US Special Forces camp at Lang Vei, only four miles southwest of Khe Sanh.

As internal Communist accounts have since made clear, quick victory wasn't the objective of the North Vietnamese at Khe Sanh. Instead, they were content to goad the Americans into rushing reinforcements to the embattled base and bleeding US forces as time passed.[3] If Khe Sanh fell at some point in the future, it would be the coup de grâce that would force the United States from the war. For now, General Giap and his troops would gradually turn up the pressure, playing on US fears of Khe Sanh becoming America's Dien Bien Phu. And while Westmoreland focused on Khe Sanh, Giap would spring his next surprise.

• • •

As at Dien Bien Phu, the North Vietnamese forces set about weakening Khe Sanh and its outposts with artillery, mortar, and sniper fire. The bulk of the damage was inflicted by two NVA artillery regiments, the 45th and 675th, now scattered through the rugged countryside west of Khe Sanh. The North Vietnamese had targeted Khe Sanh with 212 heavy weapons, including eight 152-millimeter guns, sixteen 130-millimeter guns, thirty-six 122-millimeter guns, more than one hundred 122-millimeter rocket launchers, and a supporting cast of assorted smaller guns and howitzers. To protect the artillery from American air strikes, the North Vietnamese had forty-two 37-millimeter anti-aircraft guns, twelve 57-millimeter guns, and 130 anti-aircraft machine guns.[4] Highly mobile mortar teams had completely surrounded the American outposts, and they unleashed deadly fire that was targeted and adjusted by artillery forward observers, who had established camouflaged positions around the combat base and forward posts.

On Hill 861, Dennis Mannion, the Kilo Company artillery forward observer, was engaged in the same deadly pursuit. In the aftermath of the January 21 attack, two large containers addressed to Mannion had arrived on the hill. One contained a pair of powerful naval binoculars capable of spotting NVA soldiers and other potential targets up to ten miles away. The other held a Night Observation Device (NOD). The evening of its arrival, Mannion had powered up the device and scanned the ridge-line about 500 yards to his west. In the scope's gauzy green light, he spotted about twenty North Vietnamese soldiers hard at work, digging new positions and moving supplies and equipment.[5] He arranged for one of the hill's 106-millimeter recoilless rifles to unleash a round on the NVA, the opening salvo of Mannion's relentless test of wits with the North Vietnamese forces that surrounded 861.

Sleeping in snatches, Mannion settled into a routine that began at first light and continued late into the evening. During daylight hours he would scan the nearby hills and draws with his naval binoculars in search of targets. When he found something, he would call in the coordinates to the Fire Direction Center at the combat base, then adjust the rounds as they landed. At night, Mannion would scour the area with the NOD, a more powerful version of the Starlight scope.

At the combat base and the hill outposts, an urgent effort was underway to deepen trenches and move bunkers and command posts underground. Every arriving helicopter was greeted by enemy mortars and sniper fire, and, in between, mortar rounds sporadically pounded the hill as enemy spotters called in targets of opportunity. The North Vietnamese lacked night vision devices, so the Marines moved about the hill outposts more confidently in the darkness. But night also brought fears of being overrun by the NVA.[6]

The cumulative stress of the random enemy fire and mounting casualties weighed on the young Americans.

Early in the afternoon of January 24, corpsman Larry LeClaire heard an explosion near his position on 861, followed by frantic shouts of "Corpsman up!" He hurried up the trench with his medical bag, which was packed with the usual assortment of battle dressings, tourniquets, bags of blood expander, and other items. An enemy mortar round had landed in the trench line, apparently right on top of a Marine, and all that remained for LeClaire was a bloody pile of flesh around a pair of Marine combat boots. Human brains pulsated on the trench wall. Fighting the urge to throw up, LeClaire ran back to the platoon command post. He had just informed the lieutenant about his grisly discovery when the cry sounded again: "Corpsman up!"[7]

LeClaire retraced his steps up the trench and carefully made his way past the remains he had found moments earlier. His nostrils were filled with the rusty-iron scent of blood mixed with the acrid smell of the enemy round. LeClaire found another Marine lying in the red clay at the bottom of the trench. The man was in shock, bulging eyes locked in a death gaze.

As LeClaire tended to the man, it occurred to him that this was the duty area of his friend, corpsman Christian Feit. *Where is Feit? He should be here.* LeClaire soon learned the terrible truth: his fellow corpsman had been standing about thirty feet from the enemy round when it hit, and a piece of shrapnel had struck him in the right temple. LeClaire found Feit and did what little he could.

A medevac chopper arrived and the dying Marine and gravely wounded corpsman were loaded aboard, along with the scant remains of their dead comrade. The Marine was pronounced dead by doctors at the combat base. Twenty-year-old Christian Feit died on a Navy hospital ship the following day.[8]

• • •

Around 5:30 p.m. that afternoon, January 24, the North Vietnamese unleashed the heaviest bombardment since the opening barrage three days earlier. Artillery and rockets pounded the combat base and the American outposts on 881 South and 861.

Just south of the Khe Sanh runway, the men of Bravo Company, 3rd Recon, huddled in bunkers jerry-rigged from pieces of timber, railroad ties, runway matting, and sandbags. Nineteen-year-old Dave Doehrman had worked in an International Harvester farm machinery plant back home in Fort Wayne, Indiana, before joining the Marines the previous summer. Ray Milligan, the shy son of a welder from Deptford, New Jersey, had dreamed of becoming an FBI agent or a policeman, but his grades weren't good enough for college, so he had joined the Marines. Only the day before, the wiry Milligan had celebrated his twentieth birthday.

Now, without warning, the recon bunkers were plunged into dusty blackness. Doehrman and the men around him coughed and gasped for air as blood oozed from their noses and ruptured eardrums. A few seconds passed before the Marines realized that a rocket had slammed into the trench.

Nearby, recon Marine Ray Milligan sat in the swirling dust and darkness of his shattered bunker as a friend who went by the nickname Elvis screamed and cried in fear. Milligan silently rocked back and forth. *Don't go nuts*, he told himself. *Don't go nuts.*[9]

Outside, Kevin Macaulay, a young recon radio operator from New York, and other Marines clawed at the shattered recon bunker that had taken a direct hit. Four dead and sixteen wounded were pulled from the debris.[10]

Before the day was out, NVA artillery and mortar fire had killed seven Americans and seriously wounded twenty-four at Khe Sanh.[11]

• • •

Most of Khe Sanh's defenders had been in combat prior to January 21. They had experienced night ambushes, LPs, blind patrols through elephant grass, and other assorted terrors. But the enemy artillery, rocket, and mortar barrages tested these young men like never before. Offensive skills learned in boot camp and advanced infantry training were useless in this kind of warfare. A man could dig deeper, wear his helmet, zip his flak jacket, keep one ear cocked for the sound of an enemy mortar round leaving the tube or the distant boom of a big gun—and still be killed by a lucky shot or a pea-size piece of shrapnel. This hard reality had existed since the men had set foot in Vietnam, but random terror had been woven into the fabric of daily life at Khe Sanh.

A few men broke. A distraught corpsman went to Protestant chaplain Ray Stubbe after the first day or two of shelling and said he couldn't take it. The corpsman returned on January 26 and pleaded for Stubbe's help in getting out of Khe Sanh. At Charlie Med, the main base hospital, the corpsman was diagnosed as suffering an "acute anxiety reaction" and was administered the anti-psychotic drug Thorazine. He was evacuated from Khe Sanh later that day.[12]

Most of the defenders of Khe Sanh suffered in silence.

For years afterward, Bravo Company, 1/26, rifleman Michael O'Hara would be too embarrassed to talk to his Khe Sanh brothers about the terror he had felt during the artillery bombardments, particularly in those moments when Soviet-made 152-millimeter guns hurled eighty-eight-pound shells into the base with the fearsome roar of a runaway locomotive. When he finally revealed his feelings at a Khe Sanh Veterans

Association reunion in 1993, O'Hara was astonished—and relieved—to learn that all his comrades had shared his fears.

"You just had to find a hole, get in, and hope to God it wasn't your number," O'Hara recalled. "When the shells landed, it was just like the whole earth shook. The mortars and the RPGs could damn sure kill you, but they weren't nearly as terrifying. That Russian artillery will eat your brain cells out."[13]

• • •

Amid the terror, selfless acts of courage became commonplace at Khe Sanh. On January 25, a CH-46 helicopter from HMM-262 landed on Hill 881 South for an emergency medevac mission. A wounded Marine whose head and eyes were heavily bandaged was being led to the chopper by two comrades when NVA mortar rounds dropped from the sky. The two escorts and the wounded Marine hit the ground. Aboard the waiting bird, Corporal Ernesto Gomez of Pasadena, California, looked out to see the wounded Marine blindly trying to find the chopper. Gomez dashed across the LZ, pulled the man to the ground, and shielded him with his body. When the explosions stopped, Gomez and the wounded Marine scrambled to a nearby rocket crater for cover. Another crew member ran out to help them, and together they got the wounded Marine aboard the helicopter and safely delivered him to Charlie Med.[14]

Some acts of courage demanded the ultimate price.

On Hill 861 on January 26, a two-squad patrol from the recently arrived 2nd Platoon of Alpha Company, 1/26, filed through the wire on the northern slope and headed into the draw northwest of the hill. Passing over the area in a chopper five days earlier, 2nd Platoon radio operator John Rauch had been struck by the lushness of the green jungle that cloaked its slopes. Now, the draw was a shattered moonscape of water-filled craters, splintered and scorched trees, burned grass, torn earth, and the stench of smoke and decaying bodies.[15]

The Marines of the lead squad reached the bottom of the draw and started up the western slope. From his fighting position on 861, Dennis Mannion tracked the patrol's progress through his binoculars. He had walked that route many times in the previous month, and he had called in countless artillery strikes on the area in the days since the January 21 attack.

The forest cover had been blown away, and the Marines were clearly visible through the shattered trees more than three hundred yards away.

The Marines were advancing up the western slope when Mannion's radio operator, Dave Kron, suddenly shouted, "Movement! Gooks!"[16] Mannion swung his binoculars to the right. About fifty yards from the Marines, two groups of NVA soldiers emerged from hiding and formed a line parallel to the Marines.

The Alpha Marines never saw the North Vietnamese machine-gun bunker dug into the hillside and camouflaged with toppled trees, logs, and limbs. The gun opened up, and shouts and screams filled the draw. Marines dived for cover and began to return fire. The patrol's two machine gunners moved forward as the column spread out into battle positions. Heavy NVA fire quickly pinned the Marines in place.

As he hugged the ground, John Rauch tersely briefed an officer back on 861. His lieutenant took the radio handset and read off map coordinates for mortar support, and within seconds about eight 81-millimeter rounds slammed into the NVA positions. The lieutenant shouted an order, and the Marines began to move forward again.

Still tracking the action through binoculars, Mannion watched as one Marine stood up and fired his M-79 grenade launcher at the North Vietnamese. Instead of dropping to the ground while he reloaded, the grenadier kept striding ahead toward the danger. He pumped another round into the uprooted tree trunks where the machine gun was hidden, then another, "oblivious to the bullets that were stitching the dirt around him as he progressed,"[17] as Mannion later recalled.

The grenadier was a handsome and athletic nineteen-year-old from Raleigh, North Carolina, Private First Class Dwight "Tommy" Denning. He had been in Vietnam less than two months, but Denning didn't show it. He had drawn a bead on the enemy machine gun hidden in the tangle of brush, and he continued firing and reloading as he walked directly into the teeth of the enemy fire. Denning was dropping another round into the open breech of his M-79 when an NVA bullet pierced his left eye and ripped through the back of his head. The weapon dropped from his hands, and Denning collapsed to the ground.

Minutes after the firefight began, the Marines were ordered to break contact. Covered by their comrades on 861, they pulled back across the draw and retraced their steps to the American stronghold above them. Four Marines carried Tommy Denning up the hill and laid his body on the ground near the perimeter wire.

Among the Marines trudging back inside the outpost was radioman John Rauch, and he paused over the lifeless body. He had never seen a dead Marine before. The handsome face that had been so full of life a few minutes before was now empty and gray. Rauch found his place in the trench line and sank to the red earth. His body shook. The adrenalin of combat ebbed away, leaving in its place an aching black hole. Rauch and his comrades sat quietly in the trench line, stunned by the death of their friend.[18]

• • •

Less than a week into the North Vietnamese campaign, Khe Sanh Combat Base and its outposts faced a growing challenge to meet daily needs for food, medical supplies, ammunition, and other critical items such as water purification chemicals and bunker construction materials.[19] Helicopters and transport planes braved inclement weather and enemy fire to carry out resupply sorties. Crates of C-rations and other supplies were dropped by parachute into a cleared zone beyond the western perimeter.

Most vulnerable of all were the four hilltop outposts guarding the northern approach to Khe Sanh—881 South, 861, 861 Alpha, and 558. They were entirely dependent on helicopter resupply, even for their water needs, and each arriving flight had become a magnet for North Vietnamese mortar fire. A chopper pilot had no more than thirty seconds to land, offload, take on medevac cases, and get off the LZ before the first rounds hit.

For the combat base itself, the issue of potable water loomed as a potentially crippling weakness. The base pumped its water from a stream along the Rao Quan River some 500 yards outside the northern perimeter wire. The commander of the 3rd Marine Division, Major General Rathvon Tompkins, had been aware of this Achilles heel in Khe Sanh's defenses for at least a month, but he hadn't passed the information up the chain of command.[20]

Now, in late January, General Westmoreland was appalled to learn about Khe Sanh's vulnerability. If the North Vietnamese cut the line or contaminated the source, the base would run out of water within a week.[21] As a last resort, Khe Sanh's water needs would have to be supplied by air.

Mindful that the French defeat at Dien Bien Phu had stemmed in part from a failed effort to resupply the garrison by air, Westmoreland had mobilized an impressive collection of aircraft to sustain his forces at Khe Sanh. His aerial resupply capabilities far eclipsed anything the French could muster in their losing effort at Dien Bien Phu. But Westmoreland had not counted on having to shuttle thousands of gallons of water each day to Khe Sanh. His well-laid plans were suddenly in jeopardy.

• • •

In the early morning of January 29, the expected enemy ground attack finally seemed underway when General William Westmoreland's MACV headquarters in Saigon received an urgent message from the sensor analysts in Nakhon Phanom, Thailand. "Many troop movements of large and small units from Laotian border as far S[outh] as 10 miles below Khe Sanh. All movements toward Khe Sanh. Seems to be Big Push." By dawn, two North Vietnamese troop concentrations had been identified. One of them had closed within six miles of the combat base.[22]

The commander of Forward Operating Base 3, the Special Forces compound at Khe Sanh, readied a patrol to scout enemy activity in that direction. Around 8:30 a.m., Specialist Fifth Class William Wood led a Special Forces team and a contingent of Bru fighters toward Hill 471, between the combat base and Khe Sanh village. Moving through heavy elephant grass on the hill's lower slopes, the patrol was ambushed at almost point-blank range. Sergeant Gary Lee Crone fell in the first volley with multiple wounds. Shot through both knees, Wood limped away from the kill zone and was rescued by helicopter along with one other American. Left behind were Crone, who was presumed dead, and another Special Forces operator, Michael Thomas Mahoney.[23]

Back at FOB-3, Captain Harlan "Rip" Van Winkle organized twenty-four men for a mission to rescue the two missing Americans. Their numbers included a seven-member Special Forces assault team designated as Hatchet Force Denver, and a lone Marine, Private First Class F. J. (Jim) Taylor, who knew the terrain from his time with Combined Action

Company Oscar-2 in Khe Sanh village. Rounding out the force were sixteen Bru fighters.[24]

Just minutes after four choppers inserted the men on the lower slope of Hill 471, the North Vietnamese attacked. Almost immediately, Van Winkle's second in command, First Lieutenant Grenville Sutcliffe, was hit in the throat by grenade shrapnel as he tried to direct gunships to an NVA machine-gun position.[25] Grenades rained down on Van Winkle and his outnumbered men, wounding most of the Americans with shrapnel. Sergeant First Class Charles Tredinnick fell with a mortal chest wound.[26]

In the critical minutes that followed, helicopter gunships kept the recovery force alive on Hill 471. The North Vietnamese had drawn so close to Van Winkle and his men that the choppers fired almost on top of them. On one pass, the gunships missed Taylor and Van Winkle by inches and accidentally shot a Bru fighter in both legs. The support finally allowed the embattled men to break free and maneuver to the hill's northern slope. They hunkered down while a Marine forward air controller called in air strikes from his position overhead. As helicopter gunships and fighter jets pounded the North Vietnamese with cannon, bombs, and napalm, the bloodied Van Winkle and his men walked back to FOB-3.[27]

• • •

The enemy is attempting to "dig his way into Khe Sanh [to avoid] our tremendous firepower (as he did at Dien Bien Phu)," General William Westmoreland wrote in a January 29 cable to Admiral Ulysses Simpson Grant Sharp, the American commander in the Pacific.[28] Westmoreland had just returned from I Corps, where he had conferred with senior commanders about the threat against Khe Sanh. He had ordered his staff historian to prepare a study on the lessons of Dien Bien Phu.

There were hints that General Giap had something else up his sleeve—reports from recent arrests and interrogations suggested the Communists were poised to attack South Vietnam's urban centers—but Westmoreland dismissed these as attempts to divert attention from I Corps.[29] He remained convinced that Khe Sanh was the main event.

The American commander was hardly alone in his preoccupation with Khe Sanh. Over the past month, President Lyndon Johnson had become obsessed with the subject.

For Johnson, and indeed for all Americans, the war in Vietnam had reached a critical juncture. Throughout 1967, Johnson had watched antiwar sentiment rise and his approval ratings fall. In November, he had brought General Westmoreland back home to talk up the outlook in Vietnam. Westmoreland had sounded all the optimistic notes that Johnson wanted the American people to hear. On November 19, during a National Press Club speech, Westmoreland described how the war had reached a point "when the end begins to come into view."[30]

While Westmoreland publicly hinted at victory, Johnson privately confronted the growing pessimism of one of his closest advisers. Defense Secretary Robert McNamara's doubts about the war had reached a breaking point, and on November 1, he had presented Johnson with a memo urging a cap on US troop levels and suspension of the bombing campaign.[31] Weary of McNamara's increasingly dissonant views, Johnson cut him loose. On November 29, he announced that McNamara would be leaving the Pentagon after seven years to head the World Bank.[32]

In December, Johnson had been informed that the North Vietnamese were stockpiling supplies and massing tens of thousands of troops around the DMZ. A Communist offensive was expected, with Khe Sanh the likely target. Westmoreland had assured the president that the enemy offensive was born of desperation rather than strength, but Johnson was concerned. He had been in Congress fourteen years earlier when President Dwight D. Eisenhower had briefly considered using nuclear weapons to save the French garrison at Dien Bien Phu. Now Johnson faced the haunting specter of a remote American base being besieged by Communist forces commanded by the mastermind of Dien Bien Phu.

Johnson's uneasiness over Khe Sanh escalated to alarm after he received an unsolicited warning from the capital's most influential pundit. On January 10, hawkish syndicated columnist Joseph Alsop had suggested in a lunch with Johnson's national security adviser, Walt Rostow, that US forces at Khe Sanh were poised to follow in the disastrous footsteps of the feckless French. Khe Sanh presented the North Vietnamese with their "best opportunity for a Dien Bien Phu," Alsop warned. "And the enemy is looking for a Dien Bien Phu."[33]

Johnson and Rostow now pressed General Earle Wheeler, chairman of the Joint Chiefs of Staff, to make sure that Westmoreland could handle the threat. The opening Communist attacks against Khe Sanh on January 21 had triggered more phone calls and cables, all infused with the ghosts of Dien Bien Phu.

In a January 29 phone conversation with Wheeler, General Westmoreland laid out all the preparations he had made to defend Khe Sanh: two extra Marine battalions had been moved to the stronghold in the previous week; other troops had been shifted to I Corps for use in an emergency; massive artillery support was in place; and the North Vietnamese were being hammered with about forty B-52 sorties and five hundred tactical air sorties each day.[34]

Drawing on his conversation with Westmoreland and a subsequent meeting with the Joint Chiefs, Wheeler wrote a 460-word memorandum for the president. "General Westmoreland stated to me that, in his judgment, we can hold Khe Sanh and we should hold Khe Sanh," Wheeler wrote. "He believes that this is an opportunity to inflict a severe defeat upon the enemy."[35] Furthermore, the Joint Chiefs were satisfied with Westmoreland's preparations and his rationale for standing his ground at the vulnerable American outpost. Thus, Wheeler concluded, the Joint Chiefs "recommend that we maintain our position at Khe Sanh."

Shortly after 1:00 p.m. on January 29, President Johnson convened a meeting in the White House Cabinet Room to poll his military commanders in person and make a final decision about Khe Sanh. In attendance were General Wheeler and the four service chiefs, national security adviser Walt Rostow, and Secretary of Defense Robert McNamara.

Johnson went around the table and questioned each member of the Joint Chiefs. "Have we done all we should do?"[36] he asked. "Are we convinced our forces are adequate?"

The nation's top military commanders once again reassured the president.

"Should we withdraw from Khe Sanh?" Johnson pressed.

"No," he was told. Militarily and psychologically, Khe Sanh was too important.

For the moment, Lyndon Johnson had heard enough. America would stand and fight at Khe Sanh.

PART II

CHAPTER 8

"Hell in a Very Small Place"

A s President Johnson's pivotal meeting with the Joint Chiefs of Staff was breaking up in Washington, North Vietnamese and Viet Cong forces on the other side of the world were launching the first attacks of General Giap's Tet Offensive, a series of coordinated strikes aimed at the heart of South Vietnam's urban centers. Over the next few hours, Communist troops attacked the provincial capitals of Pleiku, Khanh Hoa, Darlac, and Quang Tri, as well as the I Corps headquarters at Quang Tri and the huge US bases at Da Nang and Cam Ranh Bay.

Daylight of January 30 in Vietnam brought even worse news. More attacks were planned throughout South Vietnam that evening, reported General Phillip Davidson, chief of intelligence for Westmoreland's Military Assistance Command, Vietnam (MACV). At 9:45 a.m., the South Vietnamese government canceled the annual Tet holiday truce.[1]

At Khe Sanh on January 30, the North Vietnamese continued to punish the Americans with artillery, rockets, mortars, and sniper fire. Incoming rounds at the combat base ignited a fire in an ammunition supply point, and Sergeant Jesus Roberto Vasquez, a twenty-year-old Marine explosive ordnance disposal technician from El Paso, Texas, was among those who joined the frantic effort to put out the flames. Spotting a burning 81-millimeter mortar round, Vasquez grabbed it. Before he could hurl the shell into a bomb crater, it blew up in his arms, and Vasquez became the latest American to die at Khe Sanh.[2]

True to General Davidson's belated warning, the Communist Tet Offensive erupted in full fury in the early hours of January 31 with urban attacks launched by an estimated 84,000 Viet Cong cadre and North Vietnamese Army regulars. The fighting engulfed thirty-six of forty-four provincial capitals and South Vietnam's six largest cities, including the ancient imperial city of Hue, which was seized by Communist forces in a fierce assault. In Saigon, Viet Cong commandos breached the US Embassy compound, the presidential palace, and Tan Son Nhut Airbase.

General Giap had planned the offensive as a means of triggering an uprising against the US-backed government in Saigon, the next phase in his quest to end the war in 1968. A short-term objective was an improved position in anticipated peace talks with the Americans, part of the overall Communist strategy of fight-and-talk.

For his part, General Westmoreland remained convinced that Khe Sanh was the prize coveted by Giap. In Westmoreland's analysis, the urban attacks were a ploy aimed at drawing American forces away from Khe Sanh.

The defenders of Khe Sanh had been spared the ferocious ground attacks of the Tet Offensive, but the calibrated violence continued to kill and maim a few more Americans each day: four dead on January 31; one on February 1; another four on February 2; two on February 3. The rising death toll paled in comparison to the carnage at Hue and elsewhere, but that was little consolation to the Americans at Khe Sanh as they watched a rising number of comrades flown away in body bags.

• • •

The mounting casualties and ever-present threat of an overwhelming enemy assault had cast a pall over Hill 861 in those early days of February. Mortar and sniper fire raked the hill every day. The draw where Tommy Denning had been killed had become such a popular staging ground for enemy mortar teams that the Marines had nicknamed it "Times Square."

The sound of each mortar blast was the starting gun in a race for life. It would take about twelve to fifteen seconds for the first round to hit, so the cry of "Incoming!" would set off a desperate scramble for cover. The first impact would usually be followed in quick succession by another three or four, any one of which could be deadly in the close quarters of Hill 861.

As the hill's artillery forward observer, Dennis Mannion's job was to remain in place when the cry of "Incoming!" went up. He would spend those anxious seconds trying to fix the location of the enemy mortar team, and even as the rounds were falling, he would begin calling in artillery missions on the suspected coordinates.

Mannion had his work routine down by the second week of the enemy offensive. He would begin each day by scanning the ridgelines west of the hill to see if anything looked different—freshly turned dirt or any other sign of movement or massing of enemy troops. He would touch base with his air counterpart on the hill, Corporal Paul Knight, who returned from "R&R" (rest and recreation) in Hawaii in early February. They would compare notes with the forward air controller circling overhead in his small Cessna spotter and work up a series of strikes on the NVA-held ridgelines to the west, typically capped off with a couple of artillery fire missions, "just to shake up anybody who might be over there."[3] Afterward, Mannion would eat breakfast and write letters for a while before renewing his search for targets.

Bad weather and NVA fire had disrupted helicopter resupply missions to the hill outposts, resulting in chronic (and sometimes critical) food and water shortages by early February. Daily allotments were cut to two C-ration meals and one canteen of water. Sometimes men went without food for a day or two until supply choppers could get through.

Before the siege, Mannion had maintained an active social life on the hill. Now he spent any spare time in elaborate efforts to improve his chances of surviving an enemy assault. He and three other colleagues began work on a deep bunker that would eventually extend ten feet down into the hill and include an escape tunnel leading to a foxhole about twelve feet away. Once the bunker was completed, the men worked each night on the underground passageway, which they christened "Tom," after one of the tunnels in *The Great Escape*. It gave them a sense that they were doing *something* to even the odds.[4]

Still, spirits flagged on the hill. Most men had already experienced a few close calls, and another North Vietnamese ground attack was expected any day. The grim prospects led Mannion on January 31 to write a pair of farewell letters to his parents and his best friend back in Connecticut.

"I want to say that I'm not afraid of dying," Mannion wrote his friend. "I'll just feel sorry for my folks, brothers, and sister. And you. There's no way I can describe what good friends we two are and how much your ugly presence means to me."[5] Mannion slipped a farewell letter to his parents into the envelope and asked his friend to pass it on if he didn't make it back.

Four days later, on Sunday, February 4, Mannion turned twenty-three. Late that afternoon, he settled into the sandbag enclosure along the northern end of the hill that he and Dave Kron had used as their bomb shelter before the siege. There Mannion began to prepare his birthday meal of C-ration beans and franks.[6] He cooked off the grease with a c-rat heat tab and stirred in some melted cheese and bread he had saved from other meals. He leaned back against the northern wall of the uncovered shelter and was about to start eating when he heard a familiar sound.

Whump. Whump. Whump. Whump.

The report of the first mortar round leaving its tube had stirred an instinctive reaction in Mannion's brain. *Get to the bunker.* He had always done everything he could to improve his odds of surviving Vietnam. In recent days he had inserted extra fiberglass panels in his flak jacket and buttressed his steel-pot helmet with protective plates. Now, a flash of defiance overruled his better judgment. *My food is ready, and it IS my birthday. Fuck it.*[7]

Mannion heard the first round explode close to the LZ near the southern end of the hill. The second impacted halfway up the slope. The third landed closer still, on the crest. He waited for the last round to hit.

Mannion was airborne by the time his brain registered the deafening *Boom.* The projectile had exploded just outside the double layer of sandbags at his back and the force knocked him flying, but the sacks of red Khe Sanh soil had absorbed the brunt of the blast and shrapnel. He lay on his back, gasping for breath but otherwise unhurt.

When his head cleared, Mannion saw that his carefully prepared meal was splattered all over his filthy utilities and flak jacket. Dusting himself off, he set to work picking the chunks of red clay out of his cheesy beans and franks. Mannion wished himself Happy Birthday, then began spooning the mess off his pants and into his mouth.

• • •

In Washington, an air of crisis now gripped the White House. The onset of the Communist attack on Khe Sanh had been followed by the seizure of the US spy ship *Pueblo* and its crew by North Korea on January 23. And then came the stunning Communist attacks that engulfed South Vietnam's largest cities in combat.

The Tet Offensive had sharpened Johnson's fears of a disaster at Khe Sanh. Key members of Congress nervously questioned whether Westmoreland knew what he was doing. "Are we prepared for this attack?" Senator Robert Byrd of West Virginia had pointedly asked the president in a January 30 White House briefing for congressional Democrats.

Johnson began to ponder his nightmare scenario: a situation so dire that only the use of tactical nuclear weapons could prevent Khe Sanh from falling to the North Vietnamese. On February 1, General Earle Wheeler, Johnson's chairman of the Joint Chiefs, sent an "eyes only" cable to General Westmoreland and Admiral Sharp, America's Hawaii-based commander in chief in the Pacific theater, in which he raised the issue of using tactical nuclear weapons at Khe Sanh.[8] Wheeler asked his commanders to let him know "whether there are targets in the area which lend themselves to nuclear strikes, whether some contingency nuclear planning would be in order, and what you would consider to be some of the more significant pros and cons of using tactical nukes in such a contingency."

While General Westmoreland discreetly formulated his response, Johnson continued to fret about Khe Sanh's fragile supply line and the prospect of the American base being isolated like the French at Dien Bien Phu. He phoned General Wheeler on the evening of February 2 to ask again about Westmoreland's abilities to reinforce and resupply Khe Sanh if bad weather and North Vietnamese anti-aircraft fire shut down the airstrip. Once again, Johnson raised the prospect of being forced to use nuclear weapons to save Khe Sanh.[9]

Wheeler had spoken to Westmoreland a few hours earlier, and the Joint Chiefs chairman relayed to the president the current thinking of the MACV commander. Westmoreland believed a major ground attack on Khe Sanh could come as early as that evening and predicted "a bloody fight." But he remained "confident that the position can be held."[10]

On February 4, Wheeler formally briefed the president on General

Westmoreland's latest response to Johnson's concerns about Khe Sanh. Once again, Westmoreland had emphasized the superior US fire support and airlift capabilities in place for Khe Sanh's defense.

As for tactical nuclear weapons, Westmoreland didn't foresee the need to use them "in the present situation." However, Westmoreland allowed, a significant deterioration in the state of affairs along the DMZ could require drastic action to stave off a catastrophic defeat. "Under such circumstances," Westmoreland wrote, "I visualize that either tactical nuclear weapons or chemical agents would be active candidates for employment."[11]

• • •

By early February, Lyndon Johnson was not the only American consumed with the ominous turn of events in Asia. America's newspaper front pages and nightly newscasts were dominated by coverage of the *Pueblo* crisis, the Tet Offensive, and the siege at Khe Sanh. A steady parade of journalists and photojournalists was making the trek to Khe Sanh, and their reports painted a grim picture.

The new arrivals were stunned by the appearance of the American stronghold. The Marine combat base had become a scarred and debris-littered moonscape, its shredded tents and shattered buildings replaced by a subterranean world of sandbagged bunkers and trenches. Arriving journalists quickly learned that death lurked around the airstrip. The savvy hustled for cover with an urgency of movement that the defenders had wryly christened the "Khe Sanh shuffle."

It was perhaps inevitable, given the distrust that existed between the correspondents and General Westmoreland, that the tone of news coverage out of Khe Sanh implied doom and official miscalculation. The Dien Bien Phu analogy didn't originate with the correspondents, but it became a pervasive theme in articles bearing the Khe Sanh dateline.

In fairness to the correspondents, it was difficult to grasp Westmoreland's strategic vision at Khe Sanh. They could see and experience firsthand the jerry-rigged defenses, the dank, rat-infested bunkers and trenches, the random death and terror of enemy barrages. On the other hand, they could not see the death and terror experienced by the North Vietnamese troops surrounding Khe Sanh as Westmoreland's Operation Niagara of artillery and air strikes exacted a rising toll.

In Washington and Saigon, a debate was underway as to whether America's stand at Khe Sanh was destined to end badly. By the first week of February, President Lyndon Johnson was so engrossed by this question that he had installed a terrain model of Khe Sanh in the White House Situation Room. No assurances by General Westmoreland could allay his concerns.

Just weeks before his death while on patrol with the Marines of the "Walking Dead" in February 1967, Bernard Fall had published his much-anticipated book on the French defeat at Dien Bien Phu. Fall's critically acclaimed account was a devastating reconstruction of the debacle that ended French colonial rule in Vietnam, and its title had evoked the suffering endured by French and Viet Minh troops during the fifty-five-day siege: *Hell in a Very Small Place.*

Now, informing an American audience about the great showdown in the distant hills of South Vietnam, *Newsweek* conjured the ghosts of Dien Bien Phu. "Khe Sanh," the magazine declared, "was shaping up into another version of hell in a very small place."[12]

• • •

In the heart of the combat base, several feet beneath the ragged trench lines and scarred red earth, life proceeded at a high-octane pace in the underground bunker that housed the Command Operations Center (COC) of the 26th Marines. The COC bunker was the nerve center for the combat base and its outposts, "a labyrinth of whitewashed rooms lit by bare bulbs and bustling with staff officers and enlisted aides," as one visitor described it, a tomb-like world of squawking radios, jangling telephones, stale cigarette smoke, and unwashed bodies.

Westmoreland had anchored his quest for victory at Khe Sanh on Operation Niagara, the waterfall of artillery and air strikes that was supposed to negate the North Vietnamese advantage in numbers and decimate their ranks. But the NVA troops were masters of camouflage and concealment, and even in such large numbers as the two divisions arrayed around Khe Sanh, the enemy soldiers were hard to find.

The search for targets was endless. Reports flooded the COC each day, shards of information pouring in from patrols, artillery forward observers, aerial observers, forward air controllers, other human sources, radio intercepts, signals intelligence, and sensor readings. But the piece-meal reporting made it difficult to discern patterns of enemy movements, concentrations, and current locations. The challenge was how to shape such disjointed intelligence into a coordinated campaign of air strikes and artillery fire.

Westmoreland's subordinates had begun assembling a first-rate team to handle target intelligence and execution at Khe Sanh on the eve of the North Vietnamese attack. An energetic Army captain from Missouri named Mark Swearengen reported to the base on January 18 to co-ordinate fire from sixteen long-range 175-millimeter guns at two fire bases along Route 9 northeast of Khe Sanh: Camp Carroll and a seven-hundred-foot karst outcropping known as the Rockpile. A new regimen-tal intelligence (S-2) officer, Jerry Hudson, arrived to manage the torrent of tactical information flowing in and out of Khe Sanh. Their vital role in Khe Sanh's defense reached new heights when they were joined by a dark-skinned stranger who strode into the regimental COC on January 23 with the pretentious air of a British aristocrat.

Swearengen reacted as so many did when first confronted by Captain Munir Mirza Baig, United States Marine Corps. Baig burst into the bunker with a native kukri knife at his waist, "and spoke as though he were there to single-handedly save Khe Sanh." Swearengen wondered: *Is this guy crazy?*[13]

Now thirty-six, Baig was smart and well read in eighteenth-century siege warfare doctrine, World War I artillery tactics and techniques, even the writings of General Vo Nguyen Giap. His brilliance was rivaled by his eccentricities. Born in 1932 into a prominent Muslim family in British India, Baig was the son of a Sandhurst-trained cavalry officer who later served in the British colonial administration and foreign service. When British India was granted independence and partitioned along religious lines in 1947, Baig's father became a diplomat for the new government of Pakistan.[14]

After splitting his childhood among India, Britain, and France, Baig returned to Britain to complete secondary school and attend Cambridge University. In his early twenties, he had earned a master's degree in busi-ness in Canada, where his father had been posted as a Pakistani diplo-mat. He had briefly worked for retailing giant Sears Roebuck before being allowed to enlist in the Marine Corps as a fledgling private. Three years later, after gaining US citizenship, Sergeant Baig was discharged so he could enter Marine Corps Officer Candidates School. He emerged with the gold bars of a second lieutenant.

Harry Baig, as he was now known, logged two years in Marine artillery before expanding his expertise to include counterintelligence. In the late summer and early fall of 1964, he embarked on a daring personal reconnaissance of South Vietnam's I Corps sector, traveling by jeep up to the DMZ with only a driver. Baig spent the next three years shuttling between Vietnam and the United States in various artillery and intelligence capacities. He returned to I Corps in September 1967 to serve with the 3rd Marine Division's intelligence section. When the North Vietnamese moved against Khe Sanh, Baig was dispatched to the base to coordinate target intelligence.

Baig quickly won over his comrades in Khe Sanh's Fire Support Coordination Center. He was physically unremarkable—he wore horn-rimmed glasses and stood five feet seven inches and weighed only 125 pounds—but he possessed an iron constitution that enabled him to work eighteen-hour days. He didn't suffer fools, but his infectious energy and humor endeared him to his colleagues in the COC.[15] He bantered easily about being a Muslim in a sea of Christians, and routinely announced that he was ready to kill some North Vietnamese "infidels."

Baig's official designation was 26th Marines target information officer. Working with regimental intelligence chief Jerry Hudson, he plotted every known enemy position on note cards, one card for each 1,000-meter map grid. Baig had soon identified 3,000 targets within a 15,000-meter radius (about nine miles) from Khe Sanh.[16] He coordinated B-52 strikes and special air support missions with 3rd Marine Division headquarters, and more discreetly, he became Khe Sanh's resident expert on the electronic sensors that now blanketed the approaches to the base. Baig elevated his work to an art form, taking sensor data and other intelligence and meshing it with his knowledge of local terrain and North Vietnamese tactics to identify imminent attacks and inflict heavy blows on the enemy.

Like a mad scientist, Baig did his work at night, preferring to sleep during the day while frontline artillery and air observers called in strikes on an ad hoc basis. Baig disdained this approach as chaotic and "vulgar." As darkness fell, Baig seized the stage, and with the instincts of a maestro, he would craft a symphony of artillery and air strikes that began to take a rising toll on the North Vietnamese.[17]

• • •

Robert McNamara's electronic sensors had been derided by senior generals during the early discussions about the Muscle Shoals program, but the devices quickly proved their worth at Khe Sanh. Sensor readings not only revealed enemy troop concentrations of one hundred or more but also the speed and direction in which the troops were moving. The raw data were shared with Harry Baig in the COC bunker even as the EC-121 aircraft overhead relayed the information to the top-secret facility in Thailand known as Dutch Mill, where IBM 360-40 mainframe computers churned out spreadsheets from which analysts fashioned reports for Baig.

By early February, Baig was devouring the sensor data. He had mastered the layout of the sensor strings, which allowed him to match activation patterns with his knowledge of NVA operational doctrine. It was still an imprecise science, but the sensors pulled back the shroud of fog and darkness that the North Vietnamese used to conceal attacks and improve positions, allowing Baig to almost "see" the enemy soldiers as they moved about.

On the night of February 3, the sensors northwest of Hill 881 South erupted with activity and continued to indicate the movement of large numbers of enemy troops until the early morning hours of February 4. The enemy soldiers had appeared on the sensor grid about two and one-half miles northwest of the American outpost, then turned south and continued moving past the western flank of 881 South. When they were clear of the hill, they turned east, toward Khe Sanh. And then, they disappeared. A sensor string southeast of 881 South was never activated, suggesting the troops had sought cover nearby.

As he tracked the enemy, Baig had concluded that the column was a Vietnamese resupply convoy. He had called in artillery fire on the unseen enemy force as the sensors registered the movement, but there was no way to know whether any damage had been done.

That evening, Sunday, February 4, Baig and his comrades watched as the sensors once again crackled with activity along the same route. Midnight arrived, and the movement stretched into the early morning hours of February 5. Baig reached a chilling conclusion: rather than a resupply convoy, they were tracking an NVA regiment, and the estimated 1,500 to 2,000 troops were moving into position for an attack.[18] The sensors southeast of 881 South once again had not activated, which seemed to rule out the combat base as the objective. Baig concluded the target was 881 South. His colleagues concurred.

It was a race against time now to see whether the enemy force could be destroyed by artillery before it was able to strike. Baig projected the likely location of the enemy column. Assuming a pace of about 1.25 miles per hour—"NVA rate of march in darkness and mist"—he drew a line eastward from the last sensor triggered. It ended at a point south of the American outpost atop 881 South. Baig framed the point with a target block measuring 1,000 meters by 300 meters (roughly 1,100 yards by 330 yards), bounded on each end by 1,000-meter lines that arced across the hill's southeastern and southwestern slopes.

At 3:00 a.m., American artillery opened up on the target box Baig had drawn. For half an hour the guns blanketed the area with high explosive shells and walked rounds across the southern flanks of 881 South. Sensors south and southwest of the hill erupted with activity suggestive of urgent enemy movements. The acoustic devices captured a scene of terror unfolding inside the target box, relaying to the American analysts "the voices of hundreds of men running in panic through the darkness and heavy fog."[19]

The Vietnamese had suffered a heavy blow, and a likely attack on 881 South had been broken. But in his scramble to preempt the assault, Harry Baig had committed a rare oversight. Two NVA battalions had avoided the American trap, and they were now poised to hit the Marines on Hill 861 Alpha.

CHAPTER 9

The Battle of Hill 861 Alpha

Around 3:00 a.m. on Monday morning, February 5, Second Lieutenant Don Shanley moved in a low crouch along the northern perimeter trench of the Marine outpost on Hill 861 Alpha. After two months in Vietnam, the twenty-three-year-old platoon commander had found that his periodic line checks served two useful purposes: they kept his men on their toes, and they gave him an opportunity to get to know the forty Marines and two corpsmen under his command.

Most of the time, Shanley's men—collectively the 1st Platoon of Echo Company, 2nd Battalion, 26th Marines—were glad to see their "LT." But on nights when the enemy was about, the lieutenant could sense the agitation when he would suddenly appear in the darkness. "What the fuck are you doing this for, lieutenant?" the Marine might say. "I nearly blew you away!"[1] Now, Shanley moved cautiously to the next Marine along his line, whispering his identification well in advance so he didn't spook one of his boys and get blown away.

As he made his rounds, Shanley passed on the latest warning that battalion headquarters had relayed to his company commander, Captain Earle Breeding: there was "major movement" around their hill, or so battalion honchos claimed. Shanley was skeptical. He and his boys had heard similar warnings for days, and the false alarms were wearing them out.

Thirteen days had passed since their exhausting march to the hill, and the 150-odd Marines and eight or so Navy corpsmen of Echo Company had transformed the thickly vegetated knoll into a crude fortress. They had not been attacked in those anxious first days on the hill, but they had suffered from shortages of food and water. In desperation, the Marines tried to lick the dew off ponchos and cut open bamboo and banana trees to collect whatever water they could.

On the first day, Captain Breeding had walked Don Shanley out on a promontory overlooking the hill's gently sloping northern approach. "If they hit us, this is where they're coming through," Breeding had said. And then he had opened his arms and instructed Shanley: "This is your area, from here to here. Start setting in."[2]

Shanley and his men went to work with their Marine-issue "entrenching tools." Rocketman Dave McCall used captured Chinese dynamite to knock down three-foot-diameter trees and towering stands of elephant grass and to clear fields of fire to the west and northwest—the likeliest avenue of a North Vietnamese attack. McCall had packed a roll of concertina wire with C4 explosives and set it off, scything the grass on the southeastern corner of the hill to create a landing zone for helicopter re-supply and medevac missions.[3]

The centerpiece of 1st Platoon's critical stretch of perimeter was a salient constructed around a large bomb crater left over from the Hill Fights the previous spring and christened "Crater City" by Shanley's Marines. Shanley dug his hole on the south side of the crater, and that became the platoon command post. To his left and right, the men of 1st Platoon used their "e-tools" to scoop out fighting holes and gun pits along a four-foot-deep trench that soon looped around the hilltop. The nerve center of the garrison was Captain Breeding's company command post, carved into the crest of the hill, about sixty-five yards behind Shanley's men.

Shanley cut an impressive figure: handsome, blond hair, blue eyes, a lanky five feet eleven inches, with the easy grace of a gifted athlete. He had been a backstroke champion on the nation's top-ranked high school team in Winnetka, Illinois, and his achievements in swimming and academics earned him admission to Stanford University in 1962. He swam for Stanford while majoring in history and earned his degree in 1966. He began graduate studies at the University of California–Berkeley business school but quit to enter Marine Corps Officer Candidates School the following spring—a decision that stunned his friends, many of whom were vehemently against the war. But Shanley had a keen sense of history, and his inherent curiosity fueled within him a desire to "check out this great defining social struggle" that America had embraced in Vietnam.

Upon arriving in Vietnam, Shanley was assigned to Echo Company of the 2nd Battalion, 26th Marines. He was smart enough to know that he needed to keep his war-hero fantasies in check until he learned the ropes. "What do I need to know to stay alive?" he asked his men.[4] When he got ready to take his platoon out on a patrol or ambush in those first weeks, he would press his squad leaders, "Do you think this is a dumb way to do it? I'm open to a better way, so sound off now."

The Marines in Shanley's care were a diverse lot: black, white, and brown; Northerners and Southerners; hometowns that ranged from farming villages to big cities. Private First Class Jack Bogard, twenty-one, of Sycamore, Ohio, kept things loose around Crater City by shouting out, "Good morning, Vietnam!" (appropriated from Armed Forces Radio DJ Adrian Cronauer, as Shanley would later learn); Private First Class Martin Luther Rimson, eighteen years old, sang in nightclubs back home in Detroit, Michigan, and his comrades around Crater City were treated to silky-smooth strains of "Moon River" and other tunes; and then there was Lance Corporal Joseph Molettiere, also eighteen, who couldn't stop talking about the baby his young wife was expecting back in South Philadelphia.[5]

Now, in the predawn chill of February 5, Shanley finished his rounds about 4:00 a.m. and returned to his hole just in time to hear the three Marines in his listening post frantically keying their radio handset to sound a silent alarm. Whatever they had seen or heard, Shanley couldn't do anything without more information. He decided to grab a few minutes of shut-eye while his radioman monitored their PRC-25 unit for alarms or updates. Shanley hadn't known many pleasures in his two months in the bush, and now he decided to air out his feet for the first time since arriving on 861 Alpha. He had started unlacing one boot when Crater City erupted with explosions and gunfire.[6]

• • •

As mortar rounds, rocket-propelled grenades, machine guns, and assault rifles pounded the 1st Platoon perimeter, Shanley hurriedly tied his boot lace and sprinted the twenty yards to the northern edge of his line. He slid into one of the front holes and found himself beside a wounded Marine he didn't immediately recognize.[7] Shanley had barely processed what was happening when he was stunned and temporarily blinded by an explosion. Seconds passed, perhaps longer. When his vision returned and his head began to clear, he discovered that his M-16 rifle had been shattered beyond use, leaving him with two grenades with which to defend himself.

Peering from the hole, Shanley saw North Vietnamese soldiers all around him, dashing through the wire in twos and threes, jumping over his trench line as they headed deeper into the American outpost. One enemy soldier stopped over Shanley's hole and looked down at Shanley and the wounded Marine before continuing on his way.[8]

Shanley was frozen in place, still stunned by the shell burst and sheer terror, when a familiar voice shook him from his stupor. "One! One!" It was the call sign for a platoon commander. "One, get your ass back here!"[9] It was Shanley's tough platoon sergeant, McChurty G. Allen.

Shanley jumped up and dashed back up the hill toward the voice, diving head-first into the first hole he found. As the platoon commander popped his head out of the hole, Sergeant Allen fired several shots toward him. Three NVA soldiers fell dead around Shanley.

● ● ●

First Platoon rocketman Dave McCall was fast asleep behind the front positions around Crater City when the North Vietnamese mortar rounds shattered the night. He bolted to his fighting hole but found no sign of the two Marines who were supposed to be there. In front of the hole, McCall found a fresh mortar crater where he had left his M-16 rifle on a bipod.

Peering ahead, McCall couldn't see any NVA soldiers yet, but he figured they were just beyond the wire, waiting to force their way through the perimeter as soon as the mortars fell silent. McCall began throwing grenades as fast as he could along the perimeter wire. He realized the M-60 machine gun to his right wasn't firing, so he dashed into the pit.

The gun was on its stand, but it was twisted like a pretzel. The gunner and his assistant were lying at the bottom of the hole, moaning in agony.

McCall heard the sickening thud of a heavy object as it smacked into the dirt floor and bounced twice. He dived toward the trench line but only managed to get his head and upper body out of the pit before the enemy hand grenade exploded. Metal shards ripped into McCall's right leg, and the blast wave slammed him against the dirt wall and dropped him onto his back. He grabbed the remnants of his right leg. It felt like a wet sponge. Back home in rural Kansas, McCall had been faster than just about anyone in his high school. A thought flashed through his brain: *Well, my running days are over.*[10]

Another grenade dropped into the gun pit, a little farther away than the first. McCall pulled his helmet over his face and waited. He heard the deafening roar and felt the hot metal shred the tissue, muscles, and nerves of his left leg.

Seconds passed, maybe minutes, before a Navy corpsman he knew only by his nickname—Wild Man—darted into the hole. The corpsman checked the wounded machine gunner and his assistant first and was examining McCall's injured legs when another grenade plopped into the pit. The corpsman stepped into the blast path, and when he turned around, McCall could see Wild Man's face had become a bloody mask.

"We gotta get out of here, *now!*" McCall yelled. He dragged himself onto his left leg and hopped into the trench. The blinded corpsman felt his way out of the hole, and the two badly injured Americans helped each other through Crater City. They climbed out of the trench and slowly made their way up the grassy slope toward the center of the outpost.

The corpsman cleared enough blood and debris off his face to see out of one eye, then headed off to get help. McCall crawled deeper into the grass and dragged himself into a shallow depression. As the battle raged, the wounded rocketman lay on his back, staring up at the flare-lit sky.

• • •

First Platoon rifleman Dave Norton was asleep in a clump of grass along the northwest trench line, about thirty feet from Crater City, when the attack began. He slid into his fighting hole and ducked for cover as mortar rounds pounded the 1st Platoon positions. The barrage subsided, and one of the three Marines in Shanley's listening post outside the wire came running up the hill, shouting, "The gooks are coming! The gooks are coming!"[11]

Norton and his best friend, rifleman Joe Molettiere, peered into the darkness but couldn't see anything. The panicked voice of a Marine suddenly sounded from a 60-millimeter mortar pit about ten feet behind them. "Who's there? *Who's there?*" Norton heard the sound of boots hitting the ground, and the Marine opened fire. Two NVA soldiers fell dead between the trench line and the mortar pit.

The sounds of battle swept the hill—shouts and screams mingling with the roar of explosions and gunfire. Norton was reassured by the sound of his squad's M-60 as gunner John Ingram, a big, brawny Tennessean, sprayed the fog and darkness beyond the Crater City lines.[12]

A voice called out to Norton and Molettiere from the direction of Crater City. "Wounded man here! Wounded man here!" Norton and Molettiere reacted to the call for help and found their friend, Martin Luther Rimson, the silky-voiced singer from Detroit. A mortar had nearly severed one of his legs, but he was still conscious and alert. The two Marines dragged Rimson back to their position. Norton yelled for a corpsman, and one quickly appeared.

The corpsman had started to work on Rimson's leg when suddenly a cry carried across the hill. "Gas! Gas! Gas!" On Captain Breeding's orders, the Marines had tossed tear-gas grenades to slow the NVA onslaught, and the choking fumes had begun to settle into the trenches.

Molettiere had gotten his gas mask on and was kneeling over Rimson when the blinding red flash of a mortar round engulfed the Marines. Molettiere took the brunt of the blast and was torn apart. Rimson had been shielded from instant death by Molettiere, but he was in bad shape. The fate of the corpsman was unknown.

In the wavering light of overhead flares, Norton initially thought his right arm had been blown off at the elbow. In fact, it was still attached, but the bones had been ripped from his forearm, resulting in the grotesque extension of his hand and lower arm. A corpsman bandaged Norton's mangled limb, dressed a shrapnel gash in his knee, and gave him a shot of morphine to dull the pain.

As the soothing drug took effect, Norton stretched out along the trench line. In his good hand he clutched a knife. He was ready to die fighting.

● ● ●

From his command post about fifty yards behind Crater City, Echo commander Earle Breeding tried to make sense of the chaos. "The gooks are coming!" had quickly become "Gooks in the wire!" and then "Gooks in the trench line!" The frantic shouts had swept the lines of Echo's 2nd and 3rd platoons and circled the hill. Reports from the perimeter suggested a general attack on all sides, so Breeding ordered his troops to throw tear-gas grenades to slow the enemy onslaught.[13] To his superiors, he broadcast an appeal for all available artillery support.

Word of the attack rocketed up the chain of command, crossed the Pacific, and landed on desks at the Pentagon and the White House Situation Room, twelve time zones behind Vietnam. The question that quickly worked its way back down to Khe Sanh: was the attack the opening move in the anticipated North Vietnamese attempt to overwhelm the American stronghold?

The attack had unfolded in textbook North Vietnamese Army style, and the initial barrage had reflected the careful reconnaissance work that was a Communist hallmark in Vietnam. As soon as the initial barrage had ceased, sappers wielding Bangalore torpedoes had blasted gaps in the few strands of barbed wire the Marines had strung around the perimeter of 861 Alpha.

Lieutenant Don Shanley had reached a frontline hole in time to witness the first NVA assault teams as they dashed through the breach in his lines and spread into the interior of the American outpost. Some of the NVA soldiers went to work widening the breach by attacking 1st Platoon positions from inside the American lines, tossing grenades and firing RPGs and AK-47 rifles at fighting holes and bunkers where Marines had sought shelter. Others, like the pair of NVA soldiers Dave Norton had heard creeping up on the 60-millimeter mortar pit behind his position, had pushed up the hill to sow chaos and confusion. Still others had swept over the crest and opened fire on the 2nd and 3rd platoon lines from behind.

The enemy had gotten the drop on the Echo Marines with a ferocious first strike, but illumination rounds fired by the company's mortars quickly allowed Breeding to determine that his lines were intact along the southern perimeter and eastern and western flanks, and there was no sign of attack in those areas. Just as Breeding had anticipated, the northern perimeter was the focal point of the enemy thrust. Don Shanley had confirmed the breach in his lines and reported that small groups of NVA troops were continuing to sprint into the American outpost.[14]

As injured Marines trickled back from the 1st Platoon lines, Breeding began to reclaim the initiative. To contain the NVA soldiers inside his perimeter, Breeding had Echo's acting executive officer, Second Lieutenant Alec J. Bodenweiser, redeploy fire teams from the secure southern end of the hill to a new defensive line taking shape behind the 1st Platoon's shattered perimeter. Breeding personally took on the larger problem of shutting down the flow of enemy troops to the fight. Nine minutes after the attack began, rounds from the 105-millimeter howitzers at Khe Sanh Combat Base began screaming over the hill to pound the northwest approach to 861 Alpha and suspected NVA assembly areas nearby.

• • •

Along the northern perimeter, the remnants of Don Shanley's 1st Platoon fought for their lives. Shanley had lost more than half of his forty men in the first minutes of the fight. His trenches, fighting holes, and gun pits were soaked with the blood of his dead and wounded Marines.

Light-hearted PFC Jack Bogard, one of Shanley's favorites, had been part of the listening post outside the northern perimeter when the attack began, and he made it back to his fighting hole. He had dragged a wounded comrade back up the trench line and was trying to save another buddy when he was struck by enemy fire and killed.[15]

Some of the NVA soldiers who had dashed through the breach now stood over the trench line and fired down at trapped Marines.[16] In the fast-moving battle, Shanley and other survivors were pinned in their positions behind Crater City. Shanley managed to maintain radio contact with Captain Breeding as enemy soldiers blasted away at him with an AK-50 machine gun on the far side of the crater. The enemy gunfire and shrapnel gouged a deep groove in the back of Shanley's hole, about three inches above his head. Corporal William Johnson crouched beside the platoon leader and kept the NVA attackers from advancing with a flurry of well-placed grenades.[17]

Ignoring the heavy fire, a fearless weapons platoon corporal, Tom Eichler, headed down the trench line toward the northern perimeter to check on comrades and spread the word to fall back to a new line behind Crater City. Near the perimeter's northernmost point, he came upon three severely wounded Marines lying in the bottom of their M-60 machine-gun hole. Eichler hoisted one of the injured men on his back and headed up the trench line, but he ran headlong into an NVA soldier in the narrow passageway. Whirling around, Eichler began running back down the trench as the enemy soldier opened fire. Eichler felt the bullets smack into the flak jacket of the wounded Marine draped over his shoulder.[18]

Eichler found his way blocked by another NVA soldier who was firing a rocket at Americans farther down the trench. With the wounded Marine still on his back, Eichler grabbed the enemy soldier and strangled him with the strap of his rocket pouch.

Over the next few minutes, Eichler managed to avoid the marauding enemy soldiers while carrying three injured Marines to safety. He had returned to the front line one last time to warn any survivors to fall back when he came upon a chilling sight. Three young Marines had been blown apart in a hole, and visible in the intermittent light were "ten long, bloody marks from the top of the hole to the bottom, made by the bloody hands of one of those Marines who had attempted to crawl out before he died."[19]

• • •

On Breeding's request, supporting fire from nearly every American position in the Khe Sanh area was now blanketing the northwest approach to his hill and likely NVA assembly areas nearby. As the shells rained down, Lieutenant Don Shanley kept bringing the fire closer and closer to his line. "Drop 5-0 [fifty meters]," he would yell into his radio handset, and the 105-millimeter howitzer gunners would place more rounds that much closer to the American perimeter.

Down at Khe Sanh Combat Base, targeting officer extraordinaire Harry Baig recovered from his initial shock and embarrassment at having missed the threat to 861 Alpha and swung into action. One of the NVA battalions he had overlooked had launched the attack on Earle Breeding's Marines, so now Baig drew on his knowledge of enemy doctrine and tendencies to destroy the reserve battalion moving into position to finish off the American outpost.

In an extraordinary hourlong effort, the Americans pounded the North Vietnamese with artillery and radar-directed air strikes. Three batteries of the 1st Battalion, 13th Marines, artillery regiment at Khe Sanh laid protective fire on the slopes of 861 Alpha while a fourth battery hammered the area below the breach in Echo's perimeter "and then rolled down the slope to prevent the enemy from retiring or being reinforced."[20]

At the suggestion of Captain Mark Swearengen, the 175-millimeter artillery liaison officer assigned to Khe Sanh, the big Army guns at Camp Carroll and the Rockpile along Route 9 laid a wall of steel across the base of the hill to destroy the reserve battalion as it moved into position. The guns marched a deadly barrier of 174-pound high-explosive shells to within 200 meters (220 yards) of Echo's northern perimeter. Inside that buffer, the smaller Khe Sanh guns dropped a rolling barrage on the North Vietnamese troops that were poised to enter the American perimeter or had just been thrown back by Breeding's defense.

Radar-directed air strikes pounded the area beyond the "wall of steel," dropping bombs on enemy mortar clusters and possible assembly areas for NVA reinforcements. Marines on Hill 558 pounded away with 106-millimeter recoilless rifles while Bill Dabney's three 105-millimeter howitzers and two 81-millimeter mortars delivered crucial fire from 881 South.[21] While bracing for the NVA to hit their outpost, the Kilo 3/26 Marines on Hill 861, only about 200 yards southwest of 861 Alpha, bled the NVA assault force with 106-millimeter recoilless rifles and machine-gun fire.

While their comrades on the ground and in the skies kept North Vietnamese reinforcements at bay, Earle Breeding's Marines carried the fight to the Communist forces inside the wire and those still coming through the breach. Echo's 60-millimeter mortar section leader, Corporal Billy E. Drexel Jr., led a squad down the hill and set up a tube behind Shanley's position. While fending off NVA assault troops with grenades, Drexel and his squad dropped over three hundred rounds just beyond the 1st Platoon's perimeter.

• • •

The Marines assigned to positions away from the northern perimeter were spared the brunt of the opening NVA barrage, but the terror and uncertainty of the North Vietnamese attack quickly spread through their lines. Among those listening anxiously to the sounds of battle along the northern line was one of the youngest and greenest of Echo's grunts, Private Larry McCartney, just eighteen years old. Assigned to Echo's 3rd Platoon, McCartney's fighting position on the western trench line marked the point where 3rd Platoon lines tied in with those of the 1st Platoon.

In those uncertain first minutes, the Marines along the western line braced for the NVA to come charging up out of the steep draw that separated their outpost from the American outpost on 861. Soon there were gunshots to their rear, and the Marines realized that enemy soldiers were loose in the interior of the hill. Some of the Marines turned inboard to meet that threat while others continued to watch the darkness to their front. In the pulsating light of illumination flares, the Marines along the western perimeter caught glimpses of NVA soldiers making their way northward through the draw to join the attack on the shattered 1st Platoon lines.

Further down the western trench line, near the hill's southwest corner, 3rd Platoon rifleman Jim Kaylor, a nineteen-year-old from Costa Mesa, California, was removing his boots after completing a two-hour watch when the attack hit. Kaylor and his squad mates got the news by radio that NVA troops had breached the perimeter. They soon were exchanging small arms fire with enemy troops as they moved northward through the draw.

Kaylor was focused on that area when he heard the distinctive pop of an enemy AK-47 rifle behind him, and a burst of bullets streaked by his head and ripped into his front parapet. Kaylor and other Marines swung around in astonishment and saw a lone NVA soldier, about ten feet away. By the time Kaylor fired, the enemy soldier had disappeared into the fog.

Friendly artillery rounds streaked over Kaylor's position, followed by one "short" round that exploded directly overhead. Kaylor heard the shrapnel as it whizzed by him and spattered the ground and sandbags around him. A dagger-shaped shard of metal missed Kaylor's left shoulder by a couple of inches as it speared a sandbag.[22]

• • •

After awakening to the roar of exploding mortars, Matt Walsh, a 3rd Platoon fire team leader from North Yonkers, New York, got his men in position and ready to repel the enemy attackers. When the word flashed down the western trench line that the enemy was inside the perimeter, Walsh turned two of his men inboard to make sure they didn't get hit from behind.

Almost immediately, Walsh got word to ready his fire team to help plug a breach in 1st Platoon's perimeter on the northern end of the hill. Walsh and the three men who rounded out his team set off along the western trench line toward the sound of the heavy gunfire and explosions. As they made their way forward, a flurry of mortar rounds hit the line around them. They dived to the bottom of the trench and waited for the barrage to taper off, then started moving forward again.

Walsh and his men finally reached the area that had been pounded by the North Vietnamese mortars and RPGs at the onset of the attack, and they began to carefully work their way closer to the breach. The trench was clogged with bodies and pieces of bodies. As he crawled through the carnage, Walsh spotted a foot with a North Vietnamese Army boot on it. "We got NVA bodies in the trench!" he yelled back to his men. "Watch yourself!"[23]

As Walsh and rifleman Michael Worth picked their way through the mass of bodies, Private Joe Roble, twenty, from Latrobe, Pennsylvania, accidentally bumped a dark form lying at the bottom of the trench. It was a human body, and it suddenly moved. Roble dropped down to see whether it was an American or Vietnamese and how badly the man was hurt. As he knelt, an NVA soldier raised an AK-47 rifle and pressed it against Roble's forehead. Before the enemy soldier could pull the trigger, the last wisp of life left his body, and the weapon fell to the ground. "Did you see that?" Roble gasped to his comrades.[24]

The four Marines moved even more warily now. The breach came into view, and they tossed a few grenades toward the torn wire to finish off any enemy soldiers still around. An hour or so earlier, North Vietnamese had overrun this area in a vicious close-quarters battle. Now, Matt Walsh and his fire team saw no sign of life.[25]

• • •

The sounds and smells of the battle washed over Dave McCall as he lay in the tall grass up the slope from Crater City. Although he was now losing blood from his mangled leg, his practice of tying his jungle utilities to the top of his boot "to keep critters out" had probably saved his life. When McCall had hopped away from Crater City, the movement of his body had set his boot spinning, which had tightened his pants against the stump of his leg like a pressure bandage.

McCall stared up at a sky lit by illumination rounds, exploding enemy shells, and outgoing friendly artillery. The air was heavy with the pungent smell of gunpowder and artillery propellant. Above the roar of battle, he heard the dying screams of one of his closest friends, Lance Corporal Louis Franklin Staples, twenty-one, from Chesapeake, Virginia, whose legs had been blown off by the mortar fire that hit Crater City.

There was movement in the grass, and two NVA soldiers crept up beside him, whispering to each other. One held a rocket launcher and the other an AK-47 rifle. McCall lay as still as he could, feigning death. An American grenade plopped into the grass and exploded, killing the North Vietnamese and spraying McCall with shrapnel. The unseen Marine tossed another grenade, and McCall heard it smack the ground close by. He had lost his helmet somewhere, and now he had just enough time to yank his flak jacket over his head as shrapnel shredded his back and shoulder.

The grass parted and McCall looked up to see the familiar face of his weapons platoon sergeant and another Marine he didn't recognize. McCall raised his hand and called out to the Americans. The barrels of two M-16 rifles snapped in his direction.

"Who is it?" the sergeant demanded.

"It's McCall."

"How bad are you hurt?"

"Pretty bad."

The weapons sergeant and the other Marine laid McCall in a poncho and began dragging him toward the eastern trench line. Every few seconds, they would stop and fire a few rounds, then continue on. Slipping in and out of consciousness, McCall periodically awakened and called out, "Be careful with my leg!"

They finally reached the company aid station, in a bomb crater on the south side of the hill. A corpsman kept McCall alert and talking as he tied off the wounded Marine's useless leg and started to work on his assorted shrapnel wounds.

• • •

Don Shanley and the 1st Platoon survivors scattered above Crater City stayed alive long enough for help to arrive. With a nose for action, Corporal Tom Eichler arrived with a box of grenades and started pelting the NVA attackers.

While Shanley continued to work the radio, Corporal Bill Johnson maintained effective fire on the nearby NVA. When there was a lull in the enemy fire, Johnson hopped out of the hole and crawled across the twenty-five-foot crater. A flare burst, and Shanley was shocked to see his corporal standing up on the southern lip of Crater City, blasting away with his M-16. "Get your ass down!" Shanley screamed.[26] Johnson made it back to the hole unscathed.

At 5:20 a.m., about one hour and twenty minutes after the battle began, the North Vietnamese fire tapered off. For the moment, at least, Breeding's Marines had beaten back the enemy attack.

• • •

In the gray dawn, Don Shanley surveyed the carnage and destruction around him. The full extent of his losses had yet to be revealed: seven of his young Marines were dead, most of them still lying in a bloody stretch along the northern perimeter that was clogged with the bodies of Americans and North Vietnamese, and had yet to be reclaimed. "Okay," Shanley announced to his motley force of 1st Platoon survivors and reinforcements from other Echo units, "We're going to counterattack."[27]

Clutching a .45-caliber pistol, Shanley got as many as a dozen men on line above Crater City. With Shanley at the center, the line surged toward the northern perimeter.[28] At the front lip of the bomb crater, Shanley saw a couple of dead NVA soldiers. He also found a dead Marine whom he didn't recognize. In another fighting hole, he discovered the body of one of the newest men to join his platoon, Alan Ray Smith, a nineteen-year-old private first class from the central Ohio village of Sunbury, dead on his forty-eighth day in Vietnam.

On the right flank, smoke from hot shrapnel rose around 3rd Platoon rifleman Jim Kaylor and his buddy Michael Lucas as they moved northeast toward the perimeter trench, firing their M-16 rifles. Kaylor reached the trench and jumped in. He was relieved to have some cover from the enemy fire. He spotted the body of a Marine sprawled over the parapet nearby and pulled the dead American back into the trench.

At the northernmost point, Shanley directed men into fighting holes and organized the removal of wounded Marines.

Kaylor heard a shout.

"There's one right in front of your hole!"

The Marines swung their rifles over the parapet and blasted an NVA soldier crawling in front of the trench line. Kaylor stared at the dead man for a long time, until his friend yanked him below the parapet. "You want to get your head blown off?"[29]

• • •

At almost the precise moment the attack on 861 Alpha got underway, the North Vietnamese launched two hours of rocket and mortar fire on the combat base. Hill 881 South also came under fire. It was a common tactic for the North Vietnamese, an attempt to prevent the American artillery from coming to the aid of the embattled outpost.

The question of whether the combat base or other outposts were about to face a ground attack remained open for the next two hours. At 4:14 a.m., when the seriousness of the attack on 861 Alpha had become apparent, Colonel Lownds issued a "red alert" for all forces at the combat base. At 5:01 a.m., the Marines of Lima Company, 3/26, at the western end of the base, reported seeing a green star cluster in the sky about 550 yards in front of their position—a common NVA signal launching a ground attack. But the minutes passed at the base without any sign of North Vietnamese assault troops.

• • •

At 6:16 a.m., NVA troops burst from cover and once again charged the northern perimeter of 861 Alpha. The attack lacked the ferocity of the earlier strike, and it was quickly broken. The elusive battalion of NVA reserves that Harry Baig had feared might doom 861 Alpha had never appeared. In all likelihood, it had been decimated by the American artillery fire and air strikes.

In the growing light, Captain Earle Breeding left his command post atop 861 Alpha and made his way down to the northern perimeter. He found Don Shanley and congratulated the young lieutenant on a job well done. Breeding noticed that Shanley had blood on his head and asked, "Are you hit?"

Shanley wasn't even aware that he had been struck by a small piece of shrapnel at some point in the fight. "I'm okay," Shanley said. "No big deal."[30]

Breeding and Shanley made the rounds of the 1st Platoon perimeter. Dave Norton was still lying in the trench line, waiting to be carried back over the hill to await medevac choppers. "Good job, Marine," Breeding said. "We kicked their ass."[31]

• • •

Around 9:30 a.m., the first medevac choppers threaded their way through the wispy fog down to the hill. Marines were standing by with stretchers laden with their wounded comrades when NVA mortar rounds began to hit nearby. Earle Breeding quickly nixed any thoughts of ditching the wounded and taking cover. "No one moves!" the Echo commander ordered.

The first CH-34 helicopter settled onto the grassy LZ, and the casualties were loaded inside. In less than five minutes, Echo's wounded arrived at Khe Sanh Combat Base. There, Navy surgeons and corpsmen checked vital signs and packed and bandaged assorted wounds.

Even with his badly mangled arm, Dave Norton was alert enough to recognize the corpsman cutting off his clothes and boots: they both had been patients at a Phu Bai hospital a few weeks earlier. Norton's wounds were rechecked and bandaged to control the bleeding, and then he was moved to a holding area to await a medevac flight out of Khe Sanh.

As he lay on a stretcher at Charlie Med, Norton suddenly realized that the wounded Marine next to him was Martin Rimson, the friend he had helped carry back up the trench line in the fight's opening minutes. The aspiring singer from Detroit had lived through the night, but he was no longer lucid. He was talking softly and fast, but Norton couldn't understand what he was saying.[32]

A big C-130 transport plane arrived and stretchers loaded with the Echo wounded were carried inside for the short hop back to the coast. During the flight, Dave McCall, the wounded Echo rocketman, spotted Martin Rimson on a nearby stretcher. "How's my buddy, the black kid over there?" McCall asked an attendant.

The crewman checked, then turned back to McCall. "Man, he's gone. He didn't make it."[33]

• • •

Navy surgeons in Da Nang were able to save rifleman Dave Norton's arm. There was nothing that could be done for rocketman Dave McCall's leg. During the five days McCall spent in a Phu Bai hospital, a Marine colonel visited, accompanied by a captain with a box of Purple Hearts. "Congratulations, Marine," the colonel said as he laid a Purple Heart on McCall's covers.

McCall was transferred to a hospital in Japan, where he underwent more surgery. The American grenade that may have saved his life by killing the two NVA soldiers standing over him cost him part of his stomach. His various wounds had left him in bad shape.

One day in mid-February, an orderly arrived with trays of food for McCall and the patient next to him. "Huh!" the orderly exclaimed. "Dave McCall and Dave Norton—two Daves in a row!"

McCall leaned over and took a long look at the bruised and swollen face of the Marine in the bed next to him. "Norton, is that you?"

The rifleman from North Carolina raised himself with great effort before slowly turning toward the familiar voice. A faint smile lit his face. "Hey, you made it!" Norton said.

"Hey," McCall said, "you made it, too!"

McCall soon drifted off to sleep, happier than he had been in days. When he awoke, Dave Norton was gone, headed back to the States for another year and a half of medical treatment. McCall would soon follow. Decades would pass before the two wounded Echo comrades would meet again at a Khe Sanh veterans reunion in the 1990s.[34]

• • •

Back on Hill 861 Alpha, the last of Echo's wounded were flown out on helicopters that had offloaded ammunition, medical supplies, seven replacement Marines, and a tall, graying man in clean jungle utilities with two cameras hanging around his neck.

David Douglas Duncan, a former Marine and famous war photographer, had just arrived in Khe Sanh the day before, and had talked his way onto a chopper headed to the scene of the latest action. He made his way to the northern end of the Echo outpost to bear witness to 1st Platoon's savage fight. Among the enduring images he captured during his few hours on the hill was one of Tom Eichler and mortarman Billy Drexel as they surveyed the torn bodies of North Vietnamese soldiers beyond the northern wire. Another photo captured a nineteen-year-old Echo sniper, Lance Corporal Albert Miranda, squeezing off a shot at an enemy soldier; alongside Miranda in the photograph were a fellow sniper, Lance Corporal David Burdwell, twenty, of Wichita Falls, Texas, and Lieutenant Alec Bodenweiser of Portland, Oregon.

Among the wide-eyed replacement Marines who scrambled out of the back of a CH-46 helicopter and into the hellish tableau was Mexican-born Jose Luis Reyes Jr., an eighteen-year-old from the Los Angeles suburb of San Fernando.[35] Making his way through the blood-stained trenches and fighting holes of Crater City, Reyes felt the fear rising in his throat. *What in the hell have I gotten myself into?* he thought.

Reyes made his way past blood-spattered, hollow-eyed survivors of the night's battle, desperate to find someone who would teach him "how to stay alive." He looked around and saw a Marine with the name "Pancho" scrawled across the back of his flak jacket. Back home, Reyes had grown up watching *The Cisco Kid*, a television series about the cowboy-era exploits of two good-hearted desperadoes, the Cisco Kid and his sidekick, Pancho. Reading that name on the back of a Marine momentarily broke the tension for Reyes, and he yelled, "Hey, Pancho!" The Marine turned around, took one look at the scrawny Hispanic kid in the fresh jungle utilities, and replied, "Hey, Cisco!" From that moment on, Reyes was Echo's "Cisco Kid."

• • •

In the battle for 861 Alpha, Earle Breeding had lost thirty-three men, killed and wounded about 20 percent of Echo's total strength. The 1st Platoon sustained a 75-percent casualty rate. Eight young Americans were dead: former Boy Scouts and altar boys, a husband and father-to-be. The oldest among them was twenty-one, the youngest, eighteen. On the forms they had filled out before arriving in Vietnam, six had identified themselves as "Caucasian," one as "Negro," and one "American Indian." There were two Buckeyes from Ohio, a pair of Texans, one each from New York, Pennsylvania, Michigan, and Virginia. And now, they were loaded aboard choppers to begin their final journey home.

• • •

For the defeated North Vietnamese, there were no medevac choppers or transport planes to whisk them to warm beds and well-staffed hospitals out of harm's way. The survivors melted back into the jungle to regroup; the wounded were laid on stretchers and carried back to underground field hospitals across the border in Laos, where they would face the constant threat of obliteration by American B-52 strikes.

The American victory at 861 Alpha was a setback for the North Vietnamese in their ambitious Khe Sanh campaign. But patience and persistence were prized virtues in the North Vietnamese Army. As Earle Breeding and the bloodied Marines of Echo Company braced for another round, NVA forces a few miles to the south were poised to strike America's most vulnerable outpost at Khe Sanh.

CHAPTER 10

"Tanks in the Wire"

For the US Special Forces at Lang Vei, four miles southwest of Khe Sanh Combat Base along Route 9, Tuesday, February 6, unfolded in what had become familiar fashion since the North Vietnamese campaign had gotten underway in late January. There had been a North Vietnamese mortar attack at midmorning, followed by a dusk artillery barrage that had hammered the camp with fifty rounds of 152-millimeter shells. Now, an hour before midnight, the sounds of unusual enemy movements suggested another long night ahead for the twenty-four American Green Berets and nearly five hundred indigenous troops dug in at the hilltop outpost.

The Green Berets had been America's pioneers in the area, driving up narrow Route 9 to hoist the Stars and Stripes over an old French bunker at Khe Sanh in 1962. The arrival of the Marines four years later had cramped the style of the freewheeling Army irregulars, so the Special Forces boys had built a new camp further west along Route 9, less than two miles from the Laotian border.

From their new base at the Bru village of Lang Vei, the Green Berets had organized the local tribesmen into armed Civilian Irregular Defense Group (CIDG) units and patrolled the surrounding hills and North Vietnamese infiltration routes. Their work dovetailed with the cross-border activities of the clandestine MACV "Studies and Observations Group" (MACV–SOG), which operated out of Forward Operating Base 3 at Khe Sanh.

Over the past year, the war had engulfed Lang Vei with a vengeance. On March 2, 1967, two US Air Force planes had mistaken the village for an enemy enclave and dropped napalm that killed 135 Bru men, women, and children and injured 213.[1] On May 4, during the Hill Fights around Khe Sanh, the Special Forces camp had been partially destroyed in a ground attack by the North Vietnamese.[2]

Captain Frank Willoughby had arrived in the late summer to oversee construction of a new Special Forces outpost several hundred yards west of Lang Vei village, even closer to the Laotian frontier. Under Willoughby's supervision, Navy Seabees had studded the dog-bone-shaped camp with concrete bunkers and a steel-reinforced underground Tactical Operations Center (TOC).

The North Vietnamese campaign against the Marine base at Khe Sanh had put Lang Vei in the path of the massing enemy forces, and the Green Berets had braced for an attack after the Laotian border outpost at Ban Houei Sane fell on the night of January 23–24. More than five hundred soldiers of the Royal Laotian Army's 33rd Elephant Battalion fled eastward along Route 9 to Lang Vei, bringing with them 2,200 dependents. The civilians moved into the village and the Laotian soldiers took over the old Special Forces camp.

The Laotian battalion commander and his throngs of refugees had proved to be a distraction for the Special Forces at Lang Vei, and after the morning mortar attack of February 6, a helicopter had dropped off a lanky Green Beret officer with a graying flattop haircut to lend a hand. As commander of Company C of the 5th Special Forces Group (Airborne), Lieutenant Colonel Daniel F. Schungel was Captain Willoughby's direct boss, and he had arrived to manage the high-maintenance Laotian battalion commander and the tense refugee situation.

Later in the day, when the twilight NVA artillery attack had ended around 7:00 p.m., the camp bustled with night defensive preparations by Lang Vei's welter of American and indigenous forces. At the top of the pyramid was Captain Willoughby's twelve-man unit, Special Forces Detachment A-101, which worked with fourteen Vietnamese Special Forces to oversee nearly three hundred indigenous troops broken into four CIDG militia companies. Additionally, Lang Vei's capabilities had been strengthened by a mobile strike force company—a

Mike force, in Special Forces parlance—comprising six Green Berets and about 160 Hre tribesmen.

As night fell over Lang Vei, a platoon of Hre fighters from Lieutenant Paul Longgrear's Mike force company exited the main gate along Route 9 and headed west toward a fortified observation post several hundred yards away. In command was Sergeant First Class Charles Lindewald Jr., a heavy-weapons specialist from La Porte, Indiana. The thirty-five-year-old Lindewald had arrived in Vietnam with one of the first Green Beret A-teams six years earlier, and as a symbol of his veteran status, he wore around his neck the tooth of a tiger he had killed in one of his early missions.

The Mike force column was nearing the forward outpost when Lindewald's indigenous troops sensed an ambush. They blasted away at the brush before bolting back to camp, warning of "beaucoup VC."[3] After Longgrear convinced the Hre to head back out, Lindewald had barely gotten the platoon settled in their forward post when once again they began hearing unusual noises in the darkness.

As the night wore on, strange sounds kept the forces in the main camp on edge as well. In the southeastern sector, the CIDG troops of the Vietnamese 104 Company reported vehicle engines in the direction of Lang Troai, an abandoned Bru border village to their southwest. Around 9:00 p.m., three trip flares erupted along the perimeter of the Mike force post, prompting Lindewald's soldiers to take potshots at suspicious shapes and shadows. The noise panicked the main camp's four CIDG companies, and they, too, fired into the darkness for several minutes before order was restored.

About 10:00 p.m., Sergeant Nickolas Fragos, a twenty-three-year-old Greek immigrant, had started his three-hour watch in the observation tower that jutted from the subterranean command bunker.[4] The first hour proved eventful when a trip flare erupted outside the 104 Company area, and Lang Vei's defenders once again stitched the darkness with gunfire before order was restored. Midnight arrived, and a few minutes into the new day, Wednesday, February 7, one of the Green Berets at the Mike force outpost west of camp radioed the command bunker: "I think I have VC below me."[5]

Another trip flare burst into brilliant light outside the 104 Company lines, and this time Nick Fragos could see it was no false alarm. Two

North Vietnamese soldiers were clearly visible as they snipped away at the perimeter wire, but not for long. The alert 104 troops dropped the pair with a flurry of gunfire.

A vehicle behind the fallen NVA soldiers switched on its spotlight and scanned the camp's defenses for a few seconds, then smashed through the wire. Fragos yelled into his radio handset, "They've got tanks!"[6]

•   •   •

In the minutes that followed, North Vietnamese infantry backed by eleven Soviet-made PT-76 light tanks hit the Special Forces camp from the south, east, and west. Simultaneously, the Mike force observation post west of Lang Vei came under heavy mortar and automatic-weapons fire, followed by tanks and infantry.

Inside the command bunker, Captain Willoughby radioed the Marines at Khe Sanh and requested artillery fire on preregistered targets along the camp's southern approach. He also called the Special Forces in Da Nang to get a forward air controller overhead and arrange for air strikes, gunships, and illumination. The Marines reacted skeptically to the report of tanks, and seventeen precious minutes ticked by before the Khe Sanh batteries began firing.[7]

Meanwhile, Lieutenant Colonel Schungel took charge of ground defenses around the command bunker. Working with Fragos and another Green Beret, Schungel began firing M-72 light anti-tank weapon (LAW) rounds at two NVA tanks that were wreaking havoc along the camp's southeastern perimeter. As Schungel sent LAW rounds down the slope, a boom reverberated from a nearby 106-millimeter recoilless rifle position. On his own, Sergeant First Class James William Holt of Hot Springs, Arkansas, the thirty-two-year-old chief medic of A-101, began pumping out deadly fire. A thirty-seven-pound armor-piercing shell smashed into a tank with a burst of flames. Holt was joined by Staff Sergeant Peter Tiroch, and he found his mark with another round. Fire and smoke boiled from the crippled tank.

A third tank churned up the dirt track from Lang Troai, wheeled around the two burning carcasses, and blasted away at the bunkers defended by 104 Company fighters. Holt disabled this adversary as well, then finished it off with his final armor-piercing round. The Green Beret medic headed off to the ammo bunker to retrieve more armor-piercing shells and was never seen again.

Two more NVA tanks pulled up and began pounding the 104 Company bunkers and trenches. Forty-five minutes into the fight, North Vietnamese tanks and infantry overran the camp's southeastern sector.[8]

• • •

When the attack began, Lieutenant Paul Longgrear, twenty-four, was asleep in his bunker near the Tactical Operations Center. The young Mike force commander roused Sergeant John Early, then pumped out four or five illumination rounds from an 81-millimeter mortar before switching to high-explosive projectiles, which he blindly fired toward the likely enemy staging points to the south and west.[9]

Longgrear cut a Hollywood casting director's image of a Green Beret: six foot one, square-jawed, athletic, cocky. Less obvious was the rootless, restless rebel that lay within. He had lived much of his pre-Army life along America's impoverished back roads, from his birth in the struggling southern Illinois river town of Cairo in 1943, to his hardscrabble childhood in southeast Missouri and northeast Arkansas. His father had abandoned his mother the day Paul was born, and the boy grew up rudderless, "trying to figure out who I was and how to become a man."[10]

By high school, Longgrear had embraced hell raising as his life's calling. He got his first fake ID when he was fifteen, and while other teenagers in Jonesboro, Arkansas, were attending church socials and school dances, Longgrear was sneaking into juke joints, dancing and drinking. From his sophomore year of high school on, he lived by himself. He was a star football player, until he clashed with the coach and got kicked off the team.

Longgrear spent the next five years drifting from Arkansas to Oregon to California, working as hard as he played—making glass, building roads, bending iron, harvesting potatoes. He dabbled at college, but his rebellious ways would always get him into trouble and he'd hit the road again. He was working construction in West Sacramento, California, hanging out with his friends at the local Hell's Angels motorcycle club, when his draft notice arrived.

From his first day in the Army in June 1965, Longgrear felt at home. He rose to sergeant, then earned a coveted slot in Officer Candidate School. He taught infantry tactics at Fort Benning, Georgia, and got married at the end of 1966. But his restless streak won out, and he completed Special Forces training and left for Vietnam in October 1967.

Now, as Longgrear pumped mortar rounds skyward to slow the North Vietnamese attack, a familiar figure darted into the pit. "Uh, what's up, doc?"[11] Staff Sergeant Dennis Thompson, a twenty-five-year-old from Portland, Oregon, said in his best Bugs Bunny voice.

"In case you haven't noticed, we're under attack," Longgrear nonchalantly replied.

"Oh, I wondered what all the noise was!" Thompson joked, as he joined Sergeant Early in preparing mortar rounds for the jaunty Mike force lieutenant.

They were still cranking out rounds a few minutes later when an NVA tank clanked over the crest of the hill, no more than one hundred feet away. Longgrear hoisted an anti-tank weapon and squeezed the trigger, but nothing happened. He tried another LAW, and it, too, misfired. He fired a third. The round deflected off the tank's armored hull and disappeared into the night sky; the tank had been too close for the round to arm and explode.

Longgrear hadn't destroyed the enemy tank, but he had gotten its attention. With a chilling mechanical whine, the gun turned toward the Green Berets. "Hey guys," Longgrear shouted, "I think it's time we got out of here."[12] The three Americans scrambled out of the mortar pit before the tank could fire. They would carry on the fight elsewhere.

• • •

NVA tanks backed by infantry now pressured Lang Vei's defenses from all sides. Small-arms fire rose in a roar, punctuated by the explosions of tank rounds, LAWs, mortars, satchel charges, and grenades. In the east, the Bru fighters of the 101 Company battled enemy tanks and infantry to their front and rear. In the west, the 102 and 103 Companies were in the process of being overrun by tanks and ground troops.

The Mike force observation point, along Route 9 west of the camp, had been quickly surrounded in the battle's opening minutes. Sergeant

First Class Kenneth Hanna provided a grim situation report by radio: Charles Lindewald had been gravely wounded in the chest by automatic-weapons fire, and the encircled outpost was "under heavy attack." And then, as the outpost was overrun, the radio line went dead.[13] Inside the Lang Vei command bunker, Captain Frank Willoughby's radios crackled with tank sightings: one coming up Route 9 from the east, three from the west, two in the drop zone between the old and new camps.

As the attack entered its second hour, friendly artillery and air strikes had barely slowed the attack. Casualties were mounting, and the perimeters collapsing. By 2:00 a.m., only the inner compound around the Tactical Operations Center bunker was still holding out.

• • •

After his brush with the enemy PT-76 gunner, Paul Longgrear had headed to the command bunker to join several tank-killing teams organized by Lieutenant Colonel Schungel. The Americans concentrated fire on a tank grinding up the hill from the southeastern sector, and LAW rounds exploded against the welded-steel hull with a "great shower of orange [sparks]."[14] The tank finally lurched to a halt, and three crew members armed with AK-47s crawled out. Schungel and a South Vietnamese lieutenant killed them with grenades and small-arms fire.

When they had exhausted their supply of anti-tank weapons, Schungel and his handful of Green Berets prepared to make a last stand around the command bunker. Longgrear was watching the eastern approach when four NVA sappers draped with satchel charges came into view about thirty yards to his front. Longgrear dropped the NVA soldiers with a burst of seven or eight rounds from his CAR-15 rifle. The Mike force medic, Specialist Fourth Class James L. Moreland, tossed a grenade into the bodies to make sure they were dead.

The grenade flash caught the attention of a nearby tank, and it began moving toward the Green Berets. As the tank approached the TOC, its main gun slowly turned toward the Americans. Longgrear ducked into the bunker entrance and was on his way down the stairs when a tank round knocked him to the floor.

At point-blank range, the North Vietnamese tank had fired a shell from its 76-millimeter gun at Schungel and a handful of other men crouched behind a barrier of weighted barrels. The barrier had saved their lives, but the men had sustained assorted injuries. First Lieutenant Miles Wilkins had been crushed by the barrels; Schungel had been concussed by the blast and tossed several feet; and Specialist Fourth Class William McMurray had been temporarily blinded by the explosion, and his hands were mangled.

As the injured Americans huddled outside the TOC entrance, the tank destroyed the bunker's steel observation tower with a blast from its main gun. A LAW round fired from up the hill smashed into the tank at almost the same instant that Schungel tossed two hand grenades. The tank's hatch popped open and flames billowed out, but no crew members emerged.

Schungel dragged the injured McMurray behind some sandbags, and then he and Wilkins hobbled away from the TOC, toward Route 9. Near the northern perimeter, they slipped inside the wooden structure that served as the main living quarters for the A-101 team—and waited for daylight.[15]

• • •

On the north side of the camp, four Green Berets led by Sergeant First Class William Craig had formed one of the final pockets of resistance. A savvy, forty-one-year-old Korean War veteran and the senior enlisted man in Detachment A-101, Pappy Craig had become the vital eyes-on-the-ground for an air controller circling overhead, helping direct air strikes on hotspots and relay Lang Vei's requests for artillery missions and illumination.

As the minutes passed, Craig's transmissions grew more desperate. In his final broadcast at 2:45 a.m., he called in an air strike on a tank sitting on top of the TOC. Craig signed off and prepared to exit the camp with four Green Berets and forty Bru fighters.

The breakout was underway when machine-gun fire from the east blocked Craig and Sergeant Peter Tiroch in their tracks. They waited for the overhead illumination to fade, then sprinted across Route 9 and settled into a bamboo thicket about one hundred yards beyond the perimeter. When a friendly air strike hit close enough to spray them with shrapnel, the two Americans put another hundred yards between them and the camp. Satisfied they were out of the line of fire, they hid in a dry creek bed to wait out the night.[16]

• • •

At 1:50 a.m., as dire reports from Lang Vei worked their way up the various chains of command within the Marines, Special Forces, and MACV headquarters in Saigon, Major General Rathvon Tompkins, commander of the 3rd Marine Division at Dong Ha, ordered his men at Khe Sanh to break out new anti-personnel "controlled fragmentation munitions" (COFRAM) that had been rushed to the base for use against an NVA ground assault. But the word came back from the Special Forces at Lang Vei: hold off on the artillery to allow air strikes to continue.[17]

In the critical hour that followed, Tompkins continued to press for the use of the "firecracker" rounds. Speaking by phone with Captain Harry Baig in the 26th Marines command bunker at Khe Sanh, Tompkins asked that his recommendation be conveyed to the Special Forces commander at Lang Vei: halt the air strikes long enough to allow the anti-personnel "firecracker" rounds to be fired on the embattled camp, and then resume the air coverage.

At 2:45 a.m., a Lang Vei radio transmission was relayed to General Tompkins. "All troops above ground are enemy. Request arty and air. Tanks on hill south and southwest of us."[18]

About fifteen minutes later, the first "firecracker" rounds fired by gunners at Khe Sanh Combat Base exploded over the Lang Vei Special Forces camp. Twenty-eight rounds of the anti-personnel munitions were fired during a five-minute period, followed by five minutes of high-explosive and variable-timed rounds designed to detonate about twenty to thirty feet above the ground. The artillery was halted, and air strikes on the Lang Vei perimeter resumed.

At 3:15 a.m., Khe Sanh informed General Tompkins that communications with Lang Vei had been lost again.

• • •

Only one island of resistance remained inside the Special Forces camp: the underground Tactical Operations Center, a reinforced concrete bunker measuring thirty-nine by twenty-five feet and located in the heart of the outpost. Inside the bunker were eight Americans: Captain Frank Willoughby, Lieutenant Paul Longgrear, Sergeant Nickolas Fragos, radio operators Franklin Dooms and Emanuel Phillips, Sergeant John Early, Sergeant Arthur Brooks, and Mike force medic James Moreland. There were also about fifteen South Vietnamese, including Lieutenant Pham Duy Quan, commander of the CIDG militia forces at Lang Vei.

The tank that had nearly killed the Green Berets outside the TOC had also destroyed the bunker's radio tower and generator. In the initial scramble to secure the bunker, Early and Moreland had been wounded when they had tried to retrieve an M-60 machine gun from the observation tower. Now, as the sounds of battle faded, the silence inside the bunker was broken only by occasional whispers, hissing radios, and the groans of the badly injured John Early.

Sometime after 3:00 a.m., North Vietnamese soldiers attacked the TOC by dropping fragmentation and tear-gas grenades, satchel charges, and incendiaries down the main entrance, observation tower, and air shafts along the bunker's opposing walls. As the bunker occupants wept and gagged from the noxious fumes, they heard shouts from outside. A voice called out in Vietnamese, warning that the bunker was about to be blown up and ordering the occupants to come out.[19] Before the Americans could react, the South Vietnamese had scrambled to the surface and surrendered. Shortly afterward, the Americans heard shots fired outside the TOC but never learned the fate of their South Vietnamese comrades.

As dawn approached, a massive explosion ripped the north wall of the TOC. The North Vietnamese had dug a shaft beside the air vent and detonated explosives, tearing a sizable hole in the bunker wall. The blast battered the Green Berets with chunks of concrete and hurled them around the room. All but Sergeant Fragos were knocked unconscious.

When Paul Longgrear awakened, North Vietnamese soldiers were swarming around the blast hole and other openings, "throwing hand grenades, pouring gasoline down the breathing ports and setting the place on fire."[20] Longgrear and Fragos scrambled around the bunker to revive injured comrades and prepare the room for a last stand.

Already bleeding from cuts to his head and wrist, Longgrear was wounded again by a grenade that drove a metal shard into his ankle. Another grenade exploded about eighteen inches from Captain Willoughby.

Hot metal pierced his torso, but he saved himself by shielding his upper body with a flak jacket.

As the bunker filled with choking smoke and toxic fumes, the Green Berets sought cover behind pillars and debris and shielded themselves with flak jackets, chairs, and tables. Six of the eight Americans were now wounded. Unable to see or breathe, Longgrear crawled into a corner, covered his mouth, and prepared to die. Radio operator Franklin Dooms managed to raise a forward air controller flying overhead. "They're killing us!" he yelled. "Somebody help us!"[21]

• • •

Circling more than 1,000 feet above Lang Vei, Covey 688 sat in the cockpit of his twin-tailed Cessna O-2A aircraft and listened to the dying pleas of the eight Green Berets. The forward air controller had joined the fight to save Lang Vei about two hours earlier, after a short flight across Laos from his base in Ubon, Thailand. Sporadic radio transmissions had revealed that there were several Green Berets in the command bunker and three others at the old camp, but not much else was known.

Around 7:45 a.m., a pair of Navy A-1H Skyraiders had arrived from the carrier USS *Coral Sea* and checked in with Covey 688. The lead A-1 pilot, Lieutenant Commander Rosario "Zip" Rausa, knew the tricky terrain and the bad weather in this area all too well. A native of Utica, in upstate New York, the thirty-two-year-old Rausa had lettered in football, basketball, and baseball at Middlebury College in Vermont while earning an English degree in 1957. He had enlisted in the Navy and earned his wings two years later.[22] He was already on his second combat deployment to Vietnam, well on his way to 150 missions and 498 carrier landings.

Rausa and his wingman, Lieutenant Larry Gardiner, were part of Navy Attack Squadron (VA) 25, the last such unit still flying Douglas A-1 Skyraiders—squat, single-engine, propeller-driven fighters. The Spad, as it was dubbed, after the famed World War I fighter, could fly "low and slow" while carrying up to 8,000 pounds of ordnance, and it could take considerable battle damage and remain airborne. Right now, Zip Rausa, Larry Gardiner, and their lumbering Skyraiders were the last hope of the Green Berets in the TOC—if only the controller could somehow get the A-1 pilots beneath the clouds and into the fight.

As Covey 688 orbited a fishbowl-shaped pocket in the clouds with the A-1s in tow, another forward air controller, Covey 252—twenty-eight-year-old Air Force captain Charles "Toby" Rushforth III—arrived and began circling nearby in his O-2A. Nearly seven years earlier, when he was graduating from the University of Connecticut with a degree in international relations, Rushforth could scarcely have imagined circling a remote South Vietnamese battlefield in a tiny Cessna. But he had emerged from college at a time when President John F. Kennedy was challenging Americans to serve their country, and Rushforth responded by joining the Air Force. He earned his wings in 1963 and started flying big KC-135 tankers. He had finished a stateside tour in 1967 and considered leaving the Air Force to become a civilian airline pilot, as many of his peers were doing. But America was fighting in Vietnam, and Rushforth decided he needed to see "what wars are like."[23]

Rushforth volunteered for Vietnam and was trained as a forward air controller and assigned to the 20th Tactical Air Support Squadron in Da Nang. He had logged several dozen missions north of the DMZ by January, when he was assigned to support a new operation known as Niagara, to help American ground forces thwart a major North Vietnamese move against the Marine combat base at Khe Sanh.

When Rushforth had taken off from Da Nang on this morning at 7:10 a.m., he had been briefed about the trouble at Lang Vei. He knew that tanks and North Vietnamese troops had penetrated the compound and a number of Green Berets were trapped in the TOC, but little else. Now, circling above the camp, Rushforth quickly gathered just how critical the situation was. He listened as a Green Beret radioed from the TOC, "Get these guys off us, or it's over."[24]

As they orbited around their pocket in the clouds, Covey 688 and Rushforth searched for an opening. They both spotted the dark patch that indicated thinning clouds and a glimpse of the jungle below. "I'm going down and check it out," said Covey 688.

Rushforth watched the O-2A disappear into a "sucker hole," knowing full well the pilot could just as easily fly into the side of a hill on the other end as find clear skies. A minute or so later, Covey 688 popped back up into the fishbowl. He had found some navigable sky over Lang Vei, beneath five hundred feet. "I think there's enough room to work in here," he told the A-1 pilots. "Are you willing to give it a try?"

Under existing air wing regulations for such sketchy flight conditions, Rausa was supposed to abort the mission. But there were Americans beneath those clouds, and he knew they were probably going to die if he didn't help them. "Let's do it," Rausa said.[25]

Another desperate appeal from the Lang Vei command bunker crackled from the radio. "If you can't do anything now," said radio operator Franklin Dooms, "we're finished."[26]

Covey 688 headed down into the hole once again, this time with Zip Rausa close behind, followed by Larry Gardiner. Seconds later, Rausa broke free of the clouds above the smoldering ruins of Camp Lang Vei. He made one pass, unleashing 250-and 500-pound bombs on the NVA soldiers swarming the TOC. Gardiner followed suit. Skimming the treetops, the pilots came around for another pass, and then another, dropping their remaining bombs and scouring the camp with automatic cannon fire. Dead and dying enemy soldiers soon littered the ground around the bunker.

Inside the TOC, the Green Berets could hear the sounds of aircraft, muffled explosions, and screams. The North Vietnamese attack ended abruptly.[27]

By the time Rausa and Gardiner exhausted their ordnance, the skies over Lang Vei were clearing. Four more Skyraiders from AV-25 arrived, loaded with anti-personnel cluster bombs and napalm, and controller Toby Rushforth directed them to their targets in the camp below. The four Skyraiders completed their runs, and a pair of A-1s from the 1st Air Commando Squadron based in Nakhon Phanom, Thailand, swooped in to strafe and bomb the hilltop around the TOC and the camp's western half.

Around midmorning, Rushforth handed off to the next forward air controller and headed back to Da Nang. More A-1s were on their way from the *Coral Sea*. In all, twelve AV-25 pilots would fly sorties in support of Lang Vei during the day. For the time being, they had saved the lives of the eight Green Berets trapped inside the TOC.[28]

• • •

Daybreak had heralded the beginning of another effort to save the embattled Green Berets in the TOC, this one launched by three Special Forces medics overseeing the Laotian army troops at the old Lang Vei camp.

Sergeant First Class Eugene Ashley Jr. boasted more military experience than his two young colleagues combined, having spent sixteen of his thirty-six years in the Army. Born in Wilmington, North Carolina, Ashley had grown up in New York City. He enlisted in the Army in 1950 and after seeing action in the Korean War, decided to make military service his career. After a long infantry stint, he qualified for Airborne and entered the Special Forces.

When the attack on Lang Vei began, Ashley had dispatched one of his young comrades, Sergeant Rich Allen, to get the Laotian troops to fire illumination rounds in support of the embattled Special Forces camp to their west. The twenty-one-year-old Allen ran to the quarters of the colonel in command of the Laotian battalion to present the request. The colonel was entertaining a female companion and rebuffed the young Green Beret, so Allen whipped out his .45-caliber pistol and stuck it under the Laotian commander's chin. The colonel ordered his mortars to deliver the illumination for Camp Lang Vei.[29]

As the battle raged to their west, Sergeant Ashley helped coordinate the delivery of illumination, air strikes, and artillery support for friendly forces. When radio contact with the TOC was lost, he took the lead in coordinating air strikes against the swarming NVA soldiers. At first light, Ashley prepared to launch an effort to rescue the men trapped in the command bunker.

Around 7:00 a.m., Sergeant Ashley and Green Berets Rich Allen and Joel Johnson led a column of about sixty Laotian volunteers up Route 9 toward the Special Forces camp. The relief force was nearing the camp's perimeter when A-1 pilots Zip Rausa and Larry Gardiner pulled off their life-saving strikes. When the Skyraiders had finished, Ashley organized his two young Green Berets and their motley force of Laotian and indigenous fighters in a ragged skirmish line.

The assault force pushed westward through the 101 Company sector, past torn bodies and scorched and shattered bunkers. North Vietnamese machine guns near the TOC opened up, and the indigenous fighters broke and ran. The Green Berets fell back to the camp's eastern entrance.

Ashley coordinated more air strikes, then launched a second assault. Green Berets Pappy Craig and Peter Tiroch had emerged from hiding to join the latest attack, and the assault force surged up the hill toward the TOC until fierce NVA fire forced the attackers to the ground.

Rich Allen had sought cover behind a low dirt mound, a few feet below a bunker occupied by an NVA machine-gun team. He rolled from his hiding place and fired a three-round burst at the bunker from a Browning Automatic Rifle he had taken from a dead soldier, then rolled back behind the mound. Twice more Allen performed the maneuver. Machine-gun rounds began to kick up around his hiding place, followed by grenades. Allen clutched the rifle to his chest, then log-rolled down the hill as grenades exploded behind him. He dropped into a trench and was still plotting his next move when a grenade bounced down the hill and stopped an arm's length from his body. Allen braced for the explosion, but the grenade was a dud. He scrambled down the trench and found the remnants of the broken assault force.[30]

After more air strikes, Sergeant Ashley mounted a third assault, this one aided by 60-millimeter mortar fire laid down by Green Berets Peter Tiroch and Joel Johnson. Once again they were driven back. A fourth attempt met with the same result.

Around 10:50 a.m., Ashley radioed the TOC and asked the trapped Green Berets to hit the NVA from behind as the relief force approached. A fifth assault got underway. Ashley and his men had fought their way to within about thirty yards of the TOC when Rich Allen dropped down to change magazines. A burst of automatic rifle fire flashed past him and slammed into Sergeant Ashley's midsection, piercing Ashley's chest and exiting his back. Allen slapped a battle dressing on the entry wound, then hoisted his 220-pound comrade over his shoulder and started down the hill. He ran until his legs gave out, then dragged and carried the wounded Green Beret on a makeshift litter.

When they reached Route 9, Allen and others laid Sergeant Ashley in a Jeep, and they roared down the hill to the old camp. They had just skidded to a halt when an incoming round hit nearby. A piece of shrapnel ended the life of Sergeant First Class Eugene Ashley Jr.—the only recipient of a Medal of Honor during the 1968 fighting at Khe Sanh.

Rich Allen survived the battle unscathed.

• • •

After escaping the NVA tanks outside the command bunker, Lieutenant Colonel Schungel and Lieutenant Wilkins had found sanctuary in the A-101 team house along the camp's northern perimeter. Around 3:30 a.m., Schungel killed five NVA as they approached the house, but an explosion had wounded Schungel in the right leg, so the two Americans crept away and crawled beneath the camp dispensary further to the west.

Around 9:30 a.m., Wilkins was slightly wounded in the leg during a strafing run by friendly aircraft. The two Americans hobbled across Route 9 and headed east. They survived another strafing by US aircraft, and Schungel was wounded again by North Vietnamese fire, but they made it safely to the old camp.

• • •

As the desperate struggle for Lang Vei played out, acrimony between the Marines and Special Forces at Khe Sanh came to a head. Three weeks earlier, General William Westmoreland had asked the Marines to confirm a contingency plan that called for Khe Sanh Combat Base to support the Special Forces at Lang Vei with artillery and ground troops in an attack. In fact, the Marine command at Khe Sanh had concluded weeks earlier that it would be foolhardy—if not suicidal—to attempt an overland relief of Lang Vei.[31] For reasons that have never been explained, the Marines failed to warn Westmoreland of their concerns. Instead, the American commander was assured that the Lang Vei contingency plan would be honored.

In the early morning hours of February 7, facing a widening attack by North Vietnamese tanks and troops, Captain Willoughby had radioed the Marines at Khe Sanh to ask for execution of the relief plan. Separately, the commander of Special Forces in Vietnam, Colonel Jonathan Frederic Ladd, had awakened General Westmoreland in Saigon to request assistance for Lang Vei. When Westmoreland informed Ladd that the decision remained in the hands of the Marine command in I Corps, the Special Forces commander on his own began organizing a force to save Lang Vei.[32]

Around 3:40 a.m., the air center at Khe Sanh Combat base reported that a C-130 was inbound with about one hundred Special Forces personnel aboard. Colonel Lownds alerted the 3rd Marine Division commander, Major General Rathvon Tompkins, who lodged a complaint with his boss. The III Marine Amphibious Force commander, Lieutenant General Robert E. Cushman Jr., ordered the plane's diversion from Khe Sanh around 4:00 a.m.[33]

At almost that exact moment, a conference call got underway in I Corps, and one of Ladd's officers formally asked III Marine Amphibious Force headquarters to dispatch a relief force to Lang Vei at first light. General Tompkins rejected the request, declaring that such an attempt by the Marines at this critical moment, when the combat base itself might be facing an imminent attack, "would be a lot of foolishness." General Cushman, and then General Westmoreland, supported the decision.[34]

Shortly after daybreak, having twice deferred Colonel Ladd's request for the relief of Lang Vei, Westmoreland flew to Da Nang for a previously scheduled conference with Marine and Army commanders in I Corps. When Westmoreland once again parried the question of a Lang Vei relief mission, Ladd phoned Westmoreland's deputy. General Creighton Abrams gave Ladd the green light to work with the Marine air commander in I Corps to devise a rescue plan using Special Forces personnel.[35]

At the FOB-3 compound at Khe Sanh Combat Base, word was passed to twenty-seven-year-old Army major George Quamo to find fifty volunteers to rescue their comrades at Lang Vei. "Look, it's a suicide mission," Quamo told his senior noncommissioned officer (NCO), Sergeant Skip Minnicks. "I don't think we're coming back, but I can't leave those fellows over there."[36]

• • •

Through the morning, and into the early afternoon, the trapped Green Berets were in sporadic radio contact with Sergeant Ashley, and they had listened with rising hopes as he mounted successive rescue attempts. After the fifth assault, Colonel Schungel broke the bad news in a radio transmission from the old camp: Sergeant Ashley was dead, the Marines weren't coming, and there would be no further attempts to retake the hill until the following day.

In the TOC, Paul Longgrear "went crazy." He screamed and swore and cursed those responsible for their abandonment. "Look," the Mike force commander announced, "you people can stay down here and die like worms if you want, but I'm going up and die like a man."[37]

Captain Willoughby announced, "If he goes, we all go." He radioed Schungel, "Sir, we're coming out."

A plan was devised: An incoming flight of A-1 aircraft would make three passes, bombing and strafing the bunkers occupied by NVA troops. The Green Berets would then emerge from the TOC and escape to the northeast as the aircraft made simulated passes to freeze the NVA in place.

About 2:30 p.m. the Skyraiders began to pound the camp with bombs, napalm, and 20-millimeter cannon. The Green Berets prepared to make their break. Medic James Moreland, delirious from his head wound, reacted violently when Longgrear tried to get him on his feet. After huddled discussion, the Green Berets made the hard decision to leave Moreland behind.

Longgrear picked his way up the command bunker's ruined staircase as the Skyraiders completed their third pass, emerging into daylight as the aircraft began their decoy runs. The other Green Berets exited the bunker and began hobbling toward the camp's northeastern corner.

Trailing behind his comrades as the rear guard, Longgrear spotted a North Vietnamese machine-gun nest to his right and charged the position, firing a burst from his CAR-15 as he ran. As the NVA gun team crumpled to the ground, Longgrear's rifle jammed and his injured ankle gave way. He flipped through the air and fell on his back. It appeared to his colleagues that he had been gunned down by the North Vietnamese.

As he lay on the ground, Longgrear prepared to shoot himself rather than be captured. His wife's voice played in his head, repeating her parting words when he had left for Vietnam: "I'll be praying for you." An A-1 Skyraider roared overhead, and Longgrear made fleeting eye contact with the pilot. The pilot dipped his wings in encouragement. The gesture energized the wounded Green Beret, and he heard his wife's voice again, "I'll be praying for you," and then another voice—God himself, as

Longgrear tells it. The hell-raising Green Beret resolved that he would not die on this hill.

Longgrear dragged himself to his feet and limped after his comrades. He cleared the crest of the hill, then started down toward the gate along Route 9, where the other Americans were about to roar away in a Jeep. They spotted Longgrear and shouted encouragement. He reached the vehicle and dived inside. The driver, a brave Vietnamese Special Forces comrade, navigated the enemy-infested stretch of road to the old camp and rolled to a stop, safely delivering the seven Green Berets who had made it out of the command bunker.[38]

• • •

North Vietnamese mortars and automatic weapons were pounding the old Lang Vei camp around 5:00 p.m. when the helicopter-borne rescue force took off from the FOB-3 compound at Khe Sanh Combat Base. Major George Quamo had pulled together about a dozen US Special Forces operators and forty indigenous Montagnard fighters for the operation. As A-1 Skyraiders and jet fighters prowled overhead, the armada of Army and Marine gunships and transport helicopters circled the old Lang Vei camp.

An Army UH-1D transport chopper dropped from the formation and settled onto the old camp's shell-torn airstrip, amid a swarm of panicked Laotian soldiers. Big Paul Longgrear—his head bandaged and body rejuvenated by intravenous fluids—waded into the mob and enforced order with menacing glares and the butt of his jammed CAR-15. A path was cleared and the most seriously injured Green Berets were helped aboard the Huey, which thundered away toward Khe Sanh.

Four Marine CH-46 helicopters landed and disgorged Major Quamo's security force, which quickly fanned out to safeguard the landing zone. The remaining Americans boarded one CH-46, while the other helicopters were filled with the camp's ranking Vietnamese officers and NCOs, interpreters, and seriously injured indigenous fighters. The Marine helicopters clattered off into the twilight.

Up the hill at Camp Lang Vei, First Lieutenant Thomas E. Todd, an engineering officer from Da Nang, had spent a harrowing night dodging NVA tanks and troops before hiding in the emergency medical bunker.

In the late afternoon he had made his way to the TOC, hoping to find other Americans, but they were gone. Amid the bomb-shattered ruins, Todd saw the body of one Green Beret: the mortally injured medic, Specialist Fourth Class James Moreland. As Todd turned away from the bunker, he glimpsed a helicopter over the old camp. He sprinted down the hill, arriving just in time to board one of the last choppers that had returned to extract Major Quamo's relief force.[39]

Other live Americans remained on the ground at Lang Vei. Dennis Thompson, the wisecracking Mike force member, had already been captured once by the North Vietnamese and had escaped over the past hours. He made radio contact with a forward air controller as the evacuation was underway and tried to make it to the old camp's airstrip. When the choppers took off, the forward air controller was preparing to land his Cessna on the airstrip to rescue Thompson. But NVA troops arrived and chased the Green Beret back into the brush. Shortly afterward, Thompson was captured a second time.

Two other Green Berets had been taken prisoner by the North Vietnamese: Sergeant First Class Harvey Brande of Long Beach, California; and Specialist Fourth Class William McMurray of Scottsdale, Arizona. Over the coming days, the three captive Green Berets would be marched up the Ho Chi Minh Trail into North Vietnam. They would remain there until their release with other American prisoners of war in 1973.

• • •

The Green Berets and their indigenous troops had fought bravely at Lang Vei, but in the end they could not overcome the North Vietnamese armor. Fourteen of the twenty-four Green Berets at Lang Vei were rescued; all but one—Sergeant Rich Allen—had been wounded. In addition to a Medal of Honor posthumously awarded to Sergeant Eugene Ashley, the Distinguished Service Cross was bestowed on Lieutenant Colonel Daniel Schungel and Major George Quamo, leader of the rescue effort. Nineteen Silver Stars and three Bronze Stars were also awarded to the Green Berets who defended Lang Vei.

America's indigenous allies at Lang Vei also paid dearly: 209 of the nearly 500 South Vietnamese and tribal fighters who began the battle were listed as killed or missing, and another 75 were wounded. Over the next twenty-four hours, some 160 Montagnard soldiers who had been left at the old camp evaded NVA forces as they made their way overland to Khe Sanh Combat Base. The Marines feared there were Viet Cong or NVA infiltrators among them and disarmed the men, refusing to allow them inside the base. The Green Berets at FOB-3 were furious, and they arranged to fly their allies to Da Nang.

The North Vietnamese had attacked Lang Vei with eleven Soviet-made PT-76 tanks, the first Communist use of armor against the Americans in South Vietnam. US ground and air forces destroyed seven of the tanks during the battle and the following day. Estimates of NVA losses at Lang Vei range between 80 and 250 killed and nearly 200 wounded.[40]

● ● ●

At Lang Vei, the North Vietnamese Army had scored its biggest victory thus far in the Khe Sanh campaign. Its forces now controlled Route 9 from the Ho Chi Minh Trail in Laos to the foothills east of the Marine base.

Much later, there would be Marines such as Captain Bill Dabney, commander of US forces on 881 South, who would claim that the North Vietnamese had blundered by seizing Lang Vei, clearing the way for unrestricted B-52 strikes along the Route 9 corridor west of the combat base.[41] But such tactical nuances mattered little to the Americans on the ground as night fell over Khe Sanh Combat base and its outposts on February 7.

Despite their bravery, American forces had been defeated, and in stunning fashion. In command posts and communication bunkers around the Khe Sanh area, Marines had huddled around radios to follow the battle at Lang Vei—the frantic shouts of "tanks in the wire," the desperate pleas for help, and the chilling sounds of an American outpost being overrun. Now, the Marines at Khe Sanh Combat Base listened intently for the sound of enemy tanks clanking down Route 9, and they anxiously awaited the waves of North Vietnamese ground troops that seemed certain to follow.

CHAPTER 11

The Battle of Hill 64

In the foggy predawn of Thursday, February 8, Second Lieutenant Terence Roach Jr. prowled the tiny hilltop outpost that was home to the sixty-odd men of Alpha Company's reinforced 1st Platoon, a unit of the 1st Battalion, 9th Marine Regiment—the hard-luck Walking Dead. "Stay alert," he exhorted his Marines as they peered into the darkness from their football-shaped perimeter, just over a mile west of Khe Sanh Combat Base. "We've got movement all around."[1]

For a young Marine Corps officer, just starting day sixty-two in his Vietnam tour, Roach was swimming in deep waters. As if commanding a Marine rifle platoon in I Corps at this critical juncture in the war wasn't perilous enough, Roach and his men were stuck on an exposed knob, more than 500 yards from the nearest friendly troops, between the two North Vietnamese Army divisions closing on Khe Sanh Combat Base. Only a day earlier, their neighbors some three miles to the southwest—the US Special Forces at Lang Vei—had been overrun. And now, Terry Roach and his men were hearing movement all around them in the dark.

Colonel John Mitchell had envisioned the Alpha-1 outpost as an early warning system for the rest of his battalion, which was positioned to the southeast of Roach and his men, on high ground where rock had been quarried for the runway improvements at the combat base the previous August. Mitchell had ordered Roach's risky deployment without consulting Alpha Company's commanding officer, Captain Henry "Mac" Radcliffe, who had been delayed in transit to Khe Sanh. When Radcliffe arrived a day or two later, he tried to persuade Mitchell to bring Roach and his men back into the main lines. "It's like dangling bait," the young captain had protested, but the battalion commander would not relent.[2]

Radcliffe did what he could to give the outpost a fighting chance. He added three M-60 machine-gun teams to the pair of guns already on the hill and assigned two 60-millimeter mortar crews, pushing the strength of the outpost to about sixty-four men. For that reason, not its elevation, it would become known as Hill 64.

Terry Roach hadn't asked for the assignment, but it was exactly the sort of challenge he relished. Growing up in a big Irish Catholic family in Birmingham, Michigan, a suburb of Detroit, young Terence had been steeped in American history by his father, and together they donned homemade period costumes and participated in Civil War battle reenactments and black-powder musket competitions.[3] Tall and lanky, with a long, angular face, Roach played baseball in high school and filled a scrapbook with news clippings about his beloved Detroit Tigers. He had enlisted in the Marine Corps reserve while working part-time and studying at Wayne State University. He completed boot camp at Parris Island, and after earning his history degree from Wayne State, entered Marine Officer Candidates School at Quantico, Virginia. In May 1967, just days after the Hill Fights around Khe Sanh, Roach returned home in the uniform of a Marine second lieutenant and married Lynn O'Connor, a darkhaired beauty he met at Wayne State. He completed Basic School training with Class 6–67 that fall and left for Vietnam on November 30.

Stepping off the plane in Da Nang on December 9, Roach was eager for action. At Phu Bai, he slipped away from his Quantico classmates and jumped on a Marine truck headed to Camp Evans, where he was given command of Alpha Company's 1st Platoon.[4] He saw his first action around Christmas along the "Street Without Joy," the scrubby coastal strip near Hue that had bedeviled French forces in Vietnam. On December 27, during a patrol, Roach made a rookie mistake when he aggressively ordered his platoon beyond a creek that was supposed to be the outer boundary of his operations that day. His men were ambushed, and the platoon sergeant and a corpsman were killed.[5]

Roach learned fast, and he impressed Captain Radcliffe with his maturity.[6] He was tough but fair with his men, an optimist by nature. Around Camp Evans, Roach brightened the mood by singing Irish folk songs and rowdy ballads about gunrunning Irish Republican rebels. The death and uncertainty that hung over his daily life was tempered by thrilling news from home: Lynn was six months pregnant.

At Khe Sanh, Roach had embraced his dangerous assignment. He dubbed his tiny forward outpost "Radcliffe's Roost" and pushed his men hard to prepare for the coming battle.[7] The stronghold measured only about sixty by forty yards and was ringed by a trench that the men studded with sandbagged bunkers about every ten or fifteen feet. Concertina wire coiled around the lower slope. The area between the wire and the trench line was seeded with command-activated Claymore mines, each positioned to scythe an attacking force with seven hundred steel balls sprayed in a 60° arc.

After long days spent improving trenches and bunkers, filling and stacking sandbags, and clearing fields of fire from the surrounding brush, Roach's men were worn out. Nightfall brought the demands of watch duties, and so the men were lucky to get three hours of fitful rest.[8]

By the first week of February, the North Vietnamese had become brazen in their movements around the hill. At night, roving enemy soldiers probed the concertina wire, occasionally triggering warning flares. Sometimes the Americans would awaken to find logs laid across their perimeter wire or Claymore mines reversed toward their lines.[9]

On Monday and Tuesday, February 5 and 6, the North Vietnamese pounded the main battalion lines and Hill 64 with mortar and recoilless rifle fire, wounding ten Marines.[10] On Wednesday, as North Vietnamese forces attacked the US Army Special Forces at nearby Lang Vei, Corporal James Feasel led a patrol that found matted grass beneath the northwest perimeter of Hill 64, where enemy soldiers had been watching the outpost.[11]

Now, after an unnerving night of enemy activity around the hill, Lieutenant Roach stopped along the western trench line, outside the bunker of his eighteen-year-old 2nd Squad leader, Corporal George Chapman. "There's a lot of activity out there," Roach said to Chapman, one of thirteen children born to a West Virginia coal miner and his wife, the fifth boy in his family to join the Marine Corps. "Keep an eye on your bunkers."[12]

Chapman checked his four bunkers along the western line of Hill 64 one more time and returned to the sandbagged hooch he shared with a twenty-two-year-old Navy corpsman from Michigan, Mike Coonan. Without warning, recoilless rifle rounds and rocket-propelled grenades slammed into the hill, followed by screams and heavy gunfire. It was 4:15 a.m. on the morning of February 8.

• • •

The initial North Vietnamese barrage shattered the 1st Platoon's western perimeter, destroying bunkers and killing or wounding about twenty Marines in an arc that stretched from Corporal Feasel's 1st Squad in the south to the edge of Sergeant Joseph Sutherland's 3rd Squad in the north. Four of the hill's five machine guns were either knocked out or quickly overrun. Recoilless rifle and RPG rounds destroyed two of Chapman's four bunkers and badly damaged a third. Chapman emerged from his bunker to see North Vietnamese troops charging up the slope toward the hill's northwest corner. He squeezed the clacker to detonate his Claymore mines, then began throwing grenades and firing his M-16 at the advancing enemy.[13]

Along the northwest perimeter, the speed and ferocity of the enemy attack shocked the Marines. Amid smoke, explosions and the sing-song chatter of Vietnamese voices, some Marines headed for the trench line and others stayed behind. Among those left in the bunkers were one of Chapman's fire team leaders, nineteen-year-old Lance Corporal Jeffrey Walsh of Bethel Park, Pennsylvania, and he paid with his life. In the next bunker to the east, Private First Class Gerry Clemson, a twenty-year-old from Geneva, Ohio, who had been in Vietnam only fifty five days, and twenty-three-year-old PFC William Colegate, from Red Bud, Illinois, died in the defense of the collapsing American line.[14]

As NVA soldiers poured into the breach and overran the northwest trenchline, some survivors fell back in the face of the surging attack. Chased by enemy gunfire and grenades, the retreating Marines reached the hill's northeast bend, then started down the eastern trench line.[15]

In the M-60 machine-gun bunker anchoring the northern line,

eighteen-year-old Arnold Alderete had been awake when explosions erupted to his left. Alderete had grown up in San Antonio, Texas, near the Alamo, and had moved to Southern California with his mother when he was fifteen. He dropped out of high school two years later, joined the Marine Corps, and had been in Vietnam since mid-October. Now, as explosions and gunfire rattled across the hill, Alderete heard the sound of running feet and terrified shouts: "Gooks in the trench line!"[16]

Alderete and his assistant gunner, Private Allen McKinley, an eighteen-year-old from Gary, Indiana, prepared to join the retreat. Alderete grabbed his M-60 and was moving toward the bunker entrance when a thunderous explosion ripped the trench line where McKinley had just disappeared. Alderete crawled out to the trench and spotted the muzzle of an AK-47 just before a Chicom grenade clanked off his helmet. Smothering the grenade with his helmet, Alderete lunged back toward the bunker. The blast wave swept over him, spraying his legs with shards of hot metal.

Fortified by a jolt of adrenalin, Alderete grabbed his M-60 and jumped into the trench. Two North Vietnamese soldiers stood facing him, a few feet away. Alderete fired first, ripping the NVA soldiers apart in a spray of 7.62-millimeter rounds. Still firing on full-automatic, he backed down the trench line to the east. He tripped over something, and a hand grabbed his leg. It was McKinley, his assistant gunner, badly wounded but alive. "Don't leave me!" McKinley pleaded.

"Hang on to me," Alderete said. With the wounded Marine clutching his leg, Alderete awkwardly backed down the trench line, firing bursts toward the west to discourage any pursuing enemy soldiers. They curved around the northeast corner and headed down the eastern line.[17]

• • •

In the minutes before the attack, Lieutenant Roach had stopped along the northeast perimeter to warn the 3rd Squad leader, Sergeant Joseph Sutherland, to keep his men alert because of the movement around the hill. He moved on down the eastern side, toward Feasel's 1st Squad sector along the southern perimeter.[18]

A pair of privates, rifleman Michael Barry and grenadier Ronald Rountree, were on watch duty at the front of the bunker they shared with

Sutherland and fire team leader Edward O'Connor when they heard an explosion and a scream from the area of Chapman's squad, to their left. Barry already had his helmet and flak jacket on, and he quickly snapped on his cartridge belt, grabbed some M-16 magazines, and dashed through the trench to his fighting position, a few yards to the west. Clutching his M-79, Rountree found his place about three yards beyond Barry as heavy gunfire and explosions crashed to their left.

As Barry searched for a target, Lieutenant Roach came running up from the south. He spoke briefly with someone behind Barry, then moved past, toward Rountree's position, and began firing his M-16 rifle and throwing grenades in the direction of the NVA attack. "I'm out of grenades," Roach yelled at one point. "Barry, you have any grenades?"[19]

Barry tossed two grenades to Roach, one after the other, and the lieutenant hurled the explosives toward the brunt of the NVA attack rolling in from the west. Seconds later, three or four grenades smacked into the ground around Roach. The platoon commander dived for a bunker as explosions ripped the trench line.

Almost simultaneously, a dark object banged into Barry's helmet with enough force to drop him to his hands and knees. He grabbed the object—a hissing Chicom grenade—and jumped to his feet to hurl it beyond the trench line. The grenade had just left his right hand when it detonated.

Hundreds of metal fragments and splinters ripped into Barry's body, dropping the young Marine to the bottom of the trench in a paroxysm of pain. His head throbbed. Gingerly raising his right arm into the flare light, Barry was relieved to see his hand. It was blackened and smoking, the skin on his little finger flayed to the bone, fingernails and flesh studded with metal splinters, but still more or less in one piece. His flak jacket bristled with metal shards. From Barry's right calf to his armpit, blood seeped from dozens of lacerations.

As Barry lay there, someone jumped into the trench beside him. Barry recalls that the Marine was Private Lawrence Cioffi, assigned to the hill as an artillery scout observer earlier in the week. Now, Cioffi didn't have a helmet, flak jacket, or weapon. Cioffi asked if Barry had seen Lieutenant Roach. Barry pointed in the direction of the approaching enemy attack, where he had last seen the platoon leader before the flurry of enemy grenades. Cioffi mumbled something and bolted in the opposite direction, as Barry recalled it.[20]

Cioffi—who later changed his name to Seavy Cioffi—disputes Barry's account. Seavy Cioffi says that Barry's identification of him as the weaponless and disheveled Marine he encountered in the trenchline is "absolutely a mistake."[21]

Shortly after his encounter with the forward observer, Barry heard a familiar voice. "Barry, are you okay?" It was his fire team leader, Corporal O'Connor.

"I've been hit," Barry said.

"What about the lieutenant?"

"He's up there," Barry said. "I think he's dead."

"Can you get to him?" O'Connor asked.

Barry crawled forward until he spotted a body. He could see Marine combat boots, but not the man's face. "Is anybody in there?" Barry yelled at the bunker just beyond the body.

There was no answer.

Barry came under fire, and dirt fell on him from enemy bullets gouging the trench wall by his head. Scuttling like a crab, he retreated back down the trench until he could see Corporal O'Connor, standing in the short trench that linked their bunker to the main line. "I didn't see the lieutenant," Barry said. "I don't see anybody else."

The words had just left his mouth when a grenade smacked into the short trench near O'Connor. Barry flattened himself along the main trench wall as the grenade exploded. Seconds later, O'Connor barreled into the main trench, one hand clamped over his bloody face. The wounded fire team leader turned left and disappeared down the hill to the south, away from the surging enemy attack.

Barry turned back toward the north and scanned the no-man's-land he had just escaped. His eyes spotted movement, and then his blood ran cold. Just beyond the bunker where Lieutenant Roach had fallen, Barry saw helmets bobbing up and down. They were the distinctive headgear of the North Vietnamese Army.[22]

• • •

Captain Mac Radcliffe was awakened in his bunker at the rock quarry within seconds of the first shots. "Alpha-1 is under attack," the watch officer said. The Alpha Company commander could hear the rattle of gunfire and boom of mortars, RPGs, and recoilless rifles. He radioed for Lieutenant Roach but got 1st Platoon radioman Jimmy Rizzo instead.

"What the hell is going on out there?" Radcliffe demanded.

"We're under attack," Rizzo said. "They're in the wire."[23]

"Let me speak to your actual," Radcliffe said, using radio code for the unit commander.

"The 1-actual [platoon commander] isn't here," Rizzo replied. "He's checking out what's going on."

"Get the 1 and tell him to give me a sitrep," Radcliffe ordered.

A short time later, Rizzo and Radcliffe spoke again by radio. The enemy was overrunning the hill, the radioman said. "You gotta come get us, Skipper. They're all over the place. Alpha-6, come get us."[24]

• • •

On the south side of the hill, Corporal James Feasel, the eighteen-year-old leader of Roach's 1st Squad, grabbed his M-16 and a bag of magazines, slapped on his steel-pot helmet, and stepped from his bunker into the trench.[25] His first instinct was to find Lieutenant Roach to coordinate their defense, so he headed west, toward the auxiliary trench leading to the platoon command post near the middle of the hill.

A streetwise New York City native, Feasel had taken only a step or two when a bright flash about twenty yards ahead stopped him in his tracks. Two North Vietnamese soldiers had set up a mortar on the roof of a gutted Marine bunker, and they were firing on American positions to the east. Feasel waited until the mortar flashed again to make sure they weren't friendlies, then dropped the NVA team with a burst of rifle fire. He found the cutoff to the command post and hurried up the hill.

By February 1968, Jimmy Feasel had been in Vietnam for seven months, and he knew how to handle himself. He had grown up in the rough Hell's Kitchen neighborhood of Manhattan's West Side, a lanky kid who lived to play hockey. When he was sixteen, his parents divorced, and Feasel decided it was time to find his own way in the world. He finished tenth grade, then enlisted in the Marine Corps.

For a boy who had never been out of New York City, boot camp at Parris Island was like a voyage to another planet. Feasel arrived with seventy-eight recruits from the Northeast, but he wound up being assigned to a newly formed platoon from the Deep South. He had never met a Southerner before, so he got a quick schooling in Dixie language and culture, black and white. After Parris Island and advanced infantry training in North Carolina, he drew a six-month assignment to the US naval base at Guantanamo Bay, Cuba. He turned eighteen in April 1967, and three months later began his tour in South Vietnam.

A rifleman by Military Occupational Specialty (MOS), Feasel arrived in Vietnam a sinewy six feet one and 175 pounds. He was assigned to Alpha Company of the 1st Battalion, 9th Marines and in his first month at Con Thien took a piece of shrapnel in his leg. After three weeks in the hospital, he returned to duty. During his second tour at Con Thien in the fall, Feasel experienced his first firefight and the loss of his platoon leader and company commander in one well-placed shot from an enemy recoilless rifle. Captain Mac Radcliffe took over Alpha Company and impressed Feasel as "a good man, good leader, and good combat officer."[26]

Feasel was still sizing up his new platoon commander, but right now he only wanted to find Terry Roach so they could head off the NVA attack that seemed to be hitting Hill 64 from at least three sides. Feasel reached Roach's L-shaped command bunker, ducked inside, and made a right turn into the main room. It was empty. As he turned to leave, gunfire sounded just outside and radioman Jimmy Rizzo hurled himself through the entrance. Enemy soldiers were in hot pursuit, so the radioman and Feasel scrambled into the bunker's main room.

The attackers began pounding the bunker with AK-47s, Chicom grenades, and RPGs. Bullets smacked into the walls of stacked sandbags, and explosions shook the squat structure, bursting one of Feasel's eardrums. Feasel and Rizzo took turns defending the bunker entrance. When one emptied a magazine, the other jumped into place and started firing. Each grenade or burst of rifle fire from the Marines provoked a fusillade from the North Vietnamese. At one point, a Chicom grenade exploded in the entrance as Feasel craned his head around the corner. He jerked back, but not before three tiny pieces of shrapnel embedded in his eye.

As the minutes passed, the trapped Marines debated their next move. Rizzo suggested they try to shoot their way out. Feasel insisted they fight on until help arrived.[27]

Feasel had just fired another magazine and stepped away to reload when Rizzo bolted outside. Rifle and machine gun fire crackled, and Rizzo staggered back inside the bunker entrance, his chest and abdomen pierced with bullets. Feasel dragged the radioman into the main room, then resumed his fire. Behind him, Rizzo lay on his back, dying.

"Jimmy," the radioman called to Feasel. Then again: "Jimmy."[28] They were Rizzo's last words.

Feasel was on his own now, out of grenades and running through his M-16 magazines. Every few seconds he would peep around the corner, fire a few rounds out the entrance, and yank his head back. He could hear heavy firing and explosions outside, but he had no idea how the battle was going. He was wary when a voice called out in English, "Is there anybody in the bunker?" Fearing a ruse, Feasel said nothing. And then the same voice: "If somebody's in there, you better yell, because I'm going to throw a grenade in."

Feasel hesitated, and then he replied, "Yeah, I'm in here." The New Yorker eased his head around the corner. Standing in the bunker entrance was a big Marine.[29]

• • •

The NVA had punched through the western perimeter, and assault troops were now moving into the interior of the American outpost, gaining ground along the northern and western lines. Chapman's 2nd Squad had been reduced to a pocket of wounded survivors in the care of corpsman Mike Coonan. Along the northern line, one of the few Marines still alive was Corporal Robert Wylie, who played dead as NVA soldiers rifled his pockets.[30]

Private Michael Barry was one of the last Marines near the northeast corner, and after spotting the bobbing NVA helmets, he tried to shoot two enemy soldiers looking in his direction. The rifle exploded, knocking Barry backward. He picked himself up and started backpedaling down the trench line to the south. He was trying to make sense of everything that had happened in the past few minutes when a sharp command snapped him back to the moment: "Get the guys out of that bunker. We're pulling back."[31]

The bunker in question housed an M-60 team led by a gunner known as Scotty—Lance Corporal James Frank Scott of Mobile, Alabama. Over the past few nights, Barry had heard Scotty telling stories about a wild week of R&R he had just enjoyed. Now Barry stood at the back of Scotty's bunker and called out, "Hey, we're pulling back. Can you guys come out?" Barry pulled the poncho back from the entrance and found the barrel of Scotty's machine gun in his face.

Scotty tried to bolt down the hill, but he rammed into Barry, and both men fell to the bottom of the trench. The M-60 gunner was trying to wriggle free when a Chicom grenade bounced off Barry's chest and dropped between Scotty's legs. The brunt of the blast ripped into Scotty's lower body. Hot shrapnel tore into Barry's left forearm, and the blast wave slammed him into the trench wall.

Barry lay on his back, his brain processing this latest shock, when a body lunged onto his chest. "Get away!" Barry shouted, shoving at the form that he feared was an NVA soldier trying to kill him. Then he realized it was Scotty, screaming and clawing in his agony. Staggering to his feet, Barry lurched down the trench. Spotting a cut in the trench wall, he climbed inside.

Just south of Barry, several Marines had piled into bunkers that looked out on the main battalion lines, more than 500 yards away. Some were wounded, others overcome with fear. Whatever their reasons, they had checked out of the fight, leaving about twenty or fewer Marines to battle on.

• • •

While the NVA attack progressed, two Marines were launching an extraordinary effort to deny the enemy control of the interior. Private David Ford, a 2nd Squad rifleman, and machine gunner Arnold Alderete met in the eastern trench line and roughed out a plan. Stuffing their pockets with grenades and clutching automatic weapons, they headed into the hill's interior.[32]

From the area around Roach's command bunker, the two Marines stormed over the crest toward enemy-held positions along the northwest corner. They raked the area with automatic fire and grenades, then sprinted back over the hill amid a flurry of NVA fire and grenades.

The 1st Squad grenadier, George Einhorn, spotted the familiar lope of his close friend Dave Ford and another Marine as they pulled off one John Wayne–style charge after another over the hill. Einhorn joined the pair and tried to drop an M-79 round onto the NVA, but the grenade landed dangerously close to the Marines and the muzzle blast attracted enemy fire. After Einhorn had fired two or three rounds, Ford leaned toward his friend. "George," he yelled, "don't shoot that thing again."[33]

When Alderete and Ford began to run low on ammunition, they threw grenades. When they ran out of those, they scampered down toward the 1st Squad area to rearm.[34]

• • •

By the time Jimmy Feasel made his escape from the platoon command post and returned to the southern trench line, the battle for Hill 64 had reached a critical juncture. The attackers were still gaining ground across the hill, and more than half of the sixty-odd American defenders were dead or wounded, including the platoon commander and platoon sergeant.

Command and control inside the outpost had collapsed, a fact that Captain Radcliffe had quickly gathered as he tried to get a situation report from the hill.[35] Unable to reach Lieutenant Roach or even his radio operator after their initial exchanges, Radcliffe had contacted the other commissioned officer on the hill, weapons platoon lieutenant Francis Beirne Lovely. Radcliffe wanted Lovely to get the hill's two 60-millimeter mortars firing and adjust rounds from the battalion's 81-millimeter mortars onto the attackers. Lovely was talking nonstop, but Radcliffe couldn't get answers to his questions. The Alpha Company commander finally cut him off. "Put somebody on the damn radio that can talk to me!"[36] Someone in the bunker took the line—probably Sergeant Joe Miller—but he, too, shed little light on the situation.

In fact, the situation was even worse than Captain Radcliffe imagined: Lieutenant Roach, radio operator Jimmy Rizzo, and platoon sergeant Bernard B. McKinney were dead; and Lovely's 60-millimeter mortar teams were hiding in their bunkers rather than firing on the NVA. A similar state of disarray existed in two of the hill's three rifle squads: Chapman's 2nd Squad had been virtually wiped out in the west; the 3rd Squad had been driven from its northern positions and its leader, Sergeant Joe Sutherland, had joined Lovely and Miller in their bunker.

Feasel found his squad largely unscathed and swelling in size as survivors from the shattered 2nd and 3rd Squads asked what they could do to help. Feasel huddled with grenadier George Einhorn and one of his fire team leaders, Corporal Roy McDaniel, a twenty-year-old from Kansas City, Missouri, and laid out his plan: they would set up a half-circle defensive perimeter—a "180," as their advanced infantry training instructors had called it—that would stretch from the hill's northeast corner to the southwest. Strongpoints would block the NVA advance down the eastern and western lines. Arnold Alderete and Dave Ford would shore up the center of the hill.[37]

As Alderete and Ford headed into the hill's interior once again, Feasel made other assignments. Fire team leader Roy McDaniel headed off with nineteen-year-old PFC Guy Leonard to secure the right flank, near the hill's northeast corner. The outpost didn't seem to be getting mortar or artillery support other than illumination rounds, so Feasel asked his grenadier, George Einhorn, to fire 40-millimeter grenades to slow the flow of NVA troops into the fight from the west.[38]

As Einhorn pumped rounds into the western sky, Alderete and Ford took up positions behind the platoon command bunker and engaged NVA soldiers firing from the western trench line and bunkers they had overrun. When Alderete and Ford ran low on ammo, they threw their last grenades and began hurling rocks. As they braced for another NVA push before dawn, Alderete and Ford made a pact: when the final assault hit, they would fight to the death.[39]

• • •

The 60-millimeter mortars that Captain Radcliffe had placed on Hill 64 were silent, but a young lieutenant in charge of the battalion's 81-millimeter mortars back at the rock quarry had sprung into action. In short order, the mortars were pumping out illumination and high explosive rounds in the hill's defense.[40]

Back home in Illinois, Maurice Casey had been teaching fourth grade at an elementary school in the Chicago suburbs when he enlisted in the Marines in 1966. After dropping out of pilot's training, he had entered the Basic School at Quantico as part of Class 6–67. Among his classmates was Terry Roach. Casey and Roach had arrived in Vietnam on the same flight in December, and they were at Phu Bai drawing their combat gear when Roach had taken off and beat Casey to the temporary 1/9 headquarters at Camp Evans. Roach's zeal earned him the coveted command of a rifle platoon, leaving Casey with a less glamorous billet: 81-millimeter mortars. Now, Roach and his rifle platoon were in trouble, and Casey was doing all he could to keep his classmate and his men alive.

Casey was in constant communications with a Marine radio operator who had been assigned to the artillery forward observer sent to Hill 64 a few days earlier. When the observer had left their bunker behind the northern trench line, his radio operator, a Marine known as Smitty, had remained in place as the North Vietnamese attack had smashed through the American line and driven the remnants of Sutherland's 2nd Squad back down the slope in disarray. Smitty had radioed the 81-millimeter mortars at the rock quarry and began performing the artillery observer's duties on his own.[41]

Now, as Casey listened over the open radio line, Smitty called in missions on targets along the likely enemy avenues of attack to the west and northwest. Smitty's bunker had been partially collapsed by enemy fire, but he had threaded his radio antenna through a crack in the jumbled sandbags. As marauding NVA soldiers roamed the American trench line only a few feet away, Smitty called in mortar rounds closer and closer to the hill.[42]

As the rounds neared the American perimeter on Hill 64, Casey and the Marine running the plotting board grew increasingly concerned that they were going to kill their comrades. Casey finally ordered a cease-fire. He told Smitty that he needed to talk to his forward observer, but the radioman explained that his forward observer had left him. Casey radioed battalion headquarters for guidance. "It's your call," he was told.

As precious seconds ticked by, Smitty pressed the case for close-in fire. "The bad guys are up and running around killing people, and they're the only ones that are going to get hit," he said. "If you don't [fire], they're going to finish off the guys that are here."[43]

Casey gave the order to his men: fire away.

• • •

Assigned to anchor the right flank of the new defensive line, 1st Squad fire team leader Roy McDaniel had set off up the hill with one of his men, Private First Class Guy Leonard. As they passed the 60-millimeter mortar pit closest to the east side of the hill, McDaniel heard a sound inside the mortar team's bunker. He yelled a challenge: "If you're American, you better answer up or we're going to throw a grenade inside."

A voice called back, "Wait! We're in here! We're Marines!"[44]

A member of the mortar team emerged. "Come on," McDaniel told the frightened mortarman. "We're going to get online and try to push them back."

The mortarman protested, "I don't have a weapon."

"Go on back to the rear there and get a weapon," McDaniel commanded, "There are plenty of them."

McDaniel and Leonard began crawling up the slope. Explosions ripped the night and showered them with shrapnel, dirt, and debris. They passed a few yards to the east of the platoon command bunker and continued on. Moving past the second 60-millimeter mortar pit, they saw no sign of the American weapons team. (The mortarmen had sealed themselves inside their bunker with sandbags and would survive the battle.)

McDaniel and Leonard crawled over the crest of the hill and stopped when they were within easy grenade range of the northern trench line. From their vantage point, lying behind some sandbags near the second mortar bunker, the two Marines could see North Vietnamese soldiers firing from the trench, and from inside and behind abandoned bunkers. Occasionally, an enemy soldier would dash to another position, his uniform and distinctive helmet visible in the light of explosions and flares.

The Americans began countering the enemy fire with their M-16 rifles and grenades. McDaniel had spooked Leonard with his first grenade toss. The fire team leader had rolled onto his back and pulled the grenade pin, then let the spoon fly with his hand cocked in the throwing position, about six inches from Leonard's head. Leonard counted to himself—*one, two*—while stifling an urge to yell: "Throw that thing!" But McDaniel didn't want to give the enemy time to throw the grenade back, so he took his time before chucking the explosive at an enemy soldier he had spotted. Much to Leonard's relief, Corporal McDaniel finally threw the grenade, and an explosion ripped the trench line nearby.

After perhaps an hour in their exposed position, McDaniel and Leonard noticed a flurry of movement to their left, in the western trench that had been held by George Chapman's squad when the battle began. The two Marines unleashed a fusillade of M-16 fire at the fleeting shapes, and the movement stopped.

On McDaniel's signal, Leonard began crawling in that direction. The two Marines slid into the trench, almost on top of the enemy soldiers they had gunned down. One of the NVA fighters was coiled at the bottom. "He's still alive," Leonard said to Corporal McDaniel, grabbing the wounded man's AK-47 rifle.

"Finish him off," McDaniel ordered.

Leonard raised his M-16 and fired a three-round burst into the back of the enemy soldier's head.[45]

Before the two Americans could contemplate their next move, a grenade exploded between them, knocking them to the bottom of the trench in a burst of hot shrapnel. Another explosion blew Leonard's rifle and helmet down the hill, and Leonard collapsed onto the NVA soldier he had just killed.

A Marine emerged from a bunker a few feet away and, with the assistance of another American, dragged Roy McDaniel to safety. The rescuer was George Chapman, the 2nd Squad leader, aided by corpsman Mike Coonan.

Guy Leonard staggered to his feet and wiped enough blood from his eyes to survey his surroundings. His gut told him that he was a dead man if he stayed on this side of the hill. Armed with only a mess-kit knife, Leonard lurched down the trench toward the south, in search of his comrades in the 1st Squad.[46]

• • •

When Sutherland's 3rd Squad pulled back in disarray, the NVA had missed an opportunity to attack down the eastern trench line. Private Mike Barry took up a position in the trench with two Marines who were part of Feasel's new defensive line. Unlike the disheveled men Barry had seen from the overrun areas, these Marines had helmets, flak jackets, and rifles. One of them handed Barry an M-16 and a couple of sandbags.

After a few minutes, a Marine came into view from the north. His face and movements embodied the fear that Barry had seen so many times during the fight. The man didn't have a weapon, and he was bleeding from a gash in his right jaw. A short time later, another wounded Marine hobbled down the trench and continued past. The Marine with the injured jaw reappeared and joined Barry and the other two men at their makeshift strongpoint.

Barry was sitting with his back against the trench wall, looking north, when an American M-26 grenade arced through the air in their direction and dropped into a supply area just off the line. When the explosion passed, he aimed his rifle to the north, expecting to see charging NVA soldiers. Instead, a Marine sprinted out of the supply area, blood streaming from his face.

The North Vietnamese attack that Barry and his three comrades expected didn't materialize, and it soon became apparent that the grenade had been tossed by a lone enemy soldier. One of the Marines could see the NVA soldier when he popped up from the area where Lieutenant Roach had fallen. The Marine kept up a running commentary as he matched wits with the enemy fighter, squeezing off a round each time the man hurled a grenade.

"Almost got him!"[47] "Damn, almost got him!"

Barry fired a few rounds up the hill in an attempt to distract the NVA soldier long enough for the other Marine to get off a kill shot, but their adversary was too wily. As night gave way to half-light, the deadly cat-and-mouse game on the eastern trench line played out.[48]

• • •

In the battle's opening minutes, Captain Radcliffe had picked up his land-line telephone and informed his battalion commander that the Alpha-1 outpost was under attack. Colonel John Mitchell ordered Radcliffe to sit tight until the situation became clearer.[49] More conversations followed, and Radcliffe's frustration grew with the rising fury of the North Vietnamese attack. When Mitchell ordered the Alpha Company commander to wait until daylight to mount a relief mission, Radcliffe fumed, "That will be too damn late."[50] He hung up the phone, then turned to his executive officer. "Tell Mitchell I'm out checking the lines if he calls," Radcliffe said. He headed outside to round up volunteers for a relief force.

At 7:40 a.m., Radcliffe led a force of about twenty men through the wire of his lines at the rock quarry. He and his men passed through a minefield and started down into the little valley, toward the embattled American outpost.[51]

• • •

As day broke, the Alpha-1 survivors were greeted by a surreal sight: Their comrades at the rock quarry were at their positions and ready for battle, but they weren't firing. Some were sitting on top of their bunkers, observing the fight on Hill 64, like spectators "watching a movie."[52]

It wasn't by choice.

Delta Company rifleman George Gregory Rudell, a wiry twenty-year-old from Little Rock, Arkansas, had been awake most of the night. A little after 4:00 a.m., Rudell saw an explosion near the crest of Hill 64, followed by the twinkling of gunfire that gave the appearance of "hundreds of lightning bugs up and down the hill."[53]

As flares burst over the outpost of Alpha Company's 1st Platoon, about 500 yards away, Rudell prepared to open fire on the NVA soldiers he could see scrambling up the slopes. But his platoon commander ordered the Marines to hold fire, for fear of hitting their own men.

The Marines at the rock quarry watched in horror as the battle raged. Rudell and his comrades cursed the nameless bastards somewhere up the chain of command who prevented them from going to the aid of their brother Marines, or even firing in their defense.[54] Even more inexplicable, there didn't seem to be any mortars or artillery firing in support of Hill 64, or at least none that Rudell could see or hear.[55] Finally, after daylight, Delta Company was given permission to fire. Rudell and his comrades picked out targets among the NVA moving up and down Hill 64 and opened up with their M-16s and M-60s.

Nearby, a pair of M-48 tanks at the rock quarry had also been denied permission to put fire on the slopes of Hill 64 during the predawn hours.

The light of day gave tank commander Joseph Harrigan a better appreciation of the close combat on the hill. Following the action through his 40:1 power telescope, Harrigan spotted a pair of Marines up the slope exchanging fire with NVA soldiers inside the perimeter. The Marines scrambled around, throwing grenades and even rocks at the enemy soldiers. Harrigan rolled his tank around, trying to get a clean shot, but the protagonists were too close.[56]

Around 8:30 a.m., Harrigan was finally allowed to fire his main gun at targets outside the Marine perimeter. He spotted about thirty North Vietnamese soldiers at the base of Hill 64, breaking off the fight. Harrigan's tank and its twin each unleashed six 90-millimeter shells at the retreating enemy.[57]

Forward air controller Charles "Toby" Rushforth, flying overhead after his adventure over Lang Vei the previous day, inadvertently stumbled onto the battle underway on Hill 64. Khe Sanh Combat Base hadn't informed him that a firefight was underway in that area, much less that a Marine outpost was fighting for its life. Rushforth arranged for some A-1 Skyraiders from the *Coral Sea* to be diverted from another mission around Khe Sanh. Dropping down through the overcast, they made strafing runs off the west side of the hill and dropped a few bombs on NVA troops they spotted.[58]

• • •

As small groups of enemy troops began to stream away from the hill, Corporal Jimmy Feasel and the Marine who had aided his escape from Lieutenant Roach's bunker retrieved an M-60 from the destroyed machine-gun bunker nearby and set it up in Feasel's bunker. When a group of about thirty retreating NVA appeared in their field of fire, a Marine opened up with the M-60 while Feasel and others along the southern line blasted away with M-16s. Still other Marines exchanged fire with the dwindling numbers of NVA soldiers sniping at the Americans from the western trench line.

Hunkered in the southern line a few minutes later, Feasel heard shouts and turned to see the Marine who had rescued him, inexplicably sitting exposed on top of a bunker. As other Marines yelled for their comrade to take cover, a shot rang out. The Marine tumbled to the ground, one of the last Americans to die on the hill.[59]

Shortly afterward, Feasel was in the entrance to his bunker, talking to one of his men in the trench line, Corporal Henry York, when the crack of another shot carried across the hill. A bullet hit York just below his right eye. Seconds later, another bullet ripped through Feasel's ear. York's wound was fatal, and grenadier George Einhorn feared that Feasel was soon to follow. As blood spurted from Feasel's ear, Einhorn wrapped a large bandage around his squad leader's head.

Stunned, but still very much alive and cranky, Feasel barked, "Georgie, how do you expect me to see? You got my eyes covered."[60]

The red-stained bandage was adjusted and Feasel returned to the fight, looking like a character in Archibald McNeal Willard's iconic painting of bloodied-but-unbowed American patriots in 1776.

• • •

After surviving two grenade blasts with Roy McDaniel, Private First Class Guy Leonard embarked on his perilous journey down the western trench line as he tried to make it back to friendly territory. Working his way down the zigzag line, Leonard surprised two NVA soldiers from behind and killed or incapacitated them with his mess-kit knife. It was a final test of fortitude, and Leonard emerged from the foggy dawn like a bloody apparition and rejoined the Marines along the southern perimeter.

Leonard's fire team leader, Roy McDaniel, wasn't as fortunate: he survived the grenade blasts without serious injury but was killed by enemy fire in the bunker along the western line where George Chapman and corpsman Mike Coonan were holding out.[61]

Small firefights and sniping were still flaring across the hill when a barrage of automatic weapons rounds erupted from the south. Marines along the southern line wheeled toward the sound, bracing for a renewed attack. But the gunmen were Marines at the rock quarry, and their target appeared to be some unseen enemy forces along the hill's southern base.

As he scanned the western trench line for NVA troops, Jimmy Feasel heard a commotion behind him. He turned and saw a Marine jump into his section of the trench, with others close behind. It was Captain Mac Radcliffe's relief column.

Radcliffe's point man, Corporal Robert Genty, a plumber's son from the Chicago suburb of Oak Park, was due to leave Khe Sanh, but he kept finding reasons to remain with the Walking Dead. Now he headed toward a Marine who wore a bloody bandage around his head and seemed to be in charge. "Which way are the gooks?" Genty asked Jimmy Feasel.[62]

Feasel pointed toward the west.

As Genty and other Marines headed across the southern trench line toward the enemy-held area, Captain Radcliffe sent more Marines up the eastern trench to press the counterattack around the north. Radcliffe, meanwhile, pushed into the middle of the hill with a handful of men. Under fire from NVA troops scattered along the western rim, Radcliffe ducked behind the platoon command bunker. An NVA soldier in a southwest bunker took Radcliffe under fire, and bullets smacked into sandbags next to the company commander's head. When a Chicom grenade sailed through the air toward him, the left-handed Radcliffe caught it in his right hand and awkwardly tossed it back toward the thrower.[63]

Radcliffe tried to take his tormentor out with grenades, but the fire continued. He yelled to Feasel, "Got any more grenades?"[64] Feasel tossed one to the captain, and Radcliffe hurled it toward the NVA soldier. The enemy fighter still would not die. Feasel threw another grenade to Radcliffe, and this time the captain threw a perfect strike. An explosion ripped the area around the NVA soldier, and a human leg flew into the air.[65]

Radcliffe and his men turned their attention to other NVA holdouts. Robert Genty moved up from the southwest corner and cleared out a bunker with a grenade and a burst of rifle fire. He reclaimed the next bunker with the same combination. One by one, the Americans took out the remaining NVA positions.

As the American counterattack swept across the hill, the welcome voice of Captain Radcliffe reached the ears of squad leader George Chapman and corpsman Mike Coonan, still trapped in their battered westside bunker. Chapman and Coonan had survived repeated attacks and probes as they kept watch over three wounded comrades who couldn't be moved. At one point Chapman heard the chilling sounds of NVA soldiers beating to death two Marines in an adjacent bunker. Unable to save his men, Chapman tossed a grenade inside to avenge their deaths.

Spurred by the sound of Radcliffe's voice, Chapman and Coonan sneaked out of the bunker to get help. As they ran down the trench line toward the south, a rifle cracked and a bullet slammed into Chapman. Coonan and rifleman Dave Ford pulled the 2nd Squad leader around a bend, and the corpsman went to work. A bullet had penetrated Chapman's flak jacket, punched through his chest, and exited his back. One lung had been punctured, and he was gagging and choking on blood that gurgled up from his chest. Coonan dressed the wounds and leaned Chapman up against the trench wall. The tough West Virginian would live.[66]

• • •

Twenty minutes after the American counterattack got underway, and nearly five hours after the battle began, there were no more enemy soldiers left to kill. Bodies and parts of bodies clotted the trenches and shattered bunkers. In places, broken young men, American and Vietnamese, lay atop one another in their final repose.

Twenty-seven Americans had been killed in the fighting: twenty-six men assigned to Hill 64, including platoon commander Terry Roach, and one man who fought with Radcliffe's relief force. The light casualties sustained by the relief force were a testament to the brave work done by the defenders of Hill 64 before help finally arrived.

In defeat, the North Vietnamese had paid dearly. The hill and the surrounding area were littered with the bodies of some 150 of their dead.

Across the hill, bloody and exhausted men began the grim work of carrying their dead and wounded down the southern slope to all-terrain vehicles that had arrived from the combat base. As Corporal Jimmy Feasel and corpsman Mike Coonan carried a stretcher bearing the body of twenty-year-old Roy McDaniel, the weary corpsman tripped on a tree stump and the body slid to the ground. Feasel gently placed his fire team leader back on the stretcher.

Coonan and Feasel had handed off the stretcher and started back up

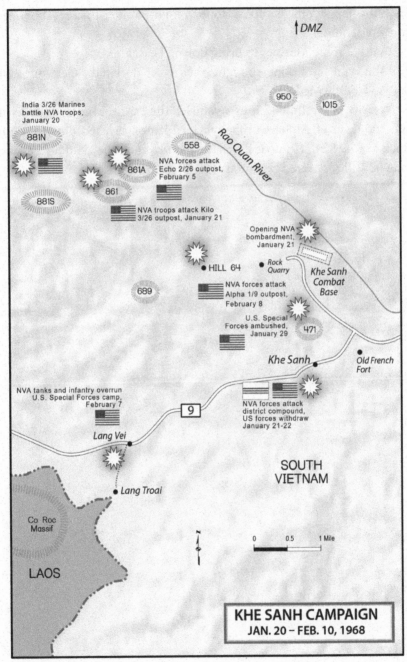

Opening attacks at Khe Sanh, January 20–February 10, 1968.

the hill when an officer's voice stopped them in their tracks. "Where are you guys going?"

"We got more Marines to bring down," Feasel said.

"You men have done enough," the officer declared. "Get yourselves over to Charlie Med."[67]

Wearily, they climbed into a vehicle. The caravan bearing the living and the dead of Alpha Company's 1st Platoon lurched down the dirt track to Khe Sanh Combat Base. The bloody knoll they had held against long odds disappeared behind them.

CHAPTER 12

"Home Is Where You Dig It"

In their twenty days at the gates of Khe Sanh, the North Vietnamese Army forces had fought five battles. They had won two, forcing the Americans from Khe Sanh village and Lang Vei, and they had lost three, failing in their attempts to overrun the Marine outposts at Hills 64, 861, and 861 Alpha. They had suffered heavy casualties and had little to show for their sacrifices.

Undeterred, the North Vietnamese now began the second phase of their Khe Sanh campaign. Bypassing and effectively isolating the American hill outposts, the NVA 325C and 304th Divisions turned their attention to the grand prize: Khe Sanh Combat Base. Under the cover of darkness, the North Vietnamese began encircling the base with a network of trenches, bunkers, and spider holes. From these positions, the NVA would be poised to launch an assault that would breach the American stronghold.

For the Americans dug in at the combat base or on one of the high points to the west or to the north, nothing had changed. NVA artillery, rockets, and mortars continued to pound their positions at random, and enemy snipers still added a personal touch to the mayhem. The chronic winter weather of low-hanging clouds made it more difficult for North Vietnamese spotters to identify targets, but it also allowed Communist gunners to operate with reduced fear of US air strikes.

Of greater concern to Colonel David Lownds and the 6,000 men under his command at Khe Sanh was the deteriorating supply situation. General Westmoreland had made the calculated gamble that enemy anti-aircraft fire and foul weather couldn't prevent his fleet of transport planes and helicopters from keeping the American stronghold equipped and provisioned, but the supply chain was already fraying. Food, water, and other essential items were in short supply on the hill outposts, and the concern was that the problem would only get worse.

The North Vietnamese had moved guns into place to cover the air approaches to Khe Sanh, and arriving American fixed-wing aircraft and helicopters now had to run a deadly gauntlet of fire on their final approach. Pilots, air crews, and ground personnel devised a frenetic routine to elude the NVA gunners, and its fundamental principle was perpetual motion. Transport aircraft never stopped moving, so cargo pallets were shoved off the back ramps of big C-130s and C-123s, and passengers jumped clear, as the aircraft trundled across the base, hounded by enemy mortars and rockets.

Stretcher bearers from Charlie Med loaded wounded aboard moving aircraft, leaving passengers trying to get out of Khe Sanh as the last priority. In a typical departure early in the campaign, Lance Corporal Keith Kapple and several other Marines who had completed their tours or were leaving for R&R sprang from a slit trench off the runway as a C-123 transport rolled past, tossed their seabags into the back, and leaped onto the heaving cargo door as the plane gathered speed and prepared to begin its takeoff sprint amid exploding shells.[1]

The Americans were not privy to the NVA's decision to shift its focus to the combat base, but they had anticipated siege tactics from General Giap. The North Vietnamese commander had claimed one of modern military history's greatest siege victories against the French at Dien Bien Phu in 1954. Oddly enough, given the American preoccupation with Dien Bien Phu, General Westmoreland had waited until the first week of February to commission his staff historian at MACV headquarters, Colonel Reamer W. Argo Jr., to analyze Khe Sanh's similarities with Dien Bien Phu and other classic sieges.

On Saturday, February 11, Colonel Argo presented his findings to Westmoreland and his staff at MACV headquarters at Saigon. Laying out the context of the showdown at Khe Sanh, Argo explained that siege warfare had produced mixed results through history, but modern weaponry had shifted the advantage to besieging forces. In all but two twentieth-century examples he and his team examined, the aggressors had prevailed over the defenders in siege confrontations. And then, narrowing his focus to the crisis at hand, Argo informed his audience, "It appears that Khe Sanh is following the pattern of previous sieges."[2] So how could the Americans avoid a disaster? Ominously, he advised that "urgent consideration be given" to dispatching an outside force to Khe Sanh to break the siege.

Westmoreland's staff was stunned.

The American commander himself rejected his aide's gloomy conclusions. He pointed to US air and artillery superiority and the availability of ground reinforcements as hedges against defeat at Khe Sanh—the same arguments Westmoreland had made in his earlier discussions with General Wheeler and President Johnson. Khe Sanh could be held, and it *would* be held, he insisted. Westmoreland closed the discussion with an emphatic declaration: "We are not, repeat, NOT, going to be defeated at Khe Sanh."[3]

• • •

The growing pessimism over Khe Sanh extended beyond Westmoreland's inner circle.

The American commander had seemingly calmed the Dien Bien Phu questions from Washington when the Communists kicked off their Tet Offensive on January 30–31. As if that hadn't jangled nerves enough in Washington, the spotlight returned to Khe Sanh with the NVA ground attacks of February 5–7. Khe Sanh "can and should be defended," General Wheeler, chairman of the Joint Chiefs, told Johnson in a National Security Council meeting at the White House on Wednesday, February 7. "It is important to us tactically and it is very important to us psychologically. But the fighting will be very heavy, and the losses may be high."[4]

Vietnam dominated the official conversation in Washington, even at social gatherings, and Khe Sanh was the top concern.[5] Johnson was now meeting daily with his military high command and senior advisers to discuss the crisis in Vietnam. Street fighting raged in Hue, and

intelligence reports pointed to a new round of Tet Offensive attacks before the week was out. The bigger question hanging over Washington
was the timing of the expected NVA ground attack on Khe Sanh Combat
Base. General Lew Walt had advised National Security adviser Walt Rostow that "all indications point to an attack on Khe Sanh in force, and
soon." But General Wheeler on February 9 suggested the enemy was "going to take his time at Khe Sanh."[6]

Other developments added to the uneasiness over Khe Sanh. The enemy's surprising use of tanks at Lang Vei had been compounded by rare
sightings of North Vietnamese aircraft in the Khe Sanh area. North Vietnamese MiG fighters had been observed practicing bombing runs, and
Wheeler told the president that General Giap might deploy his aircraft
for the first time "in support of ground action or in an effort to shoot
down our B-52s."[7]

Hanoi couldn't challenge America's air superiority over Khe
Sanh—the North Vietnamese possessed too few Soviet-made MiG fighters and Ilyushin-28 bombers to do that. But Communist air attacks could
exacerbate strains in the American resupply effort and, as Secretary Mc-
Namara warned, "have spectacular psychological impact." In response, a
US Navy guided-missile ship and other vessels armed with Terrier mis-
siles steamed into the Gulf of Tonkin.

Resupplying Khe Sanh remained the overriding concern. "How is the
supply problem at Khe Sanh?" President Johnson pressed in his February
9 meeting with the Joint Chiefs of Staff. "Will artillery and rockets knock
[the airstrip] out? Can we rely on roads?"

McNamara gently reminded the president, "There is no road available
up there." Wheeler tried to be reassuring. "As long as we use B–52s and
tactical air," he responded, "we will be able to keep our resupply up."

Johnson tried to pin his military chiefs down on what to expect at
Khe Sanh. He wanted to know whether the loss of the airfield would
force Khe Sanh's evacuation. Wheeler equivocated, leaving it to General
Harold K. Johnson, the Army chief of staff, to lay out the grim possibilities. He gave fifty-fifty odds to holding Khe Sanh and conceded that losing the air link would be a serious blow. "This is one of the hazards you
have to accept," the Army chief bluntly told the president.[8]

Saturday, February 10, brought bad news from Khe Sanh. North Vietnamese gunners had hit a Marine KC-130 transport on its approach to the Khe Sanh airstrip, and the plane burst into flames after a crash-landing, killing eight Americans. Within forty-eight hours, the Air Force quietly banned further C-130 landings at Khe Sanh Combat Base, and the Marines curtailed their use. Smaller C-123 transport and helicopters would now have to shoulder more of the burden if Khe Sanh's air link were to be maintained.

Johnson's military high command had maintained a united front in advocating a stand at Khe Sanh, but dissenting voices had begun to urge the president to reconsider. Among the influential skeptics was retired general Maxwell Taylor, the former Joint Chiefs chairman and ambassador to South Vietnam, who expressed "very deep concerns" about Khe Sanh to Johnson in a series of written communications and meetings in early February.[9]

Aware of Taylor's counsel, and perhaps sensing the growing doubts of his commander in chief, General Wheeler advised President Johnson that Westmoreland was prepared "to execute a tactical withdrawal if this becomes desirable and necessary."

Every day, it seemed, the conflicting opinions on Khe Sanh mounted.

On February 13, the CIA had a tabletop terrain model of Khe Sanh delivered to the White House to aid the president in his deliberations, and he began holding briefings around the mock-up in the White House Situation Room. The following day, Maxwell Taylor made his final case to Johnson in a blunt letter. "I know that Khe Sanh is very much on your mind as it is on mine," the former general and ambassador wrote. "It may be too late to do anything about the situation; if so, we should put doubts behind us and prepare for the fight." But if there was still time to avoid a showdown at Khe Sanh, "we should move quickly."[10]

Adding to Johnson's burden, news stories speculated that the United States had "stockpiled" nuclear weapons in South Vietnam for possible use at Khe Sanh. The White House and Pentagon vigorously denied the stories and insisted, untruthfully, that the issue hadn't been discussed. Privately, President Johnson ordered General Westmoreland to stop his secret deliberations on the possible use of nuclear weapons at Khe Sanh.[11]

Johnson was torn. "Frankly, I am scared about Khe Sanh," he told his national security team in a White House meeting. A nightmare scenario haunted him: the Khe Sanh runway gets knocked out, blocking the landing of fixed-wing aircraft; helicopters become Khe Sanh's lifeline; and then NVA gunners "pick off the helicopters." Underscoring the obvious, Johnson told his advisers, "I have a mighty big stake in this. I am more unsure every day."[12]

•   •   •

By the first week of February, the defenders of Khe Sanh Combat Base had settled into a grim routine, each new day a variation of the one before. In between the NVA rockets, shells, and sniper fire, enlisted men filled sandbags, improved or repaired trenches and bunkers, burned excrement, and performed other menial tasks. After two weeks of shelling and rocket barrages, the base had taken on the ambience of a post-apocalyptic shantytown. To dig deeper was to live, or at least improve one's chances of living, and so they dug. The grunts topped their trenches with sandbag parapets and layered bunker roofs with the sturdiest scraps they could scavenge, working on the theory that if their ramshackle shelters didn't collapse under the sheer weight of the protective layers, they could survive all but a direct hit.

Black humor flourished amid the madness. Among the more colorful displays was the pair of Bravo 1/26 grunts, Calvin Bright and Lloyd Scudder, who would run into the open and taunt NVA gunners, then dive for cover just before the mortar rounds started to hit.[13] Wry handwritten signs adorned the jumbled piles of sandbags and rubble that passed for bunkers. "Home Is Where You Dig It," read one sign, and so it was. Private First Class John Corbett, assigned to an 81-millimeter mortar team, found an incongruous metal street sign in a pile of rubble and erected it over his foxhole: "W DICKENS AV."[14]

In defiant acts of provincial pride, Marines flew flags from bunker roofs—city flags, state flags, Confederate flags, even a Scottish standard, salvaged from the abandoned Combined Action Company Oscar-2 outpost at Khe Sanh village, and now fluttering over the FOB-3 bunker of its original owner, Marine F. J. Taylor. Shrapnel-pierced *Playboy* pinups hung from latrine doors and bunker walls. In between explosions, the sounds of Motown and the Beatles blared from battery-powered turntables and reel-to-reel tape recorders.

America's supreme commander in Vietnam, General William Westmoreland (left), confers with President Lyndon B. Johnson at Cam Ranh Bay, South Vietnam, on December 23, 1967. Westmoreland sought a decisive showdown with his Communist adversaries in 1968. *(LBJ Library photo by Yoichi Okamoto)*

North Vietnamese General Vo Nguyen Giap defeated the French by encircling and overrunning a remote outpost at Dien Bien Phu in 1954. Giap's move against Khe Sanh was part of a larger plan to humble US forces in South Vietnam in 1968. *(VA001466, Douglas Pike Photograph Collection, The Vietnam Center and Archive, Texas Tech University)*

By early 1968, 20,000 North Vietnamese Army troops were converging on isolated Khe Sanh Combat Base. The US Marine base is viewed here from the south, looking north toward the Demilitarized Zone.

(source unknown)

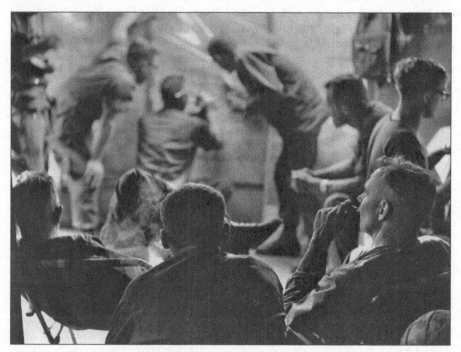

With his trademark cigar in hand, Colonel David Lownds (seated, at right) watches from a comfortable folding chair in his smoke-filled command bunker at Khe Sanh as his men plot fire-support missions against enemy forces. Lownds had 6,000 Marines under his command to defend Khe Sanh and its forward hill outposts.

(David Douglas Duncan/The Harry Ransom Center at University of Texas at Austin)

The first line of defense for Khe Sanh was a Marine outpost on Hill 881 South, under the command of Captain William Dabney (below). The Americans kept a wary eye on 881 North (above), a base for North Vietnamese infantry, mortars, and rockets throughout the siege.
(David Powell)

In the weeks prior to the siege, US Marines launched patrols from 881 South and nearby Hill 861 in an attempt to find the elusive North Vietnamese Army forces infiltrating the Khe Sanh area. The patrols honed the skills of young platoon commanders like India Company's Mike Thomas (top), seen with his men during a westward sweep toward the border with Laos. Above, the Marines of Kilo Company 3/26 move through lush elephant grass on the northern slope of 861 on the final day of 1967. At right, an India 3/26 squad leader, Corporal Ken Warner, dries his feet on 881 South.

(Richard Dworsky/Dennis Mannion/
Courtesy of Ken Warner)

North Vietnamese forces attacked the Kilo 3/26 outpost on Hill 861 in the early hours of January 21, 1968. Two days later, the Marines of Echo 2/26 established an outpost on 861 Alpha, seen at the right edge of this photograph.
(Ray W. Stubbe)

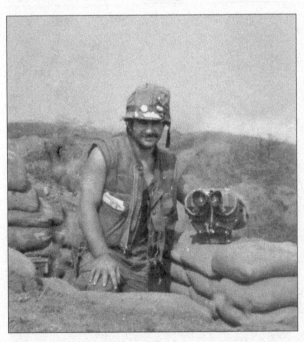

Artillery forward observer Dennis Mannion called in critical fire support during the attack on 861 and in the weeks that followed. He located targets during daylight hours with the powerful naval binoculars seen here, and employed a sophisticated Night Observation Device after nightfall.

(Courtesy of Dennis Mannion)

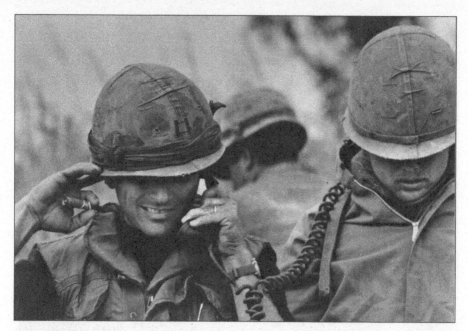

The North Vietnamese struck 861 Alpha on the morning of February 5, 1968, and penetrated the northern perimeter of the Echo Marines. Captain Earle Breeding (above) appears in good spirits as he works his radio in the aftermath of the attack. Daylight revealed enemy dead strewn around 861 Alpha.

(David Douglas Duncan/Harry Ransom Center at University of Texas at Austin)

Marine helicopter pilots and crews helped sustain Khe Sanh's hill outposts at considerable personal risk. The CH-46 Sea Knight shown here is preparing to transport American casualties from 861 Alpha down to Khe Sanh Combat Base after the February 5 battle.
(David Douglas Duncan/The Harry Ransom Center at University of Texas at Austin)

"My Staff on Radcliffe's Roost," Second Lieutenant Terence Roach (fourth from right) wrote on the snapshot he sent his pregnant wife, Lynne, in Michigan. A few days later, on February 8, 1968, Roach and twenty-five of his men were killed in an attack on "Radcliffe's Roost," better known as Hill 64. New York City native James Feasel (far right) was twice wounded as he helped organize the hill's defense. West Virginian George Chapman (third from right) was seriously wounded but survived a harrowing night amid bands of marauding enemy soldiers. Two other Marines shown here were among the dead: Corporal Jerry Burkhead (second from left), a machine gunner, and platoon sergeant Bernard B. McKinney (fifth from left, wearing glasses).
(Courtesy of Lynn Roach Fifer)

North Vietnamese gunners exacted a rising toll on US Air Force and Marine aircraft and crews flying in and out of Khe Sanh. On February 22, Captain James T. Riley and his copilot, Lieutenant Cary C. Smith, were taking on wounded Marines under enemy shellfire at Khe Sanh Combat Base when the main rotor on their CH-53 snapped and smashed through the cockpit, killing Riley and Smith. An injured crew member is being laid on a stretcher in this photograph.

(Cpl. L.F. George, US Marine Corps/National Archives)

A crash crew at Khe Sanh Combat Base sprays fire-retardant chemicals on a burning C-123 damaged by enemy fire.

(David Powell)

More than 2,500 casualties were treated at the main medical facility at Khe Sanh Combat Base, Charlie Med. The commander of Charlie Med, Dr. James Finnegan (right), is seen here operating on a casualty with the assistance of his close friend and comrade, Dr. Edward Feldman (left). The surgeons, corpsmen, ambulance drivers, and stretcher bearers of Charlie Med (below) performed heroically during the siege.

(David Powell/Courtesy of Dr. James Finnegan/Courtesy of Daniel Sullivan)

The Marines led the defense of Khe Sanh Combat Base, but Army, Navy, and Air Force personnel played crucial roles. The guns of Lieutenant Colonel John Hennelly's 1st Battalion, 13th Marine Regiment provided vital support to the hill outposts during the seventy-seven days of siege.

(David Powell)

Among the heavy weapons anchoring the northern perimeter at Khe Sanh Combat Base were Lieutenant Bruce Geiger's US Army "Duster" light tanks and "Quad Fifty" guns, which were mounted on Army trucks.

(Bruce Geiger)

Lieutenant John Dillon, a platoon commander with Bravo 1/26, looks out over the company's lines along the southeastern perimeter at Khe Sanh Combat Base.

(Michael O'Hara)

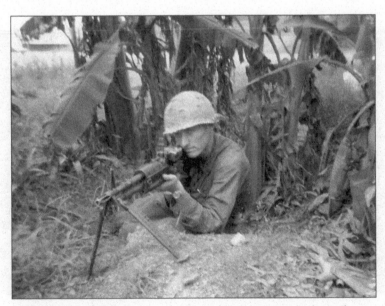

Californian Steve Wiese was one of Bravo's most experienced squad leaders at Khe Sanh. His combat skills helped him survive the devastating ambush of a February 25 patrol and the March 30 "payback assault."

(Courtesy of Steve Wiese)

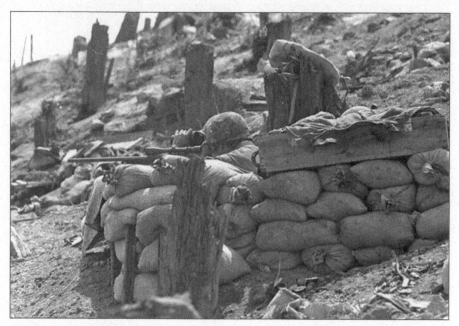

The Marines on the hill outposts sparred constantly with the North Vietnamese, exchanging small arms fire, mortars, and grenades. Photographer David Powell chronicled the work of a Marine sniper team on 881 South.
(David Powell)

The North Vietnamese around 881 South took a pounding from artillery missions and air strikes coordinated by Corporal Robert Arrotta, seen here in his bunker on 881 South.
(David Powell)

The defenders of 881 South defied the North Vietnamese siege forces with their daily flag-raising ceremony (above), timed to the second to avoid incoming mortar rounds. Concealed by the morning fog, the Americans could stretch their legs, shoot the bull, and savor their C-rations. Lieutenant Chuck Schneider serenaded the defenders of 881 South with his guitar and was joined in song by comrades such as Lieutenant Tom Esslinger (at left), commander of Mike Company on the hill.

(David Powell)

When the Air Force suspended C-130 landings at Khe Sanh in February, supplies were delivered by air drops (above) and parachute-rigged pallets shoved off the rear ramps of transport planes as they skimmed a few feet above the runway.
(David Powell)

In late February, CH-46 helicopter pilot David Althoff and his superiors devised an elaborate operation to improve the success rate of supply missions to the hill outposts. When the Super Gaggle got underway on February 24, support aircraft smothered suspected enemy positions with napalm, high explosives, tear gas, and smoke (above), allowing transport helicopters to drop thousands of pounds of badly needed supplies to the outposts (left).
(David Powell)

The siege was in its final days in late March when India 3/26 squad leader Ken Warner joined the exodus of Marines who had completed their combat tours. By the time he reached this transit barracks in Da Nang, Warner's face radiated joy and relief at having survived Khe Sanh. He left Khe Sanh, and then Vietnam, with his close friend Fulton "Fuzzy" Allen, an India Company machine gunner.
(Courtesy of Ken Warner)

In recent decades, survivors have renewed cherished ties at annual reunions of the Khe Sanh Veterans Association and private gatherings like this one in April 2012, hosted by Echo 2/26 commander Earle Breeding at his home in Ruidoso, New Mexico. Standing, from left to right, are: rifleman Jim Kaylor; artillery forward observer Bill Maves; company commander Earle Breeding; rocketman Dave McCall; rifleman Larry McCartney; and mortarman Jim Carmichael. Kneeling, from left to right, are: rocketman Jose (Cisco) Reyes; platoon commander Don Shanley; and sniper Al Miranda.
*(Sue Hutchison/*Ruidoso Free Press*)*

One of the many distinct groups at Khe Sanh Veterans Association reunions is comprised of men who served with Bravo 1/26, steeped in so much heartbreak and heroism at Khe Sanh. From left are: corpsman John "Doc" Cicala; rifleman Michael O'Hara; and company commander Ken Pipes.
(Courtesy of Michael O'Hara)

In his crisp dress-blues, his chest adorned with medals and ribbons, Ken Pipes honors the service of America's fighting men and women at public events.
(Ken Pipes)

While the grunts worked and waited along the perimeter trenches, staff officers went about their duties in the subterranean bunkers that sprawled beneath the scarred red clay. As base commander, Colonel David Lownds found himself besieged from outside by the North Vietnamese, and from inside by a growing troupe of American news reporters and photographers who had converged on I Corps to chronicle the showdown at Khe Sanh. Overnight, the journeyman colonel found himself in the world spotlight. In a *New York Times* "Man in the News" profile, published on February 12, the mustachioed Lownds was seen bustling about his besieged stronghold in flak jacket, steel-pot helmet, and rumpled utilities—resolute and ready. "My mission is to stay," Lownds declared, "and I intend to stay."[15]

Almost overlooked in the kinetic bustle of Lownds's command operations center was the work of Captain Harry Baig and his comrades of the Fire Support Coordination Center. Out of the limelight, they continued to pore over intelligence reports from the hill outposts and scrutinize sensor readings and topographic maps as they planned each day's air and artillery strikes under the rubric of Operation Niagara. In the round-the-clock struggle to deny General Giap his objective, the Americans were giving as good as they were getting. Niagara's rising toll was difficult to quantify, given the elusive nature of the North Vietnamese Army, but American air observers skittering overhead and close-in patrols out of the combat base spotted enough NVA bodies and blood trails to conclude that enemy losses were not insignificant.

But one question continued to haunt the Americans: Could Operation Niagara eliminate the NVA threat before Khe Sanh's fragile supply line snapped?

• • •

Despite worsening supply problems, spirits remained high for most at Khe Sanh Combat Base. But the mood was tense after the events of the past week—the bloody assault on 861 Alpha, the loss of Lang Vei, and the still-closer attack on Hill 64. Recon Marine Dave Doehrman knew Green Berets at Lang Vei from past missions, and he had followed the battle on his team's PRC-25 radio. Bravo Company, 3rd Recon, had been designated the quick-reaction force that would try to plug any breach in the combat base perimeter when the NVA struck. *It shouldn't be long now*, Doehrman concluded. *They're getting ready to overrun the base.*[16]

Along the southwest perimeter, radio operator Ron Smith had listened to the radio chatter during the Lang Vei attack. The twenty-year-old son of a Michigan truck driver had been on guard duty at the southwest gate on the morning of February 7 when a gunnery sergeant came by and gave him and another Marine a satchel charge and showed them how to use it. "If a gook tank shows up, shove this up under the turret, pull the pin, and run like hell," the gunny instructed. Smith thought, *I'm going to run like hell before that.*[17]

Anxieties soared when scores of Vietnamese and Laotians, some of them armed, started showing up at the gate. They were refugees from Lang Vei, and their numbers included soldiers from the sketchy Royal Laotian battalion and their families. But the Marines, Colonel Lownds chief among them, once again feared there were local Viet Cong or NVA mixed in with them, and so hard-and-fast orders were given to Ron Smith and others on guard duty: nobody gets in the gate.

The attack on Hill 64 on the morning of February 8 brought the NVA offensive within earshot of the American combat base, and for Marines along the line, every nocturnal probe and movement now became a harbinger of the big attack. Reports of revving tank engines, the movement of tracked vehicles, sappers at the wire—everything imaginable (and imagined) filtered back from the front lines. Rumors swept the base that the NVA was massing for human-wave attacks, "like Korea and Pork Chop Hill."[18]

The Marines scoffed at the Seabees and their soft Navy ways, but the onset of the siege meant that the once-mundane tasks performed by the Seabees had become life-and-death matters. Sam Messer was reminded of that one February day as he drove a forklift across the airstrip to pick up some cases of C-rations. An enemy mortar round nearly picked him out of his seat, and it knocked him flying. Messer crawled into a bunker, where he came face-to-face with a visiting general. "Marine, are you okay?" the incredulous senior officer asked, staring at the jagged schrapnel bristling from Messer's flak jacket.

The siege had thrust upon the Seabees the challenge of keeping the runway open, which required venturing onto the airstrip as soon as the shells and rockets stopped falling to clear debris and patch any holes. The runway was constructed of interlocking aluminum mats, each about three feet by eight feet and weighing one hundred pounds. The Seabees initially tried to expedite the work by cutting the sharp edges off torn mats and filling the holes with plaster, but the patches were unsatisfactory. Then they began tearing out the sections around a shell crater, filling the hole (sometimes big enough to stand in), and laying new matting—a painstaking process that gave the NVA snipers and mortar teams even more time to find the range.[19]

Charlie Med ambulance driver Danny Sullivan was driving along the airstrip on February 10 when a smoking KC-130 transport dropped from the skies on its approach to Khe Sanh. The plane's cargo hold was filled with huge fuel bladders needed to power generators at critical facilities around the base, and enemy machine-gun fire had pierced the fuselage and ignited the gasoline.

The pilot managed to land the aircraft but careened off the side of the runway. The aircraft exploded into flames. Sullivan jumped out of his ambulance and ran to the burning craft, pulling one man to safety through a rear hatch. A figure engulfed in flames appeared at the hatch, and Sullivan helped him to the ground and put out the fire with his hands. Lance Corporal Jerry W. Ferren had been badly burned over most of his body, and he screamed in agony. "We're going to get you to Charlie Med," Sullivan said. "You're going to be alright."[20]

Sullivan laid the injured man in his ambulance and roared off to Charlie Med. Behind him, other Marines tried to save men still trapped inside the wreckage. Three crew members and five passengers died from burns or other injuries.

The incident profoundly affected the men who had witnessed the crash or helped rescue the men trapped inside. Danny Sullivan resigned himself to a grim fate: he wasn't going to leave Khe Sanh alive.[21]

• • •

Almost to a man, the surviving American wounded (and several North Vietnamese) from the battles in and around Khe Sanh shared one common experience: they had received emergency treatment at Charlie Med, the main medical facility at Khe Sanh Combat Base, before being evacuated by air to military hospitals and hospital ships along the coast. Charlie Med was a collection of tents clustered near the center of the base, about thirty yards south of the helicopter pad alongside the runway. When the fighting began, a waist-high wall of sandbags was hastily erected around the triage and treatment tents, which afforded doctors and corpsmen some protection from flying shrapnel if they worked in a low crouch over wounded men laid on the floor.

The problems at Charlie Med did not end there, and an energetic Navy surgeon named James Finnegan was hastily ordered to Khe Sanh to take charge. A twenty-nine-year-old native of Pittsburgh, Pennsylvania, Finnegan had logged two years of general surgery in the States before spending four months as a combat surgeon in Delta Med at Dong Ha Combat Base. He arrived at Khe Sanh on a Huey helicopter gunship, door gunners banging away at the jungle below them during their approach. As soon as the bird touched the ground, the gunners shouted at Finnegan, "Get the hell out!" He did, and within minutes Jim Finnegan was awash in the blood of the first of more than 2,000 casualties he would treat at Khe Sanh.[22]

At Charlie Med, Finnegan led a team that included twenty-six corpsmen and three Navy surgeons: Joseph W. Wolfe, from Rutledge, Tennessee; Donald John Magilligan Jr., of Brooklyn, New York; and Edward Feldman, the New Yorker who had removed a live mortar round from a Marine's midsection while on temporary duty at the 1/26 aid station. Their facility was bereft of the X-ray machines and other sophisticated equipment found at rear-area hospitals, for Finnegan's team had one mission: resuscitate and stabilize the wounded, then get them on medevac flights as fast as possible.

Ed Feldman's first full day at Charlie Med was Saturday, February 10, a day that took a dire turn after the KC-130 crashed and burned off the Khe Sanh runway. The work of stabilizing the injured continued into the night. Late that evening, Feldman volunteered to oversee the evacuation of casualties on a medevac chopper due to arrive shortly after midnight.

The drill called for stretcher bearers to time their thirty-second dash so they met the chopper as it settled onto the helicopter pad. As Feldman and the others made their way to the pad with their casualties, mortars began to explode nearby. As the rounds came closer, two stretcher bearers panicked and prepared to bolt for cover. Feldman chambered a round in his .45 and announced, "We don't abandon our wounded."[23] The medevac flight arrived, the wounded were carried aboard, and the helicopter thundered off into the night. Only then did Feldman and the others run for cover.

The surgeons at Charlie Med had learned much about combat medicine in their months in Vietnam, namely, that high-explosive shells and flying shrapnel caused much more tissue damage and blood loss than the gunshot wounds they had seen back in America's urban emergency rooms. Head-wound cases were immediately directed into the treatment tent, where a tracheotomy was performed, breathing tube inserted, and intravenous drip placed in the groin area. A close inspection would follow to find any other wounds. Chest wounds were intubated to remove blood or fluid from the thoracic cavity, and then a large-bore IV tube would be inserted to replace the lost blood and fluid in the patient's body as fast as possible.

The doctors walked from station to station, supervising the work of corpsmen, stepping in only to perform intrusive procedures. Surgery was performed as a last resort. Once bleeding was controlled and vital signs were passable, a patient was readied for evacuation.

Finnegan did what he could to ease the strain at Charlie Med. Shortly after arriving at Khe Sanh, he had convinced the 26th Marines brass to approve construction of an underground bunker. The Seabees were working on it, but it wouldn't be ready until the end of the month. In the meantime, they would have to sweat out the NVA incoming while they worked on casualties.

By mid-February, Finnegan had brought order to the chaos at Charlie Med. He and his surgeon-teammates set a calm and collegial tone. The four doctors shared a small bunker, where they slept on cots and sat around in utilities stiffened by mud and blood, cooking C-rations and shooting the bull. Feldman had become Finnegan's indispensable wingman, skilled at his work, cool under fire, wickedly funny, and popular with the Marines.

As the commanding officer at Charlie Med, Finnegan attended the regimental briefing in the Command Operations Center bunker every morning, listening intently as various staff officers reported on the latest developments. After Lang Vei, all the reports from the front lines pointed to an imminent NVA attack. At the morning briefing, a large topographic map was unveiled to show five possible assault paths the North Vietnamese would take—five huge red arrows, punching through the perimeter and into the heart of Khe Sanh Combat Base. One arrow caught Finnegan's attention, as it plunged from the northern perimeter down through Charlie Med.

When the briefing was over, Finnegan pulled aside a staff officer. "What am I supposed to do if that's the arrow they pick?" he asked.

Not to worry, the major said. The reaction force would stop the enemy advance.

But how long would that take? Finnegan pressed.

Hard to say, the major conceded. "I would suggest that you arm all your people with M-16s and bayonets and dig fighting holes."

Finnegan was incredulous.

"Doc," the major said, "you gotta do your best until we get there."

Back at Charlie Med, Finnegan lightened his briefing with gallows humor. "They're talking about the NVA overrunning the base," he said. "If it happens, we could crawl under some parachutes and lie still until the NVA pass."[24]

• • •

For the NVA to reach Charlie Med from the north, they would first have to breach the northern perimeter held by Charlie Company of the 1st Battalion, 26th Marines. The 1/26 had been Ed Feldman's outfit during his temporary assignment to Khe Sanh in January, and he had forged friendships with its young company commanders and their beloved battalion CO, Lieutenant Colonel James B. Wilkinson. Feldman had accompanied the battalion on a reconnaissance operation along the Laotian border January 8 through 12, and it had been the greatest adventure of his life.

At the 1/26, Feldman had gotten to know a storied Marine who had recently joined the battalion, Sergeant Major James Thomas Gaynor. A mustachioed forty-seven-year-old from Louisiana, Gaynor had joined the Marines when he was seventeen and had been captured by the Japanese at Corregidor in 1942. He had survived the Bataan Death March and four years in a Japanese prisoner of war (POW) camp, and later fought in Korea. Nearing retirement, he had passed on a cushy rear-area billet to join the 1/26 at Khe Sanh on January 2.

The reconnaissance operation hadn't made contact with the NVA, and in mid-January, with growing signs that the enemy was out there and closing on Khe Sanh, Charlie 1/26 had been given the northern perimeter to defend. Under Captain David L. Ernst, the Blue Sector, as the area was known, was in good hands. A native of upstate New York, Ernst was tough but good humored, "one of those skippers you'd follow anywhere."[25] He had proven himself during the January operation, and once again when the shells started falling on the morning of January 21.

In his bunker along the Charlie Company lines, Ernst grew close to his two young radio operators, Lance Corporal Joseph Bailey, who carried the battalion radio, and Lance Corporal Chuck Chamberlin, who monitored the company net. Like Ernst, Bailey was from upstate New York, but he was the antithesis of the tough Marine—a short, witty, and affable young man of Irish Catholic heritage, with a shock of dark hair that wouldn't have passed muster back in the rear. He knew his stuff when it came to communications and had taught Chamberlin the ropes—how to handle the battalion and company radios, communications between platoons, the landline phone system. When he got a package from home, Bailey was unfailingly generous, and he recently shared his latest bounty with Chamberlin and other buddies: Lipton soup in a bag; chocolate chip cookies, Spam, and Tabasco sauce.

The twenty-year-old Chamberlin had grown up all over the place as an Air Force brat—Alaska, California, Illinois, Washington—but his parents split up when he was a high school junior, and he moved with his mother and younger sister to the Bay Area of Northern California. He quit school in his senior year and went to work for a funeral home that had the contract for deceased Army personnel coming back from Vietnam. He would drive to the Oakland Army Terminal, unload shipping cases bearing dead soldiers, and roll the remains to waiting morticians, who would prepare the bodies for shipment home to their families. It was gruesome work, and it factored in his decision when he received his Army draft notice in the fall of 1966. With memories of all those dead Army boys in his head, Chuck Chamberlin joined the Marines.

Chamberlin had arrived in Vietnam in late 1967. By mid-February, the days at besieged Khe Sanh had begun to run together—the artillery barrages and the sniping, the endless waiting for the NVA attack, the constant shadow of random death. That was how it was, one day blurring into another, until something bad happened to you or someone close to you. For Chamberlin, that day was Thursday, February 15.

A week had passed since the fall of Lang Vei and the attack on Hill 64, and everyone at Khe Sanh was on edge, waiting for the big assault. Just after 3:00 p.m., Joseph Bailey was on radio watch in the Charlie Company command bunker, and Chamberlin was asleep on a cot ten feet away. About ten minutes after the hour, Bailey reminded Chamberlin that it was his turn on the radio. Like everyone at Khe Sanh, Chamberlin was worn out, and it took him another minute or two to drag himself off the cot. He stood up to put on his flak jacket and helmet, and in that instant an NVA rocket slammed into the bunker.[26]

The world around Chamberlin went dark, and there was a terrible buzzing in his head and a ringing in his ears. A thick log column had shielded him from the blast, but not Bailey. Through a curtain of dust and smoke, Chamberlin could see that his friend was face down on the wooden bench he had been straddling, arms dangling at his side. Chamberlin started across the bunker, but tripped on a body. Sergeant Major James Thomas Gaynor, the legendary Marine, had been checking the Blue Sector lines and had just stopped by the Charlie Company CP to check in with Captain Ernst. Now he was lying at Chamberlin's feet.

Chamberlin took Joe Bailey by the shoulders and gently leaned him against a wall of sandbags. The back of Bailey's head was wet. His eyes had rolled into his head, and his skin was cold and clammy. Bailey vomited, and his legs started shaking. Chamberlin didn't know what to do, and so he hugged his friend.

Captain Ernst appeared, and he shoved Chamberlin aside and began wrapping a field bandage around Bailey's head. Ernst was oblivious to his own serious injuries, including a severed artery in his arm that spurted blood. Chamberlin grabbed a bandage and cinched it around the captain's wound.

At Charlie Med, Ed Feldman was dismayed to see Captain Ernst and Sergeant Major Gaynor among the six casualties brought in from the rocket attack. Lieutenant Colonel Wilkinson arrived, and he exhorted the unconscious Gaynor. "Talk to me, Sergeant Major. Talk to me, Sergeant Major."[27] Finally, Feldman gently said, "He can't hear you, Colonel."

Around dusk, a CH-53 set down on the Khe Sanh helicopter pad, and the Charlie Company casualties were loaded aboard. Lieutenant John M. Kaheny, a rising 1/26 staff officer, had lived with Gaynor for the past month and they had grown close. Kaheny had just been granted leave to return home to visit his dying father, and now he helped carry Gaynor's stretcher aboard the helicopter. The CH-53 headed east into the waning daylight, with Kaheny cradling the sergeant major's head in his lap. As the helicopter neared the Delta Med hospital at Dong Ha, Gaynor died.[28]

Captain Dave Ernst would lose his arm, but he would live. His war was over. Lance Corporal Joseph T. Bailey, the sweet-natured radioman, died at a hospital four days later. His friend, Lance Corporal Chuck Chamberlin, escaped serious injury. He remained at Khe Sanh to carry on.

CHAPTER 13

"What the Hell Is Out There?"

Throughout February, a trickle of men came and went from the Khe Sanh hill outposts as helicopter flights braved winter rains, fog, and enemy fire to keep the Marines alive. Among the new arrivals on 881 South was radioman Ron Smith, who got orders transferring him from the combat base and on Friday, February 9, boarded a CH-34 helicopter bound for the western anchor of the Khe Sanh defensive line. "When I give you the sign," the crew chief instructed, "get the hell off." Smith did as he was told and then heard somebody on the ground yelling, "Get down! Get down!" He threw himself into a shallow ditch as NVA mortar shells crashed nearby. When the barraged ended, Smith asked the nearest Marine, "Where can I find Bob Arrotta?"[1]

Mortar fire had wounded the forward air controller on 881 South in the early days of the siege, and Corporal Robert Arrotta, twenty-one, had taken over the job. The diminutive Marine from Bethesda, Maryland, quickly impressed Bill Dabney with a coolness and professionalism far beyond his years. Dodging enemy fire as he prowled the hill with his team, Arrotta worked his radios (call sign India 14), identified targets, verified map coordinates, and deftly synchronized close-air strikes with artillery fire and incoming helicopter flights. As high explosives and napalm summoned by Arrotta rained down on NVA troops and weapons sites around 881 South, the bearded controller was hailed by comrades as the "Mightiest Corporal in the Marine Corps."[2]

Ron Smith found his way to Arrotta's bunker, where he quickly discovered that life on the hill outposts was even worse than what he had experienced at the combat base since January 21. Food and water were harder to come by, and enemy fire was more concentrated. The Marines had limited their exposure to incoming rounds by moving underground, transforming their shallow trenches and slapdash above-ground shelters into deep passageways, underground bunkers, and "bunny holes" carved into the trench walls.[3]

Bob Arrotta was living in a bunker that he and two other Marines had hacked deep into the hillside of 881 South. They had covered the floor with wooden pallets and furnished the bunker with three cots. They rigged a bunk for Smith by hanging a stretcher from the ceiling with communications wire. Illumination was provided by a flashlight bulb wired to a spare radio battery.

By the second week of February, supply problems caused by bad weather and NVA fire had reached critical levels on all the hill outposts. The caloric intake of the men had been reduced to two C-ration meals a day, and hungry scavengers combed the garbage dumps on all the hills with renewed urgency.

Well-intentioned efforts by rear-echelon supply officers to boost morale sometimes went awry. In February, a cargo net packed with supplies was dropped onto 881 South during the afternoon. When the Marines ventured out to retrieve the supplies after dark, they were chagrined to discover hundreds of cups of ice cream among the usual cartons of C-rations and other items. The ice cream had melted, but the Marines were not about to discard the rare treat. Everyone on 881 South slurped down their share, then suffered through the resulting diarrhea.

Beleaguered as they were, the Marines on the hill outposts remained upbeat and defiant. On 881 South, Bill Dabney had added a flourish to his daily flag-raising ceremony by having a lieutenant bugle an up-tempo rendition of "To the Colors" while two Marines raised the Stars and Stripes on an RC-292 radio antenna. It was all over in less than thirty-five seconds, timed precisely so the Marines could dive for cover just before the first NVA mortar rounds hit.[4]

On 881 South, the American outpost farthest from Khe Sanh and closest to the NVA infiltration routes, Dabney tried to preempt an attack with random "mad minutes," in which his Marines on cue would blast away to their front for sixty seconds. It kept the NVA off balance while letting the Americans blow off steam and make sure their weapons were in good working order. Dabney also encouraged his men to act on their hunches if they heard movement or saw something suspicious. His ammo bunkers were full and well protected, so Dabney was generous in his use of mortars, automatic weapons, and grenades to prevent his stealthy adversary from massing around him.[5]

The NVA had positioned their big artillery and rockets on both sides of the Laotian border, so 881 South and 861 took on the added role of early warning system for Khe Sanh Combat Base. At the first sound of fire, Dabney's radiomen would alert the base with a cry of "Rockets! Rockets!" or "Arty! Arty!" Down at the base, a horn would sound, giving men about five seconds to find cover before the first explosions.[6]

Operation Niagara's deadly toll had forced NVA soldiers to revert to stealth in their movements around the hill outposts and the combat base, and sightings of the enemy became rarer as February wore on. The grunts on 881 South were startled one day to see an NVA soldier running along a ridgeline several hundred yards away. Several Marines opened fire with their M-16s, and the enemy soldier fell, then jumped up a second or two later and started running again. He fell a second time, but once again broke into a sprint. His legs churned furiously as M-16 bullets streaked by, until the soldier collapsed into a bomb crater. The Marines were laying odds on whether he was dead or not when a few seconds later a head popped above the rim of the bomb crater. In grudging admiration of their wily adversary, the Marines burst out laughing.[7]

• • •

On 861, the men in Kilo Company, 3/26, were dealing with the same hardships: too little food, too little sleep, too much incoming, and too much anxiety as they waited for the enemy to attack. The Marines were reminded every day of the near miss they had experienced in the predawn North Vietnamese attack of January 21: several of the NVA dead had remained tangled in the concertina wire along the hill's northern perimeter, and the flesh of the fallen enemy troops blackened and decayed, until all that remained were uniformed skeletons.[8] Dennis Mannion, the Kilo company artillery forward observer, found himself wondering as he looked out at the NVA skeletons: *Is that what's going to happen to me?*

The North Vietnamese had occupied a ridgeline about 500 yards west of 861, and from there, as well as from other positions on the slopes and draws north of the American outpost, the enemy had continued to pepper the hilltop with mortar and recoilless rifle rounds. Mannion knew the terrain well from the daily patrols off 861 he had accompanied in the three weeks prior to the siege, and his hunt for targets with his air counterpart was well informed by that knowledge.[9]

Nineteen-year-old Paul Knight was a rail-thin six-footer from Missoula, Montana, and he had undergone forward air controller training with Bob Arrotta before winding up at Khe Sanh. Knight had missed the early days of the siege while he was burning some R&R with his girlfriend in Hawaii, and he had returned to 861 in early February, armed with some new Rolling Stones and Aretha Franklin records for his battery-powered record player. As the music played, Knight and Mannion went to work pounding the NVA around 861 with a powerful one-two punch of artillery and close-air strikes.[10]

By mid-February, daily artillery and air strikes had burned and pulverized everything from the once-lush gulch at the western base of 861 on up and over the NVA-held ridgeline to the west. Yet hardy North Vietnamese soldiers somehow survived the cataclysm. Mannion and Knight watched in amazement one day as a lone NVA soldier stood up and blasted away with his AK-47 rifle at an American jet on its napalm run. The soldier kept firing until he was obliterated in a ball of fire.[11]

At least three times a week until the end of February, American aircraft would bomb the ridgeline west of 861 at some point during the night. Some nights a Spooky gunship appeared overhead with its moaning mini-guns and hosed down suspected NVA positions. If the close-air strikes were spectacular, the B-52 Arc Lights were like a window into the apocalypse. The massive air strikes and artillery lifted spirits on the hills, but they caused Dennis Mannion to contemplate the extreme nature of the enemy threat that demanded such an unprecedented American response. Mannion wondered: *If they're using this much firepower, what the hell is out there?*[12]

• • •

Along the northern line of Hill 861, Sergeant Miguel Salinas—Korean War veteran, merchant seaman, and incumbent M-60 gunner—filled the long stretches of down time by holding court with a cast of young understudies. He organized such crude competitions as farting and smelly-armpit contests and games of "fly poker" (grab the most flies from a crumb-sprinkled table and you win the hand). Food became currency in the raunchy competitions.

Salinas told stories about his stint as a machine gunner in Korea and his travels as a merchant seaman. "Hey, Pop, you ever been to Italy?" a young Marine from the sticks would ask the worldly Salinas. And Salinas would regale the pimply, sex-starved teenagers with wild stories about his carnal escapades in various Italian ports of call.[13] As food and water became even more scarce, the Marines stopped dreaming of sex and beer and became obsessed with food and water. Pop Salinas merged his fantasies in a recurring dream in which he was sitting nude under a waterfall, a cold beer in his hand and a naked woman at his side.[14]

From the *Time* magazines his father sent him, Dennis Mannion knew that Khe Sanh was big news back home, so he started writing American companies to tell them that the Marines on Hill 861 wanted them to know how *great* their product was. As Mannion and his buddies had hoped, packages eventually started arriving on the hill: bottles of premium gun oil, packets of "Funny Face" powdered drink mix, boxes of M&Ms, Tabasco sauce, and Necco wafers.[15]

On the southern perimeter of Hill 861, Jim Thomas performed the dual role of corpsman and sanitation officer. It was a nearly impossible assignment, given the tropical climate and the lack of water for personal hygiene or even washing wounds.[16] One young Marine with a minor shrapnel wound came to Thomas with red streaks running up his arm. Like many on the hill, he was terrified of risking a medevac flight to Khe Sanh. Thomas took one look at the spreading infection and ordered the Marine onto the next chopper that made it in.

Doc Thomas did what he could to ease the burden on his young Marines. He stood watch at night to give the worn-out grunts a break and built them a sheltered outhouse in a demolished bunker so they could perform bodily functions without getting shot. The waste was collected in halved fifty-five-gallon drums, which were regularly burned off along with the rats that Thomas snared in a network of traps.

Practical jokes leavened daily life, and the soft-spoken corpsman was a frequent target. Thomas retaliated one day by shoving a deactivated grenade down the back of a habitual joker. When the shaken Marine finally calmed down, he plotted his revenge. Thomas had carved a two-room "hooch" into the hillside. He had papered the earthen walls with *Playboy* and *Penthouse* centerfolds and had even built a chimney to vent smoke from his kerosene lantern. One day he emerged from his shelter to find a pipe sticking out of his chimney, with a handwritten sign: "Urinal."[17]

• • •

By mid-February, the NVA troops arrayed against the hill outposts had settled into their own routine, which revolved around sniping and mortaring, and firing an occasional recoilless rifle round into the American strongholds. The Americans had dug deep and had learned to live with the incoming, for the most part. But it was a game of chance, and the unlucky died.

On 881 South, Lieutenant Tom Esslinger had aged well beyond his twenty-four years since taking command of Mike Company, 3/26, on February 1. The early days had been especially harrowing as the NVA pounded away at 881 South with their Russian-made 120-millimeter mortars and 130-millimeter artillery pieces. As Esslinger walked his lines, he kept his anxieties to himself but was reassured to find that he wasn't the only one scared out of his mind. Some days the cacophony of rockets, heavy artillery, and mortars was more or less constant, and other days it was just two or three rounds. The only thing the Marines on the hill outposts could predict was the fire that would greet an incoming helicopter.

On 861 Alpha, young Private Jose "Cisco" Reyes had been among the handful of reinforcements rushed to the hill on the morning of February 5. Seasoned hands like rocketman Barry Fixler taught him the ropes in those first days, and Reyes settled into the precarious existence that passed for daily life on the hill. He had never smoked back home in Los Angeles, but he started on the hill. There was so much stress from the incoming, the probes, the long night watches, and the constant threat of death. Most of the men were hollow-eyed and exhausted. Reyes would light a cigarette to keep himself awake on watch duty, cupping his hands around the stick of burning tobacco to avoid giving away his position. When he invariably dozed off, the cigarette would burn his fingers and wake him up.

Reyes also learned hard lessons about the fickleness of fate. Huddling in his fighting hole as mortar rounds crashed around him, he reached for his 3.5-inch rocket launcher and found it shredded with shrapnel. A friend took shrapnel to the head from an incoming round and then thrashed about in agony. "Oh, my God!" the Marine gasped. "What's going to happen to my wife?" And then he died.[18] Another Marine was guarding the chow cache on 861 Alpha when two mortar rounds came in and sheared off both legs and one arm. "They're not good enough to kill me," the gritty Marine told a comrade.[19]

On a typical day on 861, Jim Thomas responded to the cry for a corpsman after mortar rounds hit the hill. He found a distraught Marine standing over a lifeless comrade. "Doc, that's my best friend—can you help me?" Thomas examined the fallen Marine, a handsome kid with blond hair. There was hardly a mark on his body, but he was dead. Thomas put the Marine in a body bag and helped carry him up to the LZ for transport to the combat base. But a winter front moved in, cloaking the hill in mist and fog, and the body lay beside the LZ for five days. By the time the decomposed corpse finally reached Graves Registration down at Khe Sanh, Thomas knew the family would be denied the solace of an open-casket funeral.[20]

The foul weather that rolled across the hills in mid-February made it even more difficult to deliver supplies and evacuate the wounded and the dead, piling more stress on all concerned. The wounded and dying men stuck on the socked-in hill outposts stood to lose the most, of course, but the psychological toll reverberated outward, from distraught comrades who could only watch their brothers-in-arms suffer and sometimes die, to the air officers at Khe Sanh Combat Base coordinating the desperate pleas for emergency medevac flights, to the helicopter crews who made heroic attempts to reach the hills in almost zero-visibility conditions, sometimes with nothing but aching failure to show for their exhausting hours in the air.

Captain Rich Donaghy was the regimental air officer for the 26th Marines, and it was his job to advise Colonel Lownds and his staff and coordinate the use of fixed-wing aircraft and helicopters in support of Khe Sanh Combat Base and its hill outposts. A native of New York City, born in Brooklyn and raised in Queens, Donaghy knew the climatological vagaries of the area all too well, having arrived at Khe Sanh in October, at the height of the rainy season. He had turned twenty-five at Khe Sanh on February 10, and now, operating with the call sign Intrigue 14 Actual, he found himself having to weigh the lives of wounded Marines on the hill outposts against the lives of helicopter pilots and crews trying to evacuate casualties in extremely treacherous flying conditions.[21] Sometimes, as if Donaghy wasn't already painfully aware of the life-and-death nature of his decisions, an air officer or someone else on a hill outpost would come on the line to underscore the stakes: "If you don't get somebody up here soon, this guy's not going to make it."[22]

Such was the case with Corporal Homer Taylor Jr.

At 5:30 a.m. on Friday, February 16, Taylor, a twenty-one-year-old Marine squad leader from Memphis, Tennessee, was walking along the trench line on 881 South when a mortar drove shrapnel into his temple and shoulder. A corpsman prepped the wounded Marine for the short medevac flight down to the combat base, but thick fog enveloped the hill. All day Saturday the fog never lifted, but Taylor was still hanging on.

Later in the day, Taylor's condition worsened. His comrades stood on the LZ into the night, waving handheld flares and strobes as they tried to talk a chopper down through the fog, but the pilot finally had to give up. In the early hours of Sunday morning, February 18, the fog lifted and a helicopter took off for 881 South. Before it could land, a radio operator on the hill informed the pilot that the medevac status had been downgraded from "priority" to "routine." Homer Taylor had died.[23]

Two days later, helicopters were inbound to the hill outposts when Lance Corporal Terry Smith, another radio operator who worked with Bob Arrotta, broke from cover on 881 South to wave an incoming bird away from an LZ that had been registered by NVA mortar teams. As the pilot veered away, a round hit the zone and Smith fell with a severed femoral artery.[24]

While corpsman Ronald V. Bowling tried to stanch the blood flow, crack CH-46 pilot Dave Althoff swooped back to the hill to pick up the wounded Marine. Althoff rushed the casualty down to Charlie Med, but Terry Smith's wounds were too severe. "I grew up a lot today," Bob Arrotta wrote afterward. "My best friend died in my arms."[25]

• • •

The Marines at Khe Sanh Combat Base had spent the two weeks after Lang Vei strengthening their defenses against a human-wave assault supported by tanks. The perimeter was ringed by fields of anti-personnel mines—M14 "toe-poppers" that cracked the bones in a man's foot and leg but usually weren't lethal, and M16 "Bouncing Betties," a nasty German invention that sprang up about waist high before spraying steel balls in all directions. Powerful anti-tank mines were added, along with barrels of *fougasse*, a potent napalm mix that would be detonated as enemy troops closed on the perimeter.

A work party from Lieutenant William Gay's detachment of combat engineers was outside the eastern wire one day in February, laying more anti-personnel mines, when South Vietnamese Army Rangers on the perimeter started screaming. The Americans dived to the ground as the ARVNs opened fire over their heads at North Vietnamese nearby. When the firing eased, one of the team members, John Pessoni, raised his head. A buddy flashed Big John a look of horror, and Pessoni choked back a wave of fear. "Oh shit, did I get hit?"[26] His friend started laughing. "No, you got a turd on your face."

In the middle of a minefield, Big John had managed to find a chunk of human excrement.

The fear and tension dissolved into howls and hoots, and soon the entire team was convulsed with laughter. The shooting died away, and the giddy Americans made their way out of the minefield and back through the Ranger lines. The South Vietnamese didn't know what to make of their crazy allies.[27]

• • •

On Wednesday, February 21, Khe Sanh began its second month under siege. Two weeks had passed since the North Vietnamese Army's stunning assault on Lang Vei. After so many false alarms and sleepless nights, the Marines once again concluded the Communists had completed their careful preparations and were poised to launch the big attack. At 12:45 p.m., as if in confirmation, the North Vietnamese launched a rare daylight probe against the eastern end of the base. As artillery, mortars, and rockets slammed into the stronghold, about a company of NVA troops—perhaps one hundred men in all—advanced to the edge of the treeline and opened fire on the ARVN Rangers.

The fighting reverberated across the Khe Sanh plateau as opposing snipers, mortar teams, and artillery batteries exchanged fire. At 1:00 p.m., a rocket smashed into the airstrip, closing Khe Sanh's lifeline for the remainder of the day.[28] Meanwhile, the formidable forces of Operation Niagara crisscrossed the skies over Khe Sanh, killing the North Vietnamese in their trenches, spider holes, bunkers, and gun emplacements. From 9:00 a.m. on February 20 to 9:00 a.m. the following day, forty-eight US Air Force B-52 bombers hammered the Khe Sanh area with sixteen Arc Light strikes—a staggering 1,200 tons of ordnance. By Thursday morning, another thirty B-52 bombers had dropped an additional 750 tons of high explosives on the North Vietnamese around Khe Sanh.[29] Low-flying Marine, Navy, and Air Force attack jets dumped 256 tons of napalm and high explosives on NVA positions in eighty-two close-air sorties on February 21 alone.

Meanwhile, the battle to maintain Khe Sanh's fragile lifeline hung in the balance.[30] The combat base and its outposts devoured as much as 235 tons of supplies daily, and by February only a fraction of that amount was getting through on most days. Parachute drops off the western end of the base had become the safest means of delivering supplies to Khe Sanh. On February 16, the Americans had introduced a hybrid method known as "low-altitude parachute extraction system," or LAPES, in which parachute-rigged pallets were pushed off the back ramp of a C-130 as it swooped low over the airfield. The pallet would careen down the runway like a runaway sled until slowed by the parachute.

The winter *crachin,* a constant fine mist, had closed in around the hill outposts, and food and water supplies were growing critically short. On 861, rations had been reduced to one canteen, and then half a canteen of water and one C-ration meal per day. On 861 Alpha, Marines sucked on pieces of bamboo they gathered in the draw off the hill's western flank.

The daily rations for some men consisted of a can of C-ration peaches.[31] A platoon of Alpha Company, 1/26, on Hill 950 had run out of water. And on 881 South, food and water supplies were so low that Captain Bill Dabney convened a council to consider whether the Marines should abandon the post and fight their way to the combat base or some other point.[32]

On February 21, 143 tons of supplies reached Khe Sanh by air, but not without the sort of drama that had become an almost daily occurrence. A C-130 flying low over the airstrip came under NVA fire as it was executing a LAPES supply drop, and its tail section clipped a bunker, burying two Marines beneath a heap of sandbags and debris. Marine Reggie Lee Vance died shortly after midnight from his injuries.

• • •

The North Vietnamese pressure increased on Thursday, February 22, with a massive barrage of artillery fire, rockets, and mortars. Captain James T. Riley of Zeigler, Illinois, a thirty-two-year-old pilot with Marine Heavy Helicopter Squadron 463, had already flown two resupply missions to Khe Sanh during the day when he heard a radio request for a medevac mission at the combat base. Riley volunteered to take it. The wounded Marines were readied near the airstrip's freight ramp for a quick evacuation, and around 4:45 p.m., Riley maneuvered his chopper into position to take the casualties aboard.

As heavy mortar and rocket fire crashed around his aircraft, Riley held in place until the wounded were loaded. A shell-burst critically damaged the chopper before he could pull away, and Riley ordered the casualties removed while he tried to save his aircraft and crew. He coaxed the aircraft off the ground, but severe vibrations quickly forced him back down. As the chopper settled onto the tarmac, the main rotor blade broke away and sliced through the cockpit, killing Riley and his co-pilot.[33]

• • •

Among the Americans seeking shelter in a trench line off the western end of the runway during the February 22 barrage were Father Robert Brett, the 2/26 battalion chaplain, and his assistant, Private First Class Alexander Chin. Brett had spent the previous day on 861 Alpha and

861, administering communion and granting plenary indulgence to Marines. (Kilo Company forward observer Dennis Mannion was among those receiving a plenary indulgence from Father Brett on Hill 861.) Brett and Chin had flown back down to the combat base at the end of the day and were trying to catch a flight to Hill 558 as the barrage raged. Nearby their companions in the trench was Lance Corporal Julius "Corky" Cartwright Foster, a twenty-nine-year-old Marine reservist who had advertised his desire to be sent to Vietnam by walking 404 miles from his West Virginia home to reenlist at Camp LeJeune, North Carolina.[34]

Just before 5:30 p.m., an NVA rocket screamed in from the west and dropped into the narrow trench line, killing six Americans and wounding nine. Among the dead were Father Brett, Alexander Chin, and Corky Foster, the inspired West Virginian who had fulfilled his wish to fight in Vietnam.

CHAPTER 14

"Proud to Be a Marine"

Friday, February 23 was the most hellish day of all for the defenders of Khe Sanh. Over seven terrifying hours, beginning in the late morning, more than 1,300 shells, rockets, and mortar rounds pounded the combat base and the hill outposts.[1] Casualties would prove light for such a ferocious bombardment, a testament to the digging and fortifying the men had done in the month since the siege began. Still, twelve Americans were killed—eight at the combat base, three on 881 South, and one on 861—and nineteen wounded seriously enough to require evacuation.

The butcher's bill could have been worse, but that was little consolation for the comrades of the fallen. Charlie Med surgeon Ed Feldman lost his friend Lieutenant Kim Johnson, who had been with him the night he removed the mortar round from the Marine's abdomen. Tall and blond, a gentle twenty-seven-year-old reserve officer from Fresno, California, Johnson was also a devout Mormon, a husband and father. His bunker took a direct hit and his neck was broken, but there wasn't a mark on his body when they dug him from the rubble.[2]

On Hill 881 South, Lieutenant Tom Esslinger had been in command of the Mike Company sector for a little more than three weeks. He had seen his young Marines conquer the "nearly paralyzing fear" of the early days of the siege and transform their piece of the hill into an impregnable fortress. The twenty-four-year-old Esslinger had been greatly aided in his leadership of Mike Company by two savvy gunnery sergeants un-

190

der his command: Eugene Charles "Gene" Wire, the classic tough-love gunny, a mantle earned after devoting eighteen of his thirty-seven years to the Marine Corps; and thirty-two-year-old Paul Edward Robitaille, a fourteen-year Marine veteran, more soft-spoken in his role as commander of Mike Company's weapons platoon.

Robitaille had begun his Vietnam tour of duty as the siege at Khe Sanh was getting underway, and after arriving on 881 South, he became close friends with Gunny Wire. They had dug a hole beneath the rim of a bomb crater left over from the Hill Fights, and they would meet there to have a smoke, sip coffee, and talk about their lives back in the world.

Around midday on February 23, Esslinger was in his bunker when several large-caliber enemy artillery shells slammed into his area. It wasn't long before his radio crackled with a terse casualty report: "007 has been hit, over," a voice announced.

Esslinger's heart sank: the number seven was a reference to any company gunnery sergeant, and "007" was Mike Company's inside joke for identifying their pair of gunnies. Esslinger steeled himself, then asked, "Which one?"

"Both," came the reply.

"How bad?" Esslinger asked.

"K."

Esslinger felt sick. *K? Killed in action? No way.*

The lieutenant sprinted from his bunker to the crater that had become the refuge of the two gunnies. Just inside the lip, where Robitaille and Wire had dug their hole, Esslinger spotted a new shell crater. There was plowed up dirt and shrapnel, but no sign of either man.

A team was organized to dig out the blast hole while Esslinger radioed all stations on his company net to request a position report on both gunnies. But no one had visual contact with them, and an examination of the blast hole soon confirmed the worst: an incoming round had landed squarely on Paul Robitaille and Gene Wire, and they had left the world together, leaving behind only a blood-soaked patch of earth.

For Tom Esslinger, February 23 would be the worst day of his life.[3]

• • •

The shell fire eased by nightfall, and the defenders of Khe Sanh settled in for another long vigil. On Hill 861 Alpha, Echo Company, 2/26, rifleman Jim Kaylor had drawn straws with a pair of lance corporals and close friends, nineteen-year-old Gerrie George Jefferies and twenty-year-old Carlos Cruz Aguirre, to decide who would sleep inside their bunker along the western side of the hill. Kaylor lost, so he stretched out in the trench line about ten feet away.[4]

Around midnight, friendly "harassment and interdiction" artillery fire from Khe Sanh screamed low over the hill, toward some unknown target to the north. Fifteen minutes into the new day, February 24, two rounds "of unknown origin" slammed into the Echo Company outpost on 861 Alpha. One hit the bunker where the two M-60 gunners, Aguirre and Jefferies, were sleeping, burying the two Marines beneath sandbags, rocks, and dirt.[5]

Jim Kaylor and other Marines rushed to the pile of rubble and began tearing it away to reach their comrades. About fifteen minutes later, the lifeless bodies of Aguirre and Jefferies were finally pulled from the debris.

• • •

As the weeks passed and the Marines analyzed their intelligence and tried to anticipate where the North Vietnamese would attack, the southeastern perimeter had become an area of intense focus. It was the Gray Sector in the Khe Sanh Combat Base defensive scheme, held by the ARVN Rangers and the Marines of Bravo Company, 1/26, and aerial photographs had revealed an expanding network of NVA trenches in the adjacent jungle.

The southeastern sector was a logical avenue of attack for the North Vietnamese. It was close to Khe Sanh village, which the NVA had occupied, and Route 9, which now bustled with Communist truck convoys after dark. The North Vietnamese activity in the area had been closely tracked by Harry Baig and his comrades at the Fire Support Coordination Center, and the Americans had devised "mini Arc Lights" and "micro Arc Lights" for the North Vietnamese siege forces in that area—carefully plotted saturation bombing carried out by low-flying American attack aircraft as close as 500 meters (about 550 yards) to the combat base.

The North Vietnamese took the punishment and continued to extend their siege lines and bunker complexes closer and closer to the American and South Vietnamese lines on the east. As the days passed, aerial photographs revealed wide assault trenches leading toward the southeastern perimeter of Khe Sanh Combat Base.[6]

The men of Bravo Company, 1/26, had waited for weeks to mix it up with the North Vietnamese. During the attack on Lang Vei, the company commander, Captain Ken Pipes, had gotten his men ready for battle, but nothing had happened. Bravo radioman Tom Quigley and his buddies had come across a story in *Stars and Stripes* that quoted Colonel Lownds as saying, "We will defend Khe Sanh to the last man," and they had laughed about that. "Glad *he's* confident," Quigley had quipped. Ever so quietly, Quigley had stockpiled grenades and ammo in his hooch "for an Alamo-style last stand."[7]

On February 13, a Bravo platoon had gone outside the wire to provide security for a mine-laying detail while the ARVN Rangers pushed several hundred yards southeast of the base in search of NVA forces. The Bravo Marines had set up in a lush bamboo thicket, beyond the heavily mined swath of cleared terrain that stretched about two hundred yards beyond the perimeter wire. Small-arms fire crackled to their front, and the Bravo boys waited nervously. The wide-eyed Marines had watched the triumphant ARVN Rangers file past them on their return to the base, clutching a recoilless rifle they had captured from the North Vietnamese. It had been a good day for the much-maligned ARVNs, and the boys of Bravo had gotten an increasingly rare glimpse of the world outside the wire.[8]

That night, Lance Corporal Ken Rodgers and another Bravo Marine had been called down to their platoon command post. There were two ARVN Rangers carrying a body—in the darkness it wasn't clear if he was a South Vietnamese or an NVA soldier—but Rodgers and his buddy were ordered to walk their ARVN counterparts over to Graves Registration. It was pitch black and they stumbled around for a while, but they finally reached their destination, near Charlie Med, and the two Americans and the two ARVN Rangers carried the stretcher inside and set it down.

A sergeant came over to handle the transfer of the corpse, and as Rodgers was explaining the situation, he heard somebody running down a hall. A young man popped into view, yelling to someone behind him, "Hit me! Hit me!" A second later he reached up, smoothly caught a severed foot in a boot, and yelled, "Touchdown!" Rodgers laughed, but the eyes of the ARVN Rangers widened with horror and they quickly left. For the Graves Registration personnel who spent their days handling the torn bodies of young Americans at Khe Sanh, black humor helped keep them sane.[9]

• • •

Down on the Bravo Company lines, Corporal Steve Wiese was ready for the North Vietnamese to make their move. In the meantime, the lanky Californian perfected his time-honored Marine Corps skills as a master scavenger. Wiese had overseen the construction of the bunker he shared with three other Marines, a structure made of stacked sandbags that measured six feet by eight feet, and about six feet deep. The floor was covered with sandbags and layers of empty bags to make it more comfortable for sleeping. A poncho hung over the entrance. Wiese's prized possession was a cot he had commandeered.

The four Bravo Marines had spent the past weeks strengthening their bunker to the point where it would survive a rocket strike, and Wiese was confident they had succeeded. He and his buddies had chopped down a tree outside the wire and used a section of the thirty-inch trunk as the roof, then layered it with runway matting. On top of that they stacked a layer of 105-millimeter howitzer ammo canisters packed with dirt, capped with two alternating layers of sandbags and runway matting. In mid-February, Wiese and his comrades had been in their bunker when an NVA mortar exploded outside. It sounded close, but only after the barrage ended did Wiese discover that they had survived a direct hit. It was a proud moment for Wiese and his comrades.

Wiese didn't fear death, but he was terrified by the prospect of being maimed. He had seen too many mangled bodies in Vietnam, and he didn't want to wind up like that. One of his buddies in the bunker, a Mexican American named Miranda, lived in fear of getting blown up by an NVA rocket. He had dug a hole in the bottom of their bunker that he hoped would save him if they took a direct hit. Wiese gave him a hard time about it: "Hey Miranda, I don't know if we would find you down there." Miranda would reply, "I don't care, man. If I get killed I get killed. I just don't want to get blown up."[10]

Around February 23, as the NVA stepped up the pressure on the combat base, Bravo's executive officer, Lieutenant Ben Long, stopped by to let him know that the latest intelligence indicated an imminent attack. Long mentioned that higher-ups wanted prisoners if the line was overrun, so they could interrogate them to learn more about NVA plans.

Wiese began to plot. Once in a while he could hear the NVA digging at night—the *clink* of metal as a pick or shovel hit rock—and so he decided: *I'm going to go out there and capture a gook.* He gathered his squad and shared his idea. They would sneak out of the wire with nothing more than a K-bar knife and a pistol, find the NVA trench line, grab a gook, and drag him back to Bravo's lines. During the course of the day, every Marine in Wiese's squad came to him to volunteer for the mission.

Another Bravo squad leader pulled Wiese aside. Corporal Ken Claire hailed from the Sierra foothills of Northern California, and he was known for his trademark Tarzan yell and other antics, but he was also one of Bravo's finest Marines. "I hear you're going on a suicide mission tonight," Claire said to Wiese. "I want to go."[11]

Before nightfall, Wiese was summoned before a senior officer who knew all about his plan. He threatened Wiese with charges if he led anybody outside the wire. As the chastened squad leader turned to leave, the colonel stopped him short. "Corporal Wiese," the officer barked, "it is men like you that make me proud to be a Marine."[12]

Steve Wiese and his band of would-be raiders stood down, but their opportunity to go head-to-head with the North Vietnamese would come soon enough. Late on the afternoon of February 24, Wiese and the other squad leaders of Bravo's 3rd Platoon were put on notice: Get your men ready. We're going outside the wire in the morning to have a look.[13]

CHAPTER 15

Super Gaggle

B y February 1968, a typical day in I Corps had taken on a well-worn routine for Marine CH-46 helicopter pilots like Dave Althoff: up at 5:00 or 5:30 a.m., swig some coffee, wolf down some dry scrambled eggs, stash some C-rats in the chopper, and then head into the morning briefing before hitting the skies.

Marine Aircraft Group 36 and its three hundred-plus pilots and 2,100 air crewmen and mechanics were on their way to a historic month, and they could scarcely meet the demand for helicopter transport, assault, resupply, and medevac missions in I Corps. In addition to supporting Marines locked in fierce street fighting at Hue, MAG-36 bore primary responsibility for the perilous work of resupplying the hill outposts at Khe Sanh.

For the defenders of Khe Sanh, their lives quite literally depended on the Flying Tigers of HMM-262 and Purple Foxes of HMM-364 in their twin-rotor Boeing Vertol CH-46 Sea Knights, and the Ugly Angels of HMM-362 in their smaller Sikorsky UH-34s. Over the course of the month, MAG-36 choppers would log 5,337.7 flight hours, fly 15,782 sorties, carry 14,566 passengers and 3,100 tons of cargo, and evacuate 2,872 casualties—and they would do all this in some of the foulest weather that Vietnam had to offer, while facing the heaviest enemy fire of the war.[1]

Nearly every landing zone in I Corps these days was hot, but the Khe Sanh runs had become especially dangerous. The approaches to the combat base and the hill outposts were now covered by NVA soldiers firing everything from AK-47 rifles to quad-.50-caliber machine guns, and the landing zones were locked in by enemy mortar teams. The rising risk of getting shot down in runs to the hill outposts had forced the helicopters to start carrying supplies in external nets, so they might dump their loads more quickly and escape the enemy's gun sights. It wasn't possible to do that with medevac missions, so the helicopter pilots needed nerves of steel to sit in place for agonizing seconds, mortar rounds and machine gun bullets scouring the landscape around them, while wounded Marines were carried aboard.

It was all in a day's work for Dave Althoff.

• • •

Born in Illinois in 1932, the son of an insurance broker and a housewife, Althoff had moved with his family to Chandler, Arizona, when he was sixteen. An accomplished football and baseball player in high school, he studied business at Arizona State University before dropping out to become a Navy pilot in 1952. He spent the first years of his career flying fixed-wing aircraft, including nuclear-armed patrols over the Korean Peninsula in the Lockheed Douglas AD-1 Skyraider, before learning to fly helicopters at Pensacola (Florida) Naval Air Station. He later spent nine months in the South Pacific, flying radiation-monitoring missions over Bikini Atoll during US nuclear weapons tests, before shifting to the Marine Corps to fly helicopters.

In the late summer of 1963, Althoff headed to Vietnam as part of Operation Shufly. Based in Da Nang, he taught South Vietnamese pilots and crews how to fly H-34 helicopters on combat missions. The war had a leisurely nine-to-five quality to it, with nights and weekends free. Every Wednesday, Althoff would fly down to Saigon to pick up fresh fruits and vegetables, squeezing in lunch at his favorite floating restaurant. But it wasn't all fun and games, and by the time he left Vietnam in the spring of 1964, Althoff had flown sixty combat missions.[2]

The war in Vietnam went on without Althoff for three years as he logged tours that took him to Okinawa and the Caribbean, went through amphibious warfare school back in North Carolina, and celebrated the birth of five children. By the time he returned to Vietnam in June 1967, the "gentleman's war" was a distant memory.

Althoff was sent to I Corps and began flying CH-46 Sea Knights with Marine Medium Helicopter Squadron 262 (HMM-262), part of Marine Aircraft Group 36. Settling in at Quang Tri Air Base in August 1967, Althoff and his fellow pilots and crews in HMM-262 did it all: troop assault, resupply, medevac, reconnaissance team insertions and extractions.[3]

At thirty-five, with sixteen years of military service under his belt, Althoff was older and more experienced than most of his comrades in HMM-262. He was the pilot everyone wanted to be: highly skilled, courageous, and "so damned cool when the going got rough."[4]

He perfected an aggressive flying style, which he summed up in sports terms: "The best defense is a good offense." For recon team insertions and extractions—dropping a team of six or eight Marines in the middle of an enemy-infested area—he would go in as low and fast as possible, skimming the jungle canopy as he picked his way through the fog-shrouded hills. He preferred to kill his adversaries rather than run, so a favorite tactic was to turn head-on into trouble. He got shot down four times and took so much battle damage that some days he needed three choppers to finish his missions, but he was there for the Marines, night and day, seven days a week. He would be named Marine Corps Aviator of the Year for 1968, but his proudest achievement may have been the nickname he earned from his peers: "Balls to the Walls" Althoff.

• • •

Althoff had burnished his growing legend on February 2 when he had led an emergency mission to extract a Marine recon team surrounded by an estimated one hundred NVA troops near Dong Ha. His copilot was Captain Charles Crookall, and the second aircraft in Althoff's two-ship section was flown by Captain W. L. Barba and Captain Bill Englehart. Althoff and his wingman had nearly gotten shot out of the sky as they maneuvered their Sea Knights into the LZ hacked from the jungle, but they kept their battered birds in the air long enough for the bloodied Marines to dive aboard, then shot their way out of the closing cordon of enemy soldiers.

On February 13, Althoff and Englehart had another narrow escape during a resupply run to Khe Sanh. Accompanied by a Sea Knight flown by Captain Robert Yeager and Lieutenant Doug Morrison, Althoff's first scheduled stop was Hill 881 South. The NVA opened up with machine guns and small arms, and a rocket exploded in the LZ, seriously wounding three Marines on the ground. Althoff landed in the maelstrom to medevac the injured Marines and sat on the LZ as shrapnel and bullets tore into his Sea Knight while the casualties were loaded aboard. He got shot up some more getting away from the hill but safely delivered the wounded men to Charlie Med.[5]

That was followed by Althoff's ill-fated February 20 mission to 881 South, when he ended up sitting in a hot LZ for more than a minute until Marines could get the mortally wounded Corporal Terry Smith aboard. Althoff had taken heavy damage getting away from the hill and had barely coaxed his aircraft down to the combat base. While stretcher bearers hustled the dying Marine off to Charlie Med, Althoff switched out his battle-damaged bird for another helicopter and took off on his next mission.

Once again, it was all in a day's work for Althoff.

• • •

As American pilots and air crews struggled to sustain the remote combat base and hill outposts, a dire snapshot of the worsening supply situation at Khe Sanh worked its way up the chain of command. Major General Rathvon Tompkins, commander of the 3rd Marine Division, had laid out the grim equation for his superiors: Khe Sanh needed sixty pounds of supplies per man per day (including artillery support), which meant a total daily requirement of about 180 tons for the current population of about 6,000 fighting men. By February 19, Khe Sanh's supply shortfall was a staggering 1,172 tons.[6]

The I Corps helicopter pilots were doing their best to chip away at the deficit, but the loss of more than a dozen helicopters in missions to the hill outposts during the first month of the siege had pushed the effort to a crisis point. At Quang Tri Air Base, there was an urgent sense that something had to be done.[7]

Around February 21, Dave Althoff huddled with Lieutenant Colonel William J. White, commander of Marine Observation Squadron 6

(VMO-6), which provided gunship support for the Khe Sanh helicopter missions, and Major Arthur C. Crane, VMO-6 operations officer. The three Marines roughed out a plan to smother the NVA gunners with smoke screens, artillery, fixed-wing aircraft, and helicopter gunships during resupply and medevac missions. White laid out the idea for the MAG-36 commander, Colonel Frank E. Wilson, and then briefed the commander of the 1st Marine Aircraft Wing, Major General Norman Anderson.

At Anderson's direction, Lieutenant Colonel White fleshed out the details with the wing's operations staff, and Lieutenant Colonel Richard E. Carey suggested a name for the operation: Super Gaggle, a fighter-pilot term for massive confusion. If the American plan worked, confusion would be the best possible outcome for the North Vietnamese lying in wait around the Khe Sanh hill outposts.[8]

• • •

About an hour before noon on Saturday, February 24, a single-engine Cessna O-1 Bird Dog entered the air space above Khe Sanh and began circling the skies to the west, over Hill 881 South and Hill 861. The aircraft was joined by a TA-4F, a modified single-engine Skyhawk jet, with a tactical air controller in the second seat. A Marine KC-130 arrived and began orbiting high above.

Operation Sierra—the Super Gaggle—was underway.[9]

At H-minus-one hour, the first of ten Marine A-4 Skyhawks swooped down and dropped high-explosive bombs and napalm on suspected enemy anti-aircraft positions and automatic weapons sites around 881 South. As smoke and flames billowed from the hillsides, the Skyhawks made repeated strafing runs, blasting the scorched terrain with their 20-millimeter cannon.

At H-minus-ten-minutes, a pair of Skyhawks with tanks dangling from their wings streaked low over the smoldering NVA positions. A fine mist floated down from the Skyhawks, soaking the terrain with tear gas. Strike aircraft dumped more high explosives and napalm on the North Vietnamese. Finally, at H-minus-four-minutes, another pair of A-4s roared over 881 South, spewing a thick smoke screen from wing tanks.

With a clatter of rotors, four UH-1E helicopter gunships escorted eight CH-46D Sea Knights into the clear skies behind the curtain of smoke. Dangling beneath the Sea Knights were external nets packed with ammunition, food, water, and medical supplies.

In less than five minutes, some 24,000 pounds of badly needed supplies lay on the landing zones of 881 South. One of the eight Sea Knights was hit over the hill, by North Vietnamese gunners firing blindly through the smoke, and it was forced to make an emergency landing at the Khe Sanh airstrip. The others headed back to their home base as the A-4 Skyhawks capped off the performance by pounding North Vietnamese positions around 881 South with high explosives, napalm, and 20-millimeter cannon.[10]

The Super Gaggle had made a nearly flawless debut.

"Today was a small victory," wrote General Norman Anderson, commander of the 1st Marine Aircraft Wing. But it was just the beginning. To outlast the North Vietnamese at Khe Sanh, the spectacular resupply mission of February 24 would have to be replicated "again and again in the next few weeks."[11]

PART III

CHAPTER 16

"Why Are You Leaving Us Out Here to Die?"

Fog cloaked Khe Sanh Combat Base on Sunday morning, February 25, as Bravo 1/26 platoon leader Don Jacques prepared his men for a two-hour patrol beyond the southeastern perimeter. Twenty years old, from Rochester, New York, Second Lieutenant Jacques didn't turn heads with his physical makeup in the manner of brawny Marines like Bill Dabney. Nothing about his height, build, or looks really stood out. But stand out he did, and that distinction spoke to the passion Don Jacques brought to his work as an officer in the United States Marine Corps.

Jacques had quit college to enlist in the Marines, and he had survived the grind of boot camp at Parris Island. He caught the eye of his drill instructors and was plucked from the ranks and sent to Officer Candidates School at Quantico. In the late summer of 1967, he became the youngest graduate of the Basic School in nearly two decades.[1]

After arriving in Vietnam on October 9, Jacques had joined Bravo 1/26 and had won the trust of skipper Ken Pipes. Given the reins of Bravo's 3rd Platoon, he had further impressed when his men ambushed an NVA reconnaissance unit in late December. The New Yorker was confident and raring to go—too much so for some who encountered him at Khe Sanh.[2]

But an officer's reputation counted for nothing with the North Vietnamese soldiers looking to kill Americans around Khe Sanh. Jacques would have to be on his game this morning as he led his platoon outside the wire to see what was up with the NVA.

The night before, Jacques had scribbled letters to his parents and his sister, Jeanne. "The days go by quite quickly but the nights are long around here," he wrote his mother and father. "I haven't been getting much sleep." To his sister, he hinted at the looming showdown that everyone expected at Khe Sanh. "We're just sitting here waiting for all hell to burst loose. . . . With each day that passes by the incoming increases and the [3rd Platoon] digs deeper." He ended on a reassuring note. "I'm fine, and still kicking. I'll write again soon. Love, brother Don."[3]

• • •

The patrol was to be a textbook diamond pattern, and Jacques was to hew closely to the plotted route so friendly artillery would know exactly where he was in the event of trouble. He was to check in by radio at three designated points and remain within 1,000 meters (about 1,100 yards) of the base.[4]

Corporal Steve Wiese, leader of the platoon's 1st Squad, had been told to get his men ready for a short recon to look for enemy tunnels and trenches, and to expect trouble. Wiese was on his second tour in Vietnam, and he had learned that troops in combat burned through ammo in a hurry. He instructed his men to take at least five magazines and four grenades.[5]

High spirits and apprehension coursed through the column as the patrol headed out through the southeastern wire just after 8:00 a.m. The fog was burning away, and after weeks of getting pummeled in their trenches, the forty-odd Marines and corpsmen welcomed the opportunity to stretch their legs. They were a mix of seasoned veterans and rookies on their first patrol. Among the former were Wiese and Ken Claire, big, athletic men from California, both squad leaders, both outstanding Marines, the kind of guys you wanted beside you in a fight. Corpsman John Cicala—"Motown Doc," he had written on his helmet—knew his way around, too, and the contents of the Unit 1 medical bag he carried in one hand reflected the wisdom of his months in combat: pressure bandages, blood expander, bags of IV fluids, and the cellophane wrappers from cigarette packs used in the emergency treatment of a sucking chest wound.[6]

Among the rookies was Private First Class Calvin Bright, a wide-eyed eighteen-year-old farm boy from a family of Marines back in Jackson, Michigan. After arriving at Khe Sanh on the eve of the siege, Bright and his regular partner, PFC Lloyd Scudder, had made a zany game of the loathsome chore of cleaning the platoon's latrines. As NVA spotters watched through field glasses, one of the Marines would pour gasoline into the halved-barrels that served as Marine toilets and burn the foul-smelling mix. Within seconds, North Vietnamese mortars would begin firing, but Bright and Scudder would not be rushed. While one of the pair timed the incoming rounds, the other would perform a spastic chicken dance. At the last possible instant, they would dive into the nearest trench, just ahead of the exploding mortars.[7]

Moving beyond the perimeter wire, the patrol almost immediately discovered a trench the North Vietnamese had dug up to the garbage dump outside Bravo lines. The trench angled down a slope to the south, then continued beyond a creek and disappeared in the direction of the NVA stronghold on Hill 471, about 2,200 yards due south. After following the trench for a short distance, the Marines climbed out and headed southeast on their planned route.

Their path was roughly parallel to the dirt road that wound along the southern perimeter of the combat base, past the garbage dump and into the coffee trees and scrub jungle of an old French plantation that had seen better days. The Marines crossed a small creek and picked their way through a landscape shorn of vegetation and cratered by bombs and shells. They completed the first leg without incident, and Jacques checked in by radio with the Bravo command post.[8]

The patrol continued in a southeasterly direction. Just after 9:00 a.m., the Marines were about 275 yards south of the garbage dump road and more than 200 yards north of the main access road that connected the combat base to Route 9. At the head of the column, the men in Steve Wiese's squad spotted a flash of movement to their right, near the access road. Three NVA soldiers jumped from cover, ran along the road until the Marines opened fire, then ducked into a treeline along the southern edge of the dirt track.

Something about the movement didn't seem right to Wiese: *Why would the gooks reveal themselves by running along the road, where we would be sure to see them?*[9]

Jacques radioed Captain Pipes and requested permission to pursue the NVA soldiers. Battalion and regimental headquarters badly wanted prisoners for interrogation, a fact well known to the Bravo skipper and his young platoon commander. Pipes gave his qualified approval. "You can go," he said. "But don't get in something you can't handle."[10] A spirited discussion ensued between Jacques and his squad leaders. The patrol's Kit Carson scout, a Vietnamese defector familiar with enemy tactics, warned the Marines not to proceed. "Bad, bad," he said, over and over again.[11]

Jacques ignored the scout and ordered Wiese to send one of his fire teams after the NVA.

"It's a bad idea," Wiese said. "I think it's a trap."

The lieutenant didn't want to hear it. "Okay, take your entire squad," Jacques ordered.

Wiese erupted. "Are you out of your mind? There's something wrong here!"

Ken Claire tried to defuse the tense situation. He made clear his concerns, but diplomatically added: "It's your call, Lieutenant."[12]

The confrontation would have made for a lively case study in small-unit command back at Quantico, but this wasn't a classroom. Don Jacques was a rising young officer with a promising career and promotions ahead. Steve Wiese didn't have anything to prove, and he didn't give a damn about promotions and medals. He wanted to survive his tour, and preserve the lives of the men under his command and the comrades he had come to love in Vietnam.

Lieutenant Jacques came down hard. He relieved Wiese of command and told him to "take a knee," then ordered Wiese's assistant to pursue the NVA. The Marine refused.

Jacques now faced a near-mutiny, and it was playing out in full view of his platoon in the middle of an operation. Aggressive by nature, he chose to ignore the warnings of his scout and squad leaders. If Wiese and his men wouldn't pursue the NVA as a fire team or a squad, everyone would go. He ordered the entire platoon on line. Raising his pistol, Don Jacques gave the order to advance. "Let's go get them!" he yelled.[13]

• • •

Moving at a trot and spread out along a line about 100 yards across, the

Marines pushed south through a field toward the access road and the treeline where the three NVA soldiers had disappeared. The Americans came to an empty trench line and jumped over it.[14] They crossed a second trench, and somebody saw movement. A shot rang out.

Almost instantly, a devastating barrage engulfed the Americans. NVA soldiers hiding in trenches, bunkers, and camouflaged spider holes to the front and right flank fired automatic rifles, machine guns, mortars, and rocket-propelled grenades into the Bravo patrol. The North Vietnamese were arrayed in the shape of the letter "L," with the long leg of the ambush in the treeline along the road. From positions in trees and brush that formed the short leg along the west, the enemy troops ripped the Americans with enfilading fire.[15]

Jacques and his command group had sought shelter in a small trench, and from there the lieutenant ordered Corporal Claire to flank the North Vietnamese in the enfilading position to the west. Accompanied by Staff Sergeant George B. McClelland, Claire led about a dozen Marines to the right in an attempt to get behind the NVA. But the Americans turned too soon, and they charged headlong into devastating frontal fire.

Rifleman Edward Rayburn fell to the ground, his lower jaw ripped away by an enemy bullet. Claire helped the wounded Marine into a trench, then stood in the hail of NVA fire as he directed the rest of his squad to take cover. Americans were dying across the field, screams and shouts piercing the roar of automatic-weapons fire and exploding grenades.[16]

• • •

Back at the combat base, roughly 1,000 yards to the north, Bravo skipper Ken Pipes was tracking the patrol's progress from his command bunker when he heard the first shots.

It was clear to Pipes almost immediately that Jacques and his men were in big trouble. If Bravo-3 had stumbled onto an NVA observation post or recon team, or even a squad or platoon, Pipes would be hearing the chatter of AK-47 rifles punctuated by an occasional RPG and Chicom grenade explosion. Instead, the sound that carried from the south was a terrible cacophony of machine guns, mortars, RPGs, and small arms firing simultaneously.

Jacques was on the company radio net almost immediately, summing up the tactical situation for Pipes, which wasn't easy amid the deadly chaos. Pipes tried to pinpoint the location of Jacques and his men. Patchy fog and the rolling terrain obscured visual contact with the American patrol. Still unknown to Pipes and 1/26 battalion fire support officers was the fact that Jacques had strayed from his plotted route and was now more than 400 yards south of the garbage dump road.[17]

Pipes ordered Second Lieutenant Peter Weiss, commander of Bravo's 1st Platoon, to move to the aid of Jacques and his men, but an NVA blocking force was waiting. The 1st Platoon Marines were still more than 300 yards from the ambush site when a burst of machine gun fire hit the relief force, killing a squad leader and corpsman and wounding several others. Weiss and his men could go no further.

At the 1/26 battalion command post, Lieutenant William Smith called up his friend, artillery forward observer Hank Norman, at the Bravo command bunker. Norman explained that the patrol wasn't where it was supposed to be. It was maddening: Marines were dying, and the one thing that could save them was a well-placed artillery mission or air strike, but that couldn't happen because nobody knew where the friendly forces were and where the bad guys were.[18]

Pipes, meanwhile, asked his battalion commander, Lieutenant Colonel James Wilkinson, for permission to lead the remainder of his company to the aid of his men. The request went up to Colonel Lownds at regimental headquarters, but Wilkinson and Lownds agreed that pouring more men into an ambush that had probably run its course would only weaken the defense of the combat base. Pipes argued that they couldn't just leave his Marines to die, but he was overruled.[19]

Don Jacques had made a tragic mistake, but he was fighting hard, trying to find a way to get his platoon out of this awful mess. Given the desperate situation, the young officer's fury was understandable. "Why aren't you doing something to help us?" Jacques demanded of Captain Pipes. "Why are you leaving us out here to die?"[20]

• • •

At the instant the North Vietnamese sprang the ambush, corpsman John Cicala was charging ahead behind the line of Marines. An American fell to the ground ahead of him, and Cicala dashed to his side. Lance Corporal

Jerry Lee Dodson of Collinsville, Illinois, was alive and conscious when Cicala reached him, despite the fact that a bullet had entered his left eye and blown out the right side of his head. Cicala dressed the massive wounds, knowing full well that the twenty-year-old Marine didn't have long. He was about to move to the next casualty when Dodson said, "Doc, put another magazine in for me."[21] Cicala popped a magazine into the M-16 lying beside Dodson and handed it to the dying Marine.

Cries of "Corpsman!" sounded from all sides as wounded men fell to the ground. Cicala sprinted toward a Marine who dropped a few yards ahead, but he never made it. An NVA soldier popped from a hole and fired two rounds from his AK-47.

The bullets slammed into Cicala's chest like a hammer blow and knocked the corpsman onto his back. One round ripped through his flak jacket, punctured a lung and exited Cicala's back. The other struck a bundle of metal objects dangling from his neck—dog tags, a can opener, a St. Christopher's medal, and other jewelry. The bullet drove hot metal shards into Cicala's neck and chest but flattened out against the metal objects and fell harmlessly to the ground.

Gasping for air, Cicala realized that his lung was slowly deflating from a sucking chest wound. As he began to prepare a dressing, he heard corpsman Frank Calzia call out to him. "J. C., are you okay?"[22] Just then, Cicala felt something hit his leg. He spotted the enemy grenade and managed to curl into a ball just before the explosion ripped into his body.

Cicala was still dazed by the blast when Doc Calzia sprawled beside him. The wounded corpsman could see his friend's lips moving but couldn't hear a thing. Cicala began a quick inventory of his limbs and felt sick when he saw that one leg was twisted behind him at an impossible angle. He was relieved to discover that his foot still moved. The grenade had blown off part of his kneecap and riddled his torso and legs with shrapnel, but everything was still attached. He waved Calzia away. "Get the hell out of here. Go take care of the other guys."[23]

The wounded corpsman was preparing a battle dressing for his mangled knee when Lieutenant Jacques ran past. "Doc, get out of here any way you can!" the platoon commander yelled to Cicala. "Everybody's getting killed!"[24] Jacques took a few more steps before collapsing to the ground, cut down by a burst of NVA machine-gun fire.

Cicala crawled to the stricken lieutenant. Two rounds had ripped through Don Jacques's groin, tearing the femoral arteries in both legs. Cicala applied dressings, but blood continued to gush from the wounds.

Glancing around, the corpsman didn't see anyone still alive around him. With agonized effort, the Motown Doc began crawling to the north, away from the field of death.[25]

• • •

On the left side of the advancing Marines, Steve Wiese heard two rifle shots and then a deafening barrage. He had been mentally prepared for the ambush, so he instantly dropped to the ground and rolled into a bomb crater as murderous North Vietnamese fire swept the field. Wiese heard yelling and screaming rise with the roar of gunfire and grenade blasts. He periodically popped above the crater rim to throw grenades and fire at NVA soldiers in a nearby trench line. Every time, heavy fire chewed up the ground around him.

The Marines couldn't match the firepower of the enemy force, and they were doomed if they remained in place. Wiese yelled to the few surviving Marines within earshot: "Every man for himself! Get yourself out of here! Get out of the kill zone!"[26]

Scrambling from one hole to the next, Wiese began moving toward the northeast, away from the deadly fire.

• • •

Elsewhere in the kill zone, Corporal Robert E. Matzka held his squad together as best he could before the deadly enemy fire proved overwhelming. And then, he, too, found a way out of the maelstrom and made his way northward.

Corporal Gilbert Wall, an 81-millimeter mortars forward observer assigned to the patrol, had moved away from Lieutenant Jacques in the opening minutes of the ambush and became pinned behind a tree. He weighed whether to call in mortar fire from Khe Sanh but decided the risk of hitting his scattered comrades was too great, so he held off.[27]

When the firing eased, Wall began making his way out of the ambush area. He came upon the blood-soaked body of Lieutenant Don Jacques, dying, if not already dead. Hoisting the young officer over his shoulder, Wall set out for the Khe Sanh perimeter.

• • •

Corporal Ken Claire and the shattered remnants of his squad were among the last Americans alive in the kill zone. Claire's clownish antics had sometimes obscured his superb qualities as a Marine, and on that terrible morning, in a blood-soaked field south of Khe Sanh Combat Base, no American performed with greater bravery. Claire had collected his wounded in one of the many trenches that stitched the ambush zone, dashing into fire again and again to pull men to safety. He continued to resist the murderous NVA fire for the better part of an hour, even after he was twice wounded. A third North Vietnamese bullet finally ended the life of the twenty-one-year-old Marine from Redwood City, California, silencing forever the Tarzan yell he had perfected on Sierra Nevada summits as a boy.[28]

Two of Claire's men, the grievously wounded rifleman Edward Rayburn and machine gunner Thomas A. Detrick, waited until the firing dropped off, then began their harrowing trek back to the base.

Three Marines from Claire's squad—Ronald Ridgeway, James Bruder, and Charles Geller—had remained hidden in a trench until the firing stopped. Ridgeway and Geller had killed three NVA soldiers who approached their trench, but Bruder had been mortally wounded. As the two surviving Marines tried to run out of the kill zone, Geller came upon a Marine lying on his back with a broken arm and dropped to his side. A bullet ripped through Geller's face, and another round broke Ridgeway's arm. The three Americans—Geller, Ridgeway, and twenty-five-year-old Willy Ruff of Columbia, South Carolina—decided to lie low until dark.[29]

Late in the afternoon, Geller became delirious, and his cries alerted NVA soldiers around them. Grenades exploded among the Marines, and Geller was hit and killed.

The NVA troops began firing from their trenches into bodies they could see, and Ruff and Ridgeway were wounded still again. Friendly artillery pounded the area, and shrapnel hit Ruff in the head. As Ruff lay bleeding from his head wound, Ridgeway passed out.

• • •

Through the late morning and early afternoon, wounded survivors made their way back to the combat base. Bravo's 1st Platoon collected as many men as possible before withdrawing inside the wire, but other Marines slipped back outside to watch for their comrades. Freelance news photographer Robert Ellison had become fond of the Bravo Marines after spending time with them, and he now led a handful of men through a minefield into the nearby brush to look for survivors.[30]

Corporal Gilbert Wall arrived from the battlefield, still carrying Lieutenant Jacques over his shoulder. Two other Marines began dragging the lifeless body of the young platoon leader back through the tall grass. With the click of his camera shutter, Ellison captured the heartbreaking scene.

One of the Marines in Ellison's photograph was Lance Corporal Edward I. Prendergast, a 60-millimeter mortarman who had been positioned in the Bravo lines to provide supporting fire for the patrol. Around 4:00 p.m., Prendergast heard gunfire from the Bravo trench line to his right, and he spotted a man near the garbage dump. Yelling for the Marines to cease fire, Prendergast ran out to see if the new arrival was a friend who hadn't returned from the patrol. When he reached the bloody form, Prendergast saw it was the corpsman he only knew as the Motown Doc. After more than six hours of agonizing struggle, John Cicala had dragged himself back from the ambush site.

During his painful trek, Cicala had managed to elude roaming bands of NVA soldiers. He had lost a lot of blood and struggled to breathe with his collapsed lung, but he had willed himself on with visions of his girlfriend back in Michigan, and the promise he had made: "I won't die in Vietnam."[31]

Now Cicala lay just outside the Khe Sanh wire, "white as a ghost." When Prendergast reached his side, Cicala tried to convey the enormity of the tragedy. "Everyone is dead," he mumbled. "Everyone is dead."[32] Prendergast hoisted the wounded corpsman to his shoulder and tossed him over the wire to a pair of waiting Marines. A long and painful recovery awaited the Motown Doc, but he would make good on his promise to survive Vietnam.

• • •

Private First Class Edward C. Rayburn had been saved by Ken Claire in the opening moments of the ambush, and he had witnessed the death of his courageous squad leader and most of his comrades. He had been greeted outside the Khe Sanh wire by corpsman Thomas E. Casey and others, but the badly wounded Marine refused to go inside for medical attention. With the ghastly wound to his jaw, Rayburn was unable to speak, but he kept looking to the south, in the direction of the ambush. Casey finally asked him if there was something he was trying to tell them. Rayburn nodded his head up and down. "Are there others still alive out there?" Casey asked. Rayburn emphatically nodded yes. With that vital information communicated, Rayburn finally agreed to go inside.[33]

Rayburn would undergo many surgeries, and he would endure painful complications with the efforts to rebuild his jaw and restore his face to a semblance of the handsome Marine who had marched out of Khe Sanh Combat Base on the morning of February 25. He visited the family of his squad leader around 1970 and told the Claires how their beloved Ken had died, and how heroic and selfless he had been in his final minutes on earth. In time, the physical and emotional burdens that Rayburn carried away from the ambush became too great, and on January 23, 1976, at a time of the year when the men who served at Khe Sanh always remember the beginning of the great battle, Edward Rayburn took his own life.[34]

● ● ●

Private First Class Calvin Bright had watched in horror as his first Marine patrol had disintegrated into slaughter. His fire team leader was cut down, along with the unit's other two members. Soon, every American within sight was dead or dying.

A PRC-25 radio strapped to the back of a dead Marine crackled to life: "Hello! Hello! Can anybody hear me?" Bright crawled to the radio. In a low voice, he informed the unidentified Marine officer on the other end that everyone was dead, and that he was surrounded by North Vietnamese. With Bright's assistance, the officer called in artillery, and the shells were adjusted until they rained down on the enemy trenches.[35]

Bright crept away toward the combat base, sometimes crouching in silence as NVA troops combed the brush around him. He finally emerged into a clearing outside the Khe Sanh perimeter.

Breaking into a run, Bright began to hear the shouts of South Vietnamese Rangers along the eastern perimeter, and he thought they were urging him on. Then he began to hear cries in English, and he saw Marines frantically gesturing. When he reached the outer wire, Bright discovered what the ruckus had been about: he had just run through a minefield.[36]

• • •

Steve Wiese's escape from the kill zone unfolded in a series of short sprints, two-second bursts from one bomb hole to the next as NVA fire sliced the air and kicked up the dirt around him. As he moved out of grenade range, Wiese saw low-flying American jets streak overhead, dropping bombs and napalm. One pilot seemed to be checking him out. Wiese waved his arms, fearing he was about to get blown away. The pilot wagged his wings and pulled off.[37]

Wiese started to time his movements to the jet passes. He would crouch like a sprinter at the starting block, wait for the bombs or napalm to hit, then dash to the next hole he had scoped out. When he finally reached the area along the garbage dump road, he decided to lie low and wait for reinforcements. He sat in a hole for a few hours, but his comrades never came. With shadows lengthening, Wiese set out for the base.

Night was falling over Khe Sanh when he finally reached the gate where the high-spirited Marines had set out that morning. Wiese had one question for the comrades who greeted him: "How many guys made it back?" There was no response, and so he repeated himself: "How many guys made it back?" He had to ask the question once or twice more before somebody finally spoke up. "Not many," came the reply.[38]

• • •

At the Bravo command post, Captain Ken Pipes waited by his radios most of the night. He prayed for a miracle, a call from other men who had made it out of the kill zone and were only waiting for daylight to return. But the call never came.

The next day, and then the next night, and for a few days and nights afterward, Pipes kept his solitary vigil. He would sit by the radios, and the tears would stream down his cheeks as he mourned the loss of his men.

• • •

As it turned out, the vigil of Captain Pipes was not in vain: one of his boys *was* still alive out there.

Rifleman Ronald Ridgeway had passed out between the NVA trenches, and he awoke with a start on the morning of February 26 as a North Vietnamese soldier tried to pull his wristwatch from his arm. The NVA surrounded their prisoner, and Ridgeway was led into captivity in North Vietnam.

Nearly five years would pass, and Ridgeway's name would be among those chiseled into a marble headstone placed over the grave of nine casualties from the February 25 ambush, Marines who were buried as a group at Jefferson Barracks National Cemetery in St. Louis, Missouri.

At 1:15 a.m. on Sunday morning, January, 28, 1973, the phone rang in the Houston, Texas, home of Mildred Ridgeway. The caller identified himself as a Marine Corps officer. "It's my son," Mrs. Ridgeway interrupted. "He's alive, isn't he?"[39]

Indeed, he was.

Ken Pipes was assigned to the Marine Corps base at Quantico, Virginia, in January 1973, and he, too, got a phone call, notifying him that a young Marine who had been under his command at Khe Sanh, a Marine who had been listed as killed in action on February 25, 1968, was alive in a North Vietnamese prison.[40] Three months later, Private First Class Ronald Lewis Ridgeway stepped off a plane with other prisoners of war released by North Vietnam. It was the miracle for which Ken Pipes had waited so many years.

• • •

Lieutenant Don Jacques had led more than forty young Americans outside the Khe Sanh wire on the morning of February 25, 1968. Fewer than half made it back alive. The only body that had been recovered from the Bravo patrol was that of Jacques. Twenty-three Americans lay at the scene of the ambush or nearby, killed by North Vietnamese fire, or by the friendly air strikes and artillery that followed. For the Marines of Bravo 1/26, it had been a day of unimaginable heartbreak and loss.

CHAPTER 17

"A Military Challenge Unprecedented in This War"

As the dying echoes of gunfire and explosions from the Bravo ambush swept across the combat base at midday on February 25, a Marine aerial observer flying overhead in a small plane spotted further cause for alarm. The trenches and bunkers in which the North Vietnamese had lain in wait for Lieutenant Jacques and his men were part of an intricate complex that an ARVN Ranger patrol had stumbled onto nine days earlier. Now, enemy soldiers had extended long tentacles from those fortifications. The Marine observer noted a new trench, more than 700 yards long and wide enough to funnel assault troops two-abreast to the outer Khe Sanh wire, as well as another trench that ran parallel to the Khe Sanh wire for about fifty yards—cover for enemy troops to form a skirmish line before charging the wire.[1]

As he orbited overhead, the Marine observer came under heavy automatic-weapons fire from the trenches and surrounding jungle. About thirty minutes after his initial discovery, he identified more enemy fortifications nearby, including two assault trenches that ended only about fifteen yards from the southeastern Khe Sanh wire. Huddled inside one of these trenches were about fifty to one hundred North Vietnamese soldiers.[2]

The Bravo ambush and the discovery of the new assault trenches tripped alarms up the American chain of command. Artillery, mortars, and attack jets pounded the NVA positions that now completely encircled the combat base. A request from General Westmoreland to bring B-52 Arc Light strikes closer than the mandated buffer of 3,000 meters (about 3,200 yards) around friendly troops had been approved by higher authorities on February 18, and now target boxes were plotted to within 1,000 meters (about 1,100 yards) of the base. A test strike was readied for Monday, February 26.[3]

The predawn hours of February 26 pulsed with the sounds of enemy vehicles and troops southwest of the base. A listening post manned by Special Forces out of FOB-3 reported a tracked vehicle moving in the darkness, as well as other movements and sounds coming from a village about 500 yards beyond the access road that connected the base to Route 9. The Green Berets requested a fire mission, and a 4.2-inch mortar unleashed several rounds that exploded in the vicinity of the noises.

Daylight brought more air strikes on the North Vietnamese lines. Among the Americans watching and cheering were the Marines of Combined Action Company Oscar. The survivors of the fight at Khe Sanh village had been adopted by the Special Forces after their withdrawal from the Huong Hoa district headquarters on January 21, and now they were dug in along the FOB-3 perimeter. Oscar-2 corpsman John Roberts, the folksy Baptist preacher from the Texas Panhandle, watched the air show unfold with Lance Corporal Billy Dale Livingston of Alma, Arkansas, and another Marine. Around 11:00 a.m., a Navy attack jet approached and fired a pair of rockets, but the pilot's aim was off. The rockets ripped into the FOB-3 trench line, killing the eighteen-year-old Livingston. Doc Roberts was hurled into the air but escaped injury. He grabbed a rifle and tried to shoot at the Navy jet before a sergeant hit him in the head and calmed him down.[4]

For more than a month now, death and gore had been staples of daily life for the defenders of Khe Sanh, and there was no end in sight. Stories about the terrible fate of the Bravo patrol had spread through the trench lines, and if that wasn't bad enough, word got around that the bodies of some twenty-five Marines were still out there, and their comrades had been told to stand down because an enemy division or two was out there, waiting to strike.

On February 27, General Westmoreland cabled a pep talk to Colonel Lownds and his embattled men. "You, your Marines, and the associated U.S. Army and Vietnamese troops are at the center of the international stage," Westmoreland said. "You are faced with a military challenge unprecedented in this war. I want you and your troops to know that I have the utmost confidence in your fighting spirit, professionalism, and alertness. These essential qualities, plus the indomitable courage of the U.S. Marines, are destined to prevail over the enemy."[5]

• • •

Like an extended drum roll, the maneuvering continued through February 27 and into the next day—enemy artillery, rockets, and mortars; friendly artillery and air; NVA movements around the wire under the cover of darkness; and the enemy's relentless digging of new trenches and bunkers. The eastern perimeter of Khe Sanh, defended by the ARVN Rangers and the Marines of Bravo 1/26, continued to be a focal point of the enemy activities.[6]

Daylight on Thursday morning, February 29, revealed the industry of NVA sappers hard at work in that area. Overnight they had ventured into the minefields set out by the American combat engineers, removing trip flares and cutting the eastern perimeter wire in three places—all without setting off a single mine or flare.[7]

Nightfall of February 29 unleashed a flurry of North Vietnamese activity. Around 6:45 p.m., sniper fire streaked into the Bravo 1/26 positions. Next, the Special Forces at FOB-3 reported trip flares going off and movement to their front. Seismic and acoustic sensor reports pouring into the 26th Marines command bunker indicated heavy enemy vehicle and troop activity along Route 9. A regiment or more of the NVA 304th Division—at least 1,500 men—was on the move.

Amid the controlled chaos and crackling radios of the 26th Marines command bunker, Colonel Lownds and his staff now executed their carefully drawn plans for the long-awaited enemy ground assault. Lownds urgently requested the diversion of inbound B-52 bombers from their scheduled targets so they could pound North Vietnamese assembly areas about 1,100 yards south and southeast of the base. Frontline units prepared to repel enemy assault troops, while further back, reaction forces

FIGHTING AROUND KHE SANH COMBAT BASE
FEBRUARY 13 – MARCH 30, 1968

USMC

KHE SANH
COMBAT BASE

USA
MACV-SOG

BRAVO 1/26
ARVN 37TH RANGERS

GARBAGE
DUMP

MILITARY ROAD (UNUSED)

March 8
ARVN Rangers attack
NVA siege positions

Feb. 29-March 1
NVA forces attack
ARVN Ranger lines

Feb. 13
ARVN Rangers
attack NVA siege
positions

Feb. 25
Bravo 1/26 patrol
ambushed

MAIN ACCESS ROAD

March 30
Bravo 1/26 Marines
attack North Vietnamese
lines

N
500 Feet

FRENCH
PLANTATION
HOUSE

TO ROUTE 9

NVA TRENCHES AND BUNKERS

The battle for Khe Sanh Combat Base, February 13–March 30, 1968.

stood ready to plug any breaches in the perimeter. Artillery and mortars thundered and whooshed as rounds blanketed preplanned targets.[8]

In a section of the command bunker crammed with radios and acetate-overlaid maps, the Fire Support Coordination Center set in motion a massive air and artillery response. The guns of Lieutenant Colonel John A. Hennelly's 1st Battalion, 13th Marines, at the combat base—105-millimeter and 155-millimeter howitzers—and the big 175-millimeter guns to the east at the Rockpile and Camp Carroll poured fire into prearranged target boxes. Radar-directed fighters joined the attack on the fringes, and the night flashed with thunderous explosions along an arc that curled several thousand yards through the countryside south of Khe Sanh Combat Base.[9]

Inside the target boxes, NVA troops came under a devastating fire. The Americans unleashed the same rolling barrage that had shattered the February 5 attack on 861 Alpha, trapping the enemy troops in a deadly box of artillery fire and air strikes that ripped their flanks and then rolled up behind them like a scythe, swinging back and forth over the NVA as they tried to position themselves to strike the American stronghold. The North Vietnamese were being driven toward the minefields and concertina wire along the outer perimeter of Khe Sanh Combat Base, and into the guns of the waiting ARVN Rangers and US Marines.[10]

• • •

At 9:30 p.m., the first wave of North Vietnamese assault troops hit the ARVN Ranger positions from the east and southeast. Many carried Bangalore torpedoes or satchel charges to blast holes in the perimeter wire. One enemy soldier actually penetrated the perimeter, and six others were killed in the wire before the South Vietnamese troops beat back the attack.

Fog now engulfed the combat base, cloaking enemy movements and adding to the anxieties of the men in the trenches. At 10:05 p.m., the commander of the ARVN Rangers requested a Spooky gunship to break up the large enemy force to his front. The gunship arrived over the southeastern perimeter in two minutes, but a layer of fog precluded firing so close to friendly lines. For the North Vietnamese who had survived the first rounds of American air strikes and artillery, it was a temporary reprieve.[11]

At 11:30 p.m., an NVA battalion mounted a second attack on the ARVN Ranger positions, but the combined firepower of the radar-directed air strikes and rolling artillery barrage shattered the surge. Midnight arrived, and in the early hours of March 1, the North Vietnamese survivors regrouped in the trenches and bunkers that studded the rolling terrain beyond the southeastern Khe Sanh perimeter.

As the night wore on, North Vietnamese gunners weighed in with modest counterfire in support of their ground forces. Between midnight and 6:00 a.m. of March 1, ninety-five rounds of artillery, rockets, and mortars fell on the combat base, killing one American and wounding five.

The final attempt to break through the ARVN Ranger positions came at 3:15 a.m., and it ended quickly with the shattered North Vietnamese survivors slipping away into what remained of the fog-shrouded night.[12] American artillery and fighter jets continued to harass the bloodied NVA forces until dawn of March 1 broke over Khe Sanh Combat Base.

Daylight revealed the bodies of seventy-one NVA dead left behind by their comrades, most of them cut down by the American air strikes and artillery. A patrol east of the base confirmed the deadly effectiveness of the new American "firecracker" artillery rounds that had been introduced during the attack on Lang Vei and were fired again during the attacks of February 29–March 1. "The dead were still huddled in trenches," the patrol reported, "many in the kneeling position, in three successive platoon lines, as if they had been caught in the assault position."[13]

The ARVN Rangers had ably defended their stretch of the Khe Sanh perimeter, surviving the night with the loss of only one man.

• • •

As the second North Vietnamese probe was being driven back from the Khe Sanh wire in the closing minutes of February 29, a crowd gathered in cold rain and sleet on the other side of the world, outside the Pentagon's Potomac River entrance. It was late morning in the nation's capital, and the shivering men and women were there to bid farewell to the haunted man at the helm of America's war in Vietnam.

Robert Strange McNamara had been summoned to the nation's capital in the winter of 1961, one of President John F. Kennedy's "best and brightest," the Ford Motor Company president bringing his business acumen and analytical savvy to America's global Cold War against the Communists. Vietnam had been a backwater in that struggle when McNamara had taken the reins at the Pentagon, an asterisk in Kennedy's idealistic crusade in which Americans would "pay any price, bear any burden, meet any hardship, support any friend, oppose any foe, in order to assure the survival and the success of liberty." McNamara had presided over America's expanding footprint in Vietnam as the conflict metastasized from a guerrilla brush fire into the full-blown war that was now draining the United States of its youth and treasure, and destroying the administration of Kennedy's successor, President Lyndon Johnson.

On this final day of February 1968, Vietnam consumed Americans—the siege at Khe Sanh, the street fighting in Hue, the military draft at home, the antiwar demonstrations, the ballooning federal budget, even the fledgling 1968 presidential campaign, already shaping up to be a referendum on the war. Every week there was a rising butcher's bill to be paid, and McNamara's voracious war machine required a constant infusion of human capital. Just a few days earlier, his spokesmen had announced that 48,000 young Americans would be drafted in April—the highest monthly total since October 1966. Even the Marine Corps, a proudly all-volunteer force in normal times, needed more bodies to fend off the North Vietnamese in I Corps, so 4,000 of the new draftees had been earmarked for its ranks.[14]

President Johnson's limousine pulled into the Pentagon's basement parking garage just before noon. McNamara greeted his commander in chief, and they stepped into an elevator for the short ride up to the second floor, to the river entrance, where the crowd waited on the lawn that looked out on the Potomac River and Washington, DC, beyond.

The war had inextricably bound McNamara and Johnson, two very different men from very different worlds. Together they had soared to the heights of their power and promise in the triumphant days following Johnson's 1964 election victory, and together they had fallen from grace. Johnson and McNamara had tried to win the war in Vietnam with incremental escalations—more troops, then bombing, followed by still more troops—but the Communists matched them, chip for chip. By 1967, Johnson and McNamara were left to wonder how they had gotten themselves into such a mess, and how they could get out without being the first US administration to lose a war.

As Khe Sanh began, and then Tet, and the fighting and dying and bombing and destruction reached unprecedented levels, McNamara and Johnson found themselves in a nightmare of their own making. In the privacy of the White House, Johnson sobbed uncontrollably in the presence of his closest friends.[15] McNamara, too, broke down with increasing frequency, but he had learned to hide his tears from visitors to his Pentagon office by turning away, "to appear to be looking out the window."[16]

Americans were stunned with the escalation after being told for months that the war was winding down. Johnson bore the brunt of the public backlash, and approval ratings for his management of the war and overall job performance plummeted. For the first time, the leading Republican presidential candidate, former vice president Richard Nixon, pulled even with Johnson in a Gallup poll released on February 24.[17]

Vilified at home and abroad, and facing questions in Congress about whether he had taken America to war under false pretenses by lying about the Gulf of Tonkin incident in 1964, Johnson sought solace in the company of the young men he was sending to fight and die in Vietnam. On Saturday, February 17, on the spur of the moment, he flew to North Carolina to address Vietnam-bound soldiers of the 82nd Airborne Division, then winged cross-country to El Toro, California, to rally Marine reinforcements who were being rushed to the battles underway in I Corps. Standing before young Marines heavily laden with full combat kit, Johnson declared, "At Quang Tri, at Hue, at Da Nang, at Khe Sanh, tonight United States Marines stand squarely in the path of [the North Vietnamese] plan. Freedom's defense could not be in better hands."[18]

Afterward, Johnson walked the ranks of the departing Marines, shaking hands, making small talk about their hometowns and families. He watched them board their C-141 Starlifter, then followed them inside the cabin for a few more minutes of awkward conversation, as if he couldn't bear to let these boys head off to their fate. He finally took his leave and then watched as the plane rolled down the runway and disappeared into the California night, another ninety-four young Americans bound for Vietnam.[19]

During Johnson's brief absence from Washington, Vietnam had been engulfed in a second wave of Communist attacks. A new CIA assessment forwarded to Johnson on February 22, as he spent the Washington's Birthday holiday on his Texas ranch, warned of more stiff challenges ahead in Vietnam: continued Communist pressure on South

Vietnam's urban areas and a general escalation of the war, with more NVA troops and supplies flowing into the south, and the possible introduction of North Vietnamese aircraft, tanks, and advanced rockets in future battles.[20]

On February 28, after a quick fact-finding trip to Vietnam, General Earle Wheeler delivered a pessimistic report to Johnson and other senior advisers. Wheeler predicted heavy fighting ahead, and he urged approval of an explosive request from General Westmoreland for 206,000 reinforcements—or risk losing I Corps.[21]

Johnson and his advisers had begun a wide-ranging discussion about the political, economic, and military implications of Westmoreland's request and the path forward in Vietnam. McNamara had remained engaged to the end, even as his last day at the Pentagon approached, and he argued forcefully against further escalation and the idea that the United States could bomb its way to victory in Vietnam.[22]

McNamara had found his voice, behind closed doors anyway, but his role in charting America's course in Vietnam had come to an end. Johnson directed McNamara's successor, Clark Clifford, to give him a new plan for Vietnam by the following week.

At a White House ceremony later that day, February 28, Johnson had presented McNamara with the presidential Medal of Freedom, praising the outgoing secretary of defense as a "brilliant and good man." Overcome by his emotions, McNamara could not deliver his prepared remarks.[23]

And now, on February 29, midday in Washington, as the Marines and South Vietnamese Rangers battled the NVA troops on the eastern perimeter of Khe Sanh Combat Base, McNamara's tenure came to an end.

Like the war in Vietnam, the sendoff did not unfold as planned. The ceremony began twelve minutes late because McNamara and Johnson had gotten stuck in a Pentagon elevator, and a fly-by of Navy and Air Force jets was canceled by a low cloud ceiling that evoked the foul winter weather in Khe Sanh. When President Johnson finally stepped to the podium to pay tribute to the broken man who had devoted seven years and one month of his life to managing America's military affairs, the sound system failed, and few were able to hear Johnson praise McNamara as "the textbook example of the modern public servant." And then it was over. With tears rolling down his cheeks, McNamara walked back inside the massive building one final time as secretary of defense.[24]

McNamara's final month had been dominated by bad news, but in his final hours at the Pentagon, a heartening dispatch had clattered across the cable machines. South Vietnamese forces in Hue had retaken the Imperial Palace in the Citadel, and the Communist flag that had flown over Vietnam's ancient seat of power since January 31 had been torn down.

At Hue, if not at Khe Sanh and the rest of Vietnam, there was light at the end of the tunnel.

CHAPTER 18

"I Just Came from Hell"

The beginning of the Super Gaggle on February 24 had been a turning point in the supply crisis for the hill outposts at Khe Sanh. Spirits rose, along with stockpiles of food and water, as great air convoys rose in the east and thundered into the hills in clearing skies. Helicopter losses and battle damage dropped dramatically, so the external load carried by each of the eight CH-46 Sea Knights assigned to a Super Gaggle mission was increased by one-third to 4,000 pounds. On some days, as many as four runs per hill were mounted. During the five weeks of the Super Gaggle, only two Sea Knights were shot down on resupply runs.[1]

With their supply lines secure, the Marines on the hill outposts braced for further ground attacks. Their defenses were much improved after six weeks under siege, their weaponry supplemented with Starlight scopes, powerful Navy binoculars, and other devices aimed at neutralizing the NVA's expertise in the arts of stealth and camouflage.

Nightfall brought on a test of nerves and stamina as North Vietnamese sappers tried to pick off Marine listening posts and probe for weaknesses in the outer defenses. Sometimes the enemy soldiers would set out their own directional mines or plant a C-ration can with a grenade inside or some other crude booby trap. When the enemy sappers made too much noise, the Marines would respond with grenades and small arms, and illumination rounds would *whoosh* into the sky as the NVA tried to disappear into the shadows.

Like their adversaries, the North Vietnamese tried their hand at propaganda and psychological operations aimed at demoralizing Khe Sanh's defenders. The NVA set up loudspeakers in their trenches near the ARVN Ranger positions on the east end of the combat base and blasted clumsy Vietnamese-language surrender appeals.[2]

On a quiet morning in the first week of March, artillery forward observer Dennis Mannion heard the *whump* of an enemy mortar, and then a pop several hundred feet above Hill 861. Hundreds of paper leaflets scattered across the sky and fluttered to the ground. On the front was a famous World War II photograph of an Asian baby in a devastated city, framed by a popular US antiwar chant: "Hey, hey LBJ! How many kids have you killed today?" The back photograph showed the burned ruins of a riot-torn American ghetto, with the message: "Black brothers, why are you supporting your white oppressors in this war? Come over to our side and you will be treated equally!"[3] Toilet paper was scarce on the hill, so Mannion and his buddies collected a wad of leaflets and stashed them outside their latrine for use.

The North Vietnamese had demonstrated time and again their ability to penetrate the typical American field defenses of tangle foot, concertina wire, trip flares, and Claymore mines, but American technology was leveling the playing field with weapons like Starlight scopes. As the siege wore on, the North Vietnamese were finding it increasingly difficult to move about without detection, even at night. At the regimental level, the Marines had continued to make good use of the electronic sensors scattered along the roads and tracks that laced the hills and draws around Khe Sanh. At the company level, frontline Marines were equipped with the AN/TPS-25 ground surveillance radar, which allowed them to identify small groups of enemy soldiers moving about in the darkness, then hit them with mortars or artillery.

Since receiving his powerful naval binoculars and Night Optical Device scope early in the siege, Dennis Mannion had called in artillery missions on dozens of targets he otherwise might have missed. He kept the NVA-held ridgeline about 500 yards west of 861 under nearly constant surveillance and exacted a rising toll on the North Vietnamese. Mannion would scan the ridgeline and other areas at night with his NOD scope, find a group of enemy soldiers, and then have a gunner mark the spot the next day by firing a tracer round from the .50-caliber machine gun mounted on the bore of a 106-millimeter recoilless rifle. The 106 would be locked onto the spot and later fired at the unsuspecting NVA that night when they resumed their work under the cover of darkness. The first time the Marines on 861 tested the setup, Mannion counted about ten enemy soldiers lying on the ground.[4]

In the daylight hours, Mannion continued to team up with Corporal Paul Knight, the 861 forward air controller. As "Green Tambourine" and "Love Is Blue" blared in the background over Armed Forces Radio, Mannion and Knight hammered the enemy ridgeline and other positions with coordinated packages of artillery and air strikes.[5]

• • •

As the Americans exacted a rising toll on the North Vietnamese siege forces, the NVA continued to respond in kind with mortars, artillery, and rockets. By early March, the volume of enemy fire had dropped off from the worst days of February, but was no less deadly.

On 861 Alpha, rifleman Matt Walsh had settled into siege life after leading his fire team into the breach at the northern end of the hill during the February 5 attack. The former A&P grocery clerk and Yankees baseball fan from Yonkers, New York, had celebrated his twentieth birthday on the hill on February 21. His best friend, Joe Roble, made him a birthday cake by melting C-ration chocolate bars over a C-ration pound cake.[6]

Walsh had sized up his odds of surviving Khe Sanh, and he was confident that he would get out alive—but not unscathed. On Tuesday, March 5, Walsh and his buddies were doing some work on their bunker, reinforcing the roof with a piece of runway matting they had snagged. Walsh was standing in the no-man's-land beyond the trench line, making sure the bunker blended in with the rest of the line, when he heard the dreaded *WHUMP-WHUMP* of two enemy mortars firing. As he was about to dive for cover, one of the rounds hit just behind him and hurled him into the trench. When he regained his senses, he was lying at the bottom of the trench, woozy and covered with blood, with pieces of shrapnel embedded in his legs, arms, left shoulder, back, and head.[7]

A corpsman dressed the worst wounds, and four Marines eased

Walsh onto a stretcher and hustled him to the LZ at the southern end of the hill. A resupply helicopter had just dropped its load, and within seconds Walsh was hustled aboard with a wounded comrade and the aircraft darted off to the east. Aboard the chopper, Walsh was relieved to learn that their destination was Dong Ha. *Any place but Khe Sanh.* As he was carried inside the Delta Med hospital and readied for emergency surgery, he heard somebody grouse, "This place is hell."

"No," Walsh corrected him. "I just came from hell."[8]

• • •

The Super Gaggle had swung the odds back in favor of the Marine helicopter pilots in their supply runs to the hill outposts, but fixed-wing and chopper flights into Khe Sanh Combat Base remained a perilous proposition as March began. The North Vietnamese carefully tracked comings and goings at the base, positioning anti-aircraft guns to cover the preferred routes of American pilots. In the early weeks, helicopters had climbed to about 3,000 feet as they followed Route 9 westward into the hills, then looped around to sneak into the stronghold from the south. The North Vietnamese took note and placed guns on both sides of the valley used by the Americans in their southern approach. The pilots countered by flying 2,000 feet higher until they arrived over the base, then executing a steep corkscrew descent to land.

The helicopter pilots soon noticed they were taking fire within seconds of touching down at Khe Sanh. NVA spotters were obviously alerting the gunners around the base, enabling them to start firing the moment the Americans arrived. In mid-February, the helicopter pilots tried to reclaim the advantage by charting a new route to Khe Sanh that wound through the valleys north of the stronghold. The "back door route," as it was known, gave the pilots some breathing room, but within a few days they were taking fire on that passageway as well.[9]

In the early afternoon of February 28, two CH-46 Sea Knights from Marine Medium Helicopter Squadron 262 took off from Quang Tri, picked up forty passengers at Dong Ha, and set out for Khe Sanh. The twenty-nine-year-old commander of the flight, Major Edwin Meixner of Alva, Oklahoma, had picked the northern route for the journey. Flying low because of fog and overcast, Meixner's aircraft was hit by automatic weapons fire shortly after leaving Route 9. The Sea Knight plunged into a riverbed, killing all twenty-three Americans aboard.[10]

Since mid-February, the rate of damage and destruction sustained by American aircraft flying into Khe Sanh had soared to an "unacceptable" level, the III Marine Amphibious Force headquarters observed in early March. The new month had seen an alarming continuation of the trend.[11] The previous Friday—the first day of March—an Air Force C-123 had been clipped by mortar fire as it departed Khe Sanh, and it crashed and burned off the airstrip. On March 5, a C-123 had been grounded by a flat tire from either enemy fire or runway damage, and enemy mortars blew the aircraft apart before it could be repaired.

Air drops had helped offset the supply shortfall caused by reduced fixed-wing landings at Khe Sanh, but chronic runway closures and aborted flights had created a growing backlog of passengers. The airfields at Dong Ha and Phu Bai were crowded with Marines, Navy corpsmen, and others trying to get into Khe Sanh.[12]

Such was the case on March 6 when a Fairchild C-123 Provider made the short hop from Da Nang to Phu Bai to pick up passengers and cargo before continuing to Khe Sanh. At the controls of the Air Force transport was Lieutenant Colonel Frederick J. Hampton, a fifty-year-old West Point graduate from Gainesville, Florida, whose distinguished career had included flying bombers over postwar Korea and Strategic Air Command flights back in the States at the height of the Cold War. Now assigned to the 311th Air Commando Squadron, Hampton waited while cargo was offloaded at Phu Bai and supplies for Khe Sanh were taken on, along with forty-three Marines, one Navy corpsman, and one civilian headed to the combat base.[13]

The loading complete, Hampton took off from Phu Bai on a flight designated Mission No. 702.

• • •

The one civilian aboard Hampton's aircraft was Robert J. Ellison, the twenty-three-year-old freelance photojournalist who had captured the tragic aftermath of the February 25 Bravo Company ambush. Quiet and reserved, Ellison was not one to boast about all that he had accomplished in three years of work as a professional news photographer. In 1965, while still a student of herpetology at the University of Florida, he had caught the eye of the top New York photo agencies and news magazines with his striking images from civil rights marches in the South. He quit school to become a full-time freelance photographer and began showing up at major news events, including the US military intervention in the Dominican Republic. In 1967, Ellison turned his focus to Vietnam.

Ellison had been shooting an assignment in South Korea when the Tet Offensive began, and he returned to Vietnam and flew to Khe Sanh in early February. Slim, with a thin mustache and shock of dark hair, he had roamed the trench lines, putting himself in harm's way as he documented the terror and strain of the daily lives of Khe Sanh's defenders. Frozen in time on the rolls of 35-millimeter film he shot were the face of a weary Navy corpsman, frightened riflemen in a trench during an NVA bombardment, and the death of Lieutenant Don Jacques.

He had captured the essence of the human drama at Khe Sanh and flew back to Saigon to process his film and forward it to the States. *Newsweek* editors in New York had been blown away by Ellison's images from Khe Sanh, and they had sent word to the rising star that they would be running an eight-page spread of his photographs in the March 18 issue. It was a tremendous achievement for a young freelancer, and Ellison could have headed off to Bangkok or China Beach to celebrate. But he felt a bond with the Marines at Khe Sanh, so, on the afternoon of March 6, he bartered some beer, Coke, and cigars for a seat on Fred Hampton's C-123.[14]

•   •   •

Among the forty-three Marines aboard Hampton's aircraft were Corporal Ron Ryan, who had rallied Bravo 1/26 Marines with well-placed kicks on January 21, and was a pair of battle-tested radio operators assigned to Second Lieutenant William (Bill) Smith, the fire support coordinator for the 1st Battalion, 26th Marines, at Khe Sanh. Private First Class George L. Elliott III, a nineteen-year-old from Norfolk, Virginia, was a tough-talking inner-city kid who loved to play Smokey Robinson records on the turntable he lugged around Vietnam. Corporal Larry Scott Kennedy was a soft-spoken twenty-year-old from Charleston, West Virginia, a country boy who embraced the top-down culture of the Marine Corps.

One of the radio operators would accompany Smith everywhere he went, and that included regular forays to the regimental command bunker to confer with Harry Baig. Elliott would jaw at the lieutenant every step of the way as they performed the "Khe Sanh Shuffle," dashing from hole to hole and dodging the enemy incoming as they made their way from their quarters to the regimental bunker. In his jaunty moods, Eliott would call out, "Hey, Lieutenant Smith, you feelin' lucky today?"[15]

During the madness of February 23, Smith and Lieutenant Hank Norman, the artillery forward observer attached to Bravo Company, were running all over the east end of the base with their radio operators to analyze craters in an attempt to fix the origin of incoming rounds.[16] Afterward, Smith's radiomen asked for a break to burn off some R&R time. Smith agreed, and off they went. Now they were seated in the back of the Khe Sanh–bound C-123 that took off from Dong Ha just before 2:00 p.m. on March 6.

A few minutes into the flight, pilot Fred Hampton was cleared to land by the control tower at Khe Sanh. He had started his final approach when he spotted a small aircraft on the runway ahead. Aborting the landing, Hampton circled around the north end of the base for another approach. Small-arms fire from the jungle struck an engine, and, seconds later, the C-123 crashed into the rugged hills east of Khe Sanh. There were no survivors.[17]

• • •

The victims of the C-123 crash lay where they fell until April 25. On that day, helicopters thundered into the hills about two miles east of Khe Sanh Combat Base, and a company of Marines from the 2nd Battalion, 3rd Marine Regiment, poured into an LZ hacked from the jungle. They found the wreckage of Fred Hampton's C-123 in minutes and spent the next five hours gathering decomposing bodies and scattered bones, as well as service record books, medical records, and personal items.[18]

The recovery operation of April 25 was less than thorough, and on June 25, a Marine patrol found another fifteen sets of remains. Still another operation on July 3 found more remains inside the aircraft and surrounding underbrush. On November 5, one more casualty of the March 6 crash was recovered by a Marine patrol.[19]

Eighteen days later, on November 23, 1968, Taps sounded and an honor guard's volleys echoed across the wooded bluffs of Jefferson Barracks National Cemetery, overlooking the Mississippi River south of St. Louis, Missouri. As a crowd of family members, service personnel, and others paid their respects, the skeletal remains of thirty-five men recovered at the crash site of Fred Hampton's Mission No. 702 were buried in a mass grave.[20]

CHAPTER 19

"Bitter Hardships and Blood"

As the record bombardments of late February hammered Khe Sanh Combat Base, the days became even more arduous for the surgeons and corpsmen of Charlie Med as they went about their bloody work. During a lull in the shelling one day, the four Charlie Med surgeons cobbled together a whimsical recruiting ad: "Wanted, General Practitioner to assume a diversified medical and surgical practice in a small, quiet, mountain setting. This sylvan community provides relief from all disadvantages above urban areas and assures inexhaustible appreciation of nature's beauty." They signed it "the doctors of Khe Sanh," and sent it off to the *New England Journal of Medicine*.[1]

The Charlie Med surgeons patched up casualties as best they could, and they laughed and bantered with each other, leaving unsaid their darkest thoughts or banishing them to their diaries. "Hope there is no attack but believe that there will be one," surgeon Ed Feldman scribbled on Tuesday, February 27, the day after marking his twenty-seventh birthday. "I think we will win, but it will be costly. Want to come out of this alive."[2]

On February 29, Charlie Med officially moved into its new underground treatment and triage bunker. During the day, the cry "Casualties!" had gone up, and surgeon Jim Finnegan and his comrades had sprinted down a walkway of wooden pallets to the triage bunker. Finnegan had just reached the entrance when an incoming mortar round hit, hurling him into the bunker and spattering his left arm, neck, and buttocks with shrapnel. The injuries weren't serious—salt-and-pepper wounds, they called them at Charlie Med—and so Finnegan went back to work as though nothing had happened, enduring good-natured ribbing from his comrades.[3]

By early March, one of the most valued members of Finnegan's Charlie Med team was a slight, nineteen-year-old preacher's son from Florida. Private First Class Jonathan Nathaniel Spicer served as a stretcher bearer, carrying wounded Marines from arriving helicopters or ambulances to the Charlie Med triage area and then shuttling stabilized casualties to the helicopter pad for evacuation—all under enemy fire. Spicer had earned a reputation for bravery and selflessness, shielding the wounded with his own body as enemy shells rained down.[4]

After all that Spicer had done to prove himself, it was easy to forget the controversy that had accompanied his arrival at Charlie Med a month earlier. The trouble had started when he arrived at Khe Sanh and refused to carry a rifle in his assignment with the supply unit of Bravo 1/26. Spicer explained that he was a conscientious objector and couldn't kill anyone. He had loved animals growing up in Florida and had hoped to be assigned to a canine unit when he joined the Marines. But Spicer was designated a rifleman, and at every stop in the Marines, he was told to take up his claim of conscientious objector status at his next duty station.

Spicer heard that line all the way to Vietnam, and the next thing he knew, he was in Bravo Company, enduring torment from his comrades for his pacifism, his Bible reading, and his rejection of the rough language that was a rite of passage in the Marine Corps. Spicer sought out Protestant chaplain Ray Stubbe at Khe Sanh in late January, and Stubbe came away from their conversation convinced that the Florida teenager was for real. He arranged for Spicer to be attached to Charlie Med as a stretcher bearer.

Spicer was only about five foot seven and 140 pounds, but he impressed everyone at Charlie Med with his courage and hard work. He was pleasant and soft-spoken, fond of talking about the home and family he missed. He had written the name of his girlfriend—Carla—on his helmet. He felt bad about his time at Bravo Company and wanted to prove he wasn't a coward. But he wasn't going to fight, even if the NVA overran the base. "I don't have any problem with dying," he would say to ambulance driver Danny Sullivan. "But I will not kill anyone."[5]

On the afternoon of Friday, March 8, medevac flights arrived at the Khe Sanh helicopter pad during an intense North Vietnamese bombardment.[6] Spicer and other stretcher bearers headed into the fire with litters loaded with wounded Marines and carried them aboard the waiting aircraft. Spicer had gotten his wounded aboard and had dashed back to get the final casualties out of the shell fire and onto a chopper. A mortar round burst among the knot of stretcher bearers and casualties, and shrapnel sliced into Spicer's chest, face, and legs. He had left his flak jacket unzipped, and a small metal fragment found the opening and pierced his heart.

Down in the Charlie Med bunker, someone stuck his head into the entrance and yelled, "Spicer's hit!" Seconds later, the young Marine was carried inside and laid on a gurney. Almost immediately Spicer's heart and breathing stopped. He was clinically dead.

Ed Feldman was performing triage on other casualties, and so his three comrades went to work. John Magilligan cut open Spicer's chest while Joe Wolfe inserted a breathing tube into the wounded Marine's throat. Magilligan surmised that Spicer's heart had stopped because of pressure from blood that had filled the surrounding membrane, so he made a careful incision that released the blood. He started a transfusion while Jim Finnegan reached into Spicer's open chest and performed a heart massage technique he had perfected on countless casualties. The young Marine's heart fluttered to life.

The shrapnel hole in Spicer's heart still had to be addressed, so Finnegan put his finger in the opening and deftly sutured it shut with three stitches. After fifteen minutes of intense work, Spicer's heartbeat was robust, his blood pressure had stabilized, and he was breathing on his own.[7]

A medevac helicopter arrived, and Danny Sullivan and three others carried Spicer aboard. The aircraft clattered away to the east.

For six days, Nat Spicer clung to life. He was transferred to a military hospital in Japan, and late on the evening of Wednesday, March 13, his parents in Florida received a telegram, informing them that their son was not doing well. The following morning, March 14, Spicer's father,

William, a substitute teacher since retiring from the Methodist ministry, was standing before a world affairs class at Shenandoah Junior High School in Miami when two Marines came to the door. Private First Class Jonathan Nathaniel Spicer, United States Marine Corps, had died of wounds received in combat in the Republic of Vietnam.[8]

• • •

Over the first three weeks of March, North Vietnamese ground forces continued to challenge the ARVN Ranger positions that anchored the eastern perimeter of Khe Sanh Combat Base, mounting seven probes of varying strength and intensity.[9] Since the discovery of the maze of bunkers and trenches off the east end of the base in late February, the American command had braced for large ground assaults originating from this area. But another concern nagged at the Americans: tunneling by the North Vietnamese.

Colonel Lownds had been on the lookout for tunnels since the early days of the siege, sending Navy corpsmen out at night with stethoscopes, which they would place on trench walls and engineering stakes driven into the ground to detect enemy digging.[10] Nothing turned up, aside from the ambient noise of artillery and air strikes, and music from record players and tape recorders.

The concern about tunneling was raised anew in late February, when an enemy rocket exploded along the northwest perimeter and revealed a recently dug shaft six feet below the surface. There were fears that the NVA might pack a tunnel with explosives and blow a hole in the Khe Sanh perimeter, as Union soldiers had done to Confederate lines at Petersburg, Virginia, in 1864.

When word filtered up from the ranks about the usefulness of divining rods, Lownds concluded that even the tools of American backwoods folklore were worth a try. Marines were sent out to walk the perimeter with brass divining rods, without success.[11] In March, the Pentagon dispatched a team of men armed with a new seismic detection instrument to check for tunnels, but they, too, found nothing to validate the fears.[12]

On March 8, South Vietnamese Rangers attacked the enemy trenches east of their positions and in two brief engagements killed several NVA soldiers as they emerged from tunnels and trenches. An Associated Press dispatch about the incident emphasized the tunnel angle, and suddenly comparisons were being made to the Viet Minh's tunneling at Dien Bien Phu. "100 Reds Caught Tunneling Toward Khe Sanh; 27 Killed," screamed the front-page headline in *Stars and Stripes*.[13] The AP dispatch concluded on an ominous note: "The new development and earlier discovery of tunnels under the Khe Sanh barbed wire perimeter indicates that the communists are following the same siege techniques used at Dien Bien Phu. There they drove mine shafts under the French positions, loaded them with explosives, and set them off at opportune times in the fighting."

The suggestion that the North Vietnamese were tunneling "toward" Khe Sanh was debatable, but one error in the article wasn't. In a situation report the Marines at Khe Sanh had prepared for division headquarters, the number of North Vietnamese dead from the ARVN Ranger attacks on March 8 was reported as eight. That same number had been forwarded to III Marine Amphibious Force headquarters, and then on to General Westmoreland's staff in Saigon. When Westmoreland's MACV press officers released the story to reporters, the number of NVA dead had soared to twenty-seven—more than triple the actual count.[14]

• • •

Although the tunneling concern was real enough to the besieged defenders of Khe Sanh, the burrowing by the North Vietnamese soldiers in all likelihood was nothing more than an attempt to escape the escalating American air raids. With the improved March weather, the skies now throbbed with American B-52 bombers and attack aircraft dumping high explosives, anti-personnel bombs, and napalm on the North Vietnamese positions.[15]

The Marines in I Corps and Westmoreland's MACV headquarters churned out remarkably precise data on enemy soldiers killed, secondary explosions detected, bunkers destroyed, and trenches reduced to rubble. But they couldn't answer one lingering question: What was the North Vietnamese endgame at Khe Sanh?

As the weeks of February had passed without the major enemy ground assault, US military intelligence and the CIA had begun to rethink their conclusions that Khe Sanh Combat Base was on the brink of a winner-take-all battle. On March 7, the *New York Times* revealed that the US military command in Vietnam "has revised its opinion and now thinks that an attack on Hue—rather than on the Marine encampment at Khe Sanh—is the enemy's next objective."[16] The "senior military official" who had briefed the *Times* reporter and other correspondents was none other than General Westmoreland.[17]

NVA intentions remained murky, but the US military command and intelligence agencies knew that General Giap had shifted some troops from Khe Sanh to Hue around February 10. The withdrawal of NVA forces from Khe Sanh had accelerated in early March, and on March 9, General Westmoreland informed President Johnson that the NVA forces around Khe Sanh "had dropped to between 6,000 and 8,000 men."[18]

Whatever their numbers, the North Vietnamese who were dug in around Khe Sanh in mid-March faced a nightmarish existence in the face of the relentless American air strikes and artillery. Bloody bandages, blood trails, scattered grave sites, and even unburied bodies—some burned by napalm, others with horrible shrapnel wounds—littered the surrounding jungle. Defectors and prisoners of war spoke of terrible suffering and high desertion rates.[19] The misery of the siege forces at Khe Sanh was captured in the diary entry of a North Vietnamese soldier on March 23, "a day full of bitter hardships and blood," he wrote.[20]

The NVA soldiers lived in mortal fear of B-52 strikes, which hit without warning. "From the beginning until the 60th day of the siege at Khe Sanh, B-52 bombers continually dropped their bombs in this area with ever growing intensity and at any moment of the day," a North Vietnamese soldier wrote in his diary. "If someone came to visit this place, he might say that this was a storm of bombs and ammunition which eradicated all living creatures and vegetation whatsoever, even those located in caves or in deep underground shelters."[21] Some NVA soldiers used the chaos following a B-52 strike as cover to desert. A captured North Vietnamese document dated February 29 stated that one unit, Doan 926, had three hundred desertions en route to Khe Sanh, with B-52 strikes cited as the main cause.[22]

Private First Class Hai Van Phan, drafted into the North Vietnamese Army in March 1967, was an illiterate country boy with only two years of schooling. In January 1968, he had headed south down the Ho Chi Minh

Trail with his unit: the 11th Company, 3rd Battalion, 1st Regiment of the 330th Division. The soldiers arrived in the Khe Sanh area in March and spent two days digging trenches in their assigned position south of the combat base. Phan and his comrades had been told they would be held in reserve for an impending assault on the American stronghold.[23]

In mid-March, the sixth day after their arrival, explosions engulfed Phan and his comrades—the first of seven B-52 strikes they would endure. Nine of the company's one hundred men were killed in the first strike. The NVA soldiers frantically deepened their trenches and fortified them with wood, and that saved them when more Arc Light strikes hit the area. But they could not escape the relentless sorties of the low-flying American attack jets, and Phan lost many more comrades to their bombs and napalm.

Phan's company remained in place in the jungle south of Khe Sanh Combat Base until April 9, when US forces attacked their trenches. The nineteen-year-old farm boy survived the fight but was wounded and taken prisoner by the Americans. Unlike so many thousands of his comrades, Private Hai Van Phan survived Khe Sanh.[24]

• • •

On Tuesday, March 12, the US Marines and South Vietnamese Rangers at Khe Sanh were put on alert on the eve of the fourteenth anniversary of General Giap's opening ground attacks on the French stronghold at Dien Bien Phu. The day passed without incident, but Hanoi's propagandists stepped up the psychological war on Khe Sanh. "Preparations for new attacks" are underway, Hanoi radio declared, warning that Khe Sanh's "days are numbered."[25] Hanoi's bluster was accompanied by continued digging by North Vietnamese soldiers around the base, and the sound of whirring machinery that ratcheted up the uneasiness of the Americans.[26]

The North Vietnamese did more than bluster in the early hours of Monday, March 18. An estimated battalion of NVA soldiers, about six hundred strong, emerged from trenches and bunkers east of the combat base and advanced toward the Khe Sanh runway. Unleashing heavy fire on the ARVN Ranger positions, they managed to blow holes in the perimeter wire before the attack stalled. A flare ship revealed the location of the enemy troops, and air and artillery fire broke the North Vietnamese attack around 6:00 a.m. The body count was eighty-three enemy dead.[27]

Throughout the day, American air observers in the skies overhead picked out new targets, and artillery missions and air strikes rained down on NVA anti-aircraft weapons positioned around the base. In the early evening, the North Vietnamese launched another probe against the ARVN Ranger lines, but it was a halfhearted effort, and the gunfire sputtered to a close as night settled over the combat base.

• • •

Supplies and mail now flowed nearly unhindered into the hill outposts, courtesy of the Super Gaggle's sky-borne forces, and visions of victory replaced the grim fears of an Alamo-like fight to the death. The volume of enemy mortar and rocket fire had dropped significantly, along with the sightings of enemy troops. On Hill 861, Dennis Mannion didn't even bother to fire up his scope on some nights.

By mid-March, the Americans on the hill outposts looked like shipwrecked castaways—dirty, ragged, bearded, and bedraggled. Water was still too scarce for bathing, so bodies remained caked with sweat and grime, skin tinted red by Khe Sanh's laterite soil. Utilities had rotted off at the knees, and blouses and sweatshirts were torn and tattered.[28]

The rough conditions had resulted in a relaxation of Marine regulations, so Mannion had adorned his battered helmet with a button his mother had sent him: "Kiss me, I'm Irish." The late Gunny Melvin Rimel's replacement on 861, Charles Perkins, had a harder edge than his revered predecessor, and he hounded Mannion constantly about the button. "Goddammit," Perkins would yell, "you're going to get yourself shot. Get that off your helmet!"[29]

Mannion laughed it off. In a tragic twist of fate, Perkins was shot by a sniper on March 28. He clung to life for several weeks, and on May 17 died aboard the hospital ship *Repose*.[30]

• • •

Forward air controller Paul Knight had continued to direct air strikes on any suspected NVA targets around 861 that surfaced. One day in mid-

March, an airborne controller radioed Knight and offered a flight of four F-4 Phantoms armed with napalm, so Knight gave the controller the co-ordinates of a tree line north of 861, which the NVA had been using as a staging point for probes and harassment of the Americans on 861 Alpha. The first Phantom roared over 861 Alpha along a southeast-to-north-west vector and toggled his canisters, but the napalm exploded about 500 yards northwest of the target. The second F-4 followed, and his canister also hurtled past the target. The third Phantom roared in and unleashed its load.

Watching from his perch atop 861, about 300 yards to the west, Knight realized the napalm was headed for Captain Earle Breeding's Echo Company outpost. "Abort! Abort! Abort!" Knight screamed into the radio handset. But it was too late. He could only watch in horror as the first canister hit and jellied gasoline boiled across the American trench line in a burst of fire and smoke. Another canister slammed into the ground and Knight feared he had killed everybody on the hill. An anxious hour passed before he was informed that the Marines on 861 Alpha had gotten advance notice of the incoming aircraft and were in their trenches and bunkers when the napalm hit. A few men had suffered singed hair, but no one had died or even been seriously injured. It had been a very close call.[31]

● ● ●

Most Marines were counting the days until they left Khe Sanh, but Corporal Ken Warner couldn't wait to get back there. After he was wounded in the assault on 881 North on January 20, the India 3/26 squad leader had required multiple surgeries on his shrapnel-torn shoulder and other wounds. During his nearly three weeks on the hospital ship *Sanctuary*, he couldn't stop thinking about his comrades, wondering how they were do-ing in the big battle underway at Khe Sanh. His parents hoped he would come home when he was discharged from the hospital on February 12, but the Southern Californian wanted to rejoin his India Company broth-ers. He headed to Da Nang to catch a flight to Khe Sanh.

Bad weather and enemy fire had created a logjam of passengers trying to get to Khe Sanh, so after a few frustrating days, Warner gave up on Da Nang. He flew to Phu Bai, and then Dong Ha, but found the same passenger backlog at each air strip. "Here I sit in Da Nang AGAIN," Warner wrote home in late February. He knew how desperately his parents wanted to see him, so he explained to them how low he felt about not being with his buddies at Khe Sanh. "I'm scared to go back," he wrote. "But this is very important to me. I hope you understand."[32]

When Warner finally got on a flight, the aircraft was forced to abort its landing at Khe Sanh because of heavy NVA fire, so he started the process all over again. Finally, on March 5, Warner made it to Khe Sanh on a C-130. He and his fellow passengers jumped off the back ramp as the aircraft slowed for its turnaround at the end of the runway, and they ducked into nearby trenches to wait out the incoming fire. Fate had spared Warner once again: he arrived one day before the C-123 crash at Khe Sanh.

Warner was stunned by the transformation of the combat base since he had left in January. It looked as though it had been ravaged by a killer tornado: buildings were flattened, trees splintered, and vehicles in pieces or riddled with shrapnel. All around were craters and churned earth, and an endless maze of sandbagged trenches and bunkers.

After two days at the combat base, Warner finally got a seat on an H-34 helicopter headed up to 881 South. Enemy rounds smacked into the fuselage as the aircraft descended to one of the hill's landing zones, and Warner emerged and sprinted to a trench. Stretcher bearers carried medevac cases aboard the bird for the return trip to the combat base, and the H-34 veered away from the hill amid exploding mortar rounds. When the barrage ended, Warner found his way to the 1st Platoon command post and checked in with Lieutenant Rick Fromme.

Warner took over his old squad and familiarized himself with a world turned upside down in his absence. Only two of the dozen men in his squad on January 20 were still there; the rest had been wounded or killed or had completed their tours. Because of the threat of NVA snipers and mortars, Warner and his men spent their days in underground bunkers and two-man "bunny holes" bored into the trench walls. The trenches themselves were now seven or eight feet deep, more than twice the depth when Warner had left.

Equally striking were the smell and appearance of his comrades. Their hair was long, at least by Marine standards, and they were unwashed and unshaven. Artillery forward observer Bob Arrotta had grown a beard; Captain Bill Dabney sported a Sergeant Pepper–worthy mustache.

One thing hadn't changed: morale was high, a tribute to the tight operation run by Dabney. Men kept busy, working on the trenches and bunkers and bunny holes when it was too dangerous to go topside, and checking the wire or performing other tasks when there was fog or cloud cover to shield their activities.

Dabney's daily flag-raising ceremony had become a pep rally for the defenders of 881 South, an act of group defiance directed at the North Vietnamese surrounding the hill. Ken Warner reveled in the routine, standing at attention in the trench line with his squad, his middle finger raised in a Bronx salute to the enemy, as Lieutenant Owen Matthews bugled "To the Colors" and the Stars and Stripes rose into the sky to welcome the new day.[33]

● ● ●

On Thursday, March 21, America's war in Vietnam marked a painful milestone: 336 Americans had been killed in action in the previous week's fighting, pushing the total of US deaths in the conflict over 20,000.[34]

At Khe Sanh, the signs of the decisive battle that once seemed inevitable had waned, but the North Vietnamese still possessed the ability to hurt the Americans. Long-range artillery fire from camouflaged positions in the Laotian massif known as Co Roc continued to inflict death and misery on the combat base and outposts, and in the late afternoon of March 22, the big enemy guns opened up with the heaviest barrage since February. The word passed along the Khe Sanh perimeter: be ready for a ground assault.[35]

In the Charlie 1/26 command bunker, radioman Chuck Chamberlin tried to read a letter he had just received from his grandmother in Montana, but the barrage was building in intensity and tensions were rising, so he slid the envelope into his pocket. As a survivor of the direct hit on the Charlie 1/26 bunker on February 15, Chamberlin carried a heavier burden than most at Khe Sanh. He had lost three comrades—two had been killed, and his company commander had been maimed. The Seabees had built a new command post, and Captain Walter J. "Jack"

Egger had arrived to take the reins of Charlie Company. Now, with the growing sense that something big was afoot, the command post bustled with the company's officers and noncoms.

In the flickering light of a kerosene lamp, Egger conferred with his highly regarded executive officer, the slight, blond lieutenant Paul W. Bush, while Gunnery Sergeant John Joseph Grohman stood by.

A few feet away, Chamberlin worked the radio, checking with platoon commanders for situation reports. Beside him was the junior radioman, Corporal John Mattern, who had replaced Chamberlin's friend Joseph Bailey, after his death in the February 15 attack. Frantic calls for corpsmen crackled across the net and then an appeal from a nearby unit of Army light tanks and "Quad 50" guns: "We need a corpsman down here. We got a man who's almost cut in half."[36]

About 8:45 p.m., without warning, a shell smashed into the Charlie Company command bunker. Knocked unconscious by the explosion, Chuck Chamberlin awoke to find himself engulfed in flames and choking smoke. A piece of shrapnel had torn open the lantern, drenching John Mattern with kerosene and igniting a smoky fire. Chamberlin had been shielded from instant death by the bunker's bank of PRC-25 radios.

The bunker had collapsed in a heap of logs, sandbags, and runway matting, but most of the debris had fallen away from Chamberlin. Through the smoke, he could see bodies trapped in the rubble. John Mattern screamed in agony from his painful shrapnel wounds and the flames billowing from his jungle utilities. Choking and gasping for breath, Chamberlin tried to move, but his shoulder was broken and his legs pinned by debris. The noxious air reeked of burning hair and human flesh. His eyes suddenly locked on an object protruding from the rubble: it was a hand and arm, torn from one of his comrades and dripping blood.

As his brain shut down, Chamberlin lost consciousness a second time. He awoke, suffocating, death closing in, and began thrashing and clawing wildly at the debris. Somehow his legs came free, and he pulled himself upward through the rubble with his good arm.

Outside, Marines tore at the burning debris. Three of them—Private First Class Terrell E. Fitzgerald, Corporal Michael Gallagher, and Private First Class Dominic Parisi—opened a passageway through the flames.

Chamberlin caught a glimpse of sky and lunged toward it. His left hand broke the surface, and Staff Sergeant Arnold Jay Ferrari of Napa, California, only eleven days in Vietnam, pulled Chamberlin from the death trap.[37]

Lieutenant Bruce Geiger, the twenty-three-year-old commander of the adjacent squad of Army light tanks and guns, had seen the round smash into the Charlie Company command post. Dodging shells and rockets, he had sprinted across the airstrip to Charlie Med and led two corpsmen back to the shattered bunker. Chuck Chamberlin and the badly burned John Mattern had been pulled from the ruins. The corpsmen field-dressed their wounds, and comrades carried the two injured Marines across the airstrip to Charlie Med.[38]

At the shattered Charlie Company command post, the full extent of the carnage soon became apparent: Captain Jack Egger, First Lieutenant Paul Bush, and Gunnery Sergeant John J. Grohman were dead or dying. Two Charlie riflemen were killed in an adjacent bunker.

More than 1,100 shells would hit Khe Sanh Combat Base and the hill outposts on the night of March 22–23—the second worst barrage of the entire siege. The defenders of Khe Sanh would spend another sleepless night, waiting to see if the bombardment was the prelude to a ground assault, but the attack never came. In all likelihood, the barrage was cover for the North Vietnamese as they withdrew more troops from the costly confrontation at Khe Sanh.

• • •

At Charlie Med, Jim Finnegan's team of doctors and corpsmen worked through the night to save scores of wounded men. Chuck Chamberlin could hear the corpsmen and surgeons talking as they hovered over him, cutting away his bloody and fire-blackened flak jacket, utilities, and boots before tending to his injuries. Morphine dulled Chamberlin's pain, but it could do nothing for the agony of the badly burned John Mattern, and his bloodcurdling screams forced Chamberlin to continue reliving the horrors of the burning bunker.

An emergency medevac flight arrived, and Chamberlin and Mattern were among the critically wounded whisked to Dong Ha. It had been a bad day for Americans along the DMZ, and the carnage had converged on Delta Med. In the triage area, blood covered the tiled floor, lapped along the gutters, and poured into drains.

When the doctors at Delta Med had done all they could for one day, Chamberlin was put on a stretcher for removal to the ward where he would spend the night. A few North Vietnamese rockets screamed overhead, and the orderlies abandoned the wounded Marine to scramble for cover. Chamberlin laughed. *This is nothing.*[39]

The barrage eased, and Chamberlin was taken into a room and laid in a bed. The drugs had dulled his senses, but not enough to diminish the thrill of clean sheets, electric lights, and running water. He heard one or two more rounds explode, and then fell into a deep morphine sleep. For the first time since it all began in January, he let go of Khe Sanh.[40]

CHAPTER 20

"The Agony of Khe Sanh"

The deadly barrage of March 22–23 was especially unnerving for an envied subset of Khe Sanh defenders: "short-timers" nearing the end of their tours. They became more superstitious, more reluctant to step outside their bunker or bunny hole, more unwilling to risk a chance rendezvous with a random enemy round. With the threat of a climactic battle diminishing, Khe Sanh had devolved into a grassroots drama of individual triumphs and tragedies—the completion of one's tour and safe passage back to the world, as opposed to departure from Khe Sanh in a body bag.

After one of the most harrowing nights of the Khe Sanh ordeal, Seabee Sam Messer was fortunate enough to be getting out on March 23. He scrambled aboard a departing CH-46 Sea Knight, "scared to death to get on that bird," and even more scared when the crew chief ordered everyone to get down on the armored deck and hug their seabags. The chopper headed east, through a gauntlet of enemy machine-gun fire.[1] Messer's parting memory of Khe Sanh was watching bullet holes appear in the helicopter fuselage where he and his fellow passengers had been sitting. He had made it out alive, and so had the others, and by nightfall they could laugh about it over a beer.

• • •

Fixed-wing flights and helicopters continued to deposit arriving passengers at Khe Sanh, including a steady stream of journalists drawn to chronicle "the agony of Khe Sanh," as pronounced by the March 18 *Newsweek* cover story that featured Robert Ellison's photographs. Associated Press correspondent John Wheeler had taken up residence at Khe Sanh Combat Base. Others were in and out, seasoned veterans like *Washington Post* correspondent Peter Braestrup, and unproven talents like the twenty-seven-year-old magazine writer who had arrived in Vietnam three months earlier, convinced that he had found "the time and the place and the subject" to make his mark.[2] Michael Herr would soon validate his hunch in the pages of *Esquire*.

Twenty-six-year-old freelance photographer David Powell purposely steered clear of the journalistic pack when he arrived in Khe Sanh in late March for his second crack at the story. A barrel-chested Army veteran, a loner by nature, Powell had quit his job as a security guard at Bob Hope's Southern California estate the previous summer to experience firsthand the war in Vietnam. He wasn't trained as a reporter or photographer, but he figured the best way to play war tourist was to show up with a camera and a notebook and act like he knew what he was doing. He arrived in Saigon on August 5, 1967, with $50 in his pocket, a cheap camera, and letters of introduction from two tiny California newspapers.[3]

Powell joined the Army's 5th Cavalry Regiment—the Black Knights—for operations near Bong Son and quickly developed a taste for combat. He headed up to I Corps to check out the Marines, and ended up at Con Thien, where he witnessed young Americans getting torn apart by shells. He shot only a couple of rolls of film in three months, but he had the time of his life.

When he ran out of money in late October 1967, Powell wandered down to the Saigon waterfront and signed on as a seaman with a United Fruit Company refrigerator ship. He hauled vegetables around Southeast Asia for three months, then flew to Hong Kong to buy a pair of cheap cameras and get accreditation with some English-language newspapers. By the time he returned to Vietnam around February 20, Hue and Khe Sanh were the big stories. He showed up at the United Press International (UPI) offices in downtown Saigon and landed a freelance assignment to Khe Sanh.

Powell flew into the besieged combat base on February 25, and before the day was out was nearly killed when a burning pallet of artillery powder charges blew up as he was photographing it. The blast hurled Powell through the air, and he landed next to a bunker, smoke curling from his blackened clothes. He looked up to find a pair of Marines staring at him as if a space alien had just landed on their doorstep.[4]

Powell dusted himself off, found his cameras, and went back to work.

After about two weeks, he flew back to Saigon with the film he had shot. UPI put his best images on their wire, and two US newspapers ran Powell's work on their front page.

The UPI photo editor in Saigon, a veteran newsman named Bill Snead, mentioned to his eager young shooter that no reporter or photographer had made it to the dangerous Khe Sanh outpost known as Hill 881 South. Powell took the bait.

At Phu Bai, he had to convince helicopter pilot Dave Althoff and his comrades in HMM-262 that he wasn't crazy and that they wouldn't be sending him to his death if they allowed him aboard one of their flights to 881 South. Around midday on March 25, Powell bounded off a Sea Knight as it touched down on Bill Dabney's hill.

Over the next three days and two nights, Powell barely slept. He was no stranger to the adrenalin-stoked intensity of combat, but 881 South exuded a visceral, end-of-the-earth vibe like no place that Powell had ever been in Vietnam. Against a backdrop of shell bursts and sniper fire, he prowled the trench lines, chatting up Marines and corpsmen in underground bunkers and bunny holes. He chronicled their precarious world with his Minolta and Miranda cameras—the fatigue and fear, the camaraderie and shared sacrifice, and the professionalism and steely resolve. He only shot about a dozen rolls of film, but many of his shutter clicks would become unforgettable images of Khe Sanh: portraits of the swashbuckling Bill Dabney and soulful Bob Arrotta; a starkly silhouetted flag-raising ceremony; a sniper team at work; and the world inside the hill's subterranean shelters and passageways.

When it was time to leave, Powell dived into the back of a CH-46 as it departed 881 South. Skidding across the helicopter's armored deck on a layer of .50-caliber shell casings, Powell ended up beneath the door gunner as he blasted away at the North Vietnamese. The gunner flashed a reassuring smile at Powell before resuming his duel with the enemy soldiers trying to shoot them from the sky.[5]

• • •

Leaving 881 South that same day was Corporal Ken Warner, the Southern California surfer and India Company squad leader who had survived his share of heartache and harrowing moments during his months at Khe Sanh. It was a bittersweet departure after all the brotherhood and loss that he had known in this place, and he was glad that he was sharing the journey with one of the best friends he had made during his thirteen months in Vietnam, machine gunner Fulton "Fuzzy" Allen.[6]

After the hugs and tears and gruff farewells, the white kid from Southern California and the black kid from New Jersey headed to one of the landing zones to catch their ride down to Khe Sanh. As Warner waited in a trench off the LZ, he started to hyperventilate. The helicopter arrived, and Warner and Fuzzy Allen dashed up the ramp with their gear and braced themselves against a bulkhead. Warner didn't like helicopters, and he feared getting shot down anytime he was on one, especially around Khe Sanh. He prayed and pleaded throughout the short flight. *Please, God, please, just get me to Khe Sanh. I'm so close. Come on, I'm so close.*[7]

The Sea Knight safely deposited Warner and Allen at Khe Sanh Combat Base, and now they had to sweat out their layover while awaiting seats on a fixed-wing flight back to the coast. They finally got on a C-130 on April 6, and Warner took one last look at the battered runway and blood-stained hills. He fought back tears as memories of his time at Khe Sanh flooded his thoughts.

As the ramp of the C-130 slowly shut, Warner watched the cratered hills disappear in the distance. He and Fuzzy looked at each other, too overwhelmed to speak. It was all over for them. They had survived Khe Sanh.

• • •

With each passing day, the bloodlust rose in the hearts of the men of Bravo 1/26.

Since February 25, the Marines killed in the ambush of the Jacques patrol had remained where they had fallen. Day after day, aerial observers photographed their decomposing bodies. From his lines, Captain Ken Pipes kept watch on his lost boys, gazing through binoculars on the terrible scene.[8]

The sense of shock and loss permeated the Bravo ranks. Virile young grunts like Ken Rodgers had been shaken to their core. They couldn't go outside the wire to help their own men? They couldn't even retrieve the bodies of brother Marines? Rodgers didn't voice his darkest thoughts: *If things are so desperate that we couldn't go save thirty guys, then we're doomed.*[9]

Among the angriest of the Bravo Marines was Corporal Ken Korkow. The son of a self-made man who had become wealthy breeding rodeo horses, Korkow was a hard worker and fearless horseman growing up in Pierre, South Dakota, but he could never please his demanding father. Korkow graduated from high school when he was sixteen and started college at South Dakota State University, but he had inherited his father's appetite for risk. So, with the war in Vietnam heating up, he quit college and joined the Marine Corps.

Korkow wanted to be a rifleman, the greatest test of manhood he could imagine, but he wound up in mortars. He joined Bravo 1/26 at Khe Sanh in the first week of January 1968. After losing close friends in a rocket attack in early February, Korkow vowed that he would never again allow himself to feel such pain. He nurtured a pathological hatred of the North Vietnamese.[10]

On February 25, Korkow watched Lieutenant Jacques lead his patrol through the wire and listened to the ambush unfold. He begged to be allowed to help save the patrol but was ordered to stand down. Korkow was furious—with the NVA, as well as with the officers who had let Jacques and his Marines die rather than risk the loss of more men.

Korkow craved vengeance.[11] He would lure an NVA sniper into taking a shot, then put a white phosphorus round from his 60-millimeter mortar on the position, visualizing the agonizing death he had inflicted on the men who had killed his friends. Scarred before he arrived at Khe Sanh, Korkow had become hard as stone. He had lost his religion, and his belief in a just God. Khe Sanh had driven Ken Korkow into the darkest place he had ever known, a place where he was tormented by his demons and mocked by a question he could not answer: *If there is a God, why would he let good men die?*[12]

CHAPTER 21

"We Made Them Pay"

In the foggy predawn of March 30, 1968, the men of Bravo 1/26 prepared for battle. Like any Marine rifleman worth his salt, Corporal Michael O'Hara of the 2nd Platoon checked his grenades and M-16 rifle one final time. Corporal Tom Quigley, the company radioman, fiddled with a broken strap on his PRC-25 field unit. "Guess I can't go out this morning," he joked with Captain Ken Pipes, the Bravo Company skipper. Wordlessly, the wiry former football halfback cinched the dangling radio strap to Quigley's cartridge belt.[1]

For two months, President Lyndon Johnson had watched with growing frustration as his forces in Vietnam reacted to enemy attacks rather than dictate the action. At long last, General William Westmoreland was poised to seize the initiative at Khe Sanh with an operation that would reopen Route 9 from the coastal plain westward to the Laotian border and drive enemy forces from their positions around the embattled American stronghold. As a prelude, Bravo 1/26 had been cleared to launch the first offensive action by the Americans at Khe Sanh since the siege began in January—a "movement to contact" aimed at engaging the North Vietnamese forces east of the combat base and recovering the bodies of the Marines killed in the February 25 ambush of the Bravo platoon.

After five agonizing weeks, haunted by the knowledge that their fallen brothers were lying unburied in a killing field nearby, Ken Pipes and his men had been unleashed to settle some unfinished business.

At 5:37 a.m., a platoon of Special Forces operators assigned to the morning's operation slipped out of the FOB-3 compound along the southwest perimeter of Khe Sanh Combat Base. Twenty-three minutes later, at 6:00 a.m. sharp, the fifty-odd Marines and corpsmen of 2nd Platoon of Bravo 1/26 marched through the southeastern perimeter wire and disappeared into the fog-shrouded gloom. The rest of the company followed, taut young Marines and corpsmen moving silently through rows of razor-sharp concertina wire and minefields, in search of a battalion or more of North Vietnamese Army soldiers dug in a short distance away to the east.[2]

O'Hara and the rest of the 2nd Platoon fanned out to secure the jumping-off point for the designated assault forces, Bravo's 1st and 3rd platoons. When everyone was in place, Ken Pipes issued a command that sent a chill through the ranks. "Fix bayonets," he ordered.

It was time for payback.[3]

• • •

To avoid the mistakes of the February disaster, the operation had been meticulously planned by Lieutenant Colonel Frederick J. McEwan, who had taken the battalion reins from James Wilkinson in mid-March, and McEwan's operations officer, Major Charles E. Davis III. Harry Baig, and his fire support colleagues had crafted a massive package of coordinated artillery missions and air strikes aimed at softening enemy defenses and suppressing the NVA fire.

The morning's fog had grounded the air strikes, but the artillery barrage got underway around 7:30 a.m. Variable-fused explosives burst above the ground to suppress enemy infantry forces, while smoke rounds dropped along ridgelines to blind and isolate enemy troops and artillery. Tear-gas rounds were mixed in to incapacitate the North Vietnamese forward observers directing mortars and artillery. Every depression and ravine, every knoll and ridgeline, was blanketed with a sophisticated combination of high explosives, anti-personnel munitions, smoke, and gas.[4]

Just before 8:00 a.m., using the fog as cover, the ground attack got underway. The assault forces surged ahead like two halves of a diamond—Bravo's 1st Platoon arrayed in a wedge, followed by 3rd Platoon in a V-formation. As Ken Pipes and his Marines pushed southeast toward the North Vietnamese lines, artillery fire moved in a rolling barrage to protect their flanks and maintain a wall of steel a little more than half a football field to their front.

A Bravo fire team moved briskly toward the first line of North Vietnamese trenches and bunkers as enemy mortars crumped and automatic-weapons fire rattled across the field. The two assault platoons spread out in a long skirmish line and attacked by squads, one fire team moving forward while two others covered them, leapfrogging ever closer to the enemy lines. Marines began to fall from the enemy fire, but the pent-up anger over the fate of the Jacques patrol now erupted in a collective fury. A detachment of combat engineers attached to Bravo for the assault began to pick off NVA machine-gun bunkers with flamethrowers and satchel charges. The Marines surged over the enemy fortifications, burning and blowing up the North Vietnamese defenders.

Behind the assault platoons, Captain Pipes and his command group hurried to keep pace with the fast-moving attack. At one point they piled into a bomb crater—Pipes, radioman Tom Quigley, artillery forward observer Hank Norman, and two other Marines—but North Vietnamese mortars quickly zeroed in on their position. "Get the hell out of here," Pipes yelled. "They've got us spotted."[5]

The Bravo command group bolted toward the front line of North Vietnamese trenches. Out of shape after the long inactivity of the siege, Quigley sweated heavily and gasped for breath under the weight of his radio. He was trying to run and fire his rifle at the same time, eyes scanning the ground around him for danger. A good buddy from training had been killed in an earlier fight when an NVA soldier had popped out of a hole and shot him in the back, and that thought now preoccupied Quigley.[6]

As Pipes led the command group forward, enemy mortar rounds clotted the sky, like a medieval battlefield darkened by arrows. The Bravo skipper was in midstride when he saw a blurred shape swoop toward him and heard a sound: *shooom*. A mortar round hit between his legs but didn't explode.[7]

It was a stroke of incredible good fortune for Pipes, but the triumph was short-lived. An NVA sniper took aim and squeezed the trigger. The bullet slammed into Pipes's helmet and pierced the manganese steel outer shell but stuck in the plastic liner, a fraction of an inch from penetrating the Bravo commander's skull. Pipes dropped to the ground, unconscious but not seriously injured.[8]

• • •

As Bravo Company pushed into the rolling terrain to the southeast, the Special Forces platoon out of FOB-3 moved toward the high ground to the south to block any flanking move by North Vietnamese forces around the base of Hill 471, an enemy stronghold since the early days of the siege.

Back inside the base, Lieutenant Bill Smith, the 1/26 battalion artillery officer, was following the action from the Bravo Company command post. From a bank of squawking radios he could make out the voices of Ken Pipes and radioman Tom Quigley, as well as a stream of transmissions from the artillery tactical network.

NVA mortar teams began firing blindly through the curtain of smoke and gas into the Bravo assault forces, and Smith heard someone on the receiving end of the enemy fire call in the development. He recognized the voice: it was his good friend, artillery forward observer Hank Norman, with the Bravo command group.

"We're taking incoming," Norman said above the roar of battle. He gave Smith a rough fix on the NVA gunners. Smith had just ordered a fire mission on the suspected location of the enemy mortars when he heard the telltale *shooom* of an incoming round over Hank Norman's open mike. The line went dead.[9]

• • •

Ken Pipes wasn't sure how long he was out after taking the sniper round through his helmet, but he awoke to find his command group intact and resumed the push forward. He and his group had reached the NVA trenches around 8:30 a.m. when the concentrated fire from twenty enemy 82-millimeter mortars exploded around them. Several pieces of metal ripped into the body of the Bravo commander, including one that tore into his chest and stopped an inch from his heart. Radioman Tom Quigley fell with shrapnel wounds to his torso and hand. First Lieutenant

Marion H. "Hank" Norman was killed instantly, and his radioman was severely wounded.[10]

Shaking off the pain and shock of his injuries, Ken Pipes grabbed Quigley's radio and asked for reinforcements. When the request was denied, the Bravo skipper ordered forward his reserves, Bravo's 2nd Platoon, under the command of First Lieutenant John W. Dillon. Bravo's assistant artillery forward observer, Ted Golab, reached the shattered Bravo command group, and with his radio operator helped restore communications with the battalion command post.

Under the direction of the badly injured Ken Pipes, the Bravo Marines forged ahead into the NVA defensive complex. In fiercely personal fights within the battle, the Americans set to work clearing every enemy trench, bunker, and spider hole.[11]

• • •

Corporal Steve Wiese, Bravo squad leader and February 25 ambush survivor, had been booked to leave Khe Sanh a few days earlier when he got bumped from his flight. As Wiese and his men began gearing up for their operation in the predawn of March 30, a Bravo sergeant had come by to inform the squad leader that a plane was coming in, and he should be on it. Wiese wouldn't hear of it.[12]

With bayonets fixed, Wiese and his squad had surged toward the North Vietnamese trenches. Screened by the fog, the Marines caught the enemy by surprise and rolled over the NVA soldiers. The North Vietnamese recovered quickly, and Wiese and his men found themselves under heavy automatic-weapons fire from enemy trenches and bunkers.

One of Wiese's men, a twenty-one-year-old machine gunner, Lance Corporal Wayne Moore of Plymouth, Massachusetts, jumped up and charged an enemy machine-gun bunker. He was hit three or four times and fell to the ground but somehow dragged himself to his feet. He was hit again and fell dead. Nearby, a twenty-year-old lance corporal from Glen Allen, Alabama, bearing the literary name Author C. Smith, jumped up and sprinted toward the enemy fire. Smith fought his way through an NVA trench and finished the job that Moore had started, taking out the machine-gun bunker, but he would fall before the morning was out.

Eighteen-year-old PFC David Bruce Anderson of Avoca, Iowa, and one other Marine—either nineteen-year-old PFC Ted Britt of Decatur, Georgia, or nineteen-year-old PFC Donald Rash from Pocahontas, Virginia—jumped up and screamed at the enemy, and the entire line surged forward. Anderson, Britt, and Rash were all killed, but the line of Marines continued ahead—screaming, running, throwing grenades, and firing. The North Vietnamese broke and ran, with the Americans on their heels.[13]

• • •

Corporal Ken Korkow had jumped at the chance to go out and kill NVA troops face-to-face, and he had demonstrated his improvisational skills earlier in the fight by using his 60-millimeter mortar tube and a modified round to pick off a couple of enemy soldiers firing at the Marines from a spider hole. As the battle was winding down, Korkow began dashing into harm's way to retrieve wounded Marines and carry them back to an aid station set up in a bomb crater by Bravo's executive officer, Lieutenant Ben Long, and Corporal Steve Wiese.

Korkow was poised to retrieve yet another Marine calling for help when Long ordered him to take cover in the intensifying NVA fire. Standing his ground on the crater rim, defiantly exposing himself to the enemy, Korkow shouted a devil-may-care challenge down to Long and Wiese: "Come out and enjoy the war!"[14]

The words had barely left his mouth when three NVA 61-millimeter mortar rounds slammed into the ground nearby, shredding Korkow's body with hot metal shards. Ben Long and Steve Wiese rushed to their grievously injured comrade and walked him back to a triage area in the rear as bullets whizzed around them.[15] A corpsman offered Korkow morphine to dull his pain, but he waved it off with a wisecrack. "You trying to make a hippie out of me?" As he lay on the ground, his face and body drenched with blood, Korkow still seethed with bloodlust toward the NVA. "Kill them," he exhorted his comrades. "Get those bastards."[16]

• • •

Lieutenant John Dillon's 2nd Platoon reached the rows of NVA trenches and found dead enemy soldiers piled on top of each other, the work of Wiese's squad and other Bravo Marines who had gone before them. Corporal Michael O'Hara ran ahead to a bomb crater and found four or five North Vietnamese dead, along with a wounded Navy corpsman, Dick Blanchfield, whose arm had nearly been severed by a mortar shell. O'Hara dressed the corpsman's injuries and resumed his advance. Blanchfield would survive.[17]

Radioman Tom Quigley was on his feet but was growing faint and nauseous from the loss of blood. "How bad is it, doc?" he asked a corpsman examining him. "Not bad at all," the corpsman lied, as he tried to stanch the blood flow from Quigley's numerous shrapnel wounds. Quigley dropped to his knees, and a pair of Marines helped him back to a casualty collection point. Around him wounded and dying Marines lay on the ground, some moaning in agony.[18]

At 9:45 a.m., the Bravo Marines began to execute an orderly withdrawal from the devastated NVA positions. A tracked utility vehicle rumbled out of the base to collect the wounded. Ignoring his own severe wounds, Tom Quigley grabbed an M-16 with a full magazine and climbed aboard to provide security. The vehicle, filled with injured Marines and corpsmen, began the slow trek back to Charlie Med.

As bloodied Marines fell back to the base, scattered gunfire continued to crackle and artillery shells roared overhead. Michael O'Hara came upon Captain Pipes, soaked in blood from head to toe, shrapnel above his heart, but still working two radios and barking orders. Beside him was the lifeless body of Lieutenant Hank Norman, the affable artillery observer.

O'Hara picked up Norman's body, raised him to his right shoulder, and set off for the combat base. An armored personnel carrier had emerged to gather up dead Marines, and O'Hara made his way to it. Ever so gently, he placed Hank Norman's body in the back.

Despite his injuries, Ken Pipes remained on his feet, overseeing the pullback of his men until its completion at 11:30 a.m. Only then would Pipes agree to have his wounds treated at Charlie Med.

Ten Marines had died in the Bravo assault, and two were missing. Another one hundred Americans had been wounded, including fortynine whose injuries were serious enough to require evacuation. On the other side of the battlefield, 115 North Vietnamese soldiers had been killed, and an unknown number wounded. The Bravo Marines had driven the North Vietnamese from their doorstep, but another objective—recovering their dead from the February ambush—had not been achieved. There had been too much fighting, so only two bodies had been brought back to the base. Completion of that grim task, the final piece of unfinished business from the February 25 tragedy, would be left to another day.

For Ken Pipes, the anguish of the Jacques ambush would never diminish. But the hatred and anger that had fueled the extraordinary assault his men carried out to ruthless perfection on March 30, 1968, would fade with time. "Those guys on the other side were following orders, just like we were," Pipes said forty-four years later, as he recalled the two days at Khe Sanh in 1968 that had left such a deep imprint on his life. "It was our job to make them pay, and we made them pay—as much as they could pay."[19]

• • •

The following morning, March 31, a Bravo sergeant stuck his head in Steve Wiese's hooch. "There's a plane landing as we speak," the sergeant said. "Get your shit, get down there, and get on it."[20]

Wiese had survived seventeen months of combat in Vietnam. He had survived the ambush of February 25 and the March 30 assault. Over half the Marines killed the previous day were from Wiese's squad, a testament to the courage of Wiese and his men as they charged headlong into NVA fire. Khe Sanh had taken its toll on Steve Wiese, and it would continue to do so in the decades ahead. But he was a survivor, and now he was going home.

CHAPTER 22

Breakout

As Steve Wiese exited Khe Sanh on Sunday morning, March 31, President Lyndon Johnson was contemplating his own dramatic departure.

March had been another dismal month for the American president. The crew of the US Navy spy ship *Pueblo* remained in captivity in North Korea, with Johnson seemingly powerless to secure their release. The potential for disaster at Khe Sanh had eased, but looming enemy threats elsewhere in Vietnam had led General Westmoreland to request more than 200,000 additional troops—a dramatic escalation in a war that the president and his commander on the ground had claimed was winding down.

The siege at Khe Sanh and the Tet Offensive had accelerated the president's plummeting approval ratings: by late March, only 26 percent of Americans approved of Johnson's handling of the war, and 36 percent approved of his overall job performance.[1] Westmoreland's troop request had become another political debacle for Johnson, splashed across the front page of the *New York Times* on Sunday, March 10, chipping away further at the president's credibility. If the Tet Offensive had been a last-ditch gambit by the Communists, as Johnson and Westmoreland claimed, why were an additional 200,000 troops needed in Vietnam?

In any other year, Johnson might have shrugged off his sagging poll numbers, but a presidential election was looming, and the war had galvanized a serious primary challenge. On March 12, Senator Eugene Mc-

Carthy of Minnesota had ridden antiwar sentiment to a stunning second-place finish in the New Hampshire primary, polling 42 percent to Johnson's 49 percent. Four days later, Johnson's greatest political fear became reality when Senator Robert F. Kennedy announced his candidacy for the Democratic nomination.

Political concerns, however, were secondary to the life-and-death decisions Johnson now faced in Vietnam. He had poured more than 500,000 American troops into the war, and now he was being asked to raise that amount by another 40 percent. Should he bow to the pressure from hawks and authorize still more manpower, more bombing, and more extensive ground operations, including strikes into Cambodia, Laos, and North Vietnam?

Burdened by those questions, and battered by a flurry of critical news articles and broadcasts calling for a reassessment of his Vietnam policy, Johnson flew to Minneapolis, Minnesota, on the spur of the moment on March 18 to deliver a speech calling for a "total national effort to win the war."[2] But his appeal had fallen flat, and political advisers warned Johnson of a disaster in his upcoming Democratic primary test in Wisconsin. Scrambling to contain fallout from the setbacks in Vietnam, Johnson scheduled a nationally televised address on the war for Sunday evening, March 31.

As Johnson debated his advisers over what to say, he took steps to give himself more flexibility in Vietnam. He revealed to reporters that he had decided to bring General Westmoreland back home to become Army chief of staff in the summer and retire his hawkish military chief in the Pacific, Admiral U. S. Grant Sharp.

Behind closed doors, Johnson continued to reject pressure to dial back the war, a position now advocated vociferously in the White House inner circle by new Defense Secretary Clark Clifford, a hawk on Vietnam whose views had been changed by Khe Sanh and Tet. On March 25 and 26, Johnson had convened a supergroup of advisers known informally as the "Wise Old Men." At Johnson's behest, the men had met in November to discuss Vietnam and had given unanimous support to the president's prosecution of the war. Now, the former generals, ambassadors, and cabinet secretaries recommended by a two-to-one margin that the president avoid further escalation and rethink his strategy in Vietnam. Lyndon Johnson was stunned.

At 9:00 p.m., on Sunday night, March 31, with his wife, Lady Bird, and daughters, Lynda and Luci, looking on, Johnson cast his tired gaze across his Oval Office desk into a bank of television cameras and radio microphones set to relay his speech across America, and throughout Vietnam, via Armed Forces Radio. "Tonight I want to speak to you of peace in Vietnam and Southeast Asia," Johnson began. "No other question so preoccupies our people."

Johnson continued as he had so often before, condemning Communist aggression, denouncing the Tet Offensive as "a savage assault on the people, the government and the allies of South Vietnam." The enemy had "failed to achieve its principal objectives" Johnson flatly declared, but he warned that "the Communists may renew their attack any day."

Abruptly shifting gears, Johnson turned to the new centerpiece of his radically rewritten speech: an olive branch to the leaders of North Vietnam. Johnson offered to ease the US bombing campaign, if only the Communists would engage in serious negotiations.[3]

Johnson concluded the remarks released in advance to news organizations and US diplomats around the world, and then began reading from a carefully crafted postscript. His closest advisers knew the burdens weighing on Johnson—the stress and sleepless nights that had mounted as the campaign against Khe Sanh played out and the Communist attacks against the South Vietnamese cities unfolded, the anguish that had beset Johnson as he watched his presidency crumble amid the soaring costs and political divisions unleashed by the war. He faced almost certain defeat in his looming political tests—if not in the primaries, then in the general election in November. He had come to feel as though he were facing "a giant stampede coming at me from all directions."[4]

Publicly, Johnson cast in noble terms the stunning announcement that capped his speech: "I shall not seek and will not accept the nomination of my party for another term as your president." He would walk away from the White House in January.[5]

During the seventy days that had passed since January 21, Khe Sanh had been a nagging preoccupation for Johnson. He had feared that Khe Sanh would become a military disaster that would sink his administration, so he had been drawn to the White House basement Situation Room on the restless nights that increasingly haunted him. He would read the latest cables and casualty reports and gaze on the terrain model of the Khe Sanh plateau and surrounding hills, a landscape now consecrated with American blood, sweat, and tears. Again and again, Johnson had asked his generals: Can Khe Sanh hold?

Khe Sanh *had* held. Lyndon Johnson's presidency was in ruins, but the hard and bloody work of the American and South Vietnamese fighting men at Khe Sanh had spared the president the final indignity of "another damn Dien Bien Phu."

• • •

As Lyndon Johnson began speaking to the American people, it was already Monday morning, April 1, in Vietnam, and the operation to retake Route 9 and drive North Vietnamese forces from their positions around Khe Sanh had been underway for four hours.[6]

Operation Pegasus, as it was christened, was under the command of Major General John J. Tolson III, US Army, and the forces at his disposal were his 1st Air Cavalry Division, the 1st Marine Regiment, and the 3rd ARVN Airborne Task Force. Operational control of the 26th Marine Regiment at Khe Sanh had also passed to Tolson—one of several developments that had not pleased the Marines, who had never wanted to be tied down at Khe Sanh in the first place and now bristled at the implication that the Army had to bail them out.[7]

Pegasus had grown out of contingency planning undertaken by General Westmoreland in late January, amid Washington's fears of a looming disaster at Khe Sanh. The Tet Offensive and bad weather had pushed an overland relief operation to the back burner, and Tolson's 1st Air Cavalry troopers had been thrown into the fight at Hue. After the battle of Hue ended, plans for Pegasus had been finalized in March, and a staging base known as Landing Zone Stud was constructed at Ca Lu, nine miles east of Khe Sanh.

The operation began at 7:00 a.m. on April 1 with two battalions of Marines—the 2nd Battalion, 1st Marine Regiment, and 2nd Battalion, 3rd Marine Regiment—pushing west along Route 9 in an armor-supported thrust. The Marines fanned out to secure the high ground north and south of the road, and their comrades of the 11th Engineer Battalion went to work rebuilding Route 9 between Ca Lu and Khe Sanh.

As the Marines advanced overland, elements of Tolson's 3rd Brigade, 1st Air Cavalry Division, thundered into the skies in helicopter assaults aimed at driving the North Vietnamese from key terrain features that dominated Route 9 and the eastern approach to Khe Sanh. By April 4, Tolson's cavalrymen were in combat with North Vietnamese forces that remained south and southeast of the combat base.

● ● ●

As Pegasus progressed, restrictions on offensive operations by the defenders of Khe Sanh were lifted, and the Marines pushed outward in search of the North Vietnamese.

At 6:00 a.m. on April 4, three companies of the 1st Battalion, 9th Marines, moved southeast from their positions at the rock quarry to challenge the NVA forces still holding Hill 471, south of the Khe Sanh perimeter. Command of the Walking Dead had passed from Lieutenant Colonel John Mitchell to Lieutenant Colonel John Cahill only three days earlier, and now, after American artillery had pounded the hill, Cahill led his men up the slopes of 471. An NVA mortar round hit in the middle of Cahill's command group, wounding the battalion commander and several others and killing two men, but the 1/9 overwhelmed the light enemy resistance around 5:20 p.m.

During the night, the NVA battered the Marines on 471 with mortars and artillery, and at 5:15 the following morning, April 5, a North Vietnamese battalion charged up the hill. The men of the 1/9 held, just as they had at Hill 64, and the bodies of 122 North Vietnamese soldiers lay scattered on the slopes. One Marine was killed and nineteen wounded.

At 1:50 p.m. on Saturday, April 6, a company of South Vietnamese soldiers from the 3rd ARVN Airborne Task Force became the first troops of Operation Pegasus to enter Khe Sanh Combat Base. The ground and skies around Khe Sanh, meanwhile, boomed and crackled with the sounds of artillery duels, air strikes, and ground engagements throughout the day.

Among the American units on the move was a platoon from Captain Ken Pipes's Bravo 1/26. With the men of Delta 1/26, the Bravo Marines

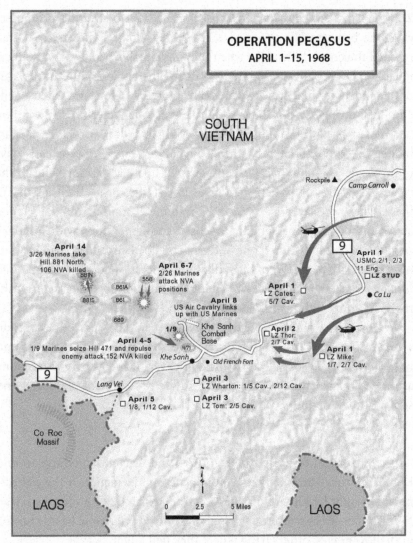

OPERATION PEGASUS
APRIL 1–15, 1968

SOUTH VIETNAM

Rockpile ▲   Camp Carroll ●

9 April 1
USMC 2/1, 2/3
11 Eng.
☐ LZ STUD

● Ca Lu

April 14
3/26 Marines take
Hill 881 North,
106 NVA killed
881N

861A   558
861

April 6-7
2/26 Marines
attack NVA
positions

April 1
LZ Cates:
5/7 Cav.

881S

April 8
US Air Cavalry links
up with US Marines

689

April 2
☐ LZ Thor:
2/7 Cav.

1/9   Khe Sanh
Combat
Base

April 4-5
1/9 Marines seize Hill 471 and repulse
enemy attack, 152 NVA killed

471

April 1
☐ LZ Mike:
1/7, 2/7 Cav.

Khe Sanh   ● Old French Fort

9

Lang Vei

☐ April 3
LZ Wharton: 1/5 Cav., 2/12 Cav.

☐ April 5
1/8, 1/12 Cav.

☐ April 3
LZ Tom: 2/5 Cav.

Co Roc
Massif

LAOS

0   2.5   5 Miles

LAOS

Operation Pegasus, April 1–15, 1968.

returned to the scene of the Jacques patrol to recover the remains of twenty-one fallen comrades.

• • •

From his perch on Hill 861, artillery forward observer Dennis Mannion witnessed one of the actions of April 6. The Marines of Golf Company

2/26 had moved from their outpost on Hill 558 to secure a prominent ridgeline between Hill 861 and Khe Sanh Combat Base, and they had reached the crest of the ridge when they were ambushed by NVA soldiers in camouflaged bunkers. Mannion watched the battle unfold through his naval binoculars and witnessed a terrible moment in the fight when an enemy shell dropped from the sky and blew up two Americans.[8] Mannion had moved back to his bunker around 3:00 p.m. when two NVA mortars hidden in a draw about a mile away opened fire on 861. In the early days of the siege, Mannion had pushed pieces of fiberglass armor beneath the camouflage cover of his helmet to give himself extra protection, and one of these plates now saved his life. An 82-millimeter mortar round exploded above and behind him, spraying his head and upper body with shrapnel. A chunk of metal shattered one of the fiberglass plates and dented his steel helmet but stopped short of his skull. Other pieces of hot metal punctured his flak jacket, and one sliver ripped into his right bicep. Once again, Mannion had come within a few inches of death.

A corpsman suggested a trip down to Charlie Med, but Mannion wanted no part of the risky journey. The corpsman probed the wound until he managed to pull an inch-long sliver of metal from Mannion's arm. He stitched the hole, applied a sterile dressing and bandage, and sent Mannion on his way.[9]

• • •

As the American forces pushed through the scarred landscape around Khe Sanh, they stumbled onto more gruesome evidence of the punishment wrought by Operation Niagara. The remains of hundreds of dead NVA soldiers were scattered through the hilly jungle, some hastily buried in shallow graves, others lying where they had fallen.

On April 7, after three days of fighting, troopers of the 2nd Brigade, 1st Air Cavalry, captured the old French fort near the intersection of Route 9 and the access road leading to the combat base. At the same time, 3rd Brigade troopers completed the work of clearing Route 9 around Khe Sanh village and Lang Vei.

At 8:00 a.m. on April 8, the official linkup between the US Army cavalry troopers of Operation Pegasus and the Marines who had successfully defended Khe Sanh Combat Base through seventy-seven days of siege occurred with an improvised flourish. As the lead cavalrymen marched into the combat base, a twenty-four-year-old trooper, Lieutenant Joseph E. Abodeely, blasted "Charge!" on an old French bugle captured from one of the North Vietnamese units that had laid siege to Khe Sanh.[10]

Three days later, crews of the 11th Engineers completed the work of rebuilding Route 9, and Khe Sanh's overland lifeline was opened for traffic.

•   •   •

As trucks and tracked vehicles rolled into the Marine combat base and back down Route 9 for the first time since the previous summer, the quixotic "lion of Khe Sanh" took his leave. Colonel David Lownds had spent nine months at Khe Sanh, and the mustachioed, cigar-smoking commander of the 26th Marines had become the face of the siege for many Americans. He had angered the Army advisory team at Khe Sanh village and the Special Forces at Lang Vei by refusing their pleas for relief when they came under attack, and he had disappointed some of his own men by failing to do more to save the ambushed Bravo patrol on February 25. But for all the criticism he would face, then and later, David Lownds delivered on his vow to defend Khe Sanh Combat Base. Now, on April 12, Lownds handed off command of the 26th Marines to Colonel Bruce F. Meyers and left Khe Sanh for good.

That same day, word flew through the trenches of Hill 861: pack your gear, and be ready to leave in less than an hour.[11] There was no word on their destination, but it was somewhere away from this blood-stained hill that had been their home since late December.

Artillery forward observer Dennis Mannion scrambled aboard a CH-46 along with several other Marines, and the helicopter cleared the hill and banked to the right. Within seconds, it became clear their destination was 881 South. The bird descended to an LZ, and Mannion and his comrades bolted left and right into the nearest trench.

The weary Marines of India Company didn't bother to welcome their guests or invite them into their bunkers and bunny holes, so the men of Kilo Company sought shelter wherever they could find it. Feeling like a hermit crab pulled from its shell, Mannion crawled beneath the carcass of a wrecked CH-46. He lay there for a while, disoriented by his abrupt departure from the hill that would be part of him forever.

Later in the day, Mannion went to Bill Dabney's command bunker to listen to a briefing that laid out why they were there. When he heard they were going to assault 881 North, a North Vietnamese base for infantry, mortars, and rocket batteries throughout the siege, Mannion immediately recalled news stories about the bloody Hill Fights the previous spring. He thought, *This is going to be really bad.*

At nightfall of the following day, April 13, the Marines of Kilo Company filed through the wire of 881 South and made their way down the northern slope. Around an hour later, they reached their destination, a terrain feature known as Hill 800, nearly 900 yards north of 881 South. They dug in as best they could with machetes and knives, then waited nervously for the night to pass. At first light, they would attempt to retake the North Vietnamese stronghold that had caused so much misery for the Marines since January.

• • •

In the predawn darkness of Easter Sunday, April 14, 1968, six hundred Marines of the 3rd Battalion, 26th Marines, began their ascent up the shell-cratered slope of 881 North. The NVA soldiers who waited in camouflaged bunkers and holes had been pounded with explosives and napalm for weeks on end, and now they faced the wrath of Kilo, Lima, and Mike companies of the 3/26.

As the Americans advanced, air strikes pounded the ridgelines above, followed by friendly artillery rounds that marched up the slopes ahead of the surging Marines. In the fog-shrouded dawn, the Marines of India Company joined the battle, sweeping the hillside ahead of their comrades with .50-caliber machine guns and eight recoilless rifles.

The fire rattled and roared over the heads of the Americans as they scrambled up the scarred slope. The *pop-pop-pop* of AK-47 rifles sounded, signaling the presence of enemy soldiers.

On the far right, Dennis Mannion was in constant radio contact with Charlie Battery 1/13 at the combat base, keeping the artillery fire just ahead of Kilo's Marines as they surged up the slope. The men of Kilo Company met only light resistance, and when they reached the summit of their objective, a lone NVA holdout bolted from his hiding place about fifty yards ahead of the Marines. Mannion and at least five other Marines opened fire, and the enemy soldier collapsed to the ground.

As the Kilo Marines swarmed the right flank of the hill and set up a 360° perimeter, the acrid smell of gunpowder and artillery propellant hung heavily in the morning air. Ten or twelve NVA dead were sprawled on the ground, some half out of their spider holes or at the door of bunkers, apparently killed by artillery fire or air strikes. Someone in the Kilo command group had an American flag, and Mannion and a comrade hoisted a Marine into the skeleton of one of the few remaining trees. The flag was tied in place, and a breeze unfurled the Stars and Stripes over the far right of the enemy stronghold.

• • •

On the American left, the Marines of Lima Company, 3/26, ascended a series of undulating slopes on the southern face of 881 North in a flurry of enemy rifle fire and Chicom grenades. Among those experiencing close combat for the first time was nineteen-year-old Neil Kenny, a salty-tongued high school dropout from Brooklyn, New York. Kenny had joined Lima 3/26 at Khe Sanh in January, and in March, he had celebrated his birthday in the Lima Company lines along Khe Sanh's western perimeter. Now, shaking off his fear, Kenny charged ahead, dropped behind the slender remains of a shell-scarred tree, and sprayed the slope to his right and left with M-16 fire.[12]

Kenny's squad piled into a large bomb crater and scanned the slope above them as another Lima platoon surged past. Ahead, an NVA soldier popped from a hole and stitched a passing Marine with AK-47 fire, knocking the young American back down the hill. "Holy shit! Look at those cartwheels!" Kenny yelled, unable to stifle his horrified amazement at the acrobatics a human body could perform when hit by a burst of 7.62-millimeter projectiles traveling at 715 meters a second. Kenny was still processing the shocking image when nineteen-year-old artillery forward observer Philip Francis Sheridan, a handsome, well-built Marine from Long Island, New York, sprinted past with his .45-caliber pistol drawn. Within a few steps, Sheridan collapsed to the ground with a mortal wound.

As the squad of Lima Marines clambered from the bomb crater and closed on the final crest, they passed the young American whose violent cartwheels had mesmerized Neil Kenny. He was propped against a tree, his torso pierced by at least four AK-47 rounds. A corpsman was trying to keep him alive, shaking him, yelling, "Stay with me! Stay with me!" But the young Marine was slipping away fast, and his lifeless eyes were already locked on some distant place, far beyond the horrors of Khe Sanh.[13]

• • •

Across the enemy stronghold, Marines enraged by months of punishment at the hands of the North Vietnamese boiled up and over the crest, overrunning bunkers and trenches, shooting and bayoneting NVA soldiers who had survived the American air strikes and artillery. When a group of terrified NVA survivors fled their crumbling bunkers and crowded into a patch of open ground, an officer ordered the Marines to allow air and artillery to finish the bloody work. But the Marines plunged ahead, shooting and bayoneting the last North Vietnamese on the hill.

Kilo Company reported its objective secured at 2:28 p.m. on April 14, 1968, and a short time later the rest of Hill 881 North was officially reclaimed by US Marines. The three companies of the 3/26 had lost twenty-seven men in the Easter assault, including six dead. They had killed more than one hundred North Vietnamese troops and captured two soldiers of the 8th Battalion, 29th Regiment, 325th NVA Division.

• • •

The Marines savored their victory for barely thirty minutes, and then the order was passed: prepare to pull back. It didn't make any sense to the men who had spent the day driving the enemy off the hill, but they retraced their steps back down the slope. It was the second time in less than twelve months that Marines had died in the conquest of 881 North, only to give it up without a fight.

• • •

The withdrawal plan called for Captain Paul Snead's Kilo Company to reoccupy Hill 800 in between the two dominant peaks and act as a blocking force against any NVA counterattack, while the Marines of Lima and Mike Companies completed the hard slog back up 881 South.

The men of Kilo Company reached their assigned positions about 4:30 p.m. and set to work deepening the fighting holes they had dug the previous night. Fog and mist rolled in, and the night came alive with shapes and shadows. Time slowed, and then stopped, as the Marines peered into the impenetrable night, rifles and machine guns at the ready, awaiting the expected NVA counterattack.

But the North Vietnamese never appeared, and the Marines of Kilo Company lived to welcome another foggy Khe Sanh dawn. It was April 15, 1968.

• • •

As the Kilo Marines prepared to move out, the epic battle marked another milestone: at 8:00 a.m., General Tolson declared the relief of Khe Sanh complete, and Operation Pegasus terminated. Officially, 205 Americans died in Operation Scotland, which entailed the defense of Khe Sanh, from November 1967 through March 31, 1968. During the two weeks of Pegasus, the Americans lost another ninety-two men killed in action, 667 wounded, and five missing. South Vietnamese forces reported thirty-three men killed in action and 187 wounded. North Vietnamese Army losses were estimated at 1,100 killed, with another thirteen captured.

• • •

The official declaration that the siege had been broken and Khe Sanh secured was an administrative fiction, a fact readily apparent to the men still in harm's way. For six Americans scattered about the Khe Sanh plateau, April 15 would be their last day on earth. For Dennis Mannion, it would be the saddest day of his Vietnam tour.

Four CH-46 helicopters had been summoned to ferry Kilo Company from Hill 800 down to Khe Sanh Combat Base. As the first Sea Knight came into view and settled into the LZ hacked from the rubble, Mannion lay sprawled in a crater nearby, shooting the breeze with one of his favorite people in Kilo. First Lieutenant Benjamin Stephen Fordham had spent his formative years in Monterrey, Mexico, where his father was an executive for an American multinational corporation. Returning to the States for college, Steve Fordham, as his friends knew him, had graduated from Baylor University in Waco, Texas, then entered the Marines.

Mannion and Fordham had worked closely together on Hill 861 after Fordham's platoon had occupied the hill's northwest perimeter, and in the process they had become good friends. They shared books their families sent them and had good-natured arguments about college football—Mannion the diehard Notre Dame stalwart, Fordham the Texas Longhorn surrogate. Most nights they would head over to the Kilo command post together to go over call signs and other protocol and then make their way back to Mannion's bunker to share a cup of hot chocolate and conversation. They had survived their hard time on 861, and they had survived the charge up 881 North, and now, with a little luck, they were going to survive Hill 800 and have one more story to tell about their days together at Khe Sanh.

Unknown to the Marines, a North Vietnamese artillery spotter had drawn a bead on them, and as the first Sea Knight lifted off with one of Kilo's rifle platoons, two mortar rounds streaked from the sky and smacked into the hillside nearby. The NVA mortar team was adjusting its aim as a second helicopter arrived and swooped away with another Kilo platoon. Mannion was preparing to scramble aboard the third chopper with the Kilo command group when Steve Fordham squeezed his hand and called out above the roar of the rotors, "See you at the combat base."[14]

The third CH-46 had pulled away with Captain Snead and the command group when a pair of mortar rounds hit the hill, killing three men: Lieutenant Steve Fordham, Lance Corporal William Matthews Jr., and PFC Patrick Patterson. PFC Charles McLaurin died of his wounds on April 24. They were the final Khe Sanh casualties for Kilo 3/26.

● ● ●

The 26th Marines had completed their work at Khe Sanh, and responsibility for the combat base now fell to the 1st Marine Regiment. Most of the Marines who had survived the siege would be gone by the third week of April, enjoying their first hot meals and showers in three months at bases near the coast. But death continued to stalk the defenders of Khe Sanh until the moment of their departure.

In mid-April, Captain Earle Breeding's Echo 2/26 had made its way from its outpost on 861 Alpha down to the combat base to await transportation out of Khe Sanh. On April 17, several Echo men were bathing in a stream north of the perimeter wire when NVA rockets or artillery rounds landed among them. Two Navy corpsmen were killed and several men wounded. Rifleman Michael Worth held the hand of corpsman Charles T. Langenfeld as he died, calling for his mother in his final moments.[15]

•　•　•

The end of Operation Pegasus on April 15 marked the beginning of Operation Scotland II, and a new ledger of the fighting and dying around Khe Sanh was begun.

On April 16, the ill-fated Alpha Company of the 1st Battalion, 9th Marines, stumbled into a North Vietnamese bunker complex on the slopes near Hill 689, and a disaster ensued. Two companies of the Walking Dead were fed piecemeal into the fight, and before the Marines could break contact, another forty-one Americans were dead, thirty-two wounded, and fifteen missing—some inadvertently left behind in the confusion. One Marine left by his comrades managed to elude marauding bands of NVA soldiers as they executed American wounded, and at dawn on April 17, and again the following day, his cries for help could be heard by comrades several hundred yards away. The intrepid Marine and one other American were finally rescued by an Army helicopter crew.

•　•　•

Bloody fighting between American and North Vietnamese forces continued to flare along Route 9 and nameless ridgelines around Khe Sanh through the late spring. By the end of June, another 308 Marines had been killed in Operation Scotland II around Khe Sanh.

Back home, Khe Sanh remained in the news. On May 23, Colonel David Lownds and the regimental sergeant major of the 26th Marines were the guests of honor at a White House ceremony. President Lyndon Johnson presented Lownds with a Presidential Unit Citation for the work of his men in holding Khe Sanh.

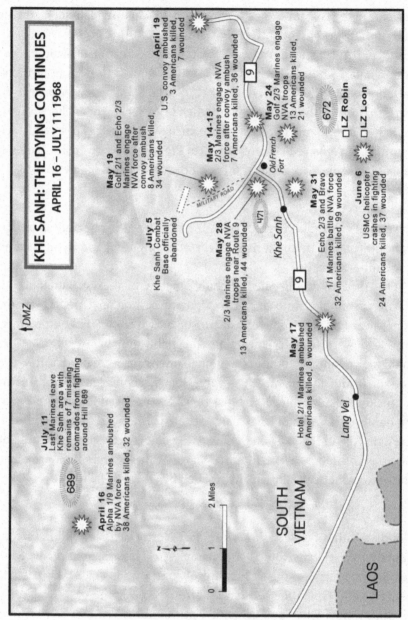

KHE SANH: THE DYING CONTINUES
APRIL 16 – JULY 11 1968

↑DMZ

July 11
Last Marines leave Khe Sanh area with remains of 7 missing comrades from fighting around Hill 689

689

April 16
Alpha 1/9 Marines ambushed by NVA force 38 Americans killed, 32 wounded

April 19
U.S. convoy ambushed 3 Americans killed, 7 wounded

April 19
Golf 2/1 and Echo 2/3 Marines engage NVA force after convoy ambush 8 Americans killed, 34 wounded

May 19

May 14-15
2/3 Marines engage NVA force after convoy ambush 7 Americans killed, 36 wounded

May 24
Golf 2/3 Marines engage NVA troops 13 Americans killed, 21 wounded

9

672

□ LZ Robin

□ LZ Loon

Old French Fort

MILITARY ROAD

July 5
Khe Sanh Combat Base officially abandoned

471

May 28
2/3 Marines engage NVA troops near Route 9 13 Americans killed, 44 wounded

Khe Sanh

May 31
Echo 2/3 and Bravo 1/1 Marines battle NVA force 32 Americans killed, 99 wounded

June 6
USMC helicopter crashes in fighting 24 Americans killed, 37 wounded

9

May 17
Hotel 2/1 Marines ambushed 6 Americans killed, 8 wounded

Lang Vei

SOUTH VIETNAM

LAOS

2 Miles

N

Final Actions, April 16–July 11, 1968.

From the beginning, the Marines had questioned General Westmoreland's decision to tie down a combat company, and, eventually, a rein-

forced regiment, at such a remote location. The siege had amplified the questions about the strategic wisdom of Westmoreland's commitment to Khe Sanh, and those questions flared into open debate when a young American reporter for the *Baltimore Sun*, Army veteran John Carroll, broke the story that Khe Sanh Combat Base would be abandoned. The explanation given by MACV spokesmen in Saigon was that changed tactical conditions had reduced Khe Sanh's importance to American strategic plans.

On June 11, General Westmoreland left Vietnam. Eight days later, his successor, General Creighton W. Abrams, commenced Operation Charlie—the destruction and evacuation of Khe Sanh Combat Base. North Vietnamese forces harassed and bled the Marines to the end, shelling the base and launching a company-strength infantry probe on July 1 that claimed the lives of two Marines.

The base was officially closed on July 5, and the Marines withdrew down Route 9. Several hundred Marines remained in the area, searching for the bodies of comrades who had disappeared in the fighting of the previous months.

In the days that followed, another ten Marines died in clashes with the North Vietnamese. Among them was Private First Class Robert Hernandez of Alpha Company, 1st Battalion, 1st Marines, killed when an NVA mortar hit his position. The following day, July 11, 1968, the last US Marines left Khe Sanh with the remains of seven missing comrades.[16]

EPILOGUE

Dennis Mannion was still in I Corps, near the DMZ, in the early summer of 1968 when a buddy threw a copy of *Stars and Stripes* at him. "Hey, you were at Khe Sanh," the Marine said. "Take a look at this shit!" Mannion was stunned when he saw the headlines about Khe Sanh Combat Base being closed.

"It was almost too hard to believe," he says. "My immediate thought was: we never gave back Tarawa or Iwo Jima, so why this? It made all that we had endured and sacrificed seem almost trivial or unnecessary. Why go through all those months of misery just to have someone decide some months later the place wasn't worth it? I wasn't angry so much as stunned—like I had been punched in the jaw."

Mannion walked to a small observation bunker at the top of a sand dune to be alone with his thoughts as he stared out into the DMZ. "I felt sad and pretty isolated from everyone else and from the war itself," Mannion says. It was the emotional end for him, the moment when he reached the hard conclusion that the war in Vietnam, at least the way it was being run, "was not worth it."

The abandonment of Khe Sanh bothered Mannion for years. In time, he would take a more philosophical view, concluding that "the military higher-ups do what they want, when they want, for the bigger picture. The troops just pay the price."

As a nineteen-year-old rifleman with Bravo 1/26 at Khe Sanh, Michael O'Hara didn't have any sense of the war's strategic or political goals. He learned all that in the decades that followed, but he never wavered in his belief that America's intentions in Vietnam were just. In walking away from Vietnam, he says, America's political and military leaders "not only let down the Vietnamese people, but they broke faith with those brave young men who believed in something larger than themselves: Freedom for all the world's people. President Kennedy called and we answered."

Still, O'Hara speaks for many, if not most, Khe Sanh veterans when he says that he would do it all again. "Khe Sanh, and the men who defended the combat base and the surrounding hills, made me who I am today and I am happy with that outcome."

• • •

The debate about Khe Sanh commenced on the eve of the battle in January 1968, with columnist Joseph Alsop conjuring the ghosts of Dien Bien Phu, and it continues to this day.

Who won? Who lost? Was General Westmoreland duped by his North Vietnamese nemesis, General Vo Nguyen Giap? Were the North Vietnamese serious about seizing Khe Sanh or merely drawing American forces away from urban areas before the Tet Offensive? Was Khe Sanh an American "fiasco," as journalist Stanley Karnow concluded?

Khe Sanh and Tet weighed heavily on the war-weary American psyche in the winter and spring of 1968, and the abandonment of the combat base and outposts less than three months after the siege helped foster the perception of Khe Sanh as a defeat. But these facts are indisputable: the American stronghold at Khe Sanh was successfully defended against a much larger North Vietnamese force, with losses only a fraction of those sustained by the North Vietnamese (even after allowing for the padded body counts of Westmoreland's MACV headquarters). These are not the elements of defeat, much less a fiasco.

The abandonment of Khe Sanh Combat Base was a propaganda victory for the North Vietnamese, but the Americans pulled back only a few miles along Route 9 to a new base at Ca Lu, which was easier to supply and defend. Just as they had at Khe Sanh, US forces operating out of Ca Lu continued to carry out mobile infantry and reconnaissance operations against the North Vietnamese along the border with Laos, as noted by Khe Sanh veteran and scholar Peter Brush. Nothing had changed, except for public perceptions of the war back home in America.

• • •

Nearly fifty years later, Khe Sanh remains wrapped in riddles and mysteries. Beyond the overarching mystery about NVA objectives, one of the most baffling questions is this: Why didn't the North Vietnamese cut Khe Sanh's water supply? Legendary Marine Lieutenant General Victor H. Krulak interpreted the North Vietnamese failure in this regard as an indication that the enemy may have "had no intention of undertaking an all-out assault on the base."[1] But Westmoreland's intelligence chief at the time, General Phillip Davidson, concluded that "the simplest explanation—and probably the most valid—is that neither Giap nor the local NVA commander ever realized the vulnerability of the Marines' water supply. Stranger oversights have happened in war."[2]

It's plausible, but I doubt we will ever know with any certainty.

The same is true about the debate over whether Khe Sanh was a North Vietnamese ruse.

General Giap's comments about Khe Sanh to the Italian journalist Oriana Fallaci are exactly what one would expect. "Oh, no," he was quoted as saying, "Khe Sanh didn't try to be, nor could it have been, a Dien Bien Phu. Khe Sanh wasn't that important to us. Or it was only to the extent that it was important to the Americans—in fact, at Khe Sanh their prestige was at stake."[3]

Acclaimed Vietnam War correspondent Neil Sheehan, who was given the National Book Award and Pulitzer Prize in 1988 for his epic narrative about the conflict, *A Bright Shining Lie*, is outspoken in his belief that General Giap wasn't serious about seizing Khe Sanh. Writing in the 1997 book *Requiem*, Sheehan declared Khe Sanh "the biggest ruse of the war." His view was based in part on his postwar conversation with General Hoang Phuong, the Vietnamese chief of military history. "General Westmoreland fell into a strategic ambush," Phuong told Sheehan.[4]

If true, the North Vietnamese paid dearly for any advantage gained. The fact is that the North Vietnamese devoted considerable resources to the Khe Sanh campaign, suggesting more than a feint or passing interest. A possible explanation is that the North Vietnamese envisioned Khe Sanh as both a ruse and, eventually, a coup de grâce that could end the war. But, like so many other questions about Khe Sanh, definitive answers will likely remain elusive, even if documents were suddenly to emerge from Hanoi's archives, purporting to shed light on the debate.

In any discussion about North Vietnamese intentions, one fact is worth highlighting: the NVA had never faced a coordinated air and artillery campaign on the scale of Operation Niagara. It is hardly far-fetched to conclude that the staggering losses the North Vietnamese sustained in the opening days of the campaign forced a change of plans. Also unknown is the impact of the leaked US deliberations on the use of tactical nuclear weapons, and the possible concerns expressed (and pressure applied) by Hanoi's patrons in Moscow and Beijing. One intriguing possibility is that the potent combination of electronic sensors and concentrated US firepower simply prevented the North Vietnamese from massing their forces for a climactic attack. Internal NVA historical accounts in recent decades have highlighted the frustrated efforts of Giap's men to draw in more American troops at Khe Sanh, and the failure of North Vietnamese commanders to mass sufficient forces for the early attacks on the American hill outposts.[5] Perhaps these early failures, and the casualties and command disruption caused by US bombing attacks in the opening days of the campaign, forced Giap and his generals to look elsewhere for a decisive victory. The debate, no doubt, will continue.

As it stands, the case for Khe Sanh as a thwarted North Vietnamese coup de grâce is circumstantial. But so is the self-serving contention of General Giap and his lieutenants that they never intended to seize the American stronghold.

• • •

For the men who served at Khe Sanh during the siege of early 1968, life became an epic written in two volumes: the years before, and the years after. The red clay dust that coated their bodies would wash off, but Khe Sanh had seeped into their souls.

In the spring and summer of 1968, fate guided Khe Sanh's survivors along a thousand paths. Some, like Hill 861 Alpha survivor Joe Roble, died in combat before they finished their tours. Most survived Vietnam and headed home, changed men trying to find their place in a changed country.

Some, like Bravo 1/26 survivor Steve Wiese, endured the vitriol of antiwar protesters, and the indignities of being cursed, spat upon, and denounced as "baby killers."[6] Many, like India Company squad leader Ken Warner, struggled with post-traumatic stress disorder (PTSD) as they tried to come to terms with the violent, dehumanizing world they had known in Vietnam. Alcoholism, drug use, divorce, and depression became common threads in the lives of many Khe Sanh veterans, even as they began careers as postal workers, preachers, teachers, university professors, policemen, FBI agents, business executives, entrepreneurs, school custodians, car salesmen, and construction workers.

Most endured, as they had at Khe Sanh, and became productive citizens. But Khe Sanh was always there—a defining moment in their lives, for better, and for worse.

Hill 881 South survivor Robert Tipton for years battled sleep disorders, exaggerated startle reflexes, and other psychological and physiological challenges. He changed jobs about twice a year, changed apartments, changed relationships, trying to stay one step ahead of the demons. Around 2000, Tipton got a phone call from a long-lost India Company buddy who invited him to a battalion reunion, and it was a turning point. Tipton rediscovered the brotherhood that had gotten him through Khe Sanh, renewed friendships with the living, and remembered the dead—writing articles, posting on Khe Sanh websites, savoring the company of men who had been there and understood. Bob Tipton had found a path forward.

Navy corpsman Robert Topmiller found a path after Khe Sanh, first as a businessman, and, twenty years later, as a Vietnam War scholar and veterans' advocate. But Khe Sanh never let go—even after he found Terri Nicks, the perfect life partner to help him conquer his demons, a Navy corpsman herself who had treated badly wounded Vietnam casualties; even after the cathartic experience of writing two books about his experiences in Vietnam; even after winning acclaim as a history professor and a peacemaker with devout Buddhist beliefs.

Topmiller had been through it all—the anger and alcoholism, the flashbacks and nightmares—and it seemed he had broken through to the other side, beyond the "grotesque hell full of death and destruction that took lives in a random, horrifying manner," as he had described Khe Sanh in one of his books. But the war in Iraq knocked him back into that dark place, and in August 2008, at the age of fifty-nine, as he was completing a book about the struggles of America's veterans, Doc Topmiller succumbed to the "grotesque hell" of Khe Sanh and took his own life.[7]

Michael Archer and Steve Orr had become best friends as radio operators in the 26th Marines command bunker at Khe Sanh, and that friendship became their path forward after Vietnam. They had gotten out of the Marines in 1970 and were going to attend college together, but Orr decided to travel around the country with his girlfriend for three months and visit some of his buddies from Vietnam. Archer and Orr remained close, and when Orr's girlfriend became his wife, and then his ex-wife, Archer was there for him. Orr would return the favor over the years, and the friendship they had forged amid the horrors of Khe Sanh became the rock that anchored their lives. It still is, and at Khe Sanh veterans reunions they are inseparable as they reconnected with comrades like Mike Reath, Raul "Oz" Orozco, and Cliff Braisted, who shared their time in the regimental communications unit.[8]

The families and friends left behind by the men killed at Khe Sanh have borne their own lonely burdens over the decades. Their pain has found an outlet in recent years on websites like the Vietnam Veterans Virtual Memorial Wall or Together We Served, where the children, siblings, or classmates of the fallen can pay their respects and share their memories of loved ones who will be forever young, with lives of promise still ahead of them.

Three months after Lieutenant Terry Roach gave his life in the defense of Hill 64 on February 8, 1968, his widow, Lynn, gave birth to a daughter. As Lynn forged ahead with her life as a single mother, she came to hate the war that had claimed the gregarious, kilt-wearing Irish balladeer who had stolen her heart back at Wayne State. In 1971, Lynn marched against the war, and in time, her daughter, Mary, would become an outspoken critic of the Iraq invasion launched by President George W. Bush.

Terry Roach may or may not have agreed with his daughter's politics, but he surely would have approved of the strength of her convictions, and her fearlessness in expressing them—the very freedoms that Terry Roach had believed he was defending by serving in Vietnam.

Mary named her son for the father she never knew, and young Terry's questions eventually led Lynn to search for answers about her late husband's time in Vietnam—how he lived, how he fought, and how he died.

She came across a website about Hill 64 created by the Alpha-1 corpsman Mike Coonan and began corresponding with a few men who had served under Terry Roach that night.

"I've been reading online about Hill 64 lately, pulling some pieces together . . . something I avoided for the first 40 years," Lynn wrote me in late 2012. "It's not easy to think about or talk about even now, but with grandson Terry, 13, now getting interested I felt I needed a few more facts."

Lynn has never wavered in her belief that the Vietnam War was not a wise use of America's youth and treasure, and that men like Terry were sacrificed in a misguided quest. "That does nothing to dull the gleam of my husband's personal honor," she says. "I will always, always, be proud to have been his wife."

• • •

General William Childs Westmoreland would always claim Khe Sanh and Tet as victories. Indeed, in his memoirs, he cited his decision to stand and fight at Khe Sanh as his finest hour in the Vietnam War, and he may be right.

Whereas Westmoreland was left to defend his controversial record in Vietnam, General Vo Nguyen Giap basked in the glow of his eventual victory in 1975, seven years after Khe Sanh. He, too, would claim Khe Sanh and Tet as victories, but he would get the last word: Westmoreland died in 2005 at the age of ninety-one. Giap outlived his American adversary by nearly a decade before his death in Hanoi on October 4, 2013, at the age of 102.

For Colonel David Lownds, Khe Sanh was the pinnacle of his four decades as a Marine. On behalf of the 26th Marine Regiment, he accepted a Presidential Unit Citation from President Johnson in a White House ceremony in May 1968. He was also honored with a Navy Cross for his successful defense of Khe Sanh.

In 1997, twenty-nine years after the battle, Lownds made a rare appearance at a reunion of Khe Sanh veterans, in St. Louis, Missouri. He received a long and warm ovation from the men who had served under him. In his remarks, he offered a brief glimpse of the burden he had carried away from Khe Sanh. "If you don't think a commander suffers when he loses people, you're sadly mistaken, because it goes deeply into your heart," he said. "It never leaves."

Lownds died in Naples, Florida, on August 31, 2011. He left behind his wife of sixty-nine years, Jean, seven children, nineteen grandchildren, twenty-three great-grandchildren, and thousands of Marines who fondly remember the cigar-smoking commander who led them through the fires of Khe Sanh.

• • •

Bill Dabney, commander of the American outpost on Hill 881 South, returned to the Khe Sanh area in 1971 as an adviser to a South Vietnamese unit involved in Operation Lam Son 719, in which ARVN troops pushed into Laos in an attempt to cut the Ho Chi Minh Trail—one of the reasons that General Westmoreland had wanted a base at Khe Sanh in the first place. Lam Son 719 ended badly, with the loss of many fine South Vietnamese troops, and Dabney left Vietnam with little doubt about the war's eventual outcome. He finished his career in the Marine Corps as a colonel, then served as the senior naval science instructor and, later, as commandant of cadets at his alma mater, Virginia Military Institute.

In retirement, Khe Sanh became a focal point of Bill Dabney's life. He attended Khe Sanh veterans' reunions and wrote articles about the battle for *Marine Corps Gazette* and other publications.

His health was failing in April 2005 when he was awarded the Navy Cross for his actions at Khe Sanh. In a ceremony at Virginia Military Institute, Dabney rolled into the hall in a wheelchair, tethered to an oxygen tank. But when his moment came, he rose to his feet, and in a strong, clear voice, paid tribute to the defenders of Khe Sanh, about seventy of whom were on hand to honor their former commanding officer. "I wear this honor today only symbolically," Dabney said. "It is they who earned it."[9]

On February 15, 2012, Bill Dabney died at his Virginia farm, at the age of seventy-seven. His funeral attracted Khe Sanh veterans from all over the country.

In his final decades, Dabney had never missed an opportunity to honor his Khe Sanh comrades. "Through it all, the troops did their duty," he wrote. "They stood their watches, flew their aircraft or serviced helicopter zones, manned outposts, engaged the enemy and raised the flag as zealously at the end as at the beginning. They were never asked to stand back-to-back against the flagpole with fixed bayonets, but rather to endure. By enduring, they triumphed. They were magnificent!"

• • •

Bravo 1/26 skipper Ken Pipes retired from the Marines as a lieutenant colonel. Now in his mid-seventies, he lives in Fallbrook, California, near Camp Pendleton. Ever the Marine officer and gentleman, beloved by the Bravo veterans who have scattered across America, Pipes addresses audiences on Memorial Day and other occasions, recalling the sacrifices of the men who served in Vietnam and honoring Marines who have fallen in America's more recent wars in Afghanistan and Iraq. In May 2011, Pipes flew across the country for a ceremony in the Atlanta suburb of Decatur, Georgia, to honor one of his Marines, nineteen-year-old Private Ted Britt, who gave his life in the March 30, 1968, "payback" assault at Khe Sanh.

The loss of so many of his men in the ambush a month earlier, on February 25, 1968, still haunts Pipes. "For all of us, that was a terrible, terrible day," he says. "Time doesn't make it any better—at all. We'll carry that with us the rest of our lives, however long that may be."[10]

• • •

The commander of the Echo Company Marines on 861 Alpha, Earle Breeding, left the Marine Corps in 1971 to become an FBI special agent. He specialized in foreign counterintelligence before his retirement from the FBI in 1991, then moved to Roswell, New Mexico, where he worked as a contract private investigator for various US government agencies for eleven years.

In 2002, at the age of seventy, Breeding "gave it all up" and retired to the Sacramento Mountains around Ruidoso, New Mexico, where he and his wife live "among ponderosa pines, pinions and mesquite, deer, bear, coyotes, fox and skunks," as he describes it. He has stayed active in retirement, serving as a volunteer investigator for the National Center for Missing and Exploited Children and as a docent at Fort Stanton, New Mexico.

Breeding was a key figure in the early years of the Khe Sanh Veterans Association, serving as founding treasurer and president. In April 2012, a few months before Breeding's eightieth birthday, nearly a dozen men who served under him on 861 Alpha converged on his house in Ruidoso for an Echo Company reunion. Among those in attendance was rocketman Dave McCall, who lost his leg on 861 Alpha during the battle of February 5, 1968. In his home state of Kansas, McCall has worked as a youth counselor for more than twenty-five years, fulfilling a promise he made on the hill that terrible, bloody morning.

Traveling to the New Mexico gathering from his home in Northern California was a man that most of the Echo regulars at Khe Sanh reunions hadn't seen since Vietnam: Lieutenant Don Shanley, the commander of Breeding's 1st Platoon.

After surviving Vietnam and completing his obligation to the Marine Corps, the former Stanford swimmer disappeared into the counterculture that had taken hold across America. He smoked marijuana and spent "a very reflective and meditative year," hitchhiking across the country and back three times and hanging out along the Northern California coast. He worked as a lumber mill hand and a lifeguard, dived for abalone, gardened, and tried to forget Vietnam.

Shanley spent a decade working through his self-described "hermit period." He worked as a gardener at an elegant inn along the Northern California coast, landscaped, wrote critically acclaimed poetry, and became caretaker at Kris Kristofferson's ranch.

In 1983, Shanley found his life's work when he started a business that specialized in landscape restoration and erosion control. Building the enterprise from scratch, he earned a reputation for high-quality work and won state and federal contracts. He married a botanist he met through his work, and they carved out a homestead in Mendocino County.

As Shanley found peace by beautifying lands scarred by road construction and other human activities, death stalked the countryside around Khe Sanh. From 1985 to 1995, 4,000 Vietnamese, many of them children, were killed or maimed by stray ordnance from the battle of Khe Sanh and US bombing missions.

Shanley heard about the tragedy, and the work of an American organization called PeaceTrees Vietnam. It had been founded by the sister of a US Army helicopter pilot killed in Vietnam and was helping the people of Quang Tri Province clear unexploded ordnance and regenerate the war-torn landscape. Shanley volunteered for a PeaceTrees mission and returned to Vietnam in 2000—to pay tribute to his fallen comrades and adversaries, and to vanquish one more heartbreaking legacy of the battle of Khe Sanh.[11]

• • •

Over the decades, Steve Wiese has fought and refought the battle of Khe Sanh in his head, trying to understand why he lived.

In 2009, the Bravo 1/26 Marine watched the movie *Taking Chance*, about the honor and respect accorded a Marine killed in Iraq, Lance Corporal Chance Phelps, as his body is escorted to his Wyoming hometown for burial. One line in the movie, about the importance of keeping alive the memories of our war dead, struck Wiese like a thunderbolt: "Without a witness, they just disappear."

Wiese finally understood why he had lived.

"If you had called me four years ago, I would have just told you, 'I have nothing to say,'" Wiese said to me near the end of one of our interviews. "But these guys don't deserve to disappear. These guys died for their country, and they died for their fellow Marines."[12]

And so, like many of the other survivors of Khe Sanh, Steve Wiese bears witness to his comrades, young Americans who fell in battle in the red clay hills of South Vietnam in early 1968.

• • •

It has been a long, hard journey for Ken Warner since those carefree days of Southern California baseball and surfing before Vietnam. He was lucky to have survived his close encounter with the North Vietnamese on the eve of the battle, luckier still to have survived NVA ambushes on back-to-back days. Like so many Khe Sanh veterans, Warner struggled to make sense of the random cruelties of war, and the question that really can't be answered: Why had he lived when so many others had died?

At heart, Ken Warner was—and still is—a gentle soul, and his disorientation after Vietnam was profound. His compass shattered, he found himself adrift in a raging sea.

"After returning home from Vietnam, I spent years fighting PTSD by self-medicating and working odd jobs, along with stays at the VA [hospitals]," he writes. "In 1984, I married my wife Donna, who immediately filled a shadow box with my medals and ribbons. It was hung by the front door so all could see it, and she told me never to be ashamed of what I had done in Vietnam."

With the love of Donna, and their two children, Margo and Jesse, Ken found his bearings. Like his father, Jesse enlisted in the Marines. He served two tours in Afghanistan, the first as a machine gunner, and the second as a scout sniper. He is twenty-six now and attending college. Margo is twenty-eight and studying psychology, with a particular interest in post-traumatic stress disorder.

"My family was the turning point that gave me a life I thought could never exist," Ken Warner says. "They continue to support me and help me to cope with the events of Vietnam and Hill 881 South."

• • •

Several times a year, Tom Esslinger travels from his home in the Virginia suburbs to the black-granite wall of the Vietnam Veterans Memorial in Washington, DC. Every year, on February 23, he makes his way to Panel 41E and finds two names: Paul E. Robitaille, on Line 2, and Eugene C. Wire, on Line 6—the two gunnery sergeants whom Esslinger lost in one awful moment on this date in 1968.

With whispered words and private thoughts, he honors the two men who helped him through some of his hardest days during the siege at Khe Sanh.

In 2003, Esslinger returned to Vietnam to visit 881 South and commune with the spirit of his gunnies. He found a local guide and, with other veterans of 881 South, headed up the hill that had taught him so much about duty, honor, loyalty, and loss.

"While the rest of our party explored the larger India Company part of the hill, I returned alone to the Mike Company sector," he wrote afterward. "It was not difficult to find my old bunker and the nearby bomb crater. I was pleased to find purple flowers growing on the spot where the gunnies were last seen. Tears and time passed as I visited and chatted with Gunny Wire and Gunny Robitaille."[13]

• • •

Navy chaplain Ray W. Stubbe continued to battle the demons of Khe Sanh long after he left Vietnam. As part of his treatment for post-traumatic stress disorder, he began writing a book about Khe Sanh and started tracking down men who had served there. In time, his list of names became the Khe Sanh Veterans Association, with more than 3,000 members. The veterans and their families gather each year, to spend time with one another and remember the comrades who fell at Khe Sanh.

Every three or four years, the Khe Sanh Veterans Association holds its annual reunion in Washington, DC, so members can visit the Marine Corps Museum in Quantico, Virginia, and pay their respects to fallen comrades at the Vietnam Veterans Memorial and Arlington National Cemetery. Such was the case in 2012, when the group gathered in late August in Arlington.

Khe Sanh veterans from around the country met at the conference hotel, a short walk from the southern edge of Arlington National Cemetery. Tom Eichler, one of the heroes of 861 Alpha, now retired from the Chicago Police Department, had flown in from Illinois to preside over the gathering. In a time-honored tradition, Dave "Bulldog" Smith, a senior Special Forces officer at FOB-3, and Marine combat engineer "Big John" Pessoni were riding herd over the hospitality room and the "post exchange" (PX) that sells Khe Sanh T-shirts, mugs, books, and other memorabilia.

Gunnery Sergeant Bill Martin strode into the marbled lobby of the conference hotel from Dallas, Texas, carrying a suit bag with the dress blues he dons for each reunion banquet as he presents and retires the colors with parade-ground precision. Navy corpsman John Cicala, one of the survivors of the February 25 ambush, was there from Michigan. Steve Wiese had flown cross-country from California to see old friends and try to sit through a heartrending documentary film on Bravo Company made by Bravo veteran Ken Rodgers and his wife, Betty.

For hours on end, the survivors of Khe Sanh would eat and drink, tell stories, laugh, and remember—the defenders of 881 South at this table, 861 over there, Bravo 1/26 here, Echo 2/26 across the room, and so on. Conversations were laced with references to comrades who died at Khe Sanh, or in the intervening years. Come Saturday night they would put on business attire or dress blues for the banquet, where they would remember their deceased comrades with silence and prayer. And then, after dinner and other ceremonies, they would recall the days of their youth and let loose on the dance floor as Eichler belted out Motown tunes on a karaoke machine.

Among the veterans at the Washington gathering was a regular who rarely misses a Khe Sanh reunion: Dennis Mannion, the artillery forward observer on Hill 861 during the siege. Mannion had returned home to Connecticut after completing his enlistment, then earned his college degree and took a job at a local high school, teaching English literature and coaching football. Over time, he became renowned for his passion and dedication, and for teaching his students about what a group of committed Americans had experienced at a place called Khe Sanh in 1968.

In 2000, Mannion returned to 861 with his old friend from the hill, forward air controller Paul Knight. They made the pilgrimage back to Khe Sanh with two buddies who had served on 881 South, forward observer radioman Glenn Prentice and air officer Bob Arrotta. One of Mannion's former students, David C. Kniess Jr., accompanied the men and made a documentary film about their journey, *Khe Sanh: A Walk in the Clouds.*

In November 2009, Bob Arrotta died suddenly, and Prentice escorted his dear friend's casket from Southern California to Arlington National Cemetery for burial. Now, nearly three years later, on August 31, 2012, Mannion, Prentice, and Knight made the short drive from the reunion hotel to the cemetery to spend a few minutes with their beloved comrade.

They found their way by memory to Section 9, and descended a steep slope near the cul-de-sac of McClellan Drive, a few hundred yards north of the Tomb of the Unknown Soldier. The trio of Khe Sanh veterans stopped before Grave 5899-A-LH, marked by a bone-white headstone engraved with the name Robert James Arrotta. They touched the smooth marble slab, whispered greetings, and told Arrotta how much they missed him. They recalled a few shared memories, then bade farewell until their next visit.[14]

• • •

Early the next morning, September 1, Dennis Mannion awoke before daybreak and drove across the Potomac River into Washington, DC.

He parked his car along Twenty-second Street, just north of the Mall, crossed Constitution Avenue, and walked the short distance to the Vietnam Veterans Memorial.[15]

Mannion makes a point of coming here every time he visits the nation's capital, and the location of certain names on the wall is fixed in his memory. The entire history of the war is here, if only the names carved into the black granite could talk. So, too, is the story of the 1968 battle and siege at Khe Sanh—names scattered across fifty-five of the memorial's 140 panels, from the east wall to the west, from the January 20 fight on 881 North to the abandonment of Khe Sanh Combat Base in July 1968.

The events of January 20–21, 1968, had marked the beginning of the confrontation, but Americans had been dying at Khe Sanh since 1964, when Captain Richard Lebrou Whitesides was shot down in his small observation aircraft after taking off from the Special Forces camp at Khe Sanh. The spring of 1967 had seen the violent episode in Khe Sanh's history known as the Hill Fights, which had claimed the lives of 155 Marines. But things had gotten quiet again, with only sporadic death from combat and accidents around Khe Sanh, until January 1968.

Dennis Mannion had not forgotten the first Marine that Kilo Company lost at Khe Sanh, on December 22, 1967, during the sweep westward from the combat base to the Laotian border in search of the North Vietnamese. Lance Corporal Michael Edward Suniga was a nineteen-year-old mortarman from Ojai, California, and he had been in Vietnam only forty-two days. It was cold that morning, and Suniga's fingers were probably stiff, and, in all likelihood, he was sleep deprived. Those factors might explain how he dropped a live hand grenade, and then compounded his error by trying to grab it with his hands instead of turning away and absorbing the blast with his flak jacket. Whatever the explanation, the grenade exploded, blowing off the young Marine's arms, and Michael Suniga became one of thirty-six Americans to die in Vietnam that day.[16]

Forty-four years later, in the half-light of the Washington dawn, Dennis Mannion stood before Panel 32E of the reflective black-granite wall, traced his finger across Michael Edward Suniga's name on Line 48, and remembered those days leading up to the great battle.

Like hieroglyphics, the story of Khe Sanh emerges in other names carved into the wall as it slopes gently upward toward the rising sun. On Panel 34E, nine lines from the bottom, is the name of James S. Collins, the India Company point man from the cornfields of Illinois, the first to fall on January 20 when he walked unaware into the line of North Vietnamese dug in on the slopes of 881 North. One line above, side by side, are the names of Thomas D. Brindley—the hockey player from Minnesota who had so impressed Bill Dabney as a platoon leader—and reconnaissance Marine Charles W. Bryan, the Texan who died trying to save his men on the right flank of the American line. At the bottom of 34E, second from the far right, is the name of the brave young Oklahoman Michael H. Thomas, the other platoon leader whom Dabney lost that day.

The confrontation at Khe Sanh plays out across the panels, day by day, revealed in names that evoke far more than battles and barrages, but also dreams unfulfilled and promising young lives cut short.

Mannion's revered Gunnery Sergeant Melvin Lewis Rimel might have seemed old to the grunts under his care, but he was only thirty-three, and he had left a wife and four young children back in the States so he might shepherd young Marines in battle. And now his name was on the wall, Panel 35E, Line 9, frozen in time, and in Mannion's memory, from the moment of his death in the early hours of January 21, 1968.

All around Rimel on the wall are the names of the young men of Kilo Company who fell in the desperate fight for Hill 861: rifleman Paul R. Bellamy; assistant machine gunner Curtis B. Bugger; rifleman Michael D. Cruitt; rifleman Clifton R. Jones; corpsman Malcolm G. Mole; and weapons man David T. Rozelle. Scattered among them are the dead from the fight for the district government headquarters at Khe Sanh village later that day, among them Jerry W. Elliott, the young helicopter crewman from Greenville, Mississippi, who selflessly jumped to the ground to save his comrades from a downed chopper and was never seen again.

A few steps to the east, on Panels 37E and 38E, are inscribed the names of the men who died in the pivotal battles along Khe Sanh's western flank in early February. One can almost hear the cry of "Good morning, Vietnam!" from Jack E. Bogard—Panel 37E, Line 31—as he put a smile on the face of his weary comrades on the northern perimeter of Hill 861 Alpha; scattered below Bogard are the names of his Echo Company comrades killed in the savage fight, including Joseph A. Molettiere, the proud father-to-be from South Philly, and Martin L. Rimson, who soothed his frazzled comrades with his silky rendition of "Moon River."

Along the bottom of panel 37E and the top of 38E are the seven fallen defenders of Lang Vei: Medal of Honor recipient Eugene Ashley Jr.; Earl F. Burke; Kenneth Hanna; James W. Holt; Charles W. Lindewald Jr.; James L. Moreland; and Daniel R. Phillips.

Further down Panel 38E, on Line 20, the casualties of the February 8 attack on Hill 64 begin with corpsman Michael B. Barrett of Los Angeles, California, and continue on through Line 42, with Henry York, the rifleman from North Babylon, New York, killed beside squad leader James Feasel near the end of the fight. In between, side by side, are radioman James P. Rizzo and platoon commander Terence R. Roach Jr.

For the survivors of Khe Sanh, Panel 41E is the most painful of all, for it bears more names of comrades than any other: seventy-one men who died at Khe Sanh, from the terrible bombardment of February 23 through the CH-46 helicopter crash of February 28. It is the panel that Tom Esslinger visits to salute his gunnery sergeants, Paul E. Robitaille, Line 2, and Eugene C. Wire, Line 6. Beside Gunny Wire is the name of Carlos C. Aguirre, killed on 861 Alpha in the first minutes of February 24, his smiling face forever etched in the memory of his platoon leader, Lieutenant Nick Elardo, as he called out, "Hey, Lieutenant, my mother sent me some peppers. Would you like to have a contest?"[17] Further down, beginning with Line 15, is the tally of dead from the February 25 patrol led by Bravo Company Lieutenant Don Jacques—twenty-seven names in all, every one remembered by their skipper, Ken Pipes.

Another sixty-three names of Khe Sanh dead reside on Panel 43E, among them the victims of the C-123 crash on March 6; on 47E are those who fell in the March 30 assault led by Ken Pipes and the men of Bravo 1/26; and on 49E and 50E lie the names and memories of those young Americans who died while retaking 881 North on April 14.

The siege had ended, and the headlines about Khe Sanh had begun to fade by then, but the names on the wall bear witness to the dying that continued unabated at Khe Sanh, long after General Westmoreland and the news correspondents and the American people had moved on. The final panel of the east wall, 70E, bears the name of Khe Sanh casualty Nicholas Samuel Vrankovich, one of thirteen men of Golf Company, 2nd

Battalion, 3rd Marines, killed on May 24, 1968, in an ambush off Route 9, just east of Khe Sanh village and the old French fort.

From that date, the story of Khe Sanh resumes at the far western end of the wall and moves toward the center of the memorial. On Panel 64W, the names recall one of the scores of largely forgotten stories in the Khe Sanh saga. It was the early morning of May 28, about 2:00 a.m., and an NVA force surged up a rugged ridgeline more than a mile east of Khe Sanh village and overran an outpost of Foxtrot Company, 2nd Battalion, 3rd Marines. The savage fighting lasted more than eight hours, until late morning, when American attack aircraft incinerated the final wave of North Vietnamese troops just a few yards from the Marine lines. The worst was supposed to be over at Khe Sanh, but another fifteen Marines were dead.

There were more ambushes and attacks and firefights around Khe Sanh in the days that followed, more names scattered across the wall from west to east, until Panel 52W, when the American withdrawal was completed on July 11, and the curtain fell on the epic saga of Khe Sanh.

In the rising light of an early September morning, standing before the gleaming walls of the Vietnam Veterans Memorial, with all the profound loss these granite panels embody, questions about who won or lost at Khe Sanh and whether it was a ruse seem indecent. So, too, are the political debates over why America lost the war, and who is to blame. It is enough to know that the hundreds of Khe Sanh dead whose names are etched into the wall heeded the call of their country, and they went to Vietnam with the best of intentions. In the company of their brothers-in-arms at Khe Sanh, they found a kinship that transcended a nation's bitter divisions, and with their blood, toil, and tears, they earned a place of honor in American history.

NOTES

PROLOGUE

1. Jack Shulimson et al., *U.S. Marines in Vietnam: The Defining Year, 1968* (Washington, DC: History and Museums Division, Headquarters, U.S. Marine Corps, 1997), 10–11.

2. Ken Warner, author's interview, March 26, 2012.

3. Ibid. As it turned out, Warner's harrowing patrol of January 17, 1968, was only the beginning of the four most intense days of his life. Even after all that happened to Warner and his men over these four days, those few minutes at the base of 881 South on January 17 rate as his "spookiest" experience at Khe Sanh. Warner said, "To this day, telling this story gets my heart racing. I knew we were being watched, and it's just a matter of somebody pulling a trigger."

4. These conclusions about the fate of Ken Warner's patrol on January 17, 1968, are based on my interviews with Warner, my analysis of the events that played out that week, various intelligence assessments, and the ruminations of key participants in the decades since.

CHAPTER 1

1. The entire US military experience in Vietnam was metric. Topographic maps were laid out on 1,000-square-meter grids, and artillery fire and adjustments were made in metric increments. Also, as just noted, hills were designated by their height in meters. As a convenience to readers, metric measurements in this book have been converted to feet, yards, and miles, unless the measurement denotes specifics for targeting, buffer dimensions, and the like, or is given in quoted material.

2. Mike Ray, author's interview, August 6, 2013.

3. Tom Esslinger, author's interview, March 12, 2012.

4. Neil Sheehan, *A Bright Shining Lie: John Paul Vann and America in Vietnam* (New York: Random House, 1988), 649.

5. William Dabney, Virginia Military Institute (VMI hereafter) Oral History interview, September 8, 2005.

6. Michael Pike, author's interview, March 26, 2012.

7. Ibid.

8. Robert Tipton, author's interview, April 17, 2012.

9. Robert Pisor, *The End of the Line: The Siege of Khe Sanh* (New York: Norton, 1982), 27.

10. Ronnie Foster, *One Day as a Lion: True Stories of the Vietnam War* (Plano, TX: Entry Way, 2007), 51–66.

11. Private First Class James A. Collins, Silver Star citation.

12. Mike Ray, author's interview, August 6, 2013.

13. Ibid.

14. Ibid.

15. William Dabney, VMI Oral History interview, September 8, 2005; Richard Dworsky, author's interview, August 5, 2013; Mike Ray, author's interview, August 6, 2013. Dabney said he also had trouble getting enough artillery support for his men on January 20. "You know, you're talking to the staff officer back in the regimental bunker and you feel like saying, 'God damn it, colonel or major, you come out here and look! I'm standing in the middle of it. Get on with it and give me what I ask for!'"

16. Ken Warner, author's interview, March 26, 2012.

17. Corporal Michael C. Elrod, USMC Oral History Collection, Tape No. 2809.

18. Ken Warner, author's interviews, March 26–27, 2012.

19. Ibid.

20. Ibid.

21. Ken Warner, author's interview, March 27, 2012.

22. Michael Pike, author's interview, March 26, 2012.

23. Ibid.

24. Robert (Bob) Ropelewski background from obituary, http://www.rootsweb.ancestry.com/~paerie/newspaper/BTKMoreFamObits.htm; James E. Schemelia, quoted in Ray Stubbe, *Khe Sanh Chaplain: A Historical Summary of Activities While Assigned to 1/26, 3d Recon., and 3d Shore Party BNs, July, 1967, Through June, 1968, Including the Khe Sanh Seige [sic] of 1968, of LT Ray W. Stubbe, CHC, USNR*, unpublished manuscript dated April 1, 1970, 333–334, Ray Stubbe Papers, U.S. Marine Corps Archives, Quantico, Virginia.

25. James E. Schemelia, interview with Ray Stubbe, July 1984, quoted in Stubbe, *Khe Sanh Chaplain*, 333–334.

26. In addition to pilot Bob Ropelewski, the other three crew members of *Frosty Gold* were: the co-pilot, Steve R. Stegich; the crew chief, Curtis Larson; and the gunner, M. J. Norman.

27. Marine Medium Helicopter Squadron 262 (HMM-262) Command Chronology, narrative written by Lieutenant Colonel Neil Allen, http://www.hmm-262combatvets.com/chronology.htm; Stubbe, *Khe Sanh Chaplain*, 333–334; Michael Pike, author's interview, March 26, 2012; also see Beth Crumley, "The Siege of Khe Sanh Begins," January 24, 2012, blog post on Marine Corps Association and Foundation website, http://www.mca-marines.org/blog/beth-crumley/2012/01/24/siege-khe-sanh-begins. Michael Pike ended up next to two members of the downed chopper crew—probably Ropelewski and Stegich—in the bomb crater.

28. Ken Pipes, author's interview, July 23, 2012, and William Gay, author's interview, August 15, 2013.

Official records credit Captain Ken Pipes, commander of Bravo Company, 1st Battalion, 26th Marines, and his men with handling the surrender of the NVA defector who appeared outside Khe Sanh Combat Base on the afternoon of January 20, 1968. The 1/26 Command Chronology for January 1968 states: "At 201400H [2:00 p.m., January 20] Company B, at (XD 854421), observed one NVA waving a white flag. 'Chieu-Hoi' [defector] was turned over to ITT [Interrogator/Translator Team]. Prisoner was wearing green utilities and a bush hat and carried an AK 47 rifle. ITT reported that 'Chieu-Hoi' was a NVA Lieutenant."

In the daily log of 1/26 activities, also found in the 1/26 Command Chronology for January 1968, the incident was similarly described: "At 201400H a Fire team from B-1-26 providing security on end of airstrip observed one (1) NVA waving white flag. The fire team captured one (1) AK 47 with Magazine. The POW wearing green utilities, bush hat, was turned over to ITT for interrogation. Also weapon was [turned] into Regt S-2. The POW was also carrying a bottle of pills and one (1) cigarette lighter."

Ken Pipes described his memories of the incident to me in our interview of July 23, 2012. He recalled that he had been walking his lines with his radio operator when he had received word that an apparent NVA had been spotted waving a white flag or object beyond the northeastern end of the runway. Pipes said he and four other Marines walked out to the area where the NVA had been spotted, a few hundred yards beyond the perimeter wire. Pipes said he repeatedly shouted, "Marine dai-uy" ["Marine captain"] and "Chieu hoi!" ["Open Arms"], the name of the U.S.-South Vietnamese program for encouraging the surrender of Communist soldiers in Vietnam. As Pipes recalled, the North Vietnamese soldier appeared over a low rise in the rolling terrain east of the perimeter, "and we motioned him on and we took control of him."

The North Vietnamese defector was taken inside the base, where he was interrogated by personnel of the 17th Interrogator Translator Team, including Gunnery Sergeant Max Friedlander and Sergeant Jimmy Brown.

William Gay has a different recollection of how the North Vietnamese lieutenant was captured. Gay was a second lieutenant in command of a platoon of combat engineers posted at Khe Sanh, and on the afternoon of January 20, he and his men were in the cleared buffer east of the runway, putting in another minefield to strengthen the perimeter defenses. Marine grunts from one of the line companies were assigned as security for the detail. Gay said he was near the jungle's edge, lying on his stomach as he carefully armed a "Bouncing Betty" anti-personnel mine, when a North Vietnamese soldier armed with an AK-47 rifle stepped from the elephant grass about thirty feet away. Before Gay could react, the North Vietnamese soldier dropped his rifle and thrust his hands into the air. Gay said he grabbed his own rifle, jumped to his feet, and motioned the man forward. He steered the enemy soldier around the live mines and ordered a Marine to hustle the prisoner inside the base for interrogation. Thus ended his involvement with the incident, Gay told me.

Discrepancies also surround the identity of the North Vietnamese soldier. The official Marine Corps history, *The Battle for Khe Sanh*, was written by Captain Moyers S. Shore II later in 1968 and published the following year. In early drafts, Shore identifies the NVA defector of January 20 as "Lieutenant La Thanh Ton." In the version that was published, Shore only identifies the defector as an "NVA first lieutenant who was the commanding officer of the 14th Antiaircraft Company, 95C regiment, 325C Division." Shore describes the information revealed by the NVA lieutenant but says nothing about his motivations for surrendering, or his fate.

In November 1970, the incident was recalled by Major General Rathvon McC. Tompkins in his testimony before the US Senate Electronic Battlefield Subcommittee, and the former commander of the 3rd Marine Division during the siege of Khe Sanh identified the North Vietnamese defector as "Lieutenant La Thanh Tonc." Tompkins offered some additional details about the defector: he "was a Regular with 14 years service and had recently failed to be selected to promotion to captain," Tompkins told the subcommittee. "This so incensed Lieutenant Tonc that he deserted." See United States Senate, *Hearings Before the Electronic Battlefield Subcommittee of the Preparedness Investigating Subcommittee of the Committee on Armed Services* (Washington, DC: Government Printing Office, 1971), 82.

From that time on, correctly or not, history has referred to the North Vietnamese defector as "La Thanh Tonc." But the name is problematic: Ton is a common Vietnamese family name, but Tonc is not. Veteran Southeast Asia news correspondent Seth Mydans, who has spent much time in Vietnam over the past three decades, notes that Tonc "is definitely not a Vietnamese name." Also, "Le Thanh" rather than "La Thanh" would be the common spelling.

Historian John Prados, whose expansive work on Khe Sanh and the larger war has been thoughtful and thorough over the years, has argued that the NVA lieutenant might have been a plant intended to redirect American attention to Hill 861 rather than the imminent attack on Khe Sanh village. But like so much about Khe Sanh, there is a dearth of hard evidence to support his case. In any event, General Tompkins, among others, consistently hailed the revelations of the North Vietnamese lieutenant as an intelligence windfall for the Americans on the eve of the Khe Sanh attack.

The NVA lieutenant himself could lay to rest many of these questions, but just as suddenly as he strode onto history's stage, he disappeared. He is believed to have been flown out of Khe Sanh on January 21, but what became of him afterward remains one of many enduring mysteries of the siege.

29. Ken Pipes, author's interview, July 23, 2012; statement of Major General Rathvon Tompkins, November 19, 1970, US Senate Electronic Battlefield Subcommittee, printed in United States Senate, *Hearings Before the Electronic Battlefield Subcommittee of the Preparedness Investigating Subcommittee of the Committee on Armed Services* (Washington, DC: Government Printing Office, 1971), 82–83; also see interrogation notes of Gunnery Sergeant Max Friedlander of the 17th Interrogator/Translator Team, reprinted in Eric Hammel, *Khe Sanh: Siege in the Clouds* (New York: Crown Publishers, 1989), 57–58.

30. Mike Ray, author's interview, August 6, 2013, and Robert Pagano, author's interview, August 20, 2012.

31. Robert Pagano, author's interview, August 20, 2012.

32. Major Matthew P. Caulfield, USMC Oral History Collection, Tape No. 6157.

33. Private First Class Kenneth O. Brewer, written statement in Navy Cross file of Second Lieutenant Thomas D. Brindley.

34. Robert Pagano, author's interview, August 20, 2012.

35. Ibid.

36. Ibid.

37. Mike Ray, author's interview, August 6, 2013.

38. Robert Pagano, author's interview, August 20, 2012.

39. Mike Ray, author's interview, August 6, 2013.

40. Robert Pagano, author's interview, August 20, 2012.

41. Robert "PJ" Pagano didn't know the identity of the Marine who found him, but Marine records indicate it was Sergeant Daniel Jessup. Robert Pagano, author's interview, August 20, 2012; and Sergeant Daniel Jessup, Silver Star citation.

42. Robert Pagano, author's interview, August 20, 2012; also Lionel Guerra, interview with Ronnie Foster, quoted in *One Day as a Lion*, 75–76. Sergeant Daniel Jessup was awarded the Silver Star for his actions in rescuing Lionel Guerra and PJ Pagano.

43. Tom Esslinger, author's interview, March 12, 2012, and Richard Dworsky, author's interview, August 5, 2013. Esslinger and Dworsky listened to the radio exchanges between Dabney and the regimental command staff on 881 South, as well as other radio traffic. "About 1500 [3:00 p.m.] the order came in for Dabney to break contact and get his men back on the hill," Esslinger told me. "Dabney was unhappy with the order. There was some

discussion between the battalion staff on the hill and back on the base, and the regimental staff. Dabney was overruled and his men returned to the hill."

44. Richard Dworsky, author's interview, August 5, 2013.

45. Tom Esslinger, author's interview, March 12, 2012.

46. Ibid.

47. Ibid.

CHAPTER 2

1. Miguel Salinas, author's interview, May 2, 2012.

2. Dennis Mannion, author's interview, November 29, 2011.

3. Miguel Salinas, author's interview, May 2, 2012.

4. Dennis Mannion, author's interview, November 29, 2011.

5. Miguel Salinas, author's interview, May 2, 2012.

6. Dennis Mannion, author's interview, November 30, 2011.

7. Miguel Salinas, author's interview, May 2, 2012; Dennis Mannion, author's interview, November 30, 2011.

8. Ibid.

9. Dennis Mannion, author's interview, November 30, 2011.

10. Ibid.

11. Ibid.

12. Miguel Salinas, author's interview, May 2, 2012. The term "fog of war" has been much overused in recent years, but I believe it aptly applies to the confusion that still exists over when the North Vietnamese attack on Hill 861 got underway. In my interviews and examination of various documents, including command chronologies, the beginning of the attack was fixed at anywhere from midnight to 3:30 a.m. Dennis Mannion and Miguel Salinas are adamant in their recollections that the attack began between midnight and 1:00 a.m. on the morning of January 21, 1968. Ted Mickelson recalled the attack beginning around 2:00 a.m. Kilo Company commander Norman Jasper insists that the attack began around 3:00 a.m. "I looked at my watch," Jasper states in an account of the battle he wrote for the Virginia Chapter of the Military Order of the Purple Heart. In a Marine Corps oral history interview, Second Lieutenant Linn Oehling of Kilo Company's 2nd Platoon stated, "About 12:30 that night we began to take incoming rounds." Oehling went on to say that 2nd Platoon "received word at 2 o'clock in the morning that they had broke through our lines." Private First Class Michael R. James, a 1st Platoon rocket squad leader who was on the north end of the hill, stated in his oral history interview that same day, "The troops started hitting us around 3 o'clock approximately."

13. Miguel Salinas, author's interview, May 2, 2012. The official Marine Corps account, *The Battle for Khe Sanh*, states that "enemy soldiers penetrated the K/3/26 lines on the southwestern side of the hill and overran the helo landing zone." I found no evidence of this, and conclude that the only breach occurred on the north side of the hill.

14. Ibid.

15. Ibid.

16. Ibid.

17. Dennis Mannion, author's interview, November 30, 2011.

18. Ibid. Some accounts have depicted Melvin Rimel as dying in the arms of Dennis Mannion. In our interviews, Mannion stated emphatically that Rimel was already dead when he found the gunnery sergeant's body.

19. Ibid.

20. Ibid.

21. Ibid.

22. Norman Jasper, author's interview, January 27, 2012.

23. Ibid.

24. Ted Mickelson, author's interview, January 15, 2012. "You could truly say about Dave [Rozelle], he was one in a million," Mickelson told me, in his poignant recollections of his friend and assistant gunner who died on Hill 861. "I've thought of Dave every day of my life, ever since. Sometime during the day I'll think about Dave."

25. Ibid.

26. Gerald F. O'Neal, letter to Ernie Spencer, November 25, 1992, printed in *Khe Sanh Veteran* (Summer 1993).

27. Norman Jasper, author's interview, January 27, 2012.

28. Ibid.

29. William Dabney, VMI Oral History interview, September 8, 2005.

30. Matthew P. Caulfield, USMC Oral History Collection, Tape No. 6157.

31. Tom Esslinger, author's interview, March 25, 2012. Esslinger was in Bill Dabney's command bunker on 881 South at the time and heard the radio exchange between Matt Caulfield and Jerry Saulsberry.

32. Dennis Mannion, author's interview, November 30, 2011. Mannion said at least five or six 105-millimeter howitzer rounds from Khe Sanh inadvertently hit 861 during the night. He wasn't aware of any Marines who were injured by the errant rounds.

33. William Dabney, VMI Oral History interview, September 8, 2005.

34. Ibid. Some estimates state that 1,400 81-millimeter mortar rounds were fired from Hill 881 South in support of Hill 861 during the assault of January 21, 1968. The Marines on 881 South suffered only one casualty: an 81-millimeter mortarman was badly burned in a flash fire when he inadvertently tossed a cigarette butt in a pile of propellant bags (known as increments).

35. Matthew P. Caulfield, USMC Oral History Collection, Tape No. 6157.

36. Miguel Salinas, author's interview, May 2, 2012. Salinas kept the wallet and later had the letter translated by a North Vietnamese defector who was serving with the Marines as a Kit Carson scout.

37. Dennis Mannion, author's interview, December 1, 2011.

38. Ted Mickelson, author's interview, January 15, 2012.

39. Dennis Mannion, author's interview, December 1, 2011.

40. William Dabney, VMI Oral History interview, September 8, 2005.

41. William Dabney, conversation with Ray Stubbe, May 28, 1996, quoted in Ray Stubbe, *Battalion of Kings: A Tribute to Our Fallen Brothers Who Died Because of the Battlefield of Khe Sanh, Vietnam*, 2nd ed., rev. (Wauwatosa, WI: Khe Sanh Veterans, 2008), 124.

42. Dennis Mannion, author's interview, December 1, 2011. Mannion also stated that the North Vietnamese did not fire rockets from 881 North in the initial barrage of January 21, 1968. The 1/26 Command Chronology for January 1968 states that "the battalion received approximately 100 82mm mortar rounds and 20 1 [sic] 122mm rockets throughout its assigned sector within the Khe Sanh Combat Base." There is no mention of heavy artillery. Some accounts have stated that heavy artillery was not used against the base until January 24. But other men I interviewed who were at the combat base on the morning of January 21 also concur with Mannion and told me that heavy artillery rounds were fired in the opening barrage, along with mortars and rockets.

CHAPTER 3

1. Phillip Davidson, interview with Ray Stubbe, April 19, 1989, quoted in John Prados and Ray W. Stubbe, *Valley of Decision: The Siege of Khe Sanh* (Boston: Houghton Mifflin, 1991), 228.

2. Phillip Davidson recalled this scene in his book *Vietnam at War: The History, 1946–1975* (New York: Oxford University Press, 1991), 554–555. Davidson described briefing General Westmoreland on the night of January 20 upon his return from Khe Sanh. According to Davidson, Westmoreland became so upset after hearing Davidson's descriptions of what he had seen and experienced at Khe Sanh that he ordered Lieutenant General Creighton Abrams to establish himself in I Corps to keep an eye on the situation at Khe Sanh. Westmoreland's staff historian, Colonel Reamer W. "Hap" Argo Jr., provided an equally harsh assessment of Colonel Lownds after visiting Khe Sanh around the same time. In Argo's caustic view, Lownds was "a complete loser." See Lewis Sorley, *Westmoreland: The General Who Lost Vietnam* (Boston: Houghton Mifflin Harcourt, 2011), 169.

3. Michael O'Hara, author's interview, April 26, 2011.

4. Ibid.

5. Ibid.

6. Ibid.

7. Tom Quigley, author's interview, April 23, 2011.

8. Ibid.

9. Michael O'Hara, author's interview, April 26, 2011.

10. Ken Rodgers, author's interview, July 21, 2011.

11. John Cicala Jr., author's interview, May 24, 2011.

12. Tom Quigley, author's interview, April 23, 2011.

13. Ibid.

14. Edward Feldman, author's interview, April 11, 2012.

15. Edward Feldman, author's interviews, April 11 and 13, 2012.

16. Edward Feldman was awarded a Silver Star for his extraordinary actions in saving the life of Robert Mussari. Mussari was evacuated to the Philippines, where American reporters chronicled his incredible story, which ran in the *New York Times, Time* magazine, and other publications across the country. Feldman was hailed as a hero. After the war, Feldman was in private practice in northern New Jersey when he received a phone call from Mussari, inviting Feldman to his wedding. Feldman not only attended the wedding of Mussari but a few years later delivered Mussari's son. Feldman also recommended the awarding of Silver Stars to every other man who assisted him in the operation, and he was disappointed when the men were given Bronze Stars instead—an injustice, in Feldman's view. Edward Feldman, author's interviews, April 11 and 13, 2012.

17. Ken Rodgers, author's interview, July 21, 2011.

18. Ken Warner, author's interview, March 27, 2012.

19. Daniel Sullivan, author's interview, April 16, 2012.

20. Dave Doehrman, author's interview, April 6, 2012.

21. Ray Milligan, author's interview, April 6, 2012.

22. Billy Ray Hill, author's interview, April 5, 2012.

23. William Smith, author's interview, March 8, 2012.

24. Ibid.

25. Lewis "Sam" Messer, author's interview, April 10, 2012.

26. Ibid.

27. Steve Wiese, author's interview, April 20, 2012.

28. Michael O'Hara, author's interview, April 26, 2011.

29. Steve Wiese, author's interview, April 12, 2012.

CHAPTER 4

1. Project CHECO Report, Khe Sanh (22 January–31 March 1968), September 13, 1968, 92–93, in RG 472: Records of the U.S. Forces in Southeast Asia, 1950–1976, National Archives and Records Administration (hereafter NARA); and "Effects of B-52 Airstrikes near Khe Sanh," Interrogation Report of captive Hi Van Phen, PFC, 11th Company, 3rd Battalion, 1st Regiment, 330th Division, April 30, 1968, Combined Military Intelligence Center Reports, RG 472, Records of the U.S. Forces in Southeast Asia, 1950–1975, NARA.

2. North Vietnamese Army documents published in *B5-T8 in 48 QXD* (Wauwatosa, WI: Khe Sanh Veterans, 2006), ed. Khe Sanh chaplain Ray Stubbe and trans. Sedgwick D. Tourison Jr., 10–11. The documents in *B5-T8 in 48 QXD* appear to present a reasonably accurate and straightforward account of the movement and disposition of forces in the Khe Sanh campaign. They also appear to provide a credible snapshot of NVA casualties, the nature of the injuries sustained, and whether they occurred from ground fire, artillery, or air attacks. The documents tend to lapse into hyperbole and propaganda when reporting the strength and casualties of opposing American forces. These numbers are invariably skewed to show the North Vietnamese Army units inflicting far greater casualties against much larger forces than were actually involved in particular incidents. This problem was not limited to NVA forces during the war: numerous Americans at various levels of command in Vietnam, including several of the men I interviewed regarding their experiences at Khe Sanh, have described how they were pressured to inflate the enemy body count in operations. But the exaggerations in the North Vietnamese documents when describing US troop strength and casualties in various engagements are particularly pronounced.

3. Ibid., 10–11.

4. My description of the opening of the attack on Khe Sanh village is drawn from the following: Bruce B. G. Clarke, author's interviews, September 17–18, 2012; Jim Perry, quoted in Bruce B. G. Clarke, *Expendable Warriors: The Battle of Khe Sanh and the Vietnam War*, Stackpole Books edition (Mechanicsburg, PA: Stackpole Books, 2009), 53; George Amos, written account in Clarke, *Expendable Warriors*; Michael Archer, author's interview, August 20, 2013; and Archer's memoir about his Vietnam service, *A Patch of Ground: Khe Sanh Remembered* (Central Point, OR: Hellgate Press, 2004), 84–85.

5. Bruce Clarke, author's interview, September 16, 2012. Some published accounts have incorrectly stated that Clarke had been leading a patrol outside the Huong Hoa district compound on the morning of January 21, 1968, and had just gotten back inside the wire before the North Vietnamese attack began. Clarke led a patrol south of the compound the previous day, January 20, but did not leave the compound again until January 22.

6. I am grateful to F. J. "Jim" Taylor, CAC Oscar Marine and unofficial historian, for his insights as I wrote about CAC Oscar and the events at Khe Sanh village on January 21–22, 1968. The product of Taylor's research can be viewed at https://sites.google.com/site/usmc-caposcar/home.

7. Jim Perry, quoted in Clarke, *Expendable Warriors*, 53.

8. Howard McKinnis, author's interview, September 24, 2012; Bruce Clarke, author's interviews, September 16–17, 2012.

9. Bruce Clarke, author's interviews, September 16–17, 2012.

10. Verner Russell was awarded a Silver Star for his actions.

11. Howard McKinnis, author's interview, September 24, 2012.

12. Ibid.

13. Ibid.

14. John Roberts, author's interview, September 21, 2012.

15. Ibid.

16. Ibid.

17. Ibid.

18. James E. Perry, Silver Star citation.

19. Bruce Clarke, author's interview, September 16, 2012.

20. Ibid.; also see "Operations of U.S. Marine Forces, Vietnam, January 1968," Fleet Marine Force Operations, U.S. Marine Forces Vietnam, NARA, RG 127.

21. Bruce Clarke, author's interview, September 16, 2012. It was Clarke's recollection that the jet called in by the Marine forward air controller was an F-4 Phantom, but Marine Corps records identify it as an A-6A.

22. Ward Britt, Silver Star citation; Bruce Clarke, author's interview, September 16, 2012.

23. Bruce Clarke, author's interview, September 16, 2012.

24. Ward Britt, Silver Star citation.

25. Ibid.; Bruce Clarke, author's interview, September 16, 2012; also see Britt, quoted in Clarke, *Expendable Warriors*, 62.

26. Tom Stiner, quoted in Clarke, *Expendable Warriors*, 75–76.

27. Jerry Elliott's sister, Donna, has spent years trying to learn the fate of her brother. Her investigation has included trips to Vietnam, where she has followed leads and searched the Khe Sanh battlefield for her brother's remains. She recounts her quest in *Keeping the Promise: The Story of MIA Jerry Elliott, a Family Shattered by His Disappearance, and His Sister's 40-year Search for the Truth* (Ashland, OR: Hellgate Press, 2010).

28. Tom Stiner, quoted in Clarke, *Expendable Warriors*, 77.

29. Bruce Clarke, author's interview, September 16, 2012.

30. Steve Orr, author's interview, August 19, 2013.

31. Miguel Salinas, author's interview, May 1, 2012.

32. Dennis Mannion, author's interview, December 1, 2011.

33. Larry LeClaire, author's interview, April 18, 2012.

34. Ibid.

35. 3rd Marine Division, Situation Reports, Operation Scotland, No. 327 and No. 328.

36. Ibid., No. 328.

37. John Roberts, author's interview, September 21, 2012.

38. Bruce Clarke, author's interview, September 16, 2012. Clarke said he learned several days later that a North Vietnamese defector had revealed that the B-52 strike during the night of January 21–22 inflicted heavy casualties on his NVA unit as it moved north to join the battle against Khe Sanh.

39. John Roberts, author's interview, September 21, 2012.

40. These seven medevac flights to Khe Sanh village on the morning of January 22, 1968, were flown by Captain Glenn Wayne Russell Jr. He would make another four flights to the village to evacuate the CAC Oscar Marines under fire. For these and other actions that day, Russell was awarded the Silver Star. See Captain Glenn Wayne Russell Jr. Silver Star citation. Also see Marine Medium Helicopter Squadron 362, After Mission Reports for January 22, 1968, at After Mission Report, 01 January 1968, Folder 099, US Marine Corps History Division Vietnam War Documents Collection, The Vietnam Center and Archive, Texas

Tech University. Accessed October 9, 2012, at http://www.vietnam.ttu.edu/virtualarchive/items.php?item=1201099069.

41. Bruce Clarke, author's interview, September 17, 2012.

42. Colonel Lownds would later say that he didn't intend to exclude the South Vietnamese and Bru from the helicopter evacuation operation at Khe Sanh village. Whether it was a misunderstanding or not, witnesses during the evacuation said the Marine helicopter crews didn't allow South Vietnamese and Bru fighters aboard their helicopters even after they had been disarmed.

43. Bruce Clarke, author's interview, September 17, 2012.

44. Robert Brewer, quoted in Ray Stubbe, *Battalion of Kings: A Tribute to Our Fallen Brothers Who Died Because of the Battlefield of Khe Sanh, Vietnam,* 2nd ed., rev. (Wauwatosa, WI: Khe Sanh Veterans, 2008), 131.

45. People's Army of Vietnam, 304th Division after-action report on the battle for Khe Sanh, quoted in *B5-T8 in 48 QXD,* 72.

CHAPTER 5

1. Adam Alexander, author's interview, December 17, 2011. Alexander was one of the twelve VO-67 pilots in Muscle Shoals, and he described in detail for me how the squadron came about and its preparations for its top secret work.

2. Also see Jacob Van Staaveren, *History of Task Force Alpha, 1 October 1967–30 April 1967,* United States Air Force, 1969, 49.

3. Phillip B. Davidson, *Vietnam at War: The History, 1946–1975* (New York: Oxford University Press, 1991), 558.

4. I drew on several primary sources for this account of Defense Secretary Robert McNamara's plan to build an anti-infiltration border barrier that included the use of electronic sensors. Among the most useful were: *Report of the Office of the Secretary of Defense Vietnam Task Force, compiled 06/1967–01/1969, documenting the period 1940–1967* (better known as the Pentagon Papers), Part IV, c.7.a, "Evolution of the War. Air War in the North: 1965–1968," vol. 1, 145–169, Records of the Office of the Secretary of Defense, 1921–2008, RG 330, NARA, hereafter referred to as the Pentagon Papers; "Bugging the Battlefield," Department of Defense training film, 1969, Motion Picture Films and Video Recordings on Four Decades of U.S. Military Activities Around the World, ca. 1950–ca. 1990, Records of the Office of the Secretary of Defense, 1921–2008, RG 330, NARA; and USMACV Command History 1968, vol. 2, 911–34, RG 472, NARA.

5. Pentagon Papers, Part IV, c.7.a, "Evolution of the War. Air War in the North: 1965–1968," vol. 1, 148.

6. The Strong Point Obstacle System (Dyemarker/Duel Blade) and its electronic sensor component, Muscle Shoals/Igloo White, are described at length in *United States Military Assistance Command, Vietnam (USMACV) Command History 1968,* vol. 2, prepared by the Military History Branch, Office of the Secretary, Joint Staff, MACV, and archived in RG 472, "Records of the U.S. Forces in Southeast Asia, 1950–1976," NARA. See Annex B, "Anti-infiltration Barrier," 911–934.

7. Adam Alexander, author's interview, December 17, 2011.

8. "Bugging the Battlefield," DOD film; also see USMACV Command History 1968, vol. 2, 911–934, RG 472, NARA.

9. Adam Alexander, author's interview, December 17, 2011.

10. *MACV Command History 1968*, vol. 2, 921.

11. Jacob Van Staaveren writes in his *History of Task Force Alpha* (p. 50) that the sensor-laying missions at Khe Sanh began on January 20 with flights by the CH-3 aircraft of the 21st Helicopter Squadron. Van Staaveren writes elsewhere that the fixed-wing aircraft of VO-67 began laying sensors around Khe Sanh on January 22. See Van Staaveren, *Interdiction in Southern Laos, 1961–1968* (Washington, DC: Center of Air Force History, 1993), 291. The *MACV Command History 1968* (vol. 2, p. 922) fixes January 21 as the date when sensor-laying operations began at Khe Sanh. Adding further to the confusion, the undated Navy Commendation Medal Citation of VO-67 pilot L. W. Gire states that he flew a mission to Khe Sanh on January 19.

CHAPTER 6

1. These details are drawn from daily situation reports. See 3rd Marine Division, Situation Reports, Operation Scotland, Nos. 329–332.

2. Lance Corporal Billy R. Moffett, USMC Oral History Collection, Tape No. 2589.

3. 3rd Marine Division, Situation Reports, Operation Scotland, No. 332.

4. Ibid., Nos. 329, 330, and 331.

5. Ray Stubbe, *Khe Sanh Chaplain: A Historical Summary of Activities While Assigned to 1/26, 3d Recon., and 3d Shore Party BNs, July, 1967, Through June, 1968, Including the Khe Sanh Seige [sic] of 1968, of LT Ray W. Stubbe, CHC, USNR,* unpublished manuscript dated April 1, 1970, 539.

6. The two Marines killed were Corporal Howard Leon Johnson of Memphis, Tennessee, and Lance Corporal Thomas Lee Cottrell of Los Gatos, California. Combat Area Casualties Database, RG 330, NARA.

7. John Prados and Ray W. Stubbe, *Valley of Decision: The Siege of Khe Sanh* (Boston: Houghton Mifflin, 1991), 274–275.

8. Command Chronology, January 1968, 1st Battalion, 26th Marines, entries for January 22, 1968, RG 127, NARA.

9. 3rd Marine Division, Situation Reports, Operation Scotland, No. 332.

10. "5,000 Men Massed at Khe Sanh," *New York Times*, January 24, 1968.

11. The two Marines who died with Bernard Fall were Lance Corporal Glenn A. Harris, eighteen years old, from Chicago, Illinois, and Gunnery Sergeant Byron G. Highland, thirty-three years old, of Detroit, Michigan. Highland, a Korean War veteran, was a combat photographer who was working with Fall.

12. Earle Breeding, author's interview, May 10, 2012.

13. Ibid.

14. 3rd Marine Division, Situation Reports, Operation Scotland, No. 334; Jim Kaylor, author's interview, February 15, 2012; Dave McCall, author's interview, February 16, 2012; Larry McCartney, author's interview, January 3, 2012; Dave Norton, author's interview, February 13, 2012; Matthew Walsh, author's interview, February 12, 2012; Michael Worth, author's interview, February 13, 2012.

15. Dave Norton, author's interview, February 13, 2012.

16. Ibid.

17. David McCall, author's interview, February 16, 2012.

18. Dave Norton, author's interview, February 13, 2012.

19. Earle Breeding, author's interview, May 10, 2012.

CHAPTER 7

1. Phillip B. Davidson, *Vietnam at War: The History, 1946–1975* (New York: Oxford University Press, 1991), 443–444. As the senior US military intelligence chief in Vietnam at the time of the Tet Offensive, Davidson had a stake in defending General Westmoreland's contention that Communist forces sought a decisive confrontation at Khe Sanh. In his book, he vehemently rejects the Khe-Sanh-as-ruse school of thought that has flourished among journalists and scholars over the decades. Davidson contends that Giap "had some important purpose in mind for the use of this corps-size force" deployed against Khe Sanh in early 1968. That purpose, Davidson argues, is that Khe Sanh "had to be the set-piece battle of Phase III."

2. The North Vietnamese buildup around Khe Sanh is discussed in Willard Pearson, *The War in the Northern Provinces* (Washington, DC: Department of the Army, 1975), 30–31, and in various North Vietnamese documents in *B5-T8 in 48 QXD* (Wauwatosa, WI: Khe Sanh Veterans, 2006), ed. Ray Stubbe and trans. Sedgwick D. Tourison Jr., 4–16 and 30–35.

3. *B5-T8 in 48 QXD*, 15.

4. Ibid., 14 and 26–28.

5. Dennis Mannion, author's interview, December 8, 2011.

6. Larry LeClaire, author's interview, April 18, 2012. "That first week, everybody was nervous as a cat," LeClaire told me. "Everybody thought we were going to get hit again. A lot of times at night you would be off watch and the word would be passed, 100 percent alert, and you'd have to get up and be ready."

7. Ibid.

8. The two Marines killed on Hill 861 by the mortar round that mortally wounded Christian Feit on January 24, 1968, were PFC Kenneth Virgil Goodman, twenty years old, of Stewart, Minnesota, and Lance Corporal Francis Pennetti, also twenty, of Philadelphia, Pennsylvania.

9. Ray Milligan, author's interview, April 7, 2012.

10. Dave Doehrman, author's interview, April 6, 2012; Kevin Macaulay, author's interview, May 17, 2012; Ray Milligan, author's interview, April 7, 2012. The four men killed by the rocket that struck the Bravo, 3rd Recon bunker at Khe Sanh Combat Base on January 24, 1968, were: corpsman Charles W. Miller; Lance Corporal Gregory F. Popowitz; Lance Corporal Juan Antonio Rosa; and Lance Corporal Gary David Scribner.

11. Also killed in the North Vietnamese barrages of January 24, 1968, was Corporal George Ralph Castillo of Lima Company, 3/26, 3rd Marine Division, Situation Reports, Operation Scotland, No. 337 and No. 340.

12. Ray Stubbe, *Khe Sanh Chaplain: A Historical Summary of Activities While Assigned to 1/26, 3d Recon., and 3d Shore Party BNs, July, 1967, Through June, 1968, Including the Khe Sanh Seige [sic] of 1968*, of LT Ray W. Stubbe, CHC, USNR, unpublished manuscript dated April 1, 1970, 566.

13. Michael O'Hara, author's interview, April 26, 2011.

14. Ernesto Gomez, Navy Cross citation, undated.

15. John Rauch, author's interview, March 22, 2012.

16. Dennis Mannion described this incident in our interviews and also provided me with his written account of the Alpha Company patrol of January 26, 1968, entitled "Wishing Upon a Silver Star," undated.

17. Dennis Mannion, "Wishing Upon a Silver Star," undated.

18. John Rauch, author's interview, March 22, 2012. A brief account of the engagement is contained in 3rd Marine Division, Situation Reports, Operation Scotland, No. 347.

Dwight T. Denning was awarded the Silver Star for his heroic actions that cost him his life on January 26, 1968. The citation states that Denning's companions "aggressively continued their assault and quickly destroyed the enemy force." In fact, the Marines withdrew from the draw and left it to supporting arms—air and artillery—to destroy the North Vietnamese positions.

19. "CO of 3rd Engineer Battalion to commanding officer of the 3rd Marine Battalion," January 28, 1968, 3rd Engineer Battalion Command Chronology for January 1968, RG 127, NARA.

20. Phillip B. Davidson, *Vietnam at War: The History, 1946–1975* (New York: Oxford University Press, 1991), 570.

21. Ibid.

22. MACV Command History 1968, 2:911; and Item 15 0900, January 29, Daily Journal Files, MACV J-2 Command Center, RG 407, NARA; also see James J. Wirtz, *The Tet Offensive: Intelligence Failure in War* (Ithaca: Cornell University Press, 1991), 217.

23. Ray Stubbe, *Battalion of Kings: A Tribute to Our Fallen Brothers Who Died Because of the Battlefield of Khe Sanh, Vietnam*, 2nd ed., rev. (Wauwatosa, WI: Khe Sanh Veterans, 2008), 144.

24. I am grateful to F. J. "Jim" Taylor for sharing with me his recollections and written account of the January 29, 1968, rescue mission to Hill 471. He also shared with me the written account of Captain Harlan "Rip" Van Winkle, US Army Special Forces, "Action on Hill 471, January 29, 1968," which Taylor edited. Also see Stubbe, *Battalion of Kings*, 146–147.

25. Van Winkle, "Action on Hill 471, January 29, 1968."

26. All three Americans who died on Hill 471 on January 29, 1968, were Pennsylvanians. Thirty-three-year-old Charles Tredinnick left behind a wife in the northeastern borough of Dallas. The remains of twenty-six-year-old Gary Crone of York and twenty-two-year-old Michael T. Mahoney of Towanda were recovered several weeks later on Hill 471.

27. Ibid.

28. General William Westmoreland to Admiral Ulysses S. G. Sharp, cable dated January 29, 1968, quoted in James J. Wirtz, *The Tet Offensive: Intelligence Failure in War* (Ithaca: Cornell University Press, 1991), 218.

29. Ibid.

30. William Westmoreland, quoted in Robert Mann, *A Grand Delusion: America's Descent into Vietnam* (New York: Basic Books, 2002), 570.

31. Robert McNamara to LBJ, November 1, 1967, quoted in David M. Barrett, ed., *Lyndon B. Johnson's Vietnam Papers* (College Station: Texas A&M University Press, 1997), 515–522.

32. Mann, *A Grand Delusion*, 566.

33. Walt Rostow recounted the January 10, 1968, lunch at Joseph Alsop's house in a memo to Lyndon Johnson later that day, Walt Rostow to President Lyndon B. Johnson; Meeting with Joe Alsop, January 10, 1968; Folder 35, Box 01, Veteran Members of the 109th Quartermaster Company (Air Delivery) Collection, The Vietnam Center and Archive, Texas Tech University, accessed at http://www.vietnam.ttu.edu/virtualarchive/items .php?item=0010135002.

34. "The Situation at Khe Sanh," Memorandum from the Joint Chiefs of Staff to President Lyndon Johnson, January 29, 1968, JCSM-63-68, *Foreign Relations of the United States: 1964–1968, Volume 6, Vietnam, January–August 1968* (Washington, DC: Government Printing Office, 2002), 69–70.

35. Ibid.

36. It has been erroneously reported over the years that President Johnson forced each of the Joint Chiefs to sign a statement promising that Khe Sanh would be held. In fact, the only written assurance from the Joint Chiefs was Wheeler's memo of January 29, 1968, in which the military chiefs endorsed "General Westmoreland's assessment of the situation" and recommended that US forces remain at Khe Sanh. See "Notes of the President's Meeting with the Chiefs of Staff," January 29, 1968, 1:04–1:40 p.m., *Foreign Relations of the United States: 1964–1968*, 6:71–72. The following day, January 30, 1968, in a meeting with Democratic congressional leaders, Lyndon Johnson described the questions he put to the Joint Chiefs and their answers. See "Notes of the President's Meeting with the Democratic Leadership, January 30, 1968, 8:30–10:06 a.m., *Foreign Relations of the United States: 1964–1968, Volume 6*, 77–79.

CHAPTER 8

1. Military Assistance Command, Vietnam (hereafter MACV) Monthly Report, January 1968, 50.

2. Sergeant Jesus Roberto Vasquez, Navy Cross citation, undated.

3. Dennis Mannion, author's interview, December 9, 2011.

4. Ibid.

5. Dennis Mannion provided a copy of his January 31, 1968, letter to the author.

6. Dennis Mannion, author's interview, December 15, 2011.

7. Ibid.

8. General Wheeler first raised the issue of President Johnson's concern about the possible use of tactical nuclear weapons in his February 1 telegram, JCS 1154, to Admiral Sharpe at CINCPAC and General Westmoreland at MACV in Saigon. See *Foreign Relations of the United States: 1964–1968, Volume 6, Vietnam, January–August 1968*, 120. This telegram and other related messages between Westmoreland and Washington regarding the nuclear issue can be found in Walt Rostow's files at the Lyndon Baines Johnson Presidential Library, filed under "NSC History of the March 31st Speech, Vol 2. Tabs-A-Z and AA-ZZ."

9. General Wheeler communicated President Johnson's latest concerns in a cable to General Westmoreland, JCS 01272, February 3, 1968.

10. Ibid.

11. General Wheeler quoted extensively from Westmoreland's assessment in "Memorandum from the Chairman of the Joint Chiefs of Staff (Wheeler) to President Johnson," Washington, DC, February 3, 1968, CM-2944–68, *Foreign Relations of the United States: 1964–1968, Volume 6, Vietnam, January–August 1968*, 117–20.

12. "Drawing the Noose?" *Newsweek*, February 5, 1968, 39–40.

13. Mark Swearengen, author's interview, August 16, 2013.

14. The background material on Mirza M. "Harry" Baig is drawn from the monograph by Ray Stubbe, *Khe Sanh and the Mongol Prince* (Wauwatosa, WI: Self-published, 2002), 9–12.

15. Ibid., 14.

16. Major Mirza M. Baig, letter to Colonel F. C. Caldwell, Head, USMC Historical Branch, December 23, 1968, found in *The Battle for Khe Sanh* Comments File, at the U.S. Marine Corps Archives in Quantico, Virginia.

17. Along with Ray Stubbe's monograph on Harry Baig, *Khe Sanh and the Mongol Prince*, Michael Archer paints a vivid portrait of the extraordinary targeting officer in his

memoir, *A Patch of Ground: Khe Sanh Remembered* (Central Point, OR: Hellgate Press, 2004), 131–136.

18. Baig, letter to Colonel F. C. Caldwell, December 23, 1968.

19. Ibid.

CHAPTER 9

1. Don Shanley, author's interview, February 20, 2012.

2. Ibid.

3. Dave McCall, author's interview, February 16, 2012.

4. Ibid.

5. Joseph Molettiere obituary, *Philadelphia Daily Inquirer*, February 20, 1968; also Dave Norton, author's interview, February 13, 2012.

6. Don Shanley, author's interview, February 20, 2012.

7. Ibid. A useful timeline of the battle for 861 Alpha on the morning of February 5, 1968, can be found in the 3rd Marine Division, Situation Reports, Operation Scotland, No. 385.

8. Don Shanley, author's interview, February 20, 2012.

9. Ibid.

10. Dave McCall, author's interview, February 16, 2012.

11. Dave Norton, author's interview, February 13, 2012.

12. Ibid.

13. Earle Breeding, author's interview, May 10, 2012.

14. Ibid.; Don Shanley, author's interview, February 20, 2012. Shanley refutes accounts that have described a massive human-wave assault hitting the Echo lines on 861 Alpha. The North Vietnamese troops he witnessed coming through the breach in 1st Platoon lines arrived in groups of two or three men, Shanley said.

15. Don Shanley, statement of February 18, 1968, in Bronze Star medal file on PFC Jack C. Bogard, quoted in Ray Stubbe, *Battalion of Kings: A Tribute to Our Fallen Brothers Who Died Because of the Battlefield of Khe Sanh, Vietnam,* 2nd ed., rev. (Wauwatosa, WI: Khe Sanh Veterans, 2008), 160.

16. Richard Lynn Woodard, April 1968, comments in USMC Oral History interview No. 2775.

17. Don Shanley, author's interview, February 20, 2012.

18. Tom Eichler, letter to Ray Stubbe, September 1986, quoted in Stubbe, *Battalion of Kings*, 161.

19. Ibid.

20. Major Mirza M. Baig, letter to Colonel F.C. Caldwell, Head, USMC Historical Branch, December 23, 1968. I'm also grateful to Mark Swearengen for his vivid recollections of how the extraordinary artillery barrage was executed in defense of Hill 861 Alpha in the early morning of February 5, 1968. Mark Swearengen, author's interview, August 16, 2013.

21. Earle Breeding, author's interview, May 10, 2012.

22. Jim Kaylor, author's interview, February 15, 2012.

23. Matt Walsh, author's interview, February 12, 2012.

24. Ibid.; Michael Worth, author's interview, February 13, 2012.

25. Matt Walsh, author's interview, February 12, 2012; Michael Worth, author's interview, February 13, 2012.

26. Don Shanley, author's interview, February 20, 2012.

27. Ibid.

28. Jim Kaylor, author's interview, February 15, 2012. Don Shanley doesn't recall much enemy resistance during the counterattack. Jim Kaylor remembers extremely heavy enemy fire, and he feared that Shanley was going to get killed as he led the charge.

29. Jim Kaylor, author's interview, February 15, 2012.

30. Don Shanley, author's interview, February 20, 2012.

31. Dave Norton, author's interview, February 13, 2012.

32. Ibid.

33. Dave McCall, author's interview, February 16, 2012.

34. Ibid.

35. Jose Luis "Cisco" Reyes, author's interview, February 23, 2012.

CHAPTER 10

1. See Major Gary L. Telfer, Lieutenant Colonel Lane Rogers, USMC, and V. Keith Fleming Jr., *U.S. Marines in Vietnam: Fighting the North Vietnamese, 1967* (Washington, DC: History and Museums Division, Headquarters, U.S. Marine Corps, 1984), 33.

2. The Special Forces detachment commander killed in the May 4, 1967, attack on Lang Vei was Captain William Anderson Crenshaw, twenty-seven years old, of Mobile, Alabama. Also killed was the detachment's twenty-seven-year-old executive officer, First Lieutenant Franklin Delano Stallings, of Washington, DC.

3. Paul Longgrear, author's interview, January 27, 2012.

4. Statement of Nickolas Fragos, "Combat After Action Report—Battle of Lang Vei," 5th Special Forces Group, February 22, 1968, RG 472, NARA.

5. There are discrepancies between the various witness statements and the radio transmission logs as to whether the attack on Lang Vei began in the minutes before or after midnight of February 6–7. See "Combat After Action Report—Battle of Lang Vei," including the eyewitness accounts. Also see William R. Phillips, *Night of the Silver Stars: The Battle of Lang Vei* (New York: St. Martin's Paperbacks, 2004), 107–110.

6. Nickolas Fragos radio transmission, quoted in Phillips, *Night of the Silver Stars*, 110.

7. "Combat After Action Report—Battle of Lang Vei."

8. Statements of Lieutenant Colonel Daniel F. Schungel and Staff Sergeant Peter Tiroch, "Combat After Action Report—Battle of Lang Vei." Paul Longgrear provided insights into the fate of James William Holt, based on his conversations with his Special Forces operators present at Lang Vei during the fight. Paul Longgrear, author's interview, September 23, 2013.

9. Paul Longgrear, author's interview, September 23, 2013.

10. Ibid.

11. Ibid.

12. Ibid.

13. Like so many aspects of the battle of Lang Vei, uncertainty has surrounded the fate of the two Americans at the Mike outpost, Charles Lindwald and Kenneth Hanna. Paul Longgrear told me that his Mike force outpost had been overrun within minutes. These were Longgrear's men, and his efforts to shed light on their fate has stretched over decades. He has maintained close contact with most of the Americans who survived the battle at Lang Vei, and he has met some of his former adversaries in recent decades in Vietnam, further deepening his knowledge of what happened that night. Radio operator Emanuel E. Phillips was the last American to have contact with Lindewald and Hanna, and in his statement in

the "Combat After Action Report—Battle of Lang Vei," Phillips writes: "As A-101 radio supervisor, my alert position and sleeping quarters were located in the TOC. I was awakened at approximately midnight and told that there were tanks advancing on the camp's southern perimeter. I first made sure That [sic] all the USASF were alerted. Then contacted Marine artillery and requested fire on our southern perimeter, reference the camps night defensive fire plan. Simultaneously, SFC Hanna reported the OP as being under heavy mortar and automatic weapons attack. Two artillery missions were called in defense of the OP before radio contact was lost. At last radio contact was regained with the OP. SFC Hanna reported that SFC lindewald [sic] was gravely wounded, and that the OP was still under heavy attack. After losing radio contact with the OP, under CPT Willoughby's direction, all efforts were directed toward stopping the tanks and coordinating air support." The author of the definitive book on the battle of Lang Vei, William R. Phillips—the cousin of Green Beret Daniel R. Phillips, who was among the missing at Lang Vei, but no relation to Emanuel E. Phillips—writes of the two Americans at the Mike force outpost: "Lindewald had taken severe abdominal wounds, as reported by Dinh Chep, MIKE Force platoon leader. He had not seen Hanna wounded, but he had watched as Hanna and the radio operator carried Lindewald into the bunker at the OP. He then had seen a tank roll up to the wire and fire at the bunker, destroying it (and presumably killing Lindewald, Hanna and the radio operator) and the machine gun behind it." The radio operator referred to as Dinh Chep must have been an indigenous fighter, as there were no other Americans at the outpost when the attack occurred. Phillips, *Night of the Silver Stars*, 204.

14. Statement of Lieutenant Colonel Daniel F. Schungel, "Combat After Action Report—Battle of Lang Vei."

15. Ibid.

16. Statement of Staff Sergeant Peter Tiroch, "Combat After Action Report—Battle of Lang Vei."

17. In a series of USMC Oral History interviews, Major General Rathvon Tompkins, 3rd Marine Division commanding officer, and two other Marine officers involved in the events recall the real-time discussions on February 7, 1968, over whether to use the "controlled fragmentation munitions" (COFRAM) on the NVA assault forces at Lang Vei. See USMC Oral History Tape No. 2535.

18. Ibid.

19. Statement of Captain Frank C. Willoughby, "Combat After Action Report—Battle of Lang Vei."

20. Paul Longgrear, author's interview, January 27, 2012.

21. Ibid.

22. "HCS to Host Hall of Honor Induction Ceremony," *Utica Observer-Dispatch*, June 20, 2012.

23. Charles "Toby" Rushforth, author's interview, January 29, 2012.

24. Ibid.

25. Ibid.; and Paul Longgrear, author's interview, January 27, 2012.

26. Charles "Toby" Rushforth, author's interview, January 29, 2012.

27. Paul Longgrear, author's interview, January 27, 2012.

28. This account of the extraordinary efforts of the AV-25 pilots in support of Lang Vei is drawn from the following: Paul Longgrear, author's interview, January 27, 2012; Charles "Toby" Rushforth, author's interview, January 29, 2012; Captain Charles Rushforth, US Air Force interview, February 18, 1968; "Khe Sanh (Operation Niagara) 22 January–31 March," HQPACAF, Directorate, Tactical Evaluation, Checo Division; Rick Burgess and Zip Rausa,

U.S. Navy A-1 Skyraider Units of the Vietnam War (Oxford: Osprey Publishing, 2009); and President's Message, *Fist of the Fleet Association* Newsletter 8 (January 2012).

29. Richard Allen, author's interviews, February 2–3, 2012.

30. Ibid.

31. William Smith, author's interview, March 7, 2012. The difficulties inherent in an overland effort to relieve Lang Vei had been underscored about two months earlier, when the Khe Sanh Combat Base commander, Colonel David Lownds, had dispatched a company of Marines to chart the best route to the Special Forces camp. It took the Marines more than a day to hack their way through the thick jungle before reaching the Special Forces camp. Bill Smith was a young lieutenant at the time he made the march. "It was an exercise in total futility, especially for a rifle company," he said. "We were totally exposed, and it was technically unfeasible."

32. Ladd found no shortage of volunteers among the American and indigenous fighters serving with the Special Forces in eastern I Corps. Members of the elite airborne Scout unit of Project Delta volunteered to jump into Lang Vei, and Longgrear's superior in the Mike Force chain of command, battalion commander Major Adam Husar, readied a separate force to relieve the embattled camp. See Phillips, *Night of the Silver Stars*, 167; and John Cash, "Battle of Lang Vei," in John A. Cash, John Albright, and Allan W. Sandstrum, *Seven Firefights in Vietnam* (Washington, DC: Office of the Chief of Military History, U.S. Army, 1985), 130.

33. Major General Rathvon Tompkins, comments on USMC Oral History Collection, Tape No. 2535.

34. Paul Longgrear told me that he doesn't believe a C-130 with Special Forces reinforcements for Lang Vei reached the Khe Sanh area. But Major General Rathvon Tompkins describes the turnback of a C-130 that was believed to be carrying one hundred Special Forces personnel. In his interview on USMC Oral History Tape No. 2535, Tompkins reads from notes he took during the Lang Vei attack and relief requests and lays out the following timeline: "0343, FC [fire coordinator] 26th Marines reports air center has incoming C-130 in with approximately 100 men aboard; 0345, CO 26th Marines called, concerned about condition of runway; 0350, CG [commanding general] 3rd Mar Div protests to CG III MAF an incoming C-130 to land or drop Special Forces personnel; 0405, CG 3rd Mar Div said C-130 will not go into Khe Sanh; I told CG 3rd MAF that his G-3 was asking for ground relief column to go to Lang Vei at first light; I told CG we had no troops to send to Lang Vei, and he agreed that no troops should go and said to tell G-3 that he said so; I said I had no intention of sending troops unless he, General Cushman, so ordered me; 0406, told the MAF G-3, Colonel Smith, 'Negative on the relief column,' and that CG III MAF concurs; I further said that such a column at this time would be a lot of foolishness"; also see William Westmoreland, *A Soldier Reports* (Garden City, NY: Doubleday, 1976), 341.

35. In two oral history interviews several years after the war, Colonel Jonathan F. Ladd spoke at some length about his activities relating to the fall of Lang Vei in February 1968. Ladd was a brave and thoughtful American soldier who served his country with distinction in Vietnam and Cambodia. His introduction to the war in Indochina came in 1962–1963, when he served as a senior adviser to the South Vietnamese army's Ninth Division in the heart of the Mekong Delta. His friendship and frank conversations with young American reporters David Halberstam and Neil Sheehan helped shape their critical accounts of the war in the crucial days before the conflict consumed Vietnam and the United States. Unfortunately, as Paul Longgrear observed in our conversations, and as William R. Phillips has noted in his thorough book, *Night of the Silver Stars*, some of Ladd's recollections about

his visits to the camp and radio conversations with Lang Vei during the battle don't mesh with the recollections of men who were on the ground at the Special Forces camp. I have more confidence in Ladd's recollections of how the Lang Vei relief mission came about. See Jonathan F. Ladd Oral History: Abrams Story Collection, U.S. Army Military History Institute; and Jonathan F. Ladd, LBJ Library Oral History Collection, interviews conducted on July 24 and September 25, 1984.

36. William R. Phillips, *Night of the Silver Stars*, 174.

37. Paul Longgrear, author's interview, January 27, 2012.

38. Ibid.

39. Statement of Lieutenant Thomas E. Todd, "Combat After Action Report—Battle of Lang Vei."

40. Spencer C. Tucker, ed., *The Encyclopedia of the Vietnam War: A Political, Social, and Military History*, 2nd ed. (Santa Barbara: ABC-CLIO, 2011), 625.

41. Bill Dabney, VMI Oral History interview, September 8, 2005; also see Bill Dabney comments in Shulimson et al., *U.S. Marines in Vietnam: The Defining Year, 1968* (Washington, DC: History and Museums Division, Headquarters, U.S. Marine Corps, 1997), 277.

CHAPTER 11

1. Among the Marines who encountered Lieutenant Terence (Terry) Roach as he made his rounds on Hill 64 in the predawn of February 8, 1968, were Corporal George Chapman and Private Michael Barry. George Chapman, author's interview, February 23, 2012; and Michael Barry, author's interview, March 15, 2012.

2. Henry Radcliffe, author's interview, August 8, 2012.

3. I am indebted to the former Lynn O'Connor Roach (now Lynn Fifer) for sharing memories of her late husband, Second Lieutenant Terence Roach Jr. Lynn Fifer, e-mail to author, November 20, 2012.

4. Maurice Casey, author's interview, July 31, 2013. Lieutenant Colonel Casey, USMC (ret.) was a classmate of Terry Roach at Basic School. Casey arrived in Vietnam with Roach and was one of the officers whom Roach slipped away from in his eagerness to get a platoon command.

5. The two men killed in the ambush were twenty-one-year-old platoon sergeant Gene Ray Phipps of Greensboro, North Carolina, and twenty-two-year-old Navy corpsman William David Schmitz, of Duluth, Minnesota. The ambush was described to me by James Feasel, the leader of Roach's 1st Squad, who was there. James Feasel, author's interview, March 23, 2013.

6. Henry Radcliffe, author's interview, August 8, 2012.

7. Roach posed for a photograph with his squad leaders and other men on Hill 64 and sent it to his wife, Lynn. He wrote across the top, "My Staff on Radcliffe's Roost." I'm grateful to Lynn Fifer for sharing this and other photographs of Terry Roach in Vietnam.

8. George Chapman, author's interview, February 23, 2012.

9. 1st Battalion, 9th Marines, Command Chronology, February 1968; George Chapman, author's interview, February 23, 2012.

10. Ibid.; also Michael Barry, author's interviews, March 15, 2012, and March 23, 2013.

11. James Feasel, author's interview, February 20, 2012.

12. George Chapman, author's interview, February 23, 2012.

13. Ibid. In the literature of Khe Sanh, official and unofficial, probably no single incident during the seventy-seven days of the siege has been marked by as much flawed history as

the February 8, 1968, battle for Hill 64. This fact was stated to me repeatedly by Hill 64 survivors when I began my research, and, after hundreds of hours of interviews and research, I reached the same conclusion. The problems began almost immediately, with the 1/9 Command Chronology for February 1968. Among other assertions, the official 1/9 account states that the NVA didn't penetrate the Alpha-1 perimeter until more than two hours into the battle. According to this official account, "At 0610 [6:10 a.m.] the enemy regrouped and attacked again, penetrating the wire and were again beaten back. The attack continued in waves, and the enemy managed to take the northwest slope of the perimeter." In fact, as multiple accounts by survivors make clear, the NVA penetrated the northwest perimeter in the opening minutes of the attack after it began around 4:15 a.m., and the enemy soldiers overran much of the western and northern perimeters and portions of the hill's interior. The account I have written is based on interviews with key participants in various aspects of the battle: George Chapman and James Feasel were leaders of two of three squads of Alpha Company's 1st Platoon during the fight; Colonel Henry "Mac" Radcliffe (USMC, ret.) was a captain in command of Alpha Company and led a relief column that reached the hill about four hours after the battle began; Lieutenant Colonel Maurice Casey (USMC, ret.) was a young lieutenant in command of the 1/9 battalion's 81-millimeter mortars and was in radio contact with a Marine he knew as Smitty, who was in a collapsed bunker just behind the northern trench line for much of the battle; rifleman Michael Barry was one of the last men to see 1st Platoon commander Terry Roach alive, and he spent the entire battle in the northeastern and eastern trench line; rifleman Guy Leonard began the fight along the southeastern trench line and would ultimately circuit the hill during the course of the night; Arnold Alderete was an M-60 machine gunner who began the fight on the northern perimeter, fell back to the east, and spent much of the remainder of the battle in the interior of the hill; grenadier George Einhorn fought along the southern trench line and ventured into the interior of the hill for part of the battle; and Navy corpsman Mike Coonan tended to wounded Marines along a section of trench line overrun by the NVA and has devoted much effort in recent years to collecting the stories of Hill 64 survivors and displaying their accounts on a website he created. I am grateful to these men in particular for their extraordinary assistance in piecing together an accurate account of what happened on Hill 64 during the early morning hours of February 8, 1968.

14. Three Marines—George Chapman, Arnold Alderete, and Michael Barry—described the sights and sounds of the opening minutes of the North Vietnamese attack. Alderete and Barry also described the fallback of Marines across the northern perimeter, and down eastern trenchline. George Chapman, author's interview, February 23, 2012; Arnold Alderete, authors interviews, April 16, 2012 and August 13, 2013; and Michael Barry, author's interviews, March 15, 2012 and March 23, 2013.

15. Ibid.

16. Arnold Alderete, author's interview, April 16, 2012.

17. Ibid.

18. Michael Barry, author's interview, March 15, 2012.

19. Ibid.

20. Michael Barry, author's interviews, March 15, 2012, and March 23, 2013.

21. Lawrence Seavy Cioffi, author's interview, October 2, 2013; Seavy Cioffi unpublished manuscript, "Our Victory for Alpha One," which he provided to the author; and Seavy Cioffi letter to the author, July 21, 2014.

22. Ibid.

23. Henry Radcliffe, author's interview, August 8, 2012.

24. Ibid. Radcliffe doesn't recall who initiated the second radio exchange he had with Jimmy Rizzo. It was also unclear to Radcliffe whether Rizzo was able to reach the 1st Platoon commander, Lieutenant Terry Roach, between the two conversations.

25. James Feasel, author's interview, February 20, 2012.

26. Ibid.

27. James Feasel, author's interviews, February 20, 2012, and September 11, 2012.

28. Ibid.

29. Ibid.

30. Robert Wiley letter to Corporal Sutherland, February 9, 1968, quoted in Ray Stubbe, *Battalion of Kings: A Tribute to Our Fallen Brothers Who Died Because of the Battlefield of Khe Sanh, Vietnam*, 2nd ed., rev. (Wauwatosa, WI: Khe Sanh Veterans, 2008) 178.

31. Michael Barry, author's interview, March 15, 2012.

32. My account of the joint activities of Arnold Alderete and David Ford on Hill 64 is based on the following: David Ford's letter to the Marine Corps commandant, April 21, 1997; Arnold Alderete, author's interviews, April 16, 2012, and August 13, 2013; George Einhorn, author's interview, March 14, 2012; and James Feasel, author's interviews, February 20, 2012, September 11, 2012, and April 10, 2013.

33. George Einhorn, author's interview, March 14, 2012.

34. David R. Ford, letter to Marine Corps commandant, April 21, 1997.

35. Henry Radcliffe, author's interview, August 8, 2012.

36. Ibid.

37. David R. Ford letter to Marine Corps commandant, April 21, 1997; also see David Ford interview, USMC Oral History Collection, Tape No. 2803.

38. George Einhorn, author's interview, March 14, 2012; James Feasel, author's interview, February 20, 2012. George Chapman, the 2nd Squad leader, said to me: "I knew what Jim [Feasel] was doing. He was stuck right there trying to hold the men down, and having them return fire and keeping [the North Vietnamese] from advancing over the hill." George Chapman, author's interview, February 23, 2012.

39. Arnold Alderete, author's interview, April 16, 2012; David R. Ford, letter to Marine Corps commandant, April 21, 1997.

40. Maurice Casey, author's interview, July 31, 2013; and Henry "Mac" Radcliffe, August 8, 2012. Hill 64 survivors contend they didn't receive the artillery and mortar support they had been promised prior to the attack. Some maintain that only illumination rounds were fired in their support. First Squad leader James Feasel said that late in the battle he asked one of the platoon's noncommissioned officers why they weren't getting artillery support and the sergeant said he had been told by the combat base that the guns were "refusing to fire on orders from the base commander." Mac Radcliffe, the Alpha Company commander, told me that he believes Hill 64 was getting some support from mortars and artillery. Maurice Casey told me that four of his 81-millimeter mortars at the rock quarry were firing illumination and high-explosive rounds throughout the battle. Casey said that most of the high-explosive rounds would have been fired away from the hill to target probable enemy attack routes and that it's possible the Americans on Hill 64 simply weren't aware of the supporting fire because of the intensity of the fight around them. Maurice Casey, author's interview, July 31, 2013.

41. Maurice Casey, author's interview, July 31, 2013. Casey's radio operator knew the Marine, and at one point during the battle, Casey asked his radioman the identity of the voice on the other end of the transmissions. Casey's radioman replied, "Oh, that's Smitty!"

42. Maurice Casey offers high praise for the heroic work performed by the young radioman known as Smitty. "You could tell that he wasn't as experienced as an FO should be," Casey said, yet the radioman still managed to call in fire on the suspected avenues of attack. It is difficult to assess the importance of the fire called in by Smitty, but his heroic contribution to the defense of Hill 64 has gone unrecognized until now—a fact that has long bothered Maurice Casey, who believes that Smitty should have been decorated for his solitary efforts at great personal risk.

43. Maurice Casey, author's interview, July 31, 2013.

44. Guy Leonard, author's interview, August 5, 2013.

45. Ibid.

46. Ibid.

47. Michael Barry, author's interview, March 15, 2012.

48. Ibid.

49. Henry Radcliffe, author's interview, August 8, 2012.

50. Ibid.

51. 1st Battalion, 9th Marines, Command Chronology, February 1968. It is Mac Radcliffe's recollection that he led the relief force to Hill 64 before dawn, but the 1/9 command chronology, and the defenders of Hill 64 whom I interviewed, all place the time as well after dawn.

52. The quote about the Marines at the rock quarry observing the fight on Hill 64 like spectators "watching a movie" is from James Feasel, author's interview February 20, 2012; similar comments were made by George Einhorn, author's interview, March 14, 2012.

53. George Gregory Rudell, author's interview, March 12, 2012.

54. Ibid. "We knew they were getting their butt kicked," Rudell said, describing what it was like to be prevented from coming to the aid of the Marines on Hill 64. "We were cussing, raising hell, wanting to do something. All we did was sit there and watch, and there was nothing we could do. We were just so damn mad."

55. Ibid.

56. Joseph Harrigan, author's interview, May 2, 2012.

57. 1st Battalion, 9th Marines, Command Chronology, February 1968; also Joseph Harrigan, author's interview, May 2, 2012. When we spoke, more than forty-four years after the battle for Khe Sanh, Harrigan was still anguished by his inability to come to the aid of the Marines on Hill 64 during the night. "They say Normandy was the longest day," Harrigan said. "For me, February 8, 1968, was the longest day."

58. Charles "Toby" Rushforth, author's interview, January 29, 2012; also see "The Vietnam War with Spads, 1968," http://www.fisthistory.org/viet-a1.htm. Several men on Hill 64 recall seeing (and hearing) only a single bomb dropped by what they mistakenly believed was a South Vietnamese Air Force plane.

59. James Feasel, author's interview, April 10, 2013.

60. George Einhorn, author's interview, March 14, 2012; and James Feasel, author's interview, February 20, 2012.

61. Michael Coonan, author's interview, February 15, 2012; and George Chapman, author's interview, February 23, 2012. The recollections of Chapman and Coonan differ as to how Roy McDaniel was killed. Chapman said that McDaniel had been shot in the shoulder before he was pulled inside the bunker, and then an NVA soldier had thrown a grenade inside that killed McDaniel. Coonan doesn't remember the grenade incident. It is his recollection that an NVA soldier shot into the entrance of the bunker and fired three rounds that struck McDaniel in the chest, mortally wounding the fire team leader.

62. Robert Genty, author's interview, April 30, 2012; James Feasel, author's interview, February 20, 2012.

63. James Feasel, author's interviews, February 20, 2012, and September 11, 2012; Henry Radcliffe, author's interview, August 8, 2012.

64. Henry Radcliffe, author's interview, August 8, 2012; also James Feasel, author's interview, February 20, 2012.

65. Henry Radcliffe, author's interview, August 8, 2012.

66. George Chapman and his comrades differ as to when Chapman was wounded. Chapman said he was shot outside his bunker, in the minutes before Roy McDaniel was killed. Coonan and David Ford contend that Chapman was wounded in the trenchline at the end of the battle, as I have described. Given the extraordinary stress that both men were under during the hours they spent in a part of the hill that had been overrun by enemy soldiers, the discrepancies are understandable. George Chapman, author's interview, February 23, 2012; Michael Coonan, author's interview, February 15, 2012; and David R. Ford, letter to Marine corps commandant, April 21, 1997.

67. James Feasel, author's interviews, February 20, 2012, and September 11, 2012; and Michael Coonan, author's interview, February 15, 2012.

CHAPTER 12

1. Keith Kapple, author's interview, April 28, 2011.

2. William C. Westmoreland, *A Soldier Reports* (Garden City, NY: Doubleday, 1976), 338; also see Shulimson et al., *U.S. Marines in Vietnam: The Defining Year, 1968* (Washington, DC: History and Museums Division, Headquarters, U.S. Marine Corps, 1997), 68.

3. Westmoreland, *A Soldier Reports*, 338.

4. See *Foreign Relations of the United States, 1964–1968, Volume 6, Vietnam, January–August 1968*, Document 60, 141–144. The document contains the official notes of President Johnson's February 7, 1968, meeting at the White House with his national security team. The notes were taken by Johnson aide Tom Johnson (no relation) and can also be found at the LBJ Library in Austin, Texas, in "Tom Johnson's Notes of Meetings," Notes of Meeting, Washington, DC, February 7, 1968, 12:29–1:55 p.m., National Security File, NSC Meetings, v. 5, Tab 63.

5. General Lew Walt to Walt Rostow, February 8, 1968, letter quoted in *Foreign Relations of the United States, 1964–1968, Volume 6, Vietnam, January–August 1968*, Document 61, 145–46.

6. "Notes of the President's Meeting with the Joint Chiefs of Staff," Washington, DC, February 9, 1968, 11:02 a.m.–12:43 p.m., in *Foreign Relations of the United States, 1964–1968, Volume 6, Vietnam, January–August 1968*, Document 64, 158–168. In addition to the various service chiefs, those in attendance were President Johnson, Vice President Hubert Humphrey, Secretary of State Dean Rusk, Defense Secretary Robert McNamara, CIA Director Richard Helms, Joint Chiefs Chairman General Earle Wheeler, incoming defense secretary Clark Clifford, National Security Adviser Walt Rostow, Press Secretary George Christian, and Tom Johnson.

7. Ibid. In his 1977 book, *Big Story: How the American Press and Television Reported and Interpreted the Crisis of Tet 1968 in Vietnam and Washington*, Anchor Books edition, abridged (Garden City, NY: Anchor Books, 1978), on press coverage of the Tet Offensive and Khe Sanh, Peter Braestrup criticized as media hype the news accounts about the threat of North Vietnamese air attacks at Khe Sanh. In fact, declassified documents have since re-

vealed that American military commanders in Vietnam took the sightings very seriously and took substantial measures to counteract the threats.

8. "Notes of the President's Meeting with the Joint Chiefs of Staff," Washington, DC, February 9, 1968, 11:02 a.m.–12:43 p.m., in *Foreign Relations of the United States, 1964–1968, Volume 6, Vietnam, January–August 1968*, Document 64, 158–168.

9. Maxwell Taylor's behind-the-scenes role in Lyndon Johnson's Khe Sanh deliberations is discussed in some detail in John Prados and Ray Stubbe, *Valley of Decision: The Siege of Khe Sanh* (Boston: Houghton Mifflin, 1991), 357–364.

10. Ibid., 361.

11. See "White House Disputes McCarthy on Atom Arms," *New York Times*, February 10, 1968; "Query by Fulbright," *New York Times*, February 10, 1968; and "Wheeler Doubts Khe Sanh Will Need Atom Weapons," *New York Times*, February 15, 1968. In his memoir, Westmoreland makes the case for the use of tactical nuclear weapons at Khe Sanh. "Because the region around Khe Sanh was virtually uninhabited, civilian casualties would be minimal," he writes. "If Washington officials were so intent on 'sending a message' to Hanoi, surely small tactical nuclear weapons would be a way to tell Hanoi something, just as two atomic bombs had spoken convincingly to Japanese officials during World War II and the threat of atomic bombs induced the North Koreans to accept meaningful negotiations." Westmoreland, *A Soldier Reports*, 411.

12. "Notes of the President's Meeting With Senior Foreign Policy Advisors," Washington, DC, February 12, 1968, 1:45–3:08 p.m., *Foreign Relations of the United States, 1964–1968, Volume 6, Vietnam, January–August 1968*, 188–196.

13. Calvin Bright, author's interview, July 23, 2011; and *Bravo! Common Men, Uncommon Valor: The 77-Day Siege of Khe Sanh*, DVD, directed by Ken and Betty Rodgers (Boise, ID: Kingfisher Arts, 2012).

14. John Corbett vividly describes daily life at Khe Sanh in his Vietnam memoir, *West Dickens Avenue: A Marine at Khe Sanh* (New York: Ballantine Books, 2003).

15. "Commander at Khe Sanh: David Edward Lownds," *New York Times*, February 12, 1968.

16. Dave Doehrman, author's interview, April 6, 2012.

17. Ron Smith, author's interview, March 21, 2012.

18. Lewis "Sam" Messer, author's interview, April 10, 2012.

19. Two Seabees died at Khe Sanh: Charles Otto Spillman, thirty-two, of New Brighton, Minnesota, was killed in a helicopter crash on February 28; Edward Cody Adams, twenty-three, of Pennsboro, West Virginia, was killed on April 16 by an enemy artillery round just after emerging from his bunker. Spillman "had premonitions that he was going to die," said Sam Messer. "He would have nightmares." He was on a helicopter flying back to Khe Sanh on February 28, carrying mail and equipment parts for CBMU-301, when the aircraft was shot down. Lewis "Sam" Messer, author's interview, April 10, 2012; also Jack Haigwood, author's interview, April 14, 2012.

20. Daniel Sullivan, author's interview, April 16, 2012.

21. Daniel Sullivan was awarded the Bronze Star for his efforts to aid the men aboard the burning KC-130 on February 10, 1968.

22. James Finnegan, author's interview, May 13, 2012.

23. Edward Feldman, diary entries, February 10–11, 1968, and author's interview, April 14, 2012.

24. James Finnegan, author's interview, May 13, 2012.

25. Charles "Chuck" Chamberlin, author's interview, March 26, 2012.

26. Ibid., author's interviews, March 26–27, 2012.

27. Edward Feldman, author's interview, April 14, 2012.

28. John M. Kaheny, quoted in Ray Stubbe, *Battalion of Kings: A Tribute to Our Fallen Brothers Who Died Because of the Battlefield of Khe Sanh, Vietnam*, 2nd ed., rev. (Wauwatosa, WI: Khe Sanh Veterans, 2008), 194–195.

CHAPTER 13

1. Ron Smith, author's interview, March 21, 2012.

2. William Dabney, quoted in Beth Crumley, "Robert J. Arrotta: The Mightiest Corporal in the Marine Corps," *Leatherneck* (September 2010), 44–49; also see William Dabney, "Sting of Battle: Hill 881S and the Super Gaggle," *Marine Corps Gazette* 89 (4) (2005), 69; also see Crumley, "Robert J. Arrotta." Dabney had this to say about Bob Arrotta and his work as forward air controller, 881 South: "I had nothing to lose, plenty of targets, and all the CAS [close-air support] aircraft we could use, so I stood by and watched as he ran the first few missions—flawlessly. I was impressed not only with his technical knowledge but also with his demeanor as a corporal giving instructions to officers through the rank of lieutenant colonel. He was assertive and unfailingly professional."

3. William Dabney, VMI Oral History interview, September 8, 2005.

4. Ron Smith, author's interview, April 14, 2012.

5. William Dabney, VMI Oral History interview, September 8, 2005.

6. Ibid.

7. Ron Smith, author's interview, April 14, 2012.

8. Dennis Mannion, author's interview, January 23, 2012.

9. Dennis Mannion, author's interview, November 30, 2011.

10. Paul Knight, author's interviews, December 18 and 21, 2011. Knight would have to do a bomb-damage assessment after strikes in which there were suspected North Vietnamese killed in action. He was encouraged by higher-ups to report damage or enemy troops killed in action. One officer went so far as to suggest that they "would get better service from air assets if they credited them with kills," Knight said. He did it for one or two missions. "And then I said, 'To hell with it! This is stupid.'"

11. Paul Knight, author's interview, December 21, 2011.

12. Dennis Mannion, author's interview, December 19, 2011.

13. Miguel Salinas, author's interview, May 1, 2012.

14. Ibid.

15. Dennis Mannion, author's interview, January 23, 2012.

16. Jim Thomas, author's interview, December 18, 2011.

17. Ibid.

18. Jose "Cisco" Reyes, author's interview, February 23, 2012.

19. Jim Kaylor, author's interview, February 15, 2012.

20. Jim Thomas, author's interview, December 18, 2011.

21. Rich Donaghy, author's interview, August 14, 2013.

22. Ibid.

23. Ray Stubbe, *Battalion of Kings: A Tribute to Our Fallen Brothers Who Died Because of the Battlefield of Khe Sanh, Vietnam*, 2nd ed., rev. (Wauwatosa, WI: Khe Sanh Veterans, 2008), 198.

24. Ron Smith, author's interview, March 21, 2012.

25. Ibid.; also see Crumley, "Robert J. Arrotta." Terry Smith was posthumously awarded the Silver Star for his valor.

26. John Pessoni, author's interview, May 5, 2012.

27. Ibid.

28. "Khe Sanh Daily Report," February 20–21 (twenty-four-hour period from 9 a.m. to 9 a.m.), 1968, 3rd Marine Division Command Operations Center to III Marine Amphibious Force Command Operations Center, RG 127, Records of the U.S. Marine Corps, NARA; also see 3rd Marine Division daily report to III MAF, February 21, 1968.

29. Ibid. Of the 166 US Air Force B-52 missions flown over Vietnam in February 1968, 111 were in support of Khe Sanh. See MACV Monthly Report, February 1968, 24.

30. In his critical study of media coverage of the Tet Offensive and Khe Sanh, *Big Story: How the American Press and Television Reported and Interpreted the Crisis of Tet 1968 in Vietnam and Washington,* Anchor Books edition, abridged (Garden City, NY: Anchor Books, 1978), Peter Braestrup notes that the North Vietnamese never put 37-millimeter anti-aircraft guns at the end of the runway, which, he suggests, would have completely shut down landings at the combat base. But this assertion implies that the North Vietnamese could put guns where they wanted and fire them with impunity. In fact, NVA gun crews and troops faced a constant struggle to avoid detection, and, once pinpointed by American spotters, faced almost certain destruction. The only exceptions to this were the big NVA artillery pieces located at Co Roc massif across the border in Laos, which managed to confound US bombers throughout the siege.

31. Jim Thomas, author's interview, December 18, 2011; Jose Reyes, author's interview, February 23, 2012; Jim Kaylor, author's interview, February 15, 2012. On 881 South, ammunition was plentiful, but food and water supplies were so precariously low that there was discussion of whether they might have to abandon the outpost and fight their way down to the base or some other point.

32. Glenn Prentice, author's interview, February 14, 2012; Richard Dworsky, author's interview, August 6, 2013. Prentice was a forward observer radioman who was shuttling between 881 South and the combat base. It was his recollection that 881 South ran out of food for about a week and was down to fifteen gallons of water. Prentice said he witnessed and participated in the discussions that Captain Bill Dabney led about possibly abandoning the outpost. India Second Lieutenant Richard Dworsky recalls "limited discussions" about leaving the hill after going without water "for three or four days." Dworsky is unsure whether the plan to launch a breakout "was sanctioned" above Dabney. Dworsky believes "if we had tried to get off the hill, we would have all been killed."

33. James T. Riley, Silver Star citation for action on February 22, 1968, undated.

34. "Four Hundred Mile Walk into Marine Corps," *Stars and Stripes* (Pacific edition), October 2, 1967. Also see Stubbe, *Battalion of Kings*, 206.

CHAPTER 14

1. The shells and rockets that fell on the Special Forces FOB-3 compound at Khe Sanh were not included in the official tally.

2. Edward Feldman, author's interview, April 14, 2012.

3. Tom Esslinger, author's interview, April 3, 2012.

4. Jim Kaylor, author's interview, February 15, 2012.

5. Ibid. Echo Company, 2/26, was under the operational control of the 3rd Battalion, 26th Marines, at the time of the February 24, 1968, incident in which Carlos Aguirre and

Gerrie Jefferies were killed. The 3/26 Command Chronology for February 1968 reads: "At 0015H, Company E received two rounds of unknown origin. Friendly H&Is were immediately investigated and subsequently cleared of any suspicion. Analysis of artillery fragments are [sic] still being conducted. Results are 2 USMC KIA." Jim Kaylor believes the deaths were caused by friendly fire. Nick Elardo attributed the bunker collapse to an NVA rocket. Nick Elardo, author's interview, February 23, 2012.

6. Major Mirza M. Baig, letter to Colonel F. C. Caldwell, USMC Historical Branch, December 23, 1968, Comments on *The Battle for Khe Sanh*, March 23, 1969, U.S. Marine Corps Archives, Quantico, Virginia.

7. Tom Quigley, author's interview, May 6, 2011.

8. Ken Rodgers, author's interview, July 21, 2011. Rodgers had recalled the incident as occurring a few days later, around February 20, but the 1/26 Command Chronology for February 1968 fixes the date as February 13.

9. Ibid.

10. Steve Wiese, author's interview, April 12, 2012.

11. Ibid.

12. Ibid.

13. Ibid.

CHAPTER 15

1. Marine Air Group 36, Command Chronology, February 1968, RG 127: Records of the U.S. Marine Corps, NARA.

2. David Althoff, author's interview, January 25, 2012.

3. Ibid. Also see Lieutenant Colonel David L. Althoff, "Helicopter Operations at Khe Sanh," *Marine Corps Gazette* 54 (5) (May 1968), 47.

4. Beth Crumley, "Walking with Giants—The Tigers of HMM-262," Marine Corps Association and Foundation website, July 25, 2011, http://www.mca-marines.org/blog/beth-crumley/2011/07/25/walking-giants-tigers-hmm-262. A young HMM-262 CH-46 pilot, First Lieutenant Michael Mullen, said this of Althoff: "He was the squadron's idol. We all thought the world of him as a man, an officer and a pilot . . . He would never ask one of his junior pilots to fly a mission he had never flown."

5. David Althoff's mission to Hill 881 South on February 13, 1968, is described in Crumley, "Walking with Giants"; and Lieutenant Colonel Neil Allen, "Narrative of HMM-262 Command Chronology," HMM-262 Combat Helicopter Association, http://www.hmm-262combatvets.com/chronology.htm.

6. "Resupply of Khe Sanh," message from commanding general of 3rd Marine Division to commanding general of III MAF, February 20, 1968, in 3rd Marine Division Messages, February 1968, RG 127, NARA.

7. David Althoff, author's interview, January 25, 2012.

8. Richard E. Carey, quoted in Shulimson et al., *U.S. Marines in Vietnam: The Defining Year, 1968* (Washington, DC: History and Museums Division, Headquarters, U.S. Marine Corps, 1997), 483; other interviews relevant to the resupply quandary at Khe Sanh include Major William A. McGaw, USMC Oral History Collection, Tape No. 3293, Lieutenant Colonel Melvin J. Steinberg, USMC Oral History Collection, Tape No. 3423, and Major Arthur C. Crane, USMC Oral History Collection, Tape No. 3294; Lieutenant General Robert E. Cushman Jr., commander of the III Marine Amphibious Force and thus the ranking Marine in Vietnam at the time, later claimed to have conceived the Super Gaggle, in

Lieutenant General Robert E. Cushman, Comments on *The Battle for Khe Sanh*, March 23, 1969, Vietnam Comment File, U.S. Marine Corps Archives, Quantico, Virginia; Cushman's claim is contradicted by virtually all of his subordinates in Vietnam at the time, including General Norman Anderson, commander of the 1st Marine Air Wing in Vietnam; Major General Keith B. McCutcheon, who served under Anderson in 1968, singled out Colonel Joel E. Bonner, Lieutenant Colonel William J. White, and Lieutenant Colonel Richard E. Carey, a member of the 1st Marine Air Wing staff, with Carey naming the Super Gaggle, according to McCutcheon and others; see Major General Keith B. McCutcheon, Comments on *The Battle for Khe Sanh*, n.d., Vietnam Comment File, USMC Archives. In my interview with David Althoff, he laughed about the official accounts of the origins of the Super Gaggle. He recalled that after Colonel Frank E. Wilson, the commander of MAG-6, forwarded up the chain of command the resupply plan that emerged from the brainstorming session in Bill White's hooch at Quang Tri Air Base, "next thing you know there were two generals taking credit for the whole freaking works." David Althoff, author's interview, January 25, 2012.

9. 1st Marine Aircraft Wing Operations Order 303-YR, February 24, 1968, in 3rd Marine Division Messages, February 1968, RG 127, NARA; for a description of the Super Gaggle from the perspective of the Marines on the hill outposts, see Colonel William H. "Bill" Dabney, "Hill 881S and the Super Gaggle," *Marine Corps Gazette* (April 2005), http://www.mca-marines.org/gazette/hill-881s-and-super-gaggle.

10. Ibid.

11. Major General Norman J. Anderson to Major General Keith B. McCutcheon, February 25, 1968, letter No. 60, 1968 correspondent, File A, Keith B. McCutcheon Papers, USMCA; also see 1st Marine Aircraft Wing, Command Chronology, February 1968, 2–3, McCutcheon, Comments on *The Battle for Khe Sanh*, not dated (Comment File), USMC Archives, and Shulimson et al., *U.S. Marines in Vietnam: The Defining Year, 1968*, 485.

CHAPTER 16

1. Ken Pipes, author's interview, July 23, 2011; also Ray Stubbe, *Battalion of Kings: A Tribute to Our Fallen Brothers Who Died Because of the Battlefield of Khe Sanh, Vietnam*, 2nd ed., rev. (Wauwatosa, WI: Khe Sanh Veterans, 2008), 216.

2. Charlie Med surgeon Edward Feldman had met Don Jacques and pronounced the young lieutenant "a cowboy." Edward Feldman, author's interview, April 14, 2012. Within Bravo's 3rd Platoon, corpsman John Cicala sized up Jacques as a bit "cocky," and "very, very gung-ho." John Cicala, author's interview, May 24, 2011.

3. Stubbe, *Battalion of Kings*, 216.

4. Ken Pipes, author's interview, July 23, 2011; Steve Wiese, author's interview, April 13, 2012; John Cicala, author's interview, May 24, 2011; Calvin Bright, author's interview, July 23, 2011.

5. Steve Wiese, author's interview, April 13, 2012.

6. John Cicala, author's interview, May 24, 2011.

7. Calvin Bright, author's interview, July 23, 2011.

8. This account of the February 25, 1968, patrol led by Don Jacques is primarily drawn from four interviews: Ken Pipes, author's interview, July 23, 2011; Calvin Bright, author's interview, July 23, 2011; John Cicala, author's interview, May 24, 2011; and Steve Wiese, author's interview, April 13, 2012. I also consulted the USMC Oral History interview with corpsman Frank Calzia, who survived the February 25 patrol but was killed in Vietnam

in May. See Frank Calzia, USMC Oral History interview, No. 2621. Finally, I consulted Ray Stubbe's collection of interviews and personal accounts found in *Battalion of Kings*, 220–231.

9. Steve Wiese, author's interview, April 13, 2012.

10. Ken Pipes, author's interview, July 23, 2011.

11. Steve Wiese, author's interview, April 13, 2012.

12. Ibid.

13. The confrontation between Lieutenant Jacques and Steve Wiese over whether to pursue the NVA soldiers was described to me by Wiese and corpsman John Cicala in our interviews cited above. Other details were gleaned from interviews and personal accounts gathered by Khe Sanh chaplain Ray Stubbe during his decades of research. These include a letter written by 81-millimeter mortar forward observer Gilbert Wall, who accompanied the patrol. Wall had seen the sharp discussion unfold. "They looked confused," Wall wrote of the Marines involved in the discussion. "Lt. Jacques ended the confusion by shouting, 'Let's go get them' while his pistol was in the air and his hand was forward in the charge manner. Then he turned and looked at me and we both smiled at the same time. It was like the same thought went though our minds: 'This is what we want.' We started moving after them and the fire began.'" Gilbert Wall to Ray Stubbe, September 9, 1988, quoted in Stubbe, *Battalion of Kings*, 223.

14. John Cicala, author's interview, May 24, 2011.

15. There have been conflicting accounts regarding the location of Lieutenant Jacques and his men when they spotted the three NVA soldiers in the minutes before the ambush. By all accounts, Steve Wiese's squad was leading the patrol at that moment, and Wiese's testimony is clear: the NVA soldiers were about two hundred meters (220 yards) away, to his right—in other words, south of the patrol—and the NVA ran along the access road before diving into the treeline on the south side of the roadway. Official records of the 26th Marines placed the location of the ambush at map coordinates XD849409—roughly fifty to one hundred meters (about the length of a football field or slightly less) north of the main Khe Sanh access road. Air observer First Lieutenant Thomas F. O'Toole Jr., flying very low over the ambush site around midday, spotted the bodies of fifteen to twenty Marines near a trench line that stretched from XD853409 to XD854409—about two hundred meters north of the main access road. All those pieces of evidence support Wiese's account that the NVA anchored their ambush from positions along the access road, which the Americans never reached.

16. Stubbe, *Battalion of Kings*, 224–225.

17. Ken Pipes, author's interview, July 23, 2011; William Smith, author's interview, March 12, 2012; also see Stubbe, *Battalion of Kings*, 226.

18. William Smith, author's interview, March 12, 2012. More than four decades later, Smith was still pained by the memories of February 25, 1968. "It's the worst thing that I've lived through in my life," he said.

19. Ken Pipes, author's interview, July 23, 2011.

20. Ibid.

21. John Cicala, author's interview, May 24, 2011.

22. Ibid.

23. Ibid.

24. Ibid.

25. Ibid.

26. Steve Wiese, author's interview, April 12, 2012.

27. Gilbert Wall, letter to Ray Stubbe, September 9, 1988, quoted in *Battalion of Kings*, 225.

28. The death of Ken Claire was related by one of his wounded men, Edward C. Rayburn, who survived the ambush. Rayburn later shared his account with Ken Claire's brother, Richard, who recalled the conversation in a letter that was printed in the *Khe Sanh Veteran* 1 (Fall 1992), 15. Rayburn's account can also be found in Ray Stubbe, *Battalion of Kings*, 225.

29. Stubbe, *Battalion of Kings*, 224–225.

30. Ibid.

31. John Cicala, author's interview, May 24, 2011.

32. Stubbe, *Battalion of Kings*, 229.

33. Thomas E. Casey, letter to Ray Stubbe, February 2, 1995, quoted in Stubbe, *Battalion of Kings*, 229.

34. Stubbe, *Battalion of Kings*, 229.

35. Calvin Bright, author's interview, July 23, 2011.

36. Ibid.

37. Steve Wiese, author's interview, April 12, 2012.

38. Ibid.

39. "A Marine Returns from the Officially Dead," *New York Times*, January 31, 1973.

40. Ken Pipes, author's interview, July 23, 2011.

CHAPTER 17

1. The discovery of the trench is described in a message from the 3rd Marine Division to III MAF, "Trenches at KSCB perimeter 25 Feb," February 25, 1968, 3rd Marine Division Messages, February 1968, RG 127, NARA. Also see Operation Scotland Situation Report No. 471, February 26, 1968, RG 127, NARA.

2. Ibid.

3. "Special Arc Light Strikes," February 25, 1968, message from commanding general, III MAF, to commander Seventh AF, 3rd Marine Division Messages, February 1968, RG 127, NARA.

4. Biographical information on Billy Dale Livingston was drawn from the Combat Area Casualties Database, RG 330, NARA; this account of Livingston's death was drawn from John Roberts, author's interview, September 21, 2012, and Howard McKinnis, author's interview, September 24, 2012.

5. General William Westmoreland message to Colonel David Lownds, February 27, 1968, 3rd Marine Division Messages, February 1968.

6. 3rd Marine Division, Situation Reports, Operation Scotland, No. 472, February 26, 1968, RG 127, NARA.

7. Ibid.

8. The scene inside the 26th Marine Regiment command operations center was described to me by several people who were there, including William (Bill) Smith. William Smith, author's interview, March 22, 2012.

9. William Smith, author's interview, March 22, 2012; and Mirza M. Baig to Colonel F. C. Caldwell, USMC Historical Branch, comments on *The Battle for Khe Sanh*, December 23, 1968, found in USMC Archives.

10. William Smith, author's interview, March 22, 2012.

11. 3rd Marine Division, Situation Reports, Operation Scotland, No. 484, February 29, 1968.

12. Ibid., No. 487, March 1, 1968; the NVA attacks of February 29–March 1 are also described in Shulimson et al., *U.S. Marines in Vietnam: The Defining Year, 1968* (Washington, DC: History and Museums Division, Headquarters, U.S. Marine Corps, 1997), 281.

13. 26th Marines, Command Chronology, March 1968; also 3rd Marine Division, message to III MAF, March 2, 1968, in III MAF Khe Sanh Operations File, RG 127, NARA.

14. "48,000 Face April Draft, Highest Total in 18 Months," *New York Times,* February 24, 1968.

15. Robert Mann, *A Grand Delusion: America's Descent into Vietnam* (New York: Basic Books, 2001), 601.

16. Robert McNamara, quoted in Deborah Shapley, *Promise and Power: The Life and Times of Robert McNamara* (Boston: Little, Brown, 1993), 444.

17. "Johnson's Rating Declines in Poll," *New York Times,* February 18, 1968; "Nixon Catches Johnson in Poll," *New York Times,* February 25, 1968.

18. President Johnson's impromptu send-off of Vietnam-bound soldiers and Marines is described in "Johnson Confers with Eisenhower; Briefs Him on War," *New York Times,* February 19, 1968, and in "LBJ Salutes El Toro Marines," *Long Beach Independent Press-Telegram,* February 18, 1968; a copy of Johnson's prepared remarks to the departing Marines at El Toro can be found at the website of the 3rd Battalion, 27th Marines, http://www.three27.com/files/LBJ%20El%20Toro%20Speech%202-17-1968.pdf.

19. Ibid.

20. Document 83, "Telegram from the President's Special Assistant (Rostow) to President Johnson in Texas," February 22, 1968, in *Foreign Relations of the United States, 1964–1968, Volume 6* (Washington, DC: U.S. Government Printing Office, 2002), 238–239.

21. "Memorandum from the Chairman of the Joint Chiefs of Staff (Wheeler) to President Johnson," Washington, DC, February 27, 1968, in *Foreign Relations of the United States, 1964–1968, Volume 6,* Vietnam, January–August 1968, 263–266; "Notes of Meeting, Washington," February 28, 1968, in *Foreign Relations of the United States, 1964–1968, Volume 6,* Vietnam, January–August 1968, 267–275. Wheeler, it should be noted, was hardly a neutral party in the discussion over whether to honor Westmoreland's request for reinforcements: As cable traffic would later make clear, Wheeler had urged Westmoreland to make the request, almost coaching him in its formulation. Wheeler believed that overall US military troop levels were too low, and he saw the crisis in Vietnam as an opportunity to call up reserves, expand the draft, and push the numbers back to a level he thought appropriate.

22. Stanley Karnow, *Vietnam: A History* (New York: Penguin, 1984), 512.

23. "President Lauds McNamara and Gives Him Medal," *New York Times,* February 29, 1968.

24. "For McNamara, It's Efficiency to the End (Almost)," *New York Times,* March 1, 1968.

CHAPTER 18

1. Command chronologies for 3rd Marine Division, the 26th Marine Battalion, and various helicopter units for February and March 1968; also Colonel William H. Dabney, interview, U.S. Marine Corps Oral History Collection, May 20, 1982, USMCA, and Lieutenant Colonel Robert W. Rasdal, interview, U.S. Marine Corps Oral History Collection, Tape No.

2627, USMCA. Dabney described the Super Gaggle as "a massive, complex, well rehearsed, gutsy and magnificent performance and only the Marines could have pulled it off."

2. The nighttime activities of the North Vietnamese around the hill outposts and the combat base are mentioned frequently in six-hour situation reports. For one example, see 3rd Marine Division, Situation Reports, Operation Scotland, No. 494, March 3, 1968, RG 127, NARA; the NVA propaganda activities are described in 3rd Marine Division, Situation Reports, Operation Scotland, No. 525, March 11, 1968.

3. Dennis Mannion, author's interview, February 16, 2012.

4. Ibid.

5. Paul Knight, December 22, 2011.

6. Matthew Walsh, author's interview, February 12, 2012.

7. Ibid.

8. Ibid.

9. Colonel William L. Barba, letter dated June 3, 1991, quoted in Stubbe, *Battalion of Kings: A Tribute to Our Fallen Brothers Who Died Because of the Battlefield of Khe Sanh, Vietnam,* 2nd ed., rev. (Wauwatosa, WI: Khe Sanh Veterans, 2008), 236–237. Barba was a CH-46 pilot with Marine Medium Helicopter Squadron 262, flying to Khe Sanh along the routes described.

10. There were five crew members and eighteen passengers aboard, including the pilot. HMM-262 Command Chronology, February 1968. Also see Colonel William L. Barba, letter dated June 3, 1991, quoted in Stubbe, *Battalion of Kings*, 236–237. Barba was the pilot of a second CH-46 Sea Knight flying the February 28, 1968, mission, and he witnessed the crash.

11. "Aerial Resupply of Khe Sanh," March 6, 1968, 3rd Marine Division Messages, March 1968, RG 127.

12. Ibid.

13. There are discrepancies regarding the number of passengers and crew aboard Fred Hampton's C-123 when it took off for Khe Sanh on March 6, 1968. For an excellent breakdown of the casualties and discrepancies, see the web page "C-123 Down!" at http://www.virtualwall.org/units/c123down.htm.

14. I am grateful to photographer Jim Caccavo for sharing with me his memories of Robert Ellison. I also gleaned material about Ellison from his obituary in *Shrapnel,* newspaper of the Western Military Academy (Alton, Illinois), March 1968; and "Fearless," Robert J. Ellison obituary, *Ebony,* 23 (7) (May 1968), 24.

15. William Smith, author's interview, March 8, 2012.

16. Ibid.

17. Thirty-five dead from the March 6, 1968, crash are buried in a mass grave at Jefferson Barracks National Military Cemetery in St. Louis. Nearby is a mass grave containing the remains of eight Marines of Bravo Company, 1/26, recovered several weeks after the February 25 ambush of the Jacques patrol. Eight pages of Robert Ellison's photographs from Khe Sanh, including the image of the mortally wounded Lieutenant Jacques being carried back to the wire, were published in the March 18, 1968, issue of *Newsweek*. The photographs posthumously won Ellison an Overseas Press Club award in early 1969.

18. The April 25, 1968, recovery operation is noted in 2nd Battalion, 3rd Marine Regiment, Command Chronology, April 1968, and 1st Marine Regiment, Command Chronology, April 1968.

19. Stubbe, *Battalion of Kings*, 247.

20. "Mass Burial Set for Crash Victims," *Daily Capital News* (Jefferson City, MO), November 23, 1968.

CHAPTER 19

1. Edward Feldman, author's interview, April 15, 2012.

2. Edward Feldman, diary entry, February 27, 1968.

3. James Finnegan, author's interview, May 13, 2012.

4. Daniel Sullivan, author's interview, April 16, 2012; James Finnegan, author's interview, May 13, 2012; Edward Feldman, author's interviews, April 13–15, 2012.

5. Daniel Sullivan, author's interview, April 16, 2012.

6. Among the wounded during the bombardment of March 8, 1968, were news correspondent Jurate Kazickas, one of a growing number of women chronicling the war in Vietnam, and Lieutenant William Gay, commander of the detachment of combat engineers at Khe Sanh. Kazickas sustained relatively minor shrapnel wounds as she was interviewing a Marine in a trench line; Gay sustained more serious injuries when he was sprayed by shrapnel as he shoved Kazickas to safety in a bunker.

7. "Heart Surgery at Khe Sanh Saves 'Dead' Marine Hero Who Refused to Kill," *New York Times*, March 12, 1968.

8. "War Wounds Fatal to an Antiwar Hero," *New York Times*, March 15, 1968.

9. 3rd Marine Division, Command Chronology, March 1968, as well as numerous 3rd Marine Division messages and situation reports during the month.

10. "Tunnel Hunt at Khe Sanh," *New York Times*, February 16, 1968.

11. "Khe Sanh Marines on Guard for Enemy Tunneling," *New York Times*, March 4, 1968. Colonel David Lownds, the base commander, explained his decision to use divining rods in the search for North Vietnamese tunnels: "No matter how stupid anything is, and I don't say the brass rods are stupid, we use it. If some country boy from the Kentucky hills says he has a gadget that he used to hunt foxes with, and wants to try to find tunnels, I say go ahead. I try everything."

12. 3rd Marine Division, Command Chronology, March 1968, 26. The chronology states, "A team from the Defense Communications Planning Group visited the command and Khe Sanh Combat base during March and assisted members of the 26th Marines in operating the AN/PRS-1 as an aid in tunneling detection." Accompanying the team was Alex Lee, a Marine lieutenant who later rose to lieutenant colonel, and he described his tunnel-hunting trip to Khe Sanh in his comments in Eric Hammel's *Khe Sanh: Siege in the Clouds* (New York: Crown Publishers, 1989), 273, and in his own book, *Force Recon Command: 3rd Force Recon Company in Vietnam, 1969–70* (New York: Random House, 2011). Lee recalls the trip as taking place around February 12, but 3rd Marine Division records contradict that. Lee is dismissive of the tunnel hunt, which he blamed on alarmist news coverage. Comments at the time by Colonel Lownds and a Marine platoon commander, Lieutenant Marshall R. Wells, suggest the search was taken seriously by the defenders of Khe Sanh. For comments by Lownds, Wells, and others about the tunnel hunt, see the previously cited articles, "Tunnel Hunt at Khe Sanh" and "Khe Sanh Marines on Guard for Enemy Tunneling."

13. "100 Reds Caught Tunneling Toward Khe Sanh; 27 Killed," *Stars and Stripes* (Pacific edition), March 10, 1968.

14. 3rd Marine Division, Situation Reports, Operation Scotland, No. 515, March 8, 1968; also see "27 Enemy Killed at Khe Sanh," *Washington Post*, March 9, 1968, and the previously cited "100 Reds Caught Tunneling Toward Khe Sanh; 27 Killed."

15. In addition to drawing on the 3rd Marine Division and 26th Marines command chronologies and Operation Scotland situation reports for this period, I consulted the daily news dispatches out of Khe Sanh and Saigon that documented the rising air campaign. For an example, see the front-page article that ran in the *New York Times* on March 13, 1968, "Big Bombs Blast Foe at Khe Sanh: 2,000-Pounders Are Used."

16. "U.S. Command Sees Hue, Not Khe Sanh, as Foe's Main Goal," *New York Times*, March 7, 1968.

17. Westmoreland acknowledged in a telegram to General Earle Wheeler, chairman of the Joint Chiefs of Staff, that he was the source for the March 7 article in the *New York Times*. See Document 112, "Telegram from the Chairman of the Joint Chiefs of Staff (Wheeler) to the Commander, Military Assistance Command, Vietnam (Westmoreland) and the Commander in Chief, Pacific (Sharp)," in *Foreign Relations of the United States, 1964–1968, Volume 6, Vietnam, January–August 1968*, 351–353.

18. Lyndon Baines Johnson, *The Vantage Point* (New York: Holt, Rinehart and Winston, 1971), 405. Robert Pisor writes that on March 6, after General Westmoreland reached his conclusion about the enemy's focus shifting from Khe Sanh to Hue, "within hours, the vast enemy force believed to be in the siege ring around Khe Sanh, still unseen, melted away." See Pisor, *The End of the Line* (New York: Norton, 1982, paperback edition), 235. In fact, the NVA withdrawal was much more gradual, and several thousand enemy troops remained around Khe Sanh. Indeed, interrogation reports of North Vietnamese prisoners in April reveal that new NVA units were continuing to arrive at Khe Sanh in early March. See "Effects of B-52 Airstrikes near Khe Sanh," Interrogation Report of captive Hi Van Phen [*sic*], PFC, 11th Company, 3rd Battalion, 1st Regiment, 330th Division, April 30, 1968, Combined Military Intelligence Center Reports, RG 472, Records of the U.S. Forces in Southeast Asia, 1950–1975, NARA.

19. See Project CHECO Report, Khe Sanh (22 January–31 March 1968), September 13, 1968, 92–93, in RG 472: Records of the U.S. Forces in Southeast Asia, 1950–1976, NARA; and "Effects of B-52 Airstrikes near Khe Sanh"; for a description of the findings of a typical US patrol that illustrated the hardships being suffered by North Vietnamese troops, see 1st Battalion, 26th Marines, Command Chronology, February 1968, entry for February 18.

20. "More Indications Air Strikes and Artillery Preempted Khe Sanh Attack," Support Document from Project CHECO Report No. 130, April 16, 1968, Folder 0186, Box 0005, Vietnam Archive Collection, The Vietnam Center and Archive, Texas Tech University, accessed at http://www.vietnam.ttu.edu/virtualarchive/items.php?item=F031100050186.

21. Project CHECO Report, Khe Sanh (22 January–31 March 1968), September 13, 1968, 92–93, in RG 472: Records of the U.S. Forces in Southeast Asia, 1950–1976, NARA.

22. Ibid.

23. The phonetic spelling of the North Vietnamese soldier's name in his US military interrogation report is "Hi Van Phen." I have changed it to reflect conventional Vietnamese spelling. See "Effects of B-52 Airstrikes near Khe Sanh," Interrogation Report of captive Hi Van Phen [*sic*], PFC, 11th Company, 3rd Battalion, 1st Regiment, 330th Division, April 30, 1968, Combined Military Intelligence Center Reports, RG 472, Records of the U.S. Forces in Southeast Asia, 1950–1975, NARA.

24. Ibid.

25. "Khe Sanh Goes on Special Alert as March 13 Recalls Dien Bien Phu," *Washington Post*, March 13, 1968; "'Days Are Numbered' for Khe Sanh, Foe Says," *New York Times*,

March 14, 1968; "Khe Sanh 'Burial' Threat," *Washington Post,* March 15, 1968; "North Vietnam's Comments Stress New Attacks Near Khe Sanh," *New York Times,* March 17, 1968.

26. "Foe Digs Deeper Outside Khe Sanh; Dirt Piles Up as Marines Hear Machinery Whir," *New York Times,* March 17, 1968.

27. 3rd Marine Division, Situation Reports, March 1968, Operation Scotland, No. 553, March 18, 1968.

28. Paul Knight, December 23, 2011; and Dennis Mannion, author's interview, January 26, 2012.

29. Dennis Mannion, author's interview, January 26, 2012.

30. Ibid.

31. Paul Knight, author's interview, December 22, 2011.

32. Ken Warner, author's interview, March 27, 2012.

33. Ibid.

34. "GI's Vietnam Deaths Top 20,000," *Washington Post,* March 22, 1968. The date of March 21, 1968, was momentous as well for the Bravo 1/26 Marines at Khe Sanh Combat Base. At first light, the men of Bravo's 2nd Platoon emerged from concealed positions just outside the southern perimeter to begin a patrol, and almost immediately came under crossfire from friendly forces at the FOB-3 compound to their rear and NVA forces to their right-front. Around twenty Marines were wounded. Rifleman Michael O'Hara was behind squad leader Quiles Jacobs when an American .50-caliber round ripped into the back of Jacobs, shredded his flak jacket, and sliced across his flesh. Jacobs completed the patrol, and only then would he allow corpsmen to suture his injuries with more than 120 stitches. Jacobs refused to be evacuated. More than forty years later, Michael O'Hara still marvels at the bravery and toughness of Quiles Jacobs of Compton, California, who died of cancer in 1995. Michael O'Hara, author's interview, April 26, 2011.

35. "Suppression of Enemy Artillery Attacking Khe Sanh," commanding general III Marine Amphibious Forces to commander Seventh Air Force, March 22, 1968, in 3rd Marine Division Messages, March 1968, RG 127, NARA.

36. Chuck Chamberlin, author's interview, March 27, 2012.

37. Nine days later, on March 31, Staff Sergeant Arnold Jay Ferrai was killed by a mortar at Khe Sanh. In an account that has gained currency among some Khe Sanh veterans, Corporal Michael Gallagher, Private First Class Dominic Parisi, and Lance Corporal Daniel Brady tore a hole in the bunker and pulled Chuck Chamberlin to safety. Chamberlin doesn't recall this. Given the chaos and terror of the moment, such discrepancies are understandable. I have drawn the biographical information on Staff Sergeant Arnold Jay Ferrari and the date and cause of his death from the Vietnam Combat Area Casualties Database, RG 330, NARA.

38. Bruce Geiger, author's interview, April 30, 2012.

39. Chuck Chamberlin, author's interview, March 27, 2012.

40. Ibid.

CHAPTER 20

1. Lewis "Sam" Messer, author's interview, April 10, 2012.

2. E. J. Schroeder, *Vietnam, We've All Been There: Interviews with American Writers* (Westport, CT: Praeger Publishers, 1992), 34.

3. David Powell, author's interviews, March 20–22, 2012.

4. Ibid.

5. Ibid.

6. Ken Warner, author's interview, March 27, 2012.

7. Ibid.

8. Ken Pipes, author's interview, July 23, 2011.

9. Ken Rodgers, author's interview, July 21, 2011.

10. Ken Korkow, author's interview, September 1, 2012.

11. Ibid.

12. Ibid.

CHAPTER 21

1. Michael O'Hara, author's interview, May 3, 2011; and Tom Quigley, author's interview, May 6, 2011.

2. The times and certain other details in this account of the March 30, 1968, operation by Bravo 1/26 are drawn from the 1st Battalion, 26th Marines, command chronology for March 1968.

3. Ken Pipes; author's interview, July 23, 2011; Michael O'Hara, author's interview, May 3, 2011; and Tom Quigley, author's interview, May 6, 2011.

4. William Smith, author's interview, March 21, 2012.

5. Tom Quigley, author's interview, May 6, 2011.

6. Ibid.

7. Ken Pipes, author's interview, July 23, 2011.

8. Ibid.

9. William Smith, author's interview, March 21, 2012.

10. The 1/26 Command Chronology for March 1968 describes the incident in which the Bravo Company command group was engulfed by enemy fire and attributes the fire to some twenty NVA 82-millimeter mortars. I gleaned other details of the incident from Ken Pipes, author's interview, July 23, 2011, and Tom Quigley, author's interview, May 6, 2011.

11. Ken Pipes, author's interview, May 6, 2011; William Smith, author's interview, March 21, 2012; also see Shulimson et al., *U.S. Marines in Vietnam: The Defining Year, 1968* (Washington, DC: History and Museums Division, Headquarters, U.S. Marine Corps, 1997), 282.

12. Steve Wiese, author's interview, April 13, 2012.

13. Ibid.

14. Ken Korkow, author's interview, September 1, 2012.

15. Steve Wiese, author's interview, April 13, 2012.

16. Ken Korkow, author's interview, September 1, 2012. Korkow was awarded the Navy Cross for his courageous actions on March 30, 1968.

17. Michael O'Hara, author's interview, May 3, 2011.

18. Tom Quigley, author's interview, May 6, 2011.

19. Ken Pipes, author's interview, July 23, 2011.

20. Steve Wiese, author's interview, April 13, 2012.

CHAPTER 22

1. Don Oberdorfer, *Tet!: The Turning Point in the Vietnam War* (New York: Da Capo, 1984; originally published by Doubleday, 1971), 301.

2. "President Asks for 'Austerity' to Win the War; Tells Farm Union Delegates in Minnesota It's Time for 'Total National Effort,'" *New York Times*, March 19, 1968.

3. "Johnson Says He Won't Run; Halts North Vietnam Raids; Bids Hanoi Join Peace Moves," *New York Times*, April 1, 1968.

4. Doris Kearns Goodwin, *Lyndon Johnson and the American Dream* (New York: Harper and Row, 1976), 343.

5. "Johnson Says He Won't Run."

6. On March 31, Operation Scotland—the defense of Khe Sanh—was declared over, along with Operation Niagara, the massive air operations that General Westmoreland had launched to defend the American stronghold.

7. It is an enduring point of dispute between the Marine Corps and the Army as to whether the combat base at Khe Sanh was rescued by the forces of Operation Pegasus or whether there was a simple handoff of responsibilities. The Marines, then and now, do not accept the contention that they needed saving. Even the name of the operation to clear Route 9—Pegasus—irritated some Marines, for obvious reasons: in World War II, Operation Pegasus had been the Allied operation launched in October 1944 to evacuate a large number of men trapped in German-occupied territory in the Netherlands.

8. Dennis Mannion, author's interview, February 3, 2012. Golf Company was forced to withdraw with its casualties, but two companies of Marines returned the following day, April 7, and overran the North Vietnamese positions.

9. Ibid.

10. Joseph E. Abodeely, "Breaking the Siege at Khe Sanh," HistoryNet.com, August 26, 2010, http://www.historynet.com/breaking-the-siege-at-khe-sanh.htm (originally published in *Vietnam* magazine, October 2010); also see Gerald D. Swick, "Khe Sanh and Beyond: Col. (ret) Joseph Abodeely Interview," HistoryNet.com, August 26, 2010, http://www.historynet.com/khe-sanh-and-beyond-col-ret-joseph-abodeely-interview.htm.

11. Dennis Mannion, author's interview, February 10, 2012.

12. Neil Kenny, author's interview, August 13, 2013.

13. Ibid.

14. Ibid.

15. Michael Worth, author's interview, February 13, 2012.

16. The official history of the North Vietnamese Army 304th Division claims that "9 July 1968, the liberation flag was waving from the flag pole at Ta Con [Khe Sanh] airfield." The history states that on July 13 the North Vietnamese leader, Ho Chi Minh, sent a message to his troops of the "Route 9-Khe Sanh Front," congratulating them on "our victory at Khe Sanh."

EPILOGUE

1. Lieutenant General Victor H. Krulak, *First to Fight, an Inside View of the U.S. Marine Corps* (Annapolis, MD: Naval Institute Press, 1984), 218.

2. Phillip B. Davidson, *Vietnam at War: The History, 1946–1975* (New York: Oxford University Press, 1991, paperback edition), 568.

3. Ibid., 566.

4. Neil Sheehan, in Horst Faas and Tim Page, *Requiem* (New York: Random House, 1997), 519–520.

5. See Ray William Stubbe, ed., *B5-T8 in 48 QXD: The Secret Official History of the North Vietnamese Army of the Siege at Khe Sanh, Vietnam, Spring, 1968* (Wauwatosa, WI: Khe Sanh Veterans, 2006), 51–55 and 79.

6. Steve Wiese, author's interview, April 13, 2012.

7. Robert Topmiller had described his battles with post-traumatic stress disorder just weeks before his death in an interview for an article on an upcoming PTSD seminar in Florida. See Scott Satterwhite, "Wounds That Don't Heal," *Pensacola (Florida) Independent News,* May 1, 2008; also, Topmiller's heartbreaking story is rendered in beautiful fashion in the eulogy delivered by his friend and fellow Khe Sanh veteran Michael Archer, preserved by Khe Sanh veteran Mike Fishbaugh at http://mikefishbaugh.homestead.com/doc-topmiller.html.

8. Steve Orr, author's interview, August 19, 2013; and author's observations from the 2012 Khe Sanh Veterans Association reunion.

9. Beth Crumley, "In Memoriam: Colonel William H. Dabney," February 22, 2012, blog post at Marine Corps Association and Foundation website, http://www.mca-marines.org/blog/beth-crumley/2012/02/22/memoriam-colonel-william-h-dabney. Bill Dabney was an extraordinary Marine and American, and this elegant blog post by Beth Crumley is a fitting tribute.

10. Ken Pipes, author's interview, July 23, 2011.

11. Don Shanley, author's interview, February 20, 2012.

12. Steve Wiese, author's interview, April 13, 2012.

13. Tom Esslinger, "The Worst Day," undated tribute to Gunnery Sergeants Paul E. Robitaille and Eugene C. Wire. I'm grateful to Tom Esslinger for providing me with a copy of his poignant tribute to his gunnies.

14. Author's observations during the August 31, 2012, visit to Robert Arrotta's grave site at Arlington National Cemetery.

15. Author's observations during Dennis Mannion's visit to the Vietnam Veterans Memorial, September 1, 2012.

16. Dennis Mannion recounted the incident to me during our visit to the Vietnam Veterans Memorial on September 1, 2012. I drew additional personal details about Michael Suniga, his hometown, and when he began his tour in Vietnam from the Vietnam Casualty Database, RG 330, NARA.

17. Nick Elardo, author's interview, February 23, 2012.

SOURCES

This book is largely based on tape-recorded interviews with ninety men who served at Khe Sanh in various capacities in 1968. I devoted hundreds of hours to vetting these accounts, including cross-checking them against other interviews and eyewitness testimony and meshing this material with various archival resources and secondary accounts. In a few instances, I elected not to use material that I could not verify with a high degree of confidence. I am deeply grateful to the Khe Sanh veterans who entrusted me with their stories, and I have listed their names in the acknowledgments section at the front of this book, and in the bibliography at the back.

Additionally, I examined several thousand pages of primary source documents generated by the Marine Corps and other branches of the US military, the White House, the Pentagon, and the US Congress. Among the most useful documents and resources were six-hour situation reports, command chronologies, after-action reports, telegrams, cables, photographs, and maps. The official documents contain a surprising number of errors, and so I devoted many hours to sorting through discrepancies in an effort to craft the most historically accurate account possible.

In addition to my interviews and the official records consulted at the National Archives in College Park, Maryland, and the US Marine Corps Archives in Quantico, Virginia, I drew on the remarkable US Marine Corps Archives Oral History Collection at Quantico, which includes several dozen interviews with men who served at Khe Sanh. A number of the interviews were conducted at Khe Sanh Combat Base during the siege; on one of the tapes is an extraordinary series of interviews conducted on Hill 861 on January 22, 1968, within twenty-four hours of the North Vietnamese attempt to overrun the hill. It is an incredible historical record, made even more vivid by the sounds of US attack jets roaring low overhead and dropping their bombs on nearby North Vietnamese positions.

Two oral history collections outside the Marine Corps proved useful: the recorded interviews conducted by the LBJ Presidential Library in Austin, Texas, and the Vietnam Center and Archive at Texas Tech University in Lubbock, Texas. The Virtual Vietnam Archive put online by the Texas Tech center contains more than 3.2 million pages of scanned materials, and it is a tremendous resource that I tapped throughout the project.

Khe Sanh veterans have written extensively about their experiences, and I examined every published and unpublished account that I could find. I was also greatly informed, especially early in my research, by the trove of personal accounts that have been published by the Khe Sanh Veterans Association in its *Red Clay* newsletter.

Several secondary accounts have examined the events at Khe Sanh, beginning with the

Marine Corps official history, *The Battle for Khe Sanh*, published in 1969. Captain Moyers Shore II weighed in with a solid effort, produced under difficult circumstances as senior officers of the various service branches sought to shape the narrative to suit their constituencies. The official "comments file" spawned by the monograph offers a revealing glimpse into the interservice rivalries that played out with such intensity at Khe Sanh.

Throughout this project, I kept close at hand three books that covered Khe Sanh in panoramic fashion: *The End of the Line: A Narrative History of the Siege of Khe Sanh*, published in 1983 by Vietnam War correspondent Robert Pisor; *Khe Sanh: Siege in the Clouds, an Oral History*, published in 1989 by Eric Hammel; and *Valley of Decision: The Siege of Khe Sanh*, published in 1991 by John Prados and Ray W. Stubbe.

I have thanked Ray Stubbe personally and in the acknowledgments for his contributions to Khe Sanh research, but it should be noted here as well. Ray was a Navy chaplain assigned to the Marines at Khe Sanh, and *Valley of Decision* grew out of his two decades of research and writing on the battle. His knowledge and command of the archival material is unsurpassed, and I have been greatly aided in this project, by both his past efforts and his ongoing counsel.

Finally, four documentary films on Khe Sanh helped me visualize and understand various aspects of this epic confrontation: *The Battle of Khe Sanh*, released in 1969 by the Department of Defense; *Unsung Heroes: The Battle of Khe Sanh*, a 2002 film produced and edited by Tracey A. Connor for A&E Television Networks; *Bravo! Common Men, Uncommon Valor*, a 2012 film by Khe Sanh veteran Ken Rodgers and his wife, Betty, in which the men of Bravo 1/26 tell their stories in unforgettable fashion; and *Khe Sanh: A Walk in the Clouds*, by David C. Kniess Jr., a 2003 documentary by Dennis Mannion's former student, who accompanied Mannion, Paul Knight, Robert Arrotta, and Glenn Prentice on their emotional pilgrimage back to Khe Sanh.

BIBLIOGRAPHY

AUTHOR INTERVIEWS

Arnold Alderete; Adam Alexander; Richard Allen; Charles Almy; David Althoff; Joe Amodeo; Michael Archer; James Armbrust; Michael Barry; Clifford Braisted; Earle G. Breeding; Calvin E. Bright; Jim Caccavo; Maurice Casey; Charles Chamberlin; George Chapman; John Cicala; Bruce Clarke; Michael Coonan; David Doehrman; Rich Donaghy; Richard Dworsky; George Einhorn; Nick Elardo; Tom Esslinger; James Feasel; Edward Feldman; James O. Finnegan; William Gay; Bruce Geiger; Robert Genty; Lionel Guerra; Jack Haigwood; Joe Harrigan; Billy Joe Hill; Richard Hillmann; Norman Jasper; Keith Kapple; James Kaylor; Neil Kenny; Paul Knight; Larry LeClaire; Guy Leonard; Paul Longgrear; Kevin Macaulay; Dennis Mannion; Bill Martin; Dave McCall; Larry McCartney; Howard McKinnis; Lewis S. Messer II; Ted Mickelson; Ray Milligan; David Norton; Michael O'Hara; Raul Orozco; Steve Orr; Robert Pagano; John Pessoni; Michael Pike; Kenneth W. Pipes; David Powell; Glenn Prentice; Tom Quigley; Henry Radcliffe; John Rauch; Mike Reath; Jose Reyes; John Roberts; Ken Rodgers; George G. Rudell; Charles Rushforth; John Sabol; Miguel Salinas; Lawrence Seavy Cioffi; Don Shanley; James Sigman; Ron Smith; William Smith; Ray Stubbe; Daniel Sullivan; Mark Swearengen; F. J. Taylor; Jim Thomas; Robert Tipton; Craig Tourte; Matthew Walsh; Ken Warner; Steve Wiese; Michael Worth.

ORAL HISTORY INTERVIEWS

A. B. Adams; F. E. Allgood; Richard W. Ambrosio; Phillip Ballard; Michael Bradbury; E. J. Bradley; Earle G. Breeding; Calvin E. Bright; Frank V. Calzia; Patrick Carr; J. D. Cauble; Matthew Caulfield; William H. Dabney; R. M. D'Amora; Charles E. Davis III; Tom Esslinger; Edward Feldman; James O. Finnegan; Dale R. Flaherty; David R. Ford; D. A. Gidlof; R. E. Godwin; D. L. Guttormson; H. T. Hagaman; John Hargesheimer; J. E. Hawley; Frank C. Iodice; Michael R. James; R. E. Kain; John Kaheny; David R. Kelly; D. J. Kiely; Charles King; John Lewis; Francis B. Lovely; J. K. Lower; David E. Lownds; L. A. Luther; Bill Martin; Victor Martinez; Billy R. Moffett; Bruce Meyers; Linn Oehling; J. V. Ostrowski; R. N. Patrick; John J. Pessoni; Kenneth W. Pipes; Robert E. Powell; Michael Ray; Jerry N. Saulsbury; John A. Shepherd; David C. Smith; Ernest E. Spencer; Mykle Stahl; H. E. Stroud; Ray Stubbe; L. E. Tibbett; Rathvon Tompkins; Isaac Walker; D. C. Walton; L. D. Widick.

337

ARCHIVAL MATERIALS

National Archives and Records Administration (College Park, Maryland)

- Record Group 127: Records of the United States Marine Corps, 1775–1981
- Record Group 330: Records of the Office of the Secretary of Defense, 1921–2008
- Record Group 407: Records of the Adjutant General's Office, 1905–1981
- Record Group 472: Records of the U.S. Forces in Southeast Asia, 1950–1975

The Vietnam Center and Archive, Texas Tech University (Lubbock, Texas)

- Oral History Project
- Virtual Vietnam Archive

United States Marine Corps Archives (Quantico, Virginia)

- Marine Corps Vietnam War Collection
- United States Marine Corps Archives Personal Papers Collection

United States Marine Corps History Division (Quantico, Virginia)

- United States Marine Corps Oral History Collection

GOVERNMENT PUBLICATIONS

Blanton, Dwight W. *Project Corona Harvest: Airpower in the Defense of Khe Sanh.* Maxwell Air Force Base, AL: Air War College, Air University, 1969.

Callahan, Shawn P. *Close Air Support and the Battle for Khe Sanh.* Quantico, VA: History Division, U.S. Marine Corps, 2009.

Cash, John A., John Albright, and Allan W. Sandstrum. *Seven Firefights in Vietnam.* Washington, DC: Office of the Chief of Military History, U.S. Army, 1985.

Clarke, Jeffrey J. *The U.S. Army in Vietnam. Advice and Support: The Final Years 1965–1973.* Washington, DC: U.S. Army Center of Military History, 1988.

Hammond, William M. *The United States Army in Vietnam. Public Affairs: The Military and the Media, 1962–1968.* Washington, DC: U.S. Army Center of Military History, 1990.

Marolda, Edward J. *By Sea, Air, and Land: An Illustrated History of the U.S. Navy and the War in Southeast Asia.* Washington, DC: Naval Historical Center, 1994.

Nalty, Bernard C. *Air Power and the Fight for Khe Sanh.* Washington, DC: Office of Air Force History, United States Air Force, 1973.

——. *The War Against Trucks: Aerial Interdiction in Southern Laos, 1968–1972.* Washington DC: Air Force Museums and History Program, 2005.

Pearson, Willard. *The War in the Northern Provinces.* Washington, DC: Department of the Army, 1975.

Sharp, Admiral Ulysses S. Grant, and General William C. Westmoreland. *Report on the War in Vietnam (As of 30 Jun 1968).* Washington, DC: Government Printing Office, 1968.

Shore, Captain Moyers S., II. *The Battle for Khe Sanh.* Washington, DC: Historical Branch, G-3 Division, Headquarters, U.S. Marine Corps, 1969.

Shulimson, Jack. *The U.S. Marines in Vietnam: An Expanding War, 1966.* Washington, DC: History and Museums Division, Headquarters, U.S. Marine Corps, 1982.

——, Lieutenant Colonel Leonard A. Blasiol, U.S. Marine Corps, Charles R. Smith and Captain David A. Dawson, U.S. Marines Corps. *The U.S. Marines in Vietnam: The Defining Year, 1968*. Washington, DC: History and Museums Division, Headquarters, U.S. Marine Corps, 1997.

——, and Major Charles M. Johnson. *The U.S. Marines in Vietnam: The Landing and the Buildup, 1965*. Washington, DC: History and Museums Division, Headquarters, U.S. Marine Corps, 1978.

Sieg, Kent, ed., and David S. Patterson, general ed. *Foreign Relations of the United States, 1964–1968, Volume 6, Vietnam, January–August 1968*. Washington, DC: United States Government Printing Office, 2002.

Telfer, Major Gary L., Lieutenant Colonel Lane Rogers, USMC, and V. Keith Fleming Jr. *The U.S. Marines in Vietnam: Fighting the North Vietnamese, 1967*. Washington, DC: History and Museums Division, Headquarters, U.S. Marine Corps, 1984.

United States Military Assistance Command, Vietnam, History Branch, Office of the Secretary, Joint Staff. *United States Military Assistance Command, Vietnam: 1968 Command History*. 2 volumes, 1968.

United States Senate. *Hearings Before the Electronic Battlefield Subcommittee of the Preparedness Investigating Subcommittee of the Committee on Armed Services*. Washington, DC: Government Printing Office, 1971.

Van Staaveren, Jacob. *Interdiction in Southern Laos, 1960–1968: The United States Air Force in Southeast Asia*. Washington, DC: Center for Air Force History, 1993.

Villard, Erik. *The 1968 Tet Offensive Battles of Quang Tri City and Hue*. Washington, DC: U.S. Army Center of Military History, 2008.

BOOKS

Alexander, Colonel Joseph H., USMC (ret.), with Don Horan and Norman C. Stahl. *The Battle History of the U.S. Marines: A Fellowship of Valor*. HarperPerennial edition. New York: HarperPerennial, 1999.

Archer, Michael. *A Patch of Ground: Khe Sanh Remembered*. Central Point, OR: Hellgate Press, 2004.

Atkinson, Rick. *The Long Gray Line: The American Journey of West Point's Class of 1966*. Boston: Houghton Mifflin, 1989.

Barrett, David M., ed. *Lyndon B. Johnson's Vietnam Papers*. College Station: Texas A&M University Press, 1997.

Bartimus, Tad, Denby Fawcett, Jurate Kazickas, Edith Lederer, and Ann Mariano. *War Torn: Stories of War from the Women Reporters Who Covered Vietnam*. New York: Random House, 2002.

Braestrup, Peter. *Big Story: How the American Press and Television Reported and Interpreted the Crisis of Tet 1968 in Vietnam and Washington*. Anchor Books edition, abridged. Garden City, NY: Anchor Books, 1978.

Caputo, Philip. *A Rumor of War*. New York: Holt, Rinehart, and Winston, 1977.

Chanoff, David, and Doan Van Toai. *Portraits of the Enemy*. New York: Random House, 1986.

Clarke, Bruce B. G. *Expendable Warriors: The Battle of Khe Sanh and the Vietnam War*. Stackpole Books edition. Mechanicsburg, PA: Stackpole Books, 2009.

Coram, Robert. *Brute: The Life of Victor Krulak, U.S. Marine*. New York: Little, Brown (Hachette), 2010.

Corbett, John. *West Dickens Avenue: A Marine at Khe Sanh*. Mass market edition. New York: Ballantine Books, 2004.

Craig, William T. *Team Sergeant: A Special Forces NCO at Lang Vei and Beyond*. New York: Ivy Books, 1998.

Dallek, Robert. *Flawed Giant: Lyndon Johnson and His Times, 1961–1973*. New York: Oxford University Press, 1998.

Davidson, Phillip B. *Vietnam at War: The History, 1946–1975*. Oxford University Press paperback edition. New York: Oxford University Press, 1991.

Delezen, John Edmund. *Red Plateau: Memoir of a North Vietnamese Soldier*. El Dorado Hills, CA: Corps Productions, 2005.

Drez, Ronald J., and Douglas Brinkley. *Voices of Courage: The Battle for Khe Sanh, Vietnam*. New York: Bulfinch Press, 2005.

Duncan, David Douglas. *I Protest!* New York: New American Library, 1968.

———. *War Without Heroes*. New York: Harper and Row, 1970.

Edelman, Bernard. *Dear America: Letters Home from Vietnam*. New York: Norton, 1985.

Elliott, Donna E. *Keeping the Promise: The Story of MIA Jerry Elliott, a Family Shattered by His Disappearance, and His Sister's 40-year Search for the Truth*. Ashland, OR: Hellgate Press, 2010.

Ellsberg, Daniel. *Secrets: A Memoir of Vietnam and the Pentagon Papers*. New York: Viking, 2002.

Fall, Bernard B. *Hell in a Very Small Place: The Siege of Dien Bien Phu*. Philadelphia: Lippincott, 1967.

———. *Street Without Joy*. Mechanicsburg, PA: Stackpole Books, 1994.

Finnegan, James O., MD. *In the Company of Marines: A Surgeon Remembers Vietnam*. N.p: Self-published, 2010.

FitzGerald, Frances. *Fire in the Lake: The Vietnamese and the Americans in Vietnam*. New York: Vintage Books, 1989.

Fixler, Barry. *Semper Cool: One Marine's Fond Memories of Vietnam*. New York: Exalt Press, 2010.

Foster, Ronnie. *One Day as a Lion: True Stories of the Vietnam War*. Plano, TX: Entry Way Publishing, 2007.

Hackworth, David. *About Face*. New York: Simon and Schuster, 1989.

Halberstam, David. *The Best and the Brightest*. Viking Penguin paperback edition. New York: Viking Penguin, 1983.

Hammel, Eric M. *Ambush Valley: I Corps, Vietnam 1967: The Story of a Marine Infantry Battalion's Battle for Survival*. Novato, CA: Presidio Press, 1990.

———. *Khe Sanh: Siege in the Clouds*. New York: Crown Publishers, 1989.

Hendrickson, Paul. *The Living and the Dead: Robert McNamara and Five Lives of a Lost War*. New York: Knopf, 1996.

Herman, Jan K. *Navy Medicine in Vietnam: Oral Histories from Dien Bien Phu to the Fall of Saigon*. Jefferson, NC: McFarland, 2009.

Herr, Michael. *Dispatches*. New York: Knopf, 1977.

Herring, George C. *America's Longest War: The United States and Vietnam, 1950–1975*. New York: Wiley, 1979.

———. *LBJ and Vietnam: A Different Kind of War*. Austin: University of Texas Press, 1994.

Karnow, Stanley. *Vietnam: A History*. Penguin Books edition. New York: Penguin, 1984.

Krulak, Victor H. *First to Fight: An Inside View of the U.S. Marine Corps*. Annapolis, MD: Naval Institute Press, 1984.

Lehrack, Otto, Jr. *The First Battle: Operation Starlite and the Beginning of the Blood Debt in Vietnam*. Havertown, PA: Casemate, 2004.

Mann, Robert. *A Grand Delusion: America's Descent into Vietnam*. New York: Basic Books, 2002.

Maraniss, David. *They Marched into Sunlight: War and Peace in Vietnam and America, October 1967*. New York: Simon and Schuster, 2003.

McLean, Jack. *Loon: A Marine Story*. New York: Ballantine Books, 2009.

McNamara, Robert S., and Brian VanDeMark. *In Retrospect: The Tragedy and Lessons of Vietnam*. New York: Times Books, 1995.

Millett, Allan R. *Semper Fidelis: The History of the United States Marine Corps*. Revised and expanded edition. New York: Free Press, 1991.

Murphy, Edward F. *The Hill Fights: The First Battle of Khe Sanh*. New York: Ballantine Books, 2003.

Nichols, John B., and Barrett Tillman. *On Yankee Station: The Naval Air War over Vietnam*. Bluejacket Books edition. Annapolis, MD: Naval Institute Press, 2001.

Nguyen, Lien-Hang T. *Hanoi's War: An International History of the War for Peace in Vietnam*. Chapel Hill: University of North Carolina Press, 2012.

Oberdorfer, Don. *Tet! The Turning Point in the Vietnam War*. Reprint. New York: Da Capo Press, 1984.

The Pentagon Papers: The Secret History of the Vietnam War: The Complete and Unabridged Series as Published by the New York Times. New York: Bantam Books, 1971. Also accessed online at National Archives, http://www.archives.gov/research/pentagon-papers/.

Phillips, William R. *Night of the Silver Stars: The Battle of Lang Vei*. St. Martin's Paperbacks edition. New York: St. Martin's, 2004.

Pike, Douglas. *PAVN: People's Army of Vietnam*. Novato, CA: Presidio Press, 1986.

Pisor, Robert. *The End of the Line: The Siege of Khe Sanh*. Norton paperback edition. New York: Norton, 1982.

Prados, John. *The Blood Road: The Ho Chi Minh Trail and the Vietnam War*. New York: John Wiley and Sons, 1998.

———. *Vietnam: The History of an Unwinnable War, 1945–1975*. Lawrence: University Press of Kansas, 2009.

———, and Ray W. Stubbe. *Valley of Decision: The Siege of Khe Sanh*. Boston: Houghton Mifflin, 1991.

Prochnau, William W. *Once upon a Distant War*. New York: Times Books/Random House, 1995.

Puller, Lewis B., Jr. *Fortunate Son: The Autobiography of Lewis B. Puller Jr*. New York: Grove Weidenfeld, 1991.

Race, Jeffrey. *War Comes to Long An: Revolutionary Conflict in a Vietnamese Province*. Berkeley: University of California Press, 1972.

Santoli, Al, ed. *Everything We Had: An Oral History of the Vietnam War*. New York: Ballantine Books, 1981.

Schell, Jonathan. *The Real War: The Classic Reporting on the Vietnam War*. New York: Pantheon Books, 1987.

Schoenbaum, Thomas J. *Waging Peace and War: Dean Rusk in the Truman, Kennedy, and Johnson Years*. New York: Simon and Schuster, 1988.

Sheehan, Neil. *A Bright Shining Lie: John Paul Vann and America in Vietnam*. New York: Random House, 1988.

Sorley, Lewis, *A Better War: The Unexamined Victories and Final Tragedy of America's Last Years in Vietnam*. New York: Harcourt Brace, 1999.

——. *Westmoreland: The General Who Lost Vietnam*. Boston: Houghton Mifflin Harcourt, 2011.

Spector, Ronald H. *Advice and Support: The Early Years of the U.S. Army in Vietnam*. New York: Free Press, 1985.

——. *After Tet: The Bloodiest Year in Vietnam*. New York: Free Press, 1993.

Spencer, Ernest. *Welcome to Vietnam, Macho Man: Reflections of a Khe Sanh Vet*. Bantam edition. New York: Bantam Books, 1991.

Steinman, Ron. *The Soldiers' Story: Vietnam in Their Own Words*. New York: TV Books, 2000.

Stubbe, Ray William. *Battalion of Kings: A Tribute to Our Fallen Brothers Who Died Because of the Battlefield of Khe Sanh, Vietnam*. 2nd edition, revised. Wauwatosa, WI: Khe Sanh Veterans, 2008.

——, ed. *B5-T8 in 48 QXD: The Secret Official History of the North Vietnamese Army of the Siege at Khe Sanh, Vietnam, Spring, 1968*. Translated by Sedgwick D. Tourison Jr. Wauwatosa, WI: Khe Sanh Veterans, 2006.

——. *Pebbles in My Boots*. Wauwatosa, WI: Self-published, 2011.

——. *Pebbles in My Boots*. Volume 2. Wauwatosa, WI: Self-published, 2011.

Tambini, Anthony J. *Wiring Vietnam: The Electronic Wall*. Lanham, MD: Scarecrow Press, 2007.

Topmiller, Robert J. *Red Clay on My Boots: Encounters with Khe Sanh, 1968 to 2005*. Minneapolis, MN: Kirk House Publishers, 2007.

Tucker, Spencer C., ed. *The Encyclopedia of the Vietnam War: A Political, Social, and Military History*. 2nd edition. Santa Barbara, CA: ABC-CLIO, 2011.

Wallace, Terry. *Bloods: An Oral History of the Vietnam War by Black Veterans*. New York: Random House, 1984.

Wells, Jack. *Class of '67: The Story of the 6th Marine Officer Basic Class of 1967*. N.p.: CreateSpace, 2009.

Westmoreland, William C. *A Soldier Reports*. Garden City, NY: Doubleday, 1976.

Wirtz, James J. *The Tet Offensive: Intelligence Failure in War*. Ithaca: Cornell University Press, 1991.

DIARIES, LETTERS, REMEMBRANCES, AND PERSONAL NARRATIVES

Richard Allen; Mirza M. Baig; Earle G. Breeding; Michael Coonan; Tom Esslinger; Edward Feldman; Lynn Fifer; Bruce Geiger; Jerry E. Hudson; James Kaylor; Paul Knight; Lacey Lahren; Dennis Mannion; Ray Milligan; John F. Mitchell; Robert Pagano; Kenneth Pipes; Henry Radcliffe; Charles Rushforth; Ron Smith; David Steinberg; Ray Stubbe; Daniel Sullivan; Mark Swearengen; F. J. Taylor; Robert Tipton; John J. Tolson III; Craig Tourte; Edward Welchel; James B. Wilkinson.

NEWSPAPERS

New York Times
Stars and Stripes (Pacific edition)
Washington Post

PERIODICALS

Newsweek
Time

ARTICLES AND BLOG POSTS

Althoff, Lieutenant Colonel David L. "Helicopter Operations at Khe Sanh." *Marine Corps Gazette* (May 1969): 47–49.

Brush, Peter. "Big Guns of Camp Carroll." *Vietnam* (August 1997): 26–32.

Coan, James P. "Vietnam War: The Road to Khe Sanh: U.S. Marine Tanks Fight to Keep Route 9 Open." *Leatherneck* (February 2013). Available at http://www.mca-marines.org/leatherneck/article/vietnam-war-road-khe-sanh#sthash.UHV3JTRE.dpuf.

Crumley, Beth. "Robert J. Arrotta: The Mightiest Corporal in the Marine Corps." Marine Corps Association and Foundation website, blog post dated January 10, 2012. Available at http://www.mca-marines.org/blog/beth-crumley/2012/01/10/robert-j-arrotta-mightiest-corporal-marine-corps#sthash.tXUHfrF7.dpuf.

———. "The Siege of Khe Sanh Begins." Marine Corps Association and Foundation website, blog post dated January 24, 2012. Available at http://www.mca-marines.org/blog/beth-crumley/2012/01/24/siege-khe-sanh-begins#comment-1004066.

Dabney, Colonel William H. "Hill 881S and the Super Gaggle." *Marine Corps Gazette* (April 2005). Available at http://www.mca-marines.org/gazette/hill-881s-and-super-gaggle#sthash.qknwSld3.dpuf.

"Extended Interview—Scholar Lien-Hang T. Nguyen: Hanoi's Secrets." February 25, 2013. Available at http://www.historynet.com/interview-lien-hang-t-nguyen-and-hanois-secrets.htm.

Finnegan, James. "A Surgeon Remembers Khe Sanh." *Navy Medicine* (May–June 2007): 26–28.

Hammel, Eric. "Khe Sanh: Attack on Hill 861A." *Marine Corps Gazette* (February 1989). Available at http://www.mca-marines.org/gazette/khe-sanh-attack-hill-861a#sthash.Es LOGARo.dpuf.

"Interview—Jim Willbanks: Tet's Truths, Myths and Mysteries." December 5, 2012. Available at http://www.historynet.com/interview-jim-willbanks-tets-truths-myths-and-mysteries.htm.

Kashiwahara, Captain Ken. "Lifeline to Khe Sanh." *Airman* (July 1968): 6.

Mannion, Dennis. "Christmas Eve at Khe Sanh." *Marine Corps Gazette* (December 1988). Available at http://www.mca-marines.org/gazette/christmas-eve-khe-sanh#sthash.aDp uVdRs.dpuf.

Mundy, General Carl E., Jr. "A Perspective on Khe Sanh." *Marine Corps Gazette* (November 1993). Available at http://www.mca-marines.org/gazette/perspective-khe-sanh#sthash .IJ8WOnOW.dpuf.

Prados, John. "Khe Sanh: The Other Side of the Hill." *VVA Veteran* (July–August 2007). Available at http://www.vva.org/veteran/0807/khesanh.html.

Studt, Lieutenant Colonel John C. "Battalion in the Attack." *Marine Corps Gazette* (July 1970): 39–44.

Swearengen, Major Mark A. "Siege: Forty Days at Khe Sanh." *Marine Corps Gazette* (April 1973): 23–28.

Tolson, Lieutenant General John J., III. "Pegasus." *Army* (December 1971): 10–19.

FILMS

The Battle of Khe Sanh. Written by Robert C. Mack, edited by Chandler House and Joe Bettencurt. Washington, DC: Department of Defense, 1969; RG 342, NARA.

Bravo! Common Men, Uncommon Valor. DVD. Directed by Ken and Betty Rodgers. Boise, ID: Kingfisher Arts, 2012.

Khe Sanh: A Walk in the Clouds. Produced and edited by David C. Kniess Jr. Documentary film, 2003.

Unsung Heroes: The Battle of Khe Sanh. DVD. Produced and edited by Tracey A. Connor. New York: A&E Television Networks, 2002.

INDEX

LSC NC 04.05.2021 #